*A*dventure Guide

China

Simon Foster

"A thorough guide not only to traveling in China but also to the country's history and culture, this should satisfy the novice and seasoned traveler alike. Each city and region is covered from all angles, including activities for those traveling with children. An informative read for those unfamiliar with the country and an excellent way to brush up for the more experienced traveler, this is an excellent guide for planning a Chinese vacation." *Publishers Weekly*

HUNTER

HUNTER PUBLISHING, INC.
130 Campus Drive
Edison, NJ 08818-7816
☎ 732-225-1900 / 800-255-0343 / fax 732-417-1744
www.hunterpublishing.com
E-mail comments@hunterpublishing.com

IN CANADA:
Ulysses Travel Publications
4176 Saint-Denis, Montréal, Québec
Canada H2W 2M5
☎ 514-843-9882 ext. 2232 / fax 514-843-9448

IN THE UNITED KINGDOM:

Windsor Books International
5, Castle End Park, Castle End Rd, Ruscombe
Berkshire, RG10 9XQ England
☎ 01189-346-367 / fax 01189-346-368

ISBN 978-1-58843-641-2

© 2008 Hunter Publishing, Inc.

This and other Hunter travel guides are also available as e-books
in a variety of digital formats through our online partners, including
eBooks.com, Overdrive.com, Ebrary.com and NetLibrary.com.

Cover photograph: *Great Wall* (© Tom Till/Alamy)

All photos by Simon Foster, unless otherwise indicated. Special thanks
to Tot Foster, Ewen Bell (www.ewenbell.com), Magalie L'Abbé and Galen
Frysinger (www.galenfrysinger.com) for their photographs.

Index by Inge Wiesen

Contents

Maps

A Changing China

As is always the case with the information in guidebooks, things change. Hotels close down (or just get run down), great new restaurants pop up and bars, clubs and Internet cafés come and go with the wind. In a country changing as fast as China this is even more so, and new roads, hotels and even cities, seem to appear overnight. All of the information in this book was carefully researched and correct at time of going to press. If there's anything you come across in your travels that has closed or gone downhill, or any great new offerings or adventures that you think should be in the book, please contact the publishers at comments@hunterpublishing.com.

About the Author

Simon Foster was born in England. Family trips first kindled his interest in places other than his own and after graduating in geography he set off to seek what he'd been studying. Following his first extended trip, wanderlust firmly set in and Simon became an adventure tour leader in the Middle East and Asia. He soon started travel writing and has contributed to the Rough the Rough Guide's Australia, China, Egypt, Europe, India and Tunisia books. Simon has spent most of the past ten years overseas, principally in China and sunny southern Taiwan. When he's not leading tours or writing, Simon enjoys, you guessed it, travel, whether to the Philippines or just back home to Yorkshire.

Dedication

I'd like to dedicate this book to my grandfather, Maurice, who traveled the globe with the merchant navy and always followed my world wanderings on his atlas at home in Newcastle in England. May he rest in peace.

Thanks

Friends, old and new, from around the globe, have played their part in this book, and I want to say a great big thank you for all the time, effort, tips and tales. Firstly, thanks to my wife, Tot, without whom I would've surely given up several times along the way. Tot assisted with research, writing and by taking many of the book's photos. I'd also like to say a big thank you to photographer Ewen Bell (www.ewenbell.com) who was kind enough to let us use his incredible images. Next, my best mate Craig, who read through material in record time and threw in the odd amusing comment to spur me on.

As always, my family has supported me and contributed their own skills – my dad helped to manage the project as a whole, my mum (the librarian) helped with the booklist and my sister and Monty resolved computer problems as I created them! My Uncle Mick is an ornithologist and helped on the Flora and Fauna section and Jadranka, an author herself, and my Uncle Jon proffered helpful advice.

In China: *xie xie* to Ben, Leo, Nick and Su-San in Beijing, Fox in Xi'an, Lu in Shandong, John Zhang in Chongqing, Steven Huang in Tunxi, Mr. Hu in Tangkou and Pete, Selina and Chris Winnan in Guangzhou. To my friends in Guangxi who helped re-initiate me to the new Yangshuo – Alf, Bill, Chris Barclay, Dee, Echo, Forest, Ian Ford and Ian Hamilton, Jessie, Malcolm, Naomi, William, Sam, Shelly, Xu Chen Zuo and the China Climb team. A bigger thank you still must go to William and Linda Lu who nourished me well with food and information. And an enormous thank you goes to Rose Mo who assisted with the language section. In Hong Kong: Sarah Clark and Paul Etherington. In Europe: thank you very much indeed to Adi Vimal, Dara-Lynne, Henrik Rasmussen and his family, Jane and Eric and Terry and Jensia. Last, but by no means least, thanks to Michael and the team at Hunter Publishing, for letting this book happen and for breaking up my unruly sentences!

Wizened monks wearing walkmans, wooden huts topped with satellite dishes, pet dogs passing those soon to be eaten, skyscrapers smiling down on temples. China is the ultimate land of contrasts!

Introduction

China, a country of superlatives, most populous of nations, hidden for so long, is now emerging onto the world travel scene. From frozen north to tropical south, modern east to wild west, this is a huge, diverse land just waiting to be explored. It abounds in magnificent sights – some are natural like the **mystical limestone peaks of Guangxi**, while others are manmade testaments to the power and glory of China's past, such as the **Forbidden City**. Some are a combination of the two such as the **Great Wall** or the impossibly steep **Longji** rice-terraces, where man has ruthlessly crowned nature's achievements.

However, many travelers' most enduring memory of this vast country is its people. From farmers to fashion students they all have a tale to tell and, even though most don't speak your language, that won't stop them from trying. Still predominantly rural, China's massive population, though principally **Han** Chinese, is actually comprised of some **56 different ethnic groups** ranging from Central Asian horsemen such as Kazakhs in the northwest, more akin to Turks than Chinese, to the hilltribe peoples of the southwest. Long suppressed, the traditions of these minorities are now experiencing a renaissance, albeit often for tourist purposes. With such diverse people and regions comes an incredible variety of food, making China one of the

Tien'anmen Square & the Forbidden City

world's **great culinary centers** – from **ultra-fresh Cantonese** to fiery Szechuan, or Mongolian hotpot to **Beijing duck**, there is always something new to try. When you add all these elements to the fact that this is the fastest-changing country in the world, it's no wonder the race to see China is on.

The events of the last 50 years have blanketed and even physically destroyed previous images of this vast unknown land and, until recently, many people's perception was of little more than an overpopulated, oppressed, Communist country. Fortunately, China has opened up, in its own inimitable way, and is here to challenge preconceptions. A country on the move, where China will end up remains unclear, but it is definitely going somewhere – at least, some of it is.

Phenomenal wealth exists side-by-side with poverty and the **Middle Kingdom**'s growing middle class are eagerly exchanging their bicycles for motorcycles and work unit housing for smart new apartment complexes. Yet China still has one of the world's worst human rights records, and there are serious questions that need to be answered about where the current ideology is taking this giant. The system allows for capitalist money-flow, with the crushing power of communism to dictate exactly what happens where and when. Corruption aside, this system is efficient but leaves little say for the people. **The Three Gorges Dam Project**, dislodging well over a million people, is a case in point. While equality and the distribution of resources are supposedly central tenets of communism, little of the cities' new-found wealth makes its way to the impoverished rural majority. Walking past the designer shops, McDonalds and Starbucks in Beijing, Shanghai or Shenzhen, you'd be hard-pressed to guess this is the same country where pictures of Mao still adorn most village houses and farmers use buffalos to plough their fields. Such paradoxes are nevertheless a fascinating and integral part of the emerging modern China.

China is such an enormous place with so much to offer that you could spend your whole life here and never see it all, especially since previously inaccessible areas are continually opening up to foreign visitors. Thus it is best taken in bite-sized chunks or, if you have the opportunity, in an extended stay. But even on a short trip it's possible to link up several of the areas we cover in one trip (see *Top 25* and *Suggested Itineraries*, p. 132-33, for possi-

The splendor of Hong Kong Harbor (Tot Foster)

Terracotta warriors, Xi'an

ble routes). This book is designed to allow you to experience as many facets of the country as possible, while concentrating on a few, select areas that can offer a broad insight into China. These are the great cities of **Beijing**, **Shanghai** and **Hong Kong**, the **Terracotta Warriors near Xi'an**, the **Yangzi River's Three Gorges** and the majestic rural scenery around **Guilin in Guangxi Province**. A few other choice sights close to these cities are also covered, including the imperial retreat at **Chengde** near Beijing and the picturesque cities of **Suzhou** and **Hangzhou** close to Shanghai, while the freshly painted mountain scenery of **Huangshan** adds a little rural flavor to this highly developed part of the country. **Yangshuo** near Guilin makes for a lower-key introduction to this idyllic rural area and is a great place to try your hand at Chinese calligraphy or tai chi and **Longji** up in the hills is unmissable for its rice terraces.

Proceeding south, **Guangzhou** and **Shenzhen** offer many visitors their first taste of mainland China while, nestled on the western side of the Pearl River Delta, **Macau** is definitely worth the short boat ride from Hong Kong. Whether climbing, shopping, sightseeing or studying, in these places you will find adventures that stimulate the body and mind, getting you into the heart of the country and under the skin of its culture.

History

 Chinese history dates back a long, long time. The immense timeline, mythical beginnings, dynastic power struggles and divisions, not to mention the complex modern period, can make gaining a sense of scale and unity in China's history a daunting prospect. The *Quick Reference Guide* below gives a simplified overview from prehistory to the present. The bracketed sections indicate contemporaneous events in the Western world.

QUICK REFERENCE GUIDE

Era	Date	Historical Advances, Events & People
Prehistory		Peking Man
Yangshao Culture	5000-3000 BC	
Three Dynasties	2100-221 BC	First recorded Chinese characters Philosophers Confucius and Lao Zi
Qin (Ancient Greece)	221-206 BC	Emperor Qin Shi Huang Great Wall and Terracotta Warriors
Han (Roman Empire)	206 BC-220 AD	Territorial expansion Advances in agriculture, paper and textiles
Three Kingdoms	220-581	China's first alien dynasty, the Xiongnu Emergence of Buddhism in China
Sui (Dark Ages)	581-618	Grand Canal
Tang	618-907	First Empress Wei Zetian Poets Li Bai and Du Fu
Song	960-1279	General Yue Fei and poet Su Dongpo
Yuan (Feudalism in Europe)	1279-1368	First Mongol dynasty Emperor Kublai Khan Marco Polo reputedly visits China
Ming (Renaissance)	1368-1644	Construction of the Forbidden City Fine pottery Admiral Zheng He reaches Africa
Qing (Industrial Revolution)	1644-1911	Opium Wars Taiping Uprising Boxer Rebellion Empress Dowager Cixi
Republican Period	1911-1949	Dr. Sun Yatsen founds Republic of China Foundation of Chinese Communist Party The Long March Japanese invasion & the Rape of Nanjing
People's Republic	1949-1976	Mao Zedong founds PRC Chiang Kaishek founds ROC (Taiwan) Hundred Flowers Campaign
	1958	Great Leap Forward
	1966	Cultural Revolution
	1976	Mao Zedong dies
Reform Era	1976-present	Deng Xiaoping heads PRC Economic Liberalization China opens its doors to tourism
	1989	Tian'anmen Square Incident
	1992	Jiang Zemin ascends to power
	1997	Deng Xiaoping dies British handover of Hong Kong
	1999	Portuguese handover of Macau
	2002	China joins World Trade Organization Hu Jintao and Wen Jibao rise to head CCP
	2008	Beijing will host Summer Olympics (p. 139)
	2010	Shanghai will host World Expo

Taking adventure to extremes in Yangshuo (China Climb)

Prehistory

Chinese legend has it that the world was created by **Panku** and that the parasites living on his body became humans. Civilization then developed with the help of the guiding advances made by the Five Sovereigns, the last of whom, **Yu, Tamer of Floods**, is also believed to have formed the first of China's dynasties, the Xia, in the 22nd century BC.

Myth and legend aside, *homo erectus* in China has a history dating back 600,000 years before Christ, first emerging in the great river valleys. In the 1920s the discovery of skull remains, 30 miles from Beijing, reinforced the contested theory of evolution and showed that so-called **Peking Man** (see *Beijing*, p. 185) knew how to use fire and basic stone tools. *Homo sapiens* emerged between 500,000 and 200,000 BC and gradually developed into modern man. Humans began to speak during the Paleolithic Age, which lasted from 100,000-10,000 BC, but it wasn't until 5000 BC that anything resembling a culture began to develop.

Yangshao Culture (5000-3000 BC)

Centered in what are now Shaanxi and Gansu provinces, Yangshao culture was probably a matriarchal society, although the official party line interprets it as a Communist community! People farmed, fished and kept domestic animals and when they died they were buried with funerary objects, including ceramic bowls and jade ornaments.

The Dynastic Age

Xia Dynasty (2100-1600 BC)

The **Three Dynasties** (2100-221 BC) is a term used to describe the supposed first three Chinese dynasties, the Xia, the Shang and the Zhou. While much during this time still remains unclear, when Yu, Tamer of Floods, died and handed power over to his son, Qi, the Xia dynasty was born, marking the beginnings of the Chinese as a unified people. The Xia represents the transition from primitive to civilized society, a shift based on the right to ownership, with the family unit at its core and the tradition of dynastic succession.

Shang Dynasty (1600-1122 BC)

The Shang dynasty followed the Xia and, although literacy was very limited, the first records of Chinese characters come from this time, marked onto oracle bones. This was China's Bronze Age and many of the fine pieces you see in museums today were forged during the Shang and subsequent Zhou (see *Bronzes*, p. 000). Archeological finds indicate that the Shang practiced ancestor worship, a belief which continues in the 21st century AD.

Zhou Dynasty (1122-221 BC)

The Zhou dynasty saw the country divided into many states, each of which was controlled by a family relative. The Zhou also introduced the concept of **Divine Mandate** (or the Mandate of Heaven), which allowed for the succession of one ruler or dynasty over another, if it was ordained by heaven. The Zhou dynasty is divided into two periods, the Western Zhou which ran from 1122 to 771 BC, and the Eastern Zhou, between 771 and 221 BC. Toward the close of the Eastern Zhou, the increasing population and the breakdown of relations between the dynastic states led to factional conflicts in a time which became known as the **Warring States Period** (475-221 BC). This part of history was very fractured and uncertain, but from it emerged stabilizing elements that remain to this day, namely the thoughts and theories of wandering scholars like **Confucius** (see p. 48) and **Lao Zi**, the creator of **Taoism** (see p. 50).

Qin Dynasty (221-206 BC)

Throughout the Warring States Period, the state of Qin had been gradually acquiring more territory and power, and in 221 BC, **Qin Shi Huang** brought the Qin Dynasty to power. Though cruel and very short-lived, the Qin is perceived as "China's first dynasty" and has had a lasting impact, most obviously in the country's name, China (in pinyin q is pronounced as ch, thus Qin is spoken as Chin). Qin Shi Huang rejected traditional Confucian values and set about unifying and expanding China, making his mark with a number of grand schemes, most famously the completion of the earliest version of the **Great Wall**. He also implemented a system of currency

The Great Wall (Su-San Tan)

and writing. Ultimately, though, Qin Shi Huang's reign was ruthless and unpopular, forcing farmers to leave the land to work on his great projects and, when he died in 210 BC, his heirs were incapable of holding the empire together. But the 1974 discovery of his secret legacy, the **Terracotta Warriors** that guard his tomb near Xi'an, has ensured that Qin Shi Huang and the glory of the Qin will never be forgotten.

Han Dynasty (206 BC-220 AD)

The fact that the dominant ethnic group and the country's language still bear the name **Han** in the 21st century gives some insight into the power and legacy of the Han dynasty. Liu Bang (subsequently known as Gaozu, or High Ancestor), a warlord of peasant origins, was the first of 27 Lius to rule in the Han line. He established his grand capital near modern Xi'an but, for the latter half of the Han dynasty (referred to as the Eastern Han), **Luoyang** became the emperor's seat. Though Liu Bang had little time for Confucian ideals, it was during the Han dynasty that written exams on Confucian lore were introduced as necessary qualifications for official postings. To limit the power of the aristocracy, regional control was put in the hands of these officials who could be transferred or replaced as required. And to appease the peasantry, land taxation was reduced from the high levels it had reached under the Qin.

Advances, Expansion & Revolt

During the Han, substantial advances were made in agriculture, paper and textiles. This was a time of expansion which called for a strong army and led to improvements in warfare. At its peak the Han dynasty stretched as far south as Vietnam and saw the trickle of trade routes to the West develop into the Silk Road. However, all this war was expensive and when **Wu Di,** the Martial Emperor, died in 87 BC, although China was larger than ever, the coffers were nearly empty. The peasants, who had been taxed more heavily as his reign progressed, were ready to revolt and this situation allowed the throne to be temporarily usurped by the nobly born Wang Mang. In 9 AD he declared himself the first emperor of the **Xin dynasty** (New dynasty) and set about land reforms, but in 23 AD the Han reasserted its rule from its new capital, Luoyang in Shandong province. However, the Han's heyday had passed and as its power diluted the dynasty slipped into turmoil before expiring in 220 AD. Knowledge of Chinese history up to this point is greatly aided by the extensive historical record writing of **Sima Qian**, one of China's greatest historians.

Three Kingdoms Period (220-581 AD)

The demise of the Han left a fragmented China wrought with complex power struggles that would last almost four centuries. China was divided into three kingdoms: the northern **Wei**, ruled by Cao Pei, son of Han poet and general, Cao Cao; the southern **Wu**; and, in the southwest, the **Shu**. The trials of the time were subsequently recorded in the Ming dynasty work *Romance of the Three Kingdoms*. Also known as the Period of Division, this was a violent, unsettled time but one that saw the re-emergence of the aristocracy and a range of new influences reach China. China's **first alien dynasty** came into being when Liu Yuan, king of the nomadic northern **Xiongnu** tribe, captured Luoyang and declared the restoration of the Han dynasty. **Buddhism** began to take hold, particularly in the north, but, like almost everything else, was quickly sinicized.

Sui Dynasty (581-618 AD)

The Three Kingdoms Period was a dark and confused time, but its patronage of the arts laid a rich platform for the Sui and Tang to build on. The 400-year struggle for power ended when General Yang Jian of the Wei kingdom managed to unify the northern states and conquer the southern states, founding the short-lived Sui dynasty. Its brevity did not stop the Sui from forming lasting legacies, and the second emperor, **Yang Di**, ordered the construction of the 1,000-mile **Grand Canal** (see *Suzhou*, p. 340-41), linking the Yangzi rice bowl to the imperial capital in the north. But thousands died in grand projects and military expansion into Korea and it was the suffering inflicted by the regime that led to its demise. Yang Di was assassinated and a military revolt was led by none other than his cousin, General Li Yuan.

The canals of Suzhou (Tot Foster)

The Tang Dynasty (618-907 AD)

Despite the consolidation of the Sui, the re-unification of north and south was by no means inevitable. China's reconsolidation and the resultant advances in agriculture, the arts and trade grounded the concept of a united kingdom as an ideal and marked the Tang as **China's most glorious dynasty**. Territorial expansion also played a key part in the Tang's success (and ultimately, its failure). At its greatest, Chinese influence expanded from Korea to Persia. The name of the imperial capital, **Chang'an** (modern day Xi'an), means eternal peace and its million-strong population relished in the prosperity and new influences that this peace afforded.

Arts & Religion under the Tang

Early Tang camel with rider

After the previous fractious periods of division, the calm and prosperity of a unified China provided a springboard for the arts, particularly painting, poetry and pottery. Two of China's most famous poets to this day, **Li Bai** and **Du Fu** (see p. 61 for more), wrote during the Tang and the world's first printed book was published in 868. **Pottery** began to take on more color and glaze, and the tri-color techniques refined in the Tang are still in use today (see *Ceramics*, p. 57). Trade was fundamental to both economic success and the resultant thriving religious and artistic scene. The Silk Road and the maritime ports of Guangzhou and Yangzhou brought, not only foreign goods, but outside ideas to the country. A tolerant attitude to foreigners allowed for a more cosmopolitan China; other religions such as **Islam** and **Nestorianism** established themselves, but neither prospered like **Buddhism**. As imperial patronage of Buddhism increased, it was represented in cave art, which reached its peak in the Tang, although much was later destroyed in periods of religious repression. Notable Buddhist cave art from the Tang remains today at Dunhuang in Gansu, Longmen Grottoes in Shandong province and at **Dazu** in Szechuan (see p. 266).

CHINA'S FIRST EMPRESS

Wu Zetian

Thirty years into the dynasty, a power struggle for the throne led to the naming of Taizong's (624-49) ninth son as Emperor Gaozong in 649. Only 20 years old when he came to the throne and plagued by ill health, Gaozong's power was soon controlled by his consort and former concubine, **Wu Zetian**, who had managed to oust the empress and take her place. When Gaozong died, she continued to rule for their weak son. A shrewd and manipulative woman, Wu finally usurped the throne in 698 AD, proclaiming the foundation of the **Zhou dynasty** in 698 AD, and giving China its **first empress**. Her relationship with Buddhism (and with Buddhist priests) has been questioned, but the royal carvings she commissioned at Longmen Grottoes in Luoyang are a testament to her short rule, which ended with her abdication in 705.

Close of the Tang

In 712, **Xuanzong** ascended to the throne and, although he is remembered as one of the Tang's greatest emperors and his reign began gloriously, as it progressed, power was eroded. There was a military defeat by the Arabs in 751, invasions from Tibet and finally a revolt led by the Turkish general An Lushan. Although the rebellion was crushed, the power of the state was considerably weakened and Xuanzong's rule ended in 756. After Xuanzong, imperial control was further diluted by internal power struggles and several emperors were poisoned by court eunuchs. Eunuchs continued to exert influence over court proceedings and a string of weak emperors allowed them to chip away at the imperial power base. It became clear that the dynasty had lost the Mandate of Heaven and, in 907, the last of the Tang emperors abdicated.

Song Dynasty (960-1279)

In spite of a 50-year hiatus from unified rule known as the **Five Dynasties** (907-960), advances made during the Tang had laid the way for economic development. When Zhao Kuangyin (Emperor Taizu) re-united the country and founded the Song dynasty in 960, things quickly picked up from where the Tang had left off. Commerce flourished from the

Dusk over West Lake, Hangzhou

capital at **Kaifeng** and the great cities grew larger, while new ones sprung up all over the south. Agricultural and industrial success opened the doors for artistic developments and the Song is remembered as a time of great poetry, pottery and landscape painting – Su Dongpo (see *Poetry*, p. 61), one of China's greatest poets, lived during the Song. But art doesn't maintain empires and, in spite of the invention of gunpowder and the magnetic compass, the Song's failure to achieve military dominance resulted in the loss of their capital in 1126 to the Jurchen, a sinicized Manchurian tribe which founded its own dynasty, the **Jin** (1115-1234). Forced to re-locate to **Hangzhou** and burdened by humiliating and considerable indemnity payments to their new neighbors, the dynasty became known as the **Southern Song** (1126-1279). They blossomed culturally, but failed politically and militarily.

Yue Fei

The Song dynasty certainly isn't known for its military leadership but **Yue Fei** (1103-42), a young man who was instrumental in subduing rebel bands after the Song were forced south to Hangzhou, emerged as a great hero from this time. He campaigned against the Jurchen in the north but his efforts were nullified by a settlement that made the Southern Song vassals of the Jurchen Jin dynasty. Yue Fei was executed as a supposed traitor, but his determined patriotism won him a place in the hearts of the Chinese people; 20 years later he was recognized as a national hero and reburied in a grand tomb in Hangzhou (see p. 369).

Rise of the Mongols

Military heroes like Yue Fei were in the minority though, and the Song's preoccupation with the arts contributed to their demise. While the Song is remembered as one of China's great dynasties, it never exerted the military dominance over East Asia that had been achieved under the Han and Tang and it was under constant threat of attack from the north. Even after losing Kaifeng and northern China to the Jurchen, the Song still paid little heed to the dangers of outside invasion. The **Mongols**, united under the forceful leadership of **Genghis Khan** at the start of the 13th century, had become increasingly powerful and penetrated deep into Chinese territory, taking Beijing in 1215. In 1279 Kublai Khan, Genghis Khan's grandson, founded the Yuan dynasty.

Yuan Dynasty (1279-1368)

Kublai Khan

The military might of Genghis Khan's marauding Mongolian tribes enabled him to seize control of a vast swathe of land from China to Europe. By the latter part of the 13th century this subsumed the northern Jurchen Jin dynasty and then the Southern Song, making China just another Mongol outpost with Genghis' grandson, **Kublai Khan**, at its head. The Mongols' nomadic traditions were ill-suited to static urban control and they soon adopted the Chinese style of rule, establishing their capital, Dadu, on the site of modern Beijing. Chinese influences were welcomed and rejected to differing extents under the various Yuan leaders, but ultimately the conquerors were changed more than the conquered. However, the Mongol tradition of elected leaders was harder to erase and ran contrary to the Chinese concept of dynastic succession. This remained a problem throughout the Yuan dynasty – each time an emperor died there was an ensuing power struggle. Nevertheless the Yuan was not without its accomplishments and trade across Mongolian Central Asia boomed, bringing a wealth of goods, influences and outside expertise to China

Social Division & Downfall

The lavish court lifestyle of the Yuan, as described by **Marco Polo** during his purported stay, didn't sit well with nomadic traditions and gradually eroded the military might of the Mongols. Fierce resistance and typhoons contributed to military failure in Japan, while little more success was met in the unfamiliar terrain of Southeast Asia.

The reasons for the downfall of the Yuan dynasty are debatable and are manifold, but Kublai Khan's division of subjects into four racial groups certainly did little to endear him to the Chinese majority. Mongols were at the top of the ladder, followed by Central Asians and Westerners; next came the Han Chinese and, on the bottom rung, the southern Chinese. Within this structure, Muslims were granted special privileges and, in the Buddhist world, Tibetans held the key posts. This alienated and angered the Chinese population. Secret Buddhist societies, like the **White Lotus** and **Red Turbans**, emerged and plotted insurrection, which was met with oppression at the hands of Kublai's inept successors, but this only led to more sustained resistance. Finally a full-scale uprising under the monk turned rebel leader, Zhu Yuanzhang, usurped the throne from the child emperor in 1368 and instilled the Ming dynasty.

Ming Dynasty (1368-1644)

Zhu Yuanzhang took the imperial name **Hongwu**, established his capital at **Nanjing** (Southern Capital) and gave the new dynasty its name, Ming meaning brightness. The Ming certainly ruled with far more power than their Mongol predecessors and succeeded in restoring the country to centralized control after a century of foreign rule. While exerting less cultural influence than either the Han or the Tang, the Ming lasted some three centuries and during this long rule the **Forbidden City** was built after **Yongle**, the second emperor, relocated the capital to **Beijing**. Major improvements were made to the **Great Wall** and the imperial kilns at **Jingdezhen** produced the distinctive fine white and blue pottery for which the Ming dynasty is still famous today. Novels also found a place in Ming libraries and classics, such as

Hongwu

The Outlaws of the Marsh and *Romance of the Three Kingdoms*, were written in vernacular language, which made them accessible to a wider audience.

ZHENG HE

Giraffe brought back from West Africa by Zheng He

The Ming dynasty was, for the most part, an inward-looking period that saw ties severed with many old trading partners and thus decreased the amount of contact China had with other countries. But in the early 15th century this was not yet the case and the emperor **Yongle** ordered enormous fleets to explore the oceans in search of knowledge and trade. Commanded by the Muslim eunuch admiral, **Zheng He**, the armadas that set sail from Nanjing were, by far, the biggest the world had ever seen, both in the number of ships and vessel size. The largest *baochuan* (treasure ships) were over 400 feet long, dwarfing all that had come before. In his seven great voyages, Zheng He sailed as far as the west coast of **Africa**, and established trading links in **Malacca** (in modern day Malaysia) and on **India's Malabar Coast**. But, shortly after Zheng He set sail on his final voyage, the Forbidden City was struck by lightning, which was seen as a sign of the gods' displeasure and almost all records of Zheng's grand journeys were destroyed. It is only in the past few years that these ventures have surfaced again and recent research suggests that it was the imperial fleet under Zheng He that paved the way for the likes of **Vasco de Gama** and **Magellan**.

Close of the Ming

The later Ming years produced a string of weak rulers and, as before, power fell into the manipulative hands of court officials and eunuchs who bickered and squabbled but did little to support the country. By the start of the 17th century the country's frontier defenses had fallen apart and a series of peasant uprisings further weakened the Ming power base. In 1644 rebel forces under Shaanxi-born Li Zicheng stormed the capital and the last Ming emperor fled to Jingshan Park, just behind the Forbidden City, where he ended his own life and, with it, the Ming dynasty.

Qing Dynasty (1644-1911)

The **Manchu** descendants of the northeastern Jurchen Jin dynasty saw their chance and moved in, ejecting Li Zicheng and claiming the capital as their own, although it took another few decades before the whole country was under the control of the newly-formed Qing (meaning Clear) dynasty. The Qing immediately imposed their Manchu culture onto the Chinese, obliging men to wear traditional pigtails and making their native tongue the official language. While Ming officials were maintained in some ranks to appease the Chinese, the top posts were reserved for those of Manchu stock. But, as with every culture that had come before and tried to absorb China into its own mold, the Manchus were quickly assimilated into Chinese culture. By the late Qing, its emperors were so cast in the Confucian model that anti-Manchu sentiment had almost ceased to be an issue.

A Golden Age

The early years of the Qing dynasty saw some of China's most proficient leaders and the reigns of **Kangxi** (1661-1722), **Yongzheng** (1723-35) and **Qianlong** (1736-95) are remembered as a golden age. During the 18th century the Qing doubled China's territorial size. Kangxi quashed rebellions and the empire was expanded to include Mongolia, Tibet, Nepal and parts of Central Asia. Kangxi was a patron of the arts and his reign also saw the construction of the **Lama Temple** in Beijing (see p. 171) and the **Mountain Retreat** in Chengde (p. 437), whose northerly temples were added to by Qianlong. Yongzheng and Qianlong's stable periods of rule and continued expansion promoted growth in industry and commerce, while the peasantry was appeased with tax reforms and flood control measures. This was China's last age as a great imperial empire and, at the start of the 19th century, the unified country stood as one of the most wealthy and powerful nations in the world.

Lama Temple

Introduction

Foreign Encroachment & the Opium Wars

Scene from the First Opium War

Western interest in the fabulously wealthy but militarily weak Middle Kingdom grew as more and more merchants made their way to China's shores hoping for a slice of the action. **The British East India Company** was keen to stake its claim and in 1793 Lord Macartney, George III's envoy, was given an audience with Emperor Qianlong in Chengde, but his refusal to kowtow was a sign of things to come. The Qing did not see the need for Western goods or influences and were not prepared to sign any kind of trading agreements with their perceived subordinates. The East India Company wasn't about to give up on such a lucrative opportunity and began to trade Indian-grown opium, rather than silver, in exchange for silk and tea. Addiction became rife and thus demand increased, which led to a futile attempt to ban the trade. In 1840 the emperor ordered the destruction of 20,000 chests of opium under **Lin Zexu**, which provoked the **First Opium War** (1840-2). Two years of bombardment later, the Chinese capitulated and were forced to sign the humiliating Treaty of Nanjing, which included a substantial indemnity payment along with the opening up of new ports and the ceding of Hong Kong to Britain. The **Second Opium War** (1856-60) brought more losses and underlined the fact that, technologically, China had some catching up to do. Further parcels of land were ceded to Britain, France, Germany, Japan, Russia and the US. Anti-Manchu feeling, long buried just beneath the surface, began to rise.

The Taiping Uprising (1850-64)

The insult of these treaties and their crippling indemnities spurred a number of popular rebellions, the most serious of which was the anti-Manchu **Taiping Uprising**. Founded by Hong Xiuquan, who believed he was the Son of God and brother of Jesus, this quasi-Christian cult acquired a million-strong army which captured much of the fertile Yangzi valley and established a capital at Nanjing. The uprising's focus on equality has led many to view it as a precursor to communism, while its draconian laws and desire to obliterate all that had come before is comparable to the destructive might of the Cultural Revolution. The uprising was eventually quashed with European support in 1864, but it left millions dead and other revolts broke out, notably the Nien (1853-68).

EMPRESS DOWAGER CIXI (1835-1908)

Empress Dowager Cixi in 1903

It was during the Taiping Rebellion that the **Empress Dowager Cixi** rose to prominence. Originally a concubine, Cixi managed to maneuver her way to the top and manipulate the ineffective emperors, ruling from behind the scenes between 1861 and 1908. Known as "the Old Buddha," she bore a son to Emperor Xianfeng, who became Emperor Tongzhi and, after outliving him, she installed her nephew, Guangxu, as emperor. After Guangxu's involvement in the 100 Days Reform Movement in 1898, Cixi kept him under lock and key in the Summer Palace while she ruled in his name. The Empress Dowager proved to be a dominant, yet inept leader and, fearing loss of her power, she rejected all attempts at much-needed reform until it was too late. Her lack of judgment catalyzed the Qing's downfall and her most crass misallocation of funds is still there to see today – the grand marble boat that sits in Kunming Lake at Beijing's Summer Palace was built using finances intended to bolster the navy!

The Boxer Rebellion (1899)

Fifty years of foreign domination and civil unrest made for a mood that only needed harnessing in a popular rebellion to challenge the Qing dynasty. This came in the form of the **Boxer (or Righteous Fists) Rebellion**, led by a mystical group who claimed invulnerability through the righteousness of their cause and as a result of their breath-control exercises. Their aim was to overthrow the Qing dynasty and destroy foreign influence in China, causes that struck a chord with the masses. Although Cixi managed to quell the rebellion in 1899, she then tried to use the Boxers to her advantage to rid the country of foreigners. In 1900 war was declared on all foreigners within China and the Boxers were set loose on the streets of Beijing. They killed the German and Japanese ministers, along with any other foreigners they could find, but the British and others were able to hold out until an allied support force arrived and routed the Boxers.

The Fall of Dynastic China

In the aftermath of the Boxer Rebellion, Cixi and the emperor fled to Xi'an leaving her ministers to negotiate yet another humiliating peace settlement. Although Cixi clung to the throne until her death in 1908, the dynastic age had passed and plans were afoot to build a new China, without emperors. Protests against a foreign-owned railway line provided the impetus for the final rebellion against dynastic China. The child emperor **Puyi** could offer no resistance and in 1911 the provisional Republic of China was founded in **Nanjing** under Dr. Sun Yatsen.

The Revolutionary Years

Dr. Sun Yatsen (1866-1925)

Sun Yatsen

Dr. Sun Yatsen is regarded as the **Father of Modern China**. He is also known as Sun Zhongshan (the Chinese translation of his Japanese name, Nakayama, which means Middle Mountain). Sun Yatsen was born in Guangdong province and was then schooled around the globe, including a stint in Hawaii and medical training in Hong Kong. He soon developed an interest in politics and a firm belief in reform. After a failed uprising in Guangzhou in 1895 Sun fled to Europe, the US and Japan, acquiring funds and followers as he moved along. In 1905 he formed the Tong Meng Hui, or **Revolutionary Alliance** in Japan. His vision of modern China was based on the three principles of democracy, nationalism and livelihood and was modeled on the USSR, upon which the **Nationalist Party (KMT)** became increasingly dependent. After founding the republic, Sun was promptly deposed and fled the country. In 1915 he married Soong Qingling (whose sister, Meiling, married Chiang Kaishek in 1927). Returning to China in 1917, he finally gained control of the country in 1923, priming the way for Chiang Kaishek to ascend to the KMT's top spot. Sun died of cancer in 1925 and is still fondly remembered on both sides of the Taiwan Straits. Almost every town has a Zhongshan Road dedicated to him. The leagues of visitors to his mausoleum in Nanjing are further testimony to his significance in modern Chinese history.

The KMT

With the idealistic principles of Dr. Sun Yatsen at the helm, the future initially seemed bright for the republic, but continued Russian interference and China's failure to successfully unite against Japanese aggression meant that a rocky few decades lay ahead for the new China. After **Yuan Shikai** deposed the last emperor, a constitution was drawn up and elections were scheduled for 1913, but it soon became clear that Yuan wanted to establish his own power base. Rather than provoke civil war, Sun Yatsen stepped down from his position as head of the newly formed **Kuomintang** (KMT or Guomindang in Pinyin, National People's Party in English) and once again was forced into exile. Yuan scoffed at Sun Yatsen's withdrawal and in 1914 he made himself president for life. He died two years later and Dr. Sun Yatsen eventually returned to power, albeit heavily reliant on Soviet support. But foreign intervention in China continued to hinder stability and the humiliating terms of the 1919 Treaty of Versailles ignited protests in Tian'anmen Square which became known as the May

Sun Yatsen, seated, & Chiang Kaishek, 1924

Fourth Movement. Sun appointed his protégé, **Chiang Kaishek** (1888-1975, known in China as Jiang Jieshe), as his successor shortly before his death. Under Chiang, the KMT developed into a military dictatorship catering to the social elites, but did little to improve the lot of the rural majority or remove foreign control from the country.

The Emergence of Communism

Nationalism certainly wasn't the only ideology that emerged from the collapse of the imperial age but communism, showcased by the recent Russian revolution, was the only one that offered serious competition to the KMT. You can still visit the building in Shanghai where the **Chinese Communist Party** was founded in 1921 (see *Shanghai, Sightseeing* p. 307). The CCP initially comprised two groups, the first of which was led by Li Dazhao and included **Mao Zedong** among its numbers, while the second was headed by **Zhou Enlai** and was guided by Russian advisors. In 1923, following Russian advice, the CCP and the KMT united to form the **National Revolutionary Army**, which headed north to remove the threat posed by warlords. The expedition was a success but the unity between communism and nationalism was short-lived. In response to a Communist strike Chiang executed many of the CCP's top leaders in 1927, leaving the rest, including Mao Zedong, to flee for the hills.

The Long March

Chiang Kaishek perceived the Communists as a more significant threat than the encroaching Japanese and focused on trying to obliterate the CCP, forcing them deep into the countryside, where their support was strongest.

By 1934 nationalist forces had surrounded Mao Zedong's **mountainous Jiangxi base** and it seemed as if the Communists were on the verge of defeat. Instead, Mao led 100,000 troops on a year-long, 6,000-mile escape, which became known as the **Long March**. They traversed numerous mountain ranges, some of which were snowcapped and only 10,000 made it all the way to Yan'an in Shaanxi province. Although thousands died, the march became a symbol of the grit and determination of Mao and the **Zunyi Conference** along the way firmly established him as the leader of the CCP.

Japanese Encroachment & Civil War

The **1919 Treaty of Versailles** had ratified all of Japan's claims to Chinese territory and they were just waiting in the wings to swoop down on China. China's division presented this opportunity and the Japanese seized Manchuria in 1931, renaming it as the supposedly independent state of **Manchukuo** and installing the last Qing emperor, **Puyi**, as its puppet leader. Anti-Japanese sentiment ran high and in 1936 Chiang Kaishek was seized by his own officers (which became known as the Xi'an Incident) and forced into forging another doomed alliance between the KMT and the CCP. However, Manchuria was just a prelude to full-scale invasion and in 1937 Japanese forces swept into China and captured much of the east coast by 1939, forcing the government to mountainous **Chongqing**, from where they were reliant upon US and British airdrops. By 1940 the Japanese controlled Beijing, Shanghai, Nanjing and Guangzhou, while Chiang Kaishek's failure to distribute mutual arms to the Communist **Red Army** resulted in the collapse of the KMT-CCP alliance. Up to 20 million Chinese are thought to have died during the Japanese invasion and the atrocities committed during the infamous **1937 Rape of Nanjing** are reviled to this day.

Allied & Communist Victory

The Allied victory in World War II and the devastating Hiroshima and Nagasaki bombs spelled the end for Japanese rule in China and, in spite of US support for the KMT, in 1945 it was the Communists who were better placed and prepared to stake their claim on the country. Although the KMT managed to retake the cities, the rural bulk of the country lay in the hands of the Communists. When the **People's Liberation Army** (formerly the Red Army) captured a US arms consignment they had not only the weaponry, but the public support and determination to win and the KMT crumbled. Chiang Kaishek fled to Taiwan, along with much of the treasure from the Forbidden City. In **Taiwan** he established the **Republic of China (ROC)** with the now inconceivable aim of regrouping to return and reinstate the KMT in China.

CHAIRMAN MAO (1893-1976)

Early Years

One of the most iconic figures of the 20th century, **Mao Zedong** (aka Mao Tse Tung) was born in Hunan into a comparatively wealthy grain-dealing peasant family. He was schooled in Changsha and then continued his education in Beijing. In response to the humiliating terms of the 1919 Treaty of Versailles, Mao became involved in the anti-foreign **May 4th Movement**. Russia's Bolshevik Revolution and sponsorship of communist cells in China helped to convince Mao that socialism was the way forward and, when the CCP was founded in 1921, Mao was one of its key members.

Rural Revolt

Mao's time teaching at **Guangzhou's Peasant Training Institute** in the early 1920s reinforced his socialist principles, but also convinced him that revolution must come from the rural masses. After Chiang Kaishek's purge of the CCP, Mao retreated to establish a Communist Red Army base in **Jinggang Shan** in Jiangxi and managed to hold out until 1934 when nationalist forces encircled the mountain. The Communist retreat took the form of the incredible **Long March** (see above), which resulted in huge loss of life and suffering, but it cemented Mao as the resilient

Mao in 1931

leader of the CCP and helped to expand his power base. In spite of Soviet and US support for the KMT, the popular following Mao had engendered carried the CCP to victory.

Revolutionary Zeal

Mao Zedong was hardly seen in public for the first few years of the PRC and was at odds with many of the party's early policies. Reforms and successes soon gave way to failures spurred by Mao's belief that his revolutionary ideals had been usurped. The **Great Leap Forward** and the **Cultural Revolution** (see below) were both a result of ideology overruling reason and had disastrous consequences for China's people, culture and economy. Although he was never a great statesman it was the powerful personality cult that Mao developed which allowed him to implement these crass plans. He was tempered to some extent by his second-in-command, **Zhou Enlai**, but Mao's third wife, **Jiang Qing** fueled his revolutionary zeal. The Cultural Revolution only really ended with Mao's death in 1976 and he was entombed in a grand mausoleum at the center of Tian'anmen Square.

Views of Mao

To western minds Chairman Mao's catastrophic mistakes vastly outweigh his achievements, but within China he is still respected, almost revered, and, although his mistakes are now recognized, they are seen as less significant than his contribution in re-establishing a unified China. The younger generation may be freer in their criticism of Chairman Mao, but his portrait still adorns many rural village living rooms and there are enormous statues of the Great Helmsman, as he has become known, in cities around the country. What Mao Zedong would make of modern China is an interesting question. Although much of the party rhetoric remains intact, economics is at the heart of the new China and the Chairman might be shocked by the hordes of visiting capitalists eagerly snapping up Mao memorabilia, including singing lighters, waving watches and his *Little Red Book* of thoughts.

The PRC Under Chairman Mao

The Early Years of the PRC

When Mao Zedong stood atop Tian'anmen in Beijing and announced the foundation of the People's Republic of China, the world's most populous Communist state was born. Soviet experts were brought in, five-year plans introduced and, although the country was in ruins, an air of optimism prevailed, especially once industry had been nationalized, revitalized and peasants granted land. The **Korean War** (1950-53) was an unneeded distraction at this crucial time of reconstruction, but China's victory reaffirmed faith in the Communist party and the mood was buoyant.

The Hundred Flowers Movement (1956)

However, while all outwardly appeared well, Mao feared that the revolutionary zeal of the party was flagging and he sought to rock the boat a little. His famous slogan "let a hundred flowers bloom, let a hundred schools contend" was intended to draw intellectual criticism of the bureaucracy, but resulted in a torrent of direct attacks on the Communist system itself.

Posters criticizing officials and policy were plastered on democracy wall near the Forbidden City. Mao responded with an anti-rightist campaign that labeled intellectuals as enemies of socialism. Thousands of people were persecuted and sent off to labor camps.

The Great Leap Forward (1958-60)

Having rattled the bureaucracy, Mao set his sights on agriculture and industry. While industry was already thriving with the help of Russian aid and expertise, agriculture was lagging. The Great Leap Forward was introduced in 1958 and was intended to increase both agricultural and industrial efficiency with a goal of matching British steel output within 15 years. Industry was to benefit from seasonal workers and the introduction of rural industry, while agriculture was to be improved through collectivization.

But this utopian plan was flawed from the start as the peasantry, who had only just acquired their land, were reluctant to collectivize. Poor management, overplanting, unachievable quotas and the focus on steel rather than food all contributed to the Great Leap Forward's outright failure. Both the 1959 and 1960 crops failed and the resulting famine left millions dead and the economy in pieces. The situation was worsened when Mao's distrust of Khrushchev's brand of communism led to the breakup of Sino-Soviet relations and Russia's withdrawal of aid. Mao's political reputation was ruined and critics within the party elite, including **Deng Xiaoping** (see p. 25) and Liu Shaoqi, voiced their opinions. Following the failure of the Great Leap Forward, the commune policy was diluted and by the middle of the 1960s the economy had recovered.

The Cultural Revolution (1966-69)

Liu Shaoqi and Deng Xiaoping favored a liberal approach to the economy to encourage private enterprise, an attitude that Mao saw as dissension. Mao sought to crush the so-called "Pragmatists" with the **1966 Great Proletarian Cultural Revolution** which was designed to rid China of the "four olds" – old culture, old customs, old habits and old ideas. Under the guidance of Mao, students in Beijing formed a political militia that became known as the **Red Guards**. They terrorized the country, brandishing the all-empowering *Little Red Book* of Mao's thoughts and quotations. The Red Guards set about erasing any-thing connected with China's his-

Red Guards in Beijing

tory and thousands of buildings, books and businesses were destroyed. Zhou Enlai managed to save a few monuments from Mao's purge, but much of China's greatest art and architecture was lost forever during the Cultural Revolution. Society was turned against itself as quotas were set for the denouncing and re-education of those who were corrupting communism and this ultimately even led to Red Guards reporting one another. Fifteen million people are thought to have died as a result of the Cultural Revolution and millions more were traumatized. While the Cultural Revolution was disastrous in almost every way conceivable it only served to reinforce Mao's seemingly omnipotent cult status. The Cultural Revolution's inextricable link with the Great Helmsman resulted in a failure to address its tragic legacy and even now it is only spoken about in hushed tones.

Broadening the Power Base

Mao with Jiang Qing

In the years prior to his death Mao Zedong was rarely seen and was often represented by his third wife, **Jiang Qing** and her radical supporters, who became known as the Gang of Four. **Lin Biao** had been Mao's strongest supporter during the Cultural Revolution and was primed for leadership, but lost some of his power base as the army became less important. What followed is not exactly clear, but in 1972 it was reported that he had died the previous year in a plane crash en route to the Soviet Union. This might be true, but it is more likely that Lin Biao attempted a coup, was executed and then the story created in order to highlight his treachery. With his closest ally gone, Mao sought to expand his power base and Zhou Enlai's protégé, **Deng Xiaoping**, veteran of the Long March and victim of the Cultural Revolution, returned to office, while **Hua Guofeng** was preened as Mao's successor. Zhou Enlai had been pragmatically limiting the worst extremes of Mao Zedong's ideological policies since the party's inception and his tact and political skill helped China gain a **seat in the UN** in 1971 and establish trade links with the US after **Nixon's visit** in 1972.

Mao's Death & the End of the Gang of Four

However, in early 1976 Zhou Enlai died and, when radicals removed wreaths placed on the Heroes Monument in remembrance of him, a riot ensued. This became known as the **Tian'anmen Incident**, for which the recently returned Deng Xiaoping was ostensibly blamed and once more removed from office. The radicals quickly capitalized on this and gained ground, but this was to be short-lived. Two months after the massive

Tangshan earthquake in Hebei, Chairman Mao died and the Gang of Four had lost their helmsman. Just a month after Mao's death they were arrested; in 1981 they were tried and each sentenced to 20 years in prison. Jiang Qing killed herself and the other three all died under lock and key. The Gang of Four were blamed for the worst excesses of the Cultural Revolution, a factor that helped to keep the Mao cult strong.

The Reform Era (1976-present)

Deng Xiaoping

Deng Xiaoping was born into a wealthy Szechuan family and was educated overseas in France, where he met Zhou Enlai. On returning to China in 1924 he joined the Communist party. He endured the Long March and staved off some of the economic crisis of the Great Leap Forward by establishing a limited free market. During the Cultural Revolution he was publicly humiliated for his moderate ideals and had to work in a tractor factory in Xinjiang as a form of "re-education." Deng favored a capitalist approach to the economy and, on his return to politics, these views made him a target of the Gang of Four. Deng was blamed for the 1976 Tian'anmen Incident (see above) and once more forced out of politics, but Mao's death and the arrest of the Gang of Four marked a turning point which saw Deng rise to the head of the CCP. Two years later Mao's chosen successor, Huo Guofeng, was ousted and **Hu Yaobang** instated.

Deng Xiaoping

Deng quickly began the economic reforms that paved the way for a string of similar economically minded leaders to bring China to where it is today – capitalist in all but name. On a tour of Guangdong province in the early 1990s Deng famously remarked that "I don't care whether the cat is black or white as long as it catches mice," reasserting China's capitalism, albeit under the auspices of "socialism with Chinese characteristics." But economic and political reform did not go hand in hand. While Deng was praised for his economic policies, he will be remembered as the leader who authorized the **Tian'anmen Square Incident** (see below), a show of strength that resulted in worldwide condemnation. Deng died in 1997 and it was **Jiang Zemin**, groomed to be his successor, who oversaw the handover of Hong Kong.

Economic Liberalization

Deng's policies focused on economic liberalization to promote foreign investment and internal entrepreneurship and his **Four Modernizations** (agriculture, defense, industry and science) provided the platform for China's economic transformation and opening up to the world. Technological skill and competency reasserted themselves over ideological commitment as the cornerstones for development. Agricultural collectives were disbanded and farmers were allowed to sell any surplus product on the free market. The number of state-owned businesses was dramatically reduced and there was a distinct shift from heavy to light industry. **Special Economic Zones** such as Shenzhen were designated and the benefits available attracted large-scale foreign investment. Entrepreneurial capitalism was encouraged and, with its huge population and low wages, China quickly reaped the rewards of international trade and has become the **workshop of the world**. Since the start of reforms China has maintained an economic growth rate of 7% and cities like Shenzhen and Shanghai's Pudong have sprung up almost overnight.

Tian'anmen Square Incident (1989)

Confrontation at Tian'anmen Square

But political and social change didn't follow economic reform and, while artists, writers and even the press enjoyed a measure of freedom in the 1980s, the party's true hand was laid out for all to see in Tian'anmen Square in 1989. Deng had sidelined Hu Yaobang in 1987 for his liberal views and when Hu died in 1989, mourning gave way to full-scale protests in Tian'anmen Square. Martial law was ordered in May but, in spite of this, by June there were a million people gathered in the square, organized by the student leaders Wang Dan, Chai Lin and Wu'er Kaixi. Although predominantly students pushing for greater political and social freedom, there was also an urban worker contingent, who were protesting against the endemic corruption within the system, rapid inflation and the economic reforms which had cost many of them their jobs. When the protesters' demands went unanswered, a thousand-plus students went on a hunger strike. Fifty thousand PLA troops were ordered into Beijing and on June 3rd tanks rolled into Tian'anmen Square. The following day soldiers fired into the unarmed crowd and hundreds, possibly thousands, were killed, although it seems unlikely any genuine statistics will ever emerge.

Foreign journalists who had been covering Mikhail Gorbachev's visit to Beijing witnessed much of what happened and, although satellite links were shut down, the world was given a grisly insight into modern China. International condemnation was followed by arms embargoes and there were protests around the globe. The Tian'anmen Square Incident had also illustrated a rift between the hardliners and more progressive elements within the party. While premier Li Peng was in favor of using force to remove the protesters, others such as party secretary Zhang Ziyang, who was dismissed, sympathized with them. Even now the June 4th Movement, as it is known in party-speak, is seldom discussed in China, and you should be sensitive asking questions about it – only do so in private and if you know the person well.

Jiang Zemin

After the Tian'anmen Square Incident **Jiang Zemin**, the former Mayor of Shanghai, who was not connected to the events of June 1989, ascended the party ladder. He became General Secretary in 1989 and President in 1992, taking the reins of power when Deng died in 1997. Jiang oversaw the **1997 British return of Hong Kong** which had been organized in 1984 (see *Hong Kong, The Handover*, p. 489). There was a countdown clock set in Tian'anmen Square and on June 30th there were handover celebrations around the country. Two years later **Macau** followed suit, albeit less dramatically.

The World Stage

Jiang continued with the open door policy and China began to see the rewards of two decades of increased economic freedom. In spite of EU and US arms embargoes, China gained favored trade status with the US under President Clinton in 1995, although relations were strained by allegations that China was stealing **US nuclear secrets**. The situation suffered another setback in 2001 when a US spy plane collided with a Chinese F8 fighter jet and crash landed on **Hainan Island,** China's southernmost point. None of the US crew were hurt but the Chinese pilot died and the incident came at a crucial time when the Bush administration was deliberating over whether to supply Taiwan with arms. Tensions were further raised following the **accidental NATO bombing** of the Chinese Embassy in Belgrade during the Kosovo Crisis a month later. In spite of these complications, economics prevailed and Beijing secured the **2008 Olympics** in 2001 (see p. 139) and China was eventually admitted to the **World Trade Organization** in 2002.

Today's Leadership

In November 2002 a large party conference was held, the net result of which was the emergence of **Hu Jintao** as leader of the CCP and **Wen Jibao** as prime minister. Equally as committed to economic progress as their predecessors, Hu and Wen are a sign of the China to come – socialist doctrine remains only in political jargon, not in practice. Indeed Wen Jibao supported Zhang Ziyang in his sympathetic attitude with the 1989 protesters and as such there is some hope that China may proceed along moderate lines.

The Future

Life for many Chinese is undeniably better than it has ever been; the economy is burgeoning and China is becoming an ever more significant player on the world scene. In the 1970s the most people could aspire to own was a bicycle, a watch and a radio, but these days some young Chinese can shop for the same things as their counterparts in Japan or Taiwan. But modern China is plagued with disparities, which it must face if it is to progress beyond sheer material wealth for its urban dwellers. The **vast population** (see *Population*, p. 42), deterioration of the **environment** (see *The Environment*, p. 32), the threat posed by **respiratory viruses** such as SARS and bird flu (see *Health*, p. 98), **human rights** and **territorial disputes** are just some of the pressing problems facing the Middle Kingdom today.

Doubletalk, Disparities & Discontent

The most basic of China's contradictions lies between the party's anachronistic political rhetoric and the reality of everyday capitalism. Issues like petty theft, prostitution and organized crime syndicates, long thought of as foreign problems, are increasing in modern China and sooner or later the party will have to acknowledge the dichotomy between policy and parlance.

Undoubtedly there is more wealth in China now than ever before, but with more money and education people want greater social freedom and, if this is not forthcoming, it threatens to tear apart the CCP. For all the cell phones, designer apartments and luxury cars found in the cities, little of this newfound wealth has made its way to the rural masses. The gap between rich coastal cities and the poor rural interior is wider than ever and there is massive migration from poorer farming areas to the big cities, although most only manage to find work day-by-day, if at all. The shift away from heavy industry and reduction in state-owned enterprises has added to the numbers of discontented, unemployed transient workers. Their anger is further fueled by the corruption that seems to penetrate every level of the system. In 2001 a group of workers in Dongbei province staged a huge demonstration, which resulted in little but the arrest of the ringleaders. If the interests of these groups continue to be ignored they may be the greatest threat to the system.

Human Rights

Although China's economic growth is making it increasingly easy for the developed world to forget about its human rights abuses and Asian foreign policy, these issues have certainly limited its international standing. Don't be fooled by all the neon lights and Western amenities – internally, China is still a police state where media (including the Internet) is restricted, religions are suppressed and political beliefs can send you to jail. There are estimated to be hundreds of thousands of political prisoners in China's gulags in the northwest of the country, kept in harsh conditions and forced to work as slave labor.

Taiwan & Tibet

China's external outlook is another sensitive area and the continued occupation of Tibet and claim of Taiwan are regarded as internal rather than foreign policy. While the US initially supported Chiang Kaishek when he established the Republic of China in 1949, as the PRC has grown in stature, the rest of the world is succumbing to its wants and Taiwan is stifled in almost any international venture which it attempts. Financial ties remain strong and it is hoped these will win out over military might. However, the 2005 **Taiwan Anti-Secession Law**, which threatened use of force if Chen Shui-bian, Taiwan's first democratic leader, continues to move towards independence, showed China's true colors once again. Tibet, which was seized in 1950, is another tricky subject. The **Dalai Lama** fled to India in 1959 and the party proceeded to populate Tibet with Han Chinese in order to secure their border. When the Dalai Lama selected a new Panchen Lama in 1995, the chosen one was arrested and the Chinese government installed their own representative. Standing in front of Lamaism's grandest building, the Potala Palace, which overlooks Lhasa, you are confronted by the bold red flag of the PRC. Chinese guides speak of Tibet's "liberation," while impoverished Tibetans pass you on the street, and the stunning old city of Lhasa resembles a Han enclave more everyday. The 2006 completion of the China-Tibet railway has further cemented the territory's status as a Chinese province.

Money Makes the World Go Round

"Internal" problems aside, China's growing economic stature is difficult to ignore for the financial fixers of the developed world. Entry into the World Trade Organization, hosting the 2008 Olympics and flourishing Special Economic Zones are all testament to China's improved international standing, but the problems which the country must really address lie with its tremendous population. If the country is to continue supporting its meteoric growth, it is crucial to ensure that wealth filters to the discontented urban and rural sectors. If not, then the danger is that people will once again question their social and political rights and rise against the system which they see as inherently corrupt and oppressive.

However, while inequality is perhaps now more stressed than ever, China is certainly a far more tolerant place than it was even 20 years ago, looking back to its past with more pride. Many of the old beliefs and teachings are managing to find their place in the modern China and for the first time, even farmers dare to dream beyond their station. China truly has been a sleeping dragon for the past few centuries and now it is stirring as the rest of the world watches. If it can deliver the economic goods to a large proportion of the population, then the CCP looks set to survive and the world balance of power will look very different in 2020.

Geography

The Yellow River

At 3.7 million square miles China is the world's fourth-largest country (and is bordered by 15 countries, including Afghanistan to the west, Mongolia to the north, North Korea to the east and Laos to the south). As you'd expect from a country stretching over such a vast area there is enormous geographic diversity. You'll find everything from the world's highest mountains, the **Himalayas**, to one of its lowest points, the **Turpan Depression**. There are lush jungles in Yunnan, tropical beaches in Hainan, the vast **Gobi Desert** in the northwest, frozen wildernesses in the northeast and expansive floodplains in the east. All the mountains, deserts and water, along with the poor quality of much of the country's soil, means that only about 14% of China's land is cultivable. The country has had a large population for a long time and this scarcity of farmable land has resulted in every possible strip being utilized, unintentionally giving rise to some incredible scenery, such as the impossibly steep rice terraces at Longji in Guangxi (see p. 440).

Geology & Topography

Broadly speaking, with the Himalaya as the highest point in the west, the farther east you travel, the lower and flatter the land becomes, although there are mountainous outcrops across the country. Much of Xizang (Tibet) and Qinghai rest on the Tibetan Plateau, which has an average height of 12,000 feet and makes altitude sickness a serious possibility for travelers to this region. China holds half the world's limestone and the southwest's landscape is dominated by a **limestone belt** that stretches all the way from

Yunnan through Guizhou, Hunan, Guangxi and Guangdong and even extends to parts of Fujian. Here lies the inspiration for many a Chinese scroll painting, most notably in the **Li River region** of Guangxi, where you'll find magnificently eroded karst pinnacles stretching for the sky.

Rivers

China has enough mountains and rainfall to provide a water source for most areas of the country, primarily distributed by its three major watercourses, although industry and the immense population has resulted in the pollution of many rivers and lakes. In spite of the generally high rainfall, droughts do occur, particularly in the arid northwest.

The Yangzi & Yellow Rivers

The 4000 mile long **Yangzi** (known as *changjiang*, or Long River, in Chinese, an apt title for the world's third longest river) and the **Yellow River** (named for its silt-laden color) both run west to east, starting their lives high on the **Tibetan Plateau**. The Yangzi then turns south, skirting Szechuan and running through the mountains of Yunnan and makes its first bend through the 13,000-foot-deep **Tiger Leaping Gorge** near Lijiang. Little by little the river gains strength and is a mighty expanse of water by the time it reaches **Chongqing**, where it commences its journey through the famous **Three Gorges**, now dammed at Sandouping, near Yichang (see p. 278). The Long River supplies the massive **Dongting** and **Poyang lakes** with fresh water and then continues through the mighty cities of **Wuhan** and the former imperial capital of **Nanjing**, before spilling into the sea at **Shanghai**. The Yellow River's source is close to the Yangzi's, but soon diverges, running some 3,400

Tiger Leaping Gorge

miles through Gansu, Ningxia, Inner Mongolia, Shanxi, Shaanxi and Henan before emptying out through Shandong in the east.

The Pearl River

A third significant waterway, the Pearl River, starts in the mountains of southern Yunnan and flows through Guangxi, and then, joined by tributaries from the north and east in Guangdong, opens out into the Pearl River Delta which reaches the sea south of **Guangzhou**. This tropically fertile region is one of China's most intensively cultivated areas, banana palms filling seemingly every available piece of land.

Natural Resources

China has a wealth of natural resources, including coal, oil, natural gas and iron ore, mainly found in the northwest, although, as the country has developed and its energy needs have increased, it has shifted from being an exporter to a net importer of oil. Inner Mongolia, Shanxi and Shaanxi are all heavily mined for coal, while the bulk of the oil reserves are under the Taklamakan Desert in Xinjiang. The Chinese have known about the burning properties of coal far longer than we have in the West, and while it has aided the country's industrial development, recently many smaller mines have been closed in response to safety concerns. There are also precious metal and stone deposits to be found, particularly in the west, and these have been utilized since early times to produce tools and fine arts.

The Environment

Environmental degradation poses a very real threat to the nation as increasingly frequent **dust storms** sweep through the north of the country and the rivers in many cities run black. Despite reducing its heavy industry base and the grand **Three Gorges Dam hydroelectric project** (which creates as many environmental problems as it solves – see p. 278), China is one of the world's most polluted countries. The government is now starting to address these issues with projects like the **Green Great Wall** that aims to combat soil erosion in the north of the country through reforestation, and by raising taxes on environmentally damaging products, from disposable wooden chopsticks to luxury cars. But there is still a long way to go.

Climate

 Again, as you'd expect in such a vast country, there is much variety in China's weather, though away from coastal and mountainous areas it could be broadly categorized as a continental climate – that is, extremely hot in the summer and very cold in the winter.

The **north** enjoys roughly six months of heat, but has to endure cold weather for the rest of the year, with temperatures rarely creeping above freezing in Beijing between December and March. Almost all of the rainfall in this region comes in July and August. This part of the country is also subject to **dust storms** during the spring and summer months, which can last days and leave everything coated with a fine layer of dust. They are exacerbated by the deforestation and desertification of the land to the north and west.

China's **northwest** offers the country's greatest extremes, from blistering 110°F in summer, to an arctic -45°F in winter. Whenever you come, you're unlikely to see much precipitation in this extremely arid region, which is home to the deserts of the **Gobi** and the **Taklamakan**.

Central China gets exceptionally hot and steamy in the summer. The "**Three Furnaces**" along the Yangzi – Chongqing, Wuhan and Nanjing – are renowned for their Turkish-bath-like summers, though Shanghai is barely any less stifling. The same region gets bone-chillingly cold during the short winter, made all the more so by the damp and lack of central heating south of the Yellow River. Although Shanghai is warmed marginally by the sea, it can still feel bitter in the winter months. Winter is the driest part of the year, though all seasons see plenty of precipitation in this part of the country.

The **south** has something of a **subtropical climate**, with swelteringly hot and humid summers and comparatively mild winters that only last from January to March, though the farther you move away from the sea the colder it can get. The rainy season in the south varies according to exactly where you are, but generally falls between May and August. Hainan Island, nestled between China and Vietnam, lies on the same latitude as Hawaii and is warm throughout the winter and roasting in summer. The southeast coast is subject to **typhoons** (from *taifeng*, meaning great wind), the Asian equivalent of hurricanes, between June and October.

Flora & Fauna

China has a diverse range of wildlife befitting a country of its size, but if you come with great expectations you may be disappointed – there's less to see on a day-to-day basis than you'll find in some of the neighboring Southeast Asian countries. However, for those who have the time and energy to delve a little deeper, there are still treasures to be found and even a two-week city-based trip should show you some of country's offerings.

Causes for Concern

Several factors have contributed to the loss of Chinese flora and fauna. The sheer scale of humanity has meant that many species' habitats have been destroyed. The Chinese have consumed much of the original fauna, sometimes eating literally whatever they could find due to famine. Traditional medicinal beliefs relating to the efficacy of certain rare animal parts have further contributed to the demise of many species. The Communist regime has also played its part in the destruction of China's environment, often showing flagrant disregard for the laws of nature. Crazed periods such as the Great Leap Forward (see p. 23) saw attention focused on increasing short-term output to ridiculous extremes – fields were overplanted and the crops and wildlife suffered. More recently environmentally damaging activities such as logging, pollution and some questionable projects, including the Three Gorges Dam (see p. 278), have compounded the problem.

Habitats

As you'd expect from a country as vast as China, it has a diverse range of habitats, from wetland to desert, tundra to tropical forest and mountains to plains. Agriculture has replaced most of China's native forest, although there are still large expanses in the northeast that remain relatively untouched. The east is so highly developed that little of its original native habitat survives, but away from the coast there are still wild pockets, some of which have been designated national parks and forest reserves, such as Shennongjia in Hebei, which is reputedly home to a yeti-like creature! Out in the mountainous western regions there are extensive grasslands, which provide a festival of wild flowers in summer (July and August) and also support some fauna. The deserts of the northwest don't offer the same biodiversity as other parts of the country, but hold more wildlife than you might expect, including wild Bactrian camels.

National Parks & Conservation Projects

China was a late starter in the conservation race and, while the situation has certainly improved, it is already too late for some species and there is a long way to go to save those that remain. But all is not lost and hope remains. The first national park was established in Guangdong in 1956 and there are now over a thousand reserves, covering around 5% of China's land area, with dozens more planned. Reforestation projects are also starting in the hope of reducing desertification in the northwest. The work of a small number of dedicated individuals has highlighted the plight of some animal species, most notably the giant panda and this, in turn, has led to more widespread interest in wildlife and the environment, particularly among the younger generation.

The government is also realizing the severity of China's environmental situation and, after decades of abuse, seems to be coming round to a more sustainable approach to development. This is aided by the increasing importance of tourism in China, and as more and more upwardly mobile Chinese want to witness their country's native wildlife, there seems to be an economic as well as a conservation incentive. However, unless environmental tourism is responsibly managed, it could further degrade the environment (see *Eco-Travel*, p. 131, for more) and in a predominantly (and ever more polarized) poor country, people's own survival and prosperity is still the ultimate concern. Conservation areas are often poorly protected, meaning that poaching and logging still occur in these supposedly safe zones.

Conservation Organizations

If you're interested in contributing (whether financially or physically) or just learning more about some of the conservation projects around the country then try some of the organizations below. All are registered charities and staffed by volunteers so any help is welcome and if you're keen to donate to their cause you can do so online.

Friends of the Earth (www.foe.org.hk)

This successful global conservation organization runs a number of projects throughout Hong Kong and China. Some of their successes to date include preventing the building of a power station and a golf course in two of Hong Kong's country parks. They are also promoting pollution awareness and the use of unleaded fuel in the cities.

Greenpeace (www.greenpeace.org/china/en)

Greenpeace International has been publicizing issues such as environmental awareness, climate change, reusable energy and non-violent action here since 1997. Operations to date include the uncovering of illegal logging operations in Yunnan province, assistance in the development of ozone-friendly industrial technology and the promotion of sustainable energy sources, particularly wind-power.

Wildlife

While China is home to countless species you are only likely to encounter a small number of these, and to see most of them in the wild you'll have to invest some serious time and energy. This said, China has an enormous number of avian species and wherever you are you are likely to see a host of birds – even Hong Kong has its share and it's worth visiting the new **Wetlands Park** (see p. 528) and **Mai Po Marshes**. If birding is your primary interest, it's worth heading to the remote northeast of the country, which is notable for herons and cranes that abound between April and September. The northeast also offers some of China's last remaining great wilderness and is home to bears, musk deer and reindeer, moose and tigers. In terms of flora, although there are plants and flowers throughout the country, for botanists the far west is the place to go. Ever since Joseph Rock, the 20th-century explorer, made it out here and catalogued what he saw, Yunnan's incredible floral biodiversity has attracted specialists. The grasslands here and in Szechuan and Tibet also support a host of animals, including wild yaks and argali sheep. The drier climes to the north of here in Inner Mongolia and Gansu give rise to little in the way of wildlife, but are traversed by that old desert favorite, the Bactrian or two-humped camel. It's impossible to list all the creatures that there are to see in China, let alone describe them, but below I've selected some of the plants and animals you're most likely to see, along with a list of endangered animals.

Animals & Plants in Chinese Mythology & Medicine

The importance of plants and animals in Chinese culture can be seen in many aspects of the country's arts, mythology and medicine. Chinese mythology owes a great deal to its flora and fauna, both real and imagined. The Chinese Zodiac pays tribute to this allegiance, with people born under each sign supposedly exhibiting characteristics of that animal (see p. 53). Both animals and plants are deemed to hold certain attributes and these are recorded in history through statuary such as Bixi, the enduring and strong tortoise, and cranes, which represent happiness and longevity. Traditional Chinese medicine makes great use of both flora and fauna, from mountain herbs to animal parts. Ironically many of the supposed benefits are based on the perceived strengths of certain creatures – the tiger is seen as wily, virile and powerful, thus these qualities can be attained by its consumption. The talents of various creatures are also put to use in different forms of martial arts, from crane to tiger.

Cranes are symbols of happiness & longevity

Flora

Bamboo – This unique fast-growing woody grass is found all over southern China and is inextricably entwined in Chinese history, symbolizing regeneration. Bamboo is part of everyday life and is used to this day in everything from cooking to scaffolding. There are countless varieties; the graceful "phoenix tail," which you'll find around Guilin and Yangshuo, is one of the most beautiful. Walking through a misty bamboo thicket as it creaks and groans is an enchantingly Chinese experience.

Bamboo forest (Ewen Bell)

Banyan – This powerful parasitic tree begins life as a seed dropped high in the branches of another tree. It then trails roots down to the ground and in time surrounds and envelopes other trees, sometimes melding several into one and creating the shade for which they are celebrated. Banyans are associated with Buddhist history and often form the focal point of villages or temples – locals frequently take some respite from the sun and enjoy a game of Chinese chess beneath them.

Chrysanthemum – Chrysanthemum flowers are familiar in many parts of the world but here can be found almost everywhere. They bloom in late autumn and many cities have flower exhibitions during this time. To the Chinese, they are considered medicinal, used in tea and often served as a delicacy.

Lotus- The delicate lotus flower (or water lily) is striking and found in most parts of lowland China. Lotus ponds can be seen in most parks and public gardens throughout the country and the roots make for a tasty vegetarian snack commonly used in cooking. You'll also see the distinctive salt-shaker-style pod in local food markets.

Lotus flower

Orchid - The orchid is prevalent in Southeast Asia and has long evoked exotic images of the East. Its manifold varieties are appreciated by botanists and gardeners the world over and fetch high prices. Orchids have grown for thousands of years in China and can been seen throughout the seasons, particularly in the south.

Osmanthus – The tree which gives Guilin its name has a sweet-smelling blossom and adds a splash of color to the city in autumn. Its intoxicating fragrance has been written about through the ages, and the flowers are used to produce both tea and wine.

Peony – The city flower of Luoyang, the peony is also one of China's national flowers, and there are over 500 varieties in the country.

Wintersweet – As one of China's most popular floral species, the wintersweet is a common sight in Yunnan and Szechuan, where its hardiness allows flowering even in the snow.

Fauna

Yaks on the move (Tot Foster)

While China has a fascinating array of different species, many of which are very rare or endangered (see below), it's far more likely that you'll come across the country's more common birds, insects and domestic animals. Some of the more spectacular bird species include **cormorants** (see *Yangshuo, Adventures On Water* p. 429), **cranes, herons** and **kingfishers**, as well as larger birds of prey such as **eagles**. Of the insects you may encounter, the **praying mantis** is probably the most fascinating and comes in a range of colors, from dusty brown to lurid green. The insect's name derives from it's seeming to be prostrated in prayer and it is renowned for its predatory nature, especially the female, which often kills the male post-copulation. **Dragonflies** and **butterflies** are also abundant throughout China, and the south claims some of the largest in the world, including the giant atlas moth butterfly whose wingspan can measure over eight inches. In parkland areas you're likely to see **squirrels** and, if you're lucky, **deer**. For those traveling into western mountain regions, you'll likely encounter **yaks**, both wild and domesticated and, if you're southward-bound, you may see **monkeys**. China's rivers also offer an array of wildlife, including **river dolphins** (see list below), **sturgeons** and even **alligators**.

Endangered Species

Brown Eared Pheasant – China has a quarter of the world's 196 species of pheasant, including the rare brown eared variety. It is unique to China and lives in high mountain coniferous forests in Shaanxi and Hebei provinces.

Chinese Alligator – The presence of alligators in China's Yangzi River may come as a bit of a surprise to many, but these reptiles once filled the waterways. Changing environments and dam construction have all played their part in the large population decline to less than 100 in the wild. They still inhabit parts of the Yangzi in Anhui and a research and breeding center has been established to help increase awareness and numbers.

Chinese alligator

Cranes – Cranes are large and spectacular birds and have cultural significance throughout the world (symbolic of new life and of babies in the West and of longevity and happiness in China). They are noisy, colorful and like to "dance." Worldwide, there are 15 species, of which 11 are threatened. Eight of these species breed or winter in China, and three of them are endangered – the Siberian crane, the sarus crane and the red-crowned crane.

Crested Ibis – The crested ibis is among the 50 most endangered birds, with fewer than 250 mature individuals worldwide. There are none left in their native habitat in Japan, and only a handful breeding in the Qingling Mountains of China. The government has invested heavily in their preservation and, with help from the WWF, these beautiful birds may just survive.

Golden Monkey – This small golden-coated monkey's distinctive up-turned nose has earned it a nickname of the 'snub nose' monkey. By the mid-1980s it was estimated that only 200 were left in the wild, but, after successful breeding projects and aid from the government, their population has increased dramatically to over 800 in 2006.

Grey Baiji (Yangzi River Dolphin) – With only five left in captivity and probably fewer than 100 in the wild, China has all but lost one of the world's most unusual mammals. Pollution, increasing river traffic and dam construction have all contributed to the demise of the *baiji* and it seems it will soon be gone forever.

A cuddly red panda

Red Panda (Lesser Panda) – A very distant relation of its giant namesake, the red panda is a cuddly raccoon-like creature that lives in the trees of southern China, the Himalayas, India and Nepal.

Siberian Tiger & South China Tiger – These are some of the world's most intriguing big cats, but are dangerously near extinction. The fur trade, demands of Chinese medicine and a rapidly vanishing habitat have all played a part in their demise. There are only an estimated 20 wild Siberian tigers in northern China, and 60 South China tigers along the Yangzi River valley. In spite of protection efforts, the future doesn't look bright for these beautiful creatures.

Snow Leopard – The snow leopard is amongst China's most endangered animals. while their pelts fetch as much as US$50,000 on the illegal fur market, their bones are also popular as a traditional Chinese medicinal remedy, factors which when combined with decreasing

Siberian tigers

habitat have seen their numbers dwindle. Now protected, and bred in captivity, some increase in numbers is being seen, but it's highly unlikely you'll ever see them in the wilderness of their Gansu, Xinjiang, Inner Mongolia and Tibetan Plateau ranges.

The Giant Panda

The giant panda is China's most famous and one of its most endangered species. Numbers have been dwindling since they were hunted by both Chinese and foreigners at the start of the 20th century, although deforestation has been the greatest recent threat – over 50% of their habitat was lost between 1974 and 1989. However, since the plight of our furry black and white

Panda cub, seven months old, from
Wolong Nature Preserve, Sichuan (Sheila Lau)

friends was brought to the world's attention in the 1980s, some of their habitat has been protected. Their range used to extend from Beijing as far south as Yunnan, but today they are confined to parts of Shaanxi, Szechuan and Gansu. Estimates suggest that there are about 1,600 pandas left in the wild but, due to their remote habitats, the accuracy of these figures is uncertain. There are 188 pandas in captivity around the world and, with new breeding and research centers, international recognition and the WWF, things are beginning to look up for these cuddly looking creatures, but there is still a long way to go in order to rebuild their numbers. The centers aim to help breeding problems and assist research, with the ultimate goal of reintroducing the pandas in to the wild. In April 2006, the first ever captive panda was released in the Qingling Mountains in Shaanxi and more releases are planned, although the jury is out as to whether this may be premature given the limited amount of habitat.

Increasing panda numbers involves preventing poaching and protecting panda habitats, but also ensuring that newborns manage to survive. Female pandas only reproduce once every two years and high infant mortality rates both in the wild and in captivity have hindered population growth. Although roughly half of all panda pregnancies result in twins, it's rare for two to survive, since the mothers reject the weaker sibling to nurture and protect the stronger. In captivity, one twin is taken away from its mother and sibling and re-introduced to the family at a later date, although this had been unsuccessful until new techniques including "twin swapping" and an accurate simulation of panda milk were introduced. Recent breakthroughs like these have led to a record number of births and an increased survival rate. Sixteen cubs were born in 2005, including a wonderful five sets of twins; all of them are still alive and well today. Success has also been enjoyed in the US, where baby Tai Shan was born in 2005 after his mom, Mei Xiang, was artificially inseminated. If captive numbers can reach 300 individuals, then this population should be able to maintain itself and its genetic diversity, though this is no viable substitute for wild populations.

> Did you know that the first panda was taken out of China in 1938 by Ruth Harkness, who passed the cub off as a puppy! 40,000 people came to visit the baby panda Su Lin on its first day in its new home at the Brookfield Zoo in Chicago.

Visiting the Pandas

Unless you have a number of months to go trekking into the wild, your best option is to visit one of the WWF-sponsored breeding and research centers at Chengdu and Wolong in Szechuan or at the Zhouzhi center in Shaanxi (see *Sightseeing, Around Xi'an*, p. 251). Here, you can see pandas in their natural habitat and, although they are still confined, the enclosures are large and the animals are well cared for. If you're not visiting these areas there are pandas in the zoos, but this is an experience far removed from a wild sighting, and conditions leave a lot to be desired.

Animal Protection Organizations

Animals get a rough deal in many parts of Asia and China is no exception, particularly because of the predilection for exotic animal parts as remedies used in TCM. The websites listed below offer information and ways to help animals in China:

Animals Asia (www.animalsasia.org). This Hong Kong-based charity established in 1998 runs a variety of animal welfare programs in China. China Bear Rescue has helped over 200 bears in China escape a torturous life of captivity. There is still a huge medicinal market for bear bile and many undergo the horrific technique of bile extraction known as 'free dripping.'

WWF (www.wwf.china.org). Although they are most readily associated with pandas in China, the WWF is involved in wide-ranging projects throughout the country that aim to protect various animals through a variety of means, including preserving their habitats, rehabilitation and education.

Population

In 2 AD China's population was estimated at nearly 58 million by the world's first large-scale census. In spite of famine, plague, epic natural disasters and mass exodus, the population has grown steadily since then and today stands at over 1.3 billion people, making it the world's most populous nation. In spite of a quarter-century of the one-child policy, it looks as if it will maintain pole position until at least the middle of the century, when India may take the lead.

The One-Child Policy

Overpopulation led to the radical step of the one-child policy in 1979. It stated that couples had to obtain permission before trying to have a child and if they failed to do this then the pregnancy would be terminated. Minority families living in the countryside were (and are) allowed two children, but in the cities if families had more than one child they had to pay punitive taxes. Although the policy has been effective in limiting population growth, it is China's tre-

The future is brighter for China's educated urban population (Tot Foster)

mendous number of people that has allowed its meteoric development. Along with the associated problems of gender imbalance and Little Emperors (see below), the aging population has led to fears that China will lose the competitive edge afforded by its vast numbers. As people enjoy more wealth and social freedom, they also want to choose how many children they can have, with two being the popularly cited number among the urban elite. In response to these factors, regulations have been relaxed a little and couples whose first child is a girl and who meet other requirements such as waiting for four years after their first-born, can now have a second child. There are suggestions that the policy may be scrapped altogether in the near future, but the official party line says nothing of the kind.

No need for a stroller

Gender Imbalance

Boys were always favored over girls as in marriages the bride's family had to pay a dowry and the new couple would live with and help to support the groom's family. Limiting the number of children to one per family made having a boy crucial to the family line and led to thousands of **female abortions** and **infanticides**. Although ascertaining a child's sex by ultrasound is theoretically illegal, in practice this procedure is available in China for less than US$100 and is commonplace. Thus many couples wait to see the child's sex and then only proceed with the pregnancy if it's a boy. The result of this isn't yet fully recognized, but even the government admits that there are 119 boys born for every 100 girls and already China has some 60 million more men of reproductive age than women.

Little Emperors

In the countryside the policy means that there are fewer people to work the fields, a problem exacerbated by **rural to urban migration**. In the cities some families are now enjoying prosperity unimaginable in their parents' time but have to focus all the love that used to be spread among many children onto their single (or, if they're lucky, two) offspring. This is evident in the legion of overfed, spoiled young "emperors" being carted around expensive shopping centers.

People

The Han

The Han was one of China's earliest and greatest dynasties (see p. 8) and lends its name to the ethnic group which makes up 93% of the population today. One of the words for the Chinese language, *hanyu* literally means Han language. The Han are *the* people of the Middle Kingdom and for the longest time considered most of the other minority groups as insignificant but savage barbarians. Central China is the Han heartland, but in politically sensitive areas like Tibet, there are incentives to attract Han people to settle there and help maintain the region's "loyalty." Through the course of history encroachments by outside influences were subsumed into the all powerful Han culture.

The Minorities

In addition to the Han, the Chinese population also includes some 55 ethnic groups, which are as diverse as you'd expect for a land as vast as China. The southwest is where you'll find the greatest number of minorities, many of whom are more akin to the hilltribes of Southeast Asia than Han China. Guangxi, Guizhou and Yunnan are home to a number of China's most colorful ethnic groups including the **Bai**, the indigo-clad **Dong**, the **Miao**, the **Naxi**, the **Yao** and the **Zhuang**, all of whom have their own distinct culture, customs and architecture. In the north and northwest there are wilder

groups, such as the nomadic **Mongol** and **Tibetan** herders, as well as Central Asian horsemen like the **Kazakh** and the **Tajik**. While central and eastern China are predominantly Han, other groups such as the **Hakka** retain importance in the region and examples of their traditional architecture are still to be found in the southeast and Hong Kong's New Territories.

Variously feared, ignored, persecuted and condescended to through history, the minority groups' biggest threat today comes from the migration of its youth to the big cities. During the early years of communism in China, there seemed little hope for minority groups and their culture, but these days the Chinese are much more curious about their other countrymen. Guest-

houses, hiking and witnessing traditional life have all become big sellers and are, to some extent, helping to preserve minority cultures. And if you head off the beaten track (even just a few days in the valleys behind **Longji**, see p. 440) you'll find communities seemingly untouched by time where cultural traditions have been maintained for centuries. You can help preserve these traditions by buying goods made in the villages, asking for regional specialty foods and using local guides.

Naxi women in Yunnan (Magalie L'Abbé)

Religion & Philosophy

China's history is steeped in overlapping religious belief and philosophy. Starting with animist worship, religion developed through **Taoism** and **Confucianism**, the latter of which, with its hierarchical code of moral values, was more a philosophy than a religion. Outside influence brought **Buddhism** to the country and together these three belief systems are the foundation of religion in China – known as **The Three Teachings**. With the onset of communism, socialism was the new doctrine; religion in all its forms was suppressed and only practiced secretly. In the last 20 years, however, religion has reemerged, albeit in party-approved form and far from free. Indeed, several religious groups are outlawed in China, such as *Falun*

Gong (meaning Wheel of Life, a quasi-Buddhist order), but they flourish in Hong Kong and Taiwan. The Three Teachings remain the most prominent beliefs in modern China, although some would argue they come second to capitalism, albeit with socialist characteristics! **Christian missionaries** and **Muslim merchants** have also had their parts to play in China's religious history, with the result that today most cities of any size have both churches and mosques to serve their sizeable Christian and Muslim populations. It is difficult to gauge the actual size of these groups, as only "official" religions are included in statistics, meaning that the millions who worship in secret according to other doctrines aren't counted. Although there are still devout followers of each of the Three Teachings, belief among the populace can seem ambiguous and Taoist temples can show elements associated with Buddhism and vice versa.

Buddhism

Though Indian in design and containing elements of Hinduism, like so many outside influences that reached China, Buddhism was adopted and adapted to fit Chinese beliefs and needs. Aspects of Buddhist *dharma* could be likened to Taoism and the fact that Buddhism didn't outlaw recognition of other gods allowed it to incorporate facets of traditional folk religions, and to prosper in China.

History in China

Buddhism came to China in 67 AD, and the first Buddhist place of worship is believed to have been the **White Horse Temple** in Luoyang, Shandong province, founded in 68 AD, by two Indian monks who arrived on a white horse. However, the religion only really gained popularity after the arrival of **Bodhidharma**, an Indian monk who is said to have journeyed to **Shaolin Temple** in the fifth century and is also credited with the development of **Chinese martial arts** (see p. 65). The Tang dynasty was Buddhism's great era in Chinese history and monks numbered in the hundreds of thousands. It was also during this period that China's great Bud-

The White Horse Temple

dhist cave art flourished, most spectacularly at **Longmen** near Luoyang in Shandong province, at **Dunhuang** in Gansu province and at **Dazu** in Szechuan province.

Life of Sakyamuni

Buddhism is a religion borne of Sakyamuni, a Nepali prince, also known as Siddhartha Gautama. Having been sheltered from the harsh realities of life by living within a palace, Siddhartha was shocked by his first glimpses of the outside world and renounced his earthly possessions in the search for release from the earthly cycle of life, death and re-birth. After several years as an ascetic, Sakyamuni realized that physical vigilance in the form of fasting, contortion and the like were not the answer. Finally he achieved *nirvana* (enlight-

Chief statue (Lushena Buddha) from the Longmen Grottoes

enment) under the *bodhi* tree in **Bodhgaya** in Bihar, India, and became Buddha (the Enlightened One), though he never claimed to be anything more than a man. He then gave sermons at Sarnath on the banks of the Ganges, where he spoke of realizing the existence of suffering and finding the *dharma*, or path to enlightenment, through meditation and giving up the desire for all worldly things. Sakyamuni spent the remainder of his life traveling around the Ganges floodplains in northeastern India, teaching and receiving visitors.

Sakyamuni

Basics of Buddhism

Buddhism is based on realization of the **Four Noble Truths**: Life means Suffering; The Origin of Suffering is Attachment; The Cessation of Suffering is Attainable; and The Path to the Cessation of Suffering. The way to achieve enlightenment is detailed in the Eightfold Path. Pinning down exactly what enlightenment constitutes is a tricky one, but could be described as an omniscience of all beings, in all their lives, the consequences of their actions and thus the symbiosis inherent in the cosmos!

Schools of Buddhism

Yellow Hat monks

Buddhism has many forms, the most significant of which are *mahayana* (Greater Vehicle), as practiced in China, and *theravada* (Lesser Vehicle), prominent in Southeast Asia. *Theravada* is the version which originally arrived in China, but its focus on gaining *nirvana* as an individual had little hold with the regimented group mentality prominent in the Middle Kingdom. Thus, *mahayana*, which indicated that release could only come as a whole, and that *arhats* (known in China as *luohan*) and *bodhisattvas* (enlightened beings who choose to stay on earth) would remain on this earth to guide others, was far more suited to China. Over time, *bodhisattvas* and *arhats* came to be worshipped themselves and local deities were brought into the fold.

Chan (Zen) Buddhism, a school of meditation, also found its feet in China and has gained standing around the world, facilitated by its belief that you don't have to be a monk or recluse to achieve enlightenment. Tibet also managed to absorb Buddhism into its pre-existing shamanistic religion, *Bon*, greatly aided by Guru Rinpoche, an Indian Buddhist, who was invited to the kingdom in the seventh century. The various Tibetan Buddhist schools are collectively known as **Lamaism**, of which Gelugpa (or Yellow Hat) is the most prominent today and includes the Dalai Lama and the Panchen Lama among its following.

Confucianism

Confucianism is seen as the most Chinese of its belief systems and, though it was never intended as a religion, if you visit a Confucian temple and see people worshipping him, you'd struggle to see it purely as a philosophy. Confucianism has also had an effect outside of the Middle Kingdom, especially in Korea. Though there is doubt as to whether Confucius actually ever lived, what is certain is that his system of hierarchical values continues to affect modern Chinese thought and interaction.

The Life Of Confucius (551-479 BC)

Confucius (*kong fu zi* in Chinese) was supposedly born in 551 BC and experienced poverty in the early part of his life, only managing to become a junior official through hard study. Disheartened by the chaos and disorder as the Zhou dynasty declined into the **Warring States Period** (see *Zhou Dynasty*, p. 6), Confucius sought to implement a system that would restore order. To this end he opened a number of private schools where he instructed thousands of students in his code of moral values. His style of teaching was more in tune with modern methods than those of the day, promoting elicitation and student participation over traditional learning by repetition. Confucius

Confucius

traveled to the various states and gave lectures on his beliefs about hierarchy within all structures, from families to governments. After the rejection of his advice by many of the state leaders, Confucius returned to his ancestral home town, **Qufu**, in Shandong province, as an old man. He continued his teachings and his following grew. It was also during this time that he contributed his thoughts to the writings of the day, now known as The Five Classics, which includes the *Book of Songs* and the *I Ching*, or *Book of Changes*. *The Analects* is a collection of Confucius' sayings published many years after his death which, along with the rest of the Confucian canon, became required reading for civil officials.

His Philosophy

Confucius' philosophy directed that if the correct hierarchy was in place and individuals treated and respected one another according to this structure, then life would be harmonious. At the top of the scale was the emperor, moving down through scholars and officials, peasants, merchants, craftsmen, soldiers, slaves and, at the bottom of the ladder, the underclasses, which included beggars and prostitutes. He placed major importance on an appropriate obedience and sense of duty within these relationships, particularly between subjects and their emperor, a wife and her husband, children and their parents and younger and older brothers. His belief was that only between friends should there be equality. Respect was based on the **five Confucian virtues** of benevolence, propriety, righteousness, trustworthiness and wisdom. Confucius didn't advocate ancestor worship, but the emphasis on respecting one's family elders has helped to maintain its importance in Chinese culture.

Confucianism as a Religion

Confucius didn't see his dictates as religious and it wasn't until after he died that he became something of a deity, with temples around the country dedicated to him. Religion aside, his impact on the Chinese bureaucracy is evident in the fact that his teachings formed the basis of civil service examinations until the early 20th century. Though shunned during the early years of communism and the Cultural Revolution, Confucian values remain in some senses and worship has re-emerged in recent times. For proof of this, look no further than Qufu, a town devoted to Confucius, where you'll find hordes of visitors exploring a mansion complex that almost rivals the Forbidden City and a vast forest containing the graves of the entire Confucian clan (which numbers in the thousands). While often rebuffed during his lifetime, and intermittently purged through history, Confucius' theories have influenced and affected the course of Chinese thinking for over two thousand years.

Taoism

Taoism is China's only native religion (since Confucianism isn't a religion as such), and was developed by the semi-mythical figure, **Lao Zi**, who is traditionally held to have lived in the sixth century BC. Lao Zi (Old Boy) is also credited with writing Taoism's elemental work, the *Tao Te Jing* (*The Classic of the Way and Power*), though this was probably compiled some time after his death and is thought to be more of a collaboration than a book by a sole author. **Zhuang Zi** was another great proponent of Taoism, who supposedly lived in the fourth century BC, rejecting rank and luxury for a humble life of reflection. His book of parables, *The Zhuang Zi*, is Taoism's second great text.

Though Taoism began as a religion without deities, over time it acquired a plethora of them, most notably the **Eight Immortals**. It also attracted imperial patronage and established a formalized priesthood. Taoism was soon an all-encompassing religion, its flowing energy nestled somehow next to the rigidity of Confucianism. But with increasing popularity came dilution and the quest for immortality became the primary goal for some Taoists, leading purists to separate themselves from the mainstream.

Taoist Beliefs

The taiji symbol

Taoism's beliefs are difficult to express succinctly, but are based on trying to attain harmony within the natural world, balancing its hard, male *yang* aspects with the soft, fluid, female *yin* facets. The *taiji*, commonly known as the *yinyang* in the West, is a symbol of this harmony. The smaller inner circles represent the presence of *yin* within *yang* and vice versa. Taoism centers on the belief that there is a unifying force or energy which flows through everything. The Taoist aims to ride the **Tao** (the Way) to a long, healthy life and even immortality, believing that worldly possessions and desires can cause a being to lose sight of this path. This belief means that Taoists often lived reclusive existences. While Taoist harmonious ideals and the concept of *wu wei* (achievement through inaction) are pacifist in essence, the religion has also fostered its own form of martial arts, born in the mountain temples of Wudang Shan (see p. 66 for more).

Visiting Temples

Visiting a working temple in China can seem like a daunting and confusing prospect. There are a pantheon of gods and all manner of associated rituals, but as a foreigner you'll be forgiven most of your *faux pas*, and in temples popular with tourists many Chinese visitors may appear to have little more idea than you! Dress conservatively, although you may well see those who don't.

The entrances of Buddhist temples are often presided over by a pair of metal or stone lions. The entrance hall usually has a statue of the "Happy Buddha," as **Maitreya** has become known, along with menacing statues of the Four Heavenly Kings. Buddhist temples are built along a central axis with a series of courtyards and

Making an offering at Tanzhe Temple
(Su-San Tan)

The "Happy Buddha" Maitreya

lesser shrines leading to the most important and grandest hall at the rear. These halls usually hold statuary, which believers bow to with the hands clasped. The courtyards are separated by screened gateways in order to prevent bad spirits (who can only travel in straight lines) from entering. In theory you should walk clockwise around Buddhist temples but this isn't always possible and you'll see plenty of locals going the other way.

You'll see a host of gods in most Buddhist temples, though **Sakyamuni**, with his tightly knit hair, is the most significant and is often shown in past,

Incense coils spiral above a grand cauldron burner

present and future form, while **Guanyin** (Kun Iam in Cantonese), the Goddess of Mercy, is often depicted with hundreds of arms and is found in many temples. In Taoist temples you might see statues of its founder, **Lao Zi**, along with the **Eight Immortals**, and in the south the Taoist Goddess of Fishermen and the Sea, known variously as **A-Ma**, **Mazu** and **Tin Hau**, is a prominent figure with numerous temples dedicated to her in Hong Kong, Macau and Fujian. Incense and ghost money are burnt in temples to all of the Three Teachings, either in large brick ovens or in ornate metal burners, usually found in the courtyards. You'll also people divining their future at temples in all kinds of ingenious ways, the most common of which is by shaking sticks in a wooden cup until one falls out!

Best Temples & Monasteries

- White Cloud Temple, Beijing (p. 174)
- Tibetan Lama Temple, Beijing (p. 171)
- Puning Temple, Chengde (p. 229)
- Eight Immortals Temple, Xi'an (p. 243)
- Big Wild Goose Pagoda, Xi'an (p. 243)
- Luohan Temple, Chongqing (p. 266)
- Fengdu Ghost Temple, Three Gorges (p. 276)
- Jade Buddha Temple, Shanghai (p. 304)
- West Garden Temple, Suzhou (see p. 351)
- Lingyin Temple, Hangzhou (p. 371)
- Temple of Six Banyans, Guangzhou (p. 458)
- Po Lin Monastery, Lantau Island, Hong Kong (p. 522)
- Wong Tai Sin Temple, Hong Kong (p. 519)
- A-Ma Temple, Macau (p. 578)

Pond resident at Po Lin Monastery (Magalie L'Abbé)

Beliefs & Superstitions

The Chinese are inherently superstitious and this manifests itself in everything from religious interpretation to modern business practice. In Chinese certain numbers sound the same as other words and these are then taken to be lucky, or unlucky. Six, eight (which brings money) and nine (longevity) are good numbers, while four (which sounds like death) is a bad number. The importance placed on these numbers cannot be overstated and telephone numbers or addresses with favorable digits command high prices. Equally, few Chinese will want to live on the fourth floor of a building. Many Chinese believe that, although your destiny is ordained, a little luck can help you skip a few reincarnations. Gambling here can be obsessive, with people betting all they own and more (see *Macau, Gambling*, p. 589). The lunar calendar also plays a significant role in modern life, and weddings, business meetings and holidays are planned accordingly.

The Chinese Zodiac

The Chinese Zodiac is based on the lunar calendar and gives each of its 12 years an animal name. If you are born within this year you are said to possess the qualities of that animal. Note that the Chinese New Year usually falls a month or two after the Western version, so if you were born in January 1973, as I was, you are actually a rat, not an ox!

Below is a brief description of each of the animal years, but if you're interested in further exploration head to an astrologer. Astrologers can be found in markets and parks throughout China and, if you give them your time and date of birth, they should be able to give you a precise rundown of who you are, what days are lucky for you and what lies in your future – take a translator!

WHAT'S YOUR SIGN?

Rat – Usually clever, giving and diligent, but can be prone to laziness.

Ox – Independent, cool and stubborn, an ox will always finish a task.

Tiger – Self-assured and adventurous, tigers live up to their name.

Rabbit – Quiet, shy and family-loving, rabbits need reassurance and love.

Dragon – Dragons are confident and able leaders and usually gracious.

Snake – Often selfish, charismatic and hard-nosed; you wouldn't want to upset a snake.

Horse – Horses are usually witty and well motivated, but emotional.

Goat – Money-loving goats are charmers but don't often turn up on time.

Monkey – Monkeys are daring and love a challenge but, despite their intelligence, they can be erratic.

Rooster – Diligence and punctuality are important to roosters, although they can speak a little too freely and are prone to feeling emotional.

Dog – Defensive, loyal and kind, they really do make best friends.

Pig – Calm and helpful, pigs may not be very intelligent but they are sincere.

Fengshui

Fengshui (wind and water), or geomancy, is the art of alignment to create the best flow of energy and can operate on a room, building or city scale. Fengshui is based on certain precepts, such as having a mountain or hill behind the property and water flowing toward the front. Hong Kong's HSBC Tower is famous for its fengshui – the unobstructed view to the water allows money to flow freely in! In a room, certain objects, such as a correctly placed fishbowl, can improve the energy flow, while a *bagua*, mirror, will repel evil spirits. You'll see geomancy in practice throughout the country and can even arrange fengshui tours in Hong Kong (see p. 504) and Yangshuo (p. 434).

Culture

Architecture

Since the onset of dynastic times, architectural design has been of key significance as an indicator of status within the imperial structure. Buildings have been added to, altered or destroyed according to the mood of the dynasty. Outside influences have also had their part to play and there are prominent examples of Mongolian, Tibetan, British, French and German architecture found in China. In the last hundred years, wars, the Cultural Revolution and most recently the country's spectacular economic growth have eliminated much historic architecture. Despite this, a number of outstanding buildings, such as the **Forbidden City** and the **Temple of Heaven**, have survived and are currently undergoing face-lifts in preparation for the Olympics, while amazing modern structures are also being built for the event (see *The 2008 Olympics*, p. 139).

Palaces & Temples

Palaces and temples were mapped out in accordance with the principles of fengshui and were usually walled complexes containing square or rectangular buildings, with a few notable exceptions such as the circular Temple of Heaven in Beijing. Inside the city walls, an inner central walled quarter was used for the emperor and was always built on a number of rising platforms. The highest point seated the great emperor, as this brought him closer to heaven and no other building was allowed to exceed this in the city.

Traditional Architecture

Cities and the traditional buildings within them were designed using a standard set of principles. Harmony was of key importance, as was creating a balance with the environment. Fengshui was essential (see above) and architectural designs were chosen so as not to disrupt the cosmos. Buildings were usually constructed horizontally rather than vertically, in contrast to today's skyscrapers. Together, low-rise buildings formed a network of narrow streets known as *hutong*, including everything from homes to shops. The grid-like rows provided shelter from the elements and were also

Traditional Chinese architecture

believed to afford spiritual protection. Solid insulated brick was used in the north while open eaves with internal courtyards were prevalent in the south. To see some of China's best preserved *hutong*, head for **Beijing** (see p. 167).

Rural Architecture

Although the principal architectural aspects remain the same from north to south, a number of variations can been seen throughout China today. The **Dong** and **Miao** of the southwest use local cedar wood, building their houses vertically and it's not uncommon to see two- or three-story houses. They are also famous for their unique **Wind and Rain Bridges** (see *Longji*, p. 441), built to prevent evil spirits from crossing the river and entering the town. In the southeast the **Hakka** constructed vast encampments containing huge circular stone mansions. These roundhouses sometimes contained up to 600 people and provided perfect defense from both invaders and the harsh climate; a few are still inhabited today. Some outstanding examples of traditional architecture remain in the **Huizhou-style** houses of Shexian and Yixian, near Huangshan (see *Huizhou Architecture*, p. 399).

Foreign Influences

Over the ages many foreign communities have settled in China, bringing outside architectural styles and techniques with them. Islamic architecture retains some of its typical features, but also incorporates Chinese themes – look no further than Xi'an's **Great Mosque** (see p. 242), where the minaret resembles a pagoda. The 19th century saw the arrival of the Europeans. **Guangzhou**, **Hong Kong**, **Macau**, **Shanghai** and **Xiamen** still have well-preserved examples of colonial architecture and the juxtaposition of Eastern and Western styles gives a very different feel to parts of these cities. For the best of the British, head to **the Bund** in Shanghai, which is more akin to Liverpool (UK) than the Orient. Today, it houses some of the most expensive properties in Shanghai and boasts a range of architectural styles from Neo-Classical to Art Deco.

Communist Architecture

Communism also had its part to play in China's architecture and saw the development of a bland, boxy Soviet style focused on functionality. Beijing's **Great Hall of the People** and **Tian'anmen Square** remain as monuments to those days, while the ancient glory of the dynastic period looks on from the Forbidden City.

Modern Architecture

From the late 1970s onwards, China opened its economy, urbanization erupted and simple, cheap accommodation was needed for the masses. As the population swelled, buildings began to creep upwards and, today, China's urban skylines have been transformed into a lofty wash of neon. Architecture has become a highly competitive field and the tallest, biggest and funkiest all battle it out in the skylines of Shanghai and Hong Kong (see *The Sky's the Limit*, p. 508), albeit still paying homage to tradition in their use of the principles of fengshui.

Marriott Hotel, Shanghai
(Tot Foster)

Bronzes

Excavations to date indicate that bronze emerged in China during the **Shang dynasty** (1600-1122 BC). Before this time vessels for everyday use were made from pottery, but the increased stability and settlement of the Shang allowed for the melding of copper and tin to form bronze. Craftsmen soon developed sophisticated casting techniques and agricultural equipment, cookery utensils and weapons were all fashioned from bronze.

The Shang also used bronze to produce ceremonial vessels used solely by the king to make offerings to the spirits. These vessels were highly detailed and often depicted animals, although, as time progressed, the images became more abstract. By the time of the **Zhou dynasty** (1122-221 BC),

Shang Dynasty bronze

styles had become more varied and items were cast in different shapes, featuring both simple and extravagant décor. Some of the best historic bronze exhibits in the country are found in **Beijing's National Museum** (see p. 166), the **Shanghai Museum** (see p. 301) and the **Shaanxi History Museum** in Xi'an (see p. 241). Although the composition now varies greatly from Shang dynasty bronze, the alloy remains popular to this day and you'll see statuary around the country fashioned from it.

One of China's most impressive bronze collections was discovered in Henan province in 1976. The tomb of China's first female general (who was also wife to one of the Shang kings) was unearthed and over 200 bronze weapons and tools, 600 small sculptures, 7,000 cowry shells, 16 sacrificial victims and six dogs were found!

Ceramics

For centuries the Western world has been lured by the splendor of China's ceramics and it even adopted the country's name as a title for its most prized product: porcelain.

Through the ages different forms and styles evolved that reflect both internal and outside influences, along with technological advances. Some of the best examples of Chinese porcelain are found in the Forbidden City's display (see p. 155-57), at the Shaanxi History Museum (see p. 241) and Shanghai Museum (see p. 301).

Yuan Dynasty ceramic

History

China's Neolithic period saw simple techniques that used black, white and red surface painting on simple everyday utensils. By the rise of the Western Zhou dynasty in 1100 BC, a kiln style of glazing had been developed, although this wasn't perfected until the Han dynasty. It was during the **Tang dynasty** that ceramic production started to increase and become more refined. With copper and bronze being used for coin production, potters found a rise in demand for practical everyday products. They started to use top quality porcelain and were keen to make their works more colorful and creative, developing a **tri-color glaze** (*san cai*) that remains one of the Tang's greatest legacies. In addition to day-to-day ware, ornaments and statuettes of horses and other animals were modeled in tri-color, and these techniques are still in use today. During the Song, the art of ceramics was further refined and many regional styles and specialties began to develop, using a simpler and more elegant style, favoring one color rather than three. However, it was the outside influences of the **Yuan dynasty** that saw one of the greatest developments in Chinese ceramics – the **cobalt blue underglaze**. This simple blue and white glaze has become symbolic of Chinese

Ming vase

pottery and is common the world over. But, with the collapse of the Yuan and the instability of the early Ming years, both quantity and quality declined.

Once the **Ming dynasty** asserted its rule, ceramics production was reborn and the Yuan art of cobalt glaze and Tang tri-color technique were reinvented and perfected. The Forbidden City began placing large orders for top quality china and founded an imperial kiln at Jingdezhen in Jiangxi province. Only the finest quality porcelain was used and the production of each piece became highly skilled and specialized, depicting intricate scenes of imperial and everyday life, as well as phoenixes and dragons. The market grew when two Portuguese ships were captured by the Dutch in 1604 and their cargo of 20,000 pieces of Ming pottery went up for auction. Buyers included England's King James I and the French King Henri IV. Demand for this distant and exotic art form soared. Despite the collapse of the Ming in 1644, the imperial kilns continued to prosper, catering to an international market and, although they were forced to close during the Japanese occupation, they have since re-opened and still produce some of the world's most highly skilled ceramic pieces.

Jade & Lacquer

Jade and lacquer date back beyond the Shang dynasty (1600-1122 BC). Jade was used to make everything from tools to ornaments and its enduring nature led to it becoming associated with longevity. As a result of this, the Shang used jade to make *pi*, flat circular ornaments which were placed in graves. Lacquer is produced using the sap of the lac tree and was another popular decorative art, most commonly used to coat small boxes, which were then inlaid with precious metals. Both jade and lacquer were so popular that they continue to be fashioned and treasured to this day.

Painting

Classical Chinese painting has a long history and conjures up images of a mystical country with mist-shrouded peaks dropping down to waterfalls surrounded by bamboo and blossoming trees. Painting in China isn't just limited to the classical form and in the past century the art has moved through Communist Red Art to abstract modernism, although traditional styles remain popular.

Tools of the Trade

There are said to be four great treasures in traditional Chinese painting; the brush, the ink, the inkstone and the paper or silk used. Only the finest horse hair was used for the brushes and it was then glued to pieces of bamboo, a traditional method that dates back to the fourth century BC. The ink was made by combining pine soot and glue, which was then left to harden, making a solid tablet of ink. The ink was then rubbed with water on an inkstone to create the correct consistency. Silk was the traditional medium, although this restricted creativity, since it was permanent as soon as applied. The invention of paper in 106 AD changed this and allowed for more artistic freedom.

Paint brushes aplenty

Tang Dynasty Art (618-907 AD)

The Tang dynasty saw the first real development of Chinese art. Under the Tang, China was a powerful, stable empire providing a perfect foundation for the arts which were essentially produced by scholars, high officials and poets. Arts were encouraged by the court and portrait painting gained in popularity. Paintings depicted emperors and their families and also serve as excellent historical documents reflecting court life from this period.

Song Dynasty Art (960-1279 AD)

With the collapse of the Tang came the rise of the Song dynasty, whose artistic legacy has been handed down to China's modern painters. Their focus was on the landscape and they wanted to capture the vast expanse of China's geography. Huge areas of the canvas were left blank in order to create space, depth and to capture light, aspects that are clearly reflected in works by **Ma Yuan** (1165-1225 AD). Academies were established under royal patronage and a number of emperors, most famously **Huizong**, adopted the hobby.

Painting by Ma Yuan

Yuan, Ming & Qing Dynasties (1279-1911)

With the invasion of the Mongols and the rise of the Yuan dynasty, many officials were forced to retire, allowing for a change in composition and subject matter. Although the traditional brush and ink techniques remained of key importance, images became more personal, with an emphasis on experimentation. Detailed images of plum blossoms, bamboo, flowers and birds fused with color washes became common and a passion for mixing calligraphy with their canvases added to the Yuan style. However, it was the rise of the Qing dynasty in the 17th century that first saw European influences merge with the earlier traditions and Western materials and subject matter became more common.

The 1900s

The biggest changes to Chinese art occurred during the 20th century through contact with the Western world and the Communist ideals promoted by Russia. Artists began to paint their great leader, Mao, in stronger, bolder colors and used Western materials such as oil on canvas. Painting, like everything else, became a medium for political propaganda and a movement developed known as '**Red Art**' – Shanghai's Propaganda Poster Art Center (see p. 314) has an excellent collection. Zhang Zhenshi's (1914-92) portrait of Mao has become an icon from this period and copies of it have stood at the entrance to the Forbidden City since 1950. Red Art is currently undergoing a revival in China and can be seen throughout the country's galleries and markets.

Modern Art

Modern art in China has been influenced by international styles and techniques, which have been fused with deeply embedded traditions to create powerful images of life today. Modern Chinese paintings often reflect artists' frustration at the censored society in which they live and the turmoil of the last century. Good places to get a feel for China's modern art scene are at Beijing's hip **Dashanzi district** (see p. 186-87), Shanghai's **Museum of Contemporary Art** (p. 314), Guangzhou's **Guangdong Museum of Art** (p. 460) and Shenzhen's **Overseas Chinese Town** (p. 479-80).

Calligraphy

The artistic portrayal of Chinese characters has a long imperial tradition and still flourishes today. Calligraphy traditionally went hand-in-hand with poetry and was practiced by scholars, although emperors and court officials also spent years mastering the art. During the Tang dynasty, a united China allowed a standard script to emerge, and calligraphy was considered so important that the emperor added it to the list of criteria for assigning posts

Chinese calligraphy (Ewen Bell)

in the civil service. Today calligraphy is very much alive in modern China and you will see it everywhere, from the work of traditional masters in temples to artists on the street. For those hunting for exquisite ancient calligraphy, **Shanghai Museum** (see p. 301) has some of the finest examples in the country.

Literature

Early Chinese literature is defined by philosophical works reputedly written by great masters such as **Lao Zi**, the founder of Taoism (see p. 50), **Confucius** (p. 49) and their disciples. However there were exceptions to this quasi-religious theme such as **Sun Zi**'s fifth-century-BC military treatise, the *Art of War*, and the extraordinary *Historical Records*, written by **Sima Qian** in the Han dynasty. The latter was an immense tome chronicling Chinese history from Huangdi, through the Shang and Zhou dynasties and up to his time. *Historical Records* enlivened its 130 chapters with biographies and constructed conversations (based on real events); its style was so engaging that it formed the basis for imperial historic works to follow. However, until the 15th century, books were written as scholarly works and remained inaccessible to the masses. In the Ming and subsequent Qing dynasties, a new, more vernacular language emerged and classics such as *Journey to the West, Outlaws of the Marsh, The Romance of the Three Kingdoms* and *The Dream of the Red Chamber* were written. These tales are still popular today, but reading books remained an elitist activity and it was only with the arrival of the social commentaries of **Lu Xun** (1881-1936) on the literary scene that *baihua* (white language) emerged. Once the Communists emerged victorious, authors like **Sheng Congwen** (1903-86) found their literary freedom suppressed and little material of interest was produced, although Mao's *Little Red Book* is a fascinating insight into socialist doctrine. Since the 1980s, restrictions have relaxed, but many of the grittiest modern writers such as Wang Shuo don't have a legally published book to their name in China. See the booklist on p. 595 for details of some of the classics, along with various other titles.

Poetry

With its tones and rhyming nature, Chinese is well-suited to poetry and the pictographic characters themselves add further sentiment. For this reason since the earliest times, poetry has been the preferred mode of written expression. *The Book of Songs*, accredited to **Confucius**, is the original Chinese poetic work and was quoted by scholars, envoys and philosophers alike. Chinese poetry reached its pinnacle under the Tang with the works of two starkly contrasting wordsmiths. **Li Bai** (701-762 AD) was a Taoist eccentric with a passion for nature and wine who embodied the poetic values of freedom, spontaneity and defiance of convention. **Dufu** (712-770 AD) was Confucian through and through, but his failed political career led him to appreciate the hardships of the common man and his poems reflect this. Li Bai and Dufu's differing styles and stances highlight the dichotomy of China through the ages – split between the rigid conventions of Confucian conformity and the romanticism and intuitive thought associated with Taoism. Born during the Song dynasty, **Su Dongpo** (1037-1101 AD) is perhaps the most famous of all Chinese poets, and was also a skilled calligrapher, painter and politician. Su's outspoken views saw him exiled more than once, but his minute attention to detail and the graceful nature of his poems continue to earn him adulation to this day.

Music

Whether you stumble across an opera performance in the park, or are taken by a catchy Canto-pop tune while shopping in Hong Kong, you're sure to come across local music of some kind on your trip to China and if you're a keen music fan you'll find plenty of styles to search out, from classical to pop.

Traditional Music

Visitors to China most commonly experience traditional music via opera performances, but this is only the tip of the iceberg and there are countless regional styles. Music in China dates back 6,000 years, and although some traditional instruments and melodies were lost in Qin Shi Huang's purge and again two millennia later during the Cultural Revolution, today it is enjoying a renaissance. Traditional Chinese music focuses

Playing the erhu

on tone rather than melody and the scale is pentatonic, which is believed to be symbolic of the five elements of earth, fire, metal, water and wood. Instruments are divided into eight categories according to the material they are made from: bamboo, clay, gourd, metal, silk, skin, stone and wood. Regional varieties are based on one or more of the instrument types. Thus the south is famous for its silk

The pipa

strings and bamboo flutes, while the north is characterized by "blowers and drummers." Popular traditional instruments that remain in use today include drums, the *dizi* (flute), *erhu* (silk-stringed violin), gongs, *guqin* (silk-stringed zither) and the *pipa* (silk-stringed lute).

One of the most relaxed ways to enjoy traditional music in China is at one of the daily performances which you'll find in parks and teahouses across the country. These range from organized performances for which you must pay, to impromptu shows by the locals – the Temple of Heaven grounds in Beijing and Hangzhou's lakeside parks are good places to try. Temples are often filled with the sound of gongs and chanting and are another place where you'll come across traditional music.

Opera

Although opera has a lengthy imperial history in China, it has long been enjoyed by the masses, unlike in the West, and several different regional styles have developed, of which **Beijing Opera** is by far the best-known (see p. 188 for Beijing theaters).

Guquin player

Other famous styles include **Cantonese** and **Szechuanese**, the latter renowned for its deft mask changing. Stories generally focus on traditional tales such as the *Outlaws of the Marsh* and are designed to be easily understood as much through the over-emphasized actions of players as the words themselves – indicative of the fact that performances were played out in noisy teahouses and theaters. Traditionally, all roles were played by men and actors playing female characters had to wear special supports to make it appear as if they had bound feet – it took a year just to learn how to walk on these! The make-up is a work of art in itself and each actor spends hours perfecting it before the start of a performance. There are also some things you should watch out for in the characters' make-up – black represents loyalty, white is generally used for baddies, red for heroes, yellow for indecisive characters and a metallic sheen is given to those who have supernatural qualities.

Traditional Chinese opera (Tot Foster)

In the 20th century, film and then television brought opera to an even wider audience. Indeed, Beijing opera's history is closely intertwined with acrobatics and martial arts and some of China's biggest movie stars, like Jackie Chan, started their careers with traditional operatic training. Although the onset of modernity in China has detracted somewhat from interest in opera, it still features heavily on TV and radio and is hugely popular with the older generation.

Characters in the Beijing Opera

If you're in the capital, it's easy enough to catch a tourist opera show, shortened to a more convenient 90 minutes and sometimes hilariously subtitled (see *Beijing*, p. 188). Some performances are also held at tourist sites, such as the **Master of the Nets Garden in Suzhou** (see p. 352) and these are worth attending for the surroundings as well as the show itself. But for more authenticity, visit a training school (see *Beijing*, p. 189) or seek out an original production, even if you don't stay for the whole thing. Many people find an hour and a half more than enough though. While the costumes are spectacular and the acrobatics astounding, the shrill pitch of the singing can be overwhelming. It is generally worth arriving at the theater a little before the performance as you may get the opportunity to see the performers preparing. Tickets for tourist performances cost in the region of ¥40-400/US$5-50 and can be bought at larger hotels, travel agencies and the venues themselves. Local performances are a different story and cost a fraction of those prices for a much longer show.

Protest Music

Not so long ago Chinese music was confined to Beijing Opera, revolutionary songs and party anthems (no, not that kind of party anthem, the Communist one ...). In the late 70s when things started opening up, Taiwanese and Hong Kong tunes began to make their way to the mainland and they were accompanied by a trickle of foreign music tapes from returning exchange students and foreigners working in China. Little by little a new kind of music began to emerge, heavily influenced by the smuggled tapes and, all of a sudden, underground protest rock emerged. **Cui Jian** was a trumpeter who'd trained as a classical musician and joined the Beijing Symphony Orchestra, but was strongly influenced by Taiwanese Deng Lijun's (aka Teresa Teng) tunes and he diverted his attentions, formed a band and is now known as the Godfather of Chinese Rock. Cui's early songs were ostensibly about love but became anthems of democracy and his lyrics and tone have angered authorities more than once. Cui and a collection of other early pioneers opened the door for popular music in China and, while these days Canto-pop and Mando-pop tunes feed the masses, Beijing has continued its rock tradition and remains the best place in the country to see locally grown live music, in spite of its seemingly few venues. Beijing rock bands to look out for include the long-running, long-haired **Cold Blooded Animal** and neo-folk rock legends **Second Hand Rose**. Where? Bar and Yugong Yishan (see *Beijing*, p. 189) are good venues to try, but check out *that's Beijing* or *City Weekend* for upcoming gigs.

Introduction

Canto-Pop & Mando-Pop

Canto-pop is characterized by catchy tunes and romantic lyrics and, along with Taiwanese and Western pop, has heavily influenced modern mainstream Chinese music to produce mainland Mando-pop. Some of the biggest names in Chinese pop today are **Aaron Kwok**, **Faye Wong** and the multi-talented **Andy Lau**.

Acrobatics

Acrobatics have a long history in China, strongly tied to both **Beijing Opera** and **martial arts**, and even in today's cyber-struck age they never fail to confound. Students begin training as early as five to be supple, skillful and strong enough to perform the stunts you'll see and I always leave the show feeling distinctly inflexible! Shows usually involve a range of acts, including balancers, contortionists, jugglers, formation troupes and magicians, the latter of which tend to be the only weak link. Modern times have also led to modern stunts and you might also find motorcycle walls (and wheels) of death! There are regular tourist shows featuring famous troupes in Beijing (see p. 187) and Shanghai (p. 313).

Chinese acrobats

Martial Arts

History & Heritage

Kung fu (*gong fu* or *wushu*) and tai chi came to the world from China and can be traced back thousands of years. Methods of fighting were detailed during the Zhou dynasty (1122-221 BC) and Taoist monks are thought to have practiced an art similar to *tai chi* around 500 BC. However, to understand the roots of modern kung fu we must move a little forward. Legend has it that an Indian monk by the name of **Bodhidharma** (known in Chinese as Damo) arrived at Shaolin monastery in the fifth or sixth century with the intention of introducing *dhyana* Buddhism (*chan* in China, and *zen* in Japan and the West; see *Religion & Philosophy*, p. 46). However, his efforts were hindered due to the poor physical condition of the monks and so he instituted a series of physical exercises to counter the long hours spent poring over texts and meditating. These exercises then developed into forms of defense in response to attacks on monasteries. Later martial arts came in dramatic form through a fusion with acrobatics and Beijing opera. However, the Cultural Revolution (see p. 23) took its toll and instructors were driven from the country. Salvation came through movies (see *Kung Fu Flicks*, p. 68), which were initially only popular within China, but subsequently brought kung fu to the world's attention in the shape of **Bruce Lee** (see p. 69), who paved the way for modern martial arts movie stars.

Styles

Although there are hundreds of styles, Chinese martial arts can generally be categorized into two broad forms, which tie in with the Taoist concept of *yin* and *yang* (see *Taoism*, p. 50). There are hard, or external, forms that focus on *yang*, or male, aspects and involve speed, muscular strength and aggression; and soft, or internal, styles that correspond to the *yin* (female) and stress the movement of *qi* (energy) to overcome opponents. The line between hard and soft is not always clear, something which is evident in the dichotomy within two of the most influential styles: *shaolinquan* (Shaolin Fist) from the Buddhist monastery in Henan is a hard form, which nevertheless utilizes the soft art of *qigong* (breath control); while *wudangquan* (you guessed it, Wudang Fist), a soft style from the Taoist retreats of Hubei, contains elements of external forms and is famous for its sword play. What is certain is that to attain the true skills of either an internal or external form, incredible physical and mental conditioning is required, whether achieved through painful exercises such as repeatedly striking wood and brick, or by intense meditation and breathing techniques.

Tai Chi

Taiji by the lake (Tot Foster)

Taijiquan (Great Eternal Fist) takes its name from the *taiji*, the Taoist *yinyang* symbol, and is the world's most popular martial art (although its gentle, graceful style runs contrary to many people's perception of the term "martial art"). It is an internal form that uses slow, cyclical movements to promote energy flow, circulation and a sense of well being. Traditionally practiced by older Chinese, tai chi is becoming increasingly popular in the West. It is probably the easiest martial art to engage in, even on a short trip, as you can see it every morning in almost any park in China. You can simply watch, but you'll frequently find yourself being invited to participate! Even if you don't manage to master the moves, you'll have had a truly Chinese experience and had a little exercise at the same time.

Studying Martial Arts

Many foreigners come to China to study martial arts and the most famous center is **Shaolin**, although the commercialization and plethora of copycat schools at the "home of kung fu" can come as something of a disappointment. **Wudang Shan** makes for a more low-key, but equally historic alternative, but if you're serious about study, knowing which style you wish to learn will help you decide where to go. You can arrange private or group instruction, whether for a few hours or a few months, in many of the places covered in this book. **Yangshuo** makes for a particularly accessible and attractive place to study (see p. 433). Obviously, having an English-speaking teacher makes learning easier, but, as instruction tends to be quite demonstrative, this isn't as much of a problem as you might think. For more information about long-term study in China check www.educasian.com and www.shaolins.com.

Film

Chow Yun Fat is said to be one of the most recognizable movie stars in the world simply because of his importance to the billion-strong Chinese cinema audience and this gives some insight into the scale and scope of movies in modern China. Movie-making in China has a checkered history and one that reflects and often portrays the events of the time. From early on, China's political situation dictated that production was split into three geographical areas and mainland China, Hong Kong (see *Kung Fu Flicks*, p. 68) and Taiwan have all developed along their own lines.

The Beginnings

Film in China saw a promising start in Shanghai, though during the early years Beijing Opera was the focus of almost all movies. In the 1920s American expertise was called upon and overseas influences continued to play a part in Chinese film production until the Japanese invasion. In the 1930s Shanghai studios such as the Mingxing and Lianhua produced a string of silent, often anti-Imperialist movies like *Spring Silk Worm* (1933) and *The Goddess* (1934), which saw the rise to fame of China's first movie stars, notably the glamorous Ruan Lingyu. In 1942 Japanese occupation put an end to the Shanghai studios, which pushed production into the nationalist and Communist regions inland, as well as to Hong Kong. Once the Japanese had left in 1945 production started up again and *Spring River Flows East* (1947), which highlighted the suffering of the masses while the elites luxuriated in their wealth, became one of the most popular movies of this period.

Repression under Communism

Unfortunately, as soon as production re-started in earnest, movies became heavily censored during the early years of communism. The party began to harness the potential of film as a propaganda medium. Students were sent to be trained in movie-making in Moscow, and the Beijing Film Academy was opened in 1956. While America was enjoying a golden era of the big screen, most Chinese movies of the time were jingoistic stories promoting the glory of communism. Despite the storylines, it was this time that really saw the Chinese start going to the movies. But as time went on, the Communist government further tightened its reins and the Cultural Revolution (see *History* p. 23) saw Chinese moviemaking at an all-time low

The Fifth Generation

In the 1980s things finally opened up with the Fifth Generation of film-makers, so-called for the number of generations since the 1949 Revolution. **Chen Kaige** is seen as having started the ball rolling with his 1984 film *Yel-*

low Earth, which painted a beautiful but bleak picture of the futility of Communist ideology, quickly provoking controversy with the government. **Zhang Yimou**, who worked the camera on *Yellow Earth*, soon followed with his own movie, *Red Sorghum*, in 1986. The "revolutionary" sentiments of this movie went some way to appeasing officialdom and he went on to score more successes, including *Judou* (1990) and *Raise the Red Lantern* (1991), both of which star the exquisite **Gong Li**. Most recently, Zhang has made a foray into the kung fu scene with *Hero* (see *Kung Fu Flicks*, below) and *The House of Flying Daggers* (2004), and he has been busy on other projects, including choreographing Yangshuo's Liu Sanjie Cultural Show (see p. 433) and the opening ceremony of the 2008 Olympics. Gong Li also features in another of Chen Kaige's movies, *Farewell My Concubine* (1993), considered to be his finest work. The story is again indicative of the troubles of the time, told through the lives of two Beijing Opera performers, and its tragic ending wasn't well received by the authorities.

The Sixth Generation

The Tian'anmen Square crackdown sent ripples in all directions and film was not excluded. Many Fifth Generation movies had been critically acclaimed overseas and in the mid-1990s this group seemed to shift their focus to foreign audiences. Today the cutting edge of film in China rests with a new breed of gritty, urban underground directors, loosely labeled the Sixth Generation. Movies like **Zhang Yuan**'s *Beijing Bastards* (1993), which stars China's undisputed king of rock, Cui Jian, and **Wang Xiaoshuai**'s *Beijing Bicycle* (2001), have a nervy realness to them, and depict the city as they see it, warts and all. Obviously, this generation of directors has fared even worse than their predecessors with the government and sadly many of these telling tales cannot be seen in mainland movie theaters.

Hong Kong & Taiwan

Hong Kong has principally focused on martial arts movies, but has also produced outstanding directors such as **Wong Kar-wai**, who was actually born in Shanghai, and is responsible for the urban love classic *Chungking Express* (1994). Taiwan's movie industry first developed under the Japanese and then passed through a number of phases, from early escapism through to the growing pains of the island's rapid industrial development. Although the Taiwanese film industry has suffered from the increasing popularity of Hollywood movies, the island has produced the Chinese world's most famous director, **Ang Lee**, whose epic *Crouching Tiger, Hidden Dragon* (2000) received worldwide acclaim. He has subsequently successfully shifted from Eastern to Western, with his Oscar-winning film, *Brokeback Mountain* (2005).

Kung Fu Flicks

While they are often disregarded by serious critics, martial arts movies have been important in the development of China's movie industry and are the only genre to have successfully bridged the gap between East and West. Although modern Hollywood action blockbusters differ greatly from Chinese movies of old, many of their fight scenes are fresh from a kung fu flick.

Early Years

The Chinese had been making martial arts movies for decades before they reached the West. Hong Kong can be called the home of kung fu flicks and is still the third-biggest movie-producing region in the world after Hollywood and Bollywood. Many early movies focused on the legendary 19th-century master, Wong Fei-Hung, renowned for his sense of fair play. At this time storylines tended to be fairly formulaic and the heroes often did what their audiences were afraid to do – standing up for themselves and what they believed, in the face of tyrannical authority or the criminal underworld. Although these early films were popular within China, the first kung fu movies to make it onto the world stage were led by Bruce Lee.

Bruce Lee

As the man who popularized kung fu in the West, Bruce Lee, is rightly its most famous son. Known in China as Lee Xiaolong (Little Dragon), he was born in the US in1940 but soon moved to Hong Kong. Although he had already appeared on screen by the tender age of five, Bruce didn't start learning kung fu under the *wing-chun* master, Yip Man, until he was 13 years old. A year

Bruce Lee statue on Hong Kong's Avenue of Stars

later he took up cha cha dancing and won a Hong Kong competition in 1958. Aged 19, he returned to the States and in 1961 enrolled to study philosophy at the University of Washington. During this time he began teaching kung fu to fellow students, opened the Jun Fan Kung Fu Institute and met his future wife, Linda Emery. He was talent-spotted to win the role of **Kato** in the 1966 TV series *The Green Hornet*, albeit playing second fiddle to Van Williams. However, in spite of a few other bit parts, Bruce was unable to make a mark on audiences who weren't ready for an Asian movie star. After returning to Hong Kong in 1971, Golden Harvest's Raymond Chow offered him the starring role in *The Big Boss*, shot in Thailand, which was an instant box-office hit. He went on to star in *Fist of Fury* (1972), *Way of the Dragon* (1972) and the one that really brought the world spotlight, Hollywood-produced, *Enter the Dragon* (1973), although this wasn't released until after his death. An incomplete film project, *Game of Death*, was pieced together posthumously and, while not as polished as other productions (and featuring a double for much of the movie), the yellow jumpsuit worn by Bruce became a trademark, paid tribute to by Uma Thurman's costume in Quentin Tarantino's *Kill Bill* (2003).

Bruce Lee's sudden, unexpected death from a cerebral edema in July 1973 came as a shock to the movie and martial arts world. While 25,000 people attended his funeral in Hong Kong, many fans have, until recently, been disappointed at the paucity of Bruce Lee memorials or sights in the city. This has been remedied of late with a statue unveiled on the **Avenue of Stars** (see *Hong Kong*, p. 516). There continues to be speculation as to how he died and the equally early and tragic death of his son, Brandon Lee, while filming the 1993 movie *The Crow*, has only intensified this. What is certain is that during his short, explosive life Bruce Lee helped the arts of the East come to the West and his movies still bring enjoyment and inspiration to enthusiasts and moviemakers around the globe.

Comedy Kung Fu

After his early death, a string of copycat Bruce Lee's were peddled by Golden Harvest, but they failed to fill the void. Rather than try and imitate him a new group of stars chose to differentiate themselves by moving the genre into comedy. Of this group, **Jackie Chan** (aka Chen Long, meaning Dragon Chen) is the only one to have seriously broken onto the world scene. Like Bruce Lee, Jackie Chan initially had difficulty making it in Hollywood and it wasn't until he starred in *Rumble in the Bronx* (1995) that he found fame worldwide. Drawing inspiration from the likes of Buster Keaton and Harold Lloyd, Chen Long has combined his incredible kung fu ability with slapstick comedy to produce

Jackie Chan

a string of mainstream hits, including *Rush Hour* (1998) and *Shanghai Noon* (2000). The development of kung fu comedy has continued with recent movies like Stephen Chow's *Shaolin Soccer* (2001) and *Kung Fu Hustle* (2004).

Hollywood Action, Hong Kong Kung Fu

Crouching Tiger, Hidden Dragon

Comedy aside, Hollywood has been strongly influenced by kung fu and martial arts are an almost obligatory part of modern action movies, often served with some direct Chinese input. **John Woo**'s oblique camera angles and intense action scenes in movies like *Face Off* (1997) and *Mission Impossible II* (2000) have helped push him to the forefront of this international genre, while **Yuen Woo-Ping** is famous for his fight scene choreography, and made his name in the West with the Wachowski Brothers' *Matrix* trilogy (1999-2003), and more recently in Quentin Tarantino's *Kill Bill* two-parter (2003-4). Yuen Woo-Ping also played his part in Taiwanese **Ang Lee**'s martial arts epic *Crouching Tiger, Hidden Dragon* (2000), which won four Oscars, and is widely regarded as the film that put China on the world movie map. While the film was criticized within China for pandering to the needs of Western audiences, it has undoubtedly ignited mainstream interest in the beauty of China's scenery and culture.

BORDERS.

197 - 203 Oxford Street
London
W1D 2LE.
Tel: 020 7292 1600

SALE
268   6 43847   25/05/2009   19:01

Today you were served by SABINA

CHINA ADV GD
9781588436412   1x   16.99   16.99
                                     . . . .
TOTAL   ITEMS   1   16.99
                                     . . . .
Card   £16.99

Thank you for shopping at Borders.

Do you have a mobile phone?
Do you want to save £5 on your
next visit? Text 82100 to claim
your voucher.

BORDERS.

BORDERS.

BORDERS.

BORDERS.

Traditional Chinese Medicine

Long scorned in the West as a mystical load of Oriental mumbo jumbo, Traditional Chinese Medicine (TCM) and healing are now enjoying popularity around the globe – a fact recognized by the WHO's acceptance of TCM (for certain ailments). However, it is also recognized that Western medicine is more effective for certain severe conditions, especially those requiring surgery, and many Chinese today use a combination of the two.

A TCM market stall

Intrinsically linked to the concept of *qi*, an energy force that moves along meridians around the body, TCM is based on attempting to balance the ever-shifting opposites of the human system. There are perceived to be five basic elements to the body (blood, energy, essence, moisture and spirit) and any misalignment of these or within the organs of the body is thought to engender poor health. Diagnosis often seems simplistic (checking the pulse by hand and examining the tongue are the usual first steps), but is aimed at identifying the imbalances that have lead to the illness. Thus, treatment is based on measures to counteract these differences, and offers a more holistic approach to health than Western medicine, which generally just treats the symptoms. TCM treatment comes in two principal forms, **acupuncture** (and acupressure/massage/reflexology) and **herbal remedies**. Massage is the most commonly utilized form of treatment and you will find establishments in every town across the country. *Tuina* (meaning push and grasp) is the official term for medicinal massage, while *anmo* is a more general term that also includes massage for pleasure rather than health benefits. Some methods of TCM treatment involve the use of both pressure and herbal remedies – moxibustion or hot-cupping uses heated bamboo or glass cups infused with herbs to draw *qi* to the required part of the body, but note that it will leave you covered in large reddish circular marks for a few days afterwards!

TCM in Practice

In most Chinese towns you'll find TCM doctors alongside Western practices and most hospitals have TCM wings, indeed some are completely devoted to traditional medicine. But if you don't want to traipse all the way to a hospital just for a massage you'll find TCM and reflexology establishments dotted around the cities (see the *Health & Relaxation* sections in the individual chapters for listings). Reflexology or massage usually costs between ¥30 and ¥60 an hour (or as much as ¥300 an hour in upmarket hotels or spas) and will make you lighter on your feet for days! If you have a serious aliment that you'd like to try and treat with TCM, it's best to go to an English speaking doctor, or take a translator along with you.

The Downside

In spite of its natural remedies and holistic approach, Chinese traditional medicine has one serious downside for animal-loving Westerners: its beliefs about the medicinal values and use of (sometimes endangered) species body parts – from rhino horn and tiger penis for boosting male virility, to bear bile for improving cardiac condition. Animals are often kept in harsh conditions to render these body parts or fluids, or huge sums are paid for them to be poached from other countries. While animal rights groups are doing their best to substitute equally efficacious alternatives for body parts and there are TCM clinics that don't use such products, demand is still high. Although there are occasional crackdowns, as long as these health benefits are seen to be true and people have the money to pay, the trade will continue. This said, it's easy to avoid such products and, if you have a niggling medical problem that won't go away, give TCM a chance. It might just work; if not, you'll have had a genuine Chinese experience and maybe a massage as well!

Travel & Living Information

Planning Your Trip
When to Go

The two main factors to consider in planning when to visit China are the **climate** and the **number of other visitors** you'll have to share key attractions with. In terms of the weather, spring, summer and fall are the best times for a visit. While summers are hot and often wet, spring and fall see less rainfall and generally offer the clearest skies. But, in a country as big as China, if you plan to travel to more than one region, you're bound to witness both rain and sunshine, no matter when you come. For more detailed climatic information see *Climate*, p. 32.

The **tourist season** for foreign visitors starts around March or April (with the exception of Hong Kong and Macau, which are mild throughout the winter) and runs until October. If you want to avoid the crowds, you can visit in winter, but be prepared for some bitter temperatures, especially in the north. But, in a country with almost 1½ billion people, the greatest numbers of tourists are, as you might expect, Chinese, so it is their vacation times that you want to avoid (see below).

Holidays & Festivals

China's rich ethnic diversity has given it a whole host of festivals and holidays, some of which are unique to individual areas, while others are celebrated nationally. In the 1990s the government introduced so-called "Golden Weeks" to help develop the tourist industry and these week-long national holidays (**Chinese New Year, Labor Day and National Day**) see China's emerging middle classes all taking a break in the same time period. Transport services are booked beyond capacity, hotels are bursting at the seams and everyone inflates their prices. Traveling during these periods, you'll truly come to grips with the fact that China is the most populous nation on earth, and these weeks have become so troublesome that, in recent years, some Chinese families have elected to stay at home and relax, although you'd never guess that when you see the number of people visiting tourist sights.

In addition to the holidays and festivals listed below, there are also countless regional celebrations and (see individual chapters for details) and Western celebrations such as Christmas and New Year are becoming increasingly popular.

■ **Chinese New Year** (Spring Festival; Jan/Feb) – The start of the Lunar New Year is the most important of all Chinese festivals and falls between January 21st and February 20th. It will fall on February 7th in 2008 and January 26th in 2009. Each year one of the 12 zodiac animals is ushered in (see *The Chinese Zodiac*, p. 53 for more) and the whole nation

Celebrating the New Year (Year of the Dragon) in Shanghai

(and Chinese world) celebrates the week-long holiday – it's a time when people return to their hometowns to be with their families. In preparation for the holiday, it's customary to give a thorough "spring-cleaning" to the house and buy new clothes for the coming year. On New Year's Eve the whole family sits down to enjoy a feast. Among a host of dishes, fish usually takes pride of place, symbolic of abundance and prosperity. Fruits, especially oranges are seen to represent regeneration, and these are often eaten after the meal. Red is an auspicious color in China and after the meal children are given red envelopes (*hong bao*) containing money. The money is usually given in amounts that feature the numbers one, six and eight, which are lucky. People also put red banners on their doors to welcome in the New Year and there are public celebrations, often involving lion dances, pounding drums and spirit-scaring firecrackers.

- **Lantern Festival** (Feb/March) – This festival marks the end of the New Year's celebrations and is held on the first full moon of the year. Lanterns are made from paper and silk and are hung outside homes and along the streets, which makes for a magical atmosphere. Lanterns were traditionally red or yellow and of a conventional shape, but today in the cities you can see all manner of creations – from monkeys to spacecraft! During the festival glutinous rice dumplings stuffed with sweet fillings are a popular snack.

- **Tomb Sweeping Day** (Qingming Festival; April) – Ancestor worship is still popular in China and the Qingming Festival is a day put aside for cleaning family graves. In the countryside, tombs are swept, cleaned and often decorated. However, in urban areas it is law to cremate the dead, so tomb sweeping is a less common practice, although ancestors are still commemorated. The festival usually falls on April 4th or 5th.

- **Labor Day** (May 1st) – The start of another of China's three golden weeks.

- **Youth Day** (May 4th) – Youth Day commemorates the 1919 student demonstrations in Tian'anmen Square, which led to the May Fourth Movement (see p. 26).

- **Children's Day** (June 4th) – Kids go on field trips around the country, so beware if you're heading to a major sight!

- **Dragon Boat Festival** (June/July) – This is one of the most spectacular of Chinese festivals, involving teams across the country racing boats adorned as dragons, spurred on by the steady sound of an onboard drummer. The festival commemorates the suicide of the poet Qu Yuan, and the boats are re-enacting the unsuccessful chase to try and save him. Bamboo-wrapped glutinous rice parcels (*zongzi*) are the food to eat during the festival. The festival takes place on the fifth day of the fifth lunar month and races can be seen on rivers around the country. If you want to try your hand at dragon boat racing, see *Beijing*, p. 200 and *Shanghai*, p. 321.

- **Ghost Month** (Aug/Sept) – This is the time when ghosts return to earth and is regarded as an inauspicious time to travel, particularly on water. Unless you're afraid of ghosts this should make it a good time to visit China, but you'll find that plenty of Chinese don't seem too scared either!

- **Confucius' Birthday** (Sept 28th) – The Old Sage's birth is celebrated with elaborate ceremonies at Confucian temples around the country.

- **Moon Festival** (Mid-Autumn Festival; Sept/Oct) – This festival is held on the

At the Moon Festival in Hong Kong

15th day of the eighth lunar month, when the moon is at its brightest. Delicious but filling mooncakes are eaten and it's a popular time for a barbeque under the moonlight.

■ **National Day** – This week-long holiday celebrates the foundation of the People's Republic.

Organized Tours

If you have limited time, then an organized tour can help you get the most out of China, removing the hassles of booking tickets, finding accommodation and picking which of the country's manifold attractions to include in your trip. Tours can also help get you closer to the Chinese people. Tour leaders and guides should be able to facilitate communication and private transport will enable you to get to places that may otherwise difficult to reach. For potential routes see *Suggested Itineraries* (p. 133).

However, the downside of tours is that you may feel shielded from the "real world" at times, they tend to be more expensive than independent travel and you might have to put up with group members, guides and even tour leaders you don't see eye to eye with. This said, as a tour leader for several years, my experience has been that most people feel they got the most out of their time and enjoyed being in a group. Meals in China, for example, are designed to be eaten in large groups and if you dine alone or as a couple your options are more limited. Possibly the best way to travel if you have money, but not time, is on a private tour where you and a few friends or family have your own guide and can tailor the itinerary to your preference.

When choosing a tour company, make sure you pick one that's suitable for you – don't let an agent make the decision for you; carefully read about the nature of the tour and what's included. The most disappointed guests I led were those who had expectations that were very different from those detailed in the brochure. All good agents have consumer protection insurance, meaning that, if the company defaults, you should get compensation; companies affiliated under **USTOA** (United States Tour Operators Association, www.ustoa.com) or **IATO** (International Association of Tour Operators, www.aito.co.uk – they also offer tours) are covered.

Recommended Tour Companies

The letters before the comma indicate which country the company is based in, although you can book a tour from any country and all companies will arrange tailor-made packages to fit your needs.

Luxury Tours

Abercrombie & Kent (US, www.abercrombiekent.com; UK, www.abercrombiekent.co.uk)

Absolute Asia (US, www.absoluteasia.com)

★★**Audley Travel** (UK, www.audleytravel.com)

★★**Bales** (www.balesworldwide.com)

Cox & Kings (US, www.coxandkingsusa.com; UK, www.coxandkings.co. uk)

CTS Horizons (UK, www.ctshorizons.com)

Hayes & Jarvis (UK, www.hayes-jarvis.com)

Imperial Tours (US, www.imperialtours.net)

Magic of the Orient (UK, www.magic-of-the-orient.com)

Virgin Holidays (UK, www.virgin.com/holidays)

★★**Voyages Jules Verne** (UK, www.vjv.co.uk)

Adventure Tours

Adventures Abroad (US, www.adventures-abroad.com)

★**The Adventure Company** (UK, www.adventurecompany.co.uk)

Asian Pacific Adventures (US, www.asianpacificadventures.com)

Backroads (US, www.backroads.com)

★**Explore Worldwide** (UK, www.exploreworldwide.com)

★★★**Freestyle Adventures** (Taiwan, www.freestyleadventures.com)

G.A.P Adventures (US, www.gapadventures.com)

★★★**Grasshopper** (www.grasshopperadventures.com)

★**Imaginative Traveller** (UK, www.imaginative-traveller.com)

★**Intrepid** (Australia, www.interpidtravel.com)

★★**Sundowners** (Australia, www.sundownerstravel.com)

Travel Indochina (Australia, www.travelindochina.com.au)

World Expeditions (UK, www.worldexpeditions.co.uk)

Agents in China

★★★**Choice Travel** (www.choicetravel.cn)

CITS (www.cits.net)

★**China Odyssey** (www.chinaodysseytours.com)

Specialized Tours

Many of the companies listed above also operate specialized interest tours; Grasshopper runs great bike tours through **Bike Asia** (www.bikeasia.com) as well as **photographic tours**. Both Backroads and World Expeditions run **hiking** and **cycling tours** and Intrepid operates **culinary tours**. Imaginative Traveller offers tours suitable for **families** and The Adventure Company has trips suitable for **infants** over a year old. Other specialized companies include:

ACIS (US, www.acis.com) – educational trips for students.

Beijing Xinhua International Tours (China, www.tour-beijing.com/disability_travel/) – Beijing and China tours for disabled travelers.

Birdfinders (UK, www.birdfinders.co.uk) – operates a few birdwatching trips a year.

Birding Worldwide (Australia, www.birdingworldwide.com.au) – searches out rare bird species.

i-to-i (www.i-to-i.com) – two- to 12-week trips and volunteer placements, principally around Xi'an.

Kumuka Worldwide (UK, www.kumuka.com) – overland truck journeys.

Naturetrek (UK, www.naturetrek.co.uk) – wildlife-focused trips throughout China.

Oasis (UK, www.oasisoverland.co.uk) – overland truck journeys.

Saga (UK, www.saga.co.uk) – tours for over-50s.

Visas

Every foreign visitor to China needs a visa to enter the country and these **must be obtained in advance** (with the exception of arrivals to Hong Kong, Macau and Hainan Island), not at the point of entry as is the case with some other Asian countries. Visas can be obtained by either applying in person at the nearest Chinese embassy, through an agency or by mail (although this is no longer possible in the UK). Complete visa applications will need to include all required fees, a passport photo, a passport with at least one blank page, six months validity and possibly proof of onward travel. For all visa types you must enter within three months of the issue date. Standard tourist visas (**L-type**) are the most common and are usually granted for 30 days to a maximum of six months. If you're coming here to work, you can apply for an **F or Z visa** and you'll need a letter of invitation from the company you'll be working with in China. To study in China you can apply for an **X visa** and will need a letter from the college where you'll be studying. Note that citizens of most Western countries do not need a visa to visit Hong Kong or Macau for periods of under a month – see p. 491 and p. 566 for more. In Hong Kong you can easily arrange a China visa from a local travel agent or the Chinese Ministry of Foreign Affairs – see *Hong Kong*, p. 491 for more. Wherever you get your visa, it will cost between US$30 for a single entry to over US$150 for a two- to five-year multiple-entry visa – check websites for the latest prices.

Chinese Embassies Overseas

Australia: 39 Dunblane Street, Camperdown, Sydney, NSW (☎ 02-8595-8000, www.au.china-embassy.org/eng/). Consulates, Melbourne, Perth and Brisbane.

Canada: 515 Patrick Street, Ottawa, Ontario K1N 5H3 (☎ 613-7893-434, www.chineseembassycanada.org). Consulates, Calgary, Toronto and Vancouver.

Ireland: 40 Ailesbury Road, Dublin 4 (☎ 053-1269-1707, www.chinaembassy.ie)

New Zealand: 2-6 Glenmore Street, Wellington (☎ 04-4721-382, www. chinaembassy.org.nz). Consulate in Auckland (☎ 09-5251-589, www. chinaconsulate.org.nz).

Thailand: 57 Rachadapisake Road, Huay Kwang, Bangkok 10310 (☎ 02-2247-7554, www.chinaembassy.or.th/eng/). Consulate in Chiang Mai.

UK: 49-51 Portland Place, London W1B 1QD (☎ 0207-7631-1430, www. chinese-embassy.org.uk; visa applications Mon-Fri 9 am-noon). Consulates, Manchester and Edinburgh.

USA: 2300 Connecticut Avenue NW, Washington DC 20008 (☎ 202-3282-500, www.china-embassy.org/en). Consulates, Chicago, Houston, Los Angeles, New York and San Francisco.

Vietnam: 46 Hoang Dieu Road, Hanoi (☎ 0845-3736, www.vn.china-embassy.org)

Extending your Visa

If you need to extend your visa while in China, this can be done by visiting the local **Public Security Bureau** (**PSB** – see *Emergency Services and the Public Security Bureau*, p. 102). Visa extension applications will need to be supported by justification, more passport photos and payment. Costs, duration of processing and length of extension all vary from city to city – visa extensions are by no means a right and are sometimes refused; some travelers search out small town PSBs as they are thought to be more generous with extra time granted. If the PSB won't extend your visa, the only options left are to try in another town, or head to Hong Kong to apply for a new visa, which can be issued within a day or two (outside of weekends). PSBs are generally open Mondays to Fridays from 9-11:30 am and 2-4:30 pm. If you do overstay your visa for any reason you will usually be fined ¥500 for each extra day you have spent in the country, although long overstays can incur harsher penalties.

Insurance

As a rule travelers should certainly have **medical insurance** and, ideally, **possessions insurance** for any trip. China is no exception and while no-one will ask to see your documentation unless you are seriously sick or injured, the peace of mind afforded is worthwhile, regardless of any actual reimbursement. Before booking any insurance, check the coverage your existing homeowners or medical policy offers. You can often buy medical insurance only, but in order to get possessions coverage you'll usually have to purchase medical. Make sure your policy includes all activities that you'll be involved in during your trip – if you are going to be climbing, jet skiing, whitewater rafting or even just hiking, check that it's covered. If you're on a guided tour, the travel company may have their own insurance which should be sufficient for all activities undertaken on that trip, although you may not be insured if the company goes bankrupt – ask before buying.

Travel & Living Information

While possessions insurance can be seen as less of a necessity, it is still recommended. As people take ever more technical tiny gadgets away with them, and move from place to place in unfamiliar, exciting new surroundings, there is always the risk of leaving something behind and that is before you consider the fact that petty crime is on the rise in China.

Insurance policies come in many different forms and can cover just a few days or a whole year. If you're going to be traveling a lot in a year, it's worth considering a yearly package, which normally covers you for as many journeys as you'd like, as long as no single trip is over 31 days. When you're buying your insurance, check the comparative amounts on offer in case of **serious emergency** (hospitalization, repatriation, etc.), along with catches such as "single item limits" on your possessions (if your camera's worth US$1,000 and the limit is US$500 per piece, it's no good for you, even if it is cheap!) Once you have your insurance policy, photocopy it, leave one copy with relatives at home and put another somewhere separate from the original in your baggage.

Below are some recommended insurance agents – the letters before the commas indicate where the company is based.

Access America (US, www.accessamerica.com)

Association of British Insurers (UK, www.abi.org.uk)

Columbus (UK, www.columbusdirect.com)

Insurance Council of Australia (Australia, www.ica.com.au)

Insurance Council of New Zealand (NZ, www.icnz.org.nz)

Insureandgo (UK, www.insureandgo.com)

Royal Bank of Canada Insurance (Canada, www.rbcinsurance.com)

Wexas (UK, www.wexas.com)

World Nomads (worldwide, www.worldnomads.com)

Making a Claim

If you have to make a claim, you'll need **receipts** for everything you're claiming for, be it medical expenses, or an electronic item. To claim for stolen items you'll also need a **police report** issued within 24 hours of the theft; make sure the PSB (see *Emergency Services and the Public Security Bureau*, p. 102) understand you need the report for insurance purposes. Otherwise, you could be in for a long wild goose chase. If possible, take someone who can speak Chinese and English along with you (or see *Language, Emergencies* in the Chinese language section at the end of this guide for helpful terms).

What to Pack

 While there are some important things you should remember to pack, in general, the less you take the better, particularly if you'll be using lots of public transport. Obviously, what you pack depends to an extent on where you're going, when and in what style. I find a **rucksack** perfect for adventure travel, but if you'll be staying in upscale hotels, taking taxis and planes and using porters at train stations, a **suitcase** may be more appropriate. In terms of clothing, you should obviously pack according to the season, although a **hat** and **waterproof jacket** can be useful any time of year. Remember that **dark colors** will hide the grime better and taking a number of layers will give you more flexibility in your attire, while still allowing you to keep warm if needed.

Remember to put any blades, scissors, lighters or liquids in your checked luggage when flying.

Aside from **TIMP** (**tickets**, **insurance**, **money**, **passport**), which you've got to have, you can find most things you need more cheaply in China than at home, although the following may come in handy:

- Alarm clock
- Adaptor
- Business cards
- Camera
- Comfortable hardwearing shoes or sneakers
- Deodorant (difficult to find in China)
- Earplugs
- First aid kit and basic medicines (see *Health, Before you Leave*, p. 98)
- Flashlight
- Hat
- Insect repellent
- Lipbalm
- Mandarin phrasebook or dictionary
- Photocopies of your important documents
- Pictures of home (to show people you meet)
- Plastic ziplock and garbage bags
- Pocket knife
- Reading material
- Rubber sandals
- Sewing kit
- Small padlock
- Sunglasses
- Sunscreen
- Travel bathplug
- Waterproof jacket

Female travelers should note that tampons are difficult to find and expensive. Moisturizers without whitening agents are equally rare, so it's worth taking both with you.

Travel & Living Information

Information Sources

i As China becomes an increasingly popular destination (for both travel and work), there are more sources of information found on the country, both at home and in China. While the concept of tourist information is still finding its feet on the mainland, **Hong Kong** (www.discoverhongkong.com) and **Macau** (www.macautourism.gov.mo) have excellent tourist offices. As the most important cities in the country, Beijing and Shanghai also have good information resources, some of which are government-run, while others are private and include a host of ex-pat magazines and webzines. *That's Magazines* have printed magazines and websites with useful listings and well-researched reviews of **bars, clubs, restaurants** and **cultural events**. The main website is www.thatsmags.com, where there are links to its **Beijing, Shanghai and Pearl River Delta** pages, or you can pick up copies of the magazine in bars and hotels. The Ismay Network produces equally useful magazines to many of the cities in this book – *Beijing Talk, Shanghai Talk, South China City Talk* (Guangzhou, Shenzhen and Zhuhai) and *Macau Talk*. *Talk* and *that's Magazines* are available in bars, restaurants and hotels in the relevant cities. In addition to those listed here, there are other websites that are helpful for specific cities – see the *Information Sources* sections in individual chapters for listings.

China Excursions (www.chinaexcursions.com) – brief histories and descriptions of destinations around the country.

China Travel News (www.chinatravelnews.com) – the latest on everything to do with travel in China.

Travel China (www.travelchinaguide.com) – information on travel and a host of Chinese destinations.

Travel Advisories

The following governmental websites offer the latest information on the potential hazards of travel to countries around the world, including China.

Australian Department of Foreign Affairs (www.dfat.gov.au)

British Foreign and Commonwealth Office (www.fco.gov.uk)

Canadian Department of Foreign Affairs (www.dfait-maeci.gc.ca)

Irish Department of Foreign Affairs (www.irlgov.ie/iveagh)

New Zealand Ministry of Foreign Affairs (www.safetravel.govt.nz)

US State Department (www.travel.state.gov)

Maps

Having a good map of the country always helps in envisioning your trip and the type of landscapes it will encompass. A good map of the whole of China is *GeoCenter World Map* but, other than providing an interesting overview, maps that cover such a large area are of little use, although some include city plans for major cities. Throughout this guide there are maps to help point you in the right direction (see the map list in the table of contents for details). However, for more detail, it's worth buying a local city map once in China. Up-to-date city maps are available from vendors who operate outside train and bus stations; these usually cost around ¥5 and may include some English. Another place to find city maps (usually for free) is in upscale hotels – if you're staying, there will probably be one in your room; otherwise just ask at reception.

Customs & Immigration

However you arrive, you'll have to go through immigration and customs, which can be a lengthy process and you'll need to fill in an arrival card and a quarantine form. Note that if you have any particularly valuable items (or over US$5000 cash) you are supposed to declare them upon entry. You're not allowed to bring more than ¥6000 in Chinese money, 400 cigarettes or two liters of alcohol. Firearms, recreational drugs and animals are all prohibited items and, theoretically, you can't bring in media material critical of China, though this is seldom enforced. Note that if you buy any antiques over 100 years old during your trip, you must obtain an export form (available from Friendship Stores) before departing. It is illegal to take anything home that dates from before Qianlong's death in 1795.

There are also restrictions on what (and how much) you're allowed to bring back to your home country, which generally allow at least for a bottle of spirits, 200 or more cigarettes, some cologne or perfume and up to a certain value of souvenirs – check the following websites for the latest:

- **US** – www.cbp.gov
- **Canada** – www.ccra.gc.ca
- **UK** – www.hmce.gov.uk
- **Australia** – www.customs.gov.au
- **New Zealand** – www.customs.govt.nz

Getting Here & Away

China is accessible through the major international transport hubs of Beijing, Shanghai and Hong Kong. Airplane is the usual mode of entry, but arrival by boat or overland is also possible.

By Air

Beijing, **Hong Kong** and **Shanghai** are China's best-served international airports, receiving direct worldwide flights. But **Guangzhou** is seeing increasing international traffic and can offer some of the cheapest flights. While many of China's other city airports can

Travel & Living Information

take international traffic, they are predominantly served by flights from within the country and Asia. In recent years a number of **budget Asian carriers** like **Air Asia** (www.airasia.com) and **Tiger Airways** (www.tigerairways.com) have emerged, flying to airports such as Macau, Guangzhou and Shenzhen, which have substantially reduced prices from destinations such as Bangkok and Singapore.

Peak travel times (and therefore the highest flight prices) include the run up to Chinese New Year, midsummer and, in Hong Kong, the few weeks before Christmas. There are airlines listed under the relevant regions below, but if you want to look for the cheapest details the following online booking agents are worth checking out:

- www.bootsnall.com (US)
- www.cheaptickets.com (Worldwide)
- www.ebookers.com (UK & Europe)
- www.expedia.com (Worldwide)
- www.flightcentre.com (Worldwide)
- www.flychina.com (Worldwide)
- www.gonomad.com (Worldwide)
- www.hotwire.com (US)
- www.lastminute.com (UK)

The following airlines fly from the US, Canada, the UK, Europe, Australia and New Zealand to China and Hong Kong:

- Air China (www.airchina.com)
- Cathay Pacific (www.cathaypacific.com)
- China Airlines (www.china-airlines.com)
- EVA Air (www.evaair.com)

From the USA & Canada

Direct flights from the West Coast to China take about 13 hours and will cost between US$700 and US$1,500 round-trip, depending on the season and routing. From the East Coast, you'll need to add a few hours and a couple of hundred dollars.

The airlines listed below all operate direct flights from the US and Canada.

- Air Canada (www.aircanada.com)
- American Airlines (www.americanair.com)
- China Southern Airlines (www.cs-air.com/en)
- JAL (Japan Airlines, www.jal.co.jp/en)
- Korean Air (www.koreanair.com)
- Northwest Airlines (www.nwa.com)
- United Airlines (www.ual.com)

From the UK & Europe

Many of Europe's capital cities are linked by direct flights to China, which take between 10 and 12 hours and cost £350/€518 to £1,000/€1,480 round-trip, although a new Hong Kong-based long-haul budget carrier, Oasis Air (see below) has slashed these prices to as little as £160 for a single fare (or £470 for business class) from London. Airlines that fly from Europe to China include:

- Aeroflot (www.aeroflot.ru/en)
- Air France (www.airfrance.com)
- British Airways (www.ba.com)
- Gulf Air (www.gulfairco.com)
- KLM (www.klm.com)
- Lufthansa (www.lufthansa.com)
- Oasis Air (www.oasishongkong.com)
- Virgin Atlantic (www.fly.virgin.com)

From Australia & New Zealand

Direct flights from Australia take between nine and 12 hours to reach China and should cost around AUS$1,500 to $2,000. New Zealand is less well-served but there are still direct flights, although you may want to travel to Australia and then on from there.

- Air New Zealand (www.airnz.com)
- Jetstar (www.jetstar.com)
- Qantas (www.qantas.com)

CARBON MILES

When traveling by plane, it's important not to forget the damage that increased air traffic is causing to the environment, and a number of organizations, including www.climatecare.com, have been established to help you counterbalance your carbon miles. The website allows you to calculate the total carbon emissions for your journey and then make a proportionate contribution to be used on projects such as tree-planting to offset the environmental damage. While this could be seen as simply a way to alleviate one's guilt without actually doing anything to reduce carbon emissions, at least it raises awareness of the issue and attempts to redress some of the damage.

Overland

The most popular overland routes into China are from the north through **Mongolia**, from the south through **Vietnam** and **Laos**, and from the west through **Nepal into Tibet**, but it's also possible to get into Xinjiang from Pakistan and the Central Asian Republics along the old **Silk Route**. Note that for most of these countries you'll need to obtain a visa in advance.

You can book train tickets for the **Trans-Mongolian** and **Trans-Siberian Expresses** in Beijing (see p. 87), but to be sure of a berth it's worth booking in advance. **Monkey Business** (www.monkeyshrine.com – see p. 143 for Beijing office details) and **Sundowners** (www.sundownerstravel.com) can

Travel & Living Information

both arrange train tickets and connections online and can also help you obtain a Mongolian or Russian visa.

Heading to or from Laos or Vietnam there are several border crossings through Guangxi and Yunnan provinces that are open to foreigners. There are trains to Hanoi from Beijing, Guilin and Nanning or you can take a bus to Jinghong and then on to Mengla to cross into Laos.

By Water

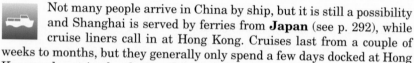 Not many people arrive in China by ship, but it is still a possibility and Shanghai is served by ferries from **Japan** (see p. 292), while cruise liners call in at Hong Kong. Cruises last from a couple of weeks to months, but they generally only spend a few days docked at Hong Kong and cost in the thousands of dollars. Cruise companies that run to Hong Kong include:

- Clipper (www.clippercruise.com)
- Cunard (www.cunard.com)
- P&O (www.pocruises.com)
- Princess (www.princess.com)
- Seabourn (www.seabourn.com)
- Star (www.starcruises.com)

Getting Around

China is a vast country with an ever-improving transport network, especially between principal cities, but it is also still a developing country and, while some services are ultra-modern, others are super-slow. Some regions are ruled by the road, while others are served better by rail. Travel by any mode of transport tends to be good value, especially when the distances covered are considered, although bus is usually the cheapest and flying the most expensive. The duration and scope of your itinerary and the amount of money you have to spend are deciding factors in how you travel. To get to smaller or more out of the way places you may have to take a bus (often from a railhead town), although for anything longer than a few hours, if it's an option, the train is preferable, unless you have the money to fly. Even if money is no object, **I'd recommend at least one long distance train journey** for the experience. Indeed, implicit in the term "traveling" is the journey itself and, for some, getting from A to B is the best part of the adventure. China has an abundance of local transport options which, while often uncomfortable, give you real insight into the lives of the people. Wherever you're planning to travel, unless you speak Mandarin, be sure to take along your destination written in Chinese (see the Chinese language section at the end of this guide). While pronouncing the name may seem like a simple process, the tones of the language and the plethora of similar-sounding place names can cause confusion.

Below are some sample fares (quoted in US dollars) in order to give a rough idea of the costs of different modes of transport.

SAMPLE PRICE GUIDE				
Route	Miles	By Plane	By Train	By Bus
Beijing-Shanghai	630	$145 (1hr 50mins)	$70 (12hr)	$40 (14hr)
Shanghai-Hong Kong	770	$255 (3hr)	$120 (24hr)	N/A
Shenzhen-Guilin	310	$85 (1hr 10)	$30 (15hr)	$30 (12hr)

By Air

China has an extensive flight network incorporating hundreds of frequently served airports. There are several **regional airlines** (China Southern, China Southwestern, etc.), many of which are subdivisions of Air China, the national carrier. Most towns of any significance have a branch of the regional airline that can issue tickets and many hotels have travel agents who can book them for a small commission. In larger cities you'll find CAAC offices where you can buy tickets for most airlines and often get buses to the airport. Airports can be close to the city center or tens of miles away so check when you purchase your tickets. While Chinese air travel doesn't have a particularly good safety track record, things have definitely improved, both in terms of pilot ability and aircraft quality. That said, flying in China is a very different experience, from the frequent turbulence to the "lucky seat lottery," although delays seem to be a worldwide feature!

Airline Details

- Air China (www.airchina.com)
- China Eastern Airlines (www.ce-air.com)
- China Southern Airlines (www.cs-air.com/en)
- China Southwestern Airlines (www.cswa.com)
- Dragon Air (www.dragonair.com)
- Shanghai Airlines (www.shanghai-air.com/English/ehome)

By Rail

Rail is generally my favorite mode of travel in any country and China is no exception. More comfortable than by road and cheaper than air, train travel affords you some time to reflect on your travels as the countryside unfolds through the window to the gentle (and sometimes abrupt) clackety clack of the tracks below. It also offers the opportunity to meet locals (albeit, on occasion, too closely for comfort). And it can give you a look at the conflicts of modern China; the system is authoritarian in essence, with its smartly dressed, stern staff and regulated systems, but these days you can hire VCD players (some trains even have individual TVs in first-class sleeper compartments) and buy tacky toys along the way. Stations usually have shops and stalls selling all the goods you'll need for a long

Travel & Living Information

journey and there are dining carriages on many **sleeper services** along with platform snacks along the way. You'll also find **checkrooms** for luggage at stations and some stations have designated waiting rooms for first-class passengers (see *Classes*, below). China has an extensive railway network that covers all the major cities, now including Lhasa, which is the end destination of the high-altitude, ultra-modern Tibet line, part of the government's program to develop the west.

Categories of Train

Trains are categorized according to their speed. The new **D trains** are the fastest, with **Z** trains hot on their heels, followed by **T** and then **K** trains, which are still fairly speedy. Un-lettered trains are the slowest of the bunch and are worth avoiding if you have a long distance to cover, as they also tend to be older and thus less comfortable and clean. The faster the train, the more expensive the tickets will be.

Classes

Trains are divided into four classes and any train may have all or only one of these classes, depending on its route and speed. All classes have **restrooms** (though these are often squat and can get pretty filthy), a supply of **hot water** for tea, and generally some kind of **food and drink** provision, usually in the form of a buffet car and food trolleys.

The bottom of the scale is "**hard seat**" which is, on the oldest trains, literally that, just a hard wooden seat, though most of these have been replaced by (still fairly rigid) cushioned seats. This is where you'll get to mingle with the masses but, when you consider the price, it's really not that bad, although it can be taxing for longer journeys. **Soft seat** is the next level up and the seats and clientele reflect the jump in price. Soft-seat carriages are sometimes double-decker. **Hard sleeper** is the most commonly used class for longer trips and accordingly gets booked up the quickest. Although the name doesn't quite conjure up images of luxury, it's actually fairly comfortable. Here you'll have one of six bunks fitted into booths along one side of the train. Although the bottom level is the most expensive, followed by the middle level and then the top, there is debate among travelers as to which is best. The bottom obviously offers the easiest access and is the roomiest, but you'll have people sitting on your bed during the day. You get a little less room in the middle but more privacy, and on the top you feel away from it all, although you have very little space to savor this. **Soft sleeper** is the top of the line, where you'll reside in a private four-bunk compartment. As with hotels, the comfort of the train also depends on its age, thus hard sleeper on a new train can be almost as good as soft sleeper on an old one The most modern trains on major routes (Beijing to Shanghai, for example) have a new "**business**" **class** where you get a two-room compartment complete with restroom and TV! In the sleeper classes you're provided with clean bedding and a flask of hot water per compartment. On entering the train you'll need to exchange your ticket for a metal or plastic tag, which enables the attendant to make sure you get off at the right station. Indeed, you'll often be awakened a good hour before the train is due so they can turn your bed around for the next passenger. Although the incidence of crime isn't high, it's worth securing your luggage to a rail with a padlock and keeping an eye on your possessions

Buying a Ticket

Buying a ticket from the train station can be a confusing and time-consuming business, so many travelers elect to purchase them through an **agent** (often found in your hotel), for a **small surcharge**. For frequently served shorter routes it's easy enough to just arrive at the station and get a ticket for the next train. However, for longer journeys, especially during peak times or on popular routes, trains can be completely booked for days, so if you know your schedule it's worth buying your ticket on arrival in the city. If you do buy your ticket at the station, make sure you take along the **written Chinese name for your destination** (see language boxes in individual chapters), ask which line to stand in, then get ready for some pushing, culminating in the frantic decision-making process as the masses behind try to oust you from your number one spot! Some stations have **designated foreigners' ticket windows**, which are worth seeking out as the staff might speak English and the lines are often shorter. See the *Language* section at the end of this guide for the train classes in Chinese.

By Road

China's road network has undergone massive investment in the last decade and some journey times have been dramatically reduced as a result. The efficiency of the government is undeniable in making progress here. While environmental action committees and protests are often the norm when a new road is proposed in Europe, in China it's a simple case of get out of the way or face the consequences. This may show little concern for human rights, but it is certainly an efficient way of getting the job done and roads are finished in a fraction of the time it would take elsewhere in the world (safety considerations aside). New **toll highways** have been built between major cities and roads have often superseded former modes of transport (especially the rivers) as the way to get around. However, China remains an enormous country and, although some areas (the Pearl River Delta and the Yangzi Basin) have been dissected by new **expressways** in recent times, much of rural China is still connected by unbelievably bumpy **dirt tracks**, which get washed away every rainy season. Journeys on these routes can be crowded, uncomfortable, frustrating and scary. But, if you're not in a hurry, they are another great way to see the country and come face-to-face with the locals, baskets of chickens and all.

Buses

While seldom as comfortable as the train, buses are generally cheaper, more frequent and often quicker for shorter routes. In remote or **mountainous areas** buses may be the only transport option. Intercity buses are generally categorized as *putong* (**ordinary**) class or *kuai* (**express**). The latter use expressways where available and are thus faster, tend to be more comfortable and are around double the price. There are also **sleeper buses** that link cities across the country, sometimes taking upwards of 30 hours. Typically, these are rickety old affairs with flat bunk beds, but a new breed of **upmarket express sleeper buses** has recently come into being, with DVD players, fully reclinable chairs and restrooms. On shorter routes you might also find **shuttle minibuses**, which cost a little more than standard buses and are a little quicker once on the road, but you'll have to wait for them to fill up before leaving. With local services your luggage may go on the roof or have to be squeezed in with you, but on more modern vehicles it will probably be stowed beneath and you'll receive a tag to reclaim it. It's worth taking some food on long-distance services as break stops can be erratic, but on rural routes there may be a wealth of local snacks to choose from as passengers get on and off at small market towns. There are usually shops selling snacks at bus stations and there may also be luggage storage facilities.

Buying a Ticket

In smaller towns and cities there may only be one **bus station** but in larger urban areas there can often be several, which serve different regions, as well as express stations in the center. For short hops you can generally just show up and get on the next bus, but for longer journeys it's worth buying your ticket in advance or arriving in the morning as buses are less frequent in the afternoons, and often finish at sundown during winter, unless there are sleeper services. Once you're at the station you may be faced with a daunting number of ticket windows but staff are generally helpful.

Car Rental

Forbidden until recently, car rental options are still limited in China unless you're a resident with a Z visa (and a valid license from your home country), in which case you can obtain the Chinese license necessary to drive here. Otherwise, your options are restricted to hiring a car with driver, which can be arranged through major international chains such as Avis (www.avischina.com) and Hertz (www.hertz.com.cn) or local companies – rates start from around US$40 a day.

Hong Kong and **Macau** are exceptions to the rule and you can easily rent a self-drive car in either – exploring Macau's coastal roads in the Cub and Moke jeeps they offer is great fun. If you live on the mainland and choose to drive, it soon becomes apparent that the rules of the road revolve around size – the bigger the vehicle the more you need to avoid it. Outside of the cities you need to pay particular attention at night as many drivers seem oblivious to the fact their cars have lights!

By Boat

Rivers and canals used to be one of the primary transport means for both people and freight in China, but these days they have been replaced by road, rail and air. Conversely, for visitors, river travel still offers one of the best ways to see idyllic rural China, with some of the country's most spectacular scenery as a backdrop. Of particular note are the **Three Gorges** (see p. 270), **Guangxi's Li River** (see p. 402) and the **Grand Canal** (see p. 340-41). While you can organize most cruises while you're in China, if you want to guarantee a quality boat to cruise the Three Gorges it's worth booking from home – see the websites listed under *Booking from Overseas* on p. 273. There are also **ferries** between **Hong Kong** and **Macau** and to Pearl River Delta destinations.

City Travel

Getting around China's cities can seem like an overwhelming task, especially given their monumental size, legions of flyovers and the array of long and unfamiliar street names. This confusion is somewhat simplified when you realize that each street name is made up of its title and a compound of smaller words indicating its position within the city and the road's size. *Bei, dong, nan, xi* mean north, east, south and west, respectively and *zhong* means middle. *Xiang* means alley, *lu* means road, *jie* means street, *dajie* means avenue, *men* means gate and *qiao* means bridge. *Guangchang* is square, *yuan* is garden and *zhan* means station. Thus Nanjing Dong Lu means Nanjing East Road, Jianguomen Qiao means Jianguo Gate Bridge and so on.

Subway

These days many of China's major cities, including Hong Kong, Shenzhen, Guangzhou, Shanghai and Beijing, have subway systems which are sometimes known as MTRs (Mass Transit Railways) and these offer a convenient, easy and inexpensive way to get around these cities. You usually buy tickets (¥2-10) from machines, which have English instructions, and stations are marked (and sometimes announced) in English. Closest subway stations are given where appropriate throughout the book.

Bus

Every Chinese city has a cheap and extensive bus network and this often forms the backbone of the urban transport system. However, the fact that destinations are generally only marked in Chinese, and that buses can be very crowded and often aren't air-conditioned makes the subway preferable where it's an option. You normally pay (¥1-2) onboard and often need to have exact change. Show the driver your destination written in Chinese and, if you're lucky, he or she will give you the nod when it's time to get off. Bus numbers are given where appropriate throughout the book.

Taxi

Taxis are the easiest way to get around China's cities. Although drivers seldom speak English, as long as you have your destination written in Chinese (see the language boxes) you won't go too far wrong. Flagfall rates vary from ¥4 to ¥12.5 for the first two km (1.2 miles) and then rise in increments beyond this. Make sure that the driver uses the meter ("*da biao*"). In some cities you'll also find motorcycle taxis, which are a speedy way to get through the clogged city streets but it can be difficult to get a fair price – see individual chapter listings for details.

Cycle Rickshaw

China still has cycle rickshaws and pedicabs, although in some of its cities these are exclusively the preserve of tourists and you need to bargain hard before you set out on your journey. If you're in a hurry they are hardly ideal, but to soak up the pace of the city they can make a fun change. See individual cities for approximate rates.

Bicycle

Although being rapidly superseded by scooters and cars, the bicycle is the traditional mode of transport in China. In spite of modernization, China has over half a billion cycles – by far the highest ownership in the world. Although cycling around the big cities can initially seem a little daunting, there are often designated cycle lanes and, as long as you move with

Cycle rickshaws

the masses, you'll be fine. Bikes can be rented in most cities and offer an excellent way to get around, particularly in Hangzhou, Suzhou and the countryside. Rates vary from as little as ¥5 for a day, to ¥50 an hour from some upmarket hotels.

Ferry

The cities are also often best seen from the water – Hong Kong, Shanghai, Hangzhou and Suzhou are testaments to this. Although seldom very practical (with the exception of Hong Kong's Star Ferry), ferries present a different side of the city and, if you're short of funds, they can offer a cheap alternative to a river or harbor cruise.

Practicalities

Money Matters

The Currency

The currency of China is the **yuan** (¥), also known as the kwai or renminbi (RMB), which literally translates as "people's money." At the time of writing there were ¥8 to the **US dollar**, ¥10 to the **Euro**

and ¥16 to the **British Pound Sterling**. Paper money was introduced to the world by China in 806 AD and today **bank notes** come in various amounts, many of which show a portrait of the omnipresent Chairman Mao on the front and famous landscapes from around the country on the back. Denominations are ¥100 (red), ¥50 (green), ¥20 (brown), ¥10 (blue), ¥5 (purple or brown), ¥2 (green) and ¥1 (green

Money, money, money (Tot Foster)

or brown), along with the almost worthless 5, 2 and 1 mao notes (10 mao, also referred to as jiao = ¥1). The ¥2 and 2 mao notes are both green and look very similar – remember the lower value one is the smaller of the two. **Counterfeiting** is rife in China and even the smallest local store may have a UV scanner. While ¥10 notes are often copied, the one to watch out for is the ¥100 (see *Warning – Scams*, p. 101). The quality of fakes is often high, but generally you can tell by the feel of the money, which is often a little too crunchy to the touch. In Hong Kong the currency is the **Hong Kong dollar** (HK$) and at the time of writing there were HK$8 to the US$, HK$10 to the Euro and HK$15 to the British Pound Sterling. In Macau the *pataca*, or **Macau dollar** (MOP$) is roughly equivalent to the HK$, which can be used throughout the territory.

Banks & Foreign Exchange

The **Bank of China** (not the Agricultural Bank of China, Construction Bank of China, Industrial Bank of China or any of the other similarly named institutions) is the only bank licensed to exchange foreign currency or travelers' checks. Their opening hours may vary but are generally **Monday to Friday from 9 am-noon and 2-5 pm**. Upscale hotels can also change money, although their rates tend to be a little worse.

In order to change money you'll need your passport and, often, a sense of patience, as each one of your crisp greenbacks or checks is meticulously inspected. **Dollars** are by far the most readily accepted exchange currency, followed by **Euros** and then **Pounds Sterling**. When China first opened its doors to tourism in the 1980s, foreigners had to use FECs (Foreign Exchange Certificates), which led to the development of blackmarket money changing. Now that tourists use yuan like everybody else, blackmarket money changers are rare – if you are approached with rates that sound too good to be true, steer clear as there will probably be a few fake bills among your wad. Note that you can't change Chinese yuan into other currencies outside of China so budget accordingly and spend all of your cash!

Unlike Mainland China, **Hong Kong** is overflowing with exchange booths and it's quick and easy to change money. Some of the best rates are generally found on the ground floor of **Chungking Mansions** on Nathan Road in Kowloon.

Travel & Living Information

Travelers' Checks

Traveler's checks are a safer option many people choose, although you'll pay a small surcharge for each check cashed. Ideally they should be purchased from one of the better-known issuers such as **American Express**, as lesser known versions may not be accepted in smaller towns. Be sure to note down the serial numbers and keep them and the purchase agreement separate from your checks. Also don't countersign them until you're sure the bank teller is watching.

ATMs & Credit Cards

 China has an expanding number of ATMs, which will usually accept **Amex**, **VISA**, **MasterCard**, **Maestro** and **Cirrus**, though you'll pay a small flat fee for each withdrawal and, outside of large cities, ATMs may be hard to come by. Also, while plastic seems a safe and easy way to carry your cash, bear in mind that ATMs can be temperamental (or empty), so they should be used as a back-up rather than your principal source of funds. In Hong Kong, ATMs are found on seemingly every corner, although the same precautions apply. For larger purchases, **credit cards** are often a good way to go. China is increasingly geared up to finding ways for visitors to part with their money and many larger shops, chains or "factory" outlets will accept credit cards, albeit with a surcharge of around 3%.

Money Transfer

If you're really stuck for cash, Western Union (www.westernunion.com) has offices around the country, often found in post offices. The sender has to pay a surcharge and you need to take along your passport to receive funds. Western Union outlets are listed where available.

Costs

While not as cheap as some parts of Asia, China still makes for an inexpensive destination in terms of **day-to-day living costs**. The four main costs of traveling (apart from the price of airfare to and from your home country) are **accommodation, eating, transport**, and **attraction entry fees**. At the most basic, it's possible to live and travel on **less than US$20 a day**. However, this involves hunting out the cheapest lodgings, eating mainly street food, traveling by local bus or hard seat train (see *Getting Around By Rail*, p. 87) and passing up shopping and more expensive tourist sites. A more realistic figure for most travelers would be in the region of **US$50-150 a day**, which incorporates mid-range hotels, eating in good restaurants, the occasional flight and entry to all the tourist sites you'd want to visit, along with a bit of shopping. If you want a more luxurious **five-star tour**, plan on a minimum of **US$200** a day.

Tipping

Tipping is not an established practice in China and is only expected in places accustomed to dealing with tourists. Thus **tourist guides** or **drivers** are to be tipped, as are **bellboys** and **waiters** in better hotels. If you are on a group trip, tips are often arranged by the tour leader. Beyond this, any attempts to tip are generally politely refused, no matter how deserving you may feel a person is.

Keeping in Touch

Mail

 China Post is the national mail carrier and its green and yellow (or green and white) signed branches are found in every town. Here you can send and receive mail and parcels, buy **telephone cards** and sometimes **make international calls**. To receive mail, have it addressed to yourself at Post Restante, China Post, City, Province, China – you'll need your passport as ID to collect it. **Standard mail** to North America or Europe usually takes at least a week, although **EMS** (express mail service) is quicker and registers your mail. To send a postcard overseas costs ¥3.2, a letter costs ¥4.4, and parcels are around ¥85/US$10 per kilo (2.2lb) for surface mail or ¥160/US$20 per kilo for airmail. If you want to send a parcel home, you need to leave it unsealed so the items can be checked – there are packing services at post offices. China Post offices are generally **open from 8 am to 6 pm**, although in smaller settlements opening hours may be shorter, while larger cities sometimes have 24-hour branches where you might also find **Western Union** money transfer offices (see *Money Transfer*, p. 94). The staff will generally be able to decipher the destination, but to be sure you could get the country written in Chinese by your hotel (for a list of countries, see *Language*, at the end of this guide). If you can't get to a China Post, there are also a few green and yellow mail boxes dotted around some of the bigger cities. In upscale hotels you can buy stamps in the business center and they may send your mail for you too.

Telephones

China Telecom is the nation's telecommunications provider and their blue and white signs are found in all towns, very often next to China Post. Here you can make **international calls** by a variety of means as well as **send faxes**, and in some larger cities, check your **e-mail**. China Telecom business hours are usually from **9 am to 8 pm** although larger cities may have 24-hour offices. There are private booths, where you are charged by the minute (around ¥3 per minute to Europe or North America) , **IC phonecards**, which slot into public telephones (similar cost), and, cheapest of all, **Internet phone (IP) cards** where you have to dial an access number, tap in your pin and number and are then connected interna-

Travel & Living Information

tionally. You can also buy **SIM cards** for your **cell phone** here, but be sure your phone is tri-band and the SIM you purchase enables international calls if you want to make or receive them. If you buy a SIM, you'll then have to purchase "pay as you go" top-up cards as you need them (keeping the old one to show staff when buying a new one makes getting the correct card easier) and note that you generally pay to receive calls. There are also public telephones and private telephone offices found everywhere. If you're staying in a mid-range or above hotel, you'll probably have **IDD** (**International Direct Dialing**) from your room, although you'll have to give a deposit of some sort to open the line. Also be aware that the hotel may charge for a call even if you didn't actually get through, and they map slap on a hefty surcharge.

To dial internationally, you'll need to tap in the correct country code (see below) and drop the first zero of the regional code. Within China, for local calls you dial the number without the code (unless calling from a cell phone), only adding the code if you're calling from another city. In Hong Kong and Macau, local calls are free from hotel phones.

International Dialing Codes

Australia – 00 61

Canada – 00 1

China – 00 86

Hong Kong – 00 852

Macau – 00 853

New Zealand – 00 64

UK – 00 44

US – 00 1

E-Mail

The Internet is very popular in China and all towns and cities have **Internet cafés** (many of which are 24-hr) where you can check your e-mail account, although speeds, standards and rates vary considerably. Recently there have been stricter controls on Internet cafés after a fatal fire in June 2002, although some argue that this was just an excuse to introduce stronger **web filtering** and thus **restrict access** to sensitive websites (see *Media, Internet*, below, p. 97). Along with firewalls, you currently also have to register your passport to use the Internet in some cities such as Shanghai. In the cheapest cafés (¥2) connection may not be that good and you're likely to find yourself surrounded by swarms of adolescent online gamers. Better cafés charge a little more (¥5 upwards) and can offer quieter and sometimes quicker access. Many hostels and backpacker cafés also have a few computers for Internet use, and some even have wireless connection if you've brought a laptop. Big hotel **business centers** are pricier (¥20 an hour upwards) but should offer the same speeds and services as their counterparts in other countries. These days many mid-range hotels have Internet connection and maybe even wireless in their guest rooms – look for the @ symbol in the hotel listings in this guide.

Media

The media in China is **censored** in all its forms, and editors may face jail time if they communicate unauthorized material. The state-run news agency, Xinhua (www.xinhuanet.com/english/), is the principal source of information and their choices about which stories to report and how to do so can be insightful. Hong Kong is a different story, with a wide variety of uncensored media.

Newspapers & Magazines

China's main English language newspaper, the *China Daily* (www.chinadaily.com.cn/english), offers news reflecting the way the government would like foreigners to view China, along with a handy listings section, and it's available at bigger hotels throughout the country. The main Chinese language national is the *People's Daily* which is available in English

Keeping up-to-date with current affairs

online at www.english.people.com. There are also local English Language newspapers, such as the *Shanghai Daily*, which predominantly cover city and national news, but also give international round-ups. **Magazines** are principally Chinese-language and those that are in English are, as ever, heavily censored, but often contain interesting articles nonetheless – try *China Today*, which was established by Soong Qingling, wife of Dr. Sun Yatsen. In large cities you can find imported, unadulterated international magazines such as *National Geographic, Newsweek* and *Time*. Larger cities also have ex-pat-oriented magazines like *City Weekend*, which contain reviews, entertainment listings and stories that don't always toe the party line. You can find these magazines in bigger hotels and bars, restaurants and cafés popular with ex-pats, although some are available on the Internet – *that's magazines* (www.thatsmags.com) is one website to look for, with Beijing, Shanghai and Pearl River Delta editions.

Internet

In spite of the mammoth task it appears to be, the Chinese authorities are committed to controlling Internet use and thus they restrict access to certain websites, predominantly political or religious. But even Google was temporarily blocked in 2002 and has recently agreed to remove websites that feature sensitive issues from its search results. On my most recent trip, www.wikipedia.com was inaccessible and in Shenzhen icons of police officers come up on screen when you enter a website or chatroom. Incoming digital documents are also monitored through a nationwide firewall that scans for combinations of suspect words. Thus, in terms of real news, the Internet can be a disappointing medium, but it offers insight on how the country operates, and it's worth trying to find what you want, since access levels vary.

Radio

On the radio you'll mostly hear a mix of **Canto-pop** and **Mando-pop** (see *Music* p. 65), opera, **Taiwanese** tracks and **Western covers** but, beyond music, unless you can understand Chinese, your options will be fairly limited. Some of the bigger cities have English-language stations such as **Hit FM** (77.7FM) and **Easy FM** (91.5FM), but otherwise it's a case of searching out the **BBC World Service** or **Voice of America** (see www.bbc.co.uk/worldservice and www.voanews.com for frequencies and schedules).

Television

A flick through China's TV channels can be an interesting experience, encompassing Beijing Opera, old war movies, ridiculous gameshows, costume dramas and authorized news. However, for English-language programs, unless you're staying in an upscale hotel, which might have **CNN** and **international movie** and **sports networks**, you'll need to check out **CCTV9**. This state-run English channel offers culture, news, sports and travel, all of it "approved," although it can be informative nonetheless. You may even see Canadian Mark Rowswell (aka Dashan, meaning Big Mountain), arguably China's most famous foreigner, who has become a household name thanks to his flawless Mandarin, and still appears on CCTV educational shows. **CCTV6** sometimes shows Western movies in English at around 10 pm. In Hong Kong, **Pearl TV** is the English-language channel and, as with most things in Hong Kong, it is far freer in its programming, with regular Hollywood movies and hit series such as *Sex and the City* and *The West Wing*.

Health

 If you come to China for any length of time there is a chance you could get sick, and indeed, in winter, half the populace seems to be ill, but a few preparatory steps should help minimize any impact on your trip.

Minor Illnesses

Most people's fear is of **stomach illness** and in many countries around the world a change in cooking ingredients, oil and water can cause "Delhi belly," "Montezuma's revenge," "the Pharaoh's curse," or whatever you want to call it. However, this is far less common in China, where fresh ingredients are cooked very quickly, at high temperatures. You can further reduce your chances of sickness by a few basic hygiene measures – wash your hands often, keep your nails clean and try not to share eating utensils. **Water** is another area to watch – drink only boiled or mineral water and brush your teeth with it as well. If you're going well off the beaten track it's worth taking water purification tablets along with you. In spite of precautions you could still end up with an upset stomach. If so, as long as it's nothing too serious, rest, plenty of water and rehydration salts generally resolve the problem. Try not to take diarrhea stoppers unless you have to travel, as they can make the problem linger. If you have longer-lasting symptoms, or blood or mucus in your stool, see a doctor.

Far more likely in this crowded country is a **throat** or **chest infection** brought about by a combination of germs from a billion Chinese spitting (see *Etiquette* p. 104), pollution and the difference in temperatures when changing from air-conditioning to sweltering heat. If it's nothing serious, lozenges can keep your throat lubricated; cold and flu remedies and rest should bring about recovery.

Mosquito-Borne Diseases

Mosquito-borne illnesses aren't a serious problem in most parts of China, but **malaria** and **dengue fever** do occur in the south, notably in Hainan and southern Yunnan. If you're visiting these regions during the summer, it might be worth taking **anti-malarial prophylactics**. While malaria is transmitted by the *anopheles* mosquito, which tends to bite from dusk onwards, the zebra-striped *aedes aegpti*, which can carry dengue fever, strikes in the daytime. But taking a few precautions should stop you from getting bitten in the first place. Keep covered up from sundown, wear repellent (containing some, but not too much DEET), burn mosquito coils and, if you have the inclination, buy a "hunter" – an electrified fly-swat in the shape of a small tennis racket available in Chinese supermarkets which, in very non-Buddhist fashion, eliminates the bugs.

AIDS, SARS & Bird Flu

While long denied by the authorities, **AIDS** is a serious problem in China, ever more so as the country relaxes its sexual attitudes. The situation is exacerbated by high levels of **prostitution** and the refusal of many men to wear condoms (which are easily available), along with increasing drug use in the south. However, the most worrisome of China's health risks are posed by potentially fatal new forms of flu viruses such as **SARS** (Severe Acute Respiratory Syndrome) and more recently **bird flu**. Although neither has, as yet, developed into the feared global pandemic, many experts say it is only a matter of time. If there is a suspected outbreak, travel can be seriously affected and then, of course, there's the risk posed by the disease itself, so see www.cdc.gov/travel for the latest.

Getting Medical Attention

For more serious ailments or injuries, see a doctor, ideally at a hospital in a bigger city, where the chances of an **English-speaking doctor** (and better facilities) are greater. If there isn't anyone who speaks English, see *Language*, at the end of this guide. for some useful phrases. For less serious or longer-term problems it's interesting and sometimes beneficial to try some **Traditional Chinese Medicine** (see p. 71 for more).

Before You Leave

There are a few things you can organize from home to further prepare for your trip. It's worth taking a small **first aid kit** with you, especially if you'll be heading off the beaten track. The following items make for a good, basic kit:

- Antiseptic cream and wipes
- Assorted plasters
- Bandages
- Butterfly stitches
- Cold and flu remedy
- Cotton wool
- Dressings
- Insect bite cream
- Iodine
- Rehydration sachets
- Scissors
- Sterile needle and suture kit
- Surgical cream
- Throat lozenges
- Vitamin pills

Secondly, it's also a good idea to have some **basic medicinal drugs** with you. Although many drugs are easily available over the counter in China, communication may be an issue and in smaller towns you might not find what you need. So taking along **antihistamines** (for allergic reactions), an all-purpose **antibiotic**, a basic **cold and flu remedy**, **diarrhea stoppers** and **painkillers** might be useful, but check with your doctor for what's appropriate for you.

Thirdly, while you're not required to have any **inoculations** to enter China (unless you've come from a yellow fever-infected area), check that you are up-to-date with your **vaccinations**, particularly **hepatitis A and B, tetanus, typhoid, tuberculosis**. And if you plan to spend a lot of time with animals or out in the wilds, a **rabies** shot isn't a bad idea. Register at www.tripprep.com for an up-to-date list of recommended travel vaccines.

Restrooms

Restrooms in China are a far cry from North American norms, although things are no longer quite as bad as they used to be, especially in the big cities. **Public restrooms** are the lowest of the low, always squat rather than seat and often without partitions between users. And then there's the smell, which can be stomach-churning. In spite of all of these indignities there is often one more to add – having to pay (2-5 mao) to use some public toilets. You'll be able to buy tissues from the attendant since the restrooms obviously don't have them. Just one more point of note – the actual toilet is often just a trough, above which you squat and it's advisable to remove your sunglasses before you do so; many are the times as a tourleader that I heard shrieks from my guests as their expensive shades dropped into the trough, and some of them actually retrieved them! Of course if you've gotta' go, you've gotta' go, but whenever possible use restrooms in your hotel, a restaurant or a shopping center.

Safety

When compared to most Western countries China comes out as very safe, especially when you take into account the vast disparity between rich and poor. However, this isn't to say that **crime** is non-existent; indeed petty theft is increasingly common, although violent crime against tourists is almost unheard of. A few **basic precautions** should help you stay trouble-free. First, keep any valuables you have to take with you in a money-belt worn under your clothing. Second, be aware of your personal space (especially in crowded or heavily touristed areas) and if you're concerned about your other valuables such as your camera, keep them in front of you. Finally, avoid walking on unlit streets alone late at night.

If something does happen, then a few precautionary steps should at least minimize damages. **Make photocopies of your passport** including the **visa page**, **insurance documents** and **tickets** and leave one copy with friends or relatives and keep another with you, in a separate location from the actual documents. Always keep the aforementioned and your cash, credit cards and travelers' checks safely stowed in a money belt, or, if you don't need them, leave them in your hotel safe. Divide your money, only keeping a small amount out for your day's spending and keep an emergency stash of US dollars. If you have something stolen and want to make an insurance claim, you'll need a police report (see *Insurance*, p. 79, for details).

WARNING - SCAMS

While China is a reasonably safe place to travel, there are those who will perceive you as a cashpot and who have invented ingenious ways of helping you to part with your money. The most common scam in China involves a couple of young women or teenage girls approaching you on the pretense of wanting to practice their English, which is invariably fairly good. After some chatting, they'll invite you either to an art display (usually owned by their "uncle") or a café. In the case of the former you'll be pressured into buying overpriced art, while the latter will lead to you paying for the girls' food and drinks at inflated prices. If you refuse, the doors may be closed and a few heavies might appear, although I've never heard any reports of violence occurring – indeed if you stick to your guns, chances are they'll back off. But best of all is just to avoid the scenario. Another popular trick is claiming the bill you have given as payment is a fake and then demanding another, thereby sticking you with a forged note. This is particularly prevalent with ¥100 bills at phone card stalls – don't let your note out of sight.

A more alarming but less common scam is being offered some food or drink on a long-distance bus or train journey by someone you've been chatting with for a while. Later you wake up with a groggy head and no valuables. However, I must temper this tale with the fact that I've been traveling around China on public transport for years and have never fallen victim to this scam, or met anyone first-hand who has. There is a balance to be struck between caution and closing yourself off from the predominantly good and honest people of this land.

Emergency Services & the Public Security Bureau

If you need emergency assistance, the following numbers are applicable throughout the mainland: **Police** (☎ 110); **Fire** (☎ 119); **Ambulance** (☎ 120) – see *Emergency & Medical Services* for the relevant numbers in Hong Kong and Macau. Although there should be an English speaker available at these numbers, try to have a Chinese speaker make the call. The police have far more extensive powers than their contemporaries in the West and while individual officers may be helpful to foreigners, it's probably best not to cross their path unless you have to, which you will if you have something stolen and need a police report – ask for the *jing cha* (police). The **Public Security Bureau** (PSB) deals with issues relating to visas (see *Extending your Visa*, p. 78) but can also be contacted in emergencies – see individual chapters for PSB locations and telephone numbers.

Begging

While beggars are not as prevalent in China as in some other Asian or South American countries, as more and more rural Chinese flood to the cities, it is an increasingly serious problem. It's worth working out what your feelings are and how you will respond in advance as this will make situations easier to deal with. You may feel that begging begets begging and thus choose not to give anything to anyone, thereby hopefully instilling the concept that foreigners are not endless bags of money, and making the journey easier for those who come after you. Or you might choose to give food or pens rather than money, although this still ultimately leads to a form of dependency. As a tour leader, I once visited a small village that had probably never seen another foreigner. The people were a little bewildered initially but soon warmed up to be friendly and hospitable. As we were leaving, a member of my group gave a few bananas to the local kids, a seemingly innocuous gesture. On my return to this village a few months later with a different group we were immediately besieged by children demanding bananas!

If you want to be left alone, giving may seem like the easy option, but in some cases this may actually end up attracting more beggars to pounce on the "soft target." And if you do give, the big question is then, to whom do you give? The cute little girl who tugs relentlessly at your leg or the old man passed out on the sidewalk – often those who are the most needy are also the least likely to benefit. And this is to say nothing of organized **begging syndicates** that sometimes put children out on the streets to work in order to generate sympathy and thus revenue. So, heart-rending as it is, the simplest solution may actually be not to give to anyone, instead making a **charitable donation** of time or money.

CHARITABLE ORGANIZATIONS

China is the most populous country in the world and, while there are plenty of people who seem to be getting rich in the cities, there are an awful lot more who struggle to feed themselves. Access to clean water, healthcare, education and legal representation is far from universal and what is a small amount of money to you can make a big difference to those in need. There are worthwhile organizations mentioned in the individual city accounts (look for the *Putting Something Back* callouts), and the following registered charities can also provide information about other projects and will gladly accept donations.

- www.actionaid.org/china
- www.chineseredcross.org.cn/English
- www.christian-aid.org.uk/world/where/asia/chinap
- www.oxfam.org.hk

Photography

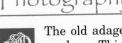 The old adage, take only photographs, leave only footprints, is a good one. This said, you should only take pictures of people who are happy to have their photo taken and also be aware that it's forbidden to take photographs at certain sites deemed of military importance (airports, bridges), and at some tourist locales like the Terracotta Warriors (although this rule is flagrantly ignored by many visitors). In popular tourist areas you may be asked to pay to take people's pictures – it's up to you whether you decide to do this, but bear in mind that, if you do, travelers who follow in your footsteps will certainly have to pay. The best way to get pictures of locals, though, is to strike up a conversation (or some kind of inter-

action) and offer to send them a copy of their picture. Make sure you fulfill your promise. For pictures of people, often you'll get the best picture by taking (or pretending to take) the posed photograph, then snapping another immediately afterwards, when the person has assumed a more natural posture or expression. While it's not always possible to coordinate your visit with the perfect time to take pictures, it's worth noting that early morning and late afternoon tend to offer the best light conditions. Mornings are also the time to catch the best street life, and many markets are at their busiest before the heat of day arrives.

When your camera memory stick is full you can take it to a photo developing shop and they'll put the images onto a CD (or print them) for you. For those who haven't joined the digital revolution, camera film is readily available and cheaper in China than at home. It's worth stocking up in reputable stores though, as stalls outside tourist sites are more expensive and the film may have suffered from sunlight exposure. Regardless of where you buy your film, you should always **check the expiration date**. There are also plenty of places, including Kodak stores, to get your pictures developed, but if you plan to have a lot of pictures processed, try one as a sample before committing yourself to rolls of washed-out photos. If you're a keen photographer and want taking pictures to be a major part of your trip then it's worth considering a **photographic tour**. **Grasshopper** (www.grasshopper adventures.com) runs excellent trips accompanied by Ewen Bell, an acclaimed photographer whose pictures are found in this book.

Etiquette

China's long history, so removed from Western civilization has left a minefield of **different social customs** that can initially be baffling to foreign visitors. Fortunately, the Chinese see foreigners as very different from themselves and in most situations cultural *faux pas* will be ignored. However, that isn't to say you shouldn't try to conform when in China – if you do your actions will be both noticed and appreciated.

SAVING FACE

While the Chinese often find Western self-flattery unseemly, they are inherently a proud people and one of the driving forces in Chinese etiquette is the concept of "**face**," which can be likened to dignity. Activities such as arguing in public will result in loss of face for both parties and thus are to be avoided at all costs. Nevertheless, in a country where private space is limited and summers are swelteringly hot, tempers can fray and you may well come across furious screaming matches out on the street – once they've started it's the one that can hold on the longest who will save most face. Face can also mean that a request or opinion (especially from a more senior employee or elder) won't be challenged, because it will cause loss of face. Thus contentious issues are often avoided or, when they are brought up, the "right" responses are given no matter what the party concerned actually intends to do.

Do's & Don'ts

Eating throws up a host of potential pitfalls for the visitor. While **breaking wind**, **burping**, sometimes **spitting** and generally making as much noise and mess as possible are all acceptable, other seemingly innocuous activities, such as **using a toothpick**, are not. If you wish to pick your teeth you should do so by hiding your mouth with your other hand. **Chopsticks** also offer more than just the problem of picking up your food with them (see *Chopsticks* callout, p. 116). Likewise, drinking has a few associated protocols; toasts are so important that at formal dinners it's rude to drink without one, and you should try to keep your companions' glasses full, for they will surely do the same for you.

When meeting people, particularly in business, it is customary to make a small **bow** while clasping one hand over the other fist, although Chinese familiar with meeting Westerners may well just plunge straight in with a handshake. When presented with anything, you should receive it with both hands and, while a business card should be scrutinized before being carefully tucked away, a gift should be opened at a later time when not in the presence of its giver.

Studying & Working in China

Since China opened up in the early 1980s, people have been curious to come and experience life in the Middle Kingdom. Many come here to study traditional arts or the language and to teach English but, since China has found its economic feet, more and more people are coming here to do business (see *Business Travel* below).

Study

If you want to study the language, universities are the best bet – your local embassy should be able to provide you with a list of suitable universities, but there are also a host of other types of schools, including some where you teach English (see below) in return for your lessons. There are also schools that use traditional arts (such as calligraphy, painting, kung fu and tai chi – see *Martial Arts*, p. 65, for the latter two) as vehicles to teach the language. Wherever you choose to study, you'll get better results if you fully immerse yourself and cut yourself off from the English-language world. There are language and cultural studies schools mentioned in the relevant chapters, although some of these are aimed at short-term visitors. Good websites for cultural studies and language studies include **www.educasian.com** and **www.worldlinkedu.com**. Officially enrolled students with school identity cards will enjoy substantial discounts at all major sights.

Teaching English

In order to legally teach you need a working visa, which can be obtained with the school's help, although some places will let you carry on teaching with a standard tourist visa. Good schools might require you to have a degree or TEFL qualification, but plenty of places just want a foreign face to look good for the parents. Salaries typically range from US$400 to US$800 per month and hours might be as few as 15 or as many as 30 a week. Many places offer accommodation, food and maybe even a bicycle as part of the bargain!

If you're serious about your teaching, then it's best to head for a high school or one of the major private schools where you should find all the teaching materials and staff support you need; some of the cowboy operations will just send you into a classroom of mixed-age, mixed-ability children with no preparation whatsoever – "OK kids, today we're going to learn about Christmas...."

Other Jobs

If you're posted to China by an international company, then many of your relocation needs are likely to be met by a specialist company that can help arrange moving, housing and domestic care. If, on the other hand, you arrive by yourself with no prospects, just a burning desire to work in China, do not despair. It's fairly easy to pick up some kind of work, perhaps teaching English, to support yourself in the beginning until you find the job you're after. Expat websites such as *that's magazines* (see *Information Sources*, p. 82) have job listings, as does *China Daily*. Speaking some Chinese will improve your prospects. In all work categories the highest wages are found in the big cities, but obviously the cost of living is also higher.

Business Travel

As China opens itself up to more foreign trade, the number of business visitors is increasing. Opportunities are predominantly in joint venture companies and, with such great potential for both manufacture and consumption, it's no wonder the race is on to grab a piece of the pie. However, doing business in China is not the same as in Europe or North America and many newcomers find these differences frustrating. The Chinese are **master business tacticians** and, while they are gracious and hospitable hosts, they are operating in their own country and have a few moves up their sleeve. Thus, the better you're prepared for your trip, the more profitable it is likely to be and, to this end, the tips below should help.

BUSINESS DO'S & DON'T'S

■ Get a **China consultant** and/or a **translator**. If this is the first time you've done business in China recruiting a China consultant can help to put you on more level footing with your new Chinese business partner. A consultant will probably speak the language, though it's also a good idea to organize your own translator (*fanyi*). Interpreters tend to be arranged by the host company and in this case you may feel you're not always getting the full picture, probably because you aren't. The Chinese know they are free to talk openly and that their translator will provide a suitably censored version for your ears. Taking your own translator won't make you any friends but it will offer you more insight into what's going on. The not-for-profit **US-China Business Council** (www.uschina. org) and the **China Britain Business Council** (www.cbbc.org) are good starting points.

■ Be aware of the importance of **personal connections** (*guanxi*). Although *guanxi* isn't the dominating force it once was, business in China is based much more on close personal ties than at home. Old friends or colleagues with suspect business practices may be preferred to an unknown newcomer with a good track record. As long as an individual is liked and trusted, business can proceed, which means it's important to make a good impression during your visit. Although part of this is clearly about your business proposal, adhering to the etiquette practices mentioned in the previous section will also play a role. In order to build up the required relationship you may need to invest much more time than you might have anticipated, so be prepared for lots of banquets and karaoke (KTV) bars before you start to head in the right direction.

■ Account for the importance of **superstition** (see *Beliefs and Superstitions*, p. 52, for more). Although it may seem crazy to you in this modern business age, some decisions may be based on how auspicious a certain date (or figure) is and production might be delayed until then. Fengshui, also known as geomancy (see *Fengshui*, p. 54) also has its part to play here and if a location is perceived to have bad fengshui (and thus future prospects) the whole deal could go sour.

■ Maintain **face**. Whoever you're doing business with will know that you'll only be in the country for a set period of time and have to make all kind of decisions while you're there; Chinese business people have an uncanny knack of knowing when you're at your most vulnerable (probably when you think the deal is signed, sealed and delivered) and will use this moment to throw a spanner into the works. What is of crucial importance is how you deal with such situations. If you can resist being confrontational and expressing anger about it, focusing instead on the bigger picture, your face-saving attitude will be appreciated and might bring about the resolution you seek.

■ **Have a banquet!** If you've spent a substantial (and successful) period of time doing business here, host a banquet, inviting all your newfound colleagues. A China consultant can help you choose a suitable restaurant and dishes. Make sure you pay ahead of time and are at the venue at least half an hour before the banquet. See *A Chinese Banquet*, p. 123, for more.

Travel & Living Information

Family Travel

Traveling as a family is becoming increasingly popular and can be a thoroughly rewarding experience if you plan your trip well. One of the most important things to think about is balancing your itinerary well so that you're not too rushed and can take in sights that appeal to all the family. While you might be fascinated by Taoist temples and historic monuments, visit more than a few with young kids and you may have a mutiny on board the family ship. The Chinese place great importance on children (even more since the one-child policy went into effect – see p. 43) and traveling as a family unit you will be warmly welcomed everywhere you go. There are some great places to visit as a family, particularly Yangshuo and Hong Kong, and the other cities have attractions kids will love, from movies to theme parks and shows. Each chapter of this guide has a "For Families" section detailing a few good options. Entry into most major sights is half-price for children under 3.9 feet high. If you'd like to go on a tour with other families, there are tour companies that run trips with itineraries which take the needs of the whole family into account (see *Specialized Tours*, p. 77). To enjoy some time away from the kids (or vice versa ...), international chain hotels often have babysitting facilities, starting from around ¥30 (US$4) an hour. Baby strollers can be a problem since access to sights, restaurants and hotels isn't always easy and sidewalks can be decidedly uneven. If you're traveling with a baby, you'll find formula, baby food and disposable nappies available at supermarkets.

Adoption

The enormous population, historic preference for boys over girls (see *Gender Imbalance*, p. 44), and the one-child policy (see p. 43) have all contributed to the large number of orphaned children in China. In 1993 several Western countries signed the Hague Convention on inter-country adoption and, later the same year, China instituted formal regulations to allow foreigners to adopt Chinese babies. Since then over 50,000 babies have been adopted, 80% of them by Americans. The children come from all over the country, but the White Swan Hotel in Guangzhou (see p. 468) is where many adoptions actually take place. If you would like to adopt a child, www.childrenshopeint.org and www. travelchinaguide.com/essential/adoption offer detailed information on the subject.

Disabled Travelers

Although there are a great number of disabled people in China, provision for the disabled is still very limited. As the country's economy booms, many cities resemble construction sites and there are countless hazards, such as uneven paving, bridges and gaping holes to negotiate. Public transport is seldom wheelchair-friendly. Wheelchairs are available from hospitals and at some tourist locations, but you can't count on these. Ensure that you bring all required specialist equipment and medication with you. Your trip will also be made smoother if you find out as much as possible about where you're going and what the facilities are before your trip. Hong Kong and, to a lesser extent, Macau, offer better provisions for disabled visitors, which are detailed in the tourist office's *Hong Kong Access Guide for Disabled Visitors* and on the web at www.discoverhongkong.com/eng/travelneeds/disabled. index. Certain hotel chains, including Holiday Inn, the Hyatt, the Sheraton, the Shangri-La and the Marriott, have facilities and rooms suitable for disabled people, although it's worth checking before you book. Listed hotels with rooms suitable for the disabled are marked DA, while those with wheelchair access mention this in the description. Going on an organized trip (see p. 76) can alleviate some of the planning, but if you want to go it alone, the following organizations can help:

- **Mobility International USA** (☎ 001-541-1343-1284, www.miusa.org)
- **Society for Accessible Travel and Hospitality** (SATH; 001-212-4477-284, www.sath.org)

Female Travelers

When compared with many other developing countries, travel for women in China presents few problems. Although you may well be stared at, this is invariably more of a curious gaze than an intimidating ogle. Indeed female travelers are more likely to be ignored than hassled. This said, in the far northwest more vigilance is advised and, as with anywhere, you'd be wise to take a **few basic precautions**, such as avoiding unlit areas late at night. Dress for women is fairly liberal and in the cities mini-skirts and skimpy tops are commonplace, though in rural areas you may feel more comfortable in conservative clothing.

Gay Travelers

Although homosexuality was long regarded a foreign peculiarity it is increasingly prominent in China, and loosely tolerated, if officially denied and illicit. The big cities have gay bars where foreigners may be approached, but be aware that public displays of affection are likely to cause a stir. Check out www.gay.com or www.utopia-asia.com for more on China's gay scene.

Facts & Figures

Electrical Current

Mainland and Macau electricity supply is **220V** through **flat two-pin** and **angled flat three-pin plugs**, although you'll also find round three-pin sockets! In Hong Kong the voltage is **200V** and plugs are of the **square three-pin** variety (the same as the UK). Thus, a **travel adaptor** is a good idea.

Time Zone

Remarkable as it seems, all of China follows the same time zone, eight hours ahead of Greenwich Mean Time, 13 hours ahead of Eastern Standard Time, 16 hours ahead of Pacific Standard Time and two hours behind Australian Eastern Standard Time.

Weights & Measures

China predominantly uses the metric system, most obvious as kilometers for road distances (one km=0.62 mile). Market goods such as fruit are measured by the *jin*, which is half a kilogram (1.1 lb) and cloth is measured by the meter (3.28 ft).

Accommodation

At the dawn of modern tourism in China in the 1980s foreigners were only allowed to stay in certain designated hotels, but these days many more options are open, from five-star splendor to five-dollar dorms. However, when compared to some other countries, hotels in China are fairly characterless and functional, although there are more and more exceptions to this, and not just in the luxury bracket (see *Escaping the Ordinary*, p. 114).

As in most countries, room rates reflect standards to an extent, but mid-range and budget hotels are generically styled and don't tend to reduce their tariff as they deteriorate. Thus the best value (and keenest staff) are often found in newer lodgings. In terms of customer service, expensive hotels may meet the standards of their Western counterparts, but equally they may not, and in many mid-range hotels you may get the distinct impression that the staff thinks customers should feel privileged for being able to stay! Worse still, in places that see few foreigners, I've witnessed reception staff hiding behind the counter to avoid serving the *lao wai* (foreigners)! Something to remember every time you check into a hotel is to **take one of their business cards**, which has the hotel's Chinese name. Then you can go out, explore and get as lost as you like, then just jump in a cab when you want to come home.

Price Codes

The price codes used in this book are based on the **cheapest double room** a hotel has in the high season (May to October). Thus, where two codes are mentioned, it means the range of rooms is such as to encompass different price brackets. Note that there's a 15% luxury tax added to room prices in upscale hotels (although this is often offset by a discounted rate). Discounts on advertised rates are almost standard and you should always try to strike a bargain. For **dormitories** the prices per bed are individually listed.

Note that hotels in **Hong Kong** and **Macau** are significantly more expensive than on the mainland and these chapters have their own price codes.

Hotel Categories

Hotels in China are are awarded stars according to their facilities and a good deal can also be ascertained from their Chinese name categories (*binguan, dajiudian, dajiulou, fandian, zhaodaisuo, luguan*, in descending order of quality), although the divide between these can be blurry. While these categories imply certain standards, you're better off making

HOTEL PRICE CHART	
¥	Under ¥150/US$20
¥¥	¥150-400/US$21-50
¥¥¥	¥401-800/US$51-100
¥¥¥¥	¥801-1,100/US$101-140
¥¥¥¥¥	Over ¥1,100/US$140

your own judgment on the room rate. To see hotel classifications in this book, look at the hotel's pinyin name in the language box. Regardless of price, in your room you'll find some source of **hot drinking water** for making tea and **a pair of plastic slippers**, along with other any other amenities afforded. Almost all upscale and some mid-range hotels offer **fitness centers** (FC), **swimming pools** (SW) and in-room **Internet access** (@), but only a few have rooms with facilities for disabled people (DA) – see individual hotels for symbols.

- **Expensive** (¥¥¥¥-¥¥¥¥¥; *binguan, dajiudian, dajiulou, fandian*). In the big cities, international chains offer the same **high standards** and (sometimes) service as they do worldwide, with prices to match (US$100 and upwards), and some of them even manage to inject a dose of flavor along with the luxury. These hotels are often well-located in the heart of the city, have all amenities, including countless restaurants, health facilities, swimming pools, Internet connection and, sometimes, a computer in the room, and front desk staff will generally speak some English. Chinese chains can offer similar services and facilities, although some of the finer points may be lacking.

- **Mid-range** (¥¥-¥¥¥; *binguan, dajiudian, dajiulou, fandian*). Almost every town of any size will have a hotel that falls into this category and, while standards and prices can vary enormously, you should at least be able to find a decent room in such a place. Rates for a double room in such hotels can start from ¥150 (US$20), although ¥300 (US$40) and upwards is more normal, especially in larger cities. If the room is too rich (or poor) for your taste, then ask at reception as many mid-range places have recently renovated smarter floors, and older, more decrepit, cheaper ones. Mid-range establishments should have rooms with attached bathrooms, TV and air conditioning, though they might be threadbare. There will also be laundry service, a restaurant, a travel desk of some sort and maybe a business center. Again, in these places you'll probably find someone who has a smattering of English.

■ **Budget** (¥). Below ¥150 (US$20) *zhaodaisuo*, *luguan*, **university rooms** and hostels (see below) form the bulk of the options, but seemingly mid-range places can creep into this category.

In *luguan* and *zhaodaisuo* **dorm beds** go for as little as ¥20 a night and there are rooms for ¥40, but these will be very basic and maybe not that clean. For a little more you can usually get a dirt-free, comfortable and secure room, possibly with a TV and attached bathroom, though you might have to look around in a few places. In the cheapest lodgings the toilets are invariably of the squat variety. Almost all places have some kind of canteen or restaurant, usually serving cheap, local fare, and the floor attendants also often have a cabinet of snacks and drinks for sale.

Budget accommodation is often clustered around transport hubs such as the bus or railway station, which is convenient for travel, but may be a long way from the town center, and not as pleasant a locale to stay in. This said, some hostels can be quite central and university lodgings, while often in the suburbs, usually have parks, gardens and trendy cafés or nightspots nearby. In some provincial cities and rural settlements budget options are still limited, since many places may not be authorized to let foreigners' stay. In such situations speaking a little Chinese can ease your path.

Hostels

As the backpacking scene heats up in China there are also increasing numbers of hostels, affiliated with HI (**Hostelling International**) or otherwise. HI places offer a slight discount to card-carrying members. You can become a member online at www.hiusa.org (US), www.hihostels.ca (Canada), www.yha.org.uk (UK), www.yha.com.au (Australia), www.yha.co.nz (New Zealand), which costs around US$30 per year.

Rooms in HI places are generally clean but cramped and cheap, and they always have dorms (*duorenjia*; ¥50/US$6 or less) and sometimes an Internet café and bar, but some places with the name hostel might be more like mid-range hotels. Hostels are often centrally located and, for solo travelers, they make amenable places to meet other backpackers. The better HI hostels and linked U-Tel Hotels generally offer organized tours to points of interest and may run more adventurous pursuits such as hiking or cultural experiences like dumpling-making. They can also book hostels in other cities for you and can arrange bus, train and plane tickets for a small commission. Hostels also often have bicycles for rent and are good places to share experiences and pick up tips for destinations farther along your route. To book hostels in advance, either look up the individual websites listed in the relevant accommodation section, or check out one of the hostel booking sites: www.hostels.com, www.hostelbookers.com or www.hostelworld.com.

Booking & Finding a Room

While those on a budget may prefer to check out a few places before deciding where to stay, in the busiest times, such as holidays, or if you're arriving late or have only a little time to spend in a place, booking ahead is advisable.

Almost all hotels listed in this book have at least a telephone number and many have e-mail or web addresses, but, outside of the better hotels or most tourist-friendly towns, you'll be lucky to find anyone who speaks any English on the telephone and websites may be Chinese-only. Therefore, if possible, have a Chinese speaker make the call (maybe someone from the hotel you're staying in), or get all your bookings made in advance through an agent such as Choice Travel (www.choicetravel.cn) or CITS (www.cits.net) – or on the Internet, which might also yield healthy discounts. Some useful accommodation booking websites include:

- www.ase.net
- www.chinatravel.com
- www.ctrip.com
- www.elong.com
- www.travelchinaguide.com

But, if you decide to check out a few places before committing, it's a good idea to store your bag in one of the **luggage lockers** or offices at the bus or train station and then head out, unencumbered, to look at some rooms. This can save you from a wild goose chase where you end up accepting any old room because you're too tired to carry your bag. Of course, if you're after a budget deal, it may well be very close to the station, but, if it's an isolated place miles away (as is sometimes the case with university accommodation), then it's worth calling ahead to check if they're open and have availability.

Room Categories

Upon arrival, bear in mind that advertised **rates are often open to negotiation,** especially out of season. First you'll need to tell the receptionist the kind of room you're after, which is not always as simple as it sounds. Upscale hotels have rooms similar to those found in Europe and North America, but in some mid-range and most budget places there are a bewildering array of standards and sizes, so if you're not happy with what you see first, it's worth asking about other types. As a single traveler you'll usually be shown rooms with one **single bed** (*danrenfang*), while couples might also initially be offered **twin rooms** (*shuangrenfang*). In either case, for a double bed request a *dachuang* (for accommodation terms see *Language* at the end of this guide). There are also sometimes larger rooms with as many as eight beds. If you're traveling in a group and want to economize, ask about these. As a single traveler it's also possible to share a room with strangers to save money (as the Chinese frequently do), although this isn't an option commonly presented to foreigners except where dorms (*duorenjia*) are involved.

Checking in & Practicalities

When you check-in you'll need your **passport** and will have to fill in a **registration form**. In cheaper places this form will be in Chinese, so you may need some assistance and the staff might need help deciphering your passport. You have to **pay in advance** and more expensive places may also request a **credit card imprint** as security, while those of a lower standard will need the equivalent of an extra night (or sometimes two) as **deposit**. At the bottom end of the spectrum (probably anything below ¥100), you may not be given a key, just a slip of paper to hand to the floor attendant who will open your room for you. But if you want a key it's often possible to pay another few yuan for this. Fear of damage, loss and theft runs high and in the room you'll find a "price list" in the event of guests breaking or stealing hotel property! Although hotels are generally fairly secure it's never worth testing this by leaving valuables lying around – more upscale rooms might have a safe, while others have one at reception. You should get a receipt for exactly what you deposit.

MASSAJEE?

An annoyance at many hotels, particularly mid-range and if the guest is a single male, is the torrent of calls to your room made by (often in-house) prostitutes. Saying no (*bu yao*) once might do the trick, but the best way not to get woken up is to disconnect the phone.

Escaping the Ordinary Hotel

After the beauty and character of some lodgings in other Asian countries, China's accommodation comes as a bit of a let down, but all is not lost – there are hotels that are more than just places to stay, at all levels of the price spectrum. Indeed some of the best are simple, but tastefully styled small hotels. While top hotels can certainly offer luxury, you often get the feeling you could be in any city anywhere in the world. The expensive options in the list below escape this uniformity and are decidedly unique.

- **Lusongyuan**, Beijing ¥¥-¥¥¥¥ (p. 205)
- **Red Capital Ranch**, Great Wall, Beijing ¥¥¥¥¥ (p. 206)
- **The Commune**, Great Wall, Beijing ¥¥¥¥¥ (p. 210)
- **Grand Hyatt**, Shanghai ¥¥¥¥¥ (p. 323)
- **Number 9**, Shanghai ¥¥¥¥ (p. 327)
- **Pingjiang Lodge**, Suzhou ¥¥¥¥ (p. 357)
- **Old Street Hotel**, Tunxi ¥¥¥ (p. 389)
- **The Hotel of Modern Art**, Guilin ¥¥¥¥¥ (p. 413)
- **Mountain Retreat**, Yangshuo ¥¥ (p. 437)
- **Jia**, Hong Kong ¥¥¥¥-¥¥¥¥¥ (p. 552)
- **The Peninsula Hotel**, Hong Kong ¥¥¥¥ (p. 554)
- **Pousada de Sao Tiago**, Macau ¥¥¥¥ (p. 590)
- **Pousada de Coloane**, Macau ¥¥¥ (p. 590)

Homestays

Staying in someone's home is a great way to really **experience Chinese life** and can be inexpensive as well. Host families often speak some English, but if they don't it's a sure way to develop your Chinese. For more information, check American International Homestays (www.commerce.com/homestays), or www.chinahomestay.org, who can also arrange longer stays.

Food & Drink

Eating and drinking is something taken very seriously in China and, while you may feel you know what to expect, based on Chinese restaurants around the globe, think again. Most overseas Chinese restaurant dishes are only loosely based on **Cantonese cooking**, one of the **four major styles**, and specialization in each one of these runs deeper than you could imagine, with some chefs spending

Noodle-making –
it's all in the wrist (Tot Foster)

decades perfecting just one dish. Thus part of exploring China should definitely involve exploring its cuisine; not only is it mouth-wateringly tasty, but it is such a fundamental part of life here that it gives real insight into the nature of the country. Food is such an important facet of the culture that a basic greeting like *"ni chi baole ma?"* which is used to mean "how are you?" translates as "have you eaten yet?" China's new economy is based on business deals cut over extravagant banquets and all the major festivals have associated snacks or dishes.

What is also striking, especially in the south, is the incredible **variety of food available** and its freshness. In this region live animals such as **bamboo rats**, **dogs** and **snakes** can be seen caged outside restaurants, just waiting to be ordered! This can be most shocking to Western eyes.

Price Codes

The price codes are based on a standard meal for one (meaning a single dish at the cheapest end of the scale, with rice and a beer or soft drink).

While cheap meals can be found in **Hong Kong** and **Macau**, eating out is generally a more expensive proposition than on the mainland and both of these destinations have their own price codes.

RESTAURANT PRICES	
¥	Under ¥25/US$3
¥¥	¥25-50/US$3-6
¥¥¥	¥51-80/US$6-10
¥¥¥¥	¥81-160/US$10-20
¥¥¥¥¥	Over ¥160/US$20

Chopsticks

Chinese restaurants are so ubiquitous that chopsticks are hardly a new thing in the West, but do you know how they came into being 3,000 years ago? Originally much larger versions were used to stir and remove food during cooking (and these can still be seen), but over time they were refined into the chopsticks we know today. The Chinese name, *kuaizi*, translates as quick (or nimble) sticks and that's exactly what they are, enabling the diner to eat comfortably using only one hand. It is normal to hold them with your right hand, which avoids clashing elbows at circular tables, and the best leverage is gained from holding them two-thirds of the way up. The bottom stick should remain immobile while the top one is held like a pen to manipulate the food. Don't worry too much about your ability (or lack thereof) with chopsticks as you'll be forgiven your *faux pas*. But there are a couple of things you should avoid doing. Passing food with chopsticks or sticking them vertically into your bowl will cause offence as these actions are associated with funeral rites. To indicate that you've finished eating, simply rest your chopsticks horizontally across the top of your bowl.

Restaurants tend to offer plastic, metal or ceramic chopsticks, and most canteens will provide disposable wooden ones, which causes hundreds of trees to be cut down daily. The cheapest places might only have washed wooden versions, so if you plan on eating in a lot of these places (and want to help the environment) it's worth carrying your own pair.

The Four Major Styles

Chinese diets were historically defined by the kind of crops grown and animals that could be reared or hunted in a given area. Thus wheat-based noodles, bread and, to a lesser extent, potatoes are the staples in the north while the balmy south is a land of rice, which has been cultivated in China since 5000 BC! Outside influences also had their part to play as you will find when sampling **Macanese and Portuguese** delights in Macau. Local cuisines further developed according to the quality and availability of particular ingredients. As you travel through the country you will be confronted by new **local specialties** at every turn, and if you take advantage of these it will add both flavor and understanding to the regional differences in your journey. But in this modern day the various styles have managed to permeate most areas of the country and, while less popular and probably less tasty than the local delicacies, **Cantonese** dim sum can be chosen in Beijing or **Mongolian hotpot** ordered in Guangzhou. The four major regional styles are detailed below, though these can be subdivided countless more times.

CULINARY CHINA

If you're keen to pick up some culinary tips while in China you can take cooking courses in Beijing (p. 202), Shanghai (p. 322) and Yangshuo (p. 433), or you could take a culinary tour with Intrepid (see *Specialized Tours*, p. 77).

Southern (Guangdongcai)

Baozi – stuffed buns (Tot Foster)

Cantonese food is the epitome of the southern style and is the most globally renowned, though it's still very different in **Guangdong** than London or New York. **Sweet and sour dishes** are a case in point, rarely offering any of their contrasting "sour" promise outside of China. **Hong Kong** and **Guangzhou** are at the **heart of Cantonese cuisine**, but the surrounding provinces, including Guangxi, are strongly influenced by the style. Southerners are famous within China for eating "anything whose back faces the sun" and as such the southern style can offer some of the most unsettling dishes the country has to offer, including dog, cat and snake. But these dishes won't come unless you order them and Cantonese food is typified by **super fresh ingredients**, lots of **seafood** and **light palatable sauces**. Best of all, dim sum (*dian xin* in pinyin) includes an astounding variety of miniature **buns**, **dumplings** and **spring rolls** served from trolleys circulating the restaurant, typically at breakfast time. The fact you can see the dishes before ordering makes dim sum an easy way for the non-Chinese speaker to choose! Other dishes to try include **sandpots** (*sha bao*), one-person pots of steamed rice, vegetables and meat.

Northern (Beifangcai)

Mandarin cuisine is the elite of the **Northern style**, derived from the **food of emperors**, and **Beijing duck** is its most celebrated offering. More generally though, Northern food is less glamorous, but no less tasty, with salty garlic, ginger and onion flavored dishes and staples of *mantou* (steamed buns), noodles (*mian*) and pancakes (*bing*), as well as numerous varieties of *jiaozi* (dumplings usually filled with pork and leek or cabbage), for which **Xi'an** is particularly famous.

DISHES FOR THE FEARLESS

A host of seemingly unpalatable foods, including cow's blood, chicken's feet, duck's tongue, rat, scorpion, snake and shark's fin, are eaten in China, particularly in the south. The reason for the amazing diversity of food consumed is partly rooted in **Traditional Chinese Medicine** (see p. 71), following beliefs about balancing the various elements of the body to improve health. Thus, dog is seen as warming in the winter, cat is cooling in summer and snake offers male virility! This variety is also partly borne of necessity –

Seahorses on sticks

Scorpions on sticks

many of the insects consumed today were initially eaten due to famine. The purported health benefits do little to encourage most visitors to try such dishes, but don't worry about mistakenly being served them – they're fairly easy to spot even on Chinese-only menus, as they tend to be the most expensive. If you're feeling adventurous, there are some tamer dishes to try which are still well out of the ordinary – try a green centered Thousand Year Old Egg (*pidan*), which has been preserved for months in straw and ash!

Eastern (Huaiyangcai)

Eastern cooking uses lots of **bamboo, mushrooms, seafood** and **freshwater fish**, although its often heavy use of oil can make it unpalatable to some. **Shanghainese** (*shanghaicai*) cuisine is at the refined end of the eastern scale and offers wide varieties of lightly cooked, miniscule treats akin to dim sum, most notably *xiaolongbao* (**steamed pork dumplings**).

Western (Szechuancai)

Szechuan and **Hunan** are famed for their **spicy dishes**, which are arguably the **hottest** you'll find anywhere in the world. In Szechuanese cooking the **meat** or **tofu** is merely a vehicle allowing the chili-laden sauce to deliver its knockout punch. Flavors are carefully constructed to produce strange-sounding but delicious dishes such as **fish-flavored pork** (which

Szechuan, Hunan and Guizhou cuisines use these fiery peppers

contains no fish), but the real trick is being able to differentiate any of the manifold tastes after your mouth has been numbed by the fragrant, potent *huajiao* (**flower pepper**).

CULINARY EXPERIENCES NOT TO MISS

■ **African Chicken** – this very un-Chinese sounding spicy dish has its roots in the Portuguese trade routes of yesteryear and can be enjoyed throughout Macau.

■ **Beggar's Chicken** (*jiaohuaji*) – this delicious eastern dish allegedly first came into being when a beggar who had no cooking utensils was given a chicken and ingeniously packed mud around the bird to cook it in his fire. To his surprise this method not only cooked the chicken perfectly, but also removed the feathers when the baked mud casing was cracked open.

■ **Beijing duck** (*beijing kaoya*) – crispy oven-roasted duck in wafer-thin pancakes with spring onions and plum sauce is the dish to try in the capital (see callout, p. 211).

■ **Caramelized Apples** (*basi pinguo*) – other than seasonal fresh fruit, desserts aren't that common in Chinese restaurants and this dish of sliced apples coated in caramelized sugar makes for a wonderfully sweet change.

■ **Mapo Tofu** (*mapo dofu*) – the spiciest tofu Szechuan has to offer.

■ **Crossing the Bridge Noodles** (*guoqiaomian*) – a kind of miniature one-person hotpot, this Yunnanese dish was supposedly devised by a Qing scholar's wife in order to keep his food warm when she carried it out to his place of study, by covering it in a layer of insulating oil.

Travel & Living Information

Sundried fish

■ **Dim Sum** (*dian xin*) – the archetypal Cantonese breakfast made up of dozens of miniature taste sensations (see *The Four Major Styles, Southern*, above).

■ **Drunken Prawns** (*zuixia*) – prawns marinated in alcohol.

■ **Dumpling Banquet** (*jiaozi yanhui*) – a northern specialty with innumerable elaborate stuffed parcels, generally served in fine surroundings.

■ **Fish-flavored Pork** (*yuxiang rousi*) – a spicy Szechuanese dish with sauce that supposedly imitates the taste of fish.

■ **Gongbao Chicken** (*gongbao jiding*) – this dish of diced chicken, peanuts (or cashews), chilies and flower peppers is at its hottest and best in Szechuan, but you'll find versions of it in restaurants throughout the country.

■ **Hotpot** (*huoguo*) – a bowl of bubbling broth (sometimes divided into a spicy half and a vegetable stock half, known as *yuan-yuang huoguo*) into which you dip wafer-thin strips of meat and assorted vegetables. This is my favorite meal to eat in a group and is popular throughout the country, particularly in Chongqing and Szechuan.

■ **Stretched Noodles** (*lamian*) – this *Hui* (Muslim) dish is usually prepared with beef, chili, coriander and leek or spring onion and is to be enjoyed as much for its preparation as its consumption. The noodles are made by continually stretching the dough

Hotpot dining (Tot Foster)

between the fingers with a wide sweeping motion of the arms. Seconds later the noodles will be dropped in to cook and just a few minutes after that you'll be tucking into them. Around the country you'll find clean, simple canteens offering a hearty bowl of beef stretched noodle soup for under a dollar, which can't be beat on a cold winter's day.

- **Sweet and Sour Fish** (*tangcu yu*) – the contrast between the two elemental flavors of this Cantonese dish has made it popular around the world, but you need to try it in southern China to experience the real deal.
- **Yangshuo Beer Fish** (*yangshuo pijiu yu*) – the specialty dish of this rural region, Beer Fish lives up to its name and is cooked in the local brew, Liquan, until it is so succulent it falls off the bone.

Where to Eat

China has a mind-boggling array of eating options, many of them ridiculously cheap. If you're on a budget, there are **tiny canteens** where you can eat for under a dollar, but for not a lot more there are private dining rooms and regional specialties just waiting. Dining in China is a social affair and, if you're traveling in a group or on business, you may find yourself in a **lavish Chinese banquet hall**. Conversely, for the single traveler, **restaurants** offer a hurdle; Chinese food is designed to be eaten by groups sharing a number of different dishes that offer a wide variety of tastes and textures. On your own you'll only be able to manage one of these dishes and thus part of the essence of eating in China is lost – indeed, sitting by yourself with your one dish in a restaurant surrounded by noisy groups, you may feel even more out of place than usual. However, there is some salvation for the single traveler – canteens and **street vendors** offer meals for one and, although choices are more limited, it's generally cheap and tasty fare and you won't be the only one dining alone. Bear in mind that people eat early in China; breakfast is from 6-9 am, lunch from 11 am-2 pm and dinner from 5-9 pm. After that you may have to hunt out a street stall or fast food joint.

Canteens

Every town in China has plenty of these small, cheap, hole-in-the-wall, places whose appearance often belies the excellent fare sold within. From **Muslim-owned beef** or **mutton noodle** ventures to **hotpot** and **dumpling joints**, canteens usually specialize in just a few tasty dishes and will also offer drinks, chopsticks and napkins, but not much else.

Restaurants

Restaurants range from **lavish affairs** (often in upscale hotels) to smaller family businesses. Traditionally they have three floors, the bottom of which may be more akin to a canteen, the middle a standard restaurant and the top housing private dining rooms (for which you may have to pay a supplement). These days private rooms often come complete with **KTV** equipment, should you want to sing for your supper! Tables are usually circular, with a Lazy Susan (rotating turntable) in the center of the table to liven things up!

Staff tend to be neatly dressed in matching uniforms and will make sure that your glass or teacup never runs dry.

Markets & Streetfood

China's streets and markets are alive with food vendors night and day and, if you're on a budget, in a hurry or traveling alone, streetfood is the way to go. What you find varies from region to region but you're sure to come across excellent **barbecued mutton skewers** (usually sold by Muslims from the northwest), **boiled or roast corn on the cob** (the latter is often chilied), **noodles**, **dumplings** and **steamed buns**, along with a host of other choices. Street vendors often have a few chairs and tables and may sell beer, while more elaborate set-ups in **nightmarkets** can resemble outdoor restaurants with all the food on display. In touristy areas always ask the price before ordering, as even though it still won't add up to much, some places will inflate prices enormously for foreigners.

Food is so cheap in China that cooking for yourself is rarely worthwhile as a traveler, but if you are here for longer, want a change or would like to stock up for a long journey, markets are packed with choices as well as great places to check out local life. Not so long ago, local produce would be all that was available, but these days you'll find **tropical fruit** for sale in Beijing's markets, even in winter.

Western Food

While China is a culinary adventure, every now and then Western food can bring a welcome shot of familiarity; just don't expect it to be exactly the way it is back home. **Dairy products** used to be very difficult to track down (outside of western and northwestern China), but in this time of the single child policy all parents want their kid to grow up big and strong, and calcium, hence milk, cheese and yogurt, are increasingly available, although you may still struggle in smaller towns and rural areas. **Breakfast** is a meal where many foreigners find Chinese food the hardest to stomach; congee (rice porridge) or noodles just don't cut it for everyone at 7 am and, though mid-range hotels may have some kind of Western fare included in their breakfast spread, the orange juice is likely to be warmed and toast and eggs may be the best you get. International chain hotels tend to offer a far better spread. For those on a budget, help is at hand in the form of a common Chinese dish that makes for an excellent Western-style breakfast – scrambled eggs and tomato (*xihongshi chaodan*).

Fast Food

When you need a Western fix, China has an ever-increasing array of options, the dominant flagships of which are predictably **KFC**, **McDonalds** and **Pizza Hut**, although there are domestic burger chains too, notably **Dicos**. Coffee shops like **Coffee Language, UBC Coffee** and **Starbucks** are also a recent phenomenon sweeping the cities, and, in addition to a good choice of drinks, they often serve reasonable Western fare such as pizzas, sandwiches and steaks. Similar items can be found at **backpacker cafés** (notably in Yangshuo in Guangxi, see p. 438) and **Western-style pubs** that have emerged in the bigger cities. Larger hotel restaurants may also have some Western options on their menus.

Vegetarian Options

Being a vegetarian in China sounds easy enough, given the sheer number of **vegetable dishes** in the country's cuisine and its Buddhist history, along with the imitation meat dishes made from **tofu** popularized since the Qing dynasty. However, it really depends on how strict you are in your definition of vegetarian, since many of these vegetable dishes will have involved meat somewhere along the way, be it in the sauce, the fat, or the small pieces of pork or shrimp you find in your "fried cabbage"! Telling your waiter that you don't eat meat (*"wo bu chi rou"*) might help, but, to be clearer, say you're a Buddhist (*"wo shi fojiao tu"*), who generally abstain from meat. Aside from the small number of purely vegetarian and Indian restaurants found in the biggest cities, the only way to be certain is to eat at one of the **Buddhist dining halls** in temples and monasteries throughout the country, although the food can be a little bland due to the lack of garlic, ginger and onion, which are considered too "stimulating."

A Chinese Banquet

In a country so overpopulated, the availability of food is something to be celebrated and the Chinese banquet is the focal point for this. If you come on business you'll almost certainly enjoy at least one of these **lavish displays of wealth**, which often involve the host paying weeks in advance to prevent anyone else trying to do so on the night of the event. Expect lots of extravagant dishes, lots of **toasts** and as much noise as possible. Indeed the Chinese word for "having a good time," *renao*, literally means hot and noisy, something all banquets worth their salt should emulate.

Ordering Food

Unfortunately, accessing China's cornucopia of foods isn't always straightforward, principally because of the language barrier. Thus, many travelers leave with less than the full picture after a trip overrun with dumplings, noodles and stir fries. However, there are several ways to combat this and ensure you get the most from your chopsticks.

Go to restaurants with an **English menu** – this is an easy way to start, although be aware that the English menu will probably have only a fraction of the dishes the kitchen can actually prepare, those that they think will appeal to foreigners, which are often blander or less exotic in their ingredients.

If there isn't an English menu, start with the **language section** at the end of this book, which gives both the pinyin and the Chinese characters for all the phrases and dishes listed in this section, along with many more. When ordering, bear in mind they're more likely to have dishes from the region which you're in (*keyi jieshao yidao cai ma* literally "can you introduce a dish?" is always a good question to ask).

Have a **look around** – seeing what other folks are eating and pointing at whatever you like the look of should do the trick. Similarly, the staff may invite you back into the kitchen (or the raw produce may be on display), in which case, pointing should once again get across your meaning and you can use the language section to explain how you would like it cooked.

Try to **order a balance of foods** for your group – one or two meat dishes, one fish and one or two vegetable or tofu dishes along with rice or noodles for a group of six to eight should suffice. This is the way Chinese food is designed to be eaten, offering contrasting flavors and textures, and it also means you're sure to find something you like.

If the above sounds like a culinary disaster waiting to happen, you could go on an **organized group tour** – if you're on a tour chances are you'll have a guide or tour leader familiar with both the language and the cuisine and who can pick the best regional specialties for you. Some companies even organize culinary tours (see *Specialized Tours*, p. 77).

A few other points are worth noting:

- Dishes will usually serve at least two when eaten with rice, although some places offer small and large plates.
- If a meat dish doesn't specify, it will be **pork**, the staple meat of the country.
- Rice tends to be served at the end of the meal (only to be used as a filler once the best dishes are consumed), unless you specify you want it at the same time as the meal itself.
- The flavor enhancer, **MSG** (monosodium glutamate), is heavily used in much of the food – indeed sometimes you are given extra should you wish to put it in! MSG can cause headaches and more serious health problems and is best avoided, especially as the food is tasty enough already. Say "*wo bu yao weijing*," (I don't want MSG) when ordering.

Drinks

It's important to make sure you **consume enough fluids** while on the road, especially during the summer months, and China offers a host of ways to quench your thirst, be it a refreshing cup of **jasmine tea** or a nice cold **Tsingtao beer** after a hard day sightseeing. You should **never drink the tap water**, but **bottled mineral water** is readily and inexpensively available throughout the country (¥1-2 for a small bottle, or ¥3-4 at tourist sights), while hotel rooms and trains will always have a supply of safe boiled water. Soft drinks are also popular and you'll find all the familiar brands along with a few of China's own such as **Jianlibao**, which is worth a try. You'll also find **fresh fruit juices**, especially in the south.

TEA (CHA)

Tea has over 2,000 years of history in China, but only gained widespread popularity during the Tang dynasty and has unquestionably become the drink of the Middle Kingdom. Originally, it was only drunk for its medicinal value, but over time tea became much more of a social drink. Teahouses sprung up around the country, particularly in temples and parks, and were the social hub of an era, featuring everything from political debate to musical performances. During the Cultural Revolution, teahouses were seen as subversive and most were closed down. These days, while coffee houses seem to be stealing some of the show, you'll find few people in the country who don't drink tea. Trains and hotel rooms are stocked with boiled water specifically for this purpose and on long train journeys almost every traveler has their individual flask close at hand at all times.

Tea (Ewen Bell)

There are hundreds of strains available around the country and they are broadly divided into green (*lucha*), red (*hongcha*) and flower teas (*huacha*). Tea is usually taken without milk or sugar (with the excellent exception of the sweetly infused *babao cha*, or Eight Treasures Tea), although the preparation process varies. The best growing areas are in the east and Yunnan in the far west and some of the most famous varieties are *longjing* (Dragon's Well), grown in the hills around Hangzhou where there is also a tea museum (see p. 372), and *guanyin* (named after the Buddhist Goddess of Mercy) from Fujian. There are also elaborate tea ceremonies performed in certain parts of the country (particularly Fujian, Guangdong, Yunnan and Zhejiang), which give an idea of the level of refinement in this aspect of Chinese culture.

Alcohol

Alcohol is widely available in China in many forms and most restaurants and cafés will serve **beer** and **spirits**, while big cities have plenty of **bars**, **pubs** and **clubs**. Beer (*pijiu*) is the most common alcoholic drink, thanks to the German annexation of **Qingdao**, which produces the country's finest beer, internationally exported **Tsingtao** (an old transliteration of the town name).

Almost every region has its own brewery and they're all fairly quaffable, all the more so due to the low price. At around 40 cents for a 640 ml bottle from a canteen or shop, beer is similarly priced to mineral water, although you'll pay far more in bars, especially for imported brands. This affordability and availability makes beer a common accompaniment to most meals, even if that's lunch served at 11 am.

While beer is most often drunk, liquor is fundamental to the banquet scene and shouts of *ganbei* (dry glass) echo around the room with alarming regularity. **Drinking games** are also popular and you'll see groups of men furiously shouting out numbers to try and guess the number of fingers their competitors will hold up. *Baijiu*, made from millet or sorghum, and *mijiu*, made from rice, are the principal liquor offerings, but in the city bars you'll find all manner of imported brands. Don't be surprised if you see a liquor bottle with a snake inside it; this is yet another alleged booster for male virility.

China also produces a few **wines**, the best-known being **Dynasty** and **Great Wall**, though if you want to drink wine you're better off splashing out on an imported European or New World bottle, available at upscale restaurants, supermarkets and department stores. This said, things could be set to change with a little help from France in the form of the Sino-French vineyard, which had its first harvest in 2003 (see *Vino China*, p. 203).

Entertainment & Nightlife

The new China offers a host of entertainment possibilities, from the ultra-modern to those that hark back to bygone days. Traditionally, entertainment came in the form of **opera** (see *Music*, p. 63) and **acrobatics troupes** (see p. 65), who performed in **teahouses** and **theaters**, but today **karaoke (KTV)** and nightclubs are equally as popular!

Bars & Clubs

There are a host of different kinds of places to enjoy a drink, from outdoor stalls to **trendy bars**, **Western-style pubs** and not so Western-style **clubs**. For a slice of Chinese life along with your beverage you can't beat a beer at one of the ubiquitous outdoor eateries in the thick of busy streetlife; owners generally don't mind if you don't eat, but a bit of nourishment can help to temper the alcohol. And while **karaoke (KTV) bars** may be a long way from your notion of a quiet place for a drink, their popularity speaks volumes about the Chinese concept of having a good time and can make for a very different and fun evening out. More upscale places have **private rooms** where you can scream your lungs out from the comfort of a couch, but be aware that some of these places are merely fronts for brothels. There are even KTV booths on the street where the spectacle of a foreigner singing is certain to cause a stir, but, no matter how bad you are, you'll always get some applause!

In the cities there are neon-lit bars serving a range of imported beers and spirits, often found clustered together in bar districts such as **San Litun Lu**

in Beijing. University areas also tend to attract bars and **coffee shops**, often with cheaper prices than their city center counterparts. **Discos** and **nightclubs** are generally found in the same locations, although the experience can be very different from the Western model! These places often have a cover charge (sometimes waived for foreigners) for which you may get a "free" drink. Once inside, you might find scantily clad women dancing on podiums to cheesy tunes and witness all manner of shows or party games! For those more serious about their music in the big cities there are also **underground venues** with the latest in dance music from around the globe and live music bars where you can see emerging bands (see *Protest Music*, p. 64). Although there are recommended bars, pubs and clubs within this book, it's a fast-moving scene, which makes it worth checking out local web magazines such as www.thatsmags.com for the latest.

Cinema

Although China has plenty of **movie theaters** to while away rainy afternoons, outside of Hong Kong, most films are in Chinese, so, unless you're into martial arts and want to catch a kung fu flick, your options can be limited. Beijing and Shanghai do have a few theaters that show movies in English and they are also popping up in other cities such as Hangzhou. Tickets cost around ¥50.

Shopping

Shopping in China has come a long way from the shortages of yesteryear and is one of the chief hobbies (and status symbols) of the Middle Kingdom's newly moneyed population. This is reflected in the country's legion of shiny **new shopping malls** and **bustling markets**, and makes China a great shopping destination. Shopping is fun in China – from **nightmarkets** to **exclusive boutiques**, there's always something to catch your eye and it's a great way to come into contact with the locals. Just remember that whatever you buy has to find its way home somehow, so it's worth concentrating your shopping at the tail end of your trip, by which time you may also have a clearer idea of what you like and how much you should pay for it. If you're buying items over 100 years old, you'll need to get an export certificate, which can be arranged at Friendship Stores and note that it's illegal to take home anything that predates the death of Emperor Qianlong in 1795. Of course, you'll also have to take into account **customs** on return to your home country – see *Customs & Immigration* (p. 83) for more information. If you plan to buy items that require shipping home, check all of the costs incurred, as cheap prices are sometimes offset by unexpected payments to have the goods delivered to your door.

What's Offered

As the biggest manufacturer on the planet, China clearly has a lot to sell and you'll find everything from **tacky Mao souvenirs**, **cheap electronics** and the latest **fashions** to quality **traditional items** such as **jade, paintings, pottery, silk** and **tea**. **Antique** items can be found everywhere from **streetmarkets** to **department stores**, but **forgery** is also rife; if something is more than 100 years old, it should have an official red wax seal, so if you're paying a substantial amount and authenticity is important to you, make sure you get one of these. Something else to note is the widespread availability of imitation products – from **designer label clothing** to pirate **CDs** and **DVDs**. Although they're very cheap and the audiovisual copies are usually good quality, they are, of course, all illegal and may be seized at customs on your return. Finally, there are also a few shopping scams that can snare the unwary – see *Warning – Scams*, p. 101 for more.

Where to Shop

China has all kinds of retail outlets, from rickety one-man stalls to **exclusive boutiques** and **emporiums** and they're all worth visiting to get a flavor for the dichotomy that is modern China. See individual chapters for prime shopping spots.

Note that returning goods is not as simple as at home. Although department stores or chains might have some kind of policy, this is usually only valid at that particular store, for a limited period (usually a week). Even with an unopened (or damaged) item and a receipt, exchange is the best you can expect to get – refunds are almost unheard of.

Markets

China abounds in markets and they make a great place to buy everything from vegetables to traditional art. In the cities you'll find **markets for everyday goods** and food, as well as those selling **antiques, clothes** and **handicrafts**. **Nightmarkets** are also popular

Market stall

and usually offer a range of stalls, along with places to eat. In the country, markets are often a social focal point, worth visiting for their snapshot of rural life, regardless of shopping. Here you'll probably see **antique coin salesmen**, **fortune tellers**, **hairdressers** and **medical practitioners**, as well as all manner of **fruits**, **vegetables** and **livestock**. Markets are always fair game for bargaining, particularly those at tourist sights.

Emporiums

If you've come on a tour you're almost certain to see at least one of these places. Emporiums are usually **government-approved** and tend to offer a variety of **crafts**, usually reflecting the specialty of the region. They are also often attached to **"factories"** where you can see the items in question being produced, although this is generally for show – the second a group leaves, the employees stop work! Groups are usually taken by a guide, who will receive a commission (as will the travel company) on anything you buy. But, if you walk into an emporium unaccompanied, you're unlikely to pay less. The advantages emporiums offer are the ease of a fixed price (though you can haggle a little) and the guarantee of quality. If you do plan to spend a significant amount, it's worth making sure the item is genuine

Anything and everything is for sale

– unless you're an expert this can be difficult, so it's easiest to buy from an approved store.

Shopping Malls & Department Stores

New **shopping malls** are springing up all the time in China's city centers and weekends see the urban elites out furiously flexing their credit cards. These giants hold **designer label outlets, bookstores, electronics** and **music stores** and they often have **food courts** and **good supermarkets** in their basements. Department stores can be a different story, especially in smaller towns, where they tend to be full of staff sitting behind glass cabinets waiting for the next victim who will have to endure reams of paperwork for the smallest of purchases. In spite of attempts to modernize, most branches of the **Friendship Store** remain similarly fusty, but it's China's most established department store (previously a foreigners' only emporium) and has quality items from all over the country, which can be a good (above average) price guide.

Everyday Needs

It used to be difficult to get everyday items such as **toiletries** and **milk** in China, but these days most products you'll need are easily available in the big cities. Foreign supermarkets such as **Wal-Mart** and **Carrefour** have established themselves and provide an interesting mix of imported and local products. For toiletries, head to **Watson's**, which can be found in Beijing, Xi'an, Shanghai, Hong Kong and Macau.

The Art of Bargaining

The Chinese are renowned for their **tactical bargaining** ability and are likely to mark up prices at the sight of a foreigner. Indeed, until recently, China had a dual pricing structure and the **overcharging of foreigners** was official policy. However, these days, while it will be difficult for you to get "local price," you can certainly aim to knock at least a third off the asking price and often much more. For cheaper purchases, amounts are negligible when converted to dollars, euros or pounds, but for bigger items a little strategy can help you to get a fair price.

First, check out a few places (ideally including a fixed-price shop) before trying to bargain anywhere.

Second, don't start bargaining unless you definitely want the item in question.

Third, have a fixed price in your head that you won't go above and ideally a back-up similar item (the one you want often suddenly becomes "unique" and hence more expensive).

Fourth, if you're not getting near your price and the vendor stops going lower, try the slow walk out – half the time you'll be called back and get your price, or negotiations can recommence.

Finally, remember that while the difference between your price and the vendor's may be minimal, chances are this amount will mean more to the vendor than you and, if you see something you like, you might regret not buying for the sake of a few dollars! Conversely, don't feel guilty if the vendor acts hurt – no matter what they say they won't sell if they aren't making money.

Finger Counting

Illiteracy and the presence of numerous mutually unintelligible local dialects has led to the development of an easy system of finger counting in China. Memorize the hand signals below (from left to right, they represent the numbers one to 10) and you're all set for a hard day of bargaining at the markets.

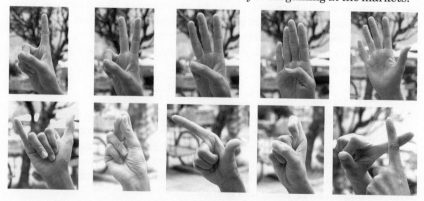

Adventures

Conventionally, you may think of adventures as being **outdoor** or **physical activities**, but travel is all about **exploration**, and in this book the aim is to allow you to experience the manifold facets of this vast, diverse country. Thus, an adventure could be a **hike** or a **bike ride**, but it might also be **learning to cook Chinese food** or **studying the ancient art of calligraphy**. For each area covered you will find an

Hot-air ballooning (Light Travels)

"Adventures" section, subdivided into the different forms of adventure for that region, such as "On Water," "On Wheels" and "Cultural Adventures." Accounts include contact details (where required), approximate costs and durations, what to expect and routes for bike rides and walks. Durations indicate the length of time walking or cycling and do not account for how long you spend at any sights en route. For physical, outdoor adventures like climbing or kayaking, be sure to check that your insurance policy is adequate. For cultural adventures you'll find background information in the *Culture* section of the book (pp. 54-73). If you're interested in one specific style of adventure and want your holiday to focus on that, then it might be worth booking a specialized tour (see *Specialized Tours*, p. 77).

Eco-Travel

Tourism is set to be the world's biggest industry, but all too often it involves destruction of both the physical and social environment. When we seek out new and unexplored locales around the globe, we are, of course, irrevocably changing that place, all the more so by telling tales of unspoiled beauty on our return. In my work as a travel writer and tour leader I feel more at fault than most. The truth is that sooner or later all the "untouched" destinations will be gone, but what we can do is make the "touch" a light one. **Eco-tourism** is really about **responsible tourism**; **minimizing negative impacts** on the physical environment and indigenous cultures while **maximizing the positive contributions travelers can make**. China doesn't yet have much in the way of eco-tourism, but you can do your bit nonetheless. Below are a few pointers (most of which are purely common sense) that will help you do the right thing.

- Try to use local, ecologically aware companies or individuals who care about the place in which they live. All too often the proceeds from tourism find their way to big travel agents who have little (if any) concern for eco-travel, so using locals will help to conserve the status quo, as well as supporting the regional economy.
- Get involved in local projects, either with direct input during your trip or financially on your return (see *Animal Protection Organizations*, p. 42, *Charitable Organizations*, p. 103, *Conservation Organizations*, p. 35 and the *Putting Something Back* sections in the destination chapters).
- Help to preserve local crafts by buying direct from the craftsmen.
- Never purchase any products made from endangered species, no matter what the vendor may tell you.
- Never leave litter – aim to leave a place cleaner than you found it.
- Recycle wherever possible.
- Try to get around under your own steam – only use fuel-guzzling transport when necessary. Offset your carbon miles (see p. 85) at www. climatecare.com.
- Keep to marked trails when cycling or hiking.
- Conserve water – don't leave the tap running and only get hotel linen washed when really needed.
- Don't use soap or detergents in natural bodies of water.

The Top 25

Below is a list of my **25 favorite places** and **pastimes** in the areas covered by this book. While by no means definitive, if you manage to see and do all that follows, you'll get a real flavor for what this giant land has to offer – contrast and diversity.

- **Beijing** – Imagine China of old at the imperial trio of sights: the Forbidden City, the Temple of Heaven and the Summer Palace (p. 153). Eat Beijing duck in Beijing (p. 211). Walk the Great Wall from Jinshanling to Simatai (p. 196).
- **Chengde** – Take a hike and a boat ride through the parkland of the imperial Mountain Resort (p. 220).
- **Xi'an** – Stare in awe at Qin Shi Huang's Terracotta Warriors (p. 247). Cycle along the top of Xian's imposing ancient city walls (p. 255).
- **The Three Gorges** – Relish a boat trip up the spectacular Lesser Three Gorges or Shennong Stream (p. 270)
- **Shanghai** – Witness the mindboggling contortions and agility of the Shanghai acrobats (p. 313). Enjoy an evening stroll along the colonial Bund, with the bright lights of China's future shining from across the river in Pudong (p. 319-20).
- **Suzhou** – Visit one of the city's exquisitely styled traditional gardens (p. 345).

- **Hangzhou** – Take a bike trip out to the famous tea-growing village of Longjing (p. 376). Enjoy a boat ride across the enduringly beautiful West Lake (p. 378).
- **Huangshan** – Ascend the majestic and mystical Yellow Mountains for scenery fresh from a scroll painting (p. 393).
- **Guilin & Around** – Enjoy a cruise along the Li River, which winds its way through the fairytale wonderland of Guangxi's mystical tower karst mountain scenery. Take an exhilarating bike ride between the forest of pinnacles (p. 425) to one of the region's bustling, colorful and sometimes disarming produce markets (p. 421). Hike up to the breathtaking Dragon's Backbone rice terraces above Ping'an village (p. 443).
- **Guangzhou** – Tuck into the finest Cantonese dim sum in the world, in Canton (p. 470). Enjoy the quiet life on the sleepy former colonial enclave of Shamian Island (p. 469).
- **Hong Kong** – Shop 'til you drop (p. 534). Take the Star ferry across the harbor seemingly adrift amidst a sea of skyscrapers (p. 504). Enjoy a day-trip to the beaches, hiking trails and fish restaurants of Lamma Island, only 30 minutes by boat from the bustling metropolis (p. 520).
- **Macau** – Forget you're in China for a while with an amble around the peninsula's stunning colonial Portuguese architecture (p. 574). Pay your respects to the Goddess of the Sea at the A-Ma Temple (see p. 578).
- **Anywhere** – Practice tai chi at sunrise in the park with hundreds of others. Soak up a traditional Chinese massage to soothe those aching traveler's limbs.

Suggested Itineraries

The following itineraries can all be completed in seven to 10 days; if you have more time you can combine any of them to make a longer trip.

The Imperial North

Arrive in **Beijing** and spend a few days soaking up the **Imperial sights** – the **Forbidden City, Temple of Heaven, Summer Palaces** and the **Great Wall**. Spend your evenings enjoying **Beijing duck, opera** and maybe a trip to the **acrobats**. If you have time, take a train up to **Chengde** and spend a couple of days enjoying the imperial retreat before returning to the capital and flying on to **Xi'an**. Allow a full day at the **Terracotta Warriors** and another day to explore the fascinating walled city. Make sure you enjoy a **Dumpling Banquet**, as well as dinner in the **Muslim markets**. Reflect on your trip in the overnight train back to Beijing.

Travel & Living Information

Cruise the Three Gorges

Fly into one of the international hub airports (Beijing, Guangzhou, Hong Kong or Shanghai) and then on to **Chongqing**. Spend a day in this mountainous city before boarding your **boat** for the spectacular **three-day trip** to **Yichang** (or **Wuhan**). Stop off at the **Ghost City of Fengdu** and take a stunning side-trip up the **Lesser Three Gorges** or **Shennong Stream** along the way. Disembark and fly on to your choice of the international hubs, where you can spend time enjoying the city and surrounding attractions before flying home. Remember that, if you choose the same hub to fly into and out of, this should reduce your ticket price.

Shanghai, Silk & Tea

Shanghai skyline (Michel_r / Wikipedia)

Fly to **Shanghai** and spend a few days in the vibrant heart of modern China. Promenade the **Bund**, shop on **Nanjing Lu**, visit **Shanghai Museum**, take a **boat trip** along the Huangpu and enjoy a drink at the top of the Jinmao Tower overlooking it all. In the evenings, see the famed **acrobats**, try some **Shangainese cuisine** and experience some of the best **nightlife** in China. Take a bus or a train to **Suzhou** for a day or two of **silk shopping**, strolling the narrow streets and **canals** and admiring the splendor of the city's famous **traditional gardens**, maybe taking a day-trip to one of the smaller water towns nearby. From Suzhou take an overnight boat journey along the Grand Canal (or a train) to **Hangzhou** for a couple of relaxing days exploring **West Lake** and the **tea-growing hills** that surround the city. Take the bus to **Huangshan** and ascend its stunning peaks, capped by lone pines and temples. If you have any extra time, you could visit the beautiful villages around **Shexian** and **Yixian** before returning to Shanghai for your flight home.

The Star Ferry in Hong Kong Harbor

Big City Lights & Rural Delights

Fly into **Hong Kong** and spend a few days discovering its diverse attractions – from shopping in bustling **Kowloon** to **hiking** along one of the **islands'** well-marked lush trails. Eat dim sum downtown and head up **Victoria Peak** for an after-dinner drink to remember. Take a boat or a train to **Guangzhou** and sample yet more Cantonese delights, along with some fine colonial architecture, maybe stopping off in modern **Shenzhen** for a peek at the new China. From Guangzhou, take a bus, train or flight to **Guilin** and spend a day visiting its mountainous and man-made attractions. The following morning take a **boat** along the **Li River** to **Yangshuo**, where you can spend the next few days **hiking** and **cycling** through the famed idyllic limestone scenery. Head back to **Guilin** for the return flight to Hong Kong. Take the ferry over to **Macau** and enjoy a day or two soaking up the splendid architecture, fine cuisine, small fishing villages, temples and beaches.

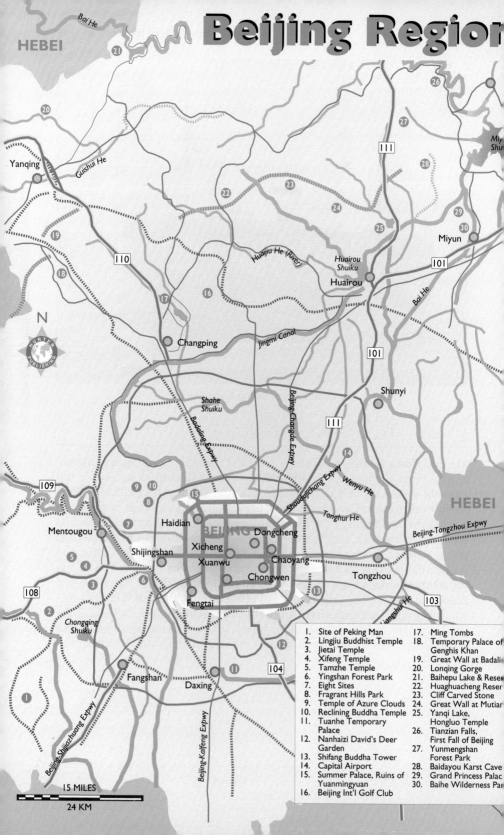

Beijing Region

HEBEI

Bai He

HEBEI

Yanqing

Guishui He

Miyun
Shuiku

Changping

Huairou
Shuiku

Huairou

Shunyi

Huajiu He (River)

Jingmi Canal

Shahe Shuiku

Badaling Expwy

Beijing-Changde Expwy

Shoudujichang Expwy

Wenyu He

Mentougou

Tonghui He

Haidian

BEIJING

Shijingshan

Xicheng
Dongcheng

Xuanwu
Chaoyang

Chongwen

Tongzhou

Beijing-Tongzhou Expwy

Fengtai

Chongqing Shuiku

Bai He

Miyun

N

HUNTER PUBLISHING

Fangshan

Daxing

Beijing-Shijiazhuang Expwy

Beijing-Kaifeng Expwy

15 MILES
24 KM

1. Site of Peking Man	17. Ming Tombs
2. Lingjiu Buddhist Temple	18. Temporary Palace of Genghis Khan
3. Jietai Temple	19. Great Wall at Badali
4. Xifeng Temple	20. Lonqing Gorge
5. Tamzhe Temple	21. Baihepu Lake & Reser
6. Yingshan Forest Park	22. Huaghuacheng Reser
7. Eight Sites	23. Cliff Carved Stone
8. Fragrant Hills Park	24. Great Wall at Mutiar
9. Temple of Azure Clouds	25. Yanqi Lake, Hongluo Temple
10. Reclining Buddha Temple	26. Tianzian Falls, First Fall of Beijing
11. Tuanhe Temporary Palace	27. Yunmengshan Forest Park
12. Nanhaizi David's Deer Garden	28. Baidayou Karst Cave
13. Shifang Buddha Tower	29. Grand Princess Palac
14. Capital Airport	30. Baihe Wilderness Par
15. Summer Palace, Ruins of Yuanmingyuan	
16. Beijing Int'l Golf Club	

Beijing & Around

Beijing, literally translated, means **Northern Capital**, a title it has held since the Ming Dynasty (see *History*, p. 13) and a name that still holds true today. Whether imagining the past or marveling at the future, this city is most definitely still the cultural, political and, to the Pekinese, geographical, heart of the Middle Kingdom. While Beijing's modern appearance owes much to the Communist era and the recent influx of capitalist cash, its most impressive and inspiring monuments are recognition of its long imperial tradition. The scale of the city, with its population of 15 million, can initially be overwhelming, but even a short meander into one of Beijing's remaining **hutong** districts brings you close to the realities of daily life and all of a sudden the city seems human again. While the vast number of construction sites, flyovers and mirrored skyscrapers can come as a shock to those hoping for a view of the years when Beijing was the emperor's seat, a visit to any one of the principal imperial sights (the **Forbidden City**, the **Temple of Heaven** or the **Summer Palaces**) easily remedies this. However, the greatest of Beijing's, if not the world's, sights lies north of the city. The **Great Wall** never ceases to amaze and it's worth spending a couple of days out of the city to fully appreciate its majesty. If you have enough time and want more imperial splendor, the rugged countryside around the capital holds Ming and Qing tombs, while, farther afield, the **Mountain Resort at Chengde** was long a popular emperor's haunt and has some wild scenery along with its subdued palaces and grand temples.

Beijing

History

The Beijing area has been inhabited for thousands of years, as illustrated by the discovery of one of the earliest known examples of *homo erectus*, the 500,000-year-old Peking Man, 30 miles south of

Yongle

the capital in the 1920s. However, Beijing's pre-eminence dates from the time of the Mongols, who conquered the city in 1264 and established it as the Yuan dynasty capital under **Kublai Khan** (see p. 12). It then prospered as the gateway to the Silk Road. The capital moved to Nanjing at the start of the Ming dynasty, but quickly returned to Beijing under **Emperor Yongle**, who was instrumental in developing some of the city's most impressive monuments as well as its grid layout. The first versions of the Forbidden City and Temple of Heaven were constructed under Yongle and Beijing remained the imperial seat through the Qing dynasty, when the vast lake park of the Summer Palace was completed.

In spite of these grand buildings the city was as dichotomous then as it is today and, while the emperor rattled around in the hundreds of rooms of the Forbidden City, people starved on the streets outside. Beijing suffered under the weak imperial rule of the late Qing and the city was routed during the **Opium Wars** (see p. 16), when the Summer Palace was burned to the ground, only to be rebuilt under the **Empress Dowager Cixi** (see p. 17), then ransacked again in response to the **Boxer Rebellion** (see p. 17). When the Qing dynasty finally collapsed in 1911, Beijing fell into the hands of **General Yuan Shikai** (see p. 19) and, after his death in 1916, it was left at the mercy of northern warlords, who weren't evicted until the arrival of nationalist forces in 1928. The Japanese took the city in 1939 and then, after World War II, an American/KMT coalition force controlled Beijing until the arrival of Communist forces in January 1949. In October 1949 Mao Zedong declared the foundation of the PRC, with Beijing as its capital.

The Communist Era

The declining Qing dynasty and the subsequent 40 years of neglect left Beijing in a pitifully backward state, something that Mao Zedong and the CCP immediately sought to rectify. Early urban planning borrowed heavily from the Soviet model and created the vast concrete desert of **Tian'anmen Square** along with the monolithic buildings that flank it. The imperial decree that no building should be higher than the Forbidden City meant that Beijing was almost entirely low-rise until the 1950s, which seems unbelievable, given the city's current appearance. Much of old Beijing, including hundreds of temples and cultural monuments, was torn down to make way for high-rise housing blocks. Industry had previously been absent from Beijing and factories were soon established to help bolster the city's economy and to fit in with the urban Communist model. It was also under Mao that Beijing's **subway system** was developed, originally only intended for use by the party cadres, but opened to the public after Mao's death in 1977.

Since Economic Reform

While the major monuments of the capital are now safeguarded by the government's recent emphasis on cultural heritage, much has already been lost. Traditional *hutong* residential districts, which were for so long an integral part of the city, are fast disappearing, and only a few have been designated for special protection. The lack of any buildings deemed of import has given an architectural freedom of sorts and since the economic reforms of the '80s there has been little to stop planners dreaming up whatever they see fit. Beijing is now awash with so many skyscrapers that it is at times difficult to know where you are in the city, while out in the suburbs ever more plush residential villa complexes pop up to cater for the newly moneyed and ex-pat population.

The 2008 Olympics (www.en.beijing2008.org)

Olympic countdown (Tot Foster)

In China, eight is a lucky number and the Zhang Yimou (see *Film*, p. 67) choreographed Olympic opening ceremony will commence on the eighth day of the eighth month of 2008, seemingly automatically securing success but, just to be sure, Beijing has been doing everything it can to prepare for its 16 days in the world spotlight. Incredible new structures are popping up all over the city (and indeed the country), none more impressive than the trio of extraordinary buildings in the **Olympic Green** – the National Stadium, the Aquatic Center and Digital Beijing. Urban planning has stepped up a notch and all the major sights are getting a facelift, along with **improvements to the transport system** and the **closing down of heavily polluting factories**. Satellite cities are being built to contain Beijing's ever-spiraling population and the **"Green Great Wall"** of trees is being planted to try and reduce the dust storms that tear through the city every summer. When researching this book, almost everywhere I went around the capital was being spruced up and everything, it seems, will open in time for the Olympics.

However, while much is being made of the advantages of this infrastructural investment, the **additional US$1 billion revenue** that will be raised during Olympic year and the **1.8 million**

jobs that will have been created during the whole project, there is an uglier side to the Olympic picture. Human rights groups around the world were appalled when Beijing was awarded the event, as it seemed to condone abuses as long as money was being made. I was here when the Olympic committee came to inspect Beijing as a potential venue in 2000 and witnessed first-hand the walls erected to hide the low-quality housing on the road from the airport and I read about how thousands of beggars were carted out of the city. These methods helped to attain the prize and it seems they will be used again during the actual event – 300,000 houses have been demolished and their residents removed (sometimes forcibly). It's also reported that mentally handicapped people and vagrants will be ejected from the capital. Over 70 new laws have been passed in order to suppress anti-government groups such as Free Tibet. Thus it's unlikely that such groups will be allowed a voice at the Olympics, but, even if they manage to protest, you have to hope that China, nearly two decades after the Tian'anmen Square Incident and ever more aware of its international standing, will refrain from any draconian action. Having seen the six years of tremendous investment that has gone into the Olympics, my guess is that the 2008 Games will only reaffirm what the world is starting to realize – China has arrived!

Factfile

Locations: Beijing (athletics, badminton, diving, judo, soccer, shooting, swimming, taekwondo, weight lifting), Hong Kong (equestrianism), Qingdao (beach volleyball and sailing), Qinghuangdao (soccer), Shanghai (soccer), Shenyang (soccer), Tianjin (soccer).

Logo: The Dancing Bear logo for the 2008 Olympics is an ingenious piece of work that uses the Chinese character *jing* (meaning capital) in traditional seal style to also portray an athletic and open-armed individual, embodying the slogan for the games, "One World, One People."

New Events: BMX, *wushu* (kung fu) and marathon swimming, among others.

Tallest Competitor: At seven feet six inches, basketball player Yao Ming is the tallest athlete ever to take part in the games.

Medal Hopes: Following promising performances in the Asian Games, China expects to win at least 20 Olympic medals.

Visiting During the Olympics

If you're thinking of an Olympic visit, be ready for a spectacle, but also for crowds – it's estimated that there will be an extra 2 million visitors to Beijing during 2008, 300,000 of whom will come from overseas. In spite of the government regulations limiting hotel prices during the Olympic period, many hotel and hostel owners are already planning their price hikes, so be prepared to pay over-the-top rates and reserve as soon as possible – tour companies are already taking bookings (www.tour-beijing.com is a good resource). Getting around should be facilitated by the new subway lines that will have opened, and the reduced number of vehicles allowed on the roads.

The Future

In spite of all this investment and positive looking future, Beijing is still beset by problems. As increasingly wealthy Beijingers exchange their bikes for Buicks and *hutong* houses for high-rises, more and more migrants arrive at the bright lights of the capital looking for work, few of whom realize their dreams. **Congestion, pollution** and **inequality** are serious issues that need addressing more effectively if Beijing is to acquire the international cultural capital status it aspires to. However, although Hong Kong, Shenzhen and Shanghai may be the economic giants of 21st-century China, Beijing is undeniably still their master and the authoritarian capital of Communist China. Yet even here the iron fist is loosening its grip – residents today enjoy far more social rights than they did 20 years ago, and, taking a drink in one of the cities' neon-lit and cosmopolitan bar districts, you'd be hard pressed to imagine that you are at the heart of a Communist empire.

Getting Here & Away

By Air

Beijing's International Capital Airport, located 18 miles northeast of the city, was only opened in 1999, but is already being upgraded to handle 60 million passengers a year in anticipation of the forthcoming Olympics. The airport is served by direct flights from major capitals around the world, along with almost every city with an airport in China. There are two terminals, a domestic (2) and an international (1), although a few internal flights operate from the latter. In the airport you'll find *bureaux de change*, ATMs and a few expensive restaurants and snack bars (including a Starbucks in terminal 1 – a prelude of the China to come). If you've got a lot of luggage, there are red-capped porters on hand to help with your bags – this is a free service but they're not averse to a tip.

Getting into Town

To get into town from the airport a taxi should cost between ¥80 and ¥100 (including ¥10 toll) and will take around 45 minutes, longer in rush hour. Unless you want to get taken for a ride, don't use any of the touts who might try to lure you into a taxi – head straight for the official line outside arrival gates 5 to 9. There are also airport buses that cost ¥16 and run from 7:30 am until the last domestic arrival, but for departures the last buses leave the city around 7:30 pm. Four routes operate from outside arrival gates 11-13 and, of these, lines #2 and #3 are of most use:

■ Line #2 runs to the Xichang'an Jie CAAC Office via the SAS Hotel, Asian Games Village, Friendship Hotel and the Shangri-La.

■ Line #3 runs to Beijing Train Station via the Third Ringroad, Lufthansa Center, Kunlun Hotel, Great Wall Sheraton Hotel, Dongzhimen subway, Swissotel, Chaoyangmen subway & Beijing International Hotel.

Beijing & Around

Domestic Flights

You can buy flight tickets through travel agents in most hotels and at the airport. Check out *City Weekend, that's Beijing* or see the websites listed on p. 87 if you want to find airline offices in Beijing.

Destination, frequencies and durations are as follows:

Chongqing (13 daily; 2 hrs 20 mins), Guangzhou (23 daily; 2 hrs 45 mins), Guilin (5 daily 3 hrs), Hangzhou (20 daily; 1 hr 50 mins), Hong Kong (38 daily; 3 hrs 40 mins), Huangshan (1 daily; 2 hrs), Shanghai (45 daily; 2 hrs), Shenzhen (20 daily; 3 hrs), Yichang (2 daily; 2 hrs).

Xi'an (17 daily; 1½-2 hrs)

By Rail

Beijing is linked to the rest of China (including Hong Kong) by rail and is also the terminus for the Trans-Mongolian and epic Trans-Siberian Expresses. Beijing has several train stations, but most destinations in this book are served by its two principal stations, **Beijing Station** and **Beijing West Station** (Xi Zhan). Generally speaking, trains to the south and west use Beijing West, while the north and east are served by Beijing Station, although there are exceptions to this. Beijing Station is fairly centrally located, a couple of miles east of Tian'anmen Square, while Beijing West lies farther out in the west of the city on Lianhuachi Dong Lu. Beijing Station is perpetually busy, but easy enough to navigate – the main ticket offices are beyond the KFC on the right of the station as you look at it, but you'll find far shorter lines at the designated foreigner kiosk, number 26, which is just to the right of the waiting hall entrance. Beijing West Station is a far grander construction, the biggest in Asia, but is well laid-out and easy enough to negotiate; buying tickets isn't too traumatic, although lines can be lengthy. To avoid this, simply buy a ticket through your hotel for an extra ¥25 to ¥50 fee. The new Tibet Railway operates from Beijing West, with daily departures at 9:30 pm, which arrive in Lhasa two days later. To go to Lhasa, you'll need a Tibet travel permit, which travel agents can help arrange.

Getting into Town

Both stations have luggage facilities, snack shops and canteens, as well as bus depots and taxis that can get you to your hotel – Beijing Train Station is also connected by subway, while bus #1 runs from Beijing West along Chang'an Jie and #52 heads to Tian'anmen Square. If you take a taxi, make sure you use the official ranks at the stations to avoid being overcharged. Although lines can seem long, they tend to move fairly quickly and the attendants will make sure the driver uses the meter and knows where you want to go.

Destinations, frequencies & durations:

Chengde (6 daily; 4 hrs), Chongqing (2 daily; 25-32 hrs), Guangzhou (2 daily; 22 hrs 20 mins), Guilin (3 daily; 22-27 hrs), Hangzhou (3 daily; 11-22 hrs), Hong Kong (every other day; 24 hrs 25 mins), Huangshan (1 daily; 19 hrs 30 mins), Lhasa (1 daily; 47 hrs 30 mins); Shanghai (9 daily; 12-22 hrs), Shenzhen (2 daily; 23 hrs 30 min-29 hrs), Suzhou (2 daily; 12-21 hrs).

If you enjoy train rides, then the Trans-Mongolian and Trans-Siberian Expresses are two of the best. If you know you're going to take the trip in advance, then it's worth booking from home as tickets can be sold out for weeks in the height of summer (see *Travel & Living Information*, p. 273, for agents). Once in Beijing you can book tickets from **CITS** (☎ 010-6515-8010; Mon-Fri 8:30 am-5 pm) in the Beijing Tourism Building at 28 Jianguomen Wai Dajie, or through **Monkey Business** at Room 35 in the Red House Hotel, 10 Chunxiu Lu (☎ 010-6591-6519, www.monkeyshrine.com). There are several trains a week, which take roughly 30 hours to Ulan Batur or five days to Moscow. Prices vary according to the class you take and whether the train is operated by Chinese, Mongolian or Russian railways.

Mongolia – The Chinese train leaves on Tuesdays and costs ¥595 hard-sleeper, ¥828 soft-sleeper or ¥999 for a two-berth cabin. The Mongolian train leaves on Saturdays and costs ¥657 for hard-sleeper or ¥1006 for a two-berth cabin.

Russia – The Chinese train leaves on Wednesdays and costs ¥2142 hard-sleeper, ¥3108 soft-sleeper and ¥3620 for a two-berth cabin and passes through Mongolia, so you'll need a Mongolian visa. The Russian train bypasses Mongolia and leaves on Saturdays, costing ¥2526 for hard-sleeper or ¥3989 for a two-berth cabin.

The trains are heated, but if you plan to do either of these trips in winter the traditional way of keeping warm is drinking vodka! At the border the trains are lifted off the tracks to change gauge and you'll have to go through border procedures – the whole process takes four to six hours.

By Road

 There are numerous bus stations dotted around the capital, serving every place from the Great Wall to Hainan Island, China's most southern extremity, but train or plane is a better bet for all destinations outside of this chapter (see *Getting Around* for buses to destinations around Beijing). Chengde (hourly, 4 hrs) is served from Deshengmen Bus Station, which is north of the city on the second ringroad, and can be reached by bus #55 or from Jishuitan subway station.

Getting Around

Once known as the city of bicycles, these days Beijing is more and more the city of scooters, cars and flyovers. Traffic can be frustratingly slow at times and, if it's an option, the subway is a good way to go. Beijing's polluted skies owe at least something to its vehicles and, although buses and taxis are going greener, skyrocketing private ownership sees 1,500 new car registrations issued every day and these are the biggest worry for planners (and cyclists) today.

By Subway

Beijing's subway is a cheap and quick way of getting around the city if the area you want has a line running through it. Although it is being expanded, the subway is still fairly limited in extent, and as the oldest subway system (constructed as party cadre transport under Mao Zedong) in China, it is also the most antiquated. Currently the subway system consists of lines #1, #2 and, bizarrely, #13, along with the Batong Light Rail Service. Apparently lines #3 to #12 are in the pipeline, of which #4 and #5 will run through Xicheng and Dongcheng respectively, and, along with the Airport and Olympic Lines, should be open by 2008. Of the present lines, #1 and #2 are the most useful. Line #1 runs from east to west and takes in the city center, including stops at Tian'anmen West and East, Wangfujing, and then the hotel districts around Jianguomen and Guomao. Line #2 takes a circular route around the city and includes stops at Beijing Train Station, Yonghe Temple and the Drum Tower. The two lines intersect at Jianguomen in the east and Fuxingmen in the west.

BEIJING Subway

- Line 1
- Line 2
- Line 5 *under construction*
- Line 13 City Rail

Services operate from 5:30 am-11 pm and tickets cost ¥2 for the Batong Line and ¥3 for other lines. Weekly passes were recently modernized to plastic passes, but single-journey tickets are still paper. If you're going to take a few subways in a day, buy several tickets (which can only be used on that day) to save yourself from lining up again. Trains aren't air-conditioned, which can make them sticky in summer, although this is set to change. Announcements are made in English and Chinese and there are English subway route maps in the carriages. Stations are marked above ground by a white square inside a C on a blue background.

By Bus

In the City

 Beijing has an abundant bus network and private minibus routes, offering cheap travel to all parts of the city for between ¥1 and ¥2. It can be confusing since most services are only marked in Chinese but, as long as you can find the right bus number and show your destination to the driver, you should get where you want to go.

Bus travel affords a look at everyday Beijingers going about their everyday business, although services can be crowded and you should be wary of pickpockets. Services numbered in the 800s are slightly more expensive luxury and tourist buses (¥3-10), which are air-conditioned in summer and heated in winter. If you have a student or working visa and will be using the buses a lot, you can buy passes at McDonalds and major bus terminals that allow unlimited travel on buses numbered below 400. Services run from 5:30 am-8:30 pm and numbers 200-212 run through the night. Some useful routes are as follows:

- Bus #52 – Beijing West Station (Xi Zhan) to Tian'anmen Square and along Chang'an Jie
- Luxury bus #802 – Beijing West Station (Xi Zhan) to Panjiayuan market
- Luxury bus #808 – Qianmen to the Summer Palace

Buses to Surrounding Sights

For buses out to sights such as the Great Wall it's easiest to go on a tour or take a tourist bus (see *Sightseeing*, p. 152), but there are also regular buses that depart from **Dongzhimen Station** on the eastern section of the second ringroad, **Deshengmen** in the north of the city and **Pingguoyuan**, way out west, all of which are connected by or close to the subway (see individual sights for listings). Tourist buses run from the **Qianmen bus depot** opposite Qianmen subway on Qianmen Dong Dajie.

By Taxi

 Taxis come in a range of different colors and are abundant in Beijing, charging ¥10 for the first two kilometers (1.2 miles) and ¥2 per kilometer (0.6 miles) after this, but the city's size makes it very easy to run up a meter fee of ¥40 and more. Although Beijing has many times more cabs than equivalent-sized cities around the world, it can still be difficult to find one when any of the capital's manifold adverse weather conditions (rain, snow, sandstorm) hit. As private vehicle ownership increases, it is planned to nearly halve the number of taxis on the street, which will make competition at peak hours that much greater. In the

Beijing

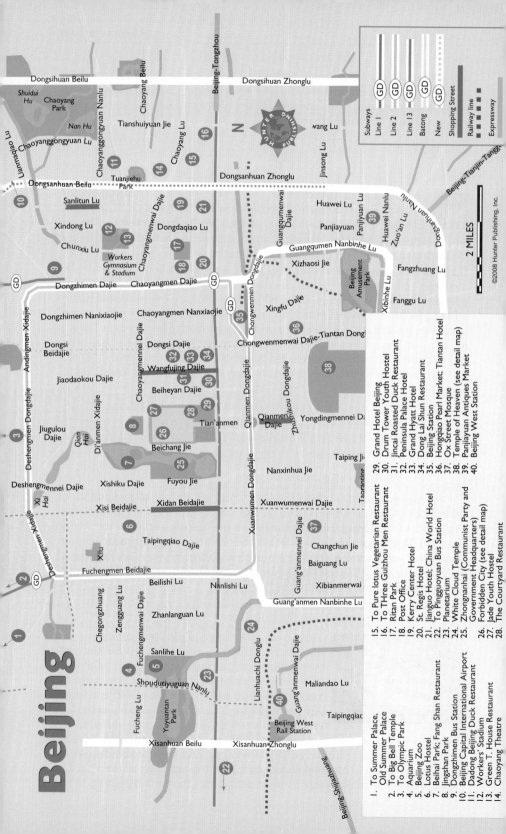

Map legend:

Subways	
Line 1	GD
Line 2	GD
Line 13	GD
Batong	GD
New	GD
Shopping Street	
Railway line	
Expressway	

2 MILES

Street labels:

- Dongsihuan Beilu
- Dongsihuan Zhonglu
- Shuidui Hu
- Chaoyang Park
- Nan Hu
- Tianshuiyuan Jie
- Chaoyang Beilu
- Beijing-Tongzhou
- ...wang Lu
- Chaoyanggongyuan Nanlu
- Chaoyanggongyuan Lu
- Chaoyang Lu
- Jinsong Lu
- Lianmaqiao Lu
- Tuanjiehu Park
- Dongsanhuan Zhonglu
- Dongsanhuan Beilu
- Sanlitun Lu
- Xindong Lu
- Chaoyangmenwai Dajie
- Dongdaqiao Lu
- Guangqumenwai Dajie
- Huawei Lu
- Panjiayuan
- Huawei Nanlu
- Paniyuan Lu
- Zuo'an Lu
- Chunxiu Lu
- Guangqumen Nanbinhe Lu
- Xizhaosi Jie
- Beijing Amusement Park
- Fangzhuang Lu
- Xibinhe Lu
- Fanggu Lu
- Workers Gymnasium & Stadium
- Dongzhimen Dajie
- Chaoyangmen Dajie
- Chongwenmen Dongdajie
- Xingfu Dajie
- Dongzhimen Nanxiaojie
- Chaoyangmen Nanxiaojie
- Andingmen Xidajie
- Dongsi Beidajie
- Chaoyangmennei Dajie
- Dongsi Dajie
- Chongwenmenwai Dajie-Tiantan Dong
- Chongwenmenwai Dajie-Tiantan Dong
- Jiaodaokou Dajie
- Wangfujing Dajie
- Zhushikou Dongdajie
- Jiugulou Dajie
- Beiheyan Dajie
- Dianmen Xidajie
- Qian Hai
- Beichang Jie
- Tian'anmen
- Qianmen Dajie
- Yongdingmennei Da
- Deshengmennei Dajie
- Xishiku Dajie
- Fuyou Jie
- Nanxinhua Jie
- Taiping Ji
- Xi Hai
- Xisi Beidajie
- Xidan Beidajie
- Xuanwumen Dongdajie
- Xuanwumenwai Dajie
- Taoranting
- Deshengmen Xidajie
- Xiru
- Taipingqiao Dajie
- Guang'anmennei Dajie
- Changchun Jie
- Fuchengmen Beidajie
- Beilishi Lu
- Nanlishi Lu
- Baiguang Lu
- Chegongzhuang
- Zhanlanguan Lu
- Guang'anmenwai Dajie
- Xibianmenwai
- Guang'anmen Nanbinhe Lu
- Zengguang Lu
- Fuchengmenwai Dajie
- Sanlihe Lu
- Lianhuachi Donglu
- Maliandao Lu
- Fucheng Lu
- Yuyuantan Park
- Shoudutiyuguan Nanlu
- Beijing West Rail Station
- Taipingqiao
- Xisanhuan Beilu
- Xisanhuan Zhonglu
- Beijing-Shijiazhuang
- Beijing-Tianjin-Tanggu
- Dongsanhuan Nanlu
- Beijing West Station

run-up to the Olympics there is a program to help drivers speak English, but this seems to have had little impact as yet. You can also hire taxis for day-trips out to Beijing's surrounding sights (see *Sightseeing*, p. 152, for prices).

By Cycle Rickshaw

You'll see cycle-rickshaws all over the city, but they have no meters so it can be very difficult for foreigners to get a fair price. Plus a ride through any of the city's busier streets on these rickety little contraptions can be a hair-raising experience, so you're better off in a cab. This said, three-wheelers make for a less perilous and fun jaunt around the old *hutong* areas, but beware that some wheeler-dealer operators might try and take you for a ride, so establish a clear price at the beginning. See *Adventures On Wheels*, p. 198 for more.

By Bicycle

Although much of the modern city is over-run by traffic and flyovers, bicycles are still used by millions of Beijingers and there are quieter areas definitely worth exploring by bike. Standard bikes can be rented from backpacker hostels and outside some subway stations for as little as ¥10 a day, but major hotels and places at tourist sights will charge more. If you're planning on heading to some rougher terrain, it's worth renting a mountain bike, which can be arranged through **Cycle China**, who also runs bike trips in and around Beijing (see *Adventures On Wheels*, p. 198).

By Car & Motorbike

Unless you live here, driving in Beijing isn't an option and, even if you do, negotiating its traffic-choked streets is easier in a cab. For tourists, options are limited to hiring a car with driver, which can be arranged through the major hotels or **Hertz**, who have outlets at the **Jianguo Hotel** (see p. 208; ☎ 010-6595-8109) and the **Lufthansa Center** at 50 Liangmaqiao Lu (☎ 010-6462-5730). Far more fun and an option open to tourists is to rent a motorbike sidecar for a spin into the surrounding countryside. Bikes, guides, insurance and license can be arranged through **CJ Motorcycle Club** (see *Adventures On Wheels*, p. 198).

Orientation

Beijing is a vast sprawling city, its grid-plan centered on imposing **Tian'anmen Square** and the **Forbidden City**, outside of which it is encircled by a series of numbered ringroads that form the city's main traffic arteries. The central city is divided into districts: west of Tian'anmen Square is **Xicheng**, to the east **Dongcheng** leads into **Chaoyang**, while to the south the Temple of Heaven lies in **Chongwen** and, west of here, **Xuanwu** contains the city's Muslim quarter. In the far northwest **Haidian** has the old and new **summer palaces** and these days it's also getting a reputation for a lively nightlife and restaurant scene. Farther out from here, things become distinctly more rugged in the **Western Hills**, where you'll find the **Fragrant Hills** and **Badachu** and, to the south, the temples of **Jietai** and **Tanzhe**.

The City Center

Tian'anmen Square (Nowozin)

Tian'anmen Square's northern end is dominated by the Forbidden City's grand entrance and, within the square itself, you'll find a number of monuments, including the concrete block of Chairman Mao's Mausoleum, and to the east and west are the stately National Museum and the Great Hall of the People. West of the Forbidden City is the party enclave of **Zhongnanhai**, while to the north are two interesting parks, **Beihai** and **Jingshan**, the latter of which gives great views out over the Forbidden City and is a good place to get your bearings. Farther north from here takes you through the trendy *hutong* nightlife areas of Houhai to the **Drum Tower**, around which you'll find some budget accommodation and tasty dining options.

The Temple of Heaven (Saad Akhtar)

One of Beijing's best shopping districts, **Wangfujing**, is just to the east of Tian'anmen Square and, from its southern end, **Dongchang'an Dajie**, which becomes **Jianguomen Dajie**, runs east past banking headquarters and some of the city's best hotels and malls. From Tian'anmen Square, **Qianmen Dajie** heads south through a popular backpacker *hutong* hotel haunt to the **Temple of Heaven**, east of which there are two worthwhile markets, **Hongqiao** and, farther out, **Panjiayuan**. Aside from those already mentioned, other trendy eating and drinking zones include the **Workers Stadium** and, not far away, the original bar street of **San Litun Lu**, which are both in the east of the city, near the second ringroad.

Street-Spotting

Negotiating Beijing's giant avenues and flyovers can seem a monumental task and isn't aided by the complex street names, although they are at least marked in pinyin. The usual directional terms (see *Street Names*, p. 91) are supplemented by two more in Beijing: *wai* means outside and *nei* means inside, which refer to the street's location in relation to the line of the now absent city walls. Thus Jianguomen Wai Dajie means Jianguo Gate Outer Avenue. *Hutong* are great to wander down and get lost in, but can be quite tricky if you actually want to find something specific. Take the name in Chinese and look for landmarks among the *xiang* (alleys).

Information Sources

Beijing's numerous tourist offices might seem like a logical place to start, but, although there are plenty of leaflets, staff aren't particularly helpful. Nevertheless, you're bound to pass by a branch, in which case it's worth popping in: there's a convenient office at **Beijing Train Station** (☎ 010-6528-8448; chezhan@bjta.gov.cn). For other branches check out www.bjta.gov.cn. Another online source of information to try is www.thebeijingguide.com. Hostels and hotels also tend to be good places to gather information, but for a more in-depth and current take on the city check out one of the city's magazines, such as *Beijing Review*, *City Weekend*, *that's beijing* (www.thatsbj.com) and *Time Out*. These free magazines can be found in bars, hotels and restaurants and offer reviews of everything from shopping to bars, clubs and cultural events, as well as items for sale and apartments for rent. If you're going to be staying in the city longer, the *Insider's Guide* series which is linked to *that's beijing*, has books and maps covering everything from individual bar districts to weekend excursions and can be found in major bookstores and in the Friendship Store (see *Shopping*, p. 195). The best easily available map of the city is the red and white *Beijing Tourist Map* (¥8), which has most sights and major hotels and shopping districts marked in English – you can buy it at the train stations, in bookstores and at some news kiosks.

Events & Festivals

All the regular Chinese holidays and festivals are celebrated in Beijing, although you're better off avoiding the three major weeklong holidays (see p. 73-76) if you can. This said, the huge celebration in Tian'anmen Square on National Day is a sight to behold and thoroughly convinces you of the might of China. If you can brave the cold, January and February offer not only Chinese New Year and the chance to see the Great Wall and Temple of Heaven in the snow, but also an ice festival out at Longqing Gorge (see p. 183).

Communications

Post Office: Chaoyangmen Nan Dajie, just north of the Jianguomen overpass, and at the airport.

Telephone code: 010

Internet access: Internet cafés are abundant and many coffee shops and hostels also have access. Prices begin at ¥3 but in such places you'll almost certainly find yourself surrounded by gangs of noisy teenage gamers – for quieter surfing there are upmarket places such as the **Qianyi Internet Café** (¥20/hr) on the third floor of the Railway Station Shopping Mall at the southeastern corner of Tian'anmen Square, or, farther out in Chaoyang, **520 Digital Technology** (¥12-15/hr) on the third floor of the Wangshi Bali supermarket at 12 Chaowai Dajie. If you have a laptop you can find **wireless** connection at many locations around the city, some where you have to pay (the Kerry Center and Starbucks, for example) and others that are free.

Money

Bank of China: 8 Yabao Lu, just north of the international post office and another on the eastern side of Wangfujing Dajie.

If you need to change money on the weekends try your hotel or you can head to the ground floor of the Friendship Store, which has an exchange office. If you need cash urgently, get some sent to **Western Union** and collect it at the post office (see above).

Embassies

Most of the embassies are found either in San Litun or the Ritan Park area, north of Jianguomen Wai Dajie.

- **Australia**, 21 Dongzhimen Wai Dajie (☎ 010-6532-2331, www.austemb. org.cn)
- **Canada**, 19 Dongzhimen Wai Dajie (☎ 010-6532-3536, www.beijing.gc. ca)
- **Mongolia**, 2 Xiushui Beijie (☎ 010-6532-1203)
- **Nepal**, 1 San Litun Xiliu Jie (☎ 010-6532-1795)
- **New Zealand**, 1 Dong'er Jie, Ritan Lu (☎ 010-6532-2371, www. nzembassy.com/china)
- **United Kingdom**, 11 Guanghua Lu (☎ 010-5192-4000, www.uk.cn)
- **United States**, 3 Xiushui Beijie (☎ 010-6532-3831, www.usembassy-china.org.cn)
- **Vietnam**, 32 Guanghua Lu (☎ 010-6532-1155)

Public Security Bureau

2 Andingmen Dong Dajie (☎ 010-8402-0101)

Medical Services

 Peking Union Medical Hospital at 53 Dongdan Bei Dajie (☎ 010-6529-5284) has a designated foreigners' wing where consultations cost ¥100-¥300. If you want an international clinic, try **SOS** (☎ 010-6462-9112), which can be found at Building C of the BITIC Jing Yi Building, 5 San Litun Xiwujie in Chaoyang – consultations are US$90.

LEARNING THE LINGO

Starting on page 598, there's an extensive language section, including useful phrases ranging from restaurant vocabulary to what to do in an emergency. These are written in both Romanized Chinese (pinyin) which will enable you to try and pronounce them, and Chinese characters, should verbal communication fail! The major transport terminals, attractions, hotels and restaurants are also shown in Chinese characters. This will allow you to get into a taxi, point at the relevant characters and get to your destination. Chinese vocabulary specific to **Beijing** begins on page 607.

Sightseeing

In spite of its mightily modern appearance, Beijing has a lion's share of China's great historic sights, each of which is worth a visit to the city in its own right. This plethora of monuments hasn't escaped the notice of the rest of China (or the world) and you'll need to be prepared for hordes of tourists at all of the key sights. In 2005, 12 million Chinese tourists and nearly four million foreigners visited Beijing, most of them during the busy summer months. If you want to see the sights at their quietest, then a winter trip is advisable – indeed the Temple of Heaven is captivating when blanketed with snow. But, if you can't face the cold, then some of the smaller sights or lesser parts of the main attractions are worth seeking out for some solitude.

There are four must-see sights in Beijing: the **Forbidden City**, the **Temple of Heaven**, the **Summer Palace** and the **Great Wall**. Although each is worthy of a full day's visit, you could just about squeeze all of them into a three-day trip. However, this would leave no room for the other areas and sights that make Beijing the dynamic dichotomy it is today. Temples, lakes, markets, cuisine and opera are all integral to the capital and a visit to Beijing would be incomplete without seeing at least some of them. So try to intersperse the big four with some smaller sights, and build in a bit of time for an aimless amble through the *hutong*.

(margin) **Beijing & Around**

A Busy Three Days in Beijing

■ **Day 1:** Start in the center and head straight to **Tian'anmen Square** and onto the **Forbidden City**. Take your time soaking up the imperial splendor and exploring its manifold courtyards, gardens and museums as well as the grand halls themselves. Emerge at the northern exit and continue to **Jingshan** or **Beihai Park**, and then take some lunch at the Courtyard or Fangshan (see p. 213). Take a taxi up to **Shichahai** and hire a rickshaw to take you around the local *hutong*, then enjoy a lakeside dinner, or if you're feeling super romantic, eat aboard a gondola courtesy of Kaorouji (see p. 214).

■ **Day 2:** Rise early for a trip to the **Great Wall** and the stunning hike between Jinshanling and Simatai (or from Jiankou to Mutianyu), stopping for a picnic and a cheeky glug of Great Wall red along the way. Return shattered and drag yourself out to for a **Beijing duck** dinner at Li Qun (see p. 213).

■ **Day 3:** Start with an early morning trip to the exquisite **Temple of Heaven**, maybe even catching the last of the sunrise tai chi brigade's morning exercises and then take a taxi to **Panjiayuan Market** for some great souvenir shopping. From here take a long taxi ride to the Summer Palace and enjoy a boat ride after checking out the palace buildings. To round off your trip, enjoy dinner at the love-or-hate-but-must-try-once experience of the **Beijing opera**, or, if this is too shrill, be astounded by the **Beijing Acrobats**.

■ **End of Day 3:** Remind yourself to come back to Beijing because there are hundreds of other sights waiting for your next trip....

Tours

Although it's perfectly feasible to get around and see all the sights by yourself, if you want to skip some of the hassle (and fun) of getting about, or have limited time, then there are plenty of agencies who arrange tours. All the major hotels have agencies, and hostels run budget versions of the same along with more adventurous trips, including hikes along the Great Wall. Some hostel trips require a minimum number of passengers to operate, but during the summer months this is seldom a problem and, as many of the hostels operate joint tours, you should always be able to get to where you want to go, even if you have to wait a day or two. Most of these tours include transport and entry fees as well as an English-speaking guide. However, while these trips are inexpensive and convenient, they can be rushed and leave little room for independent exploration. Hostel sightseeing daytrips cost ¥230 for a city tour and between ¥90 and ¥180 for trips to the wall (see *Visiting the Wall*, p. 179 for more).

If you want more of an upscale tour, try your hotel booking desk, **CITS** (☎ 010-6515-8570, www.citsbj.com) at 28 Jianguomen Wai Dajie, or **Gray Line** at 5F Grand Rock Plaza, 13 Xinzhongxili, Dongcheng (☎ 010-6417-0383, www.grayline.com/franchise.cfm). Gray Line has whistle-stop tours that, unbelievably, manage to cover Tian'anmen Square and the three big imperial sights all in a day, although you'll barely have time to appreciate them. You're better off selecting one of their tours that limits itself to a few sights, such as Historic Beijing (Tour 5), which only visits Tian'anmen Square, the Forbidden City and the Temple of Heaven (¥320).

There are also companies that specialize in taking you places which are more difficult to stumble across by yourself and these can be worthwhile to escape the crowds, particularly for the *hutong* and trips out to the Great Wall. **Cycle China** runs cycling tours in and out of the city, as well as Great Wall hikes, while **Beijing Hikers** arranges weekly Sunday trips out to the wilds of Beijing's hinterlands or, if you want the journey to be an adventure in itself, then you could consider a sidecar trip with the **CJ Motorcycle Club** (see *Adventures*, p. 198-99, for all three).

The Big Three Imperial Sights

Although Beijing's long imperial rule has left it with numerous historical monuments dating back to the dynastic age, three of them, the Ming dynasty **Forbidden City** and **Temple of Heaven** and the Qing dynasty **Summer Palace**, stand out and are must-sees on any itinerary. As a tour leader I went to each of these places many times, but, testament to their size and scope, on every visit I found something that I hadn't seen before. All three sites are big enough so that you should be able to find a quiet nook for some peaceful reflection, but, to avoid the worst crowds at the main structures, try to come as the sights open, toward the end of the day, or in winter.

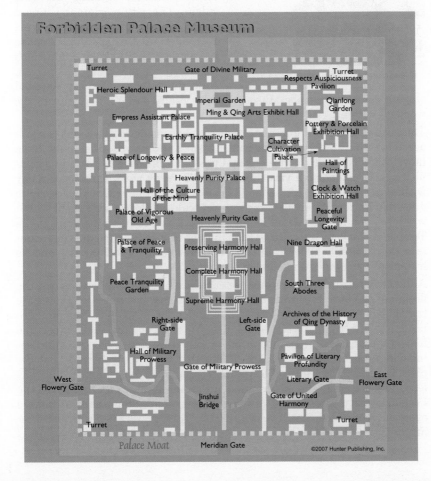

Forbidden Palace Museum

©2007 Hunter Publishing, Inc.

Beijing & Around

★★★ The Forbidden City

Soldiers at the Forbidden City

(Daily 8:30 am-4:30 pm; ¥60, ¥40 Nov 1-March 31; Tian'anmen East or West subway, line #1)

Some History

One of the world's most magnificent palaces, the Forbidden City's imposing main gateway looms large over Tian'anmen Square. Forbidden to the public from its construction until after the fall of dynastic China, the splendor of imperial life is now open for the world to see. Originally built under the Ming Emperor **Yongle**, on the site of a Yuan dynasty palace, the Forbidden City served as the imperial seat for another 23 Ming and Qing rulers. The city's original Chinese name, Zijin Cheng, means Purple Forbidden City, which alludes not to its color, but to the Polar Star, which was seen as the center of heaven. Now the city is officially entitled Gugong, meaning Palace Museum, which really doesn't do justice to the wonders within.

The term city might sound like exaggeration, considering that this is a palace, but with its **800 buildings** housing **9,999 rooms** and great halls, and a labyrinth of courtyards, gardens and passages all contained within a complex nearly a thousand yards long and 820 yards wide, it really is a city within a city. It's difficult to gauge the city's size from within, but a trip to Jingshan Park will provide some sense of scale, while a Google earth search will leave you in no doubt of its magnitude. Apart from annual trips to the Temple of Heaven (see p. 157), the Summer Palace (p. 160) and the Mountain Resort at Chengde (p. 224-27), emperors seldom left the city and its legions of concubines and eunuch servants.

Although destroyed and reconstructed several times through history, the design of the buildings remains largely the same, but to really appreciate the splendor of what the city was like under the Ming and Qing you also need to take a trip to the National Palace Museum in Taiwanese Taipei! The bulk of the treasures from the Forbidden City were smuggled out by the fleeing Chiang Kaishek in 1949 and, if you visit both, you can really put the place together. The Cultural Revolution threatened to tear apart what was left and it was only the intervention of Premier Zhou Enlai that saved the Forbidden City. These days its wonders are seen by thousands of visitors every day and at the time of writing parts of the city were being given a facelift for the 2008 Olympics.

Did You Know? The Forbidden City is struck by lightning over 100 times a year!

Visiting the City

The city is visited from south to north and there are guides (one person ¥150, four people ¥400 for a 90-minute tour) and audioguides (¥40 plus a ¥200 deposit) are available at the main entrance at the Meridian Gate. While the principal courtyards and halls on the main south-north axis hold the most impressive buildings and are all must-sees, their inhuman scale (and the crowds of tourists visiting them) can make it difficult to get a sense of what life was like here during the dynastic era; a more insight-

Rub the dragon for good luck (Tot Foster)

ful perspective (and solitude) can be found by visiting the **smaller chambers** that flank the main courtyards.

Golden lion guardian

Throughout the city you will notice a number of recurring features, including **dragons** (signs of the emperor), **phoenixes** (signs of the empress) and golden **lions**, symbolic of the natural order of things – the male has the globe at his feet, while the female tends a cub! You'll also see images of **cranes** and **tortoises** popping up from time to time and these represent longevity and immortality. Enormous **cauldrons** are also dotted throughout the city and these were filled with water (which had to be heated to stop it from freezing in winter) in order to quell fires.

From Tian'anmen to Taihemen

The main entrance is beneath the watchful gaze of a portrait of Chairman Mao (see *Tian'anamen Square*, p. 164, for more) that hangs on the imposing **Tian'anmen Gate** (Gate of Heavenly Peace), which you can ascend for good views over the square (daily 8:30 am-3 pm; ¥15). From here head straight through the large oblong courtyard, perpetually bustling with baseball cap-clad Chinese tourists trying to keep up with their flag- and

Beijing & Around

megaphone-toting guides. You'll pass through the smaller Duan Gate and into another courtyard, at the far end of which lies the **Meridian Gate**. Just before the Meridian Gate on the right hand side is the ticket office, where you may have to be pushy to avoid losing your place. There is a separate entrance lane for foreigners to the right and, once inside, you'll hear the dulcet tones of Roger Moore, who narrates the headphone audio-guides available here (¥40), which you can drop off at the northern exit. Once you're through the arduous task of getting in, you'll find another vast courtyard, bare apart from the **Jinshui (Golden Water) Stream** and the five bridges that cross it, representing the five Confucian virtues (see p. 49). At the far end of this courtyard, steps lead past grand lion statues to the **Gate of Supreme Harmony** (Taihemen).

The Big Three Halls

All three major halls were being restored in preparation for the Olympics at the time of writing. Moving through, you enter another far grander courtyard with the **Hall of Supreme Harmony** (Taihedian) at its center, sitting atop flights of steps and an intricately carved marble ramp. This grand hall was the tallest building in Beijing during the dynastic age and commoners were forbidden from building anything that exceeded its height. The Hall of

Hall of Supreme Harmony (Allen T Chang)

Supreme Harmony was the most important building in the Forbidden City and was used for events such as the emperor's birthday and coronations. It still holds the dragon throne today. Within the same courtyard, the smaller **Hall of Middle Harmony** (Zhonghedian) is the next building you'll come to and was used for events considered less important, such as receiving foreign leaders or envoys (illustrating the Ming and Qing's largely inward-looking perspective), and served as a dressing room for more important occasions, which were held in the Hall of Supreme Harmony.

The final building in the courtyard, the **Hall of Preserving Harmony** (Baohedian) was where state banquets took place and later served as an imperial examination hall. As you descend the steps that lead away from the Hall of Preserving Harmony you'll find a disturbing insight into the dichotomy of modern China – here in the heart of the Forbidden City, once the preserve of emperors, there is a Starbucks! Some might argue that the Mandate of Heaven has just swung that way and that global corporations are today's dynasties, but this small outlet caused such a stir on opening that it has had to remove its iconic sign from the wall. Whatever your feelings about the matter, if you're tired and want a coffee to perk you up, there's something to be said for a Forbidden Starbucks. Continuing right (east) from Starbucks will take you to the **Nine Dragon Screen, Jewelry Museum** and **Imperial Theater** (¥10 for all three) and the **Clock Museum** (¥10), both of which are thoroughly worthwhile side-trips, as much for the rooms they take you through as the exhibits themselves.

The Imperial Living Quarters

Moving north from here, beyond the **Gate of Heavenly Purity** (Qianqingmen), access was limited solely to the emperor, his servants, concubines and royal relatives. The next courtyard was part of the imperial living quarters and contains a further trio of halls, once again the most significant of which is the first one you'll come to. The **Palace of Heavenly Purity** (Qianqinggong) was the royal bedroom, but was later used as a state room. The **Hall of Union** (Jiaotaidian) follows and was the empress's throne room, and the third hall, the **Palace of Earthly Tranquility** (Kunninggong), was used for shamanistic rituals under the Manchu Qing emperors, but was traditionally where the emperor and empress spent their wedding night. Flanking the courtyard to the east and west there are **two museums**, dedicated to **Bronzes** and **Ceramics**, both of which are worth a wander.

A little farther to the west, the **Hall of Mental Cultivation** (Yangxindian) was a favorite place for emperors to spend time, offering a much more intimate scale and holding some original Qing dynasty furnishings.

From the end of the imperial living quarters, you enter the **Imperial Garden**, from where passages lead east to the Zhen Fei Well and lovely Qianlong Gardens, and west to the concubine's and eunuch's quarters. Straight through the Imperial Garden leads you to the northern exit at the **Gate of Martial Spirit**, where you can return your headset and there are a few benches to wait for any friends you might have lost inside!

★★★ The Temple of Heaven

(Open daily 8 am-5:30 pm; ¥35 or ¥15 for entry to the park only; bus #17 from Qianmen)

Some History

Situated in a vast park a mile southeast of Tian'anmen Square, the Temple of Heaven is unmissable and its Hall of Prayer for Good Harvests is seen as the pinnacle of Ming architecture. The temple was constructed in 1420 under Emperor Yongle, when Beijing was designated the imperial capital, at a place deemed the meeting point of heaven and earth, which is reflected in its design. Heaven was thought to be circular and the earth square, so the principal heavenly buildings are round and are set above their square earthly emplacements. As the Son of Heaven, the emperor was the primary medium between heaven and earth. Three days before the winter solstice, the emperor would abstain from meat, "stimulating" foods and spices and on the third he would travel from the Forbidden City to the Temple of Heaven's Fasting Palace. During the procession, all commoners retreated indoors to avoid laying eyes on the emperor – a crime which carried the death penalty. The following day, the emperor would move to the Imperial Vault of Heaven to meditate, before continuing to the grand domed Hall of Prayer for Good Harvests and then emerging to ritually sacrifice animals at the Round Altar and pray for a good harvest in the coming year.

The temple was continually used during the Ming and Qing dynasties and was solely the preserve of the emperor and his staff until it was declared open to the public on the first Chinese National Day in October 1912. Today, the simple grandeur of the temple makes it a must-see on any tourist's itinerary, but despite this, the size and tranquility of its grounds makes it seem less crowded than the Forbidden City. The Echo Wall and main prayer hall have both recently undergone restorations and the latter's paintwork and tiles now gleam resplendently in the sunlight.

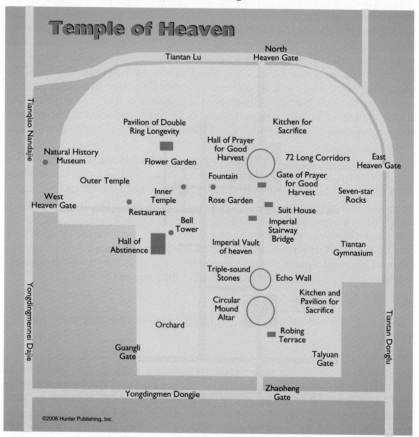

Visiting the Temple

The temple is laid out on a traditional south-north axis and is best visited in this order, although you can also enter the park at its eastern and northern gates. There are guides available at the entrances to the temple, as well as audio-guides (in English and French, ¥40) that can be dropped off at any of the gates. Although the main buildings always have a flow of visitors passing through, the temple is twice the size of the Forbidden City and the surrounding grounds, particularly those to the west, are usually quiet and are a pleasant spot for a picnic. Entering through the principal southern Zhaoheng Gate the path leads to the three-tiered **Round Altar** (Yuanqiu). The three levels represent Man, Earth and Heaven and on each numerically significant slabs of marble indicate the importance of the number nine in Chinese cos-

The Temple of Heaven (Tot Foster)

mology. The top tier was seen as the center of the Middle Kingdom and as such, the world. You can ascend the marble steps and stand on the central stone, just as the emperor did, although these days you'll have to wait your turn!

Decorative detail at the Temple of Heaven

Proceeding north from here and after passing some incredibly old trees protected by wire-mesh, you'll reach the circular **Echo Wall** (Huiyinbi). Similar to whispering walls found in Roman amphitheaters, the idea here is that you can whisper at one side of the circle and the words will quietly travel and be perfectly audible to someone on the opposite side, although the number of people testing this theory confounds most attempts. The 'sweet spot' in the center of the circle also creates great echoes. Immediately north of the wall is the octagonal wooden **Imperial Vault of Heaven** (Huangqiongyu) where the emperor would meditate and commune with the heavens before proceeding to the prayer hall.

Continuing north along the imperial way you'll start to see the fabulous sweeping azure roof of the complex's most impressive building, the **Hall of Prayer for Good Harvests** (Qiniandian). This 120-foot-high building becomes all the more amazing when you discover that not a single nail was

A winter day at the Temple of Heaven

used in its construction! Its sits atop another three-tiered marble platform and inside is supported by four central pillars and another 12 peripheral columns, which represent the seasons and months respectively. The hall was completely destroyed by lightning in 1889, which was seen (correctly) as a very bad omen, given that the Qing, and indeed dynastic China, would completely collapse within two decades. It was reconstructed immediately and has just received another facelift in preparation for its next wave of worshippers during the 2008 Olympics.

The Grounds

Walking east from Hall of Prayer for Good Harvests takes you along a covered pathway full of old folk passing the time of day by singing opera songs, playing cards and watching the world go by. It's not far from here to the eastern exit. From there you can take a taxi (or visit Hongqiao Market, see p. 192, just over the road). Or, if you might prefer to wander through the wooded grounds around the Fasting Palace (Zhaigong) to the west of the Hall of Prayer for Good Harvest. There are plenty of quiet spots for a picnic. The park is free from 6 am-8 am and, although the buildings aren't open, it's a great time to visit as every open space is full of people gently carrying out their morning exercises – from tai chi to ballroom dancing.

★★★The Summer Palace

Yiheyuan Lu, Haidian (daily 7 am-5 pm; ¥30, ¥20 Nov 1-Mar 31; bus #808 from Qianmen)

Some History

Located in the city's northwestern suburbs, the Summer Palace (Yiheyuan) isn't as grand or striking as the Forbidden City and Temple of Heaven, but its lakeside setting offers a refreshing sense of tranquility and space, along with its historic buildings. The lake upon which the palace rests dates from the 12th century, but the original versions of the buildings that surround it weren't constructed until the Qing dynasty under Emperor Qianlong. Since then the Summer Palace has been re-built twice, both times on the order of the **Empress Dowager Cixi** (see p. 17), who chose to rule from here year-round between 1903 and 1908. The palace was first destroyed by Anglo-French forces during the Second Opium War (see p. 16), and 40 years later it was ransacked by the British in response to the Boxer Rebellion (see p. 17).

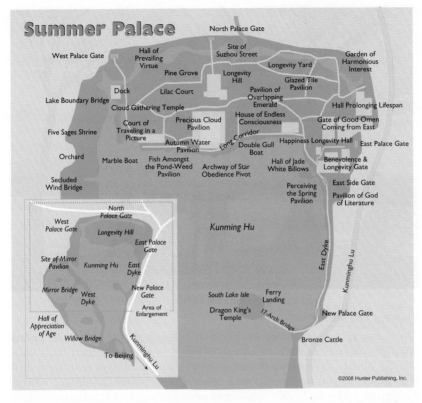

Summer Palace

North Palace Gate

West Palace Gate

Hall of Prevailing Virtue

Site of Suzhou Street

Longevity Yard

Garden of Harmonious Interest

Pine Grove

Longevity Hill

Dock

Lilac Court

Pavilion of Overlapping Emerald

Glazed Tile Pavilion

Lake Boundary Bridge

Cloud Gathering Temple

House of Endless Consciousness

Hall Prolonging Lifespan

Precious Cloud Pavilion

Gate of Good Omen Coming from East

Five Sages Shrine

Court of Traveling in a Picture

Autumn Water Pavilion

Long Corridor

Double Gull Boat

Happiness Longevity Hall

East Palace Gate

Orchard

Marble Boat

Fish Amongst the Pond-Weed Pavilion

Archway of Star Obedience Pivot

Hall of Jade White Billows

Benevolence & Longevity Gate

Secluded Wind Bridge

Perceiving the Spring Pavilion

East Side Gate

Pavilion of God of Literature

North Palace Gate

West Palace Gate

Longevity Hill

East Palace Gate

Kunming Hu

Site of Mirror Pavilion

Kunming Hu

East Dyke

East Dyke

Kunminghu Lu

Mirror Bridge

West Dyke

New Palace Gate

South Lake Isle

Ferry Landing

Hall of Appreciation of Age

Area of Enlargement

Dragon King's Temple

17 Arch Bridge

New Palace Gate

Willow Bridge

Kunminghu Lu

Bronze Cattle

To Beijing

Kunminghu Lu

©2008 Hunter Publishing, Inc.

These days it is a popular retreat from Beijing's baking summers but is equally, perhaps more, attractive during the icy winters. The whole complex has recently been spruced up in preparation for the Olympics.

Seventeen Arch Bridge at the Summer Palace

Beijing & Around

Sunset at the Summer Palace (Ewen Bell)

Visiting the Palace

There are plenty of guides on hand at the entry gates, but the palace grounds are easy enough to navigate and if you want to hear their spiel (mostly about Cixi's excesses and cruelty) you can always eavesdrop on a tour group as you make your way around. The palace is laid out around **Kunming Lake** and has a number of pretty bridges on its shores, notably the 17-arch bridge in the southeast, the Jade Bridge in the west and the Humpbacked Bridge in the south. The bulk of historic buildings (and thus visitors) are found on the north shore, while the south remains quieter and a good spot for a picnic. Though the buildings are certainly of interest and some, like the temples on Longevity Hill, offer fine views, the palace is enjoyed as much for its lake and grounds and a gentle few hours strolling or paddling a pedal boat can work wonders if you're feeling a bit overloaded with temples and palaces. Boats can be rented from below the Sea of Wisdom Temple and by the marble boat, costing ¥10 an hour. Alternatively, if you don't want to do the legwork, tourist motorboats run between the Dragon King Temple (Longwangmiao) on South Lake Island and the marble boat. In winter the lake becomes a natural ice rink and you can rent skates.

Taxi is the easiest way to get to the palace, but buses run here, or for a different approach **you can arrive by boat**, just as Cixi did over 100 years ago (see *Adventures On Water*, p. 200).

The Royal Residences & Theater

The East Palace Gate brings you into a large courtyard, which leads to the **Hall of Benevolent Longevity** (Renshoudian) where Cixi kept court. You can still see her throne, although you can't enter the hall. In the courtyard you'll see huge river-carved stones and statues of an imperial dragon and phoenix, along with a less usual offering – the mythical *qilin*, a hotchpotch hybrid of creatures. You'll also come across the longevity symbol, which features prominently throughout the palace. Just beyond here, the **Palace of Virtue and Harmony** (Deheyuan) contains a theater, which is worth the extra ¥10 to look around. Inside you'll find a grand three-tiered stage and the resplendent imperial viewing area, complete with bed, which may seem excessive until you realize that performances often lasted days! Cixi was a keen fan of theater and is rumored to have acted herself here, ironically selecting the role of Guanyin, the Buddhist Goddess of Mercy. There's also a display of operatic costumes, palanquins and paintings. Continuing on from here, the **Hall of Jade Ripples** (Yulantang) was where Guangxu was imprisoned while Cixi dealt with his affairs of state. Just to the west, looking out over Kunming Lake, the **Hall of Joyful Longevity** (Leshoutang) was Cixi's residence and has been left as she lived in it – you can still see the table where she reputedly grazed over her 108 course meals.

The Long Gallery & Longevity Hill

From here the path opens out onto Kunming Lake, created to give cool breezes during Beijing's hot summer and you'll be able to see the graceful 17-arch bridge to the south. A covered corridor, the finely painted and recently restored **Long Gallery** runs for half a mile along the lake's northern shore, backed by **Longevity Hill** (Wanshou Shan), which holds the Sea of Wisdom Temple and

Longevity symbol (Tot Foster)

is worth ascending for the views. Back at the bottom, the Long Gallery skirts the lake for a few more minutes and leads to one of the Summer Palace's most famous monuments, a hideous, but finely crafted **marble boat** built under the dowager empress, Cixi, with funds that were intended to rebuild the navy.

Marble boat at the Summer Palace (airunp)

Continuing on from here along the same side as the boat, you'll cross a bridge and the path takes you through beautiful parkland more reminiscent of Oxford in England than Beijing, eventually leading to the western exit. Behind Longevity Hill the kitschy 'Suzhou Street' leads out to the northern exit, which is a better bet for getting a taxi.

In the City

★★★Tian'anmen Square

The vast expanse of Tian'anmen Square

Some History

This is the world's largest square and is seen as the heart of Beijing and thus China. In dynastic times the square was a mere avenue between ministerial buildings, but was geographically significant as it represented the divide between the privilege of royalty and the poverty of the masses. When the nationalists came to power in 1911 they immediately cleared the square and with it the inequality which it represented, although it didn't take on its current form until after the arrival of the Communists. The square served as a focus of dissent as early as 1919 when demonstrators in the May 4th Movement protested against China's humiliation in the terms of the Treaty of Versailles. It has continued to perform this function ever since, ranging from the expressions of discontent posted here during the ill-conceived Hundred Flowers campaign to the 1989 protests, which ended with tanks rolling into the square, untold numbers of fatalities and worldwide condemnation (see p. 26).

In the 1950s the Communists enlarged the square to its current massive proportions and the flanking Great Hall of the People and museums of Chinese History and Revolution (now known as the National Museum) were built. Even after the construction of Chairman Mao's Mausoleum in its center, Tian'anmen Square still feels overwhelmingly huge and it takes a good 15 minutes to walk from end to end. The square also retains a menacing and autocratic air and you can't help but feel you're being watched (not just by the amazed out-of-town Chinese visitors). As a tour leader in the late 1990s,

I witnessed a group of seated Falung Gong (a quasi-Buddhist religious doctrine banned in mainland China) protesters being forcibly removed from the square only minutes after they had sat down. Yet somehow, in spite of its recent history and all of this control, today Tian'anmen Square manages to function as a relaxing place for a stroll, especially in the evenings (until 9 pm). You'll see locals flying kites and tourists from near and far meandering between the historic monuments. It's difficult to imagine the events of 1989 taking place here.

Visiting the Square

If you want to visit Chairman Mao's Mausoleum, you need to get here in the morning, unless it's a Tuesday or Thursday outside of July and August (see below). It's easy to combine a visit to Tian'anmen Square with the Forbidden City and Jingshan Park, in which case it makes sense to get the subway or a taxi to Qianmen.

Zhengyang Gate & Chairman Mao's Mausoleum

Use the underpass to cross into the square and the first structure you'll see is the imposing **Zhengyang Gate** (daily 9 am-4 pm, ¥10) which marks its southern limits. You can ascend the 130-foot gate, which gives a good overview of the square and some idea of its original magnitude before **Chairman Mao's Mausoleum** was built in the middle of it. From here, proceeding north will shortly bring you to the mausoleum (Tues-Sun 8:30-11:30 am, Tues & Thurs 2-4 pm, July & August mornings only, free, no bags or cameras) where you'll have to leave your bag with your guide or a friend to go inside. Every morning you'll see lengthy lines waiting for their glimpse of the Chairman, who is refrigerated overnight and then rises again in the morning! There is something very surreal in a visit to the mausoleum – from Mao's perfectly plasticated appearance to the fake flowers that people buy to offer, which are then quickly collected and returned for re-sale. There have been suggestions that the body on display is as false as the flowers but we're unlikely to ascertain the truth on that one for some time. What is striking is the adulation still shown to Chairman Mao. As the bigger picture of what happened under the Great Helmsman becomes more apparent, there is dissention within the younger generation, but the sheer numbers of serious-faced visitors to the mausoleum are testimony to Mao's enduring popularity. For more on Chairman Mao, see p. 22-24.

The Monument to the People's Heroes

A little north of the mausoleum and in the center of the square, the Monument to the People's Heroes is a 125-foot-tall marble obelisk to commemorate the martyrs who lost their lives in China's revolutionary struggle. On the obelisk itself both Mao Zedong and Zhou Enlai have inscribed mottos, while at its base you'll see scenes glorifying the country's efforts to free itself from both domestic and foreign imperialism between 1840 and 1949.

The Great Hall of the People

(Daily 8 am-4 pm, but closed during government meetings)

From the obelisk you'll see two grand buildings on the square's flanks. To your left the Great Hall of the People is an enormous, daunting building, designed to awe, hosting parliamentary meetings and state functions. You can visit and see a selection of its manifold rooms, including the purported 10,000-seat banquet hall (it's big, but not that big…). Just to the north of the Great Hall, **Zhongnanhai**, the state residences, are not open to the public – all you'll see are a wealth of black Audis bringing the big men of Chinese politics to and from their offices.

The National Museum

(Daily 8 am-6 pm; ¥30)

Across the square from the Great Hall, the former Museums of Chinese History and Revolution finally received a long overdue re-branding and became the new National Museum in 2003. The museum is currently undergoing renovation and is predictably scheduled to re-open in time for the 2008 Olympics. It will showcase some of the nation's greatest treasures displayed in state-of-the-art fashion. In the meantime the museum houses a selection of Shang dynasty bronzes, ceramics and jade work, as well as a waxworks display of some of the latest and greatest from Chinese history.

Tian'anmen Gate

Tian'anmen Gate

At the far northern end of the square there's a guarded flagpole where daily sunrise flag raising and sunset lowering performances are held, replete with plenty of pomp and ceremony. To the north the burgundy walls of the Forbidden City dominate, although even this bastion of Chinese imperialism is replete with an enormous portrait of Chairman Mao, who was left with egg on his face when protesters from his home province threw paint-filled egg-shells at the picture during the 1989 demonstrations.

★★★THE HUTONG

To step out of the modern concrete forest of skyscrapers and get a flavor of old Beijing, a trip to the *hutong* is a must. *Hutong* are the alleyways that run between the Ming and Qing dynasty low courtyard houses – still the backbone of Beijing's residential housing. To the north and south of the Forbidden City the *hutong* houses are crude and simple, while

Hutong in Beijing (Kallgan)

many of those to the east and west were formerly grand residences belonging to one family, though after the revolution they were transformed into *zayuan* or shared courtyards for the masses. Although individual houses vary significantly, they all follow the basic *siheyuan* courtyard form and typically face south in order to maximize light. In spite of much redevelopment, substantial *hutong* districts still exist around the Forbidden City and are the antidote to Beijing's inhumanly vast modern streets and flyovers. Stepping into a *hutong* you are immediately confronted with Beijing's human side and will see kids playing and old folk watching bicycles casually drifting by – nobody seems to be in a hurry here. There are small shops and restaurants and these days some of the *hutong* have become trendy places to dine and drink (Nanluoguxiang for example). Some expats have even moved in

Inside a Hutong house

and restored them to their original splendor. There are also plenty of budget and a few boutique hotel options within the *hutong* and it's definitely worth staying here to get a taste of old Beijing. All the more so now, while there are still some *hutong* left – many have been demolished over the years in the name of progress and, although some areas are now protected, many more are slated for redevelopment.

My favorite way to explore the *hutong* is simply to strike out into a promising area and get lost in the maze of alleyways. It's fairly easy to maintain a rough idea of which direction you're heading in and, when you've had enough, head along one of the major east-west *hutong* and sooner or later you'll emerge onto a road from where you can get a taxi (or subway). But if you want more direction or purpose you can go on an organized bike trip with Cycle China or hire a cycle rickshaw (see p. 147).

(see p. 147)

Beijing & Around

The North
★★★ Jingshan Park

(Daily 7 am-10 pm; ¥2; bus #5 from Qianmen)

If you're hot and bothered after a trudge through Tian'anmen Square and the Forbidden City, a short climb in Jingshan Park will bring you some cooler air and great views over the palace to the south and north to the Drum Tower. It also makes a nice place to enjoy a picnic. Try to come in the morning to get the best photos from this great vantage point. The park was first created during the Ming dynasty in accordance with the principles of geomancy to protect the Forbidden City from the chilling and evil northern winds. The hill it sits upon was made from the earth excavated to create the Forbidden City's moat. The park outlasted the dynasty and is now famous as the place where the last Ming emperor, Chongzhen, hanged himself in 1644. You can still see the spot where he ended his life, although the tree here isn't the original.

The Forbidden City from Jingshan Park

★ Beihai Park

(Daily 6 am-10 pm; ¥10 or ¥20 for access to all sites; bus #5 from Qianmen)

Set on the site of the Mongol Yuan dynasty's Dadu Palaces, Beihai (North Sea) is a continuation of the Zhongnanhai (Middle and South Sea) lakes, which were excavated at Kublai Khan's orders and run up to Qianhai and Houhai. Beihai is a lovely park, dominated by water, and it houses a grand *dagoba* (Lamaist Stupa), which was built for a visit by the Dalai Lama and sits on Qiong Island in the south of the lake. Entering the park through its southern gate, you'll immediately come to the **Round City**, the only remaining part of Mongol Dadu. Here, there is a courtyard where you'll see a jade bowl that reputedly belonged to Kublai Khan himself. From here a bridge leads to Qiong Island and the **Yong'an (Eternal Peace) Temple**. At the top of the island hill you'll see the gleaming white *dagoba*, while the north of the island holds the renowned imperial restaurant, **Fangshan** (see p. 213). You can take boats from here across to the northern side of the lake, where you'll find another of the park's key attractions, the 88-foot-long **Nine Dragon Screen**, made up of some 400 tiles and designed to confound evil spirits.

★★ Shichahai (Qianhai & Houhai)

Zhongnanhai, Beihai, Qianhai and Houhai are all part of a chain of lakes that stretch northwest from the Forbidden City. There have always been ephemeral watercourses here, appearing during times of flood and disappearing during drought, but these areas were connected and expanded under the Yuan dynasty in 1293 and formed the northern terminus for the Grand Canal from Hangzhou (see p. 340-41). The area flourished as a religious, as well as a trade, center and thus earned its current name, Shichahai (10 Temples of the Sea). It became a popular place to come and relax by the water, a function Qianhai and Houhai still serve today. Shichahai's proximity to the seat of power and waterfront property appealed to those with business in court and the area developed as an upmarket residential *hutong* district, which has housed imperial relatives like Prince Gong and aristocrats such as Soong Qingling over the years.

The *hutong* here still offer a real escape from brash modernity and are a great part of the city for a cycle rickshaw ride (see *Adventures On Wheels*, p. 198). But if you want a break from sightseeing, the area is worth a visit for the bars and restaurants that have taken over the waterfront streets (see *Where to Drink*, p. 217, and try to pick up a copy of the *Insider's Guide to Beijing Houhai Map*).

In the summer the lakes offer boating, bike rental and you'll even see people swimming; in the winter, skating is popular. You'll see boat rental places scattered around the lakes, ranging from simple paddle affairs (¥40, plus ¥200 deposit) to electric boats (¥60-120, plus deposit) and 15-person wooden crafts (¥300), which come complete with oarsmen and, if you want to add to the ambience, you can hire an *erhu* player (see *Traditional Music*, p. 62; ¥100 per hour) and even some snacks or a full-blown meal to enjoy onboard (see *Kaorouji*, p. 214).

★ Prince Gong's Palace

14A Liuyin Jie (daily 9 am-4:30 pm; ¥20; Jishuitan subway)

This grand *hutong* residence was originally built in 1777 and comprises nine courtyards, connected by covered walkways. Prince Gong was the younger brother of Emperor Xianfeng (1850-61) and was instrumental in bringing the Dowager Empress Cixi to power after his brother's death. If you come here on a *hutong* cycle rickshaw trip, you can also witness short performances of Beijing Opera while enjoying a cup of tea!

The Bell Tower and surrounding hutong (Tot Foster)

★ The Bell and Drum Towers

Di'anmen Dajie (daily 9 am-4:30 pm; Gulou Dajie subway)

Beijing's first drum tower was built in 1272, but the version you can see today dates from the Ming dynasty. In days of old the Drum Tower (¥20) was used to mark out the time and the drums are still beaten every half-hour (9-11:30 am & 2-5 pm), although these days this is purely for the enjoyment of tourists rather than to hustle along imperial servants in their duties. At the southern end of Di'anmen Dajie, the Bell Tower (¥15) was constructed at the same time as the Drum Tower, but was destroyed and rebuilt after a fire in 1747. The tower still holds its original 63-ton bronze bell (which you can gong during Chinese New Year for a price). The towers define the neighborhood, hence its name, Zhonggulou (Bell and Drum Tower), and both offer good views over the surrounding *hutong*.

★ Soong Qingling's Former Residence

46 Houhai Beiyan (Tues-Sun 9 am-4:30 pm; ¥20; Gulou Dajie subway)

The Qing mansion of Soong Qingling's former residence sits in a large, ornate garden and holds displays that detail aspects of her life, including the pistol given to her as a wedding gift by Sun Yatsen. Of the various other houses where Soong lived, her Shanghai residence is one of the most attractive (see *Shanghai, Soong Qingling*, p 000).

Confucius Temple

13 Guozijian Jie (daily 8:30 am-5 pm; ¥10; Yonghegong subway)

The *paifang* (memorial arch) decorated *hutong* which houses the Confucius Temple has long been home to scholars and the temple's quiet courtyard and few visitors make it a great place to soak up the old school ambience, surrounded by stone tablets and cypresses. As with most Confucian institutes and temples this was a place of learning and there are stelae (stone tablets) denoting those who passed the civil service exams set around the courtyard. On the western side of the grounds you'll find more tablets inscribed with the Thirteen Classic philosophical writings that were attributed to Confucius. There's also a display of ancient musical instruments, which are played on the Old Sage's birthday, celebrated annually on September 28th (National Teachers' day). **Note:** The temple was undergoing extensive restorations at the time of writing.

★★Tibetan Lama Temple

12 Yonghegong Dajie (daily 9 am-4:30 pm; ¥25, audio tour ¥20; Yonghe Gong subway)

Some History

This is Beijing's premier Buddhist tourist attraction and thus, while it's certainly worth a visit, don't come expecting monastic silence and isolation. The temple was originally built in 1694 as Prince Yong's palace (hence the Chinese name Yonghe Gong), which he renounced when he ascended to the dragon throne and became Emperor Yongzheng in 1723. The palace was converted to a lama temple in 1744 under Emperor Qianlong and offers a fusion of Lamaism, Buddhism and Shamanism. The latter fueled rumors of human sacrifice in the early 20th century! The temple's architecture reflects an equally dazzling array of styles, including original palace features, along with Manchurian, Mongolian and Tibetan design elements. The temple prospered during the Qing and there were reported to be over 500 monks from Inner Mongolia and Tibet in residence here under Emperor Qianlong. You can still see the golden urn that was used to elect the Mongolian Dalai Lama in days of old, and the temple is also the site where the puppet Panchen Lama was instated in 1995.

After the foundation of the PRC in 1949 the temple was closed for 30

Tibetan Lama Temple (Rolf Müller)

years, which may well have been its saving grace, as it completely escaped the ravages of the Cultural Revolution (see p. 23). The temple re-opened in 1981, but these days it is as busy with tourists as it is with monks, but you'll still see them chanting sutras in the morning.

Visiting the Temple

Above the entrance to the **Yonghe Gate Hall** you'll see gold inscriptions on a blue background in four languages (Mongolian, Tibetan, Chinese and Manchurian) – the Chinese characters were written by Emperor Qianlong. On entry you'll immediately be confronted by a statue of Maitreya who is accompanied by the four Heavenly Kings. Through the next courtyard you'll find the **Yonghe Palace**, which houses *arhat* statues and a stunningly decorated ceiling.

Continuing on, the Qing dynasty **Hall of the Wheel of Law** holds a statue of Tsongkhapa (1357-1419), the founder of Lamaism's Yellow Hat sect. Beyond here the **Wanfu Pavilion** contains a colossal 85-foot-tall statue of Buddha which was donated to Qianlong in 1750 by the seventh Dalai Lama and took three years to transport from Nepal. The Buddha is carved from a single trunk of sandalwood and is actually sunk 20 feet into the ground in order to prevent it from toppling over. At the very rear of the temple there is a display of Qing dynasty Tibetan articles, including dharma wheels and a multi-armed statue of Guanyin, the Goddess of Mercy.

The East

★The Ancient Observatory

2 Dongbiaobei Hutong, southwest corner of Jianguomen Bridge (Tues-Sun 9 am-4 pm; ¥10; Jianguomen subway)

Understanding the skies was perceived as fundamental to maintaining power by the rulers of dynastic China lest they lose the Mandate of Heaven (see *History, Zhou Dynasty*, p. 6). To this end they invested much time and effort in trying to predict eclipses and comets, which were seen as omens of change. The current observatory was established in 1442 and was initially guided by Muslim astrologers, reflecting the advanced state of Islamic science in the medieval world, until the arrival of the Jesuits in 1601, who took the reins until the early 19th century. The Jesuits sought to use their superior knowledge and equipment to impress the court, with the aim of eventually converting the emperor, and China, to Catholicism.

Under the guidance of a Belgian priest, Father Verbiest, the Chinese learned how to accurately predict eclipses and the astrological instruments you can see on the roof were mostly designed by Jesuits on the orders of Emperor Kangxi in 1674, although the large azimuth was a gift from Louis XIV. Today, in true Beijing style, the ancient observatory, housed in a former watchtower, is dwarfed by the modern buildings that surround it. Special evening events are held here to observe cosmic events such as comets and eclipses but modern Beijing's polluted skies means that it's hardly the best place to enjoy a stellar spectacle.

The South

Qianmen

Immediately south of the gate of the same name, Qianmen developed something of a seedy reputation during the imperial era as an area that offered all the vices lacking in the Forbidden City. Alongside the brothels and opium dens, plenty of respectable businesses also flourished in the *hutong*. These days Qianmen still holds some its shady charm and is a great place for a wander, which will reveal century-old shops and teahouses alongside more modern businesses. However, this is all set to change with Qianmen's redevelopment, which was being carried out at the time of writing. The southern part of Qianmen around the Ox Street Mosque has long been home to Beijing's Muslim population and the area retains its unique character.

★ Ox Street Mosque

88 Niu Jie (daily 8:30 am-5 pm; ¥10; bus #6 from Tiantan)

Both the street and mosque take their name for the Muslim preference for beef over pork and this area offers a distinctly different feel from other old parts of the city. The mosque, which was built in 966, sits on the eastern side of Ox Street (Niu Jie) and initially appears little different from a traditional Chinese mansion. Indeed, the main entrance (which isn't used these days) is faced by a distinctly Chinese spirit wall, designed to prevent ghosts from entering, and the color scheme is equally Chinese. However, closer inspection reveals the mosque's heritage, from the Arabic you'll see inscribed on the walls to the more obvious bearded and white-capped Hui men who come to pray here. There are some 200,000 Hui in Beijing and the Ox Street Mosque is one of the focal points of Islamic life in the capital. The mosque contains a Moon Observation Tower used to determine the start of the fasting month of Ramadan and a prayer hall, but both of these are off-limits to non-Muslims so you'll have to be satisfied with the tombs of its founder's son and those of two Persian sheikhs who traveled here across the Silk Road. If you plan to visit the mosque, you should dress conservatively (covered knees and shoulders) and avoid Friday prayer times, when you won't be allowed in (unless you're a Muslim). A trip here can be nicely rounded off with a meal at one of the *halal* restaurants that line Ox Street.

The West

★ Big Bell Temple (Dazhong Si)

31A Beisanhuan Xilu (daily 8:30 am-4 pm; ¥10; Dazhong Si subway or buses #302 & #367)

If you want to see the biggest bell in China this temple is certainly worth a visit on the way to or from the Summer Palace. The bell is almost 20 feet tall and weighs in at around 50 tons. There are nearly a quarter-million Buddhist scripture characters inscribed on its bronze exterior. The bell is only rung on New Year's Eve and during Chinese New Year, but its gong can supposedly be heard up to 25 miles away.

Beijing & Around

★White Cloud Temple (Baiyun Guan)

6 Baiyunguan Jie, Xibianmenwai, Xuanwu (daily 8 am-4:30 pm; ¥10; bus #212 from Qianmen)

Originally built in 793, this temple is a center of Taoism in Beijing and offers a sneak peek at China's only indigenous religion (given that Confucianism is a philosophy), a visit made all the more enjoyable by the fact it's more popular with worshippers than tourists. Inside, you'll see blue-clad pony-tailed Taoist monks and might even get to see them performing the art of *qi gong* (breath control) if you're lucky. The temple is a popular pilgrimage sight and it is thought to bring good luck if you find all three of the temple's monkeys and rub their bellies! There are also Taoist monk physicians on hand who can give you the once over if you're feeling poorly!

★The Old Summer Palace

(Daily 7 am-7 pm; ¥10 for the park, ¥15 for the ruins; bus #375 from Xizhimen subway)

A little east of its successor, the Old Summer Palace (Yuanmingyuan) now lies in romantically crumbling ruins and makes a great escape from the city. Transporting you halfway to ancient Rome, the European-style palace originally held some 200 buildings in its vast enclosure and was the imperial

Ruins of the Fang Wai Guan, a mansion on the grounds of the Old Summer Palace (Rolf Müller)

summer retreat until 1860. It was first constructed under Emperor Kangxi and was modeled on Versailles, but was destroyed and looted by Anglo-French forces during the Second Opium War (see p. 16). The palace is centered on a large lake where you can hire boats, go fishing

Old Summer Palace ruins (Clee7903)

as the locals do, and in the winter you can ice-skate. Although the only sight as such is the few standing columns of the **Hall of Tranquility**, the palace grounds are wonderfully atmospheric and are a popular spot for a romantic sunset *rendezvous*.

Around Beijing

The rugged countryside around the capital affords an easy remedy to the downtown blues and features a variety of attractions, the most obvious of which is the incredible Great Wall, which can be visited at a number of spots. Other sights include dramatic gorges, imperial tombs, prehistoric caves and charming temples, all of which are feasible as day-trips from Beijing. There are tourist buses from Qianmen and westerly Fuchengmen to some of the more popular sights, as well as public buses from Dongzhimen, Deshengmen and Pingguoyuan. Alternatively, you can go on a tour from your hotel or hostel. Or, if you want to see things at your own pace, you could hire a car and driver for the day.

North of Beijing

The Ming Tombs

(Daily 8:30 am-5 pm; see below for costs and transport information)

The Ming Tombs are 30 miles north of Beijing in a (once) peaceful valley and are the final resting place for 13 of the 16 Ming emperors – hence the Chinese name Shisanling, which means 13 Mausoleums. The scenic valley is on the way to Badaling (see p. 180), which has made it a popular tourist stop on day-trips out to the Great

Gateway at start of the Sacred Walk leading to the tombs (Ofol)

Wall, and, while it has lost some its tranquility in the process, it remains a worthwhile destination offering grand imperial mausoleums and pretty countryside. And there are still quiet nooks to be found if you head off the beaten track a little.

Some History: Emperor Yongle visited this valley basin nestled between the Yan Mountains in the 15th century and instantly knew this was where he wanted to be laid to rest. The valley has perfect natural fengshui (see p. 54) and construction of his grand mausoleum began shortly afterwards. Successive emperors followed suit, facilitating ancestor worship, and the tombs were tended for the remainder of the Ming dynasty. The Qing selected a different locale for their mausoleums (see *The Eastern Qing Tombs*, p. 185) and, while some emperors of this dynasty looked after the Ming Tombs, they were gradually forgotten and went to seed. By the 20th century the Ming Tombs were overgrown and unkempt, but it wasn't until the 1950s that anything was done about this and a few of the mausoleums were restored, albeit overzealously. Today, only the Sacred Way and three of the 13 tombs are open to the public, the grandest of which is Yongle's, known as Changling.

Visiting the Tombs: Once at the tombs if you have enough time it's worth visiting, not only the Sacred Way and three open tombs, but also wandering around the grounds to some off the fenced-off mausoleum compounds that offer quiet picnic spots (despite signs forbidding picnicking) and more of a sense of what the area was once like – you can buy maps at the site that indicate the location of all 13 tombs.

The Sacred Way (Richard Chambers)

The Sacred Way: Once actually at the site, the Sacred Way (¥30) is usually the first stopping-off point. This 4½-mile avenue was the route taken by imperial coffins and begins with a grand *paifang* (memorial arch), although the entrance brings you into its second significant gate, the triple-arched Dahongmen. Beyond here you'll find the Shengde Stele Pavilion, which houses a grand stone tablet borne by Bixi, the hardy tortoise. From the pavilion the way is lined by symbolic statues of humans and animals. Of the real and mythical beasts to be seen (lions, elephants, camels, horses, unicorns and *qilin*), there are four of each, two standing and two resting, while the humans represent servants, officials and generals.

The Sacred Way continues most of the distance to the tombs, but to confound evil spirits (who, it was believed, could only travel in straight lines), the mausoleums are placed at oblique angles to the avenue.

The Mausoleums: Yongle is remembered as one of China's greatest emperors and his mausoleum, **Changling** (¥45), is fittingly grand. The mausoleum is laid out as a scaled-down version of Yongle's most impressive creation, the Forbidden City, and its greatest edifice, the Hall of Eminent Favor, is supported by hefty wooden pillars brought all the way from Yunnan. It now houses replicas of the emperor's most treasured possessions, which were buried with him. In contrast, the tomb itself is a simple tree-covered mound. Emperor Wanli's mausoleum, **Dingling** (¥65), is less ostentatious than Changling, but offers the chance to descend into the burial chamber, which was opened up in 1956 and found to hold the emperor and his two wives, along with their most valued possessions, all packed neatly into 26 pieces of baggage for the trip to the afterlife! Today, the musty stone vault resembles a disused subway as much as an imperial tomb, but it holds Wanli's bright red imperial coffin and reproductions of the treasures he chose to take to the grave with him.

On your way out, you can visit the museum at the main gate which has information about the restoration of the tombs and a model of the valley basin. The last of the open mausoleums, **Zhaoling** (¥30), is the final resting place of Emperor Zhuzaigou (1567-72), and, although it is less impressive than either Changling or Dingling and you can't access the vault, it is the most authentically restored of the three. It also sees fewer visitors, which makes it

Statue on the Sacred Way

worth seeking out. The other 10 tombs nestled around the valley are fenced off, but if you want a quiet spot for a picnic they offer more of a sense of adventure and discovery.

Getting to the Ming Tombs: If you're on an organized day-trip to the Great Wall at Badaling, you'll stop at the Ming Tombs, although these trips often leave scant time for any real exploration. For a more relaxed trip, **Cycle China** (see *Adventures On Foot* and *On Wheels*, p. 196-98) run trips that combine the tombs with the Great Wall at Huanghua (from ¥300). Another alternative is to take tourist buses #1 or #5, which leave from Qianmen before 9 am, although once again you'll only get around 90 minutes at the site. For fuller exploration you can take bus #345 from Deshengmen to Dongguan in Changping and then bus #314 circuits the sites from there. Or if that sounds like too much work, a taxi should cost around ¥400 for the round-trip. How ever you choose to come here, the journey will take at least an hour.

The Great Wall

Two thousand years old and several thousand miles long, the Great Wall is China's most captivating historic site. Stretching from the Yellow Sea to the Central Asian outpost of Jiayuguan, the wall was originally built under China's first emperor, Qin Shi Huang to protect against northern invaders, a task it never really effectively served. However, a couple of thousand years later, the wall seems to make a lot more sense – there are few tourists who visit Beijing without seeing the wall and it is the country's most instantly

The Great Wall at Mutianyu near Beijing (Fabien Khan)

recognizable tourist sight. Fortunately, if you avoid the most visited section at Badaling, it's still fairly easy to appreciate the majesty of the ruggedly isolated land the wall once protected, and a hike at Jinshanling, Simatai, Huanghua or even crumbly Jiankou is both stunning and evocative.

Some History: The Chinese had historically built walled cities and regions and, in reality, the Great Wall was just a consolidation of these, focusing on the more vulnerable lowland and valleys, in the belief that the higher mountains were a natural defense in themselves. After the fractious periods that had come before, **Qin Shi Huang** was determined to maintain his empire, the newly formed China. Fearful of the threat from the north, he linked the various regional barriers to make this first, crude version of the **Wanli Changcheng** (10,000-Li Wall – one *li* is around a third of a mile) using over a million laborers. The wall was made of rammed earth but, such was the suffering incurred, that the wall's foundations were said to be made up of the bodies of those who had died making it! After the collapse of the short-lived Qin dynasty, the wall continued to serve its defensive purpose until the empire expanded under the Tang and the wall found itself several hundred miles back from the front line, although the Song quickly reversed

A Section of the Great Wall (Samuel Li)

their predecessor's gains. In contrast the Yuan had little need to protect from northern invaders – they were the northern invaders, and it wasn't until the Ming dynasty that the wall once again became of key importance. The Ming didn't have the resources for expansive forays to the north and therefore they tried to maintain the extent of their influence by reinforcing

The Great Wall near Beijing in winter (Andreas Tilly)

and improving the wall. All that had come before was made of rammed earth or piled stone at best, but the Ming began baking bricks to rebuild the wall. Most of the sections of intact wall you can see around Beijing today, including **Badaling**, **Mutianyu**, **Jiankou**, **Jinshanling** and **Simatai**, are Ming, albeit often built on the remnants of older versions. While the wall is often cited as a failure, it wasn't without its successes and, for the most part, served the purposes of the Ming. The Qing, with their stronger northern ties, had less to worry about in this direction, and as time wore on it became apparent that the principal threats were from the ocean: Japan and the Western powers wanted their piece of China and they didn't need to cross the wall to get it.

Today, historically successful or otherwise, the Great Wall has become a symbol of the greatness of China, as observed by Richard Nixon in his state visit here in 1972. Claims that it is the only manmade barrier visible from space with the naked eye may be untrue, but it is undoubtedly one of the greatest constructions the world has ever seen and continues to amaze. Don't leave without seeing it.

Beijing & Around

FACTS & FIGURES

- The Wall is really, really long (no one knows quite how long, but at least 3,500 miles).
- The Ming sections of the wall are around 23 feet high and almost as wide.
- There were once some 25,000 watchtowers.

Visiting the Wall: The Great Wall's manifold segments pepper the countryside north of Beijing and offer opportunities for quick day-trips to easily accessible and fully restored sections, as well as more adventurous journeys along its wilder stretches. Of those listed below, Badaling is the easiest to visit, but also the most touristy, while Mutianyu is slightly quieter, and farther afield, Jinshanling and Simitai are far more rugged and have fewer visitors.

If you want to see the wall at its unrestored crumbliest, Huanghua and Jiankou aren't too far from Beijing and will reward the journey with unspoiled wilderness. The wall is a great place for a picnic and, for the ultimate tacky picture, you could buy a bottle of Great Wall wine to consume on the ramparts! Tourist buses operate to Badaling (in conjunction with the Ming Tombs, see p. 175) and Mutianyu from opposite Qianmen subway station. You can also take local buses from Dongzhimen or Deshengmen stations. While hotels charge as much as ¥300 for the Badaling trip, hostels are much more reasonable at ¥180, ¥150 for Mutianyu, or ¥90 for Jinshanling and Simitai (entry fees not included for the last two). Finally, outdoor companies such as **CnAdventure** and **Cycle China** run excellent hiking trips along the wall (see *Adventures On Foot*, p. 196).

Staying at the Wall: To really appreciate the majesty and isolation of the wall, staying overnight is definitely worthwhile and there are increasingly numbers of places to do so. While tours with companies such as Cycle China might offer you the opportunity to stay in a local farming village near the wall, if you want to head out by yourself, you'll find a **hostel** at Simitai, **camping** at Jinshanling, or, if money is no object, the exclusive retreats of the **Commune** at Shuiguan, and the **Red Capital Ranch** at Xiaguandi offer unique experiences at the wall you'll never forget. See *Where to Stay*, p. 205-209, for more on these options.

Badaling (daily 6:30 am-6 pm; ¥45; bus #919 from Deshengmen or tourist bus #1 & #5 run from Qianmen; 90 mins). If you're on a standard organized tour, chances are this is where you'll visit the wall, and, despite the extensive restoration and hordes of tourists, it's still undeniably striking. This was the first section to be restored for the benefit of tourists in 1957, and its proximity to the capital has maintained its pole position as *the* place to see the wall. However, if you have the choice, then Jinshanling, Simitai or even Mutianyu will offer a quieter experience. If you do find yourself here nonetheless, once at the top try walking to the north (left) and you might just find a little peace to appreciate the majesty. Turning south (right) is more popular and will eventually bring you to the cable car (¥50). If you're coming under your own steam and are visiting Badaling in conjunction with the Ming Tombs or Longqing Gorge (see p. 175 & 183), then try to come when the site opens or closes to avoid the crowds. There's a hotel here, but, if you have enough time to stay overnight, you're better off heading to one of the quieter wall options.

★★**Mutianyu** (daily 7 am-6:30 pm; ¥35; bus #916 from Dongzhimen to Huairou and then a minibus, or on weekends tourist bus #6 runs from Xuanwumen; 90 mins). Thirty miles east of Badaling, Mutianyu offers more dramatic scenery and (slightly) fewer crowds, making it a better bet if you have the choice. The 1½-mile stretch of wall is furnished with plenty of watchtowers and was first built as far back as the sixth century, but was rebuilt under the Ming and then extensively restored in the 1980s. It's a steep hour's climb up to the wall, but if you'd prefer to save your energy, you can take a cable car to the highest point (¥35 one way or ¥50 round-trip) which offers fine vistas along the way. You can also descend in novel fashion by taking a toboggan (¥40) down the hill! President Clinton came here in 1998 and enjoyed the wall in relative solitude but, if you don't have such status, to beat the worst of the crowds try to come as early as possible.

The Great Wall at Jiankou (Tot Foster)

★★★**Jiankou** (¥10; bus #916 from Dongzhimen to Huairou and then a minibus; two hrs). Jiankou is one of the most easily accessible sections of wild wall where you'll really feel as if you've stumbled onto a lost tract of history. Note that it can be crumbly underfoot and you'll have to be careful not to trip over it. The wall here is made from a white-hued rock that clearly etches its serpentine trail over the rugged terrain, making Jiankou one of the most dramatic of all the Beijing sections, although it's a steep climb up to the wall. You can hike from here all the way to Mutianyu (four-five hrs) and then pick up transport from there back to Beijing, although the wall is in fairly poor condition for most of the way. You'll need to be very careful – better to join one of Cycle China's one- or two-day hikes along this section (see *Adventures On Foot*, p. 196). There's nowhere to buy supplies up here so make sure you bring snacks and plenty of water.

★★**Huanghua** (free; bus # 916 from Dongzhimen to Huairou and then a minibus or taxi; two hrs). The Yellow Flower Wall gets its name from the profusion of sweet-smelling flowers which characterize this remote area in summer, and the unreconstructed section here offers some fairly easygoing, beautiful hiking until you reach the steep "camel's back." However, the wall here is being restored, which will inevitably lead to tourist buses and more visitors, but for the time-being it remains a peaceful spot. The road cuts through the wall and if you turn right from where you're dropped you'll rise high above a reservoir before reaching a steep, rubbly ascent, which might be enough to make you turn around. But, if you continue, after another 10 or 15 minutes you'll come to a path leading down to the road from where you should be able to get a bus or taxi (¥20) back to Huairou and then a bus back to Beijing.

★★★**Jinshanling** (24 hrs; ¥30; board bus #980 from Dongzhimen to Miyun and then a minibus or taxi; three-four hrs). Seventy miles northeast of the city, the wall at Jinshanling is slightly less impressive than along the road at Simatai, but it also sees fewer visitors. Once you've made the 15-minute walk up to the wall, restored sections of Ming wall run in both directions, and this is the starting point for the arduous three- or four-hour hike to Simatai (see *Adventures On Foot*, p. 196). The stretch here is open 24 hours and you can camp on the wall itself, which affords the opportunity to see both sunset and sunrise on the wall using the same ticket.

Taking a break on the Wall near Jinshanling

★★★**Simatai** (daily 8 am-5 pm; ¥40; bus #980 from Dongzhimen to Miyun and then a minibus or on weekends take the 8:30 am tourist bus from Qianmen; three-four hrs). Simatai offers the wall's most dramatic scenery and is thoroughly worth the long trip out, especially if combined with the hike from Jinshanling, six miles to the east (see *Adventures On Foot*, p. 196). The snakelike wall here clings precariously to the mountain, which makes for a daunting climb, or if you don't feel up to this there's a cableway (¥20), which will take you as far as the eighth watchtower. If you're up for the climb, simply turn right from the car park and you can puff and pant your way as far as the 14th watchtower, from where you'll get stupendous views. As at Mutianyu, there's also a thrill-seeking way to get down – a flying fox zipline runs from a little below the lower section of the wall down across a reservoir! If you want to spend the night at Simatai, there's a hostel (see p. 211), but the wall here and at Jinshanling should both soon be much more accessible as a daytrip from Beijing when a new expressway is completed.

★Longqing Gorge

(Jan-Oct daily 8 am-5:30 pm; ¥40; bus #919 from Deshengmen to Yanqing and then a taxi; 90 mins). Fifty miles from Beijing and close to Badaling, Longqing Xia offers scenery fresh from the Three Gorges and makes for a great afternoon pit-stop if you've had enough of braving the crowds at the wall. Even getting to the gorge is an experience and involves taking a seemingly never-ending escalator (covered by a model dragon ...) to the largest dam in this part of the country. Beyond here, the emerald green water gives way to craggy limestone peaks and there's the option of taking a boat ride, bungee jumping or, if you come in January or February, Longqing holds a smaller version of the famous Harbin **Ice Festival**, complete with brightly lit ice sculptures and a frozen waterfall – which are worth enduring the cold for! Tickets for the festival are ¥70 and during the event the park is open from 8:30 am-10:30 pm.

West of Beijing

The Western Hills

The Western Hills stretch from the summer palaces out into Beijing's hinterlands and present plenty of opportunities for hiking and picnicking away from the madding crowds within easy reach of the city (as long as you avoid the weekends).

★**The Botanical Gardens** (daily 7 am-7 pm; ¥5, Conservatory ¥50; bus #333 from the Summer Palace; bus #331 from Xinjiekou subway or #318 from Pingguoyuan subway). North of the Summer Palace, the Botanical Gardens have the largest plant collection in China, including 300 varieties of orchids, over 1,000 types of roses, and bonsais over 1,000 years old! The predominantly northern plants and trees are spread through formal gardens and are labeled in English. If you pay an extra ¥50, there's an expansive conservatory that offers tropical and desert environments you can amble through on wooden walkways. Here you'll find cacti and even carnivorous plants hidden among the foliage.

The **Wofo Temple** (daily 8 am-4:30 pm; ¥5) is also on the grounds, originally built in the seventh century but badly damaged during the Cultural Revolution and inadequately restored afterwards. Nevertheless, the temple still contains its 16-foot-long recumbent Buddha, originally cast in 1321, which is surrounded by offerings of giant shoes for the barefoot icon!

★★The **Fragrant Hills**, near Sanjiadian (daily 6 am-6 pm; ¥10; bus #331 from Xinjiekou subway or #318 from Pingguoyuan subway). West of the Summer Palace, the Fragrant Hills were once an imperial hunting retreat and today offer wooded walks past temples, pavilions and scenic pools – a great spot for a picnic. Accessing the park from its eastern gate, it's about an hour's climb up to **Incense Burner Peak** from where, on clear days, you'll enjoy good views back toward the capital city, but if your time is limited there's also the option of taking a chairlift to the top (¥40). The walk is particularly spectacular during fall when the leaves glow warm reds and browns in the sunlight. But this beauty comes at a price, as you'll have to share the slopes with hordes of visitors, especially on the weekends.

By the park's northern exit you'll find the exquisite **Azure Cloud Temple** (Biyun Si; daily 8:30 am-4 pm; ¥10), which holds the 100-foot-tall **Diamond Throne Pagoda** and is more reminiscent of India than northern China. Inside the temple you'll also find some 500 *arhats*, each of which has its own unique expression, along with a more bizarre find – a crystal coffin that once housed Sun Yatsen and was donated by the Soviets. Sun was interred here between 1925 and 1929 before his remains were moved to Nanjing and there is an exhibition detailing the whole process. You could quite easily spend a day or two in the park and if you'd like a night's respite from the city, the Fragrant Hills Hotel is a good option (see p. 209).

★**Badachu** (daily 6 am-6 pm; ¥10; bus #347 from Xinjiekou subway or #972 from Pingguoyuan subway). A few miles south of the Fragrant Hills, Badachu has been a Buddhist retreat since the Tang dynasty but the current temples date from the Ming and Qing dynasties. Aside from the temples, it's a great place to come for a hike through the forested hills of gnarled old pines, cypresses and gingkos. Badachu means **Eight Great Sights**, paying homage to its eight monasteries and temples, including the Temple of Sacred Light (Lingguang Si), which allegedly once held one of Buddha's teeth and is the only temple with monks still in residence. The temple has a scenically placed 13-story pagoda dedicated to the tooth, although the tooth is long gone and the pagoda is a modern one, since the original was destroyed by the Allied Forces in 1900. From Lingguang Si you can walk, or take a chairlift (¥30) up the mountain past several more of the park's temples, but none of these is as impressive and it's best taken as a jaunt through the forest.

★**Jietai Temple** (daily 8 am-5 pm; ¥35; bus #931 from Pingguoyuan subway or tourist bus #7 from Fuchengmen; one hr). Set in the forested country that stretches just outside of the city proper, Jietai Temple was first constructed in 622 and gradually expanded over the ages to reach its current size. In contrast to the pretty charm of Tanzhe (see below), first impressions of Jietai are of its imposing red walls, although these were unable to repel the attentions of the Japanese or the Red Guards. Inside, the temple is far less austere, particularly in spring and summer when the courtyards are adorned with pretty flowering trees. The three impressive bronze Buddhas in the Mahavira Hall date from the Qing dynasty when the temple was greatly expanded. Another of the temple's stunning features is the serene statue of Sakyamuni seated on a lotus flower. It rests on the marble platform of the Ordination Terrace. However, in spite of this grandeur, empty niches inside the temple hint at the temple's suffering through the ages – the Japanese invasion and the Cultural Revolution both took their toll, leaving present-day visitors only to guess at its former splendor.

★**Tanzhe Temple** (daily 7:30 am-5:30 pm; ¥35; bus #931 from Pingguoyuan subway or tourist bus #7 from Fuchengmen; one hr). A little farther from the city and easily visited in conjunction with Jietai, Tanzhe Temple is said to be older than Beijing itself and, while this isn't strictly true, the place certainly has some history, dating as it does from the third century. Since its earliest days, Buddhist monks have been coming here to meditate, pray and study; today the temple continues to attract followers from around the globe. Most visitors come to see the **Guanyin Hall**, where Kublai Khan's daughter reputedly prayed so hard that she wore away the rock. But just a walk past the stupa terrace, through the courtyards, taking in the ancient gingko "Emperor Tree," which is over 1,000 years old, makes the trip to Tanzhe worthwhile.

Peking Man Site & Museum

Zhoukoudian Village, Fangshan (daily 8:30 am-4:30 pm; ¥30; bus #917 from Tianqiao near the Temple of Heaven). Locals have known about the collection of bones found on this craggy hillside 30 miles southwest of Beijing for a long time, hence the Chinese name, Longgu Shan, or Dragon Bone Hill. The Swedish explorer Johann Gunnar Andersson was the first to document the area, but it wasn't until Chinese anthropologist Pei Wenzhong's discovery of a complete skull in 1929 that Zhoukoudian really hit the headlines. This was a time when the theory of evolution was being fiercely contested by creationists and *sinanthropus pekinensis* with his stout frame and broad facial features seemed to offer definitive proof that man evolved from the ape. Peking Man, as the find became known, was actually some 40 individuals who lived in 20 caves dotted about the hillside between 700,000 and 500,000 years ago. It became clear that they had mastered fire, hunted large animals in groups, but that they had only basic tools and a limited capacity for verbal communication. However, only a few years after the discovery, the Japanese invasion in 1937 put a stop to excavations and, unbelievably, the five skulls and 147 teeth found were lost somewhere along the way! Although some partial skull casts remain and there are a few interesting bits and pieces in the museum such as a model of Peking Man and a sabertooth tiger skull (all of which are clearly labeled in English), subsequent excavations have unearthed nothing that matches the 1929 finds. Thus, while Zhoukoudian is UNESCO World Heritage listed and one of the most important anthropological sites on the planet, its story is better than the reality and is only really of interest to anthropology buffs. One can only hope that the villagers, who used to drink the ground "dragon's" bones in medicinal teas, haven't slurped the last relics of Beijing's earliest inhabitants!

East of Beijing

★★The Eastern Qing Tombs

(Daily 9 am-4 pm; ¥90; three hrs). The Qing dynasty tombs are unusually divided between two locales, equidistant to the east and west of Beijing, but the Eastern Tombs at Zunhua, 100 miles from the capital, are the more impressive. While only a paltry three of the 13 Ming tombs are open, the Qing tombs offer access to the burial compounds of all five emperors interred here as well as those of several empresses, including the notorious Empress Dowager, Cixi. The mausoleums are grander and better preserved than their Ming counterparts, but see fewer visitors and, if you have time for a full day-trip, the Qing tombs offer a more rewarding experience.

Some History: The Changduan mountain location was selected by the first Qing emperor, Shunzhi, for its excellent fengshui and his son, Kangxi fol-

Qing Dong Ling Cixi's Tomb

lowed in his footsteps. But the next emperor, Yongzheng, chose to be entombed over a hundred miles away on the other side of Beijing. It isn't completely clear why he made such a decision, but he spent much of his rule trying to justify his legitimate succession and it probably had something to do with his wish to avoid the afterlife anger of his ancestors. In any case, two of China's most famous emperors, **Kangxi** and **Qianlong** (see *A Golden Age*, p. 15), are buried here, as is the Old Buddha, the **Empress Dowager Cixi**. The tombs were well-maintained by Manchus brought to the region specifically for the purpose, but after the collapse of the Qing, some of the tombs were plundered by the northern warlord, Sun Dianying. Today the site is protected again but you can still descend into Qianlong and Cixi's opened tombs.

Visiting the Tombs: Qianlong's tomb, Yuling, has a grandeur befitting a man who ruled the country for nearly 60 years and is a three-chambered affair 65 feet below ground, covered in exquisite Buddhist carvings inscribed in Sanskrit and Tibetan. Cixi's doorbell-sounding mausoleum, Dingdongling, was re-built, as she wasn't happy with the original, and while the burial chamber itself is less impressive than Qianlong's, the tomb features the usual lavish exuberance associated with her, including a gold-threaded mattress.

Getting to the Qing Tombs: The easiest way to get here is by taxi (around ¥800 for the day-trip), but if you haven't got the cash to splash you can take the subway to Sihui station, walk a little south and take a bus to Zunhua, from where a taxi should cost ¥10 to the site.

Galleries, Shows & Theaters

Beijing is the political and cultural capital of China and is renowned for its fine Chinese arts, most famously the Beijing Opera and the acrobatics, which can be seen throughout the capital. Cultural arts aren't only historic, though, and these days the city has trendy modern art districts like Dashanzi and is also the best place in China to hear local musical talent, from Beijing rock to bands using traditional Chinese instruments.

Contemporary Art

If you're a fan of contemporary art, a trip out to the formerly industrial suburb of **Dashanzi** offers a chance to see some of China's hippest (and strang-

Exhibition at 798 Space Gallery (Lawrence Lavigne)

est) exhibits. There are also plenty of trendy cafés where you can soak up the bohemian atmosphere. Recommended galleries include the **Beijing Tokyo Art Projects** (www.tokyo-gallery.com), the **Chinese Contemporary** (www.chinesecontemporary.com) and the **Hart Center of Arts**, which are all on 4 Jiuxianqiao Lu. To get to Dashanzi, take bus #915, #918 or #934 from Dongzhimen. If you don't want to trek out to Dashanzi, there are also some contemporary art houses closer to town and the **Red Gate Gallery**, at Levels 1 & 4, Dongbianmen Watchtower, Chongwenmen (daily 10 am-5 pm) is one of the best. This hip modern gallery occupies two levels of a huge Ming dynasty watchtower and prides itself on being Beijing's first contemporary art gallery. Another gem is the **Courtyard Gallery** at 95 Donghuamen Dajie, Dongcheng (☎ 010-6526-8883), where you can combine a passion for good art with good food (see *Where to Eat*, p. 215).

★★★ Acrobatics

(See p. 65 for more on acrobatics). Beijing has a long acrobatic history and the mind-boggling assortment of juggling, cycling, contortion and balancing acts will keep you on the edge of your seat. A host of acrobatics troupes operate in the capital and a show either here or in

Beijing acrobats (Ewen Bell)

Shanghai is a must-see. Of the various offerings the best in Beijing at the moment are:

- **Chaoyang Theater**, 36 Dongsanhuan Bei Lu (☎ 010-6507-2421, www. acrobatics.com.cn; ¥180-380). They have nightly one-hour performances by acrobats (5:15 pm and 7:15 pm) and by Beijing Opera at 7:20 pm. This is definitely Beijing's biggest and slickest acrobatics performance. Highlights include 12 girls on one bicycle and a stunning lion dance.
- **Tianqiao Acrobatics Theater**, at 95 Tianqiao Market Street, Xuanwu (☎ 010-6303-7449; ¥100-200), also offers nightly performances by the Beijing Acrobatic Troupe and, although the performance is similar to the aforementioned, there's some excellent contortionism and unicycle stunts, and the smaller size of the theater allows you to get closer to the action. Nightly performances start at 7:15 pm.

Martial Arts

Beijing offers a number of exciting martial arts displays where the death-defying stunts might even persuade you to take up kung fu! **Legend of Kung Fu** at the Red Theater, 44 Xing Fu Da Jie, in Chongwen (☎ 010-6714-2473; daily 7:30-8:50 pm; ¥180 to ¥680 with dinner) offers a number of dramatic displays, including some nail-biting spear maneuvers, although it is a little heavy on the sound and light, and that's not even mentioning the fog or bubbles! The **Shaolin Warriors** at 17 Jintaili, Xiaozhuang in Chaoyang (☎ 010-6404-8781; daily 7:30-8:50 pm; ¥180-¥380) have just returned from a World Tour, and their show features beautifully choreographed performances alongside edge-of-your-seat moves.

Beijing Opera

(See p. 63 for more on opera). Beijing Opera is a love-or-loathe experience and many visitors find they don't have the patience, understanding (or earplugs) for a full-scale Beijing Opera performance, which can last for hours, and, in the past, even days. Thus the tourist-friendly, shortened, often subtitled versions available at some theaters around the capital present an easy introduction to the art. Many of these places also offer the chance to see the performers before the show, which allows you to really appreciate the detail of the makeup and costumes worn as well as to get some close-up photos. One of the best of the tourist choices is at the **Liyuan Theater** (☎ 010-6301-6688, ext. 8860) in the

Beijing Opera

Qianmen Hotel at 175 Yong'an Lu, which has evening performance at 7:30 pm. If you arrive an hour or so before the show's start, you'll find the performers out in the lobby, all ready for photographs and light conversation. Ticket prices start from ¥40 and go up to ¥280, which will give you a table near the stage where you'll be served tea and light snacks to enjoy during the performance. There are also shows at the **Chaoyang Theater** (see *Acrobats*, p. 187) where standard seats again start from ¥40 or you can indulge in front-row tables and a full Beijing duck dinner for ¥800. Shows last an hour or two and it's worth booking in advance for both of these options during the peak season. Other places to experience opera while you eat include **Jingcai Roasted Duck Restaurant** (see p. 213) in Wangfujing and the **Laoshe Teahouse** (see p. 216) in Qianmen.

If you want to see opera in its original form, away from the subtitles and shortened tourist theater versions, take a stroll around Shichahai or the Temple of Heaven's grounds in the early evening and you might well see crowds of elderly folk clustered around the local park star, enjoying a free performance. For a more intimate opera experience, try visiting the **Academy of Chinese Traditional Opera** (☎ 010-6333-7672), at 400 Wanquan Si in Fengtai district. Here, the public is invited to watch the academy's students rehearse once a week and, although the performances won't be flawless (they are students after all), it's a laid-back environment and provides a more personal experience. If you arrive early, you may even get the chance to go backstage and see the actors preparing their make-up. Rehearsals usually start at about 1:30 pm on Fridays and only happen in semester time.

Beijing's Music Scene

Beijing has a long history of music and even a stroll through the Temple of Heaven is often enlivened by performances using traditional instruments. But, more surprisingly, the capital city, so close to the prying eye of the government, has also developed a thriving live music scene, which is dominated by Beijing rock (see *Protest Music*, p. 64, and *Live Music Bars*, p. 219). If rock's not your thing, there are also jazz bars and, for classical music, there are concert halls spread throughout Beijing, offering a wide range of performances – check *City Weekend* and *that's Beijing* for upcoming events.

- **Beijing Concert Hall**, 1 Beixinhuajie, Xicheng (☎ 010-6605-7006)
- **Forbidden City Concert Hall**, Zhongshan Park, Xi Chang'an Jie, Xicheng (☎ 010-6559-8285)
- **Great Hall of the People**, Tian'anmen Square west side, Dongcheng (☎ 010-6309-6156)

Movie Theaters

If you're stuck on a rainy day, or simply want some time out from noisy Beijing, then **Star City** (Oriental Plaza, 1 Dongchang'an Jie, Dongcheng; ☎ 010-8518-5399) and **Sun Dong An Cinema City** (5F Sun Dong'an, 138 Wangfujing Dajie; ☎ 010-6528-1838) movie theaters have regular screenings in English.

For Families

Although both the Summer Palace and the Temple of Heaven have plenty of space for the kids to enjoy, Beijing's imperial attractions can be a bit boring for them and so it's best to intersperse these "serious sights" with some fun options. Other open spaces worth a visit include **Ritan Park** (north of Yong'anli subway), which has plenty of rocks for the kids to clamber over and trees to hide behind, or **Ditan Park** (north of Yonghegong subway), which has more formalized kiddies' attractions. Other kid-friendly sights in the city include:

- **The Aquarium** (daily 9 am-5:30 pm; ¥100 adults, ¥50 children), located at the northern end of Beijing Zoo at 18B Gaoliangqiao Xijie, Haidian–the zoo itself is best avoided unless you really, really want to see pandas.

- **The Planetarium** (Wed-Fri 10 am-4 pm, Sat and Sun 9 am-4:30 pm), at 138 Xizhimen Wai Dajie, isn't far from the aquarium (above) and has recently undergone a major refit. Its displays are now state-of-the-art and include a space-shuttle simulator and a 4-D movie theater! Different attractions range in cost from ¥30 to ¥45.

- **Sony ExploraScience** (Mon-Fri 9:30 am-5:30 pm, Sat and Sun 10 am-7 pm; ¥30, kids younger than six go free) in the Oriental Plaza Mall by Wangfujing MTR. Here they have cutting-edge technology presented in a fun way and you might even find yourself captivated by the robotic dogs playing soccer.

At the Beijing Botanical Gardens

Many of the excursions around the city also have a bit of fun for all the family. When visiting the Great Wall you could choose **Badaling** (p. 180, which has a wildlife park opposite), **Mutianyu** (p. 180, which has a toboggan for kids over four feet) or **Simatai** (p. 182, with a flying fox zipline suitable for older kids). Closer in, the **Botanical Gardens** make another great day-trip and could be combined with a picnic and walk (or chairlift) at the nearby Fragrant Hills. If you're going to be staying in Beijing for a while and have exhausted all the options above, the *Insider's Guide – Kids in Beijing* has lots of fun outings as well as more practical advice about living as a family in the Chinese capital.

Health & Relaxation

Beijing has an abundance of TCM clinics, hospitals, massage parlors and spas, which can help take the stress out of your days. The establishments listed below are all worth seeking out but, if you want something closer to home, there are cheap reflexology and massage outlets all over the city that are generally good and cost as little as ¥40 an hour.

White Cloud Temple at 6 Baiyunguan Jie in Xuanwu (see p. 174) has traditionally trained Taoist practitioners who can give on-site diagnoses.

Beijing Massage Hospital (☎ 010-6616-8880, www.massage) at 7 Baochan Hutong in Xicheng specializes in *tuina* therapy, but they also perform acupuncture and moxibustion (see *Traditional Chinese Medicine*, p. 71).

Bodhi Theraputic Retreat (☎ 010-6417-9595, www.bodhi.com.cn) at 17 Gongti Bei Lu, opposite the northern entrance of the Worker's Stadium in Chaoyang, offers Chinese and Thai massages in a cool, minimalist environment. Massages are ¥138, or ¥78 Monday to Thursday before 5 pm.

Dragonfly (www.dragonfly.net.cn) has a couple of outlets here offering great Chinese massages, *shiatsu* and aromatherapy for ¥60-120. There's a branch near the Forbidden City at 60 Donghuamen Jie (☎ 010-6527-9368) and another on the ground floor of the Eastern Inn on San Litun Nan Lu (☎ 010-6593-6066).

Tianhe Liangzi at the Golden Bridge Building at 1A Jianguomen Wai Dajie has a number of outlets around the city that offer quality TCM foot massages from ¥68.

Shopping

Beijing is becoming increasingly famous for its shopping and offers merchandise from all over China, though at a higher price than the point of origin. International brands certainly aren't cheap either, but this doesn't discourage the legion of newly moneyed Beijingers who saunter through the city's increasingly upmarket malls armed only with their credit cards. If this is your thing, then there's no shortage of glitzy malls and department stores, but you'll find more atmosphere at the capital's excellent markets. They sell everything from copy goods to secondhand clothing, pearls, jade and antiques. Many buyers are attracted to the markets because of their reasonable quality imitation brand-label clothing and pirated CDs or DVDs, although they also stock the usual tourist nicknacks. In spite of periodic raids and lawsuits from designers, the trade simply restarts elsewhere and the recently relocated Silk Market, a key Beijing attraction, is piled high with copied goods.

Markets

Recommended phrases for Silk Market vendors

The Silk Market (Silk Street), Jianguomen Wai Dajie (daily 9 am-9 pm; Yong'anli subway). This market's name is misleading. While there is silk sold here, it is famed as *the* place to buy fake goods in China and ranks high on many visitors hit-lists. The market was recently moved from its outdoor location to a six-story building a bit along the road, and has lost some of its character in the process – but not its bargains. In spite of recent attempts to sue the market by Burberry, Chanel, Gucci, Luis Vuitton and Prada, the stalls continue to prosper and are now officially sanctioned to the extent that you can get a receipt (which costs an extra ¥5) and can return goods within a month. Spread over the six levels, you'll find sporting goods, electronics, jewelry and occasional silk items. If you're happy with "stealing" from the likes of Calvin Klein and O'Neill then you'll find plenty to fill your shopping bags. Bargaining is the order of the day.

Hongqiao Pearl Market, Tiantan Donglu, Chongwen (daily 8:30 am-7 pm; bus #41 from Chongwenmen). Renowned as a pearl market, these days Hongqiao sells a wide range of goodies. The ground floor holds electronics and silk, while the next floor up is all about fake brand clothes and bags, with the main event, pearls, on the third floor. More upscale jewelry is sold on the floor above. If you need a break, head up to the roof where there are good views over to the Temple of Heaven. For a drink, try **Coffee Tuo**, next to the market, although you'll have to endure the potent smell of fish rising from the basement market! If you spend too much, there's an ATM to restock your wallet on the fourth floor

★★★**Panjiayuan Antique Market**, Panjiayuan Qiao, Chaoyang (Mon-Fri 8 am-6 pm, Sat and Sun 4:30 am-6 pm), This fantastic covered "antiques" market is one of Beijing's (and China's) best and is well worth a visit, particularly on weekends, whether you buy or not. You'll find traders from all over the country selling a feast of wares, including (but not restricted to) books, calligraphy, furniture, ink stones, jewelry, modern and Red Art. Make sure you don't miss the huge outdoor display of stone

Buddhas, ill at ease with the skyscrapers that surround them – they are in the far right-hand corner from the main entrance. There's also a coffee and sandwich shop in the market should you need a refueling stop. The easiest way to get here is by taxi.

Shopping Streets

Wangfujing Dajie (Wangfujing subway)

One of Beijing's original and best shopping streets, Wangfujing Dajie has every consumer item known to man. From electronics and fashion to sports and traditional Chinese medicine, you'll find it all here, including a small night-market off Xiaogongfu Lu at the southern end of Wangfujing Dajie.

**Jianguomen Wai Dajie
(Jianguomen subway)**

This busy thoroughfare is lined with hotels, shops and malls and you'll find the Friendship Store, the Silk Market and the China World Shopping Mall here.

★★Dazhalan (Qianmen subway)

This is one of the city's oldest commercial shopping streets and is the place to find Traditional Chinese Medicine shops, along

*Taking a break at
Panjiayuan Market*

with tea and herb specialists. The area has a vibrant atmosphere and is full of eager shoppers purchasing all kinds of healing remedies and ointments. You'd better visit soon though, as there are plans to convert the street into a modern commercial area, in preparation for the 2008 Olympic Games. If you do visit, don't miss **Tongrentang Traditional Medicine Shop** (☎ 010-5869-1171), founded in 1669, which now has branches around the world. If you want a consultation, it's best to call ahead.

Shopping Malls

Beijing offers plenty of opportunity to witness China's latest commodity, the shopping mall, most of them built in the last 15 years. Many cater to Beijing's newly-moneyed set who want the latest Western designer gear and pay more for it than you would at home. If you've got to get some Gucci, then try the following:

China World Shopping Mall, 1 Jianguomen Wai Dajie (daily 9:30 am-9:30 pm; Guomao subway). Shops include Prada, Louis Vuitton, Burberry, Moschino and Esprit.

Oriental Plaza, 1 Dongchang'an Jie, Dongcheng (www.orientalplaza.com; daily 9:30 am-10 pm; Wangfujing subway). Shops include Paul Smith, Nike, Givenchy, Sisley, Bally and Watson's drugstore.

Department Stores

Along with a growing number of shopping malls, Beijing has a fair selection of department stores:

Friendship Store, 17 Jianguomen Wai Dajie, Chaoyang (daily 9 am-8:30 pm; Jianguomen subway). For a broad general overview of arts and crafts available and costs you could head for the Friendship Store. The service is not great and the few tourists who venture in are greatly outnumbered by staff, but if you buy here the quality is assured and there's even a currency exchange to make sure you can afford the high prices. There's also a good foreign language bookshop which sells yesterday's international newspapers.

SOGO, 8 Xuanwumenwai Dajie, Xuanwu (daily 9:30 am-10 pm; Xuanwumen subway). This upmarket Japanese store houses a good collection of boutiques and coffee shops and also has an extensive food court offering excellent sushi.

Wangfujing Department Store, 255 Wanfujing Dajie, Dongcheng (daily 9 am-10 pm; Wangfujing subway). This is Beijing's ultimate department store and provides floor after floor of glitzy shopping. If you only visit one, then this has to be it!

Antiques, Arts & Crafts

Beijing is bursting with antiques and local crafts. The only problems you'll have are deciding where to shop, what to buy, and whether it's real or fake. Take the usual precautions (haggle hard and be aware of copies) and try to have a good look around first. One of the best areas in town is **Gaobeidian**, in Chaoyang district (Gaobeidian subway), where the main road is full of dusty old shops overflowing with Ming and Qing replicas. The craftsmen here are highly skilled and can reproduce virtually anything requested. If you're here on a weekend, **Panjiayuan Market** (see *Markets*, p. 192), is good for antiques, art work, ceramics and crafts, although its popularity has led to high prices. It's also worth visiting the **Beijing Curio City** at 21 Dongsanhuan Nanlu, a fantastic four-story market full of local arts and crafts. It also houses a number of genuine antiques stalls (try **Dong Fang Yuan**, fourth floor), and is a great place to pick up jewelry and ceramics.

Tailors

Beijing's tailors offer cheap and competitive prices. Although tailoring costs are quite low, fabric prices can be heavily inflated so be prepared to haggle over their cost. If you have the time (and knowledge) your best bet is to buy your choice of material in advance and then give it to the tailor, but make sure you get the correct amount needed for your outfit. One of the best places to try is the third floor of **Yaxiu Market** at 58 Gongti Bei Lu, near San Litun, where the whole floor is crammed full of tailors and fabric shops. Try **Ya Shi Tailor** at stall 3066 (☎ 010-6413-2432), but you'll have to negotiate hard over the cost. Another reliable tailor is **Rong Xin Tailor and Boutique** on the second floor of the Friendship Supermarket, 7 Sanlitun Lu (☎ 010-6532-7913), where friendly Toby speaks English and can make Chinese or Western clothes. **Tom's Tailor Shop**, at B218 Li Du Jin Jie, 2 Fangyuan Xilu, Chaoyang (☎ 010-5135-7768), is also a quality shop that can produce tailor-made suits for men and women in under 24 hours.

Top Tailor Tip: Although tailors are cheap throughout China, fashions vary a great deal, so to make sure you get what you want, try taking a picture of an item for them to copy.

Bookstores

Beijing's bookstores have also come a long way since the days when only a limited selection of classics was available and there are a number of good places to browse, some of which, like **Bookworm** at 4 San Litun Nan Lu, have attached coffee shops. Other places to try include the **Beijing Foreign Languages Bookstore** at 235 Wangfujing Dajie and **Cuckoo**, in the basement of the China World Shopping Mall (see *Shopping Malls*, p. 193).

Electronic Goods

Although you'll find a better selection in Hong Kong, Beijing provides a range of electriconic goods at cheaper prices than home. One of the best places to try is **Wonderful Electronic Shopping Mall**, at 12 Chaoyangmen Wai Dajie (daily 8:30 am-10 pm), which sells most international and local brand names.

Beijing street scene (Galen Frysinger)

Everyday Needs

Beijing has plenty of good supermarkets, including the French chain **Carrefour**, as well as **7-Elevens** for daily convenience goods and **Watson's** for toiletries. Carrefour has branches throughout the city, but there's a convenient one at 6B Beisanhuan Donglu in Chaoyang (daily 8:30 am-10:30 pm). You'll find Watson's (9:30 am-9:30 pm) in both the Oriental Plaza and China World Shopping Centers (see *Shopping Malls*, p. 193) and another in Lido Place. Beijing also has a growing selection of more specialized imported food stores for all the things you miss from home although prices are high – try **Jenny Lou's** at 1 San Litun Lu, Beixiao Jie (daily 8 am-midnight) or nearby **Heping Supermarket** at 3 San Litun Lu.

Adventures

Beijing itself is brimming with adventures, and the surrounding countryside offers some great escapes. If you're going to be spending a substantial amount of time in Beijing and enjoy countryside trips, it's worth buying the *Insider's Guide to Beijing – Excursion Guide* (¥40), which details dozens of great trips around the city.

On Foot

Beijing's vast size can initially make walking seem like a futile way of getting around, but between the ringroads and flyovers there are still pockets of *hutong* that are well worth exploring on foot. Outside of the city, the hills and mountains to the west and north respectively offer some great hiking opportunities, most notably along sections of the Great Wall. Several organizations in Beijing offer hikes in the surrounding countryside. **Beijing Hikers** (☎ 139-1002-5516, www.beijinghikers.com) is a walking club that meets every Sunday at Starbucks in the Lido Hotel at 6, Jiangtai Lu in Chaoyang. Walks cost ¥200 and are graded from one to five according to distance and difficulty. They also operate monthly weekend trips (¥600). **CnAdventure** (☎ 010-8621-6278, www.cnadventure.com) runs day-hikes to the wall for as little as ¥110 (without entry tickets) and **Cycle China** (☎ 010-8402-4147, www.cyclechina.com) also runs great hiking tours that cost ¥200-500 depending on the route and the number of people in your party. If you're going to be spending a lot of time here and want to explore the area's full hiking potential, then it might be worth picking up *Hiking Around Beijing* by Seema Bennett, Nicky Mason and Huilin Pinnegar (Foreign Languages Press, 2005).

Walking the Wall

Various sections of the wall run within 100 miles of Beijing and the less visited parts provide some fantastic hiking opportunities. By definition, once you get to the wall, you will do some walking, but the short stretches at Badaling or Mutianyu barely constitute a hike. Although it is becoming increasingly popular, the rugged hike between Jinshanling and Simitai remains my favorite. For more solitude, Jiankou is closer to the city and you might just have the whole place to yourself if you make the rough hike from here to Mutianyu (four-five hrs), which can be arranged through Cycle China (see above).

★★★Jinshanling to Simatai

Jinshanling and Simatai (see p. 182) are two restored sections of wall that are both worthy of a trip in their own right, but when you link them in an exhilarating hike the effect is mindblowing. The scenery here is some of the most rugged anywhere along the wall and, while stunning, this makes for some **serious legwork**. The walk takes a minimum of two hours, but more likely three or four, and offers fine picnic spots so it's worth bringing some supplies. Although you can buy drinks along the way (see below) make sure you bring some water and start the walk well hydrated – it can reach 100°F here in summer and the wall is unforgiving in its gradient. This section of wall is getting busier all the time and sees adventure tour groups and organized hikes. But, if you choose to come individually, or walk at your own pace, you should still have magical moments of solitude, especially in winter.

The Wall at Jinshanling

Most people choose to walk from Jinshanling to Simatai rather than the other way round as it's easier to find transport back from Simatai. But, if you have a driver, then it makes little difference. There's also the option of staying at Simatai's hostel or, for the hardy, camping on the wall itself at Jinshanling, which allows you to catch sunrise on the wall and then start the hike early before it gets too hot.

The Walk: The walk itself is fairly straightforward. Once you've bought your ticket (¥30) at Jinshanling. follow the path straight for a while and then turn left just before a toilet block. You'll see the wall ahead of you and the path soon starts to climb steeply up to it. Ten or 15 minutes later you should be on the wall, where there are drinks vendors and you can see all the way across to Simatai, which looks alarmingly far away. You'll pass through the first of 14 watchtowers on the walk and then you just need to

Simatai

follow the wall up and down, up and down, up and.... The wall is crumbly in places and the steps range from enormously high to rocky remnants, so take care. There are also a couple of points where you have to leave the wall as it is impassable – there are obvious tracks leading off to the side of the wall, but if you're away from the wall for more than a few minutes you've gone wrong. As you approach the end, you'll pass through a watchtower where you'll be asked to buy a ticket for Simatai (¥40), which feels like an indignity unless your poor, tired legs have the energy to make it up the scarily steep section across the water in front of you. From here, descend away from the wall and proceed across the bridge (¥5) and along the far side of the reservoir (which is mighty inviting for a swim in spite of the signs forbidding it) to the car park where there are some cafés and drinks stalls.

On Wheels

By Bike

Beijing was traditionally known as the City of Bicycles, but these days getting around by bike can be a scary prospect. This said, there are still designated cycle lanes and as long as you move with the crowd it's fairly plain (if polluted) sailing. But the best parts of Beijing to explore by bicycle are undoubtedly its *hutong*, which still offer the quiet rides of yesteryear – Shichahai and Qianmen are both great places to get lost!

If you want to see the best of Beijing by bike and not have to worry about finding your way around, **Cycle China** (☎ 010-8402-4147, www.cyclechina. com) offers guided bike tours of Beijing and the *hutong*, as well as trips to surrounding sights, including the Great Wall. Trips outside the city are often a combination of biking and hiking and are vehicle-supported so if you get too tired you can simply jump in the van. Prices vary from ¥150-500, depending on group numbers and trip length, but all are professionally operated and managed and are definitely worth the money. Their offices are at 12 Jingshan Dong Lu (daily 9 am-6 pm), opposite the east gate of

Jingshan Park, and they will provide everything you need. Cycle China also rent out both city cycles and quality mountain bikes; for other bike rental options see *Getting Around*, p. 147.

For more serious mountain bikers the **Mountain Bikers of Beijing**, who like to be known by their MOB acronym, offer challenging weekend rides outside the city on everything from roads to rubble. Trips cost ¥80 and bike rental is ¥60. If you're interested, check out www.themob.404.com.au or call ☎ 131-6129-8360.

Hutong Rickshaws

If you want to see the *hutong* on wheels, just not under your own steam, then a cycle rickshaw tour might be the answer. But make sure you're very clear about the price at the beginning as some of these guys are very unscrupulous, taking you into local houses, then demanding extortionate prices afterwards. To avoid such hassles head for the **Beijing Hutong Tour Company** (☎ 010-6615-9097,

Hutong rickshaws (Ewen Bell)

www.hutongtour.com.cn), which you'll find 200 yards west of Beihai Park's northern exit at 26 Dianmen Xi Dajie. They run tours at 8:50 am and 1:50 pm (¥180 per person), lasting approximately 2½ hours, that take you through the *hutong* as well as allowing you access to people's houses. If you want to go it alone you could head here outside of these times, or just hail a likely looking rickshaw driver and haggle with him. Beijing Hutong Tour Company also operates longer tours, which include the opportunity to enjoy a meal in a traditional home and even try your hand at making dumplings!

★★By Sidecar

Sidecar

For an exhilarating day out in the beautiful countryside around Beijing and the Great Wall you can't beat the thrill of the open road riding a 750cc sidecar. **CJ Club** (☎ 010-8456-2594; club@cjmotorcycle.com) is a new venture that offers you chance to ride these magnificent machines (based on the design of a 1930s German model) out to remote villages and crumbling sections of the wall. They organize tailor-made guided tours to wherever you please – a good place for a day-trip is Huanghuacheng (Yellow Flower Great Wall). You need your home-country driver's license and adequate insurance and can get the equipment at their office at 36

Xiaojunmiao, Xiaoyun Lu in Chaoyang. Prices are ¥200 per day plus ¥2,000 and your passport as deposit.

On the Green

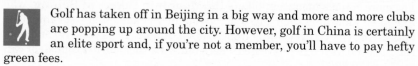

Golf has taken off in Beijing in a big way and more and more clubs are popping up around the city. However, golf in China is certainly an elite sport and, if you're not a member, you'll have to pay hefty green fees.

Chaoyang Kosaido Golf Club, Nongzhan Nanlu, Chaoyang (☎ 010-6501-8584). The virtue in this tidy little par-30 nine-holer lies in its proximity to the city and the comparatively low green fees. (¥180 weekdays and ¥240 on weekends).

★★**Beijing International Golf Club**, Changping (☎ 010-6076-2288). This is one of the finest golf courses around Beijing, with a stunningly located course and first-class facilities. The 18-hole course is tucked on a hillside overlooking the Ming Tombs (see p. 175) and incorporates a river and reservoir. As a non-member, you'll have to pay ¥800 (men) or ¥450 (women) for weekdays or ¥1,400 (men and women) on weekends. Caddy fees are a compulsory ¥200.

Beijing Golf Club, Shunyi (☎ 010-8947-0245). This golf club hosts the annual Helong Cup, the premier amateur golf invitational tournament in China. It was opened in 1987 and includes a driving range, four practice courses and even a Japanese-style bathhouse. Non-members can play for ¥800 on weekdays and ¥1,200 over the weekends.

On Water

Plenty of Beijing's sights and areas have boating opportunities, including the Summer Palace, Beihai Park and Shichahai. You can often choose between rowboats, paddleboats and electric boats. In the heat of summer being out on the water keeps you cool, offers some solitude and provides a different perspective on the sights. These boating options are described under *Sightseeing*, but note that most boat activities cease in winter – see *On Snow & Ice* below for the frozen alternatives.

If you want to try and experience some of the regal life, you can now **cruise the imperial canal to the Summer Palace**, just as the Empress Dowager Cixi did. The **Shangri-La's River Dragon** boat (☎ 010-6841-6824) offers four trips a day (April-November), which include commentary for the 30-minute journey, refreshments and a guided tour of the Summer Palace before hopping back on the boat – all at ¥420 per person. A cheaper boat trip to the Summer Palace runs from behind the Exhibition Center near the Beijing Zoo and costs ¥40 one-way or ¥70 round-trip.

Dragon Boat Racing

If you'd prefer a little more exertion than a genteel boat trip, the **Beijing International Dragons** (☎ 139-1002-5251; jxu@vokdams.cn) meet every Sunday morning (April to November) at Houhai (see p. 169). Sessions cost ¥30 and you should bring a dry set of clothes. Call for the exact practice session times.

On Snow & Ice

Ice-Skating

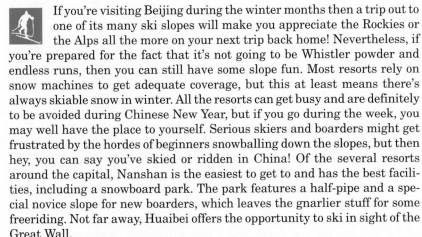

Beijing's cold winter climate may leave you feeling a little chilled, but when the lakes freeze over, rosy-cheeked skate vendors congregate around Shichahai and Kunming Lake at the Summer Palace, where you can warm yourself up with a few pirouettes. Skates cost ¥10 per day but, if you want to get ones that fit, you'd better get here early.

Skiing & Snowboarding

If you're visiting Beijing during the winter months then a trip out to one of its many ski slopes will make you appreciate the Rockies or the Alps all the more on your next trip back home! Nevertheless, if you're prepared for the fact that it's not going to be Whistler powder and endless runs, then you can still have some slope fun. Most resorts rely on snow machines to get adequate coverage, but this at least means there's always skiable snow in winter. All the resorts can get busy and are definitely to be avoided during Chinese New Year, but if you go during the week, you may well have the place to yourself. Serious skiers and boarders might get frustrated by the hordes of beginners snowballing down the slopes, but then hey, you can say you've skied or ridden in China! Of the several resorts around the capital, Nanshan is the easiest to get to and has the best facilities, including a snowboard park. The park features a half-pipe and a special novice slope for new boarders, which leaves the gnarlier stuff for some freeriding. Not far away, Huaibei offers the opportunity to ski in sight of the Great Wall.

Huaibei International Ski Resort, Hefangkou Village, Huaibei (☎ 010-8969-6677; daily 8:30 am-9:30 pm; bus #936 from Dongzhimen to Huaibei Town). Entrance to the park is ¥20 and prices then start from ¥140 on weekdays to ¥200 on weekends for a half-day.

★★★**Nanshan Ski Village**, Henanzhai Village, Miyun County (☎ 010-6445-0991, www.nanshanski.com; daily 8:30 am-5:30 pm; buses from Dongzhimen to Xi Da Qiao and then a taxi). Entrance to the park is ¥20 and prices then start from ¥100 for two hours on weekdays and ¥150 on weekends, with cheaper packages available for longer periods of time.

Nanshan

Cultural Adventures

Beijing is the cultural capital of the country and there is an array of cultural adventures available, from traditional tai chi to more recent options such as wine-tasting!

Cooking

Learn traditional Chinese dishes (especially Cantonese and Szechuanese), where else but in a *hutong* house at 3 Shajing Hutong, Nanluoguxiang. Call **Chunyi** on ☎ 010-8401-4788 or e-mail hutongcuisine@yahoo.com to arrange a lesson. Classes cost ¥150 per person and run from 10:30 am to 2:30 pm.

Language

Beijing's *putonghua* dialect is the language the rest of the country speaks and the capital is therefore one of the best places to study Chinese. Added to this, the number of expats and foreign students means that there are a plethora of study options, from full-blown university courses to private lessons and even places where you learn through traditional artistic activities. The listings below offers short-term courses and are thus suitable if you won't be spending too long in Beijing.

Ai Kun Sheng (☎ 135-5248-0411, www.akscenter.com.cn), at 3E in the Linda Tower, due south of Liufang subway (exit B), offers a unique way to learn the language while partaking in traditional Chinese activities such as calligraphy, tai chi and traditional Chinese painting. A one-week course involving 20 hours of training costs from ¥2000.

Global Village (☎ 010-6253-7737), near Wudaokou light rail station, is an international chain which offers private lessons or ¥240 for 20 hours in a group class.

My Chinese (☎ 010-6417-9553, www.mychineseclassroom.com) is conveniently located at Room 8203, Baoliyuan Building, Gongti Bei Lu in Chaoyang. Along with conventional Mandarin lessons they also offer painting and calligraphy classes.

Martial Arts

There are plenty of places used to teaching martial arts to foreigners in Beijing, although many of them are focused on long-term courses. For just a lesson or two, try the **Milun School of Traditional Kung Fu** (☎ 139-1081-1934, www. kungfuinchina.com), who give private classes (¥150) in Ritan Park. Another highly reputed school is the **Jinghua Wushu Associa-**

tion, which operates from the Kempinski Hotel (see p.000; ☎ 010-6465-3388, www.jinghuawushu.com). All of the Shaolin qualified teachers here can speak English and there are several classes each week, with Sunday tai chi sessions (9-11 am) held in Ritan Park (see p. 90). If you prefer the idea of watching kung fu rather than participating, there are some incredible shows to be seen in Beijing's theaters, or you could just head down to the nearest park or square around sunrise or sundown where you should see some tai chi.

Painting & Calligraphy

My Chinese Classroom also runs calligraphy and traditional painting classes, while **Ai Kun Sheng** (see *Language*, above for both) uses the arts as a vehicle for teaching Chinese.

★ On the Vine

VINO CHINA

For over 600 years, China has been growing and producing wine, and, with a little help from the French, its quality and variety is increasing. Wine was a common social drink during the Tang dynasty, but subsequently its popularity declined and *baijiu* (see *Food & Drink*, p. 126) has long been the drink of choice. But with China's growing middle class, a renewed interest in wine has begun, and you don't have to look far to find excellent labels. Hebei's climate is similar to that of Mediterranean Europe, with hot summer days and cool dry nights, and its thin and rocky topsoil has proved ideal for vine cultivation. Although the Great Wall of China Winery has been making wine since 1979, quality varies immensely as the grapes are grown by local farmers and are not regulated. But in 1997 the Chinese government went into business with the French, who agreed to bring quality vines, equipment and expertise to China. The first vines were planted in 2001 in Hebei province and by 2003, the vineyard saw its first harvest and the dawn of a new era in Chinese winemaking. The Sino-French Vineyard has since been producing high-grade wines and hopes to conquer both the domestic and international wine markets.

If the smell of *baijiu* and cheap beer has finally taken its toll and you long for the taste of a good Cabernet Sauvignon, then why not escape the city and head for the refreshing climate provided by Hebei's vineyards? There are

Beijing & Around

currently two vineyards to visit and both are well worth the trip for wine enthusiasts. For an excellent tour in English visit the **Sino-French Demonstration Vineyard** in Donghuayuan village, Huailai county, Hebei (☎ 0313-6849-882; call in advance). Although the tour is free, if you want to join in the wine tasting, you'll have to pay ¥150, but it's money well spent. You can also visit the **Great Wall of China Winery** (☎ 0313-623-2216; call in advance), which offers a similar deal, although they currently lack any English-speaking guides. If you don't have your own transport, or simply want to enjoy the wine tasting, then **WestChina** (☎ 1358-1682-703, www. westchina.net.cn) offers a **wine tour** (¥380) that takes in both listed wineries and includes lunch and a spa. The vines are best visited when at their fullest from late July to September, although both vineyards can be visited all year round.

Putting Something Back

For Beijing's **street kids**, life is very tough. Not only do they face living outdoors in extreme weather conditions, but many have been sold into a life of enforced begging, crime or prostitution. The **Wisdom Springs Technical Skills Training Center** (wisdomsprings@psmail.net) is a local organization that was established to help give some of these children a chance. Each child receives daily meals, Chinese and English lessons, and computer and business skills, plus a small weekly allowance. The center is funded by donations and any offers of time or money are gratefully received.

Where to Stay

Beijing's accommodation options have really improved over the past decade and, along with the predictable five-star monoliths, there are some beautifully renovated *hutong* hotels and an increasing number of cheap and central, if blandly functional, hostel options. The bulk of Beijing's hotels are east of Tian'anmen Square. Stretching along Dongchang'an Dajie, which becomes Jianguomen Dajie, you'll find some of the best hotels Beijing has to offer. If you seek something a little less impersonal than the grand establishments that line this busy thoroughfare, the atmospheric *hutong* around the Forbidden City has some hidden gems and plenty of budget choices. North of the city, out near the Great Wall, there are also escapes to be had in some of the country's most exclusive hotels.

What's it mean? FC=fitness center; SW=swimming pool; @=in-room Internet access; DA=rooms for disabled. For ¥ price codes, see page 113.

North

★**Bamboo Garden Hotel,** 24 Xiaoshiqiao Hutong, Jiugulou Dajie (☎ 010-5852-0088, www.bbgh.com.cn; Gulou Dajie subway). The Bamboo Garden's tranquil groves of greenery offer a seemingly secluded retreat from busy Beijing and the building itself has some history to boot – it was once home to a Qing dynasty eunuch, an early 20th century minister and, most recently, one of the primary advocates of the Cultural Revolution, Kang Sheng. However, charming and charismatic as it may be, the Bamboo's rooms certainly aren't cheap and they're a hotchpotch lot, so it's worth checking out a few before you decide. DA ¥¥¥-¥¥¥¥¥

Downtown Backpackers, 85 Nanluoguxiang, Dongcheng (☎ 010-8400-2429, www.backpackingchina.com; Andingmen subway). Well-located on Nanluoguxiang, a gentrified but nonetheless characterful *hutong*, this hostel is comfortable and friendly, close to a host of good eating and drinking options. Rooms are cheap, basic and functional and dorms are ¥50. The hostel also has bikes for rent and operates all the usual tours. It's a good place to base yourself, although the whole of Nanluoguxiang was being dug up at the time of writing. ¥-¥¥

Drum Tower Youth Hostel, 51 Jiugulou Dajie, Xicheng (☎ 010-6403-7702; drumtowerutels@hotmail.com; Gulou Dajie subway). This is one of the best of the new breed of Hostelling International Places popping up all over Beijing. Rooms are functional and modern, if a little small, and the hostel is well-located close to Gulou subway station, Café Sambal (see p. 214) and the Houhai *hutong* area. All the usual tours are offered. Dorm beds are ¥60. ¥¥

★★★**Lusongyuan,** 22 Babchang Hutong, Dongcheng (☎ 010-6404-0436; lsyhotel@263.net; Yonghegong subway and then a taxi or bus #104). This beautiful mid-range hotel perfectly captures *hutong* life and is worth a stay whatever your budget. Lusongyuan is housed in a Qing mansion and the elegant rooms are set around a series of pretty plant- and rockery-filled courtyards that have tables and chairs where you can sit and soak up the serenity. The hotel has Internet access, bike rental, plus transport and tour booking services. It's popular with tour groups and booking ahead is necessary in summer. ¥¥-¥¥¥¥

Lusongyuan

East

East of the Forbidden City

★**Jade Youth Hostel,** 5 Beizhide Xiang, Beiheyan (☎ 010-6525-9966, www.xihuahotel.com; Tian'anmen East subway). The Jade Hostel has an excellent location in the *hutong* right next to the Forbidden City and has basic, clean and modern doubles and dorm beds for ¥60. The hostel operates tours, has bikes for rent and also offers Chinese cooking lessons. ¥¥

★★★**Peninsula Palace, 8** Jinyu Hutong, Dongcheng (☎ 010-8516-2888, www.peninsula.com; Dongdan subway). The Peninsula is an outstanding example of how a five-star can still ooze character, seamlessly fusing state-of-the-art facilities with classic Asian style. The enormous Peninsula Suite is a favorite of visiting VIPs, but all the rooms have hardwood floors, quality furnishings and enormous plasma TVs. The lobby even has a waterfall! The shopping arcade here has designer boutiques galore, including Jean Paul Gaultier and Tiffany & Co. FC/SW/@ ¥¥¥¥¥

Peninsula Palace

Red Capital Residence

★★**Red Capital Residence, 9** Dongsi Liutiao, Dongcheng (☎ 010-8403-5308, www.redcapitalclub.com.cn). The Residence is *the* place to stay if you want your accommodation in Beijing to be more than just a bed for the night. The hotel is housed in a 200-year-old Qing mansion nestled into the *hutong* – look for #9 on its red door. There are only five suites, which are all stylishly furnished with antiques harking back to the early days of the PRC. The mansion's bomb shelter has been converted into a bar and screens Cultural Revolution movies to complete the Communist picture, although the prices are distinctly capitalist. ¥¥¥¥¥

Dongchang'an Dajie (Wangfujing subway)

★★**Grand Hotel Beijing**, 35 Dongchang'an Dajie (☎ 010-6513-7788, www.grandhotel-beijing.com). The west wing of the Beijing Hotel is a far more appealing prospect than its neighbor. Rooms on the upper floors enjoy good views of the Forbidden City, as does the appropriately named Terrace View Bar, which is worth a visit (5:30-8:30 pm) even if you're not

Grand Hotel Beijing

staying. Rooms have a slightly dated feel but are comfortable and plush nonetheless. FC/SW/@ ¥¥¥¥¥

Grand Hyatt

★★**Grand Hyatt**, 1 Dongchang'an Dajie (☎ 010-8518-1234, www.beijing.grand.hyatt.com). Although it can't outdo its famous cousin, the super-high Shanghai Hyatt, the Beijing offering still comes through with the goods. From the relaxed lobby to the modern, functional rooms, the Hyatt offers first-class comfort and service and also contains one of Beijing's finest Chinese restaurants, Made in China (see p. 216). FC/SW/@/DA ¥¥¥¥¥

★★**Raffles,** 33 Dongchang'an Dajie (☎ 010-6526-3388, www.beijing.raffles.com). In 2006 Raffles was opened in two of the Beijing Hotel's historic wings and is now Beijing's premier hotel, restoring the landmark building to its former glory. Raffles' refined class hits you the moment you enter the chandelier-lit lobby. All rooms are stylishly and luxuriously furnished and there are "personality suites" where various dignitaries have stayed over the years, although it's doubtful if even these illustrious visitors were able to watch TV while washing in the bathroom! FC/SW/@ ¥¥¥¥¥

Raffles

Jianguomen Dajie & Around

★★**China World Hotel**, 1 Jianguomen Wai Dajie (☎ 010-6505-2266, www.shangri-la.com; Guomao subway). Owned and operated by the Shangri-La, this hotel is an opulent five-star affair with spacious, comfortable and subtly

China World Hotel

understated rooms. The hotel is set amidst the China World Towers, with the upscale shopping of the China World mall, and makes for a decidedly comfortable base. The Trader's, behind the China World, is also run by the Shangri-La and is another good upmarket option. FC/SW/@DA ¥¥¥¥¥

Jianguo, 5 Jianguomen Wai Dajie (☎ 010-6500-2233, www.jianguohotels.com; Yong'anli subway). This US-Chinese joint venture enjoys a prime location and has fairly good rooms, many of which have balconies overlooking busy Jianguomen Lu, although you'll have to be fairly noise tolerant to spend any time on them! FC/SW/@ ¥¥¥¥

★**Kerry Center Hotel,** 1 Guanghua Lu (☎ 010-6561-8833, www.shangri-la.com/beijing/kerrycentre/en; Guomao subway). Another of the Shangri-La's Beijing lodgings, the Kerry Center is an upbeat and ultra-modern establishment with comfortable, spacious rooms and attractive bathrooms. The hotel has an excellent fitness center and is home to the lively 24-hour Centro bar (see p. 219). FC/SW/@/DA ¥¥¥¥¥

Kerry Center Hotel

★★**St. Regis**, 21 Jianguomen Wai Dajie (☎ 010-6460-3299, www.stregis.com/beijing; Jianguomen subway). Of the many upscale offerings clustered around Jianguomen Qiao, the St. Regis is the finest, setting the standard for five-star hotels across the city, and has attracted the likes of President Bush and Uma Thurman. Rooms are elegantly understated and each guest is assigned a butler, but all this luxury doesn't come cheap. The hotel has five restaurants, of which the Celestial Court Cantonese (see p. 216) is particularly renowned. FC/SW/@ ¥¥¥¥¥

Scitech, 22 Jianguomen Wai Dajie (☎ 010-6512-3388, www.scitechgroup.com; Jianguomen subway). The Scitech is a little more understated than some of its neighbors and, although its rooms

St. Regis

are aging and on the small side, the hotel has good facilities and is well-priced. FC/SW/@ ¥¥¥

South

Far East International Hostel, 90 Tieshuxie Jie, Xuanwu (☎ 010-5195-8811, www.fareastyh.com; Hepingmen subway). The best known of a host of budget options along this *hutong* in Qianmenwai, south of Tian'anmen Square, the Far East's location is great, but the standard rooms and dorms are bland. The hostel offers the usual variety of trips within the city and out to the wall and Ming tombs. They also have bike rental and Internet access. Dorm beds ¥45-60. ¥¥

Tiantan, 1 Tiyuguan Lu, Chongwen (☎ 010-6719-0666, www.tiantanhotel. com). The Tiantan used to be run-down and unhelpfully staffed, but since a recent renovation the hotel and staff have moved upscale. Although it's a little far from the center of town the Tiantan is close to the Temple of Heaven and Hongqiao market and is a good mid-range option. ¥¥¥

West

★★Lotus Hostel, 29 Xisi Beiqitiao, Xicheng (☎ 010-6612-8341, www. lotushostel.cn). This newly opened hostel offers the opportunity to stay in an atmospheric, traditional *hutong* home even if you're on a tight budget. The peaceful and clean rooms are set around a courtyard and are attractively decked out with traditional Chinese furniture and paintings. The helpful manager, Ben can arrange tours and onwards transport. Dorm beds ¥60. ¥¥

Lotus Hostel

Around Beijing

★Fragrant Hills, Fragrant Hills Park, Haidian (☎ 010-6259-1155). Designed by famed architect I.M. Pei (who is also responsible for the Louvre Pyramid in Paris), the Fragrant Hills Hotel offers a subtle blend of Eastern and Western styles in a beautiful environment surrounded by picturesque gardens, a large lake and a miniature stone forest. The hotel can offer a great break from Beijing's bustle and is a good base from which to explore the Fragrant Hills' hiking trails, although the rooms are past their best. See p. 183 for more on the Fragrant Hills and how to get here. ¥¥-¥¥¥

At the Wall

Options at the Great Wall near Beijing used to be limited to Badaling and a couple of low-grade hotels or a night under canvas at the more remote sections, but the scene has dramatically improved of late with the opening of some unique, if expensive, options.

★★**Camping at Jinshanling.** Camping on the wall at Jinshanling sure provides a stony bed, but, when you wake up and peer out of your tent at the sun rising over one of mankind's greatest achievements, you can't help but get out on the right side of bed! You can take your own tent and just pitch it yourself or go on a camping package through Mr. Sun (☎ 139-3244-4368) for ¥400, which includes entrance to the wall, dinner, drinks, breakfast and equipment.

The Commune

★★**The Commune,** Shuiguan (☎ 010-8118-1888, www.commune. com.cn). The Commune is as much of an architectural attraction as it is a place to stay and features 12 individually styled villas created by some of Asia's most progressive designers. Although interior designers might quibble about the quality of the workmanship, the innovative buildings undeniably stand out from, and yet somehow complement, the beautiful natural surroundings. Facilities are first-rate and include personal butlers, a lavish clubhouse, a stunning swimming pool – even a private path to the Great Wall. In September 2006 a new zone opened, offering additional villas and suites at more reasonable (but still decidedly high) prices. To get here, take a tourist bus to Badaling and then a taxi to Shuiguan. SW/@ ¥¥¥¥¥

★★★**Red Capital Ranch,** 28 Xiaguandi Village, Yanxi Town, Huairou (☎ 8401-886, www.redcapitalclub.com.cn). The latest addition to the Red Capital rostrum, the Ranch moves away from the Communist-capitalist contradiction of the Club and Residence and focuses on the wilder days of old, when the Manchu emperors tried to reclaim their roots with hunting lodges and mountain retreats, as at Chengde (see p. 220). A rural and rustic retreat is the theme here, although the luxury offered could hardly be described as roughing it. The Ranch enjoys a beautiful location out by the wild wall at Huairou and has 10 stone villas, the better ones with roof terraces to enjoy the seldom-seen Beijing spectacle of the stars. There's also a Tibetan-style spa, a cigar bar and a good restaurant – some ranch! You can easily explore the wall on foot from here, but there are also bikes for rent

(¥30 per day). To get here from Beijing there is a 10 am shuttle from the Red Capital Residence (see above). ¥¥¥¥¥

Simatai Great Wall International Youth Hostel, Simatai (www. hostelworld.com). The Simatai Hostel is comfortable, affordable, well-run and has a great location at the bottom of the hills, overlooking the reservoir. You can book through hostelworld or at Far East and Jade hostels in Beijing. ¥

Where to Eat

The one thing you have to try when you're here is **Beijing duck** (see callout below), but **Mongolian hotpot** is another specialty that will warm you up on a cold winter's day. The capital's eating options stretch way beyond duck and hotpot, though, and are increasingly cosmopolitan, featuring everything from Malaysian fare to French *haute cuisine*. Western-style coffee shops, including Starbucks, proliferate (even in the Forbidden City) and many of these places have reasonable Western and Chinese food, along with wireless Internet connection and good coffee. The usual array of Western fast-food joints also prevail, and in addition to the McDonalds, KFCs and Pizza Huts you'll also find healthier chain options such as Subway and independent sandwich shops and delis. If you're feeling impecunious or adventurous, **streetfood** in Beijing is definitely worth experiencing and offers dishes as diverse as sweet potatoes, *xianr bing* (stuffed pancakes) or scorpions on sticks – try the **Dong'anmen nightmarket** just off Wangfujing Dajie for an eye-opening selection.

Although there are restaurants and eating districts all over the city, the highest concentrations are found to the north and east of the Forbidden City, and the *hutong* contain some delightful little places worth visiting as much for their location as for the food.

If you want to accompany your meal with the local brew, Yanjing (an old name for the capital) is Beijing's beer and there are some increasingly good domestic wines available (see *Vino China*, p. 203). English menus are provided and reservations recommended at all the places below unless otherwise mentioned. The selections below focus on Beijing duck and Chinese options with a smattering of the best of the rest

See page 117 for an explanation of the ¥ restaurant price codes.

BEIJING DUCK (BEIJING KAOYA)

It's a cliché, but there really is no better place to enjoy Beijing duck than Beijing. As a tour leader, I used to start and finish tours in the capital, meaning that I'd sometimes get to enjoy a Beijing duck meal twice within the space of a few days – delicious no doubt, but it was only the lengthy Great Wall walks that saved me from packing on the pounds.

History & Preparation

Roast duck isn't unique to Beijing and you'll find a delicious pine-cooked version in Yunnan, but it is certainly the capital's most fa-

Cooking Beijing duck (Tot Foster)

mous food export, even though it actually originated in Nanjing and then moved, with the Ming dynasty, to Beijing. To become a renowned Beijing duck chef takes many years of training and each master has his own special, and sometimes secret, techniques and recipes. In the best restaurants the ducks are carefully chosen from local farms, plucked and then brought to the city. On arrival, air is blown under their skin, a process traditionally done using the chef's own lungpower, although these days it is often done with a kind of electric fan. Then the duck is scalded to tighten the skin, before being air-dried and rubbed with molasses. The duck is then filled with broth to allow it to cook from the inside while the wood-fired oven cooks the outside, with regular rotations to ensure it roasts evenly. The wood burned in the oven is also of key importance as it will affect the duck's taste, and fruit tree wood is often preferred. It is this complex process that makes the skin of the duck so delicately crispy, while the meat remains succulently sumptuous. After the broth has been drained the duck is brought directly to your table and often carved right in front of you by the chef – a great photo opportunity.

Depending upon your appetite and the size of the bird, a duck should serve three to four people, but if you tell the restaurant how many people there are in your group they will be able to recommend the right number of ducks. Duck banquets often involve consuming most of the duck – tongues, feet, bone broth soup and all, but if these more acquired tastes don't appeal, there's no shame in sticking to the tasty meat and crispy skin.

Beijing duck is usually served with finely sliced spring onions and cucumbers, wafer-thin pancakes and plum sauce, which, when combined in the right ratio, provide one of the best taste sensations you'll ever have. The pancake stuffing process can by done by chopsticks if you've got the skills but it's easier to do it by hand. Methods vary, but I like to spread some plum sauce on the pancake, then add the desired amount of spring onion slices, and the *pièce de résistance*, the duck itself, before rolling the pancake around its contents and finally popping it into your mouth. If your pancake rolling skills leave a little to be desired, fear not, for the duck will taste just as good! Although traditionalists might argue that Beijing duck is best enjoyed by itself, many people, myself included, prefer a little greenery to offset its roasted richness – a simple vegetable dish or two should suffice.

Beijing Duck Restaurants

Of the duck restaurants listed below, my favorite is Li Qun, although it seems as if "progress," in the form of urban redevelopment, may spell the end for this *hutong* hideaway, but Dadong is reliably good, Jingcai is a great newcomer on the scene, and Quanjude, while decidedly touristy, also has delicious duck.

★★**Dadong Beijing Duck**, Building 3, Tianjiehu Beikou, Chaoyang (☎ 010-6582-2892; daily 11 am-9:30 pm). This is one of the most popular duck restaurants in Beijing and with good reason – the duck is deliciously crispy and unusually light. The atmosphere is always lively. It was voted by *that's Beijing* magazine's reader poll as the best Beijing duck restaurant in the city in 2006 and you'll understand why once you've eaten there. You'll find the restaurant on the southeastern corner of Changghong Qiao. ¥¥¥¥

★★**Jingcai Roasted Duck**, 223 Wangfujing Dajie (☎ 010-6523-0483; daily 11:30 am-2 pm & 5-9:30 pm; Wangfujing subway). The stylish and modern interior is matched by the excellent cuisine, and the secret duck recipe, known only to the chef, is perfection on a platter. To complete it all, you can enjoy live performances of Beijing opera while you eat. ¥¥¥-¥¥¥¥

★★★**Li Qun Beijing Duck**, 11 Beixiangfeng, Zhegyi Lu (☎ 010-6705-5578; daily 10:30 am-1:30 pm & 4:30-10 pm; Chongwenmen subway). It's nestled into the *hutong* southeast of Tian'anmen Square and finding this place is half the fun. But you'll be thoroughly rewarded by some of the best duck in Beijing. The atmosphere is warm and convivial and the restaurant's small courtyard and surrounding few private dining rooms are often full. They only cook a certain number of ducks a night so it's worth calling in advance. Rumors of the restaurant's closure due to the redevelopment of the area are as yet unsubstantiated – if it's still open get there while you can. ¥¥

★**Quanjude Duck Restaurant**, 14 Qianmen Xi Dajie, Chongwen (☎ 010-6301-8833; daily 11 am-2 pm & 4:30-9 pm; Qianmen subway). This is an institution in Beijing and has been serving juicy Beijing duck since 1852. They now have a number of branches throughout the city and are certainly more touristy than many of the other duck restaurants listed. But they do offer a tasty traditional duck feast; every part of the duck is prepared, from cold tongue to their sautéed webbed feet and if you visit this branch you'll be together with 2,000 fellow duck lovers. ¥¥¥¥

North

North of the Forbidden City

★★**Fangshan**, 1 Wenjin Jie, inside Beihai Park (☎ 010-6401-1879; daily 11 am-1:30 pm & 5-8 pm; bus #5 from Qianmen). Fangshan was established in 1925 by three imperial chefs whose families have been preparing cuisine fit for a king over hundreds of years. However, in spite of this long imperial tradition and the striking courtyard setting on the edge of Beihai Lake, the emperors might not be so happy with the food these days, particularly if the hefty bill was being deducted from the imperial coffers. This said it's certainly authentic (maybe too much so) and is worth coming for the imperial experience. To get here enter through the east gate of Beihai Park, cross over the bridge and then turn right. ¥¥¥¥¥

★**Fish Nation**, 31 Nanluoguxiang and north of 43 Bei San Litun Nan Lu (both daily 10 am-2 am; Gulou Dajie subway). This fish and chips haven won *that's beijing*'s "outstanding late night dining" award in 2005, and with good reason. The fish and chips taste as good as in the UK and can either be enjoyed at the peaceful and larger Nanluoguxiang branch, which has wireless Internet connection and a great roof terrace, or as the perfect end to a night of drinking at the tiny San Litun branch, which mostly does take-out but has a few tables outside. Reservations aren't necessary. ¥¥

★**Source**, 14 Banchang Hutong, Nanluoguxiang, Dongchen (☎ 010-6400-3736; daily 11 am-2 pm & 5-10:30 pm; Andingmen subway). Set in a converted *hutong* house, this restaurant provides quality Szechuanese fare in a tranquil setting. It's worth visiting on a fine evening to enjoy the courtyard tables, set against a backdrop of bamboo and ancient date trees. ¥¥¥-¥¥¥¥

Shichahai

★★**Café Sambal**, 43 Doufuchi Hutong, Jiugulou Dajie (☎ 010-6400-4875; daily noon-midnight; Gulou Dajie subway). Authentic Malaysian cuisine in an attractively ramshackle *hutong* courtyard makes this a firm favorite for locals and tourists alike. The *satay* is excellent and, while straying from the Malaysian theme, the *mojitos* are the best in town. ¥¥¥

★**Kaorouji**, 14 Qianhai Dongyan (☎ 010-6404-2554; daily 11 am-2 pm & 5-11 pm; Gulou Dajie subway). This simple lakeside restaurant serves excellent Muslim food, although service can be a little slow. The ambience is relaxed and laid-back making a pleasant break from the bustle of Beijing. The roast mutton is well worth the wait. If you're visiting during summer, then you can have it all served to you on the lake from your own private gondola (see *Romantic Dinner Escape*, p. 214). ¥¥¥

★★★**Li Family Restaurant**, 11 Yangfang Hutong, Deshengmennei Dajie, Xicheng (☎ 010-6618-0107; daily 6 am-10:30 pm; Jishuitan subway). This once small imperial restaurant has become such a hit that it has been extended and now seats over 100 people. The menu consists of recipes used in the Qing court, all of them cooked to perfection. They offer well priced set menus and a lively ambience. ¥¥¥¥

ROMANTIC DINNER ESCAPE

For a touch of romance to round off your day, **Kaorouji** (see above) provides deliciously barbecued delights, served to you in the comfort of your own privately punted gondola with the backdrop of Houhai lake and the sounds of two classical Chinese musicians. To experience this at its most beautiful, leave just before sunset. You can arrange this at the lakeside or call Kaorouji in advance – the complete package costs ¥300.

★**Mei Mansions,** 24 Daxiangfeng Hutong, Houhai (☎ 010-6612-6845; daily 11 am-2 pm & 5:30-10 pm; Jishuitan subway). This traditional courtyard restaurant pays tribute to one of Beijing's greatest Chinese opera stars, Mei Fang and offers expensive, but exceptional, Shanghainese fare. Its lavish setting and decadent interior of velvet curtains, dusty antiques and old black and white photos give it a 1930s salon atmosphere and a touch of sophistication. ¥¥¥¥¥

East

East of the Forbidden City

★★**The Courtyard,** 95 Donghuamen Dajie, Dongcheng (☎ 010-6526-8883). This trendy, modern restaurant serves fantastic finely fused Chinese and European dishes, all within a stone's throw of the Forbidden City, which you can gaze out over as you relax in the romance of the Courtyard. There's a gallery below the restaurant with works by some of Beijing's foremost contemporary artists. ¥¥¥¥¥

★★**Red Capital Club,** 66 Dongsijiutiao, Dongcheng (☎ 010-6402-7150, www.redcapitalclub.com.cn; daily 6 pm-11 pm; Dongzhimen subway), Another brainchild of Laurence Brahm (see *Red Capital Residence*, p. 206, and *Red Capital Ranch*, p. 210), the delightful Red Capital Club offers a glimpse back in time and serves a number of imperial favorites. The restaurant is set in a traditional courtyard house and is filled with memorabilia and nick-knacks from the really Red years of Chinese history. The club also features a 1950s-style cigar and cocktail lounge, which is a great spot to luxuriate in the contradiction of this imperialist/Communist/capitalist combo. ¥¥¥¥-¥¥¥¥¥

★**Xiao Fei Yang**, 209 Xiaojie (middle of Gui Jie), Dongzhimen Nei Dajie (☎ 010-8400-1669; 24 hrs; Dongzhimen subway). Gui Jie has a host of hotpot establishments and Xiao Fei Yang, which means Little Fat Lamb, serves a superb spicy bubbling broth. ¥¥-¥¥¥

The Worker's Stadium

Green T. House, 6 Gongti Xilu, Chaoyang (☎ 010-6552-8310; daily 11:30 am-2:30 pm & 6 pm-midnight; Dongsi Shitiao subway). Green T provides contemporary Chinese cuisine much of which is infused with its namesake, green tea. That may sound a little strange, but it is popular within China and adds a unique and sometimes delicious flavor. The restaurant aspires to something of a romantic-industrial feel with its high ceilings, bare walls, colored lighting and towering chairs but the excellent food makes it worth putting up with the pretensions – try the wasabi prawns. ¥¥¥-¥¥¥¥

★**Pure Lotus Vegetarian,** below JVC Tower, 10 Nongzhangyuan Nan Lu, Chaoyang (☎ 010-6592-3627; daily 9:30 am-10 pm). This exquisite Buddhist restaurant retreat presents finely crafted *faux* meat dishes from vegetables using traditional methods, which avoid "stimulating" foods such as garlic and onions. The food here is 100% organic and also features herbs and mushrooms from China's holy mountains. The restaurant is run by monks and the whole statuary-laden, smoke- and alcohol-free environment will leave both your stomach and your spirit sated, although your wallet will feel less full. ¥¥¥

Wangfujing

Dong Lai Shun, 5F Xingong'an Plaza, Wangfujing Dajie, Dongcheng (☎ 010-6528-0932; daily 11 am-9 pm; Wangfujing subway). Dong Lai Shun is a local favorite and serves up excellent and well priced hotpots in an authentic environment. The mutton hotpots are particularly popular and will definitely fill the gap after all that sightseeing. ¥¥-¥¥¥

★★**Made in China**, Grand Hyatt Hotel, 1 Dongchang'an Dajie (☎ 010-8518-1234 ext.3608; daily 11:30 am-2:30 pm & 5:30-10:30 pm; Wangfujing subway). This elegantly refined restaurant serves delicious Chinese cuisine with a Szechuan slant and its crimson and dark wood latticework interior is the perfect place to enjoy old favorites such as Beggar's Chicken. ¥¥¥-¥¥¥¥

Jianguomen Dajie & Around

Bento & Berries, The Kerry Center, 1 Guanghua Lu (☎ 010-6561-8833, ext. 45; daily Mon-Fri 7 am-11 pm, Sat & Sun 8 am-7 pm; Guomao subway). For a healthy break from Chinese fare, this deli offers freshly baked breads, sandwiches and veggie wraps, wine by the glass, great coffee and organic fruit juices. ¥¥

★**Celestial Court**, St. Regis Hotel, 21 Jianguomen Wai Dajie, Chaoyang (☎ 010-6460-6688; daily 11:30 am-2:30 pm & 6-10 pm; Jianguomen subway). This top-notch Cantonese restaurant offers specialty dishes, including Bird's Nest Soup, as well as dim sum, seafood and more moderately priced dishes, all presented and served with the utmost style. ¥¥¥¥¥

★**Justine's**, 1F Jianguo Hotel, Jianguomen Wai Dajie, Chaoyang (☎ 010-6500-2233 ext 8039; daily 6:30-9:30 am, 12-2:30 pm & 6-10 pm; Yong'anli subway). This excellent French restaurant is located in the Jianguo Hotel lobby and offers exquisite French cuisine in a chic atmosphere. Prices are high but are matched by the quality of food and service and Justine's has one of the best wine lists in Beijing. ¥¥¥¥-¥¥¥¥¥

Le Café Igosso, Dongsanhuan Nan Lu (☎ 010-8771-7013; daily 11 am-2 am; Guomao subway). This small and quirky modern café serves tasty Italian food with a just a dash of Japanese influence in a cozy and convivial environment. Try the *beef carpaccio* in olive oil and lemon juice. ¥¥¥¥

Three Guizhou Men, 6 Guanghua Xilu, Chaoyang (☎ 010-6502-1733; daily 24 hrs; Jianguomen subway). To sample some of the best spicy Guizhou food available in Beijing, head to any of the five branches of this excellent restaurant. Sour fish soup and tender juicy spare ribs are some of the must-tries and can all be enjoyed 24 hrs a day. ¥¥¥

South

Laoshe Teahouse, 3 Qianmen Xi Dajie (☎ 010-6303-6506; daily 10 am-1 am; Qianmen subway). This is one of Beijing's historical teahouses and offers fine tea served by staff clad in long traditional flowing gowns in an elegant traditional setting. There are performances of Beijing Opera and acrobatics in the afternoon (Mon-Fri 2:30-5:30 pm, Sat & Sun 3-4:30 pm; ¥10-60) and evening (daily 7.40-9.20 pm; ¥40-130; reservations necessary). ¥-¥¥¥¥

Nightlife

There are those who argue that Shanghai's nightlife is where it's at, but anyone who's spent a few nights on the tiles in Beijing recently might have reason to contest this. New bars and whole new bar districts are popping up all over the place and the only way to keep track is by keeping an eye on the ever-changing listings and reviews in *City Weekend* and *that's beijing*.

Beijing's nightlife traditionally revolved around the expat embassy district of **San Litun Lu**, a fact so strongly embedded that if you get in a taxi and say *jiuba lu* (bar street), this is where you'll find yourself. What was just one street expanded to fill the surrounding alleys and has recently been extensively remodeled, but you have to pick and choose to avoid the characterless tourist bars of the main strip. However, these days San Litun Lu is by no means the only nightlife zone found in the city – other worthwhile districts include the nearby **Worker's Stadium**, **Shichahai** where you can drink overlooking the lake, **Nanluoguxiang** nestled in the hutongs, and **Haidian** out in the suburbs.

Where to Drink
North

North of the Forbbiden City & Shichahai

★**Buddha Bar,** 16 Yiding Qiao, Shichahai, Xicheng (daily 2 pm-2 am; Jishuitan subway). As one of the founding bars in the area, Buddha Bar is an institution and offers a welcome break from the pretentiousness of some of Beijing's newer watering holes. Its funky acid-jazz and Latino beats, antique furniture and lakeside setting make this one of the top spots in the area.

★★★**Drum and Bell**, 41 Zhonglouwan Hutong, Dongcheng (daily noon-2 am; Gulou Dajie subway). This quaint bar is a hidden gem in Beijing and is well worth hunting out. The roof terrace is decked out with comfy sofas, and trees provide some welcome shade for daytime summer drinks. It's also a good place to get views over the neighboring Bell and Drum Tower courtyard. Inside, you'll find a network of tastefully designed small rooms and a tranquil environment.

★**Lotus Blue**, Lotus Lane, Ping An Lu (☎ 010-6617-2599; daily 11:30 am-1:30 am; Jishuitan subway). One of a hundred bar-restaurants lining the lakes, Lotus Blue stands out not only for its *Tintin in Tibet*-inspired décor, but also its fine Thai food. In the evenings it is a popular drinking spot and hosts live bands and DJs, but if that's too rowdy for you, the outdoor tables are a great place to watch over the water while Beijing's night crowd promenades past.

★**Pass By Bar**, 114 Nanluoguxiang, Dongcheng (☎ 010-6400-6868; daily 11:30 am-midnight; Andingmen subway). This comfy little nook on backpacker Nanluoguxiang is a great place to hide away for a while, enjoying some tasty Italian food or a drink, and there's also a small bookshop on-site.

★★**No Name Bar**, 3 Qianhai Dongyan (daily noon-2 am; Jishuitan subway). Think bamboo, banana palms and tropical plants, set among rattan furniture, a laid-back atmosphere, lake views and just a hint of modern China – wireless Internet. No Name Bar is a perfect late afternoon spot to sit back and relax.

East

The Workers' Stadium, San Litun & Beyond

★**Bar Blu**, 4F Tongli Studios, San Litun Beilu (Mon-Thu & Sun 4 pm-late & Fri-Sat 11 am-4 am). Bar Blu is a popular drinking haunt and offers a tasteful rooftop terrace, pool table and private booths with a lively party atmosphere.

Goose & Duck, 1 Bihuju Lu, Chaoyang Park West (daily 24 hrs). If you're missing your sports, head to this old expat favorite run by an avid American sports fan. The Goose & Duck offers live sports coverage round the clock and, continuing the (not so athletic) theme, you'll find pool tables, a dart board and some quality pub-grub after all that exercise!

Poachers Inn, 43 Bei Sanlitun Lu, Chaoyang (daily 8 pm-late). Poachers Inn is one of the cheapest bars in town and consequently attracts a young, thrifty and up-for-it crowd. If cheesy dancing, flirting and cheap drinks are your thing, this is the place for you.

The Tree, 43 Sanlitun Beilu (Mon-Sat 11 am-late & Sun 1 pm-late). This old favorite has recently moved and now occupies a new tree, near the Poachers Inn. It's particularly popular as a result of its extensive draft beer collection and also boasts some good Belgian beers. If you need to soak up the booze then try one of their tasty wood-fired pizzas.

World of Suzie Wong, 1A Nongzhanguan Lu, Chaoyang Park (daily 6:30 pm-late). Located by the west gate of Chaoyang Park, Suzie Wong is where old meets new, and east meets west. The decor is part 1930s Shanghai and part post-modern, while the presence of a number of Ming dynasty beds gives it an old opium den feel. It's a lively spot, always bursting at the seams, and was recently voted "best place to find a date," by *that's Beijing* magazine. If the heat of the dance floor gets too much for you, then head upstairs to the outside terrace, which offers great views of Chaoyang Park and a quieter candle-lit vibe.

Jianguomen Dajie & Around

Banana, Scitech Hotel, 22 Jianguomen Wai Dajie, Chaoyang (Mon-Thu 8:30 pm-4:30 am & Fri-Sun 8:30 pm-5 am; Jianguomen subway). A banging club replete with cages and enthusiastic dancers, Banana offers everything you'd expect from a mainstream Chinese nightclub. Upstairs is a little less tacky and houses the Spicy Lounge, a sometime venue for international DJs.

★**Centro**, Kerry Center Hotel, 1 Guanghua Lu, Chaoyang (daily 24 hrs; Guomao subway). Centro's stylish, elegant and comfortable interior is complemented by its nightly live jazz and is a top spot to sip a cocktail.

★★**Stone Boat Bar**, Ritan Park (daily 10 am-late; Jianguomen subway). The quaint Stone Boat Bar is housed in a traditional Chinese pavilion in the southwest corner of leafy Ritan Park. The bar is perched on the edge of the lake and the only distractions are fishermen, kids flying kites and maybe a few locals doing a bit of tai chi. During the day it's a great place for an intimate chat (or surfing the Web Wi-Fi if you have a laptop), while in the evenings it's transformed by jazz music.

Live Music Bars

★★**East Shore Live Jazz Café**, 2F, 2 Qianhai Nanyu Lu, Xicheng (☎ 010-8403-2131; daily 11 am-late). This place may look like nothing special from the outside but, once you step in, you'll enter a world of thick cigar smoke and exquisite live jazz. The wall-to-wall windows and stylish rooftop terrace offer views over Qianhai and the café's atmosphere and classic jazz beats should have you tapping your feet in moments.

★**Hometown Bar,** 30 Huangsi Dajie, Xicheng (☎ 010-6206-4256; daily 9:30 pm-late). If jazz and Beijing rock aren't your thing and you want to expand your musical boundaries, the Hometown's Heijuma trio presents a contemporary take on traditional Mongolian songs.

★**Ice House**, 53 Xi Peilou, Dong'anmen Jie, Dongcheng (☎ 010-6522-1389; daily 5:30 pm-2 am; Wangfujing subway). This building used to be the ice house for the Forbidden City during the Qing dynasty and has since been transformed into one of Beijing's funkiest jazz dens. The central stage plays host to an excellent line-up of local and top international blues and jazz artists.

What? Bar, 72 Beichang Jie, Xicheng (daily 2 pm-late). Near the Forbidden City's west gate, What? hosts local rock bands and the venue's tiny size means that you can't fail to get close to the action.

★★**Yugong Yishan**, 1 Gongti Beilu, Workers' Stadium, Chaoyang (☎ 010-6415-0687; daily 5 pm-late). The small Yugong Yishan is rapidly developing into *the* live music venue in Beijing. Dim lighting and unpretentious decor are combined with quality equipment and a top line-up, which means that it's always buzzing and often full beyond its 300-person capacity.

Chengde

One hundred and forty miles northeast of Beijing in Hebei province, Chengde has a population of 200,000. It's an unassuming town that wouldn't be worth much attention were it not for the beautiful Qing dynasty imperial **Mountain Resort** (Bishu Shanzhuang) and the astounding collection of temples at the foot of the mountains to the north. The palaces, pavilions, pagodas, grasslands, lakes and temples of the retreat make it an ideal weekend escape for Beijingers, and the park's main attractions can get very busy. But fortunately the grounds are large enough to make finding a quiet spot easy and the northwest offers good hiking opportunities.

Bishu Shanzhuang vista

History

Chengde rose to fame when Emperor **Kangxi** (1661-1722) of the **Qing dynasty** (see p. 15) passed through the region and was bewitched by its cool mountain breezes. He ordered the construction of lodges, palaces, pavilions and temples. Chengde enjoyed continued royal patronage under **Yongzheng** (1723-35) and **Qianlong** (1736-95), who added a significant number of the buildings you'll see now.

The rugged landscape and hunting lifestyle appealed to the traditions of the Manchurian Qing rulers, but its northerly temples, built in Lamaist style, were designed to impress and, at the same time, appease the various northern vassal leaders who were entertained here during the summer months. In 1786 the Tibetan **Panchen Lama** came and must have been astounded by the imitation of Lhasa'a Potala Palace, the Putuozongcheng Temple. Seven years later the British sent **Lord Macartney,** bearing gifts provided by the East India Company, to open negotiations for trade, the first of many attempts, which would eventually lead to the Opium Wars (see p. 16). Macartney refused to kowtow and Qianlong refused to trade but the meeting was otherwise amicable enough. The imperial retreat was also popular under Qianlong's successors, but when emperors Jiaqing and then Xianfeng died here, Chengde was deemed inauspicious and went to seed, even avoiding attention during the Cultural Revolution. Since economic reform, tourism has become one of the town's mainstays and the historic buildings are gradually being spruced up, although the town itself could do with a little of the same.

Getting Here & Away

By Rail

 Chengde is served by several trains daily from Beijing Station, which take between four and five hours to reach the station on the east bank of the river in the south of town – the N211 leaves at 7:16 am. For the round-trip journey, buying tickets at the train station isn't too traumatic, but most hotels in town can book them for you for a small fee. It's difficult, nigh on impossible, to get soft class tickets, but paying a little more for one of the faster trains should put you in carriages that aren't as busy. To get into town, take bus #5 or a taxi, although it can be hard to get drivers to use the meter – the ride should cost ¥5.

By Road

 Buses from Beijing's Deshengmen depot take four or five hours to reach the Long Distance Bus Station at the southern end of Wulie Lu in Chengde, from where you can take a taxi or walk into town.

Getting Around

The town of Chengde is small enough to navigate on foot, but the usual array of transport options are on hand to get out to the temples or if you get tired.

By Bus

 Chengde is fairly small and taxis are cheap enough (if they use the meter) so buses shouldn't be necessary around town, although they can be useful for getting out to the temples. Bus #6 runs from Bishu Shanzhuang to Puning Temple and #188 heads to the eastern temples.

By Taxi

Chengde's taxi drivers have seen too many tourists and can be a little unscrupulous, often refusing to take foreigners for less than ¥10. Flagfall is ¥5 and ¥1.4 per kilometer (0.6 miles) beyond this. Most journeys around town should cost ¥5, or ¥10 to one of the northern temples. If the driver refuses to use the meter then hail another taxi.

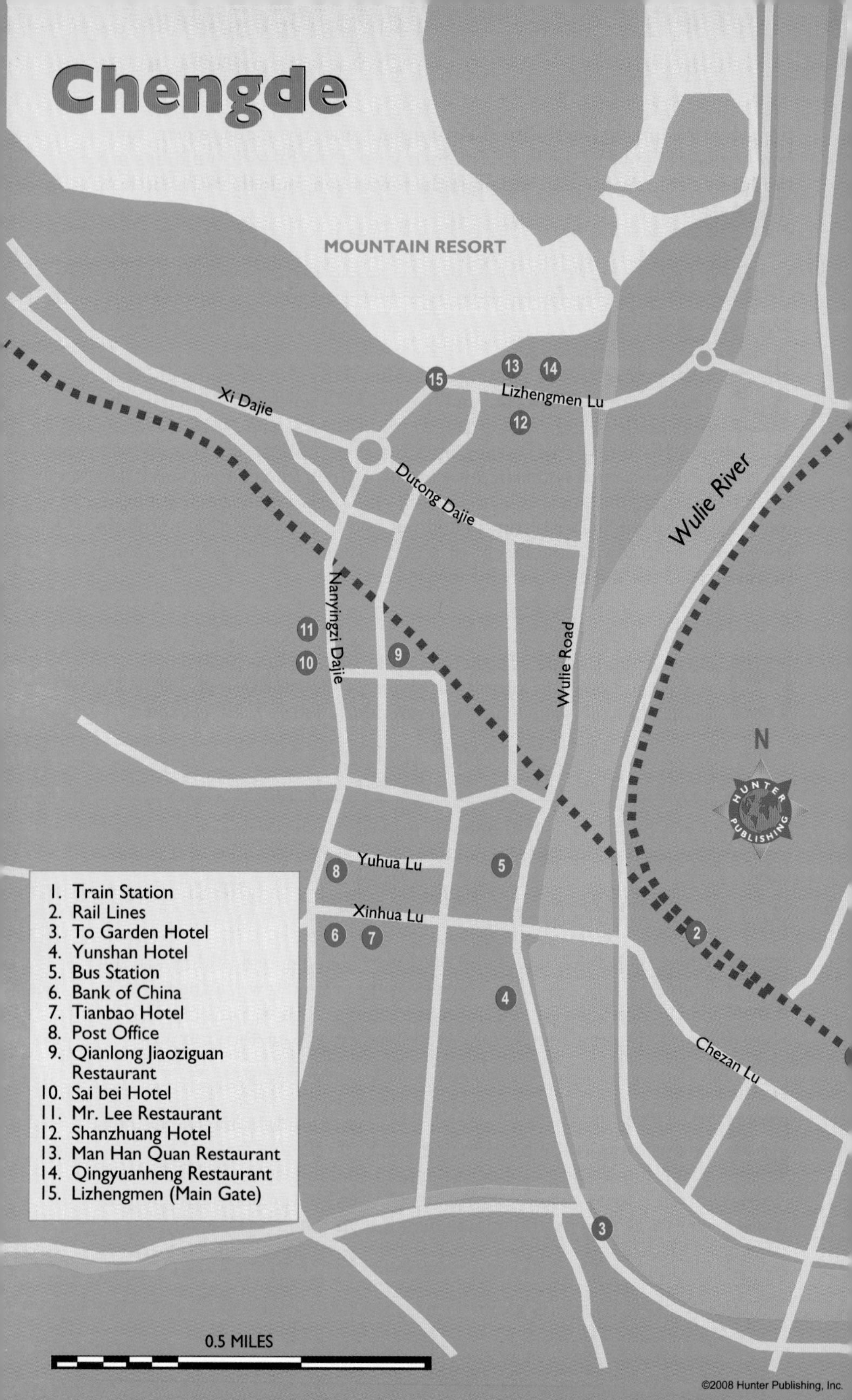

Chengde

MOUNTAIN RESORT

Xi Dajie

(15) (13) (14) Lizhengmen Lu

(12)

Dutong Dajie

Wulie River

Nanyingzi Dajie

(11)

(10) (9)

Wulie Road

N

Yuhua Lu (8) (5)

Xinhua Lu

(6) (7)

(4)

Chezan Lu

(2)

1. Train Station
2. Rail Lines
3. To Garden Hotel
4. Yunshan Hotel
5. Bus Station
6. Bank of China
7. Tianbao Hotel
8. Post Office
9. Qianlong Jiaoziguan Restaurant
10. Sai bei Hotel
11. Mr. Lee Restaurant
12. Shanzhuang Hotel
13. Man Han Quan Restaurant
14. Qingyuanheng Restaurant
15. Lizhengmen (Main Gate)

(3)

0.5 MILES

By Bicycle

Bicycle isn't a bad way to get up to the eastern and northern temples, although the main roads are far from tranquil. Ask at your hotel for bike hire.

Orientation

Chengde is, by Chinese standards, a small town and is easy to find your way around. In spite of the number of tourists who make their way here, the town remains sleepy and subdued. Its setting on the west bank of the **Wulie River** surrounded by hills and rocky outcrops is attractive, even though the town itself lacks charm. The train station is on the east bank of the river in the south of town and the long-distance bus station is over the river a little north of here on Wulie Lu, which runs a mile along the river to the entrance of Bishu Shanzhuang. The bulk of tourist amenities and services can be found a little south of the park entrance at the junction of Lizhengmen Lu, Xi and Dutong Dajie and Nanyingzi Dajie. Running south from this junction, **Nanyingzi Dajie** is the city's main shopping street and the northern end has a few stalls and street-bars in the evening. **Bishu Shanzhuang** is encircled by a six-mile wall and is almost as large as the town itself and stretches north for a couple of miles from the main entrance on Lizhengmen Lu to the temples at the foothills of the mountains. To the east, there are more temples and, farther out, the appropriately named monolith of **Sledgehammer Rock**.

Communications

Telephone code: 0314

Post Office: On the corner of Nanyingzi Dajie and Yuhua Lu.

Internet Access: Just off Dutong Dajie, two streets east of its junction with Nanyingzi Dajie.

Bank of China: Nanyingzi Dajie at the junction with Xinhua Lu and there are plenty of others (with ATMs) dotted around town, including one directly opposite the park entrance on Lizhengmen Lu.

Public Security Bureau: Opposite the river on Wulie Lu (☎ 0314-2073-775).

Medical Services: There's a hospital opposite the main post office on Nanyingzi Dajie.

Sightseeing

The reason to come to Chengde is the well-preserved imperial retreat of Bishu Shanzhuang and the collection of Lamaist-inspired temples to its north. The sights are pleasantly spread out through the park and this makes it an ideal place for some hiking (see

Adventures On Foot, p. 230) and the park is big enough that if you head out to some of its lesser sights you should find some solitude, even in the height of the peak summer season. The temples to the north and east can be reached from Bishu Shanzhuang, but there's plenty to see and you're better off dividing your sightseeing into two days – one day hiking at the retreat and another cycling or taking buses (or taxis) between the temples and the outlying and magnificently eroded Sledgehammer Rock. If you're short on time, you could take a day-tour from the train station (or your hotel), which covers the main sights, although, as usual, these are rushed and leave little time for the exploration that Chengde is all about.

An Imperial Weekend Retreat

Get the early train from Beijing and check straight into your hotel. Have some lunch and then rent a bike or take a bus or taxi out to northern **Puning Temple**. Take in eastern **Pule Temple** on the way back and then hike (or take the cable car) up to **Sledgehammer Rock** for some sunset views. Return to town and enjoy some dinner at one of Chengde's imperial restaurants. The following day, rise early and pick up some supplies for a picnic lunch in **Bishu Shanzhuang**. Visit the palaces and then proceed along the lakes and beyond to Yongyou Pagoda. Take a break from "sightseeing" and stroll to the quiet northwestern quadrant of the park, where you could enjoy your lunch on the wall by Xibeimen with views over to Putuozongcheng Temple (see *Adventures On Foot*, p. 230). Return in time for the last train (or bus to Beijing) or, if you're too tired, leave tomorrow.

★★★Bishu Shanzhuang

Some History

(Open daily 7 am-6 pm; ¥90 or ¥60 Oct 16 and April 14). Bishu Shanzhuang was designed by Emperor Kangxi (see p. 15) as a cooler summer retreat from Beijing, where he could indulge in the Manchu pastimes of horsemanship and hunting. He discovered the area accidentally while out hunting, and the majority of what remains today is the result of his passion for the landscape and scenery. Its design was inspired by the simplicity of Manchurian villages and he was heavily influenced by his imperial travels. The end result was the creation of a harmonious balance between water, landscape and architecture and a peaceful retreat from Beijing court life. Kangxi's grandson, Qianlong, also loved the resort, favoring it over his other palaces and added another 36 imperial buildings to the already vast collection. However, after Emperor Jiaqing was struck dead by lightning here in 1820, the area was considered inauspicious and fell into disrepair. The last emperor to have taken up residence at the Mountain Resort was Emperor Xianfeng, who fled here during the Second Opium War in 1860. The site was completely neglected after this, but at least managed to avoid the ravages of the Cultural Revolution. In the 1980s restoration began and in 1994 the Mountain Resort was assigned UNESCO World Heritage Status.

Lake pavilion, Bishu Shanzhuang

Visiting the Sights

On entering the retreat you'll immediately enter the palaces and, while these are certainly worth a browse, they tend to be the busiest part of the whole park. You may find yourself quickly moving on to the lakes and wilds beyond. You can visit the main sights on one of the ubiquitous golf buggies (¥40 for the complete circuit), which shuttle visitors through the park from Ruyi Island, as well as using boats (daily 7 am-6 pm) to negotiate its southern lakes – there are rowing boats (¥10 per hour, plus ¥100 deposit), paddle boats (¥20 per hour, plus ¥200 deposit) and electric boats (¥30 per hour, plus ¥200 deposit). However the greatest pleasure in Bishu Shanzhuang is walking through its tranquil northwestern corner, a wooded wonderland of quiet trails and minor sights that see few visitors. Here bees, butterflies, deer, dragonflies and squirrels will keep you company, rather than the cacophony of megaphones found back at the palaces. Although not recommended by the park staff, it is possible to walk short stretches of (or all the way around) Bishu Shanzhuang's six-mile Qing dynasty walls, from where you'll enjoy fine views. The northwestern section is stunning (see *Adventures On Foot*, p. 230).

The Palaces

The palaces are impressively subdued and fit in well with the verdant backdrops, but can get overrun with tour groups. Still, these groups tend to come and go quite quickly and, if you bide your time, you'll find moments of solitude. The *nanmu* wood palace buildings are attractively set around a series of alternately grassy and paved courtyards linked by covered lattice-lined corridors. Inside the buildings you'll find some interesting historic displays which are labeled in English and include furniture and ornaments from the Qing and models of the great emperors, resplendent in imperial yellow dress.

The Lakes

As you strike out north of the palaces you'll soon reach the lake complex of bridges, islands, pavilions and walkways, which makes for a lovely wander. Many of the buildings dispersed throughout the lake are exact copies of monuments from around southern China. The central island was a private retreat for both Kangxi and Qianlong. To the east you'll find **Ruyi Island** which

Shuixinxie, Bishu Shanzhuang

was used by Emperor Kangxi for affairs of state while his palace was still under construction. Although it's not possible to go inside the impressive imperial library, **Wenjinge**, it's worth a walk just to see it from the outside.

The library is enclosed by rockeries and pools in order to make a fire barrier. The central chamber has no windows to protect the books from the damaging rays of the sun. Today it houses a number of important books, including the *Four Treasures* (a 36,000-volume Tang dynasty encyclopedia!) There's also plenty of wildlife around here, including Bambi-cute deer and maybe the odd electric blue of a kingfisher darting by.

North of the Lakes

To get away from the crowds, head north to the towering **Yongyou Pagoda** (closed for restoration at the time of writing) and you'll see a vast swathe of flat grassland off to the west. There are usually some deer

Deer at Bishu Shanzhuang

enjoying a graze around here and you'll also

see an improbable fleet of mock yurts (traditional Mongolian tent-houses) where you can stay if you have the urge (see *Where to Stay*, p. 230). North and west of here the park stretches over low hills to the limits of its extent, denoted by the encircling wall. This area comprises quiet retreats, rocky gorges and occasional expansive views, all dotted with pagodas, pavilions and wildlife – see *Adventures On Foot*, p. 230 for walks.

The Northern Temples

(Open daily 8:30 am-5 pm; ticket prices between ¥30 and ¥50). As time progressed the Mountain Resort's northern setting was used as place to entertain leaders of vassal states such as Mongolia and Tibet. In order to appease and impress these visitors a series of nine Lamaist-style temples were built to the north of the parkland at the foothills of the mountains. In spite of the Mongolian and Tibetan Lamaist influence, the temples also pay allegiance to Chinese temple style and offer an eclectic mix of architecture. Of the nine temples, five remain today, the most striking of which is the grand Putuozongcheng Temple, designed to resemble Lhasa's Potala Palace, while Puning Temple is worth visiting for its wooden statue of Guanyin – the largest in existence.

Putuozongcheng Temple from the wall at Bishu Shanzhuang

★★**Putuozongcheng Temple** (daily 8 am-6 pm; ¥40). The vast block of the Putuozongcheng Temple dominates the area north of Bishu Shanzhuang. This is the area's largest and most impressive temple complex, built between 1767 and 1771 to celebrate Emperor Qianlong's 60th birthday. Heads of states from all over the vast empire were invited to cele-

Preceding page: Yongyou Pagoda

brate at Chengde. The Putuozongcheng was based on the Potala Palace in Lhasa, and is a striking monument, although closer inspection reveals it to be nothing more than a mock-up of the Tibetan original. It is most spectacular from afar.

★★**Puning Temple** (daily 8:30 am-4:30 pm; ¥50). This temple was built in 1755 to commemorate victory over invading northeast tribes and is the most typically Tibetan temple here. It's also the only one where you'll see practicing devotees. Of the temple's various levels of stupas, towers and halls, the highlight is without a doubt the 75-foot-tall, 43-armed wooden **carving of Guanyin**, the Goddess of Mercy. To find the statue, walk to the Mahayana Hall at the rear of the compound. You'll need to pay an extra ¥10 if you want to ascend to the upper viewing tower.

The Eastern Temples

Of the three eastern temples, ★**Pule** (daily 8 am-6 pm; ¥30) is the one to visit. Pule (Temple of Universal Happiness) dates from 1766 and combines aspects of Han and Tibetan temple architecture, the latter of which is far more eye-catching. The hodgepodge of styles incorporates everything from staid Han edifices at the front of the temple to tantric sex *mandalas* and a conical main hall and vivid ceiling designs distinctly reminiscent of Beijing's Temple of Heaven! From Pule you can hike, or take the cable car up to Sledgehammer Rock (see below). North of Pule, **Anyuan** enjoys an attractive setting on the river bank but is otherwise unremarkable, while the closest of the eastern temples to town, **Puren**, is closed to visitors.

Other Sights

★**Sledgehammer Rock** (¥20). East of town, Sledgehammer Rock's bizarrely eroded shape is another tourist draw and has a cable car (¥45 round-trip) if you don't want to make the short, steep ascent from Pule Temple (see above). Once at the top, the true scale of the 65-foot tower becomes apparent. There are tacky stalls around its base selling models of the rock, which resembles a chicken drumstick more than a sledgehammer, but is impressive nonetheless.

Shopping

Chengde has little in the way of recommended shopping, but is famous for its mountain herbs and mushrooms which can be bought from the shops opposite Bishu Shanzhuang's entrance on Lizhengmen Lu. To stock up for a picnic in the park there are a couple of **supermarkets** at the eastern end of Xi Dajie and there's a good bakery next to the Sai Bei Hotel.

Adventures

On Foot

Bishu Shanzhuang was made to be explored on foot and has an extensive network of main trails and smaller footpaths, as well as the wall which surrounds the park, which can be walked. Any stroll through the park is worthwhile, but to fully appreciate its extent and the solitary retreat for which it was intended, a hike in the northwestern quadrant is recommended. Another short trail worth hiking runs from Pule Temple up to Sledgehammer Rock and, if you want to extend your walk, from here the path leads another mile or so on to Frog Rock.

★★★ The Best of Bishu Shanzhuang (around 3 hours walking)

Enter Bishu Shanzhuang through Lizhengmen and take your time looking around the palace complexes before exiting to the east toward Shuixinxie. Cross the triple-pavilioned causeway and proceed northward across the center of Ruyi Island. At the end of the lake continue north through the parkland to the Yongyou Pagoda. From here bear southwest and you'll be able to see the pavilion of Nanshanjie Xue perched atop a hill. Proceed west along the foot of the hill and you'll reach a path leading north, which follows a small stream north through pretty, gladed woodland and you'll probably chance across some deer and birdlife. Less than half an hour later you'll find yourself at Xibeimen where you can ascend the wall for spectacular views of Putuozongcheng Temple.

From Xibeimen, a path runs east, parallel and below the wall, before bearing south via the hilltop pavilion of Nanshanjie Xue, which affords fine views. From here`, continue south to Wenjinge and then along the western edge of the lake back to the temple complexes and exit.

> **Diversion:** If you can cope with the steep ups and downs, you could continue clockwise from here along the wall as far as Wanshuyuan, a venture that takes in breathtaking views of both the northern temples and the park to the south. At Wanshuyuan you can descend the wall, continue south and then skirt the western edge of the lake to the main entrances.

Where to Stay

See page 113 for an explanation of the ¥ hotel price codes.

Chengde's places to stay are generally disappointing. At the budget end of the scale, hoteliers will try and take you for every cent you have, so be prepared to bargain hard. There are a clutch of places a little north of the train station, but these are generally overpriced and run-down. It's worth heading farther into town for more choice at all budgets.

@=in-room Internet access

Garden, 1 Banbishan Lu (☎ 0314-2259-999). If you don't mind staying a little out of town, the Garden offers some of the cheapest tolerable rooms in Chengde. The hotel has a quiet location (except for the occasional train) and rooms are clean and acceptable, although the bathrooms are a little dingy. ¥¥

Mongolian Yurts (☎ 0314-2163-580). This is the only place to stay in the grounds of Bishu Shanzhuang and certainly offers a different experience. All rooms are in the style of traditional Mongolian tents (known as yurts or gers), and offer a fun alternative to staying in a standard Chinese hotel. The yurts are all twins and comfortable enough, if a little run-down. To complete the theme, there are nightly bonfires where you can relive the wild steppe life before retreating to your air-conditioned yurt. ¥¥

★**Sai Bei**, 12 Nanyingzi Dajie (☎ 0314-2137-488). The best cheap option in the center of town, the Sai Bei has a pleasantly renovated third floor with small but comfortable twins and doubles which, unusually for this price bracket, have satellite TV. Try to get a room facing the rear as they are brighter and quieter or, if you're on a tighter budget, ask to see the older but perfectly functional rooms on the fourth floor (avoid the fifth as the KTV Bar is on the sixth). ¥¥

★★**Shanzhuang**, 11 Lizhengmen (☎ 0314-2091-188, www.hemvhotel. com). The city's best offering, the Shanzhuang has comfortable and modern, if slightly small, doubles and older twins. The hotel is well-located directly opposite the park entrance and bustles with tour groups. @ ¥¥¥

Tianbao, Xinhua Lu (☎ 0314-2090-888). This new 15-story addition to Chengde's upmarket hotels has spacious, well-equipped rooms, some of which have reasonable views, although service can be a little slow. @ ¥¥¥

★**Yunshan**, 2 Banbishan Lu (☎ 0314-2055-588). The aging Yunshan doesn't quite live up to its four-star status, but is one of the better places to stay in Chengde and there's a pleasant teahouse in the hotel. Its location is a little far from Bishu Shanzhuang, but only a 15-minute walk from the train station. @ ¥¥¥

Where to Eat

 Chengde's eating options are limited, but fun and center on the region's game produce, including venison (*lurou*) and pheasant (*shanji*), cooked in the imperial style, which you'll find at the tourist restaurants near the park entrance. The region also produces chestnuts and mountain mushrooms, which are used in the cooking, but are also for sale in shops. You'll find barbecued corn on the cob for sale across the city. The town's Western eating options are limited to a KFC at the southern end of Nanyingzi Dajie.

★★**Man Han Quan Xi**, outside Bishu Shanzhuang entrance, behind the two fountains (daily 9 am-2 pm & 4:30-9 pm). This gaudily decorated Qing-style restaurant offers the local delicacies served up by an army of waitstaff, all decked out in Manchu regalia. Beggar's pheasant and deer clay pots are specialties. ¥¥¥-¥¥¥¥

Mr. Lee, Nanyingzi Dajie, next to Sai Bei Hotel (daily 7 am-11 pm). Part of a nationwide chain, Mr. Lee is easy to identify by its sign, which shows the man himself in white, looking decidedly like a Chinese version of Colonel Sanders, on a red background. Tasty, filling and inexpensive beef noodles (*niurou mian*) are the pick here. ¥

Qianlong Jiaoziguan, Center Square, Nanyingzi Lu (daily 10 am-9 pm). This place serves the best dumplings in town in a clean and bright environment. ¥¥

★**Qingyuanheng**, outside Bishu Shanzhuang entrance, behind the large black cauldron (daily 9 am-2 pm & 4:30-9 pm). A little less glitzy than its neighbor, this restaurant offers equally good specialty dishes at slightly lower prices in an open-plan Qing-style wooden dining hall, or in private rooms above. ¥¥¥

See page 117 for an explanation of the ¥ restaurant price codes.

Nightlife

Chengde's nightlife scene is limited to an army of KTV bars and a few tables and chairs set up at the northern end of **Nanyingzi Lu**, but it can get pretty raucous.

Xi'an

Xi'an (Western Peace), population three million, has served as China's capital many times and at its peak it was described as the most prosperous city on the planet. These days, although the city is polluted, hot as an oven in summer and cold as a freezer in winter, it manages to remain one of China's most attractive and charismatic destinations, gracefully blending its historic architecture with newer developments. Although there's plenty to see within the city and the surrounding region, the main reason visitors flock to Xi'an is to stare out over the unforgettable

Terracotta Warriors which were discovered in 1974 in the district of Lintong, 20 miles outside of the city.

While the warriors deservedly attract the limelight, the city itself is certainly worth a visit in its own right and within its stunning early **Ming dynasty walls** you'll find intact **bell and drum towers**, an **ancient mosque** and a fascinating **Muslim quarter**. Beyond the walls lies another host of sights, including impressive pagodas, one of the best museums in the country, the **Shaanxi History Museum** and, just a few miles to the east, **Banpo** is one of the best pre-served examples of Yangshao Culture (see p. 5) in China. Farther to the east, **Huashan** is one of China's five holy mountains – feasible as a day trip. Xi'an is in Shaanxi

New mirrors old in Xi'an

province, which is famous as one of the regions where **pandas** still survive in the wild, and you can arrange trips to a panda reserve in the **Qingling Mountains** at Zhouzhi, two hours away. Culinary travelers will also find a feast awaits in Xi'an – the city is famous for its dumplings and there are plenty of opportunities to sample (and even make) them, while the Muslim quarter has outdoor treats aplenty.

History

Ancient Capital

Xi'an's strategic location between the loess plateau to the north and east, and the Qingling mountains to the south have seen the city and its environs serve as China's capital for 11 dynasties, starting with the Western Zhou dynasty (1122 to 771 BC, see p. 6), over 3,000 years ago. A few hundred years later, the founder of the Qin dynasty (221-206 BC, see p. 6), **Qin Shi Huang**, chose Xianyang, a little north of the modern city, as the capital of his short-lived empire, and was buried 20 miles east of the city at Lintong, guarded by his secret, but now infamous Terracotta Warriors. The succeeding **Han** (206 BC-220 AD, see p. 8) built a new capital not far from Xianyang, which they named Chang'an (Eternal Peace). The Han were one of China's most successful dynasties and under its emperors Chang'an prospered from its position at the start of the **Silk Road** across Central Asia.

When the Han fell, Chang'an was ransacked and China fell into turmoil for the next 400 years. But Xi'an remained the favorite imperial residence and the brief Sui dynasty (581-618 AD) based itself here, as did the successive and more successful **Tang dynasty** (618-907 AD), which really breathed life into the city. Under the Tang, Chang'an is said to have been **the most populous and prosperous city in the world** and the arts and religion thrived in the city. The Tang was a tolerant dynasty and, with the influx of influences coming along the Silk Road, Buddhism flourished while both Nestorianism and Islam gained a foothold and the Great Mosque (see p. 242) was built. The tremendous wealth of the city also allowed for developments in the arts, notably the tri-color pottery still produced in the region today.

After the Tang

After the Tang, things went downhill for Xi'an and it never fully regained its former imperial splendor, although the city walls, bell and drum towers that you can see today were built during the Ming dynasty (1368-1644). The city continued its decline, with occasional moments in the spotlight, such as the Empress Dowager Cixi's forced relocation here and the kidnapping of Chiang Kaishek by his own forces at nearby Huaqing Pool (see p. 245) in order to coerce an alliance with the Communists in what became known as the **Xi'an Incident** (see *Japanese Encroachment and Civil War*, p. 20).

In 1974 Xi'an received an unexpected blessing – the discovery of Qin Shi Huang's Terracotta Warriors 20 miles east of the city, near Lintong. The subsequent opening up of China to tourism has resulted in a new heyday for the city as one of China's premier tourist destinations. The combination of this new-found popularity and the city's industrial background has made Xi'an a wealthy city and today the streets are lined with shoppers busy flexing their financial muscle. However, this prosperity has led to an influx of rural migrants seeking work day-by-day, or begging on the streets, and industry has contributed to severe pollution. In spite of these problems, Xi'an remains an attractive and engaging city and its cosmopolitan blend of old and new continues to attract domestic and foreign tourists, while its manageable size and comparatively low cost of living have also made the city a popular place to study Chinese.

Getting Here & Away

By Air

Xi'an's airport is some 30 miles from the city and it takes a good hour's bus journey to get there. Airport buses leave from the Melody Hotel by the Bell Tower and the Jiefang Hotel by the train station. They cost ¥25. A taxi should cost around ¥150 to or from the airport. You can book air tickets through your hotel, hostel or the **CAAC**, west of the city wall on Laodang Nan Lu (☎ 029-8879-0042).

Destinations, frequencies & durations

Beijing (18 daily; 1 hr 40 mins), **Chongqing** (5 daily; 1 hr 10 mins), **Guangzhou** (8 daily; 2 hrs 45 mins), **Guilin** (6 daily; 2 hrs), **Hangzhou** (5 daily; 1 hr 50 mins), **Hong Kong** (2 daily; 3 hrs), **Shanghai** (17 daily; 2 hrs), **Shenzhen** (6 daily; 2 hrs), **Yichang** (1 daily; 1 hr 10 mins).

By Rail

Xi'an is near a major rail branch divide, with one line heading east to Luoyang and Shanghai and another running north to Beijing. It's a popular stop and thus it's worth buying a ticket as soon as you arrive in order to get the train you want a few days later. The train station is conveniently located just outside of the northern city wall, but the roads on the way out here can get seriously gridlocked – some taxi drivers will drop you just inside the gate to save getting snarled up, which is fine if you don't have too much luggage! The ticket office is at the eastern end of the station and, although the lines appear long, they move fairly quickly, but hostels and some hotels can also book train tickets. To get into town, take a taxi, or bus #603 runs down Jiefang Lu, west to the Bell Tower and then south to Nanmen (South Gate).

Xi'an

Xi'an Region

- Tonguan
- Dali
- Pucheng
- Yaozhouqi
- Tongchuan
- Sanyuan
- Jingyang
- Yanliangqu
- Lintong
- Xi'an
- Luonan
- Danfeng
- Shanyang
- Jhangluo
- Lantian
- Zhen
- Ankang
- Shiqan
- Zhenba
- Xixiang
- Foping
- Zhouzhi
- Maixian
- Pingdu
- Liuba
- Hanzhong
- Baoji
- Fengxian

Roads: 108, 310, 311, 312, 210, 316, 211

1. Huaqing Pool
2. Mount Huashan
3. Qin Shi Huang's Tomb
4. Terracotta Warriors
5. Zhouzhi Panda Rehabilitation Center

Railroad

N

HUNTER PUBLISHING

40 MILES

Destinations, frequencies & durations

Beijing (5 daily; 12-15 hrs), **Chongqing** (1 daily; 14 hrs 30 mins), **Guangzhou** (1 daily; 26 hrs 20 mins), **Guilin** (1 daily; 28 hrs), **Hangzhou** (2 daily; 24 hrs), **Shanghai** (1 daily; 16 hrs 30 mins), **Suzhou** (1 daily; 15 hrs 30 mins), **Yichang** (1 daily; 15 hrs 45 mins).

By Road

Destinations within a few hours of Xi'an are feasible by bus, but anything longer is far more comfortable by plane or train. Buses run from Dongguangchang Station, just south of the train station to Banpo, Huashan and Lintong.

Getting Around

The main sights within the walled city are close enough to one another so walking is an easy way to get around, but if your legs are tired or you want to head outside of the walls, taxis are cheap. Roads can be gridlocked at rush-hour within the city walls, however.

By Bus

Since taxis are cheap, there is little point in taking public buses, which are invariably crowded, but a few useful numbers are included where appropriate, notably sightseeing buses that allow you the freedom to jump on and off throughout the day – route #5 heads to most of the major sights.

By Taxi

Xi'an's army of green taxis seems to overrun the streets and (except in rain or snow) it's fairly easy to hail one. At ¥6 minimum for the first two km (1.2 miles) and ¥1.4 per km (0.6 miles) after this, Xi'an's taxis are some of the cheapest in the country and it's worth making use of them.

By Bicycle

Bicycle is a great way to get around Xi'an's backstreets and along the city walls. Some hotels and all the hostels (¥20 per day) have bikes for rent, and they are also available at the South Gate for rides around the wall. Wherever you rent, you'll need to put down a ¥100-200 deposit. For routes see *Adventures On Wheels*, p. 255.

Xi'an

Orientation

Xi'an's **ancient city walls** encircle the old city which makes it easy to navigate. Many of the main sights are within the city walls and this central zone is bisected by four major roads. They run along the points of the compass to their respective gates in the wall and are named Bei, Dong, Nan and Xi Dajie (North, East, South and West Avenues). These roads meet just south of the center at the **Bell Tower**. To cross this busy intersection you need to use the subterranean tunnel, which has access points from each of the four roads. A little west of the Bell Tower, across a large public plaza, you'll see the **Drum Tower**, marking the entrance to the atmospheric **Muslim quarter**. With its tangle of alleys, this is one of the only parts of the city you're likely to get lost in, but it's great fun. Sooner or later you'll emerge somewhere you recognize, or where you can flag a cab.

Within the Muslim quarter, the **Great Mosque** is the main sight, and it's easy to find – there are signs, but you can just follow the souvenir stalls. In the southeast of the old city there is an artist's quarter, which is definitely worth a stroll. You'll also find the **Beilin Stone Tablet Museum** here.

Outside the city walls the sights are a little more spread out. Not too far south of the South Gate you'll find the **Little Wild Goose Pagoda** and, farther south still, the **Shaanxi History Museum** and, to the east, the **Big Wild Goose Pagoda**. Although there are a few hotels out this way, you're much better off staying within the city walls, which has options for most budgets. Likewise, the best eating and drinking are within the old city, particularly the lively **Muslim markets** and **Defuxiang Bar Street**.

LEARNING THE LINGO

Starting on page 598, there's a section with useful phrases written in both Romanized Chinese (pinyin) which will enable you to try and pronounce them, and Chinese characters, should verbal communication fail! The major attractions, hotels and restaurants are also shown in Chinese characters. This will allow you to get into a taxi, point at the relevant characters and get to your destination. Chinese vocabulary specific to **Xi'an** begins on page 611.

Information Sources

There is a visitor center (☎ 029-8552-0555) on the eastern side of the Big Wild Goose Pagoda, but the best source of information in Xi'an tends to be the hostels, which are used to foreigners wanting to do things their own way. Larger hotels might be able to provide good information, but they're of more use for booking tickets and tours than anything else. For online resources, www.toureasy.net/expat has information on hotels, restaurants, shopping, sightseeing and travel. You can buy **maps** marked in English outside the train station and from vendors in the central plaza. The best map is *Xi'an Traffic and Tourist Map*.

Communications

Telephone code: 029
Post Office: On the northeast corner of the Bell Tower intersection.
Internet Access: Most of the hostels have net cafés (around ¥8 per hour), but there are also plenty of places along Dong Dajie, including Hong Shu Lin at #424.
Bank of China: Halfway down Nan Dajie street on the eastern side and another branch with 24-hour ATMs at the eastern end of Dong Dajie on the north side of the street.
Public Security Bureau: 123, Xi Dajie (☎ 029-8727-6241). Extending your visa usually takes two-three days.
Medical Services: Xi'an Number Four Hospital (☎ 029-8403-5110) on Jiefang Lu.

Sightseeing

Xi'an is overflowing with sights, from the big drawcards like the Terracotta Warriors and the History Museum to the more abstract pleasures of a wander through the Muslim markets. Many lie within the old city walls, which are an attraction in themselves, but if you have enough time there are sights outside the walls, and still more outside the city, from ancient temples, to pandas and holy mountains.

Within the city it's easy enough to walk, cycle or take taxis between the sights, but to get out to the outlying attractions you might want to take a tourist bus or join a tour. They are run by all hotels, with cheaper (and sometimes more adventurous) options run by the hostels.

THE BEST OF XI'AN

Arrive in Xi'an, check into your hotel and take a taxi down to the **Shaanxi History Museum**, which will give you an overview of Xi'an's immense history. Continue to the **Big Wild Goose Pagoda** and then take a taxi back to the south gate of the Ming dynasty city walls. Wander through the artists' quarter of **Shuyuanmen** (and maybe visit the **Beilin Stone Tablets Museum**), before ascending for a sunset **walk or bike ride around the city walls** (see *Adventures On Foot* or *On Wheels*, p. 255), which will give you a feel for the city's layout. Return to the center, freshen up and head to Defachang (see p. 258) for a **dumpling banquet** fit for an emperor.

The next morning rise early and beat the crowds to the **Terracotta Warriors**. Spend time taking in their lifelike splendor. Return to the city for a stroll to the **Drum Tower**, then through the **Muslim quarter** to the intricately designed **Great Mosque**. After your visit, do some souvenir shopping, then take a dinner of lamb skewers in the atmospheric Muslim markets. Round your trip off with a stroll through the lively central square, surrounded by the Bell and Drum Towers.

Historic Highlights

★**The Bell Tower** (daily 8:30 am-9:30 pm, 8 am-6 pm Nov 1 to Mar 31; ¥20, or ¥30 for a combination Bell and Drum Tower ticket; tourist bus #5). Drum and bell towers around the country were used to mark out the time in days of old, but Xi'an's are the most prominent of any large city and the Bell Tower dominates downtown, stranded in the middle of a large traffic circle. The original tower was located west of its current location in the old city center, but the triple-eaved, 200-foot, two-story tower you see today was built in 1582 under the Ming dynasty and restored in 1792. Inside the tower you'll see intricate roof truss work, chime displays and, as you'd expect, a large bronze bell, although this is not the original. The balcony, which runs around the edge of the tower, offers views over the traffic across to the Drum Tower. To get to the Bell Tower you'll need to take the subterranean passageway that runs under Bei Dajie.

★**The Drum Tower** (daily 8:30 am-9:30 pm, 8:30 am-6 pm Nov 1 to Mar 31; ¥20, or ¥30 for a combination Bell and Drum Tower ticket; tourist bus #5). The Drum Tower was built at the same time as the original Bell Tower and has remained in place ever since. The enormous drum was used to mark time, and in times of war, to warn citizens of impending attack. Both the Bell and Drum Towers are illu-

The Drum Tower

minated at night, and the Drum Tower offers attractive evening views over the plaza below and on to the Bell Tower. The tunnel through the center of the tower's base leads to the Muslim quarter. There are daily drum beatings at 9, 10 and 11 am and 2, 4 and 6 pm.

★★★**The City Walls** (daily 7 am-10:30 pm, 8 am-6 pm Nov 1 to Mar 31; ¥40). A wander or a bike ride along Xi'an's 40-foot-high city walls offers great vistas and, given that the walls are completely flat, it's a much easier venture than many of the other walls you might ascend in China! From the 500-year-old walls you can see the thronging new city, yet remain comfortably and quietly removed from it all. You can access the wall from any of the four major gates and can then walk, cycle or take an electric buggy (¥50 for the complete circuit of one hour and 10 mins or ¥5 for any one of the 15 sections). You can see as much or as little of its nine-mile circumference as you want. Guides are available at ¥30 for half the wall, or ¥50 for the whole thing, but there's little for them to point out beyond a basic introduction.

There are watchtowers on each of the four corners and major gates in the north, south, east and west – the East Gate is worth stopping off at to see the replicas of ancient military contraptions, including a giant catapult. See *Adventures On Foot* and *On Wheels*, p. 255, for the best parts to tackle.

The Ming city walls

Museums

★★**Beilin Stone Tablets Museum** (daily 8 am-6 pm; ¥45). While the stelae (stone tablets) are unintelligible to non-Chinese speakers, they are fascinating nonetheless, and the museum's setting, in a former Confucian Temple, is wonderfully tranquil. There are over 1,000 stelae spread through several courtyards and halls and you can have rubbings made of some of them. The tablets commemorate everything from the Five Confucian Virtues (see *Confucianism*, p. 48) to historic events such as the arrival of a Nestorian priest in the eighth century, identifiable by the cross at its top, and some are supported by the tortoise-like creature, Bixi, renowned for his enduring strength. There's also a collection of small stone posts topped with carvings, which were used to tether animals, but were also symbolic of status. When you've seen enough stelae, the pavilions and contorted trees of the courtyards make for a pleasant place to just sit and contemplate.

★★★**Shaanxi History Museum** (daily 9 am-6 pm; ¥50; buses #610 or tourist bus #5). A mile northwest of the Big Wild Goose Pagoda, the History Museum is one of the best in the country and its pavilion-style enclosure houses over 100,000 relics unearthed in Shaanxi. The museum is divided into three key sections – the permanent exhibition halls, an eastern sector that displays temporary exhibits from China and overseas and a themed section containing local Shaanxi cultural relics.

Xi'an

Posts for tethering animals at Beilin Stone Tablets Museum

On the lower floor, the **Zhou and Shang dynasty bronze vessels** (see *Bronzes*, p. 56) steal the show, but there are also weapons and ceramics here. The themed exhibitions include intricate displays of **Tang gold, silver and costume** and there's also the chance to see **terracotta warriors** up-close, a prelude for the thousands more lying in wait near Lintong. There's a lot to see here and if you want to take a moment to reflect (or relax) there's a coffee shop. There are audio headsets and English-speaking guides available. You have to leave your bag at the entrance.

Temples, Pagodas & Mosques

★★★**The Great Mosque** (9 am-5 pm; ¥12). This exquisite blend of Arabic and Chinese architecture was originally constructed in 742 AD and remains a bastion of calm in the thronging streets of the Muslim quarter. To get here, enter the Muslim quarter through the Drum Tower and continue straight on for a couple of hundred yards, after which you'll see a turn-off to the left lined with souvenir stalls, which is signposted for the mosque. Turn left again after a few yards, past yet more stalls, and at the end you'll reach the entrance where you buy your ticket, which includes a pamphlet giving a basic introduction to the mosque. Pass through the entrance *paifang*, and into the grounds of the mosque. You'll soon see a pavilion in front of you, which was actually the original minaret from where the *muezzin* would perform the call to prayer. Straight ahead of you lies the 1,000-capacity prayer hall. You can look in but not enter the hall. Note the clock showing the five daily prayer times and the dragon images on the board hanging beneath the eaves – a long way from the Islamic notion that creatures shouldn't be artistically represented in mosques!

★**The Eight Immortals Temple** (Baxian An), Changle Lane (9 am-6 pm; free; bus #300 from the Bell Tower). Northeast of the city walls, this Taoist temple is still an active place of worship, with monks and nuns in residence. The temple was first built during the Tang dynasty and expanded during the Qing, receiving regular visits from the Empress Dowager Cixi (see p. 17) after she fled from Beijing following the Boxer Rebellion (see p. 17). The Eight Immortals (see *Taoism*, p. 50) are fundamental to Taoist belief and they are depicted in a dedicated hall. There are stelae pertaining to the religion's five holy mountains, which include Huashan (see p. 251). On Wednesdays and Sundays there's a lively antiques market at the entrance to the temple (see *Shopping*, p. 253).

The Little Wild Goose Pagoda

★★**The Little Wild Goose Pagoda**, Youyi Xi Lu (daily 7 am-8 pm, 8 am-6 pm Nov 1 to Mar 31; ¥18, plus ¥10 to climb the pagoda; tourist bus #5). Less than a mile south of the South Gate, the Little Wild Goose Pagoda, originally constructed in the eighth century, is far less popular with tourists than its larger southern counterpart and this is an attraction in itself. Sitting in pretty temple grounds, the honey-colored 130-foot pagoda gracefully rises up from the bamboo that surrounds it and is very photogenic. The pagoda was originally built to store Buddhist scriptures brought from India which were translated by the famed monk Yi Jing. The pagoda was originally 15 stories high but was damaged by an earthquake, which lopped off two levels, leaving a jagged top to the otherwise streamlined tower.

You can climb the pagoda (¥10), but the staircase is very narrow and the views from the top are pleasant, but not breathtaking. There's also a temple here, Jianfu Si, which holds a 10-ton bell dating from the end of the 12th century – its toll can allegedly send out messages to loved ones! In the courtyards you'll find pretty flowerbeds and a collection of ancient carved stone pillars that were once used to tether animals. To the south there's a pond crossed by a few arched bridges, but this part of the grounds was undergoing renovation at the time of writing.

Xi'an

Sunset at the Big Wild Goose Pagoda

★★**The Big Wild Goose Pagoda**, Xiaozhaidong Lu (daily 9 am-9:30 pm, Nov 1 to Mar 31 9 am-5 pm; ¥25; bus #606 or tourist bus #5). Two miles southeast of the city center the Big Wild Goose Pagoda is much more striking than the Little Wild Goose Pagoda and so gets hordes of visitors. The pagoda's boxy bulk sits in beautiful temple grounds and was originally built in 648 as a fire-proof repository for sacred scriptures translated by the monk Xuanzang. You can ascend the seven-story, 197-foot pagoda for views over the grounds and square. Inside you'll find inscriptions made by successful imperial exam candidates who came here in the belief that it would lead to a soaring career. In the large square to the north of the pagoda enclosure you'll find a visitors center, restaurants and, on the flanks, the new Shaanxi Folk Customs Gardens (west) and the Shaanxi Opera Theme Park (east). They have an interesting collection of local arts, including papercutting and pottery, although it's all very Tang Paradise (see below). If you come in the evenings there are sometimes impressive fountain and lights displays in the square.

Other Sights

Tang Paradise (daily 9 am-10 pm; ¥50; bus #21, #24 & #610). This mammoth new tourist construction south of the Big Wild Goose Pagoda offers a glimpse of the splendor of imperial Tang Chang'an, albeit in Disney fashion. The site has become a big attraction with visiting Chinese but, given the proximity of genuine antiquity in Xi'an, it's only worth a visit after you've seen the major historic sights. The collection of Tang-style buildings is centered around the vast man-made Qujiang Lake and can make for a fun visit, especially with kids. But, despite the incredible attention to detail, it's just a bit too kitsch to take seriously. There's a nightly cultural show here (see *Galleries, Shows & Theaters*, p. 252).

Around Xi'an

Although there are a feast of sights around Xi'an, the Terracotta Warriors stand out. Terracotta Warriors tours (see below) often take in other sights such as the Banpo or Lintong Museums and Huaqing Pools, or you can hire a taxi for the day and take your pick – you can pick up unofficial taxis outside the Melody Hotel for around ¥150 for the day.

★Banpo Museum

(Open daily 8:30 am-5 pm; ¥30; bus #11, #15 or #517). Five miles east of Xi'an, the Banpo Museum houses the excavated remnants of a Neolithic village and is the best preserved example of Yangshao culture (5000-3000 BC, see p. 5) in the country. The site was unearthed in 1953, and was a keystone in understanding more about Yangshao society. It was a primitive subsistence culture and is thought to have been matrilineal, given the grander nature of the women's tombs here.

The site was devastated by severe floods a couple of years ago and has only recently reopened. The excavation site itself is less impressive than its history and leaves a lot to the imagination, but it is possible to walk over it on raised walkways from where you can see the former mud and straw dwellings surrounded by animal pens. To the north lies the burial ground and there are skeletons and funerary objects on display. From here you move into the museum, which houses ceramics and other items unearthed here, including fish-hooks and stone tools. The Culture Village is a reconstruction of the settlement and, while tacky, it helps to give a more tangible idea of what the village might have looked like. Banpo is often visited on day-trips out to the Terracotta Warriors, but if you want to come here independently you can take a taxi or one of the buses listed above.

Huaqing Pool

(Open daily 8 am-5 pm; ¥70; bus #306 or tourist bus #5). Twenty miles east of Xi'an, these mineral-laden 123°F hot springs have been attracting visitors for millennia, but until recently they were the preserve of emperors. Qin Shi Huang, and the Han and Tang emperors all numbered among the springs' patrons but, while some Tang dynasty buildings remain, the springs are best visited for their thermal pleasures rather than their architecture, although the pools can get very busy. It was here that Chiang Kaishek was arrested by his own troops and coerced into an alliance with the Communists in an event that became known as the Xi'an Incident (see

Xi'an

Xi'an

Changying Road
Changle Zhonglu
Changle Park

Hansen Road

Xingqing Road

Kanfu Road

Shiyuan Rd

S19

East Ring Road

Dongwu Road
Dongsan Road
Dongxin Street

Xiba Road
Dongqi Road

Renmin Square

Beixin Street

Tangfang

Xixin Street

Beida

East Street

Dongxianmen

Nanda

Ziqiang Road

North Ring Road

Ring Road

Yaowangdong

Qingnian Road

Lianhu Park

Miaohu St

West Street

Wuxing Street

Baoensi Street

Hongying Rd

Hanguang Rd

Xiwuyuan

Lianhu Road

Xinghuo Rd   W Huancheng Rd   N Taibei Rd

Lianhu Road

Landong Park

Tuanjie Road

East Fenggao Road

Laodong Road

S Ring Road

Fengqing Park

N Fengdeng Road

Taoyuan Road

S Fengdeng Road

West 2nd Ring Road

Jiandong St

Taiyi Rd

S Ring Road

Yanta Road

Jianshe Road

Wenyi Road

S Tiyuan Rd

Youyi Road

Chang'an Lu

S 2nd Ring Road

S 2nd Ring Road

Xiaozhai Rd

Xiying Rd

Cuihua Road

West Yanta Rd

Zhuque Street

Quijang Chunxiao Park

Zhuque Street

Railroad

City Wall

N

HUNTER PUBLISHING

1. To Silk Road
2. To Airport
3. CAAC Office
4. Ximen (West Gate)
5. Tang Dynasty Show
6. Shaanxi History Museum
7. Big Wild Goose Pagoda
8. Information Center
9. Xingqinggong Park
10. Dongmen (East Gate)
11. Tang Wangi Temple
12. Eight Immortals Temple
13. To Banpo Museum
14. To Terracotta Warriors
15. Train Station
16. Beimen (North Gate)
17. West Mosque
18. Han Tang Hostel

19. Bell Tower Hotel
20. Bell & Drum Hotel
21. Drum Tower
22. Hui Fu Restaurant
23. Shuyuan Hostel
24. Nanmen (South Gate or Yongninmen Gate)
25. Beilin Stone Tablets (Steles) Museum
26. May First Hotel & Restaurant
27. Shaanxi Local Fast Food
28. Hyatt Regency Hotel
29. Number 4 Hospital
30. Sofitel & Grand Mercure Hotel; Le Chinois Restaurant
31. Qixian Hostel
32. Dongguangchang Bus Station
33. Bell Tower; Post Office
34. Tang Paradise

Japanese Encroachment & Civil War, p. 20). A short walk from the Huaqing Pool, the **Lintong Museum** (daily 8:30 am-6 pm; ¥30) is worth a brief visit for its collection of Han and Tang dynasty funerary objects. Both sites are often included in Terracotta Warrior day trips.

Qin Shi Huang's Tomb

(Open daily 8 am-5 pm; ¥25). A little over a mile to the west of the warriors, the tomb that they were built to guard appears as little more than a mound, but reputedly holds a lethal array of booby-traps designed to further protect the megalomaniac emperor and his underground afterlife city, which was complete with rivers of mercury. According to the writings of the famed Han dynasty historian, Sima Qian, the Qin emperor was interred with a cohort of concubines and servants who were buried alive!

★★★ The Terracotta Warriors

(Open daily 8 am-6 pm; ¥90 or ¥65 from Nov 31 to Mar 1; bus #306 or tourist bus #5). The Terracotta Warriors are one of China's (and indeed the world's) premier historic sights and are worth a trip to Xi'an, even if you choose to see nothing else. From the moment you lay eyes on them it's impossible not to be spellbound by the sheer scale of the army, which is fascinatingly offset by the intricate and unique detail of each soldier.

Some Background History

Qin Shi Huang (see p. 6) founded the Qin dynasty (221-206 BC) and united China. Although his rule was short and brutal, the grand projects which he embarked upon have ensured that his name will never be forgotten. Under Qin Shi Huang, the first version of the Great Wall was built and currency and writing were standardized, which alone put his name in the Chinese history books. It was common knowledge that the first emperor was

Terracotta Warriors (Peter Morgan)

interred near Lintong, but nothing was known of his guardian army until the 20th century. In 1974 a group of farmers were digging a well when they unearthed a terracotta shard that appeared to be part of a statue. They duly reported their find and excavations were carried out, which revealed a pit of over a thousand terracotta soldiers. When they were first uncovered, many of the warriors still had remnants of their original painted coloring, but unfortunately the strong Shaanxi sun soon destroyed this. Further excavations uncovered another two pits and archeologists then began the painstaking process of putting the pieces together.

Legends & Facts

It is still unclear exactly why Qin Shi Huang ordered the construction of the Terracotta Warriors, but theories abound, among the most popular of which are that they were to guard his tomb in the afterworld, or that the soldiers were to protect him from the invading armies of the east. There are also rumored to be more pits to the north, west and south of Qin Shi Huang's tomb, but preliminary excavations have thus far revealed nothing of the sort. A similar range of tales circulate about the design of the warriors – some guides will tell you that the individual faces were modeled on real members of Qin Shi Huang's army, while others believe that the faces represent the workers who made them. What is more certain is the way they were made – kiln-baked in separate hollow sections (apart from the legs, which are solid) to avoid cracking and then put together and brightly painted. Some of the soldiers are over six-feet tall and there is yet more speculation about why they are so tall – some attribute their height to the belief that Qin Shi Huang would have only chosen the strongest soldiers for his imperial guard, while others feel that their stature was to intimidate spirits in the afterworld. The soldiers' clothing indicates their rank; some of them were originally clothed in leather armor and held metal weapons.

Visiting the Site

Hotels run tours to the warriors and nearby sites from around US$50, while hostels operate cheaper versions of the same from as little as ¥160 with a minimum of five people (¥230 if there are only two of you, although this is unlikely in the summer as there is plenty of demand). The price includes round-trip transport, lunch and entrance fees. If you want to make your own way out to the warriors, a round-trip taxi should cost ¥150, including waiting time. If you take a tour, check how long you'll spend at the site (a minimum of two hours is recommended) and what time you'll arrive. It's definitely worth getting here early to avoid the crowds; if you're the first one here you'll get a blissful few minutes to savor the splendor before the hordes come. However you arrive, from the new car park it's a 10- to 15-minute walk to the site, or you can take an electric buggy for ¥15.

Pit One

On entering through the ticket gates, the first place to head is Pit Number One, which is straight ahead of you. In spite of subsequent excavations, Pit Number One remains the most impressive and on a sunny day the finely detailed faces of the soldiers catch the light through the opaque roof. Even from above you can clearly make out the differences in stature, clothing, headdress and facial expression. There are over a thousand figures here arranged in battle formation and you can walk around the edge of the enclosure to get a little closer to them. The lines of warriors are divided by earthen walls, which originally supported a wooden beamed roof. In the center there is a collection of terracotta horses, which originally had chariots

The army lies in wait at Pit One (Ewen Bell)

behind them, and to the rear of the pit many of the figures lie shattered on the ground. In spite of signs forbidding photography, everybody takes photographs in this pit – just make sure not to use your flash.

Pits Two & Three

Pit Two was discovered in 1976 and opened to the public in 1994. Although only a small portion of the pit has been excavated, the warriors unearthed here display a much greater variety of postures than in Pit One and there are four particularly fine examples housed in glass cabinets – an archer, a cavalryman, an officer and an overbearing general who is six feet six inches tall! Pit Three is the smallest of the sites and only holds 68 warriors, but their elaborate clothing is thought to indicate higher rank – it seems as if this was the command center for the terracotta army!

Other Points of Interest

There's a small museum here which is definitely worth a visit, principally for the two ornate bronze chariots found near Qin Shi Huang's tomb. The fine workmanship of both chariots is replete with symbolism and the design incorporates elements which represent the belief that the earth was square and heaven was round. To the left of Pit One there's a movie theater that screens a show detailing the history of the warriors and their creation – ask when the next English performance will be. In the hall outside the theater there's a gift shop where you might see one of the farmers who first found the warriors busily autographing books.

Xi'an

SOLDIER SHOPPING

If you're taken with the warriors and want to take a souvenir home, you'll find copies available all over Xi'an (and China) for as little as a few yuan, but these tend not to be properly fired and smudge to the touch. If you want genuine quality it's worth buying from inside the site or from a factory, though prices are far higher. You might feel that a lifesize warrior would be a perfect garden guardian back home, but these don't come cheap – you'll pay at least US$3,000 (including shipping). You can buy these on-site, in Xi'an or at one of the "warrior factories" that tours often include in a visit. Even if you don't want to buy, these places can be fun.

★★★Pandas

(Open 8 am-5 pm; ¥20). Two hours southwest of Xi'an, the Panda Reserve at Zhouzhi in the Qingling Mountains is a good place to see the animals, along with golden monkeys, red pandas, black bears and leopards. There are currently eight pandas at the site, including one baby. Hostels run tours that cost ¥160 as long as you have a minimum of five people, or you can hire a taxi for the round-trip, which should cost ¥400-500. Try to get to the reserve for the 10:30 am or 4 pm feeding times when you'll see the pandas tucking into apples and milk along with the bamboo. For more about pandas and the other animals listed, see *Fauna*, p. 38. If you're interested in getting more involved with promoting panda conservation, **i-to-i** organizes volunteer programs at the center (which you must pay for) – check out www.i-to-i.com.

★★Huashan

(Open 8:30 am-6 pm; ¥100; tourist bus #6). Seventy-five miles east of Xi'an, Huashan is the westernmost of China's five holy Taoist mountains and is well worth a trip. The mist-shrouded mountain has long been a Taoist hermits' retreat and there are several temples and a cave dedicated to Laozi (see *Taoism*, p. 50), the religion's semi-mythical founder. Huashan is a couple of hours drive from Xi'an, which makes staying overnight preferable if you wish to climb, rather than take the cable car (daily 9 am-4 pm; ¥60 one-way or ¥110 round-trip), up the mountain.

Practicalities

Hostels run day-trips to the mountain for ¥280, which includes transport, entrance fees, cable car and meals, but these tend to be rushed and it's better to hire your own taxi (¥700 round-trip including waiting) and leave early, or take the bus and stay overnight. Buses leave from Dongguangchang station and take two hours to get to the mountain. There are plenty of **hotels** on Yuquan Jie in town, some of which have dorms, and there are also places to stay on the mountain itself. Many of these are basic affairs where you'll need a sleeping bag, but there are better options on the North Peak and the East Peak.

Facing page: A healthy bamboo snack (Tot Foster)

Xi'an

View from the North Peak (Brian Dell)

Making the Climb

The mountain is notoriously steep and there are some precipitous drops but, if you choose to climb rather than take the cable car to the 5,295-foot **North Peak**, your efforts will be rewarded with fine views (weather permitting), a tremendous sense of achievement and aching legs. The nine-mile climb takes around four hours and starts easily enough, but the route becomes increasingly steep and narrow as you ascend. Once at North Peak you can travel on to the highest point of the mountain, **South Peak**, at 7085 feet. You can continue on around the remainder of the mountain's five peaks, although it takes a good six to eight hours to complete the circuit, so you might want to stay on the mountain (see *Practicalities*, above).

Galleries, Shows & Theaters

Xi'an's cultural scene is more limited than the big cities but there are a few performances (designed for tourists) worth checking out. The 5 pm "**Dream Back to the Great Tang Dynasty**" (☎ 029-8551-1888; ¥150) at Tang Paradise (see p. 244) is the most elaborate, while the 8:30 pm ★**Tang Dynasty Show** at 75 Chang'an Lu (¥410 with dinner, ¥200 without; ☎ 029-8782-2222) lasts an hour and is accompanied by a classical Chinese orchestra.

 Afternoon Delight: In the late afternoon and early evening it's worth looking out for locals giving performances of opera around the city walls, often accompanied by drums and wind and string instruments.

For Families

Xi'an is a city brimming with historical sights but these might not always appeal to the entire family. The **Ming city walls** (see p. 240) make a good compromise which combines a bit of history with some cycling or walking, and **Tang Paradise** (see p. 244) is another fun option. In the north of the city, **Revolution Park** can offer some playtime, and in the evenings the **central plaza** is full of families flying kites (you can buy them there). Another trip that should appeal to the kids is out **Zhouzhi** to see the pandas and other wildlife (see p. 251).

Health & Relaxation

There are massage parlors all over the city – the **Han Tang Hostel** (see p. 257) offers Tibetan and *tuina* massage (see *Traditional Chinese Medicine*, p. 71). For more of a health cleanse you could try **Le Spa** (☎ 029-8792-8888; daily 10 am-4 am) in the east wing of the Sofitel, which offers massage and spa treatments, but be warned they don't come cheap. If you want to soak away your stress you could head out to **Huaqing Hot Springs** (see p. 245) and bathe in the mineral springs, but don't go expecting luxury.

Shopping

Xi'an is a great place for shopping, new or old. While ever more new shopping malls spring up, markets provide for those who want to sightsee as they shop.

Markets

At the Muslim markets (Galen Frysinger)

The ★★**Muslim markets**, as they are known, run north along Beiyuanmen from the Drum Tower and along parallel Huajie Xiang, which leads to the Great Mosque. They incorporate everything from foods (see *Where to Eat*, p. 258) to souvenirs. This is a great place to pick up all the China souvenirs you want – from singing Mao lighters to kids' toys, as well as "antique" items, although it can be difficult to determine authenticity. You'll also see replica terracotta warriors here but, while they're cheap, the quality is suspect (see *Soldier Shopping*, p. 249).

Xi'an

Xi'an has a long artistic history and this is evident in the string of shops and stalls that run east along ★**Shuyuanmen** from the South Gate. Here you'll find lots of calligraphy, scroll paintings and art equipment, including enormous paint-brushes; the market is a great place for a wander even if you're not going to buy, and, since it's on the way to the Beilin Stone Tablets Museum (see p. 241) you can combine the two in a trip.

Likewise if you're going to visit the Eight Immortals Temple, it's worth heading there on a Wednesday or Sunday to take in the ★★★**antiques market** at its entrance. You'll find all manner of goods, from genuine antiques to real bric-a-brac and the vendors themselves are often as interesting as the objects for sale. It's always difficult to ascertain authenticity, but there are still some great souvenirs. Qing dynasty opium pipes, busts of Chairman Mao, Taoist alchemy treatises, rusty old weapons, statues of Buddha and antique coins all sit incongruously next to one another.

Shopping Streets & Malls

A short stroll down frenetic **Dong Dajie** on a summer's evening is all you need to convince you that consumerism has arrived in China – everyone under 30 seems to be out picking out the latest bargains from the plethora of clothing and sports outlets. One of the first and still the best mall in Xi'an is the **Century Ginwa Plaza** (daily 9:30 am-9 pm) beneath the public square between the Bell and Drum Towers. Access is next to Starbucks on the

Traffic in Xi'an (Galen Frysinger)

northwestern corner of the Bell Tower intersection. Inside you'll find clothing stores, sportswear, electronics and a supermarket, but be warned that imported items cost as much, if not more, than at home. There's also a Kenny Rogers Roasters and a DeliFrance there in case you get hungry. For designer labels, the **Zhongda International Shopping Center** on the western side of Nan Dajie has the likes of Luis Vuitton and Prada, and the **Chang'an International Center** includes a Gucci store.

Everyday Needs

The supermarket in the **Century Ginwa Plaza** (see above) should provide for most of your everyday needs, but for a cheaper supermarket try **Nan Dajie**. For toiletries there are plenty of **Watson's** outlets, including one next to the Han Tang Hostel on Xi Dajie.

Adventures

Xi'an is so overloaded with sights that you may find little time for anything beyond a bike ride or walk around the city walls, but you could also try your hand at dumpling making, or join in with some tai chi or **kiteflying** around the central plaza above the Century Ginwa shopping mall.

On Foot

★★ Around the City Walls

You can walk around the flat city walls in about three hours, but it can get very hot in Xi'an, so many people prefer to do just a section of the walk. Don't worry about getting stranded. If you get tired you can either descend when you come to the next gate and take a taxi to your hotel, or hop on one of the electric buggies that circuit the wall. Late afternoon is a good time to start the walk as the heat of the day starts to fade and the walls are bathed in the warm glow of the setting sun – you may see local musicians performing below you as you make your way round

The city walls (Galen Frysinger)

On Wheels

★★★ Around the City Walls

Cycling makes for a speedier way of seeing the wall than walking and the whole circuit can be completed in around an hour. You can rent bikes from the South Gate of the wall – rental costs ¥20 (plus a ¥200 deposit) for 100 minutes or ¥40 for a tandem.

Cultural Adventures

★The Art of Making the Perfect Dumpling

Xi'an has a long culinary history and is particularly famous for its dumplings. There are countless excellent dumpling restaurants around town (see *Where to Eat*, p. 258), but to learn how to make them head to the **Shuyuan Hostel** (see *Where to Stay*, p. 256), which has dumpling making sessions at 7-9:30 pm every Friday. You'll be shown how to do it before trying your own, which will likely look OK until they get to the pan when they'll probably fall apart.

Making dumplings (Ewen Bell)

If it's any consolation, years of training are required to become a qualified dumpling chef and, while yours may not look great, they should still taste good, as long as you can find all of the pieces!

Where to Stay

Xi'an has embraced its modern tourist status with open arms and there are plenty of good places to stay, including an ever-increasing number of hostels, although options at the top end are mostly found outside the city walls.

What's it mean? FC=fitness center; SW=swimming pool; @=in-room Internet access; DA=rooms for disabled. For ¥ price codes, see page 113.

★**Bell and Drum**, 1 She Hui Lu (☎ 029-029-8727-5018; BDTHTL@gmail. com). This is a good mid-range choice, located right in the heart of the city between the Bell and Drum towers. Rooms are comfortable and quiet. Staff are friendly and helpful. ¥¥¥

Hyatt Regency atrium

★**Bell Tower**, 110 Nan Dajie (☎ 029-8760-0000). The Bell Tower's excellent location and comfortable (but small) rooms make it popular with tour groups. @ ¥¥¥

★**Hyatt Regency**, 158 Dong Dajie (☎ 029-8769-1234, www. xian.regency.hyatt.com). From the outside the Hyatt looks its age but, inside, the lobby is elegantly modern, as are the rooms, some of which have opaque Japanese paper screens in front of the windows to hide the poor views. Discounts of up to 50% are common. FC/@/DA ¥¥¥¥¥

Han Tang Hostel, Xi Dajie (☎ 029-8728-7772, www.hostelxian.com; buses #201, #205 & #611 from the train station). It's less atmospheric than the Shuyuan (see below), but the Han Tang's better facilities, good location and clean, bright and quiet rooms make it a popular place with budget travelers, although mosquitoes can be a problem. You'll find the usual array of hostel offerings, including laundry, Internet café, and travel and tour booking facilities, as well as the opportunity to learn how to make dumplings (see *Adventures*, above) and a small, but pleasant roof terrace. Dorms are ¥50. ¥¥

May First, 351 Dong Dajie (☎ 029-8768-1098, www.may-first.com). Located on the busy shopping street of Dong Dajie, May First is reached by walking through the restaurant of the same name (see below). It has a presentable selection of rooms, although the cheapest ones don't have windows. ¥¥

★**Qixian Hostel**, 1 Beixin Jie (☎ 029-8744-4087; gaoming55514@yahoo.com.cn; bus #610 from the train station). Of the many hostels that have sprung up around the city, Qixian is by far the most atmospheric, although it's a little farther from the center than some of the others. The hostel is housed in a historic building next to the Eighth Army Museum and the simple rooms and dorms are set around courtyards linked by moon gates. Dorm beds are ¥25 or ¥50 with a bathroom inside the room. There's also a cozy café with Internet access and tables in the courtyard outside. ¥

Shuyuan Hostel, 50 feet west of the South Gate (☎ 029-8728-7720; shuyuanhostel@yahoo.com.cn; bus #608 from the train station). Housed in an attractive building just inside the city wall by the South Gate, Shuyuan's recently renovated rooms are clean, simple, feature modern bathrooms, and are set around a couple of courtyards. There's also an Internet café/bar that hosts dumpling-making sessions and serves the usual blend of basic Chinese dishes and Western traveler fare at modest prices. The small, basic dorms are ¥50/¥30 for a/c or non a/c respectively. If you take a room go for one on the upper level; they are brighter. ¥¥

★**Sofitel**, 319 Dongxin Jie (☎ 029-8792-8888, www.sofitel.com). The recently opened collection of Accor hotels in Renmin Square are the city's most prestigious and the Sofitel is the best of the group. The hotel is divided into east and west wings, both of which have spacious rooms styled in a comfortable and hip fashion, although the service isn't qyite up to scratch as yet. The **Grand Mercure** (¥¥¥¥¥), **Mercure** (¥¥¥¥), which both have use of the Sofitel's fitness center and pool, and the budget **People's Hotel** (¥¥¥) are all here and can be booked through the same tele-

Sofitel

phone number. But given the Sofitel's frequent discounts it's worth paying a little more to stay there. The complex also holds has one of the most exclusive restaurants in Xi'an, **Le Chinois** (see below). The only downside to the hotels is their location, which is a little far from the center. FC/SW/@

Shaanxi Wenyuan, 45 Xi Dajie (☎ 029-8310-3000). A little west of the Bell and Drum Hotel, the Wenyuan is a new place, with comfortable, well-appointed rooms and helpful staff. @ ¥¥-¥¥¥

Where to Eat

Xi'an is renowned for its *jiaozi* (dumplings) and these are a must, whether you make your own (see *Adventures*, p. 256), go to a simple canteen or enjoy a full-blown banquet – for the latter try **Defachang**. Or, if you want to accompany your feast with some entertainment, the **Tang Dynasty Show** ¥¥¥¥¥ should fit (see p. 252). The Muslim markets on **Beiyuanmen** offer a host of eating options, from tasty beef (¥0.5 each) and lamb skewers (¥1 each) to flatbreads, tasty desserts and sweets. If you need some Western food, there are a few McDonalds, KFCs and Pizza Huts, along with the city's first Starbucks and a number of backpacker cafés, which are mostly in the hostels.

Lamb skewers are a popular snack at the Muslim Markets

★★★**Defachang**, next to the Bell and Drum Hotel (☎ 029-8721-4060; daily 9:30 am-9:30 pm). This specialty restaurant serves more kinds of dumplings than you ever imagined possible. The canteen downstairs has simple but tasty *jiaozi* for as little as ¥6 per plate of 15 but, for more choice and style, head upstairs to the second floor where banquet options start at ¥80 per person. That buys you an assortment of 16 different kinds of dumpling. If you've come in a group you might want to think about the private rooms on the third floor. ¥-¥¥¥¥¥

See page 117 for an explanation of the ¥ restaurant price codes.

★★**Hui Fang**, Beiyuan Lu (daily 11 am-late). In the heart of the Muslim markets, this place serves the standard skewer and flatbread fare and has an English menu to boot.

★★**Le Chinois**, Sofitel Hotel, 319 Dongxin Jie (☎ 029-8792-8888 ext. 4688; daily 10 am-2 pm & 5-9:30 pm). This refined restaurant is one of the best in the city, specializing in delicious Cantonese dishes, but they also serve a good assortment of other regional delicacies. ¥¥¥¥

★**May First**, 351 Dong Dajie (daily 7:30 am-10 pm). May First is a busy canteen-style restaurant outside the hotel of the same name. It offers a host of local specialties including *baozi* and meat skewers. ¥-¥¥

Shaanxi Local Fast Food Restaurant, 298 Dong Dajie (daily 11 am-9 pm). This clean but characterless canteen has inexpensive local specialty dishes served in its daily buffet. ¥

Tong Sheng Xiang, next to the Bell and Drum Hotel (daily 8 am-10 pm), Opposite Defachang, this Muslim restaurant serves delicious baked breads, along with lamb and beef in comfortable surroundings. ¥¥-¥¥¥

Nightlife

While nowhere near as diverse as the big cities of Beijing and Shanghai, Xi'an's blend of students and tourists makes for a fun night scene and there are plenty of bars, clubs and pubs where you can drink and dance to your heart's content. **Defuxiang Bar Street** has a number of bars – just take a stroll and see which one takes your fancy. **Tribe Bar** is cozily fitted out, while farther south the **Showtime Bar** fits its name and is a place to be seen. For a less pretentious but more fun drink, most of the restaurants and canteens in the **Muslim markets** are happy to serve you just beer (chances are you'll get hungry and order some food later anyway). If they let you put your seats outside, you'll have a fine vantage point from which to watch the crowds milling about. Xi'an also has a few thronging nightclubs – **1+1** on Dong Dajie is a popular spot.

Xi'an

Chongqing

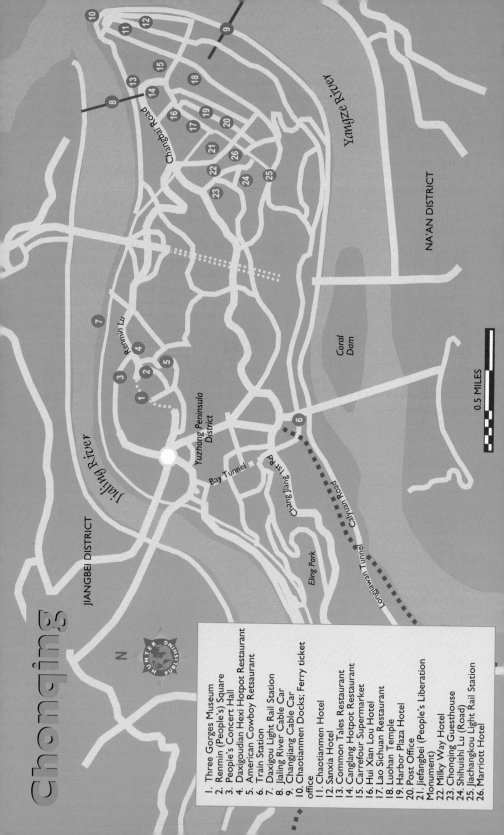

JIANGBEI DISTRICT

Jialing River

Yangze River

NA'AN DISTRICT

Yuzhong Peninsula District

Changbei Road

Renmin Lu

Coral Dam

Bay Tunnel

Chang Jiang

Chang 1st Rd

Caiyuan Road

Eling Park

Longjiawan Tunnel

N

HUNTER PUBLISHING

0.5 MILES

1. Three Gorges Museum
2. Renmin (People's) Square
3. People's Concert Hall
4. Daxigoudian Hexi Hotpot Restaurant
5. American Cowboy Retsaurant
6. Train Station
7. Daxigou Light Rail Station
8. Jialing River Cable Car
9. Changjiang Cable Car
10. Chaotianmen Docks; Ferry ticket office
11. Chaotianmen Hotel
12. Sanxia Hotel
13. Common Tales Restaurant
14. Canglang Hotpot Restaurant
15. Carrefour Supermarket
16. Hui Xian Lou Hotel
17. Lao Sichuan Restaurant
18. Luohan Temple
19. Harbor Plaza Hotel
20. Post Office
21. Jiefangbei (People's Liberation Monument)
22. Milky Way Hotel
23. Chonqing Guesthouse
24. Shihuishi Lu (Road)
25. Jiachangkou Light Rail Station
26. Marriott Hotel

The Three Gorges

The Yangzi is China's greatest river and the Three Gorges are one of its most stunning stretches, steeped in myth and legend, and, until recently, notoriously dangerous and difficult to navigate. All this is set to change with the completion of the Three Gorges Dam, the largest in the world, which it is hoped will dramatically reduce the catastrophic effect of flooding, as well as generate an enormous amount of electricity. The project is due for completion in 2009 and, despite staunch opposition regarding its environmental and social consequences and setbacks in its construction, it looks as if it will, if anything, be finished ahead of schedule. As a result of the predicted impact of the dam, the race to see the Three Gorges is on and a cruise along the Yangzi is one of the country's premier attractions. The Three Gorges are best (and most easily) appreciated heading downstream and thus are dealt with in this order, starting with Chongqing, then the cruise along the Yangzi, and finally Yichang, where you can take a plane or train to your next destination.

History

As the country's primary waterway, the Yangzi basin has been settled for a long time and remains date the first human habitation along the Yangzi to over 20,000 year ago. Many of the battles of the fractious **Three Kingdoms Period** (220-581 AD, see p. 8) were fought out on this land and are recollected in the 14th-century work, *Romance of the Three Kingdoms*. Heroes of this time, such as Liu Bei, are remembered by temples along the Yangzi which can still be visited to this day.

Despite its treacherous waters, the Yangzi has long played a fundamental role in China's internal transport network. While road, rail and air have superseded the river as primary passenger routes, the Yangzi remains important for shipping freight, and the Three Gorges are one of the country's biggest tourist earners.

The completion of the **Three Gorges Dam** will change the river and life along it forever but, while industry and transport are certain to benefit, millions of people have been displaced, environmental disasters loom and the dam's effectiveness as a flood prevention measure for the whole region is in question. Furthermore, many of the unexcavated treasures of the river are certain to be lost forever and it remains to be seen whether the Three Gorges will maintain their allure when they become part of China's largest lake in 2009.

Chongqing

Cooling off during Chongqing's furnace-like summer

Chongqing is a big, bustling and mountainous city of 31 million, located at the confluence of the **Yangzi** and **Jialing rivers**. It serves as the industrial powerhouse of inland China and is renowned as one of China's **"Three Furnaces"** (the others are Wuhan and Nanjing, both on the Yangzi) – because of its stifling summer heat and humidity. While the city isn't without character, this climatic reputation is well-deserved, and most visitors spend just a few hours here before departing downstream on a cruise boat through the Three Gorges. However, if you do end up spending more time here, you will find the streets lined with fiery **hotpot restaurants** and steep, narrow alleys alive with local flavor. There are also a few historic sights and points of interest in and around the city, most notably the new **Three Gorges Museum** and the **Luohan Temple**, as well as the exquisite Buddhist cave carvings two hours away at **Dazu**.

History

Chongqing's location on the life-giving and -taking Yangzi has seen it settled since the **Paleolithic** era, and densely populated villages existed in **Neolithic** times, but it first rose to prominence with **Ba culture**, around 1000 BC. The city was given its current name, **Chongqing** (which means "Double Celebration"), by the emperor Zhao Jiezhong and remained a stronghold against Mongol rule well after they had taken control of the rest of the country. In more recent times Chongqing was ceded as a treaty port to the British and Japanese in the 19th century and was used as the headquarters of the **KMT** after they were ousted from Nanjing by the invading Japanese. During World War II Chongqing played a crucial role as the drop zone for the resupply of Allied-Nationalist forces against the Japanese. US General Stilwell was a key figure in the joint effort until the alliance with the Nationalists failed in 1944, but much of the city was heavily bombarded by the Japanese and little of Chongqing's long history remains intact.

Chongqing's key location on this most significant of waterways has continued to serve it well and it soon developed into a center for heavy industry, which has left the city polluted, but prosperous. More recently Chongqing has emerged as a manufacturing hub for China's burgeoning automobile industry – Ford has a factory here, in partnership with local producer Chang'an and Chongqing recently produced China's first armored car.

Shopping on the modern streets around the Victory Monument, **Jiefangbei**, you can feel the wealth, but, as ever, this goes hand in hand with poverty and you'll see plenty of people struggling to stay above the breadline. The city's meteoric growth has left it with several million residents in the **Yuzhong peninsula** alone, and over 30 million in the municipal area! This gargantuan population and the city's strategic importance led to Chongqing's separation from its parent province, Szechuan, in 1997, and it was designated as a "specially administered municipality," controlled directly by the central government. Industry and tourism combine to give Chongqing its fair share of foreign visitors and the city is being spruced up little by little but, with the enticing vistas of the Three Gorges waiting just along the river, few visitors stay long. If you are willing to explore Chongqing a little you'll find a gritty but captivating slice of Chinese city life.

Getting Here & Away

As one of China's principal industrial cities, Chongqing is served by planes, trains and buses from around the country, but these can get very booked up in the peak season. It's worth buying a ticket from the travel agent you book your cruise with or, if this isn't possible, getting one as soon as you arrive.

By Air

The **airport** lies 20 miles out of the city, from where there are shuttle buses (¥15) to the airline offices on Zhongshan San Lu.

Destinations, frequencies & durations

Beijing (13 daily, 2 hrs 20 mins), **Guangzhou** (11 daily, 2 hrs), **Guilin** (2 daily, 1 hr), (3 daily, 2 hrs 10 mins), **Hong Kong** (2 daily, 2 hrs), **Shanghai** (14 daily, 2 hrs 30 mins), **Shenzhen** (10 daily, 1 hr 40 mins), **Xi'an** (5 daily, 1 hr 10 mins), **Yichang** (1 daily, 50 mins).

By Rail & Road

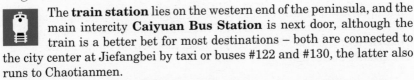

The **train station** lies on the western end of the peninsula, and the main intercity **Caiyuan Bus Station** is next door, although the train is a better bet for most destinations – both are connected to the city center at Jiefangbei by taxi or buses #122 and #130, the latter also runs to Chaotianmen.

Rail destinations, frequencies & durations

Beijing (2 daily, 24 hrs 51 min-33 hrs 12 mins), **Guangzhou** (5 daily, 30-38 hrs), **Hangzhou** (3 daily, 39-43 hrs), **Shanghai** (1 daily, 42 hrs 5 mins), **Xi'an** (4 daily, 13-19 hrs).

Getting Around

Chongqing's mountainous nature can make orienting yourself difficult, while its oven-like summer heat rules out walking for other than the shortest distances. Fortunately, speedy and cheap **taxis** are on hand (¥5 for the first 1.2 miles and ¥1.1 for each 0.6 mile after that), although empty cabs can be elusive during rush hour, in which case motorcycle taxis are an exciting option, but you'll have to bargain (within the peninsula should be no more than ¥5). **Buses** also run around the peninsula, but routes are difficult to decipher so you're better off sticking to cabs.

Chongqing's metro has finally been given the green light for construction, but won't be complete for some years to come. There is also a **light rail line** that runs from Jiachangkou in the south, up to Jiefangbei and then northwest past Daxigou, although this is of little use to casual visitors. Far more fun, though serving little functional transport purpose, there are two **cable cars** that cross from the Yuzhong peninsula to the north across the Jialing River and south across the Yangzi. Tickets are ¥1.5 each way and the services leave every 15 minutes from 8:30 am to noon and 2 pm to 6:30 pm.

LEARNING THE LINGO

Starting on page 598, there's a language section with useful phrases written in Chinese characters, should verbal communication fail! Chinese vocabulary specific to the **Three Gorges** begins on page 612.

Orientation

In spite of Chongqing's vast population and size, the principal area you need to concern yourself with is the teardrop-shaped parcel of land encircled by the **Jialing** and **Yangzi rivers** known as the **Yuzhong district**. The city center is focused on **Jiefangbei**, the Victory Monument, and includes the main business and shopping districts, as well as a good selection of hotels. Cruise boats and ferries leave from the **Chaotianmen Docks** on the eastern side of the peninsula, while **Renmin Square** in the west is the site of the new Three Gorges Museum and the People's Concert Hall. South of here you'll find the train and bus stations.

Information Sources

Chongqing has a monthly expat-oriented magazine, *Chongqing Comments*, which has a few local stories and reviews and can be found in major hotels.

Post Office: Just south of the Jiefangbei junction on Minquan Lu.

Telephone code: 023

Internet Access: There are Internet cafés dotted around the downtown region.

Bank of China: Just east of the Jiefangbei junction on Zourong Lu and another near the Hui Xian Lou Hotel on Minzu Lu.

Public Security Bureau: 1 Linjiang Lu, off Wusi Lu (☎ 023-6396-1944).

Medical Services: Chongqing Emergency Medical Center (☎ 023-6369-2147) at 1 Jiankang Lu in Yuzhong.

Sightseeing

 With a day to spare you could comfortably make the trip out to the Buddhist caves at **Dazu**, but if you just have a few hours you'll have to settle for the few sights within Chongqing. Foremost of those is the new **Three Gorges Museum**, although the **Luohan Temple** also makes for an interesting diversion. If you'd like a stroll, walk up Zhongshan Yi Lu (past the Chongqing Guesthouse) for a few minutes and you'll will find a surviving section of the **old city walls** which have been spruced up and are now adorned with a series of bronze statues that depict the siege of the city. There's also a good teahouse here.

In the City

★★**Three Gorges Museum** (daily 9 am-5:30 pm, last entry 4:30 pm; ¥40). This new museum is the showcase for many of the artifacts frantically excavated in the race against the rising waters of the Yangzi, and is housed in a grand, modern building that faces the People's Hall across Renmin Square. But, in spite of its state-of-the-art presentation and the fine quality of the museum's displays, many of the halls only have cursory explanations in English, leaving a lot to the imagination.

The ground floor focuses on the **Three Gorges Dam Project** and you'll find an impressive "cinepanorama" of the Three Gorges section of the Yangzi with shows at 10, 11 am, 2:30, 3:30 and 4:30 pm, as well as a model of the dam complete with shiplocks, lifts and lights.

The second floor has a hall dedicated to **Ba Culture** and includes a mighty mammoth's tusk, while a second exhibit traces the development of Chongqing as a settlement, complete with a mock-up of an old Chongqing

The grand People's Concert Hall

street and all the businesses along it. On the third floor the **Anti-Japanese War Exhibit** has only an introduction in English and you're left guessing for the rest, although you'll recognize the replica of the Victory Monument if you've been downtown to Jiefangbei. There's also a **Han dynasty sculpture display** and an insight into the **folk traditions of southwestern China**, as well as an ancient coin collection hall on this floor – the square space in the center of the circular coins represents the ancient belief that the earth was square and was circled by a round heaven. The top floor holds **painting, calligraphy** and **porcelain** exhibits, which are interesting if you haven't already had your fill of such in other museums.

People's Concert Hall (daily 8 am-6:30 pm; ¥5). This 1950s building, modeled on Beijing's Temple of Heaven, is far more impressive from the outside, particularly as the interior and the adjacent Renmin Hotel were undergoing renovation at the time of writing. Nevertheless, if you come to see the Three Gorges Museum, the Concert Hall dominates the opposite side of the square and can hold 4,000 people.

★★**Luohan Temple** (daily 8 am-5 pm; ¥5). This small, intriguing temple to the east of Jiefangbei is definitely worth a visit. As you approach the temple you'll see a collection of incense shops that lead to its entrance. Once inside, the first thing you'll come across is a severely eroded but fascinating collection of Buddhist figures chiseled into the bare rockface. These were originally carved in the Song dynasty and are decorated with flowers, clothing and surrounded by incense, making for an atmospheric first impression of the temple. In the main temple complex itself you'll find the *luohan* (see *Glossary*, p. 597) for which the temple is named, along with the usual collection of statuary to Sakyamuni and giant incense and candle burners. The temple is still very active and you'll see plenty of monks in attendance, along with folk from all walks of life coming to pray.

A family visit to Luohan Temple

Around Chongqing

★★★**Dazu** (daily 8:30 am-5 pm; ¥120 for both sites, see text for individual prices; buses from Caiyuan Bus Terminal in Chongqing - ¥45). If you have the time to head out to Dazu, a hundred miles west of Chongqing, then it's a thoroughly worthwhile two-hour ride. Nestled in the damp, overgrown valleys you'll find thousands of Buddhist statues carved into the rockface, resplendent in (recent) color. Dazu is one of the few southern examples of Buddhist cave art and many of the astoundingly detailed carvings date from the **Song and Tang dynasties**. The carvings are found in two principal areas, with **Baoding Shan** (¥80) the most impressive, while **Bei Shan** (¥60) has the earliest work. At Baoding Shan you'll find nearly 10,000 cliff-side figures spread around a U-shaped cove. Carvings include a grand reclining Sakyamuni at the bottom of the U and an amazing thousand-armed Guanyin. Baoding Shan can get busy so it's best to come

Reclining Sakyamuni at Dazu

around lunchtime. Or if you're looking for more solitude try quieter Bei Shan, but it's less popular for a reason and the carvings here pale in comparison. You can take a bus between the two sites for ¥3.

Galleries, Shows & Theaters

For evening entertainment you could check out the nightly hour-long shows at the **Huguang Guild Museum** in Chaotianmen. They feature a variety of acts, including acrobatics, dancing, singing and Szechuan mask-changing opera. Shows start at 8 pm and tickets cost from ¥98 to ¥288, which includes tea and snacks – call ☎ 023-6391-2798 for reservations.

Shopping

The pedestrianized streets around the Victory Monument are Chongqing's main shopping district and are lined with malls, shops, banks and fast-food outlets. For an interesting (and potentially alarming) little stroll, you could walk along **Shihuishi Lu**, home

Watermelon makes a refreshing snack

to a fresh (and live) food market. Everyday needs can be met at the **Carrefour** on Cangbai Lu, or at **Trust-Mart** which is in the shopping center to the north of the People's Concert Hall.

Where to Stay

While most visitors don't stay, if you do you'll find Chongqing's hotels generally offer good value. For an early departure you might want to stay down by the docks in Chaotianmen, but otherwise the best accommodations are in the center of town around Jiefangbei.

What's it mean? FC=fitness center; SW=swimming pool; @=in-room Internet access; DA=rooms for disabled. For ¥ price codes, see page 113.

Chaotianmen Hotel, 18 Xingyi Jie (☎ 023-6371-3370). Handy for the boats (but not for town), friendly, comfortable and with good views over the river, the Chaotianmen's downside is its price, which is above the odds. @ ¥¥¥

★**Chongqing Guesthouse**, 235 Minsheng Lu (☎ 023-6384-5888, www.cq-hotel.com). Well-located, comfortable and friendly, this is one of Chongqing's longstanding hotels and offers good value. It is deservedly popular, although the pool and health center are a little grubby. FC/SW/@ ¥¥-¥¥¥

Harbor Plaza

★**Harbor Plaza**, Wuyi Lu (☎ 023-6370-8888, www.harbour-plaza.com/hpcq). One of the more upscale places in town, the Harbor Plaza offers a central location, with good rooms and facilities, including a great fitness center. FC/SW/@ ¥¥¥¥¥¥

Hui Xian Lou, 186 Minzu Lu (☎ 023-6384-5101). If you're on a tight budget and want to stay in the center of town then this could be the place for you. Rooms are small and musty but passable and discounts of 50% are standard. ¥¥

Marriott, 77 Qingnian Lu (☎ 023-6388-8888, www.marriotthotels.com). Along with the Harbor Plaza, this is the best-situated of Chongqing's international chains, offering comfortable rooms and all the usual amenities. FC/SW/@ ¥¥¥¥¥

Milky Way, 49 Datong Lu (☎ 023-6380-8585, www.cqyinhe.com). The name hardly fits the mundane and functional rooms, but this is offset by a central location and reasonable prices. @ ¥¥

Sanxia, 1 Shaanxi Lu (☎ 023-6355-5555). The Sanxia is the best budget option by the port,

Marriott

offering a range of different kinds of rooms, all of which are clean and the better ones have views over the river. ¥-¥¥

Where to Eat

Chongqing is reputedly the home of hotpot (*huoguo*) and is a great place to sample this spicy bubbling broth. But if you can't take the heat there are regular Chinese restaurants along with the usual Western fast-food options, most of which are found around Jiefangbei. Many Chinese restaurants don't have English menus, but in hotpot places the food to be put into the pot is often on display, so you can just point at what you want.

See page 117 for an explanation of the ¥ restaurant price codes.

American Cowboy, 173, Renmin Lu (daily 11 am-10 pm). If you're visiting the Three Gorges Museum or the People's Concert Hall, then you could pop into this hotpot restaurant, where the choices are laid out buffet-style for you to select, although there are better places in the center of town. ¥¥

Canglong Hotpot, 19, Cangbai Lu (daily 9 am-midnight). A popular place, which serves the *yuan-yang* style of hotpot, meaning you can choose if you want it cooked in the spicy broth or its less potent, but still delicious, alternative. ¥¥

★★**Common Tales**, 3F Nanguo Lijing Building, 46 Cangbai Lu (daily 9:30 am-midnight). Although the décor resembles a school canteen more than a great restaurant, this place serves some seriously spicy hotpot and enjoys good views over the Jialing River. ¥¥

Daxigoudian Hexi Hotpot, 125 Renmin Lu (daily 9 am-midnight). On the northern side of the People's Concert Hall this is another hotpot place with a range of options including pots divided into four sections to make finding your food easier! ¥¥

Lao Szechuan, Minzu Lu, next to KFC and the Huixian Lou Hotel (daily 10:30 am-2 pm & 4:30-9 pm). As you might guess from the name, this place specializes in spicy Szechuan food and includes favorites such as *gongbao jiding* (diced chicken with chili and peanuts) and *yuxiang rousi* (fish-flavored pork). They have a limited English menu. ¥¥-¥¥¥

Nightlife

Chongqing's nightlife options are fairly limited, but you'll find a few bars and clubs around Jiefangbei and all the major hotels have reasonable places for a drink – the **Cotton Club** is near the Marriott and has live music from its house band six nights a week.

The Three Gorges

The Three Gorges

The Three Gorges have been hailed as one of China's greatest sights for nearly 2,000 years, and they remain undeniably spectacular. However, the building of the world's biggest dam at Sandouping has consequences not only for the people and wildlife of the region, but also for its natural beauty. In spite of the dangers, part of the allure of the gorges was their swirling currents and the sheer height of the cliff walls; when the dam is completed, the gorges will appear some 400 feet lower than they were, and the raging river will be a placid 375-mile-long lake. For these reasons the rush to see the gorges before 2009 is on and, although the government is actually predicting an increase in visitors after completion, tour operators anticipate dwindling numbers as the water level rises.

The clear waters of the Three Gorges

Cruises

Cruises operate between Chongqing and Yichang, Wuhan or even Shanghai, but the crucial Three Gorges stretch runs between Baidicheng and the dam site at Sandouping. Ferries and cruise boats both offer splendid views of the gorges themselves and also stop at a collection of temples along the way. As you'd expect, the more you pay, the classier the vessel and the onboard services and facilities should be. Cruises typically last three nights for the Chongqing-to-Yichang section, but some of the upscale boats go at a more leisurely pace and can take as long as five days for this stretch, longer if they travel as far as Wuhan.

Types of Cruise

Cruising the Yangzi (Ian Sewell)

There are three principal styles of travel along the river: international and domestic cruise boats, ferries (which stop at all the tourist sights) and, finally, the 13-hour straight-through hydrofoil, which offers no more than a fleeting visit and is only worthwhile if you have financial or time constraints.

Cruise Boats

Some international cruise boats are effectively hotels on water and offer essentially the same facilities as you'd expect in a good hotel, although rooms are understandably a little smaller. Most rooms will have river views (check when you book) and the suites can be positively luxurious. Domestic cruisers can be nearly as good, but equally may not.

Also, damp rooms and variable water temperature in the bathrooms can be issues. Facilities on the better ships might include a gym, as well as several lounges and dining areas, plus expansive viewing decks. Cruisers of all standards may offer the chance to learn something about **Chinese culture**, from tai chi to **mah jong**, and in the evenings you can usually enjoy some evening entertainment in the form of a show, disco or the ubiquitous karaoke.

On the better boats, all meals and excursions are generally included in the price. The only things you should have to pay for are drinks. Drinks are generally signed for and the bill is settled on the final evening. A few drinks are usually included with meals but, outside of these times, beverages (especially alcohol) and snacks tend to be drastically overpriced. So it's worth stocking up in Chongqing or Yichang. It's also customary to **tip the boat staff** and a recommended amount is often mentioned, but pay what you think befits the service you've received.

If you're booking a cheaper cruise, you should check exactly what is included in terms of excursions – frequently these are "extra" options which you will have to pay for. No matter what style of cruise you choose, you may find the

The Three Gorges

Yangzi tourist boat (Galen Frysinger)

schedule and guiding to be somewhat authoritarian and controlling, with musical wake-up calls and demands over the loudspeaker system that passengers assemble "immediately" for sightseeing excursions! **Guides** on the better boats should be of a good standard, but on cheaper cruises their English ability can range from excellent to unintelligible. However, given that most of what they are talking about on board relates to the perceived shapes of rocks, and that separate guides are available for onshore trips, this isn't crucial.

Ferries

Ferries are at the bottom of the line, but really not that bad given the price. They manage to zip along from Chongqing to Yichang (or vice versa) in around 40 hours. Prices are as follows:

1st Class in a two-berth cabin – ¥1,022

2nd Class in a four-berth cabin – ¥463-510

3rd Class in a six-berth cabin – ¥297-327

4th Class in an eight-berth cabin – ¥229-252

There are cheaper classes, where you simply claim a space on the floor, but these are best avoided unless you have no choice or want to take the term "adventure travel" to its limits. All excursions, meals and drinks are extra, so budget (and stock up) accordingly. In terms of the excursions, you'll be approached the second you step off the boat – see the relevant sections under *Sightseeing* for approximate prices. Make sure you arrive back at the boat by the designated time as ferries aren't averse to leaving without tardy passengers.

Booking a Cruise

The Three Gorges are one of China's premier tourist attractions and a must-see on many people's lists. Cruises sell out quickly in peak season when it's worth booking **at least a week in advance, and two months or more for the better international boats**. As a single traveler, whatever kind of boat you choose, you'll have to pay a supplement if you want a twin room to yourself.

There are flights and trains on to major destinations from Yichang but they can get very booked up so it's worth **arranging onward transport in advance** through the agent that books your cruise in order to minimize lay-over time.

Booking from Overseas

For top-of-the-line boats try:

President Cruises (www.yzcruise.com) has a range of boats to suit different budgets from US$300.

China Regal Cruises (www.chinaregalcruises.com) – US$500-650.

Oriental Royal Cruises (www.orientalroyalcruise.com) – US$700-900.

★★**Victoria Cruises** (www.victoriacruises.com) – US$800-2,100.

Booking in China

Hotels, hostels and travel agents in other tourist cities will be able to book a cruise for you, along with connecting transport needs but, if you get to Chongqing with nothing secured, head to **Chaotianmen** at the eastern end of the peninsula, where you'll find the **Ferry Ticket Booking Office** (daily 6:30 am-10 pm), which also has a plane and train ticket booking service. Alternatively, there are a host of travel agents over the road on **Xinyi Jie**, who can arrange all categories of boat and will facilitate the process by getting you to the right mooring, which can otherwise be a tricky process. **John Zhang** at Changhang Jiangshan Boat Company (☎ 023-6377-3545, cell ☎ 139-8317-7596; cqteddybear@126.com) is recom-

A market on the shore (Galen Frysinger) mended – he is friendly, helpful and can look after your luggage while you head off to explore the city before commencing your cruise. For more upscale cruises the **Chongqing Yangtze Impression International Travel Service** (☎ 023-6376-2392) on the 18th floor of the Baifu Hotel on Bayi Lu is a good bet. Cruises with these agencies can start from as little as US$150 but, for a better quality boat, expect to pay US$300-500 between Chongqing and Yichang and more for the journey to Wuhan.

Sightseeing

Cruises typically last three nights and stop at a few of the sights listed below en-route, although the highlight is the spectacle of the Three Gorges themselves. The major sights along the way are: **Fengdu** and **Shibaozhai**, both of which lie to the west of the gorges, **Baidicheng**, which marks the start of the first gorge, and the **Lesser**

Three Gorges and **Shennong Stream** between here and the **dam site at Sandouping**. Sights throughout the region have been affected by the rising waters. While some, such as Shibaozhai, have been protected and others (Zhang Fei Temple, for example) have been moved, an equal number have been lost forever. However, as cruise ship operators and the government are keen to point out, the higher water levels will facilitate access to certain sites, including Baidicheng and Fengdu and will allow greater exploration of tributaries such as the Lesser Three Gorges and Shennong Stream.

All of the attractions are worth exploring but, if you're interested in visiting a certain sight in particular, ask when you book. Most cruises stop at Fengdu, but choose only one of the Lesser Three Gorges or Shennong Stream, and might include Shibaozhai or Baidicheng temples. If you're on an upscale cruise boat, then all the excursions (including entry fees) should be included, while on cheaper boats you may have to pay for each trip. Transfer to the sights sometimes takes place by bus or ferry and a guide will be appointed for the English speakers from your boat and will take you through the main sections of the sight, perhaps giving you some free time to explore at the end. Guides often focus on the legends associated with sights; while entertaining, many of these stories are best taken with a pinch of salt. If you want to go it alone, make sure to tell your guide and arrange a time to meet and return to the boat. These stops are also a good opportunity to stock up on drinks and snacks if you don't want to pay the boat's inflated prices – you'll find shops, stalls and vendors clustered around docks and at the sight entrances. Cruises finish at Yichang (or Wuhan). But, until the lake is completely full in 2009, the locks may be closed from time to time, meaning you'll disembark at Sandouping, avoiding the intriguing **four-hour journey through the locks**.

The Gorges

The Three Gorges (Qutang, Wu and Xiling) lie between Fengjie and Yichang, and offer a stunning ride through towering peaks steeped in history and legend. All three gorges were formerly treacherous to navigate, particularly Xiling and Qutang, and the latter was famously described by Song poet Su Dongpo as "a thousand oceans in one cup." These days the gorges are far tamer and by 2009 the whole run should be smooth sailing. Passing through the gorges, you'll see bold markers denoting the water level when the lake reaches its full height. Of the three gorges, **Qutang**, at only five miles long, is the shortest, while **Wu** (Witch Gorge) stretches for some 30 miles and **Xiling** is longer still at 50 miles. Although they have lost some of their depth, the gorges remain impressive and all three have craggy, lofty peaks which have been given poetic sounding names to describe their shape. Guides will keenly tell you these names as you pass by and if you're lucky you might actually be able to see the resemblance – **Goddess Peak** in Wu Gorge and **Monk Hung Upside Down** in Qutang Gorge are both recognizable. High up on the side of Qutang Gorge, you can also just pick out a series of **four hanging coffins** dating from the Ba period.

Three Gorges

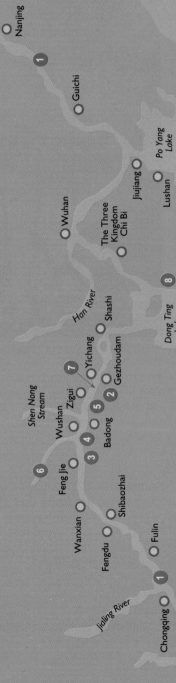

Yellow Sea

Shanghai

Yangzhou

Grand Canal

Nanjing

Guichi

Po Yang Lake

Jiujiang

Lushan

Wuhan

The Three Kingdom Chi Bi

Han River

Shashi

Shen Nong Stream

Yichang

Gezhoudam

Dong Ting Lake

Zigui

Wushan

Badong

Feng Jie

Shibaozhai

Wanxian

Fengdu

Fulin

Jialing River

Chongqing

Yibin

East China Sea

N

120 MILES

1. Yangzi River
2. Baidicheng
3. Qutang Gorge
4. Wu Gorge
5. Xiling Gorge
6. Lesser Three Gorges
7. Sandouping Three Gorges Dam
8. Yue Yang Tower

©2008 Hunter Publishing, Inc.

★★Fengdu Ghost Temple (¥80)

A hundred miles east of Chongqing, Fengdu city has been completely covered by the rising waters of the dam, and its residents have been relocated to the other side of the river, but the ghostly temple itself remains intact. The 15-minute climb up gives a little chance to stretch your legs but, if the boat has put you in a stupor, there's a cable car (¥15 one-way, ¥20 round-trip). At the top you'll be greeted by a grizzly collection of brightly colored statues that allegedly only allow the virtuous to pass – look out for the baby-munching green demon and his blue pal who's chewing on a leg!

The temple itself is dedicated to the King of the Dead, and guides will eagerly tell you a legion of macabre tales associated with the site, encouraging you to participate in an Indiana

Grizzly demons guard Fengdu Ghost Temple

Jones-style set of tests, such as crossing a bridge in only three steps and running up a staircase without taking a breath! On the way out you should make sure not to miss the display of fiendish judges of hell, keenly meting out appropriate punishments to wrongdoers – a glutton is being boiled alive in a cauldron of oil and a nagging woman is having her tongue removed!

★★Shibaozhai (¥60)

Fifty miles on from Fengdu, the 12-storey tower and temple at Shibaozhai is one of the most impressive structures along the cruise and although the town at its foot is now submerged, a coffer dam is being built to hold off the lake's waters. The pagoda-style tower and temple were built during the Qing dynasty and the rocky outcrop to which they cling was once joined to the north bank of the river, but has now become an island.

Baidicheng (White Emperor City; ¥80)

The whole of this stretch of the Yangzi is associated with the Three Kingdoms Period (see p. 8), which is recounted in the 14th-century novel, *Romance of the Three Kingdoms*, but nowhere as much so as Baidicheng. White Emperor City was established by the Shu King, Gong Sun, after he saw a white mist rising from a local well, whence he also proclaimed himself the White King. The Shu protagonist, Liu Bei, retreated here after his closest ally was killed by his own troops and Liu died here in 265 AD. There's a tablet commemorating his death in the temple, and there used to be another temple dedicated to his ally, Zhang Fei, although this has now been moved, brick-by-brick, to Yunyang, to save it from the rising waters. Poets were also inspired by the region and Tang master Li Bai (see *Poetry*, p. 61) "left Baidi amidst colorful clouds."

Tributary Trips

★★★ The Lesser Three Gorges (¥190)

A little way beyond Baidicheng, the Daning River joins the Yangzi, and there's a great five-hour trip to be enjoyed up the "Lesser Three Gorges" as this dramatic stretch of the **Daning River** is known. You'll transfer from your cruiser to smaller motor crafts and push farther upstream through some stunningly narrow gorges and, unless it's been raining heavily, you'll see the water color change from murky brown to emerald green as you progress. There's a hanging coffin to be spotted in the second gorge and you might even see monkeys if you're lucky. In days gone by you would be pulled up by men with ropes (see *Shennong Stream*, below), but as the water level has risen this is no longer the case.

Navigating the narrow Lesser Three Gorges

★★★ Shennong Stream (¥160)

There's another excellent upstream adventure to be enjoyed on the Shennong Stream, a little downstream of Wushan. This four-hour trip affords breathtaking gorge views from small wooden rowing boats, which are painstakingly pulled through the roughest parts by teams of men using ropes. The local people are famous for their singing and your trip might be accompanied by their dulcet tones. To get to the smaller boats you have to take a 40-minute ferry ride from your cruise ship. A little east of the

Boatmen taking a break at Shennong Stream

Shennong Stream, **Zigui** is the hometown of famed minister and poet, Qu Yuan, whose river suicide is remembered by the Dragon Boat Festival (see *Holidays & Festivals*, p. 75).

Three Gorges Dam Site (¥135)

Three Gorges Dam

Whatever you think of the project, it's gone ahead and is being touted as the best thing to happen in China since boiled rice. I visited the dam site several times during its construction and every time was overwhelmed not only by its gargantuan scale, but also by its popularity with domestic tourists. At the site there's an exhibition detailing construction and with a grand model of the dam. You can ascend to a viewpoint where you can overlook the whole site. If you're lucky, your guide might be able to arrange for you to take a trip along the top of the dam itself – ask in advance and note that security is tight. You can also visit the dam site from Yichang by minibus or bus #8, which takes around an hour and costs ¥25.

THREE GORGES DAM PROJECT

Throughout history, China's great rivers and particularly the Yangzi, have been both a blessing, bearing fertile soils and transport, and a curse, bringing floods, destruction and death. Since the time of Yu, Tamer of Floods (see *Xia Dynasty*, p. 6), the Chinese have been trying to reap the river's rewards, while minimizing its catastrophes, but the first serious talk of damming the river didn't come until the 20th century. Initially deemed impossible, plans were finally put into motion in 1994, and quickly provoked international condemnation on several fronts – namely damage to the environment, the human cost, the catastrophic risks if the dam fails, and the claim that the dam won't effectively serve its purpose of flood prevention throughout the region.

Fast Facts:

- Cost: US$24 billion and counting
- Number of workers: 40,000
- Number of people re-located: 1.2 million
- Length of dam: 1.4 miles
- Height: 607 feet
- Hydro-electric capacity: 19 gigawatts (10% of China's requirements)
- Number of Locks: Five, plus the world's biggest ship-lift
- Water-level rise: 400 feet across the Three Gorges

Many experts believe that the best way to address flooding along the Yangzi would be to build several smaller dams, but the energy needs and grand project mentality of the government has brushed these aside in favor of the biggest construction feat in China since the Great Wall. The dam is in a tectonic fault zone and, although it has been designed to withstand missile attack, the appearance of cracks along its walls has done little to reassure skeptics. Even if all these fears are unfounded there are further worries that the lake will silt up in a matter of decades – the river at Chongqing is already suffering from increased sedimentation and the government recognizes that it will need to address the problem. In spite of all these concerns, the coffer dam was demolished in 2006 and the project is now way past the point of no return. However, for all the negatives there are a few positive points. First, the dam should prevent the loss of thousands of lives to flooding; second, it provides a renewable source of energy which will reduce reliance on fossil fuels; and third, the dam allows the Yangzi to be safely navigable, even by large vessels, for the first time in human history.

Human & Cultural Costs

In order to construct the dam and create one of the world's biggest man-made lakes, over a million people have been forced to relocate – a gargantuan task in itself. Many of these people have lived in the same villages and towns all of their lives and are unsure how they will cope with relocation. One of the most heartbreaking things I've seen in my time in China is people demolishing their own homes along lowlying stretches of the river. The Yangzi valley is one of the cradles of civilization in China and there are also thousands of unearthed historic relics that will be lost forever. Only one percent of the dam project's budget is allocated for the protection of cultural relics, but 10,000 workers are frantically excavating 600 sites, racing against the rising water level to uncover as much as possible before it's too late. Artifacts are being found faster than they can be catalogued, but for every piece which makes its way to the new **Three Gorges Museum** (see p. 265) in Chongqing, an untold number of treasures will be lost.

Environmental & Economic Costs

Beyond human and cultural effects, the dam will also irrevocably alter the ecosystem and affect the creatures living within it. Animals such as the Chinese alligator and Yangzi River dolphin (see *Flora & Fauna*, p. 39) were already struggling for survival and the dam looks set to seal their fate. Furthermore, some of the area's inherent natural beauty will be lost and, although plans are afoot to develop designated tourist zones, there are fears that the lake will become a giant sludge-pool of polluted water. Over a million visitors traveled along the Three Gorges in 2004 and, despite government claims to the contrary, these numbers are expected to decline. If they do, the region will lose an important sector of its economy.

Yichang

Yichang is a small city on the north bank of the Yangzi which would see few visitors were it not the terminus for the Three Gorges cruise, and the nearest city to the gigantic dam 22 miles west at Sandouping. Most tourists arrive by boat from Chongqing, but you can also start the Three Gorges cruise upstream from Yichang, which takes fractionally longer. Chances are you won't need to stay in Yichang, but if you do you'll find reasonable hotel rates and a pleasant, if unexceptional small city.

Getting Here & Away

By Air

 Taxis cost around ¥60 to the airport, which is six miles east of town.

Flight details from Yichang

Beijing (2 daily, 2 hrs); **Chongqing** (1 daily, 50 mins); **Guangzhou** (2 daily, 1 hr 40 mins); **Shanghai** (1 daily, 2 hrs); **Shenzhen** (1 daily, 1 hr 30 mins); **Xi'an** (1 daily, 1 hr 10 mins).

By Rail

The train station sits on a hill immediately above Dongshan Dadao.

Train details

Beijing (1 daily, 20 hrs); **Guangzhou** (3 daily, 15-23 hrs); **Hangzhou** (1 daily, 27 hrs); **Nanjing** (1 daily, 21 hrs); **Shanghai** (1 daily, 10 hrs); **Xi'an** (1 daily, 6 hrs).

Getting Around

Yichang is small enough to negotiate on foot, but there are taxis (¥5) if it's too hot to walk.

Orientation

As a small city Yichang is fairly easy to find your way around and the bulk of amenities are within walking distance of the train station. The train station sits on a hill in the north of town and there are restaurants, hotels, shops, a post office and banks between here and the Yangzi River a mile to the south.

Information Sources

The better hotels are your best bet for information in Yichang, but the CITS at Yiling Lu (☎ 0717-6220-837) are also helpful and can arrange tours.

Communications

Telephone code: 0717

Post Office: At the intersection of Yunji Lu and Yiling Lu.

Internet access: There are Internet cafés dotted around the city, including one on the south side of Fusui Lu.

Bank of China: Shengli Lu.

Public Security Bureau: Tiyuchang Lu (☎ 0717-6499-943).

Medical services: Yichang Central People's Hospital at 127 Yiling Lu (☎ 0717-6447-894).

Sightseeing

Aside from the mammoth Sandouping Dam site an hour out of town, which has become a popular tourist sight (see the description on p. 274 for transport details), Yichang has little in the way of visitor attractions. You can take a taxi to the **Gezhouba Dam** (¥20) in the north of town, which was formerly the largest along the Yangzi, but otherwise the best thing to do is take a wander through the riverside park.

The Three Gorges

Yichang

1. Gezhouba and Three Gorges Dam
2. To Airport
3. Train Station
4. Yangzi River
5. CITS
6. Bank of China
7. Post Office
8. Yichang International Hotel
9. Heping Jia Ri Hotel
10. New Century
11. Taohualing Hotel
12. Beijing Jiaoziguan
13. Zhenjiangge Teahouse
14. Yanjiang Dadao
15. Minzhu Lu
16. Jiefang Lu
17. Taozhu Lu
18. Yunji Lu
19. Longkang Lu
20. Yiling Lu
21. Dongshan Dadao
22. Central Aquare
23. Bus Station
24. Riverside Park
25. Dagong Bridge
26. Docks

Where to Stay

If you plan your onward travel well, there's no need to stay in Yichang, but if you find yourself here for a night there are a few reasonable hotels. The functional but friendly **Heping Jia Ri** (☎ 0717-6254-088; ¥¥) and upscale **Yichang International** (☎ 0717-6222-888; ¥¥¥) are both down by the river on Yanjiang Dadao, while the **Taohualing** (☎ 0717-6236-666; ¥¥¥-¥¥¥¥) on Yunji Lu is a safe mid-range bet in the center of town. If you're on a tight budget, there are a selection of cheap places at the train station end of Yunji Lu, including the good value **New Century Hotel** (☎ 0717-6445-559; ¥¥).

See page 117 for an explanation of the ¥ restaurant price codes and 113 for a key to the hotel price codes.

Where to Eat & Drink

Yichang's restaurant scene isn't up to much, but the better hotels have reasonable fare and the **Beijing Jiaoziguan** (¥-¥¥) on Longkang Lu serves tasty dumplings and other northern fare. For cheap eats the nightmarket, which sets up along the river on Yanjiang Dadao, is popular with locals and tourists alike. You'll find a good cup of tea and some riverside retreat at the **Zhenjiangge Teahouse**, but if you crave things Western there's a McDonald's and KFC set around the square, and a few coffee shops such as Liujin Suiyue nearby. Yichang doesn't have much nightlife to speak of, but there are a few bars along Jiefang Lu.

The Three Gorges

Shanghai Region

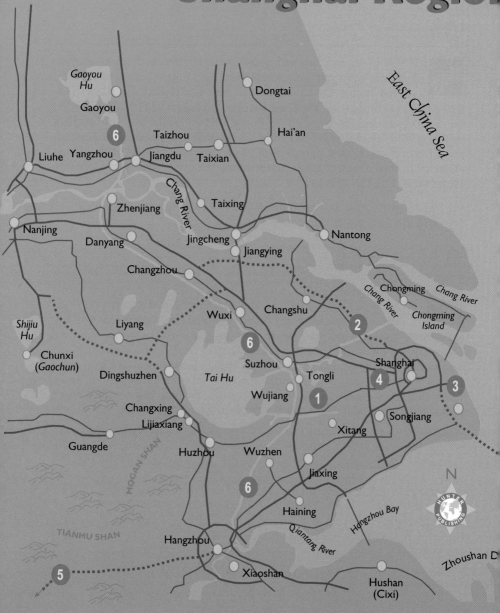

Gaoyou Hu

Gaoyou

Dongtai

Taizhou

Hai'an

Liuhe Yangzhou Jiangdu Taixian

Nanjing

Zhenjiang

Danyang

Chang River

Taixing

Jingcheng Jiangying

Nantong

Changzhou

East China Sea

Chongming Chang River

Chang River

Chongming Island

Shijiu Hu

Liyang

Wuxi Changshu

Chunxi (Gaochun)

Dingshuzhen

Tai Hu

Suzhou

Tongli

Shanghai

Wujiang

Changxing Lijiaxiang

Guangde

Huzhou

Wuzhen

Xitang

Songjiang

Jiaxing

MOGAN SHAN

TIANMU SHAN

Haining

Hangzhou

Qiantang River Hangzhou Bay

Zhoushan D

N

Xiaoshan

Hushan (Cixi)

1. Zhouzhuang
2. Zhujiajiao
3. Pudong Airport
4. Hongqiao Airport
5. To Huangshan & Tunxi
6. Grand Canal

60 KM
40 MILES

Shanghai & Around

astern China is the country's boom-belt and its heart is the Pearl of the Orient, Shanghai, a city which was recently wonderfully described to me as "Hong Kong on steroids." **Shanghai** is the country's most modern city, but manages to retain both

its Chinese and European history and its economic development is also helping a renaissance in culture and the arts, along with a shopping and nightlife scene matched only by Beijing and Hong Kong.

Around Shanghai, the Water Towns have picturesque canals lined with classic **Ming architecture** and can make for great day trips, and a little further out, the city of **Suzhou** offers more of the same, albeit on a larger scale, along with some of the country's finest gardens and the opportunity for some serious silk shopping.

Nearly 100 miles south along the **Grand Canal**, the former **Southern Song dynasty** (1126-1279, see p. 11) capital of **Hangzhou** is set on pretty **West Lake** and is a prime tea-growing region. Away from the lake the city is much like any other Chinese city, but the surrounding countryside and its smattering of temples and tea villages make for some excellent bike rides. Some 110 miles west of Hangzhou, **Huangshan** is arguably the most beautiful of eastern China's mountains and offers the region's finest scenery and best hiking. The mountain's mist-shrouded, jagged peaks, lone pines and perched temples are straight from a watercolor and it's no wonder Huangshan attracts so many visitors. But fortunately there are enough paths to ensure you can always find yourself a quiet spot.

Shanghai

Known as the **Pearl of the Orient**, Shanghai has endured a boom-bust cycle like no other city in China and is a must-see for a glimpse into the China of the future. It currently has some 20 million residents. A walk along the **Bund** on the banks of the **Huangpu River** offers a cityscape to rival Hong Kong's, taking in the glory of Shanghai's colonial past, while at the same time giving views across the river to the city of tomorrow, **Pudong**. Less than 20 years ago, this was just marshy farmland, but today it boasts

Pudong by night (Tot Foster)

countless skyscrapers, among them China's highest tower, the **Pearl Oriental TV Tower**, and loftiest lodgings, the 88-floor **Grand Hyatt**. Traditional Chinese sights are a little sparse due to Shanghai's comparative youth, but it's colonial and revolutionary history over the past 150 years has left it with a series of significant political buildings. What is more, there are modern activities aplenty, reflecting the city's dynamic and modern heart – fine dining, nightlife, shopping and a kaleidoscope of exhibition centers and good museums await.

History

The Early Years

Although Shanghai's explosion onto the world scene is comparatively recent, the city has a trading history of nearly 1,000 years. Shanghai's strategic location near the **Grand Canal** and the confluence of the **Yangzi** and the **East China Sea** made it a natural distribution point for the cotton, rice and silk grown in the region, which was first put to use during the **Song dynasty** (960-1279, see p. 11).

The Beginning of Foreign Influence

By the middle of the 19th century, Shanghai was a regional trading hub and, based on this, the **British** sought land and trading rights here after victory in the **First Opium War** (1840-42, see p. 16). They were ceded 140 acres of muddy riverbank north of the walled Chinese city, which became known as the **Bund**. Other nations soon wanted to get on the bandwagon, and the French established themselves west of the Chinese town in 1847, while the **Americans** settled north of **Suzhou Creek** in 1863. The British and American parts of town became known as the **International Settlement**, while France's sector was called the **French Concession**. The international communities within both settlements lived completely apart from the Chinese, under their own laws, and they prospered from trading opium in return for the exotic goods of the East that were exported to their home countries. The **Taiping Uprising** (1850-64) threatened Shanghai's fortunes and, in response, international forces helped to quell the revolt both in the city and throughout the country, which reaffirmed the military superiority of the colonials. With greater confidence came houses and offices in the home styles of the expat community, and Shanghai's infrastructure was developed, giving the city China's first telephones (1881), electricity (1882) and running water (1884).

Japanese Factories, White Russian Workers & Iraqi Jewish Tycoons

Defeat in the **Sino-Japanese War** led to the establishment of a **Japanese Concession** in 1895, and with it the beginnings of an industrial base in Shanghai. The Japanese had acquired not only a trading post, but the right to manufacture. Other nations quickly followed suit. Aided by its strategic location and fueled by cheap labor, Shanghai developed as a manufacturing center. However, poor working conditions and pay for the Chinese laborers in Shanghai's factories soon instilled resentment against the foreign community, which was echoed by the nationwide **Boxer Rebellion** (see p. 17) in 1899.

The collapse of the **Qing dynasty** in 1911 had little effect on Shanghai's dynamism, and likewise business went on as usual during **World War I**, although the rise of the Bolsheviks in Russia saw an influx of White Russians to the city. Refugees, rather than gentleman traders, the White Russians were resented by the existing foreign community, particularly for their willingness to work any job, which showed the Chinese a vulnerable side to the supposedly impervious Caucasians. **Iraqi Jews** such as the Hardoons, Kadoories and Sassoons, many of whom had originally worked for the British, became increasingly wealthy and powerful during this time and some of their grand buildings still dot the city today.

Gangsters & Glory

Despite increasing Japanese expansionism, Shanghai seemed unstoppable and became more cosmopolitan and raucous as the years went by. Gangsters had always been influential in Shanghai and during the 1920s the city was principally controlled by the notorious gang leader, **Du Yuesheng** (aka Big Eared Du), which seemed just fine with everybody as long as things were run efficiently. As part of a plan conceived by the nationalist party and foreign concerns, Du and his **Green Gang** carried out a full-scale massacre of Communists in 1927, which saw **Mao Zedong** flee for the hills – little wonder Du escaped from the mainland when the Communists gained power in 1949. In the 1920s the foreign communities further consolidated their holdings and many of the Bund's neo-classical buildings were constructed. The 30s were Shanghai's decade and the city became known as the **Paris of the East** – a somewhat glamorous term for the brothels, gangsters, opium dens and gold-rush feel that the city afforded. A few famous movie studios developed (see *Film, The Beginnings*, p. 67) and the international community became curious about this exotic and dangerous outpost on the other side of the world. As a result a few famous faces found their way here, including Charlie Chaplin!

Japanese Control & the End of an Era

The bubble finally burst and the Japanese, who had gradually been swallowing up more and more of northern China (see *Japanese Encroachment and Civil War*, p. 20) overran Shanghai. The Japanese controlled Shanghai until they were evicted by US forces at the end of World War II in 1945, and the Americans stayed in place for a year before handing power to **Chiang Kaishek**. However, Chiang and the nationalists were on their way out and, as the Communists gained more ground, many of Shanghai's great industrialists fled to **Hong Kong** or back to their home countries. After the formation of the **PRC** in 1949, little by little the Communists commandeered Shanghai's businesses to contribute to the development of the country.

Renaissance

Both **Mao** and **Zhou Enlai** kept houses in this former capitalist playpen and the bright lights of Shanghai's heyday were turned off for some 40 years. After the death of Mao, Shanghai continued to be neglected for its bourgeois past. It wasn't until 1990 that the party decreed the city was, once again, to be the country's **economic heart**, much to the chagrin of newly rejoined Hong Kong. Pudong was designated as a Special Economic Zone and since then Shanghai has seen unparalleled development in all areas: business, transport, tourism, culture and the arts are all flourishing in the modern city.

The Costs of Development

Aside from Hong Kong, Shanghai is China's most cosmopolitan, westernized and developed city, and is once again attracting large scale **overseas investment** and foreign residents. However, Shanghai's development has its costs. Nearly **20 million people** are thought to live in the greater metropolitan area and its purported wealth and opportunities are drawing ever more people, in spite of restrictions – there is thought to be a floating population of at least 3 million. Shanghai's vast population, industrial legacy and increasing car ownership makes for gridlocked streets, blackened rivers, smoggy skies and there are even reports that the city is sinking due to its gargantuan buildings. In this city of cell-phones, mega-malls, sleek cars and super-skyscrapers, there are still people living in abject poverty. As elsewhere in China, the greater the wealth, the bigger the social disparity.

The Future

This said, Shanghai is undeniably making progress and rags-to-riches stories are commonplace. **Environmental problems** are being addressed to some extent and Suzhou Creek is no longer quite as black and oily as it was, although it's still a long way from its projected status as a beautiful riverside promenade. **Economic growth** and rising international prominence has brought infrastructural, cultural and social development. Reflecting this, Shanghai has been awarded the **2010 World Expo**. While under more direct government control than Hong Kong, Shanghai enjoys more social freedom than anywhere else on the mainland and is set to eclipse its southern rival in the coming decades. Shanghai works hard, but it plays hard too and it has once again become the place to shop, dine and drink to your heart's content.

Getting Here & Away

Shanghai is one of China's **international gateway cities** and is served by planes and boats from around the globe, as well as by domestic flights, trains and buses.

By Air

International flights use Shanghai's impressive new **international airport** on **Pudong**, which is connected to downtown by shuttle buses (¥30), taxis (¥120-150) and the super-speedy Maglev train (¥50 one-way, ¥40 with an air ticket for that day; see callout, p. 292), although for the latter you'll have to change to the subway or taxi at Pudong's Longyang Lu station. The old airport at Hongqiao is still used by domestic carriers and is more convenient for downtown, linked by shuttle bus and taxi (around ¥50). Pudong and Hongqiao are also connected to one another by shuttle bus. You can buy flight tickets through travel agents in most hotels and at the airport. Check out *City Weekend, that's Shanghai* or see the websites listed on p. 83 if you want to find airline offices in Shanghai.

Routes from Hongqiao

Beijing (45 daily, 2 hrs); **Chongqing** (14 daily, 2 hrs 30 mins); **Guangzhou** (23 daily, 2 hrs 25 mins); **Guilin** (2 daily, 2 hrs 10 mins); **Hong Kong** (23 daily, 2 hrs 20 mins); **Huangshan** (3 daily, 1 hr 10 mins); **Shenzhen** (23 daily, 2 hrs 25 mins); **Xi'an** (17 daily, 2 hrs); **Yichang** (1 daily, 2 hrs).

By Rail

Routes from all over the region, and indeed the country, converge on Shanghai and it's generally pretty simple to arrange tickets, although for longer journeys it's worth buying tickets as far in advance as possible.

Shanghai has three stations but, unless you're coming from Inner Mongolia, you're likely to end up at the main terminus, **Shanghai Train Station**, not too far northwest of the center. On arrival, turn left out of the exit for the subway and taxis (which can be found down some steps in the center of the train station square), or turn right for city buses. Taxis should cost around ¥12-15 for Nanjing Dong Lu, ¥30 to Pudong, ¥150 to Pudong airport or ¥50 to Hongqiao.

Just another day at Shanghai train station (Tot Foster)

As you look at the station the ticket office is on the right (east) side, while departures are from the central waiting halls, unless you have a soft class ticket which means you can enjoy the greater comfort of the soft waiting rooms at the far right of the station, just beyond the ticket office. There's also a soft class ticket office just west of the station.

Trains head to locations all over the country

Beijing (8 daily, 12-21 hrs); **Chongqing** (1 daily, 41 hrs 50 mins); **Guangzhou** (3 daily; 23-28 hrs); **Guilin** (2 daily; 26-27 hrs); **Hangzhou** (15 daily; 2-4 hrs); **Hong Kong** (every other day, 26 hrs); **Huangshan** (1 daily, 11 hr); **Shenzhen** (1 daily, 24 hrs 50 mins); **Suzhou** (10 daily, 40-50 mins); **Xi'an** (2 daily, 14-16 hrs 30 mins); **Yichang** (1 daily, 28 hrs).

By Road

 Shanghai has a number of bus stations, but the one used most often is just west of Shanghai Train Station. Transport to and from the center is the same as for the train station. There are buses to: **Hangzhou** (24 daily, 2 hrs 30 mins), **Huangshan** (1 daily, 5 hrs), **Suzhou** (20 daily, 1 hr 30 mins).

Shanghai

1. The Old City
2. Confucian Temple
3. Xiaotaoyuan Mosque
4. Dajing Lu Produce Market
5. Sunday Ghost Market
6. Classical Hotel; Old Shanghai Teahouse
7. Gucheng Park
8. Fuyou Mosque
9. Old Town Bazaaar
10. Yiyuan; Huxinting Restaurant
11. Shilipu Pier
12. Grand Hyatt Hotel; Jinmao Tower
13. Lujiazui MTR Station
14. Shanghai Ocean Aquarium
15. Oriental Pearl TV Tower; Ming Zhu Park
16. Jinling Pier
17. The Bund & Sightseeing Tunnel
18. Huangpu Park; Bund Historical Museum;

Shanghai People's Heroes Monument
19. Astor House & Panorama Century
20. Suzhou Creek
21. Hiker Youth Hostel
22. Peace Hotel; Post Office
23. Captain Hostel; Cupola Restaurant, New Heights, Whampoa Club, M On the Bund Restaurant
24. Westin Hotel
25. YMCA
26. Bird & Flower Market
27. Dongtai Lu Antiques Market
28. Concert Hall
29. Renmin Square; MTR Station
30. Shanghai Museum
31. Shanghai Grand Theatre & Gallery, Library, Art Museum, Shanghai Urban Planning Exhibition Centre
32. Acrobatic Theatre

33. Renmin Hotel; Ren Ren Restaurant
34. Shaanxi Noodles
35. Suzhou Mian Gan Restaurant
36. Chun Shen Jiang Hotel
37. Hongze Jiulou Restaurant; Nanjing Hotel
38. To Jewish Refugee Museum & International Passenger Quay
39. To Pudong International Airport; St. Regis Hotel
40. Fuxing Dong Tunnel
41. Yan'an Dong Lu Tunnel
42. To French Concession
43. To Hongqiao International Airport
44. To Shanghai Train & Bus Stations
45. Junmao Dock
46. Tourist Office
47. Henan Zhong Lu MTR Station
48. Shanghai Post Office
49. To Science & Technology Museums

©2008 Hunter Publishing, Inc.

By Water

Shanghai's location has made water an important means of transport through the ages, but today this has mostly been superseded by rail, road and air. Nevertheless, cities in **Japan**, including Kobe and Osaka (¥1,300), are served from the International Passenger Quay at 1 Waihongqiao Lu, a 10-minute walk from the northern end of the Bund. Tickets can be bought at the terminal and from the China-Japan International Ferry Company on the 18th floor of Jin'an Dasha, 908 Dong Daming Lu (☎ 021-6325-7642).

Getting Around

By Subway

Shanghai's ultra-modern subway currently has four lines. Of most use are lines #1 and #2. Line #1 runs from Gongfu Xincun in the far northwest, past both train stations to Xinzhuang in the southwest. Line #2 starts at Zhangjiang in the southeast of Pudong and heads northwest to Lujiazui, close to the Oriental Pearl TV Tower, before continuing under the river, along Nanjing Lu, past Renmin Square and terminating in westerly Zhongshan Park. Services run from 5:30 am-11:30 pm and tickets cost from ¥3. There are announcements and signs in English and even videos encouraging courteous conduct on the subway!

Shanghai Maglev - The World's Fastest Train (www.smtdc.com)

Completed in 2004, the 19-mile stretch of track from Longyang Lu subway station on Pudong to the airport can now be covered in as little as eight minutes, and the train reaches some 267 miles an hour, although it has been tested at speeds up to 310 miles per hour! The train achieves these incredible speeds by the use of magnetic levitation. A system of powerful magnets controls the train and keeps it elevated a third of an inch above the rails, reducing friction to almost zero. This technology comes at a price though – US$1.2 billion, although tickets cost only ¥50 one-way or ¥80 for a same-day round-trip. The line was built in partnership with a German consortium, Transrapid, who are also involved in the construction of new Maglev lines out to Hangzhou and Beijing. Although the system is environmentally friendly and produces no emissions, some feel that the tremendous investment could have been better spent on other projects. But whatever you think, the Maglev is here and is a taste of the China to come!

By Bus

There are hundreds of bus lines across Shanghai, but while they are useful for some sights, buses get crammed to capacity during peak times and the language barrier can be a problem – you'll need to know the route number and the name of your destination in Chinese. Thus, if it's an option, the subway is far easier and, given the reasonable price of taxis, buses are best avoided, unless you're just in it for the experience. This said, there are a few places that are best served by bus and details are included in the text for these. A couple of useful routes include bus #1 from Shanghai train station to Renmin Square and #6 from Renmin Square bus station to Pudong. Fares are ¥1 and ¥2 for air-conditioned buses.

By Taxi

Taxis are abundant. Minimum rate is ¥11 (¥14 at night) for the first two kilometers (1.2 miles) and ¥2 for each additional kilometer (0.6 miles). In addition to taxi ranks at key points around the city, there are also request stations, where you push a button and a car should arrive within a few minutes. Few drivers speak much English so take your destination written in Chinese. According to the rules and regulations for cab drivers posted in the back seat, if a taxi driver spits during your journey you are entitled to a free ride!

By Bicycle

Shanghai's busy streets make cycling a scary option in many areas of the city, but there are exceptions to this, notably parts of the French Concession and Pudong. You can rent bicycles from the Captain's Hostel (¥20 for up to four hours, ¥30 for up to a day; ¥500 deposit) on Fuzhou Lu (see *Where to Stay*, below). For cycling trips out of the city see *Adventures On Wheels*, p. 321.

By Ferry

Ferries aren't the most convenient way to get around, but they are cheap at ¥0.5 for the 10-minute trip from the wharf at the southern end of the Bund (or farther south at Shilipu) across to Puxi.

Orientation

Shanghai sits on the banks of the **Huangpu River**. The city center stretches west of the river and south of the oily black waters of **Suzhou Creek**. Shanghai's fabulous colonial riverside promenade, the **Bund**, runs along the west bank of the Huangpu and meets the city's main shopping street, **Nanjing Dong Lu**, which runs west for over a mile before arriving in **Renmin Square**. Many of the city's hotels are found along Nanjing Dong Lu and its westerly extension, **Nanjing Xi Lu**, as well as around Renmin Square.

Southwest of here is one of the city's most interesting districts, the **Old French Concession**, which has some of the best restaurants and nightlife hidden in its tree-lined streets. Just to the east, **Xintiandi** is one of the trendiest areas, an evocative mix of new and old with its warren of restored (and rebuilt) 1920s Chinese *shikumen* (see p. 308) houses, many of which function today as bars, cafés, restaurants and shops. East from here, the **Old City** centers on the **Yu Gardens**, an area that has been revamped to draw in tourists, though there are still pockets of genuine antiquity close by.

Shanghai's newest district, **Pudong**, on the east bank of the Huangpu, is also its most prominent and you can see the **Pearl Oriental TV Tower** from all over the city. Pudong is the city's new business district and contains many upscale restaurants and hotels, including the world's tallest, the **Grand Hyatt**. The new international airport is also on Pudong, while its predecessor west of the city in the expat hub of **Hongqiao** operates domestic flights. Out in the southwest, suburban **Xujiahui** offers a few sights of interest, including the Botanical Gardens and the lively Longhua Temple.

LEARNING THE LINGO

Starting on page 598, there's a language section with useful phrases written in Chinese characters, should verbal communication fail! Chinese vocabulary specific to the **Shanghai** area begins on page 614.

Information Sources

i There are 30 **tourist offices** scattered across Shanghai; the **main branch** is in Century Plaza toward the western end of Nanjing Dong Lu (☎ 021-6350-3718; daily 10 am-8 pm). However, these offices offer little beyond maps, basic advice and tour bookings. Far more helpful is the **Information Center** (not affiliated with the tourist office) at No. 2, Block 123, Xingye Lu, Xintiandi (☎ 021-6384-9366; daily 10 am-10 pm), which has leaflets on most city sights, as well as interesting fact-sheets and books on the city. It also offers 30 minutes free Internet use. Expat magazines, including *that's Shanghai* (www.thatssh.com), *Shanghai Talk* (www.ismaychina.com), *City Weekend* (www.cityweeekend.com.cn) and *Metrozine*, are available at bars, hotels and restaurants. The magazines and websites offer reviews on everything from shopping to bars, clubs and cultural events, as well as items for sale and apartments for rent. To keep up to date with Chinese current affairs the local **English newspaper**, *Shanghai Daily* (¥2) is an easy read; it gives a brief scan of world news and sports along with cultural events in the city. *Shanghai Tourist Map* and *Gray Line* are among the best free maps and can be found at hotels and tourist offices.

Events & Festivals

Traditional Festivals

 Any festival in Shanghai is a memorable event and, if you're lucky enough to be there for some of the bigger holidays, it will really make your trip. **Chinese New Year** sees Shanghai at its noisiest, with fireworks and crackers going off at every turn and dragon and tiger dances at Jing'an and Longhua Temples. The colorful **Lantern Festival** is also a treat with most houses and shops displaying red lanterns and Yuyuan Gardens transformed by 10,000 lights. Another favorite is the **Dragon Boat Festival** where you'll see longboat competitors racing along the Huangpu River. See *Holidays & Festivals*, p. 73, for more information on all of these festivals.

SPRING SHANGHAI

Late March to April is a beautiful time to visit eastern China as many of the fruit trees are beginning to bloom. The Longhua Temple has abundant peach blossoms. They add a great backdrop to an already stunning temple. And the **Longhua Temple Fair** is held in the first 10 days of April. The temple (see p. 311) comes alive with merchants selling religious trinkets, books and prayer beads. It's also a time to eat fantastic vegetarian food, for which the temple is famous.

International Festivals

As Shanghai becomes rapidly becomes more international, so do its festivals. The line-up now includes a **Flower** festival (April), **Music** festival (May), **Film** festival (June), **Beer** festival (July) and an **Arts** Festival (November). All are great fun and worth a look if you're visiting, but remember that Shanghai gets very busy during these times. For art lovers, another not-to-miss event is the **Shanghai Biennale**, housed in the Shanghai Art Gallery (see p. 313) from October to November. Since beginning in 1996 the Biennale has been a great hit and now offers a chance to see ultra-modern Chinese and international art. Check the local expat websites (see *Information Sources*, p. 294) for up-to-date listings. Shanghai will host the **2010 World Expo**, which is also sure to attract attention, visitors and more investment.

Communications

 Post Office: The main branch is north of Suzhou Creek at 276 Beisuzhou Lu (24 hrs) and there are smaller branches near the Peace Hotel on Nanjing Dong Lu and in the Shanghai Center at 1376 Nanjing Xi Lu.

Telephone code: 021.

Internet Access: There are plenty of cafés around town but note that tighter monitoring laws in Shanghai mean you currently have to show your passport in order to use them. If you are in town for a while it's worth becoming a member, if possible, which removes the lengthy form-filling otherwise required. There's a large 24-hr Internet café on the 4th floor of a shopping center just to the east of the Sofitel hotel on the southern side Nanjing Dong Lu. It is signed from the street and has comfortable chairs, large screens, non-smoking sections and generally provides quick access. Another good café can be found at 379 Zhejiang Zhong Lu, on the western side of the road just north of Nanjing Dong Lu – it's on the fourth floor, but you'll have to follow a maze of corridors through a run-down theater to get there.

Money

Bank of China: Next to the Peace Hotel on Nanjing Nan Lu and with branches all around town.

Other Banks: HSBC (☎ 021-6329-1775) and Credit Lyonnais (☎ 021-6279-8661) both have branches inside the Shanghai Center on Nanjing Xi Lu and you'll find the Bank of America (☎ 021-6320-1491) and Citibank (☎ 021-6328-9661) inside Union Mansions on Yan'an Lu.

Western Union: 1337 Huaihai Zhong Lu.

Consulates

Australia, 22F CITIC Building, 1168 Nanjing Xi Lu (☎ 021-5292-5500, www.aus-in-shanghai.com).

Canada, Room 604, 1376 Nanjing Xi Lu (☎ 021-6279-8400 ext. 5597, www.shanghai.gc.ca).

New Zealand, Room 1605-1607A, The Center, 989 Changle Lu (☎ 021-5407-5858, www.nzembassy.com).

United Kingdom, Room 301, Shanghai Center, 1376 Nanjing Xi Lu (☎ 021-6279-7650, www.uk.cn).

United States, 1469 Huaihai Zhong Lu (☎ 021-6433-6880, www.usembassy-china.org.cn/shanghai).

Public Security Bureau

333 Wusong Lu (☎ 021-6357-7925).

Medical Services

Huashan Hospital Foreigners Clinic, 19F, 12 Wulumuqi Zhing Lu (☎ 021- 6248-3986 ext. 2531 for 24 hour hotline; Changshu Lu subway).

Ruijin Hospital, 197 Ruijin Er Lu (☎ 021-6437-0045 ext 668101; Shanxi Nan Lu subway).

Sightseeing

Sightseeing in Shanghai offers a break from the typical Chinese staple of ancient monuments and temples, instead providing modern attractions aplenty and a cosmopolitan feel found few places on the mainland. This isn't to say that there aren't beautiful temples and parks, it's just that the focus is elsewhere – on the army of skyscrapers and futuristic towers staking their claim here. Nevertheless, Shanghai has seen its share of history, especially in the last couple of hundred years, which has left an array of different styles of architecture, both Chinese and European. If you don't have enough time to make full trips out to Suzhou and the Water Towns (see p. 312), then there is the option of day-trips from Shanghai (see below). Although day excursions to Hangzhou are also offered, you'll spend a lot of time in the bus and, if you can't manage a longer trip, you're better off focusing on areas closer to Shanghai. See *Suggested Itineraries*, p. 134, for a good route around the region.

SHANGHAI NIGHTS

Night shopping on Nanjing Dong Lu (Tot Foster)

Shanghai is the future of China – it has the highest hotel in the world, the fastest train in the world and a dizzyingly dynamic feel to it, yet it still manages to hold on to some of its traditional and colonial legacy. Plan to spend at least three days here taking in the contradictions afforded by this charismatic city. Shanghai's greatest spectacle revels in its contrasts: the **Bund's grand colonial architecture** is faced by impossibly modern skyscrapers across the Huangpu and the sight is definitely worth seeing from both sides of the river, as well as from the water itself. Not too far away, the **Shanghai Museum** is one of the best in the country, both in terms of content and design, and is certainly worth a trip. Other highlights include the **Jade Buddha** and **Longhua temples**, drinks at Cloud 9 atop the **Jinmao Tower**, a meander around the **French Concession**, a cup of tea at the Huxinting Pavilion in the **old city**, a trip to see the incredible **acrobats** and plenty of **shopping**. Round your days off with yet more contrasts by dining in a hip hangout like M on the Bund one night and a traditional eatery such as Meilong Zhen the next.

Tours

Shanghai is easy enough to get around by yourself, but if you've got limited time it's worth booking a tour to make sure you see all the sights. Most hotels have tour booking facilities; otherwise, **Gray Line**, on the fifth floor at 1399 Beijing West Road (☎ 021-6289-5221, www.graylineshanghai.com), runs group (¥370) and private (¥800-1,000) tours of the city. They also do some interesting private insight trips where you can visit and eat in a local home or be taken to a Traditional Chinese Medicine clinic, as well as group tours to nearby towns and cities including Suzhou (¥580), the Water Towns (see p. 312) and not-so-near Hangzhou (¥860). Prices include meals, transport and entry fees; tickets can be booked online. A cheaper alternative is to head to the **Shanghai Sightseeing Bus Station** (☎ 021-6426-5555) at Shanghai Stadium (subway line #1 or buses #15, #42, #43 and #73), which operates bus tours both around the city and to surrounding attractions. Although you'll have to endure the ramblings of a Chinese tour guide on the bus, it's an easy and inexpensive way to see the Water Towns (see p. 312). For cruises on the river see *Adventures On Water*, p. 321, and for cycling tours see *Adventures On Wheels*, p. 321.

★★★ The Bund

A stroll along the Bund

Often compared to Liverpool's Merseyside, the Bund (*waitan* in Chinese) is a showcase of bold, **colonial architecture** dating back to the 1920s when this area was the **British Concession**. The Bund's very un-Chinese sounding name is also part of the colonial legacy and originates from India, where the word means a raised bank. Its sense of history is only exacerbated by the ever-growing number of bigger, brighter and taller buildings across the water in **Pudong**.

Although almost every building on the Bund is of historic significance, there are some you should be sure to check out, including the **Peace Hotel** (see *Where to Stay*, p. 324), the **Customs House** and the **former Hong Kong & Shanghai Bank** (see below). There are also some great restaurants that have recently established themselves here – a few pretensions and high prices are worth enduring for the fine food and views. Try **M on the Bund, the Whampoa Club** or, if you're feeling super-romantic, **Cupola** (see *Where to Eat*, p. 330, for all three).

Even if you don't dine, it's worth coming to the Bund in the evenings – as if the lights of the Pearl Oriental TV Tower weren't enough, there are nightly lightshows (from 7 pm) that dramatically illuminate both Pudong and the Bund. If you want to get across to Pudong in a novel fashion, then the **Sightseeing Tunnel** (daily 8 am-10:30 pm; ¥30 single, ¥40 round-trip) which runs from the northern end of the Bund opposite the junction with bustling Nanjing Dong Lu (see *Shopping*, p. 317), might be just the thing. The tunnel whizzes you under the Huangpu in glass contraptions as brightly colored lights flash by. Henan Zhong Lu on line #2 is the most convenient subway stop for the Bund.

There are also plenty of cruise operators ready to take you out onto the water along the Bund – see *Adventures On Water*, p. 321, for details.

From North to South

★**Huangpu Park**, 1 Zhongshan Dong Er Lu (Apr-Nov daily 5 am-6 pm, Nov-Apr daily 6 am-6 pm; free). At the northern end of the Bund, this park is a pleasant place for a stroll and gives views of both the Bund and Pudong. The park was constructed by the British and allegedly used to have a sign reading "No dogs or Chinese," which is paid tribute to in the Bruce Lee movie *Fist of Fury*. Although the story probably isn't true, the Chinese certainly weren't allowed in (unless they worked for a foreigner) until 1928, 60 years after the park was first opened. These days it's a popular spot for morning tai chi and inside the park you'll find an obelisk-like monument to the "Heroes of the People," beneath which lies the tiny **Bund Historical Museum** (daily 9 am-4 pm; free). The museum traces the history of the Bund as a commercial center and is worth a quick stop before you visit the buildings themselves. South of the park you'll see a large statue, which vaguely resembles Chairman Mao, but is actually Chen Yi, the first mayor of Shanghai.

★**Customs House**, 13 Zhongshan Dongyi Lu (Henan Zhong Lu subway). This architectural masterpiece is one of the most photographed buildings along the Bund, and is easily spotted due to its large bell tower. It still serves as Shanghai's Customs House and the public is prohibited from entering, although it is worth a walk past the main entrance, since you can see a number of ship-

Customs House and former Hong Kong & Shanghai Bank, at left (Miguel A Monjas)

ping mosaics in the entrance hall. During the Cultural Revolution, the building's bell (nicknamed Big Qing) was dismantled and replaced by loud speakers, blaring out a recorded version of the party anthem. In 1986, the bell was returned and the clock has chimed ever since, although it's often drowned out by the streams of traffic flowing through downtown Shanghai.

★★**Former Hong Kong & Shanghai Bank**, 12 Zhongshan Dongyi Lu. For many, this is the finest piece of architecture along the Bund and is well worth a closer look. The building currently houses the Pudong Development Bank, but was originally built by the British in 1921 as the Hong Kong & Shanghai Bank. The architects (Palmer & Turner) were given a singular directive for their design – to dominate the skyline of the Bund. But little did they know that less than 100 years later Pudong would get to dominate the skyline from the Bund! In 1949 the bank was closed and the building was used as Communist party offices. Its dome was painted over in thick white paint to conceal the 'inappropriate' mosaics. They remained covered throughout the Cultural Revolution and were consequently ignored by the Red Guards and forgotten in later years, only being rediscovered in 1997. You can visit the inside of the building during office hours and see these **Italian mosaics** dating back to the 1920s and depicting scenes from all cities around the globe that housed a Hong Kong & Shanghai Bank at that time. Bangkok, Calcutta, Hong Kong, London, New York, Paris, Shanghai and Tokyo are all represented, with the Roman goddess of abundance, Ceres, set in the center of them all.

Bund Museum, Zhongshan Dongyi Lu (daily 9 am-6 pm; free). You can't miss this small tower, uncomfortably surrounded by traffic, at the southern end of the Bund, which has been used to track typhoons and meteorological activities around the Huangpu River since 1884. Downstairs, you'll find a museum about the Bund's most famous buildings and there are a number of old photographs and maps of the area.

Renmin Square

*Shanghai Museum,
in Renmin Square (Galen Frysinger)*

(Renmim Square subway). Today, Renmin (People's) Square is in the heart of Shanghai, with the municipal offices, the Urban Planning Center, the Shanghai Museum, the Grand Theater, the Shanghai Art Museum and the new Museum of Contemporary Art all located in or around it (see *Galleries, Shows and Theaters*, p. 313, for the last three). First built in 1862, the square was originally used as a racetrack by the Shanghai Jockey Club and was a central focus of colonial life. Known as the Ascot of the East, it was the place to be seen, and when the racing season was over, it was used for training and polo matches. In 1941, Japanese occupation brought the closure of the race track and the square was used to detain Allied nationals. When the Communists ascended to power in 1949 the racetrack was obliterated and during the Cultural Revolution (see p. 23) the square was used as a propaganda point and for the humiliating self-criticism of anyone who didn't conform. In the 1990s, the municipal government buildings were moved here and the square underwent reconstruction, to emerge as the focal point of the city.

 Author's Tip: Visiting the square at dawn or dusk will reveal traditional tai chi, ballroom and fan dancing juxtaposed against the sky of gleaming skyscrapers. Kite-flying is another popular pastime in the square and if you take along some food you can also join the masses feeding the pigeons.

Qing Dynasty mask, Shanghai Museum
(Galen Frysinger)

★★★**Shanghai Museum**, Renmin Square (www.shanghaimuseum.net; daily 9 am-5 pm, last entry one hour before closing; ¥20). The Shanghai Museum sits on the southern side of Renmin Square and is another of Shanghai's architectural masterpieces. Designed by one of Shanghai's leading architects, Xing Tonghe, and completed in 1996, the shape of this US$50 million structure is based on a traditional bronze vessel. With four floors and over 120,000 exhibits, the museum houses some of the finest artifacts in China, meaning you'll need plenty of time to explore. Bronzes are the museum's pride and joy, but there are also exquisite examples of ancient calligraphy, ceramics, sculpture, jade, coins, furniture and minority handicrafts on show. It's well laid-out and all the exhibits are clearly labeled in English, but if you require more information there are audio guides available (¥40 plus ¥400 or your passport as deposit). The museum also has three temporary exhibition halls, a tearoom and an excellent bookshop and provides free bag storage if you want to take the weight off your shoulders.

Man on Bactrian camel, Shanghai Museum
(Galen Frysinger)

★★**Shanghai Urban Planning Center**, 100 Renmin Dadao, Renmin Square; Mon-Thurs 9 am-5 pm, Fri-Sun 9 am-6 pm; 9 am-6 pm, last entry one hour before closing; ¥30). Town planning museums don't usually rank high on visitors' itineraries, but you should make an exception for this fine display. The eye-catching futuristic building contains an exhibition that

Nanjing Xi Lu & the French Concession

1. Renmin Square & MTR Station
2. Shanghai Urban Planning Museum
3. Shanghai Museum
4. Grand Theatre
5. Park Hotel; Grand Cinema; People's Square MTR Station
6. Shanghai Concert Hall
7. To Old City (see Shanghai Downtown map)
8. Huangpi Nan Lu MTR Station
9. Museum of the First National Congress of the Chinese Communist Party; Xintiandi; Hotel #88: Crystal Jade Restaurant, TMSK Restaurant, Ye Shanghai Restaurant; Shikumen Open House Museum; Xintiandi Information Center
10. Former Residence of Zhou Enlai
11. Taikang Art Museum; Antiques Market
12. Ruijin Hospital
13. Ruijin Hotel: Art Deco Garden Café
14. Former Residence of Sun Yat Sen
15. Shanghai Art Museum: Kathleen's 5 Restaurant
16. Marriott Hotel
17. Godly Vegetarian Restaurant
18. Old China Hand Reading Room
19. Xiangyang Market
20. Shanxi Nan Lu MTR Station
21. Jin Jiang Hotel
22. Hengshan-Moller Villa Hotel
23. Former Residence of Mao Zhedong
24. Meilong Zhen Restaurant
25. Shimen Yi Lu MTR Station
26. To Train Station, Bus Station, Shanghai Circus World
27. To Jade Buddha Temple
28. Plaza 66: Wagas Restaurant
29. Portman Ritz-Carlton; Element Fresh Restaurant
30. Guyi Hunan Restaurant
31. Shinton Restaurant
32. Bao Luo Restaurant
33. Changshu MTR Station
34. Arts & Crafts Museu39
35. #9 Hotel
36. Yang's Kitchen Restaurant
37. Hengshan MTR Station; to Botanical Gardens, Longhua Temple, Xujiahui Cathedral, Shanghai Sightseeing Tour Bus Company
38. Former Residence of Soong Qingling
39. Propaganda Poster Art Center
40. Bali Laguna Restaurant
41. Jing'an Park & MTR Station
42. Jing'an Temple
43. Yunfeng Theatre
44. To Hongqiao Airport
45. Shanghai Opera Theatre

traces the skyline of Shanghai throughout the centuries. The highlight is an enormous model depicting central Shanghai in 2020. At 6,400 square feet, it's said to be the largest of its kind in the world. The model presents existing architectural favorites such as the Oriental Pearl Tower and the Customs House on the Bund, as well as planned additions to the city's already spectacular skyline. Don't miss the clock that sits above the entrance to the center, counting down the days until the Shanghai World Expo in 2010. If you want a drink or snack, there are a few cafés in a mock 1930s street below the museum.

Nanjing Xi Lu & the Northwest

Although Nanjing Xi Lu is more about offices, shopping and upscale hotels than sightseeing, there are a few bits and pieces worth seeking out here. A mile north of Nanjing Xi Lu, the **Jade Buddha Temple** is one of Shanghai's most visited sights and definitely worth a trip. subway line #2 runs under Nanjing Xi Lu, but for the Jade Buddha Temple you're better off taking a taxi.

Former Residence of Mao Zedong, 5-9, Lane 583, Weihai Lu (daily, 9:30 am-4:45 pm; ¥5; Shimen Yi Lu subway). This traditional *shikumen* building housed Mao, his wife, their two sons and Mao's mother-in-law on and off from 1924 and it contains a number of the Chairman's letters and photos, along with some of the family's everyday items. Although it remains a popular spot with domestic tourists, there is little of real significance or interest here and it doesn't justify a special trip.

Jing'an Temple, 1686 Nanjing Xi Li (daily 7:30 am-5 pm; ¥10; Jing'an Temple subway). Forming a contrast with the surrounding cityscape, the traditional roofs of Jing'an Temple offer a pleasant diversion from the skyscrapers of Nanjing Xi Lu. Originally built during the Three Kingdoms period (see *History*, p. 8), the temple has been rebuilt a number of times and was completely flattened in

Traffic rushes by Jing'an Temple

the 1990s. What you see today is still incomplete and you may find the gray breezeblock interior a little disappointing. Despite this, Jing'an remains one of the city's central places for ancestor worship and comes alive during festivals.

Jing'an Park, opposite Jing'an Temple, Nanjing Xi Lu (daily 6 am-6 pm; free; Jing'an Temple subway). Jing'an Park makes a welcome break from the noise and bustle of the city. Located opposite the temple, the park has a number of pavilions, picnic areas and open green spaces. There is also an attractive lily pond, on the far side of which you'll find the excellent Bali Laguna restaurant (see *Where to Eat*, p. 332).

Monks pray at Jade Buddha Temple

★★★**Jade Buddha Temple**, 170 Anfu Lu (daily, 8:30 am-4:30 pm, ¥10). This large and attractive temple in the northwest of Shanghai is well worth a taxi ride. Built as a monastery in 1882 using a Song dynasty style of architecture, the temple features symmetrical halls and courtyards with sweeping eaves. The temple was closed from 1949 to 1980 and managed to survive the terror of the Cultural Revolution by pasting portraits of Mao on the wall, an image that the Red Guards would not remove or destroy. The temple gets its name from the two jade Buddhas brought from Myanmar and housed in its halls. On the ground floor you'll see the larger of the two Buddhas in reclining position, but the seated Buddha upstairs shows finer craftsmanship. If you think of jade as always being green, think again – both statues here are carved from white jade. Often thronging with tour groups, the temple is nevertheless an active one and, if you hang around long enough, you should get to witness the monks' evocative chanting. The temple also has an excellent vegetarian restaurant.

★★★The French Concession

The former French Concession has always been a bit of a hideaway from downtown and remains so today, despite its plethora of sights, shops, hotels, bars and restaurants. In the 1920s and 1930s while the French nominally ruled the roost, the area was effectively controlled by the notorious gangster Du Yuesheng (see *Shanghai, History*, p. 287) and the French Concession was the center of Shanghai's drug and prostitution racket. Despite lax law enforcement, the district still enjoyed the security of the international com-

Facing page: The French Concession

munity and as a result it served as home to many of the Chinese revolution-
aries of the day. Today the French Concession is a charming part of town to
visit and during the day its **quiet tree-lined avenues and parks** make for
a wonderfully refreshing stroll (see *Residential Ramble*, p.000) and there
are plenty of cafés where you can stop and refuel. By night the scene is
transformed and the streets come alive to a hedonist beat, albeit with a
somewhat more restrained and chic style than in days of old. subway line #1
runs through the French Concession. The Art and Crafts Museum and Propaganda Poster Art Center are also worth checking out for a flavor of
China's diverse arts scene (see *Galleries, Shows & Theaters*, p. 313).

Former Residences

Former Residence of Sun Yatsen, 7 Xiangshan Lu (daily, 9 am-4:30 pm;
¥8; Shanxi Nan Lu subway). This gray, simple mansion sits in the southwest
corner of Fuxing Park. With a British- style lawn, flanked by tall trees and
high walls, the house seems more suited to a suburb of London than Shanghai. Dr. Sun Yatsen and his wife Soong Qingling moved to the house in June
1918, shortly after his return from Japan, and it was from here that he
became China's first leader in 1923. The contents have remained untouched
and letters, books and photos remain, while the outside has recently undergone a much needed facelift.

Former Residence of Zhou Enlai, 73 Sinan Lu (Mon, Wed & Fri, 9 am-
11 am & 1 pm-4:30 pm; ¥5; Shanxi Nan Lu subway). On a quiet street just
down from Sun Yatsen's, the façade of this three-story French mansion is
engulfed in ivy and the building is fringed by hedges. The house served as
the secret operational base of Shanghai's Communist movement in the late
1940s although little evidence remains of this today.

★★**Former Residence of Soong
Qingling**, 1848 Huaihai Zhong Lu (daily,
9 am-4:30 pm; ¥8; Hengshan Lu subway). The
most charming of Shanghai's collection of former residences, this house was built in the
1920s by a German ship owner. From 1948
to1963 this was the main residence of Soong
Qingling, widow of Dr. Sun Yatsen, and has
been left as it was, giving a fascinating
insight into one of China's most famous
women. Photos of Soong with her husband,
family and important officials (notably Mao
Zedong) hang on the walls and there are over
4,000 books, which tells you something about Soong's intellectual bent.
Soong's bedroom is also worth a look as it houses the furniture her parents
gave as a dowry. In the garage is a limousine given to the family by Stalin.
Other exhibits include a red carpet from Mao and next door you'll find a
small museum containing more photos, including Soong and Sun's wedding
pictures.

SOONG QINGLING

Charlie Soong was a wealthy Shanghai businessman and missionary. His marriage bore three daughters, all of whom married highly prominent figures in the emerging new China. Soong Qingling (1893-1981) was born in Jiangsu, educated in Shanghai and the US and in 1915, much to the chagrin of her parents, she married Dr. Sun Yatsen (see p. 18), who was 26 years her senior. Her sister Meiling wed Chiang Kaishek. Qingling was an intelligent, well-read and dedicated woman who spent her career

Sun Yatsen and Soong Qingling

trying to improve the lives of everyday Chinese people, particularly women. She became the leader of the Women's Department of the Nationalists in 1924 and, after Sun's death, sided with the Communists, albeit remaining connected to the Nationalists. When the Communists took power she was awarded the title of Vice-President of the PRC, although she didn't officially join the Communist party until two weeks before her death in 1981. Throughout her life she campaigned relentlessly for the emancipation of women and the foundation she established is continuing her work to this day. In 1949 Qingling also founded the magazine *China Today* (previously *China Reconstructs*), which is still published in six languages around the world. Qingling's commitment to the development of a new republic has earned her the title "The One Who Loved China" and she is fondly remembered throughout the country.

Xintiandi

Xintiandi literally means New Heaven and Earth and is the result of Shanghai starting to appreciate some of its historic architecture. Its *shikumen* (see callout below) houses have been gentrified to form one of Shanghai's trendiest eating and shopping districts. Although it's decidedly contrived, the area is attractive and gives some idea of what much of Shanghai looked like 80 years ago. Xintiandi also holds a couple of historic monuments of note and its location halfway between the Old City and the French Concession makes it an ideal spot to stop for a drink. It is served by Huangpi Nan Lu subway station on line #1.

★**Museum of the First National Congress of the Chinese Communist Party**, 374 Huangpi Nan Lu (daily 9 am-5 pm, last entry one hour before closing; ¥3). Easily spotted by the large numbers of Chinese tourists clustered outside taking photos, this small museum pays homage to the formation of China's Communist party. On July 23rd, 1921, 13 members of secret Communist cells (including Mao Zedong) met to discuss the founding of a new national party – the Chinese Communist Party. Opened in 1949, the contents have remained untouched, other than the addition of a wax model showing Mao and his comrades in the meeting. There is an upstairs exhibition that evokes the mood of the time and features some interesting anti-imperial propaganda.

Shikumen Open House Museum, 25 Lane 181, Taicang Lu (Sun-Thurs 10:30 am-10:30 pm, Fri & Sat 11 am-11 pm; ¥20). This small museum celebrates the *shikumen* architecture of 1920s Shanghai and sets the scene for a foray into the surrounding area. The lobby is also a good place to pick up information and listings for Shanghai.

SHIKUMEN HOUSES

Shikumen housing used to cover much of Shanghai. Developed in the 19th century, the style, which literally means "stone gate," shows a unique mix of east and west. The houses, which were originally designed as middle-class residential quarters, typically had black wooden doors set inside a stone gateway that opened up into a small enclosed courtyard. These days there are few examples of *shikumen* housing left. Xintiandi sensationalizes *shikumen* architecture with its bars, restaurants and shops, but for more genuine examples head to Mao ming Bei Lu.

The Old City

While the colonials were busy reconstructing their homelands on the Bund and in the French Concession, the Chinese lived within a walled city to the south. The Old City has a **2,000-year history** and was originally a fishing village. In the middle of the 16th century it was walled to defend against Japanese pirates, and these walls remained until 1911. During the colonial era the Old City was perceived as a strange and savage place where few foreigners ventured, until Thomas Cook began leading tours there in 1872.

These days the Old City is very new in parts – all the Ming- and Qing-style buildings in the **Yuyuan Bazaar**, which surrounds Yu Gardens, have been completely rebuilt or at least heavily restored. When combined with the legion of souvenir shops and hordes of tourists, it gives this part of the Old City a decidedly contrived and Disney feel. Still, it's a fun place to visit and the central lake, crossed by the **Bridge of Nine Turns** (impassable to ghosts who can only travel in straight lines...), is very picturesque in a kitsch way – especially as the sun goes down and the curved eaves of the buildings are illuminated.

Halfway along the bridge you'll reach the famous **Huxinting teahouse** (see p. 335), while over on the other side of the lake you'll find **Nanxiang** (see p. 336), a great dumpling restaurant. The **City God Temple** (daily 8:30 am-4:30 pm; ¥5), in the center of the bazaar, is also worth a quick peek. The temple, which pays tribute to the old city's resident god, dates from the 15th century and has been restored after a period of neglect. The reason most people come here, though, is to see the acclaimed **Yu Gardens** (see below). But a stroll through the genuine antiquity and characterful markets of some of the nearby streets, such as Fangbang Zhong Lu, and maybe a trip to **Dongtai Antiques Market** (just outside the Old City boundary), are also recommended. There are no convenient subway lines for the Old City but it's not too far to walk down from the Bund or Nanjing Lu; otherwise get a taxi.

Huxinting Teahouse, Yuyuan Bazaar

★★**Yu Gardens**, Yuyuan Bazaar (daily 8:30 am-5 pm; ¥40). Despite being one of the most frequented sights in Shanghai, the Yu Gardens make for a pleasant diversion from the bustle of the Old City. First constructed during the Ming dynasty for the governor of Szechuan (Pan Yunduan), these classical gardens contain pavilions, bridges, chambers, towers, ponds, rockeries and white-washed walls capped by fierce dragons. If you happen to be visiting during the Chinese Lantern Festival (see *Holidays & Festivals*, p. 73, for details) then you'll see the gardens beautifully illuminated by 10,000 lanterns.

Pudong

The city's newest district was, until 20 years ago, just marshy flatland. However, with the opening of the economy in the 1980s, Shanghai, long neglected by the party for its bourgeois past, suddenly sprang to life and began expanding. The result is nothing short of spectacular and Shanghai's skyline has taken on a new silhouette, which rivals that of Hong Kong, New York or Sydney.

Pudong's two most famous and dramatic structures, the **Jinmao Tower** and the space-rocket-like **Pearl Oriental TV Tower** manage to make various other impressive buildings fade into the background. While ascending these towers is great for the ride and also gives 360-degree views, part of what makes Shanghai's skyline so impressive are these two super-tall buildings. When looking out from them, I always feel something is missing from the panorama! Next to the Jinmao, a new tower is rapidly climbing skywards and, when complete, the **Shanghai World Financial Center**, at

101 floors, will eclipse its neighbor (but not Taipei's 101 Tower, the world's highest).

To appreciate the Bund from Pudong, take a walk along the Riverside Promenade which is lined with cafés (see *Where to Drink*, p. 337) which, while expensive, offers great views, especially when the sun sets and gives way to the evening lightshows (from 7 pm). The sights below can be reached by subway line #2 to Lujiazui.

Pearl Oriental TV Tower, at left (Galen Frysinger)

★★**Pearl Oriental TV Tower**, 1 Shiji Dadao (daily 8 am-10 pm; ¥35-100 – see text for details; Lujiazui subway, or the Bund Sightseeing Tunnel. Shanghai's signature building, completed in 1994 looks fresh from the set of a sci-fi movie. The three cylindrical concrete supports give the appearance that the space-rocket of a tower is poised for take-off, an apt metaphor for Shanghai's explosive re-launch as China's financial capital. The tower contains 12 "pearls" or circular constructions, the three largest housing observation areas and restaurants. To go to both the first and second pearls costs ¥85, or ¥70 to choose just one (obviously the second commands better views). To gain access to all three pearls, the highest of which is 875 feet, tickets cost ¥100, or ¥200/280 respectively, including lunch (11 am-2 pm) or dinner (5-9 pm). At the base of the tower, the **Shanghai Municipal History Museum** (daily 9 am-9 pm; ¥35 or entry with a tower ticket) is definitely worth a visit. The museum contains over a thousand exhibits tracing Shanghai's social history since the mid-19th century, including its "foreign paradise" past.

★★**Jin Mao Tower**, 88 Shiji Dadao (daily, 8:30 am-9 pm, ¥50). No trip to Shanghai would be complete without a visit to this breathtaking structure. With 88 floors, it is the tallest building in China and the highest hotel (1,575 feet) in the world. Designed by an American team of architects, Skidmore, Owings & Merril, it has become a symbol of modern Shanghai, fusing tradition and modernity, East and West. The building takes its shape from traditional Chinese pagodas, with 13 distinct tiers, and is made from steel and glass. The number of floors, 88, isn't a matter of chance – eight implies wealth and prosperity (see *Beliefs & Superstitions*, p. 54). There is an observation deck (¥50) on the 88th floor offering 360-degree views of the city (choose a clear day since visibility can be poor). For only a little more money you can enjoy the expansive vistas with a cocktail or cup of coffee at the café on the 54th floor of the Hyatt (next to reception), the numerous restaurants on the 56th floor or, better still, from Cloud 9 (see *Nightlife*, p. 360), on the 87th floor.

The Jin Mao Tower

Xujiahui & Longhua

These predominantly residential and shopping districts have a couple of treats in store – their Buddhist and Christian religious sights, and the wonderfully lush retreat of the Botanical Gardens. It's a long way from town though and, while the subway line is good for the cathedral, both the temple and the Botanical Gardens are a fairly long walk from the station, so you might be better off in a taxi (¥40-50).

★**The Botanical Gardens**, 111 Longwu Lu (daily, 8 am-5 pm, ¥10; Shanghai South Railway Station subway). Although a fair trek from downtown Shanghai, the Botanical Gardens make for an excellent day-trip. With over 9,000 plants and a number of ponds, greenhouses and *bonsai* gardens, this is a great place for a picnic. Families often bring entire toy boxes to entertain the kids while they spend the afternoon eating and playing cards. The gardens also house a great collection of orchids that is sure to impress.

★★**Longhua Temple**, 2583 Longhua Lu (daily 7 am-5 pm, ¥10; Longlao Lu subway or buses #41, #44, #73 & #87). With a history dating back nearly 2,000 years, the Longhua Temple is Shanghai's oldest and one of its most active temples. It's popular with both locals and tourists and can get very busy, especially during Chinese New Year and the annual Longhua Temple Festival in early April (see *Holidays & Festivals*, p. 73). As with most temples, the original structure has been re-built a number of times and is in excellent condition today. Along with a 1,700-year-old seven-story octagonal pagoda standing 145 feet high, there is a large bell tower containing a 14,000-lb bronze bell, rung only once a year to welcome in the Chinese New Year.

Xujiahui Cathedral, 158 Puxi Lu (Xujiahui subway or bus #42 & #43). This imposing cathedral reflects Xujiahui's history as the earliest Western community in Shanghai, established by a Chinese Catholic, Pau Xu Guangqi, who invited Jesuits to settle here in the 17th century. The cathedral was built in 1846 and was closed during the Cultural Revolution, but the large congregations at mass (Mon-Sat 7 am, Sun 8 am) are evidence of today's greater religious freedom. Xu was a dedicated meteorologist and he established a survey center here which is still used as Shanghai's weather observatory.

North of Suzhou Creek

★**Jewish Refugee Museum**, 63 Changyang Lu, Hongkou (daily 9 am-4:30 pm; ¥50; Hongkou Stadium subway). North of the center and housed inside the former Ohel Moshe Synagogue, this small museum offers a glimpse into the development of the Jewish community in Shanghai. Although the first Jewish settlers came with the British in the 19th century, during the Holocaust Shanghai was one of the only places in the world accepting Jewish refugees without the need for even a passport. Between 1937 and 1939, 30,000 Jewish refugees arrived and the Chinese are fondly remembered for their tolerant attitude, but when the Japanese seized control, Jews were rounded up and forced to live in Hongkou's ghettoes. The museum has photos and a historical video that detail day-to-day life within the ghetto community.

★**Lu Xun Park**, 146 Dongjiangwang Lu (daily 6 am-6 pm; ¥5; Hongkou Stadium subway). This pleasant park is dedicated to China's most famous 20th-century novelist, Lu Xun (see *Bibliography*, p. 595); inside, you'll find his tomb, a statue and a museum (daily 9 am-5 pm; ¥8) with an extensive collection of his works, photos and personal effects.

Around Shanghai

★★★ The Water Towns

To really take a break from the city it's worth heading to one of the region's famed water towns, where you'll find quaint old houses lining tranquil canals spanned by impossibly steep arched stone bridges. Suzhou (p. 339) is the most famous of the water towns but, for a more intimate look at the watery world of this part of the country, seek out one of the smaller settlements that can be easily reached from Shanghai or Suzhou. However, the serene beauty of these towns has not escaped the notice of the rest of the country. Many of these once peaceful havens now charge entrance fees and have become real tourist traps to be avoided on weekends. **Zhujiajiao** is the closest to Shanghai and, along with stunning ★★**Zhouzhuang** (www. zhouzhuang.net) and its canal mansions, sees the most visitors, with ★**Wuzhen** (www.wuzhen.com.cn) and its cottage industries coming in a close third. ★★**Xitang** (www.xitang.com.cn) is a little farther afield and consequently draws fewer crowds, while ★★**Tongli** (www.china-tongli. com) and its famed Tuisi Garden is best visited by bus or taxi from Suzhou.

You can quite easily head out to any of the towns by yourself, and there is simple accommodation found in many of them (see websites for details), but if you want to visit on a day-trip several agencies in Shanghai run tours, notably Gray Line and the Shanghai Sightseeing Bus Center (see *Tours*, p. 297, for details on both). The latter has several buses daily out to the towns and trips cost from as little as ¥70 for nearby Zhujiajiao, to ¥150 for those farther afield.

Galleries, Shows & Theaters

Shanghai has an increasingly international array of cultural attractions, from music (and musicals) to art galleries, but the highlight for many visitors is the spectacular acrobats.

★★★Acrobatics

The Shanghai Acrobats are renowned in China and the troupe performs around the world. You can see performances every night at various theaters around the city – Shanghai Circus World is one of the best, while the Yunfeng offers a more touristy version but, wherever you see Shanghai's acrobats, you're likely to come away mindblown! (See p. 65 for more on acrobatics.)

- **Shanghai Center Theater**, 1376 Nanjing Xi Lu (☎ 021-6279-8948; daily 7:30 pm if there are no visiting shows; ¥100; Jing'an Temple subway).
- **Shanghai Circus World**, 2266 Gonghexin Lu (☎ 021-6437-4685, www. circus-world.com/EN; daily 7:30 pm; ¥50-150).
- **Yunfeng Theater**, 1700 Beijing Xi Lu (☎ 021- 6258-2258; daily 7:30 pm; ¥150-200; Jing'an Temple subway).

Art

The bold Red Art posters at the Propaganda Poster Art Center and modern displays at the brand new Museum of Contemporary Art are a world away from the traditional handicrafts found at the Arts and Crafts Museum. If you're here between October and November it's definitely worth visiting the **Shanghai Biennale**, held at the Shanghai Art Museum.

★**Shanghai Art Museum**, 325 Nanjing Xi Lu (daily 9 am-4 pm, ¥20; Renmin Square subway). This 1930s building on the northwestern corner of Renmin Square started life as the Shanghai Jockey Club and was converted into an art museum in 1956. While the permanent collection contains calligraphy, painting and sculpture, the contemporary exhibitions offer interesting insight into the thoughts of modern day Chinese artists, although labeling in English is limited. There is also a smattering of international art and the museum hosts the Shanghai Biennale Festival in October (see *International Festivals*, p. 295). Check out *that's Shanghai* for current exhibitions.

★★**Museum of Contemporary Art**, Renmin Park (daily 10 am-6 pm, www.mocashanghai.org; Renmin Square subway). The MoCA is a dazzling addition to Renmin Square's already numerous sights. The museum's ultra-modern industrial-style architecture uses radically skewed angles to catch the eye, and its bright interior hosts both international and domestic displays of contemporary art and design. There's also a great Italian restaurant that offers alfresco dining. For current exhibitions, refer to the website or one of the magazines mentioned in *Information Sources* (p. 294).

★★**Arts and Crafts Museum**, 79 Fengyang Lu (daily 9 am-4 pm; ¥8; Changshu Lu subway). This impressive late-Renaissance French mansion built in 1905 offers an excellent opportunity to see traditional local craftsmen at work. From paper-cutters to embroiderers, the museum presents an interesting insight into the production of traditional Chinese crafts. Many of the pieces are for sale at reasonable prices and it's always nice to have watched your purchase being made!

"Red Art" at the Propaganda Poster Art Center (Tot Foster)

★★**Propaganda Poster Art Center**, basement floor, Building 4, 868 Huashan Lu (daily 9:30 am-4:30 pm; ¥20; Changshu Lu subway). Established two years ago by Mr Yang Pei Ming, the Propaganda Art Center is definitely worth hunting out, hidden in the basement of a residential complex in the leafy Huashan area. Although a challenge to locate, once there you'll see over 200 original "Red Art" prints produced between 1949 and 1979. To get there head to 868 Huashan Lu and take the right-hand entrance by number 5, rather than number 4, which is on your left. Soon you'll see building 4 on your left. Head inside and take the lift down to the basement.

The two rooms are packed with posters depicting a host of happy scenes, including an ever-jubilant Mao, Red Guards full of revolutionary zeal and children keenly brandishing *Little Red Books*. Many of the posters are for sale and most have English captions. If you want to know more, speak to Mr. Yang who is an excellent guide and will detail the history of any poster and may even show you his favorites hidden in a back office.

Music

For refined evenings the striking **Grand Theater** in Renmin Square is the cultural heart of the city. Its design was inspired by the ancient Chinese belief of a square earth surrounded by a circular heaven and it sports a dramatically curved roof. The theater's three stages show some of the best performances in China. Line-ups include ballet, opera, music recitals and Western musicals. *Les Miserables* saw its China premiere here in 2002 and in 2006 the arrival of the *Lion King* (whose cast occupied the Park Hotel across the square) caused a big stir. You can get tickets by calling the hotline at ☎ 021-6448-0898.

If you're looking for **opera**, then try the **Yifu Theater** (☎ 021-6351-4668) at 701 Fuzhou Lu, just off Renmin Square, which has regular performances of various operatic styles. For **classical music** look no further than the recently moved (brick by brick!) **Shanghai Concert Hall** (☎ 021-6386-9153) at 523 Yan'an Dong Lu, which is home to the **Shanghai Symphony Orchestra** and also hosts performers from around the world.

Movie Theaters

Shanghai has a number of movie theaters showing films in English. Tickets are generally around ¥60.

Cathay Theater, 870 Huaihai Zhong Lu (Shanxi Nan Lu subway)

This striking art-deco building was once owned by the wealthy Sassoon family. Today, while not as comfortable as its modern counterparts, it shows a mix of Chinese and Western movies.

Paradise Warner Cinema City, 6F Grand Gateway, 1 Hongqiao Lu (☎ 021-6407-662, www.paradisewarner.com/index-en.htm; Xujiahui subway).

UME International Cineplex, Xingye Lu, Xintiandi (☎ 021-6373-3333; Huangpi Nan Lu subway).

For Families

Shanghai's steamy summers can make sightseeing feel like a bit of a mission with kids, but there are increasing numbers of sights that appeal to all ages. To keep your *xiaopengyou* (small friends) happy, try the following:

★**Madame Tussauds**, 10th Floor, New World Building, 68 Nanjing Xi Lu (daily, 10 am-10 pm; ¥125; Renmin Square subway). Opened in June 2006, this is the latest addition to Madame Tussauds' worldwide collection and offers all the usual treats. Be prepared to fight your way through the crowds of tourists snapping photos of their heroes – Tom Cruise, Bill Gates and

David Beckham are local favorites The nation's heroes are also represented and include China's first astronaut, Yang Liwei, and the seven-foot six-inch basketball star, Yao Ming.

★★**Shanghai Ocean Aquarium**, 158 Yucheng Bei Li, Pudong (daily 9 am-9 pm, adults ¥110, children ¥70; Lujiazui subway). Informative and fun, the aquarium makes for an enjoyable excursion, with over 10,000 fish from all over the world on display. The highlight, without a doubt, is the 500-foot underwater tunnel that takes you on a marine

Shanghai Ocean Aquarium

adventure past sharks, turtles and tropical fish, all oblivious to your presence.

★★**Science and Technology Museum**, 1000 Shiji Dadao (daily, 9 am-5:15 pm, last entry 45 minutes before closing, adults ¥60, children ¥20; Science and Technology Museum subway). This massive structure lies halfway between the new airport and downtown Shanghai. Despite the distance, it's well worth the time and kids love the interactive exhibits, sound and light shows, two IMAX 3D cinemas (¥30) and simulated rainforest.

Health & Relaxation

Shanghai is a frenetically paced city and, whether living here or just passing through, it can all get too much at times. A break from sightseeing and shopping could help you gain more from your trip and Shanghai has plenty of places where you can switch off for a while.

Massage

Many of the top hotels have good massage and spa facilities – **Banyan Tree** at the Westin is recommended (see *Where to Stay*, p. 324). On a lower budget it's worth seeking out **Dragonfly** (20 Donghu Lu; ☎ 021-5405-0008, www.dragonfly.net.cn; ¥60-120; Shanxi Nan Lu subway), which is a citywide chain offering great Chinese massages, *shiatsu* and aromatherapy. Cheaper still are the legion of foot massage parlors, sometimes staffed by blind masseurs, where you can get reflexology for around ¥40 an hour.

Traditional Chinese Medicine

For traditional Chinese acupressure, acupuncture and herbal remedies (see *Traditional Chinese Medicine*, p. 71) try the **Xiangshan Hospital** at 11

Xiangshan Lu (Shanxi Nan Lu subway). Consultations cost ¥35 but you'll need to bring someone who speaks Chinese.

Shopping

Shanghai's shopping is second only to Hong Kong and you'll find goods from all over China and the world. The most obvious shopping street is Nanjing Lu, which gets increasingly classy as it shifts west, but there are also an army of shopping malls and markets to scour.

Markets

To escape the bright, air-conditioned malls, Shanghai's markets are as interesting for a slice of the city's life as they are for the astounding range of products they offer.

★★★**Bird and Flower Market**, Jiangyin Lu (daily 9 am-5 pm; Renmin Square subway). A lively and buzzing market, the streets around here are crammed with birds, fish, flowers and *bonsai*. Prepare for a noisy excursion as hawkers and customers haggle over the best prices to the backdrop of bird song.

★★**Dongtai Lu Antiques Market**, Dongtai Lu and Liuhekou Lu, off Xizang Nan Lu (daily 9 am-6 pm; Huangpi Nan Lu subway). This is a great place to come for a stroll, some browsing and light haggling. The market is spread over a few streets on the western side of Xizang Lu and is a treasure trove of cheap Mao nicknacks, with a few genuine antiques. Expect to knock two-thirds off the asking price.

Xiangyang Market, Xiangyang Nan Lu (daily 9 am-8:30 pm; Shanxi Nan Lu subway). For fake goods, this is the place. Hidden in its grid of stalls you'll find DVDs, handbags, sportswear, sunglasses and almost anything else that can be copied. Bargaining is essential.

Shopping Streets & Malls

China's version of London's Oxford Street, **Nanjing Dong Lu**, offers over a mile of shopping from around the world and is a great place to get a feel for the pace of the city even if you manage to avoid buying anything. Pedestrianised for over half its length, Nanjing Dong Lu is also an easy place to shop and has everything from small one-off outlets to enormous malls. It's a good place

Lanterns lead the way to Dongtai Lu Antiques Market (Tot Foster)

to pick up souvenirs like chopsticks and silk, as well as international brand clothing and sports goods, although larger-frame Westerners may have trouble finding clothes to fit. There are plenty of good restaurants in the vicinity for those all important pit-stops and, if you can't face the walk, there's even a mini-train that can take you along Nanjing Dong Lu between Henan Lu and Renmin Square for ¥2.

One of the grandest and newest malls is the shining tower of **Heng Yuan Xiang Department Store** on the southern side of Nanjing Dong Lu by Huangpu Lu and just across from Renmin Square. Some relics from the past still manage to survive on thriving Nanjing Lu, including an enormous pharmacy, the No.1 Dispensary. As you progress west past Renmin Square, the street becomes **Nanjing Xi Lu** and the shops and malls start to get more upmarket. This is Shanghai's version of Fifth Avenue and you'll find all the usual characters – Prada, Versace and friends. One of the glitziest malls is **Plaza 66** at 1266 Nanjing Xi Lu.

Arts & Crafts

Other places to try for handicrafts include the **Arts and Crafts Museum** (see p. 314) and trendy **Taikang Lu**, south of Jianguo Zhong Lu, which has contemporary shops selling paintings, pottery, jewelry and other arts and crafts.

Silk & Tailoring

Shanghai is close to the silk-growing areas of Suzhou and Hangzhou and has a long history of fine dressmaking. Cheongsams or (*qipao* in Chinese) were the cutting edge in the 1930s and have seen a renaissance of late as people re-embrace their past. You can pick up inexpensive readymade dresses just about anywhere in town (Xiangyang Market, see above, is very cheap), but if you want a quality dress made up, then head for **Silk King** at 66 Nanjing Dong Lu. Silk costs around ¥30-40 per meter (3 ft 3 inches) and tailor-made dresses can start from as little as ¥500, depending on the fabric chosen.

Quality men's suits can also be made for significantly lower prices than in Europe or North America – **Dave's Custom Tailoring** at 6, lane 288, Wuyuan Lu, north of Huaihai Lu, is recommended, although suits take 10 days to complete.

SHANGHAI FASHION

For a modern take on traditional Chinese dress, check out zesty **Shanghai Tang** (sample at left, www.shanghaitang.com), with branches at 55 Maoming Nan Lu and in Xintiandi Square, or for more *couture* styling try internationally acclaimed **Vivienne Tam** (opposite Pizza Express, just off Huangpi Nan Lu in Xintiandi).

Electronic Goods

If you've been having trouble with any of your electronic equpment or just want to pick up some new headphones, a flash-disk or even an adaptor, you can get it all at **Modern Electrical City** on the southwest corner of the junction of Fuxing Zhong Lu and Xiangyang Nan Lu (Shanxi Nan Lu subway).

Everyday Needs

Most everyday needs can be met at the ubiquitous **alldays** and **KEDI** 24-hr convenience stores, but for bigger shops it might be worth heading to **Carrefour** out in Gubei (268 Shuicheng Nan Lu, off Yan'an Xi Lu). **Watson's** is the place for toiletries – there's a branch at 787 Huaihai Lu and another on Nanjing Dong Lu.

Adventures

On Foot

While Shanghai is, in many ways, well-set up for visitors, its busy streets and the army of attendants ensuring you only cross the road when it's supposedly safe makes for a lot of waiting and traffic lights. But there are pedestrianised streets such as the western part of Nanjing Dong Lu and the riverside promenades of the Bund and Pudong, all of which are worth a stroll. To get inside Shanghai a little more, the walks listed below take you through the lively heart of the old city and the leafy streets of the French Concession and are your best foot forward. If you want to be shown around, **Cycle China** (see *On Wheels*, below) conducts guided walking tours of Pudong, the Old City and the Bund. They cost ¥150-200, depending on the number of people in the group.

From Old to New (1 hr)

This is a pleasant afternoon walk that begins in the heart of the old city, taking in temples, tea houses, markets and everyday life, ending in the center of Shanghai's trendiest area, Xintiandi. Start after lunch and give yourself plenty of time to amble along as there are markets and sights to take in on the way.

Take a taxi to **Yuyuan Bazaar** to start this walk. It's worth popping into the City God Temple, which has recently undergone restoration. At the back of the main courtyard you'll find an exit that will lead you straight into the bazaar, where you can stroll at leisure, taking in shops, exquisite Yu Gardens (see p. 309) and the traditional Huxinting Teahouse (see p. 335). If you're hungry and want a snack, try the legendary dumplings from Nanxiang, easily spotted by the lines of people eagerly awaiting their turn (see p. 336).

Exit the southern end of the bazaar, turning west onto **Fangbang Zhong Lu**. This road is lined with a collection of recently restored, picturesque traditional houses. Now selling touristy trinkets, the houses have earned the road its nickname, Shanghai Old Street. Once you cross Henan Nan Lu, the road becomes narrow and winding but its name (Fangbang Zhong Lu) is clearly marked at regular intervals. The tourist shops fade away and bicycles, carts and street vendors fill the alleyways. Continue along Fangbang Zhong Lu until you reach **Xizang Nan Lu**, where you turn right. Walk north up Xizang Nan Lu for a block before turning west onto Liuhekou Lu. This is the beginning of yet another excellent market, the **Dongtai Lu Market**. Filled with waving Mao watches, Communist propaganda posters and reproduction antiques, this market is well worth a visit. Be prepared as there's lots to buy! When you're marketed out, head south down Jian Lu, which runs along the western side of the market, before turning right (west) onto Zizhong Lu. You'll notice a change in the architecture as you approach the gentrified *shikumen* buildings of **Xintiandi** (see *Shikumen* callout, p. 000). Once here you can enjoy a well-earned beer or meal in one of the area's trendy bars and eateries before taking a taxi or subway line #1 from Huangpi Nan Lu station.

Residential Ramble (90 mins)

The former French Concession has countless tree-lined avenues and, with so many to choose from, it can be a little hard to know where to begin. This walk starts on the busy Huaihai Zhong Lu and then uses quieter roads to link a number of older buildings, former residences and parks.

Starting at Shanxi Nan Lu subway station, walk east along **Huaihai Zhong Lu** and you'll see the impressive 1930s Art Deco structure and spire of the Cathay Theater (see p. 315) on the northeast corner of the junction with Maoming Lu, almost next to the subway exit. From here head south down **Maoming Lu**, where you'll notice a cluster of shops lining both sides of the road – this is a great place to get clothes tailored. Turn left when you reach Nanchang Lu and continue east for 10-15 minutes, crossing over Ruijin and Sinan Lu, before entering Fuxing Park by its northern entrance at Yandang Lu.

Maybe take a break in the park and then head for the southwestern exit, which leads onto **Xiangshan Lu** and the Former Residence of Dr. Sun Yatsen, next to the park. From here, take the picturesque **Sinan Lu** south, passing Zhou Enlai's former residence at number 73, continuing down to cross over the large and busy Jianguo Lu before finally arriving at **Taikang Lu**. Taikang Lu offers a series of small side allies housing galleries, jewelry shops, ceramics outlets and design studios. The local community is trying to create a bohemian enclave here, and the area offers a less pretentious version of trendy Xintiandi with an eclectic and interesting selection of shops.

At the western end of the road, turn right onto **Ruijin Lu** and follow it north until you reach Yongjia Lu, approximately 10 minutes walk up Ruijin. Turn left (west) onto Yongjia, and then right (north) onto Maoming Lu. If you follow this street north you'll pass the grand Ruijin Hotel (see p. 328) and after about 15 minutes end up back at Huaihai Zhong Lu. From there you can use Shanxi Nan Lu subway station to get back to your hotel.

On Wheels

 Although Shanghai itself isn't great for cycling, you can rent bikes from the Captain's Hostel (see p. 323). But for some real biking you'll need to head out of the city. **Cycle China** (☎ 139-1707-1775, www.cyclechina.com) organizes some excellent bike trips both to the leafy French Concession (¥150 for a four- to five-hour trip on Saturday mornings) within the city and out to surrounding regions, including the rural expanse of Chongming Island, nestled in the Yangzi estuary, and the Water Towns. Private guided rides cost ¥400 for half a day.

If you want to go it alone, **Boddhisattva Mountain Bikes** (☎ 021-5266-9013, www.bohdi.com.cn), is a little far out of town, but worthwhile for serious mountain bikers as they have top-of-the-line bicycles (¥150 per day plus deposit of ¥2,500 or your passport) and advice on trips in the surrounding area. They also rent vans that can transport up to eight bikes into the region. Bodhisattva is at Suite 2308, Building 2, 2918, Zhongshan Bei Lu.

On the Green

 As in the rest of modern moneyed China, golf is taking off in Shanghai, with some clubs charging tens of thousands of US dollars for lifetime membership, but for the casual visitor who just wants to keep in swing there's a **driving range** in Pudong at 501 Yingcheng Lu, Lujiazui (☎ 021-5882-9028; ¥20 for 30 balls during the week, ¥120 per hour on the weekend).

On Water

Shanghai from the water is definitely worth seeing, particularly at night, offering the spectacle of both its sleek, modern east bank and the colonial splendor of the Bund on the west bank. River trips can be arranged through hotels or from the **Jinling Pier** on the Bund. To get an idea of Shanghai's scale, take one of the longer trips that follow the river all the way to its mouth. Trips depart from 10 am-9 pm and cost ¥35-70 for an hour, or around ¥100 for a three-hour trip, dependent on the quality of the boat and whether food is included. If you don't have the time or money for this, then the ¥0.5 ferry from the wharf at the southern end of the Bund or farther down at Shilipu, which run to Jinmao docks on Pudong can give you a glimpse of Shanghai from the water as well as some local flavor.

If you want something a bit more energetic you can try your hand at **dragon boat racing**. Practices are held every Sunday morning out at Dian Shan Lake and cost ¥50, which includes transport out to the lake. The group meets at 8 am at Starbucks on Shuicheng Nan Lu, near Guyang Lu. For more information you can e-mail dragonboatsh@yahoo.com.

Cultural Adventures

As a comparatively new Chinese city, Shanghai isn't famed for its cultural legacy, although with more foreigners flocking to the city there is more scope for learning traditional arts.

Cooking

Captain Hostel (☎ 021-6323-5053, www.captainhostel.com.cn; see *Where to Stay*, p. 323) runs hour-long sessions teaching you how to try (and I mean try – mine always fall apart) to make dumplings. Classes are on Tuesdays, Thursdays and Sundays at 5 pm.

Language

With the ever-increasing number of foreigners relocating to Shanghai, language schools are big business and there is a good selection to choose from. If you just want a few lessons in the basics try **Creative Methodology** (☎ 021-6289-4299, www.talkingchina.com) at 200 Zhenning Lu (Jiangsu Lu subway), who charge ¥45 for hour-long group classes or ¥125 for a private tutor. For long-term courses it's worth checking out a few places to see what fits your needs. **Ease Mandarin** (☎ 021-5465-6999, www.easermandarin. com) at no.2, lane 25, Wuxing Lu (Hengshan Lu subway) is a well-reputed and popular school (¥80 per hour).

Martial Arts

Of the many martial arts schools in Shanghai, **Longwu International Kung Fu Center** (www.longwukungfu.com) is one of the best. They teach *shaolinquan* and tai chi (see *Martial Arts*, p. 65) and are conveniently located at 1 Maoming Nan Lu. Another place used to teaching foreigners is **Mingwu International Kung Fu Club** (www.mingwukungfu.com) at floor 3, building 1, 359 Hongzhong Lu in Hongqiao. They conduct classes around the city taught by national champions.

Painting & Calligraphy

If you want to try your hand at these fine arts, then call **Chen Li Fan** (☎ 1300-4153-602; newpiacaso@hotmail.com) in advance of his Friday class (9:30-11:30 am; ¥100) at Demarco Restaurant on Yandang Lu, near Huaihai Lu (Changshu Lu subway). See p. 58-60 for more on painting and calligraphy.

Paper-Cutting

The **Captain's Hostel** (☎ 021-6323-5053, www.captainhostel.com.cn; see *Where to Stay*, p. 323) organizes short lessons on the traditional arts of paper-cutting and making dough figurines on the weekends. Check their website or the noticeboard at the hostel for the latest.

Tea Ceremony & Guqin

You can join in a Chinese tea ceremony or even learn to play the *guqin* (see *Music*, p. 62) from **Zhen Qin Guan** (☎ 021-5404-8779; zhenqinguan@

Shanghai & Around

hotmail.com) at 167 Anfu Lu, off Wulumuqi Lu (Changshu Lu subway). Lessons cost ¥300 an hour.

Where to Stay

As you'd expect for a city of Shanghai's stature, there are plenty of places to stay. However, if you're on a budget, finding a room in the center of town can be something of a mission. International chains abound and offer their usual array of facilities, but these days Shanghai is also embracing its chic 1930s history and there are a few remnants of this era where you can stay, for an escape from the uniformity of most Chinese hotels. Pudong, while less convenient for most of the tourist sights, has the world's highest hotel, the Grand Hyatt, which is definitely worth a visit, even if you don't stay.

As long as you don't arrive during a national holiday you should expect a discount of 10-20% on the rates below, and greater reductions in winter. Nearest subway stations are mentioned where appropriate.

What's it mean? FC=fitness center; SW=swimming pool; @=in-room Internet access; DA=rooms for disabled. For ¥ price codes, see page 113.

The Bund & Around

★**Captain Hostel**, 37 Fuzhou Lu (☎ 021-6323-5053, www.captainhostel.com.cn; Henan Zhong Lu subway). More akin to a hotel than a hostel, Captain offers a range of comfortable, modern twins and doubles, all decked out in a maritime theme, although the staff seldom smiles. There are also dorm beds (¥50) in the basement and on the fourth floor, the latter preferable as they're closer to the bathrooms. The hostel has an Internet café and a rooftop bar that shows

Lobby of the Captain Hostel

movies and sports games and there are good views over to Pudong (see *Where to Drink*, p. 337). The hostel also runs a few cultural programs such as learning how to make dumplings and the traditional art of paper-cutting. ¥¥¥

★★**Westin**, 88 Henan Zhong Lu (☎ 021-6335-1888, www. westin.com/shanghai; Henan Zhong Lu subway). You can see the distinctive crowned cap of the Bund Center that houses the Westin from all over the city. Although the hotel's setting isn't great, it makes up for this with super-friendly service, an interesting blend of traditional Asian and modern styling and excel-

The Westin

lent facilities, including a first-rate spa, the Banyan Tree. Rooms have wireless Internet connection and are very comfortable with great beds and showers. FC/SW/@ ¥¥¥¥¥

Nanjing Dong Lu & Around

★**Chun Shen Jiang**, 626 Nanjing Dong Lu (☎ 021-6351-5710; Henan Zhong Lu subway). The best moderately priced option actually on Nanjing Dong Lu, the Chun Shen Jiang offers comfortable, spacious twins and doubles with baths, although some rooms are a little damp. ¥¥¥

Hiker Youth Hostel, Jiangxi Zhong Lu (☎ 021-6329-7889; Henan Zhong Lu subway). Set in the backstreets just south of Suzhou Creek and much

Peace

more a real hostel than the Captain, the hiker has dorms (¥50, ¥5 discount for HI members), comfortable, if damp, twins, and some plusher doubles (¥300) as well as a Net bar. It's definitely on the backpacking scene and is a good place to meet travelers from around the globe. ¥¥

Nanjing, 200 Shanxi Lu (☎ 021-6322-2888, www.NJ-Hotel.com; Henan Zhong Lu subway). Located just north of Nanjing Dong Lu, this is another inexpensive central choice. The cheapest rooms (Standard A) are a little cramped, but the better rooms (Standard B or C) are good value and comfortable. @ ¥¥¥

★★**Peace**, 20 Nanjing Dong Lu (☎ 021-6321-6888, www.shanghaipeacehotel.com; Henan Zhong Lu subway).

Unmissable on the corner of Nanjing Dong Lu and the Bund, this Renaissance-style Shanghai landmark hotel was known as the Cathay, Shanghai's most prestigious accommodation. The hotel has just celebrated its centenary and is still one of *the* places to stay in Shanghai, in spite of its mediocre service and ever increasing competition. The hotel has a North and South Wing, the former of which is a little newer, dating from 1929. Although the hotel's rooms are still elegantly furnished, the cheaper ones (especially in the North Wing) can be a little gloomy and don't live up to the opulence of the lobby. However, it's a different story if you can afford the deluxe national rooms that have been kept in their original style, albeit with a few necessary modernizations (¥5880). There are numerous restaurants, a lively jazz bar and a museum tracing the hotel's history (Mon-Fri 9:30 am-5 pm). The Peace Hotel is definitely worth a visit, but maybe not a stay. The hotel has wheelchair access. FC/@ ¥¥¥¥¥

Renmin, 500 Tianjin Lu (☎ 021-6351-7636; Renmin Square subway). Tucked just behind the hubbub of Nanjing Dong Lu, this place offers the best budget bargains in this part of town and is popular with budget tour groups. Although there's no elevator and the carpets could certainly do with a clean, the rooms are well-furnished and not too noisy, and the staff is friendly. The hotel also owns the excellent Ren Ren Restaurant next door (see *Where to Eat*, p. 332). ¥¥

Renmin Square & Nanjing Xi Lu

Marriott

★★**Marriott**, 399 Nanjing Xi Lu (☎ 021-5359-4969, www.marriotthotels.com/SHAJW; Renmin Square subway). The gleaming pointed tower of the Marriott is well-placed between the business districts of Nanjing Xi Lu and the shops of Nanjing Dong Lu. The interior is tastefully decked out in bamboo and pine and the hotel provides the usual high standards of service, accommodation and facilities and also claims to have the highest library in the world on its 60th floor! FC/SW/@/DA ¥¥¥¥¥

Park, 170 Nanjing Xi Lu (☎ 021-6327-5225, www.parkhotel.com.cn; Renmin Square subway). Another relic from Shanghai's past, this 24-story Art Deco hotel was once the city's tallest and one of its best. These days, while the Park retains its grand architecture and views, its services and accommodations have taken a turn for the worse, with small bathrooms and musty rooms. FC/@ ¥¥¥¥¥

★**Portman Ritz-Carlton**, Shanghai Center, 1376 Nanjing Xi Lu (☎ 021-6279-8888, www. ritzcarlton.com; Jing'an Temple subway). Well-located for the business and shopping districts of Nanjing Xi Lu, the Portman Ritz-Carlton remains a hub of expat life in Shanghai. The hotel lives up to the group's usual high standards of service and has excellent facilities, but the rooms are perfunctorily five-star, nothing more. FC/SW/@/DA ¥¥¥¥¥

Portman Ritz-Carlton

YMCA, 123 Xizang Nan Lu (☎ 021-6326-1040, www. ymcahotel.com; Renmin Square subway). Close to Renmin Square, the bizarre temple-like exterior of the YMCA holds another budget haven. Its spacious but musty rooms have good coffee-making machines and baths, but this doesn't make them worth the money. The three- to four-bedded dorms (¥100) are what draws in backpackers, although even these are on the expensive side. FC ¥¥¥

The French Concession & Xintiandi

The tree-lined streets of the French Concession offer a pleasant escape from the bustle of downtown and yet still have great shopping, restaurants and nightlife in the vicinity. Many of the hotels in this region are former residences and are almost worth staying in for their architecture and sense of history alone.

Anting Villa

★★**Anting Villa**, 46 Anting Lu (☎ 021-6433-1188, www.sinohotel. com; Hengshan Lu subway). This grand Spanish Baroque villa was built in 1934 and has served as the Mayor of Shanghai's residence. It was opened as a hotel in 2000 and is popular with visiting officials with good reason. Set in secluded grounds yet only minutes from the bars of Hengshan Lu, the hotel exudes a refined ambience, in spite of its mix of styles which includes stained glass window scenes of bullfighting. FC/@ ¥¥¥¥¥

Number 88, 380 Huangpi Nan Lu (☎ 021-5383-8833, www.88xintiandi. com; Huangpi Nan Lu subway). This boutique hotel in trendy gentrified Xintiandi has tasteful and luxurious rooms with beds on raised platforms as well as suites complete with kitchens, balconies and lake views. However, the ambience feels a little too contrived and reception can be chaotic. Number 88 tries hard, maybe too hard, but it doesn't quite manage to justify its room rates. FC/SW/@ ¥¥¥¥¥

Bedroom in
Hengshan-Moller Villa

★**Hengshan-Moller Villa**, 30 Shanxi Lu (☎ 021-6247 8881, www.mollervilla.com; Shanxi Nan Lu subway). Stepping into the grounds of the Moller villa is like stepping back in time, and place, to a Bavarian fairytale. The villa was constructed in 1936 for a British Jew, Eric Moller, and supposedly represents a dream that his daughter had, complete with patterned brickwork and turrets. The interior is almost as over-the-top as the outside, with garishly opulent deluxe rooms (¥4,000), although the business rooms (¥2,400) are a little subtler. The standard rooms in Building number 2, however, manage to be boringly ordinary and are overpriced (¥816). There is also a pleasant café where you can enjoy a cup of tea on the lawn. FC/SW/@ ¥¥¥¥¥

Jinjiang, 59 Maoming Lu (☎ 021-3218-9888, www.jinjianghotelshanghai. com; Shanxi Nan Lu subway). Originally built in 1931 as upscale residences for the French, these three Art Deco mansions are now jointly run as a government hotel. In 1931 Zhou Enlai and Richard Nixon signed the 1972 Shanghai Communique here. The hotel has good facilities and is trying to recapture some its former glory, though the rooms are plain and, despite its history, the building is a little ugly. FC/SW/@ ¥¥¥¥¥

★★★**Number 9**, 9 Lane 355, Jianguo Xi Lu (☎ 021-6471-9950; ad50192907@online.sh.cn; Hengshan Lu subway). This hidden jewel takes some locating, but if you're looking for a place with character that's not too expensive, it could be just right. Number9 is housed in a 1937 Art Deco mansion and decked out in a tasteful mix of original and contemporary fur-

Number 9

nishings. The hotel has only five rooms and feels more like an upmarket homestay than a hotel, with laid-back, friendly service. Rooms are large and some have peaceful balconies, although make sure to specify you don't want the room that has a bathroom across the corridor rather than in the room. To get here, find number 355 on the southern side of Jianguo Xi Lu, just east of

Taiyuan Lu. Walk through the entrance gate and continue past a line of pretty houses to the end of the lane, where you turn left. At the end you'll see a large wooden gate where you buzz for entry. Or, if you want to save the hassle, call before you arrive and someone from the hotel will come and meet you on Jianguo Xi Lu. @ ¥¥¥¥

★★**Ruijin**, 118 Ruijin Er Lu (☎ 021-6472-5222; Shanxi Nan Lu subway). Set in beautifully tended gardens and housed in a 1920s mock Tudor mansion, the Ruijin certainly wins the prize for elegance. Once home to one of Shanghai's wealthiest expats, the Ruijin aims to evoke the heady days of the '30s. Rooms in building number 1 and 3 succeed, although those in the other two buildings lack character. The Ruijin is also well-placed for the amenities of the French

Ruijin Building 1

Concession but, if you don't want to leave the hotel, Face Bar is one of the city's most indulgent and there are also quality Chinese, Indian and Thai restaurants on the grounds. @ ¥¥¥¥¥

The Old City

There aren't many hotels in this part of town but, if you want to stay here, the **Shanghai Classical**, 242 Fuyou Lu (☎ 021-6311-1777, www.laofandian.com) is in the heart of the newly renovated "old city" bazaar. The hotel's subdued, low-lit and well-furnished rooms are a good value and popular with tour groups. FC ¥¥¥

North of Suzhou Creek

Astor House

There are a cluster of recently revamped Art Deco hotels just north of the creek, along with a few newer options, all of which are just a 10-minute walk from the Bund. The nearest subway line is 20 minutes walk away at Henan Zhong Lu.

Astor House, 15 Huangpu Lu (☎ 021-6324-6388, www.astorhousehotel.com). Once known as a budget retreat, this grand old building which dates back to 1826, has gentrified itself and moved up a couple of price notches in the process. The hotel has a famous guestlist, including Albert Einstein, and it's wonderfully atmospheric in the lobby. The rooms, however, are a disappointment. @ ¥¥¥

Panorama Century Court, 53 Huangpu Lu (☎ 021-5393-0008, www.panorama-sh.com). In contrast to the historic hotels around it, the Panorama is a newer Accor Group affair which, as its name suggests, affords great views. Well-priced modern rooms and a host of one- to three-bedroom suites are all well-equipped, which makes the hotel popular with business travelers. Wheelchair access. FC/@ ¥¥¥

Pudong

There are some excellent hotels in Pudong and the airport is close by, but the drawback of staying here is the distance to most of the city's attractions (Jinmao and Pearl Oriental Towers notwithstanding). However, it's worth making an exception (especially if you're doing business on this side of the river) for the two outstanding hotels listed below. Pudong can be reached by subway line #2.

★★★**Grand Hyatt**, Jinmao Tower, 88 Century Boulevard (☎ 021-5049-1234, www.shanghai.grand.hyatt.com). This is the world's highest hotel, a landmark building in the city's modern history which has let the world (especially rival Hong Kong) know that Shanghai is back with a boom. The hotel's physical height is matched by its standard of service and accommodation and is recommended for a treat. In addition to its excellent restaurants and bars (including Cloud 9, see *Nightlife*, p. 336, and the suave 53rd-floor Piano Bar), the hotel also has one of the highest fitness centers in the world, where you can enjoy the bizarre sensation of running on a treadmill looking straight down 57 floors to the river and Puxi in the distance. FC/SW/@/DA ¥¥¥¥¥

Grand Hyatt

★★**St. Regis**, 889 Dongfang Lu (☎ 021-5050-4567, www.starwood.com/stregis/index). Although its location 15 minutes from Pudong's riverside makes the St. Regis feel a little out of the way, it makes up for this with its outstanding service and range of amenities. Rooms are super-size, everything reeks of quality and butlers attend to your every need (well almost...). FC/SW/@/DA ¥¥¥¥¥

St. Regis

Where to Eat

Shanghai's distinctive cuisine is famous within China, but these days you can also find food from almost every country in the world here. It's difficult to choose which culinary delights to sample in a short stay. In the listings below I have focused on Chinese and Shanghainese restaurants with a peppering of international offerings – for more check out *that's Shanghai* or *Shanghai Talk*. Unless otherwise mentioned, all restaurants listed below have English menus. Aside from local eateries and canteens, reservations are recommended, particularly on weekends.

The Bund & Around

The Bund is home to a new order of Shanghai dining, where historic buildings, fine views and excellent contemporary cuisine are blended to create some of the city's finest and most expensive restaurants. Many of these restaurants are found in the exclusive Three on the Bund Development. Reservations are advised at all of the following, other than New Heights for lunch. Henan Zhong Lu on line #2 is the nearest subway station.

See page 117 for an explanation of the ¥ restaurant price codes.

★★★**Cupola**, 3 The Bund (☎ 021-6329-1101, www.threeonthebund.com; from 7 pm). Rightly touted as Shanghai's most romantic restaurant, Cupola is part of the exclusive Three on the Bund development. Housed in the former bell tower of the 1917 building, Cupola has only two eating spaces. The lower room seats eight while the upper, which enjoys panoramic views of the city, has room enough for only two and has a divan on which to relax. Food can be ordered from three of the building's restaurants (Jean Georges, Laris and the Whampoa Club, see below). For a truly special meal this is the place to come, but make sure you bring your wallet. There is a minimum charge of ¥1,500 per person. ¥¥¥¥¥

★★★**M on the Bund**, 7F, 20 Guangdong Lu (☎ 021-6350-9988, www.m-onthebund.com; Tues-Sun 11:30-2:30 & daily 6.15-10:30). The first of the Bund's new wave of elite dining options, M has a cool elegance, excellent views and is wildly popular for its blend of Mediterranean and Middle

M on the Bund

Eastern dishes – try the slowly baked lamb. During the week, set lunches cost ¥118/138 for two/three courses, while on the weekend brunch comes in at ¥188/218 and dinner runs more. There's a charming terrace from where you can savor the flavor of the new Shanghai – ambience, food and skyline. If you just want a drink, the Glamour Bar is next to the restaurant (see *Nightlife*, p. 337). ¥¥¥¥¥

New Heights

★★**New Heights**, 7F, 3 The Bund (☎ 021-6321-0909, www.threeonthebund.com; daily 10 am-1 pm & 5:30-10:30 pm). Occupying the upper floor of the Three on the Bund, New Heights is a far more laid-back eatery than the other restaurants in the development and enjoys an outdoor terrace with unsurpassed views. There's a selection of Asian dishes or, for a taste of home, there are burgers, sandwiches and even fish and chips. In the evenings the space becomes a club, with DJs from around the globe, but while the night views are stunning, New Heights seems more comfortable as a restaurant than a bar. ¥¥¥¥¥

★★**Whampoa Club**, 3 The Bund (☎ 021-6321-3737, www.threeonthebund.com; daily 5:30-10 pm). Another of the restaurants in the Three on the Bund development, this dining club offers exquisite décor, good views across the river and, most importantly, fine cuisine prepared by the youthful master chef, Jereme Leung. Dishes are modern reinterpretations of

Whampoa Club

traditional Shanghainese and Chinese recipes. Specialties include bird's nest soup. Every detail of this place has been thought about and some of the dishes are even served on jade plates. However, all of this fine food and splendor is heavy on the pocket and set meals cost ¥588. ¥¥¥¥¥

Nanjing Dong Lu & Around

If you want a cheap snack close to Nanjing Dong Lu, head for Guizhou Lu, where you'll find an array of dumplings, noodles and breads for under ¥10.

Hongze Jiulou, 187 Shanxi Lu (☎ 021-6352-1133; 11 am-11 pm; Henan Zhong Lu subway). This restaurant doesn't look like anything special from the outside but serves good Szechuanese cuisine and its upstairs has a little more character than the ground floor. The *yuxiang rousi* (fish-flavored pork) and finely sliced potatoes with green pepper are both tasty. ¥¥

★**Ren Ren**, 488 Tianjin Lu (☎ 021-6351-0431; daily 7 am-midnight; Renmin Square subway). A couple of minutes walk north of Nanjing Dong Lu, this spacious, friendly old favorite serves inexpensive dishes from around the country with an emphasis on Shanghainese cuisine. The beef with pineapple (¥22) is excellent. ¥¥

Suzhou Mian Guan, Guangxi Bei Lu (daily 11 am-10 pm; Renmin Square subway) .This standard Chinese canteen manages to differentiate itself by its bright color scheme and is full to bursting at lunchtime. It can make a good place for a breakfast of scrambled eggs and tomatoes, or for a cheap dinner try the pork and onion. No reservations are required. ¥¥

★★**Shaanxi Noodles**, 113 Guizhou Lu (daily 7 am-10 pm; Renmin Square subway). For cheap eats you can't go wrong with this tiny canteen which is often full to bursting. They serve tasty dumplings (an unbelievable 30 per plate), good shaved noodles and vegetarian "chicken" noodles. No reservations but you might have to wait for a table! ¥

Renmin Square & Nanjing Xi Lu

★★**Bali Laguna**, Jing'an Park, 189 Huashan Lu (☎ 021-6248-6961; daily 11 am-2:30 pm & 6-10:30 pm; Jing'an Temple subway). A tranquil retreat from the streets, Bali Laguna is beautifully situated on a lily pond in Jing'an Park. The minimalist restaurant slowly serves up tasty Indonesian fare with a wide Southeast Asian smile. The *satay* chicken and *nasi goreng* are recommended. The restaurant also functions as a bar from 11 am-1 am and, sitting outdoors, enjoying a cold beer by the water, you can forget about all the traffic and chaos of downtown. You might even find yourself ordering some tasty snacks. ¥¥

Bali Laguna

★**Element Fresh**, Shanghai Center, 1376 Nanjing Xi Lu (daily 7 am-11 pm; Jing'an Temple subway). A light and bright sandwich and healthy snack stop, Element Fresh was established by an American and serves Asian, Middle Eastern and Western dishes. They also do great juices and smoothies that can be energized with nutrition boosters such as ginseng to give your legs some get-up and go for the shops and sights. Reservations aren't necessary. ¥¥¥-¥¥¥¥

★**Godly Vegetarian Restaurant**, 445 Nanjing Xi Lu (☎ 021-6327-0218; daily 11 am-3:30 pm & 5-9 pm; Shimen Yi Lu subway). One of Shanghai's most renowned vegetarian restaurants, Godly is famed for its five-course set-meal (¥144) and also has a range of imitation meat dishes such as diced sautéed chicken and beancurd (¥18). ¥¥¥-¥¥¥¥

Kathleen's 5, 5F 325 Nanjing Xi Lu (☎ 021-6327-2221 www.Kathleens5. com.cn; daily 11:30 am-2:30 pm & 5:30-10:30 pm; Renmin Square subway). The rooftop of this historic building has great views of Renmin Square, a relaxed atmosphere and friendly staff. Cuisine is New World with a European twist – the Australian Beef Rossini is a house specialty but, if you just want a drink, Kathleen's is also popular for its bar. ¥¥¥¥

Meilong Zhen

★★**Meilong Zhen**, 1081 Nanjing Xi Lu (☎ 021-6253-5353; daily 5-10 pm; Shimen Yi Lu subway). This historic and modestly-priced restaurant is housed in a former Communist party building and is famed as one of Shanghai's best traditional eateries. Inside, the dining halls still have original woodwork and mahogany furniture that retains its grandeur. Szechuan dishes are particularly tasty but Meilong Zhen also does good line in Shanghainese cuisine. Booking is advised. ¥¥

Wagas, CITIC Square, 1168 Nanjing Xi Lu (daily 7 am-11 pm; Shimen Yi Lu subway). Another trendy modern citywide pasta and sandwich chain, Wagas (meaning pure in Filipino) also has great Western breakfasts, from muesli, fruit salad and Greek yogurt to a less healthy but equally delicious big breakfast of bacon, eggs, baked beans, mushrooms and toasted *panini*. All breakfast meals are half-price before 10 am. Wagas also does good coffee and there are sofas inside as well as a pleasant outdoor area to take some time out if you're not as rushed as most of the office workers who come here. Reservations aren't necessary. ¥¥¥-¥¥¥¥

The French Concession

★**Art Deco Garden Café**, Building 3, Ruijin Hotel, 118 Ruijin Er Lu (daily 8:30 am-midnight; Shanxi Nan Lu subway). A great place for that oh-so-British pastime of tea on the lawn (8:30-noon & 1-6 pm; ¥35), albeit in the French Concession! ¥¥

★★**Bao Luo**, 271 Fumin Lu (☎ 021-6279-2827; daily 11 am-6 am; Changshu Lu subway). From the outside, this place appears tiny and you'll need to look carefully for the narrow entrance, but its vast backroom is a banqueting hall that can seat hundreds and there are more rooms upstairs. If you come at peak dining hours you'll find Bao Luo crammed to capacity with diners noisily working their way through a feast of Shanghainese specialties and reservations are essential. Dishes to try include the aubergine sandwich, which comes with minced pork and pancakes, the crab and pork meatballs or just good old *xiaolongbao* (steamed pork dumplings). ¥¥¥

Guyi Hunan, 87 Fumin Lu (☎ 021-6249-5628; daily 11:30 am-10:30 pm; Jing'an Temple subway). This simple but stylish restaurant offers classical fiery Hunanese cuisine. Recommended dishes include fried prawn skewers (¥118 for 500 g / 1.1 lb), chili and garlic pork ribs and, one of the mainstays of western cooking, spicy hotpot. ¥¥¥

★★**Old China Hand Reading Room**, 27 Xiaoxing Lu (daily 10 am-midnight). To brush up on your knowledge of Shanghai with a cup of tea (¥35) and some cake, there is no better place. Antique furniture and walls lined with bookshelves housing hundreds of books on Shanghai give a relaxed and unhurried air to the Reading Room, and you'd do well to check your watch as it's easy to unwittingly pass hours here. Reservations aren't required. ¥¥

Entrance to Shintori

★★★**Shintori**, 803 Julu Lu (daily 5:30-10:30 pm; ☎ 021-5404-5252; Jing'an Temple subway). Finding this unmarked Japanese restaurant only adds to its appeal and as you walk along the bamboo-lined concrete corridor, which leads to its oversized automatic sliding doors, you feel as if you're entering a James Bond villain's secret lair. Inside, the cool, industrial minimalism of the converted warehouse doesn't disappoint and neither does the food. Superb sushi is served by black-clad staff at stone bars and there are a host of other treats to try, including rock and roll salad and beef sashimi. To find the restaurant, head for the southwestern corner of the junction of Fumin Lu and Julu Lu. Just west of the junction walk down the unmarked open-air corridor next to number 803. ¥¥¥¥-¥¥¥¥¥

Yang's Kitchen, Number 3, 9 Hengshan Lu (☎ 021-6445-8482; daily 11 am-11 pm; Hengshan Lu subway). A couple of minutes walk up a lane off Hengshan Lu brings you to Yang's Kitchen, which serves up great and well-priced Shanghainese cuisine in a pleasant, airy environment. The lemon chicken is tangy and succulent and the Mandarin fish is excellent. ¥¥

Xintiandi

Xintiandi's gentrified old 1920s buildings make for a refreshingly different, if contrived, bar and restaurant scene. If you blur the architecture, Xintiandi's outdoor eating areas feel almost European and are massively popular with Shanghai's international crowd. You won't find any cheap options here but amid the pretensions of many of its establishments are a few hidden gems. All the restaurants listed below are served by Huangpi Nan Lu subway station on line #1.

★★**Crystal Jade**, 2F South Block, Xintiandi Plaza (☎ 021- 6385-8752; daily 11:30 am-3 pm & 5-10:30 pm). This upmarket restaurant in the modern Xintiandi Plaza is part of a Singapore-based chain and is popular for its reasonably priced but delicious Cantonese and Shanghainese specialties –

try the pork buns. Main courses start from ¥30. Reservations are advised. ¥¥¥

★★**TMSK**, 11, Xintiandi Square (☎ 021-6326-2227; 2 pm-midnight). TMSK is a trendy dining and drinking establishment on Xintiandi's thronging square. The upstairs restaurant serves fine Western fare. The roasted pistachio-crusted rack of lamb with ginger gravy is recommended. Downstairs you can enjoy a pre- or post-dinner cocktail (from ¥50) on a funky glass sculptured bar. ¥¥¥¥¥

★★**Ye Shanghai**, 338 Huangpi Nan Lu (☎ 021-6311-2323; daily 11:30 am-2:30 pm & 5:30-11 pm). This sophisticated, low-lit restaurant also has branches in Hong Kong and Tokyo. As the name suggests, the cuisine is Shanghainese and the décor also pays homage to the city's roots. Average main courses are around ¥40-50, but if you're on a tight budget you can get a bowl of noodles for as little as ¥18. At the other end of the scale, sweet and sour fish which feeds four to six people costs ¥580. The restaurant is also particularly proud of its vegetarian duck. ¥¥¥

The Old City

There are no convenient subway stops near the Old City so taking a taxi is the easiest way to get there.

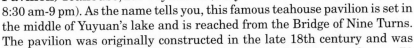

Ye Shanghai

★★★**Huxinting (Heart of the Lake Pavilion) Teahouse**, 257 Yuyuan Lu (daily 8:30 am-9 pm). As the name tells you, this famous teahouse pavilion is set in the middle of Yuyuan's lake and is reached from the Bridge of Nine Turns. The pavilion was originally constructed in the late 18th century and was converted into a teahouse 70 years later. The teahouse has served the likes of Queen Elizabeth and continues to be popular with dignitaries and tourists alike. Sit on the upper floor. While fractionally more expensive, it affords views of the lake and the price of tea includes light snacks. As you'd expect, there are a wide range of green and flower teas and they also hold a traditional Chinese tea ceremony every evening at 8.30 pm. ¥

Huxinting

Lu Bo Lang, 115 Yuyuan Lu (☎ 021-6328-0602; daily 7:30 am-11 pm). Right in the heart of tourist central Yuyuan bazaar, this traditionally styled restaurant is enduringly popular for its Shanghainese specialties, although the service is ordinary at best. The sweet and sour fried Mandarin fish is excellent. ¥¥-¥¥¥¥

Lining up outside Nanxiang

★★★**Nanxiang**, 85 Yuyuan Lu (☎ 021-6355-8507; daily 10 am-9 pm). Located on the alley leading to the entrance of Yu Gardens, you'll probably see the lines on the street before you see the restaurant itself, which is always a good sign. The Nanxiang has three floors, with differing opening hours, but if you come between the hours specified above you'll always find a section that is serving. On the ground floor a kiosk turns out thousands of pork dumplings (¥8) a day, while the upstairs dining areas offer a wider range of fillings. Reservations aren't required. ¥-¥¥

★**Old Shanghai Teahouse**, 385 Fangbang Zhong Lu (daily 8:30 am-11 pm). This quaint teahouse serves a range of teas (¥25) and coffees (¥30), as well as dim sum and light snacks. They play subdued jazz tunes and the teahouse is kitted out with photos and paraphernalia from Old Shanghai. ¥¥

Nightlife

After more than half a century of being stifled by authority, Shanghai's club scene is once again coming of age, albeit slowly. The city once renowned for its rowdy sailor bars, opium dens and good time gin joints dances to the beat of another drum these days, but has a few clubs worth checking out, including:

The lost-world feel of **Mural** (¥100 cover, including the unbeatable offer of all you can drink on Fridays) at 697 Rongjia Lu (Hengshan Lu subway).

Japanese hip-spot, **Rojam** (¥50 cover) on the fourth floor of the Hong Kong Plaza at 283 Huaihai Zhong Lu (Huangpi Nan Lu subway).

Both clubs are open until at least 2 am, but neither really gets going until 11 pm. As in most cities, the club scene in Shanghai is fast-moving and fickle, so check *Shanghai Talk* and *that's Shanghai* for the latest.

Where to Drink

Like the club world, Shanghai's thriving bar scene is constantly morphing, so it's worth checking out the local magazines (see above) for the latest. Traditionally, the French Concession has been the bar district, but nearby Xintiandi's redevelopment, the new string of upmarket bars on the Bund and some high-flying options over in Pudong have diversified the scene. Many of the places listed below also serve food and some also function as clubs later in the evening.

The Bund & Around

★**Captain's Bar**, 6F, 37 Fuzhou Lu (daily 11 am-2 am; Henan Zhong Lu subway). For the backpacker version of the Bund's trendy bars, look no further than the Captain's Bar on the sixth floor of this upscale hostel. There are comfortable loungers indoors but the Captain's treasure lies on its small terrace which enjoys excellent views over to Pudong, free from the social constraints of the bars and restaurants of the Bund. Live sports are shown indoors and a few snacks are on offer along with the draught beer (¥35).

★★**Glamour Bar**, 7F, 20 Guangdong Lu (daily 5 pm-midnight; Henan Zhong Lu subway). The antithesis of Captain's, Glamour provides what its name suggests in abundance and has a dress code of no shorts or jeans. Cocktails are deftly prepared by the smooth bar staff and there are sometimes jazz performances.

Glamour Bar

Nanjing Lu & Renmin Square

This part of town is more about shopping than partying but has a few good places to take a break and watch the crowds drift by.

Big Bamboo, 132 Nanyang Lu (daily 10 am-2 am; Shimen Yi Lu subway). A comfortable and popular expat bar with pool tables, live sports and good pub food – try the fish and chips (¥75).

Chez L'Ami, Century Square, Nanjing Dong Lu (daily 11 am-11 pm; Renmin Square subway). Serves tea, coffee, beer and snacks right on Nanjing Dong Lu.

★**Mojo Café**, 505 Nanjing Dong Lu, next to the Sofitel (daily 8:30 am-1:30 am; Henan Zhong Lu subway). Slightly raised above the street, the outside deck here makes a great spot for people watching.

The French Concession

★★**The Blarney Stone**, 5 Dongping Lu (Mon-Wed 4 pm-1 am, Thur-Sun 11 am-1 am; Hengshan Lu subway). Of the many Irish pubs I've sampled in China, the Blarney Stone is the most authentic. Its dark, wooden interior, genuine Irish live music and, of course, the mainstay, a pint of Guinness (¥60), take you on a journey to the Emerald Isle and they also serve good pub-food, including the heart-attack inducing Dublin Fry (¥95), which includes lamb chop, bacon, sausage and egg. There's a pool table and terrace upstairs.

Blue Frog, 207 Maoming Nan Lu (daily 10 am-2 am; Shanxi Nan Lu subway). On a bar-filled stretch of Maoming Lu, the Blue Frog is a peaceful place for a drink during the day and livens up at night. It also serves a range of south-of-the-border dishes.

Cotton Club, 8 Fuxing Xi Lu (☎ 021-6437-7110; Changshu Lu subway). This smokey bar has a devoted following and its house band presents silky jazz tunes as patrons enjoy their bargain-price drinks.

★★**Face Bar**, Building 4, Ruijin Hotel, 118 Ruijin Er Lu (Sun-Thurs noon-1:30 am, Fri & Sat noon-2 am; Shanxi Nan Lu subway). One of Shanghai's most stylish bars, set in the colonial Ruijin Hotel, Face is a great place to come and enjoy a pricey drink overlooking the lawn, envisioning life as it was here for the privileged some 75 years ago.

Lounge on an opium bed at Face Bar

★**Freelance**, 45 Yueyang Lu (Mon-Fri 4 pm-4 am, Sat & Sun noon-4 am; Hengshan Lu subway). This brand new bar opened by a Los Angelino aims to bring a bit of California's laid-back lifestyle to Shanghai. The bar is low-lit and friendly and has a tree-shaded beer garden where live sports are shown. Draft Heineken (¥45) and Guinness (¥60) are served and inexpensive bar food is also available – favorites include the range of filling burgers (¥65).

Pudong

Pudong has a few bars that are worth a visit, principally for their views. The nearest subway is Lujiazui on line #2.

★★★**Cloud 9**, 87F, Grand Hyatt Regency Hotel, Jin Mao Tower (Mon-Thur 6 pm-1 am, Fri 6 pm-2 am, Sat 11 am-2 am & Sun 11 am-1 am). This bar truly does sit among the clouds and is worth a visit for the spectacular vistas alone. Ambient music, studded steel support beams and different seating levels seamlessly complement the celestial cool. Cloud 9 offers an unsurprisingly expensive range of beers, wines (from ¥320) and cocktails (¥80) and also

Cloud 9

serves light Asian snacks (¥45 upwards). There is a minimum charge of ¥120 after 8 pm on the weekends.

★★**RBT Garden**, Pudong Riverside Promenade, a little south of Lujiazui subway station (daily 11 am-midnight). After a hard day's sightseeing there are few better places to enjoy a drink than sitting on a sofa on a wooden terrace just yards above the river watching the sun set and the lights of the Bund appear. Sure, the drinks are a little pricey, but the scenery is priceless and, if you get hungry, they also serve food (¥45 upwards). Cocktails from ¥45.

Suzhou

With a population of one million and hailed as the **Venice of the East**, Suzhou is famous for its canals, gardens, silk and beautiful women. As you approach through the industrial suburbs, you might begin to doubt the hype, but visit one of the enchanting **traditional gardens** or take a **canal cruise** and you'll soon get back on track. With entire blocks of traditional old housing lining the canals, Suzhou's streets can take you back to another time. If you want to take the experience one step further, Tongli, Wuzhen, Xitang, Zhouzhuang and Zhujiajiao (see *The Water Towns*, p. 312), while touristy, offer idyllic scenes free from the clamor of the city.

History

Supposedly founded by the mythical emperor, He Lu in 600 BC, Suzhou didn't really begin to develop for another thousand years. The construction of the **Grand Canal** (see callout below) under the **Sui dynasty**, which runs from **Hangzhou** straight past the city, transformed Suzhou from a sleepy backwater into an industrial hub. With the arrival of the **Tang dynasty** in 618 AD came the development of the **Silk Road** across Central Asia, and Suzhou prospered as a result of its silk production. The establishment of the **Southern Song dynasty** in 1126 brought the formation of a new capital in nearby Hangzhou. The resulting influx of academics, merchants and government officials to the new capital directed yet more wealth to Suzhou. That laid the foundations for the development of Suzhou's Chinese gardens. During the **Ming dynasty**, Suzhou continued to flourish. It became a center for the arts, especially wood-block carving and silk weaving. The already established gardens were expanded and it is estimated that, in Suzhou's heyday, the city had as many as 200 of these exquisite retreats.

Despite the **Taiping Uprising** in the 1860s, which destroyed much of nearby Hangzhou, and Japanese occupation during **World War II**, Suzhou remained well preserved. Its 2,500-year-old **city walls** provided excellent protection from attacks and it wasn't until 1949 that they were totally demolished. Although a large amount of Suzhou's old city still remains, it is being lost at a rapid rate. Today, some of the best examples of Ming architecture are found lining the canals, while the waterways themselves remain a focal point for everyday life in Suzhou, despite their foul-smelling slickness.

THE GRAND CANAL

Built during the short-lived Sui dynasty (581-618 AD), the Grand Canal is seldom visited, yet it rates as one of China's greatest achievements. Like that other massive construction of old, the Great Wall, it actually came about through linking countless pre-existing shorter sections. It now stretches 1,000 miles from Hangzhou to Beijing. The original canal only extended as far as the former capital of Luoyang in Shandong and was created to supply the north with rice or, if need be, troops. Building the canal was no small feat and millions were forced into slave labor to work on it. The canal was extended to Beijing under the Yuan dynasty (1279-1368). It continued to be used until the Qing dynasty (1644-1911), transporting food, building materials, silk and tea, but suffered from floods and the Taiping Uprising, gradually falling into disrepair. The advent of new modes of transport such as trains and planes hastened its decline. These days some stretches are completely silted up, but the section between Hangzhou and Suzhou is navigable and you can take an overnight boat trip between the two (see *Getting Here and Away*, p.000). Bear in mind though, that, as impressive as the canal is, it was designed with transport, rather than beauty in mind. While it certainly has a gritty charm, there are plenty of factories along the way.

Getting Here & Away

By Air

There is no airport in Suzhou, so you'll have to fly to Shanghai's **Pudong** or **Hongqiao airport**, from where you can take a bus (¥80 and ¥50 respectively). Buses arrive and depart from the Water Garden Hotel on Ganjiang Lu and run every 30 minutes. The buses for Pudong run to Hongqiao airport, from where you will be transferred by shuttle bus to Pudong – the trip takes a couple of hours. A taxi should cost about ¥500 for Pudong and ¥400 from Hongqiao. For airline reservations, there's a CAAC office (☎ 0512-6510-4881; daily 8 am-7 pm) at 943 Renmin Lu.

By Rail

Most visitors arrive in Suzhou by train. Suzhou lies on the main Shanghai-Nanjing line so there are plenty of trains and it's easy to get a ticket, despite the hordes of visitors. However, it is still worth buying your onward ticket in advance, particularly if you have a tight timescale. The ticket office is on the eastern side of the station, as is the soft seat waiting room. There is also a ticketing office at 8 Taijian Jie (☎ 0512-6523-3027), just off Guangqian Jie, or you can arrange your ticket through your hotel for a small fee. The station is at the north end of Renmin Lu and is connected to the city center by a number of buses. Buses #2 and #20 run along Renmin Lu, and #2 stops on Shiquan Jie, close to the Master of the Nets Garden and a cluster of hotels.

Destinations, frequencies & durations

Beijing (1 daily, 12 hrs 40 mins); **Guangzhou** (1 daily, 29 hrs); **Guilin** (1 daily, 28 hrs); **Hangzhou** (2 daily, 3 hrs 40 min-4 hrs 20 mins); **Shanghai** (10 daily, 40-50 mins); **Xi'an** (1 daily, 15 hrs 45 mins).

By Road

There are two main bus stations in Suzhou, one in the north and the other in the south. Most of the buses you'll require leave from the **North Station** which is just east of the train station. Minibuses from both stations head to **Tongli,** while **Zhouzhuang** is served from the South Station. The North Bus Station (☎ 0512-6753-0686) is the terminal for buses to Hangzhou (12 daily; 4 hrs) and Shanghai (every 20 mins, 1 hr 30 mins).

By Canal

For the adventurous, it's possible to take a steamboat along the **Grand Canal** to Hangzhou. Boats depart daily at 5:30 pm from the passenger dock on the southern side of the moat on Renmin Lu, and you should arrive in Hangzhou at 6:30 am the following day. Cabins are for two (¥88-95 per person) or four people (¥30-65) and have bathrooms and air-conditioning. It's best to get tickets in advance and they can be obtained from the ferry jetty or from the ticketing office at 1606 Renmin Lu (☎ 0512-6729-0093). Take bus #1, #101 or #102 and get off by Renmin Bridge; make sure you arrive 30 minutes before departure.

Getting Around

Suzhou's small size makes it simple to get around and with a number of local buses, taxis and cycle-rickshaws plying the streets, you'll always find an alternative for aching legs.

By Bus

Local buses are a cheap way to get around Suzhou and cost either ¥1 (non a/c) or ¥2 (a/c). Bus #202 is a good choice and runs past the Master of the Nets Garden in the south, the Twin Pagodas in the east and up to the Humble Administrator's Garden in the northeast. Buses #1 and #2 drive out to Tiger Hill and bus #691 will take you as far as Taihu (Lake Tai). For more comfort, there are also tourist buses (T services), which you buy a day-pass for, although the onboard guides tend to be in Chinese only – see *Sightseeing*, p. 343 for more information.

By Taxi

The base rate is ¥10 for the first 3 km (1.86 miles) and ¥1.8 per kilometer (0.6 mile) thereafter. Although there are taxis everywhere in Suzhou, they often seem to be full whenever you need one! Drivers rarely speak English, so make sure you take your destination written in Chinese.

By Cycle Rickshaw

You will see a number of brightly colored cycle rickshaws weaving their way along the streets. They are a fun way to travel around the city, keeping you close to the sights, sounds and smells of Suzhou! Always fix your price before departure and haggle hard – a trip from Shiquan Jie to Guangqian Jie will take about 15 minutes and should cost ¥5 or less, although the starting price is usually ¥20.

By Bicycle

With a number of excellent bike rides (see *Adventures on Wheels*, p. 355) offered in Suzhou, cycling is a good choice. There are a number of shops along Shiquan Jie that rent bikes. For good quality bikes and reasonable prices, look near the Suzhou Hotel, where you should pay around ¥10 per day. You may be asked to leave a deposit, although usually your name, hotel and room number will suffice. Try **Long Feng Xuan** at 390 Shiquan Jie, which has a collection of well-maintained and colorful bikes.

By Boat

For Suzhou canal cruises see *Adventures on Water*, p. 356.

Orientation

Central Suzhou is enclosed within the square of canals that make up its moat, and is further dissected by countless smaller waterways within this. The **train station** is on the north side of the moat at the top of **Renmin Lu**, with the **North Bus Station** to its east. Renmin Lu is Suzhou's main artery and runs north to south through the middle of the city, passing the commercial center at **Guangqian Jie**. **Accommodation** is available all over the city, but there are a host of good options clustered around the Master of the Nets Garden on **Shiquan Jie** in the south. In the east, **Pingjiang** has some of the prettiest canals and an excellent collection of traditional houses. Many of the main sights are within walking distance of here. The **Grand Canal** runs along Suzhou's western flank, turning east to exit in the south east.

Information Sources

Unlike many cities in China, Suzhou has an excellent **tourist information center** at 495 Shiquan Jie (☎ 0512-6520-3131; daily 9 am-5 pm). The center offers a number of leaflets, maps, guidebooks and free Internet use. The staff speaks excellent English and is happy to help with any questions you may have. You can also pick up information on neighboring towns and sights. The center publishes a comprehensive city guide, imaginatively entitled *Suzhou Travel Guide* (¥48), which is full of useful information. You can also pick up a free copy of a local expat publication, *What's on in Suzhou*, at hotels and bars. It is published once a month and, despite its diminutive size, manages to give listings for courses, festivals, tours, restaurants and musical and theatrical performances.

Communications

Post Office: Close to Shiquan Jie – just head north up Fenghuang Jie and it's on the second street off to the west.

Telephone code: 0512

Internet Access: You can check your mail or surf the web for free at the tourist information center on Shiquan Jie, but for longer stints head to the eastern end of Shizi Jie near the university.

Bank of China: To the east of the Suzhou Hotel on the southern side of Shiquan Jie. There's another branch at 50 Renmin Lu.

Public Security Bureau: 1109, Renmin Lu (☎ 0512-6522-5661).

Medical Services: Hospital #1 (☎ 0512-6522-3637) is on Shizi Jie in the southeast of the city near the university.

Sightseeing

For a comparatively small city, Suzhou has a lot to see. The **gardens**, a **canal cruise** and some **silk shopping** are taken as givens and, if you'd like to get deeper into the world of silk, the **museum** is also worth checking out. As far as the **gardens** go, there are so many that you're better off choosing a few from the list below and taking your time to

Suzhou

Chezhan Lu
Bei Huan Lu
Qimen Bridge
Outer Moat
Pingqi Lu
Qimen Lu
Donghuan
Renmin Lu
Dongbei Jie
N
Taohuawu Dajie
Xibei Jie
Guangji Lu
Dong Zhongshi
Baita Xilu
Baita Donglu (East Road)
Xi Zhongshi
Shi Lu
Yipu Garden
Lindun Lu
Changxu Lu
Jingde Lu
Zhonglie Lu
Jingde Lu
Crane Garden
Guanqian Jie
Yangyu Xiang
Yiyuan Garden
Tieping Xiang
Renmin Lu
Ganjiang East
Wusa Lu
Fenghuang Jie
Daoqian Jie
Changxu Lu
Laodong Lu
Panmen Lu
Siqian Jie
Dong Dajie
Shizi Jie
Renmin Lu
Shiquan Jie
Xinshi Lu
Zhuhui Lu
Meijiaqiao Long
Xujiang Lu

0.5 MILES

©2008 Hunter Publishing, Inc.

Nanmen Lu
Renmin Lu
Nanmen Lu
Outer Moat

HUNTER PUBLISHING

1.	Train Station	13.	Zoo	26.	Hospital #1	38.	Canglang Pavilion
2.	Tourist Boat Dock	14.	East Garden	27.	Old Campus, Suzhou	39.	Foreign Language Bookshop
3.	North Bus Station	15.	Couples Garden		(Soochow) University	40.	Friendship Hotel
4.	The Silk Museum	16.	Suzhou Opera Museum	28.	Dongwu Hotel	41.	Bamboo Grove Hotel
5.	North Temple Pagoda	17.	Pingjiang Lodge Hotel	29.	Yang-Yang Shui Jiao Restaurant	42.	South Bus Station
6.	Suzhou Arts & Crafts Museum	18.	Temple of Mystery	30.	My Hotel; Tudori Restaurant	43.	To Precious Belt Bridge
7.	Suzhou Museum	19.	Songhelou Restaurant	31.	Suzhou Hotel; SuCa Café	44.	Renmin Bridge
8.	The Humble	20.	Suzhou Garden View Hotel	32.	Suzhou Youth Hostel	45.	Nanmen Wharf
	Administrator's Garden	21.	Lexiang Hotel;	33.	Tourist Information Center;	46.	Long Distance Bus Terminal
9.	To Tiger Hill		Antique Bookstore		Master of the Nets Garden	47.	Sheraton Garden Hotel
10.	Lingering Garden;	22.	Buddhism Museum	34.	Yunnan Noodles Restaurant	48.	Ruigang Pagoda
	West Garden Temple	23.	Grand Park	35.	Sarawak Restaurant	49.	Panmen (Pan Gate)
11.	Lion Grove Garden	24.	Post Office	36.	Indian at the Cross Restaurant	50.	Wumen Bridge
12.	Beiban Garden	25.	Twin Pagodas	37.	Library		

appreciate these, rather than trying to rush around all of them. The **peak season** runs from April through October and if you visit during off-season, ticket prices are around 25% less. Free **English-speaking guides** are available at most of the sights, although you may have to wait for a number of people to gather. Although free, it's customary to tip the guide at the end of the tour (¥5 per person).

Much of Suzhou is best enjoyed on foot, by bike or cycle rickshaw, but regular buses, tourist buses and taxis are on hand when you run out of steam. Tourist buses are more comfortable than regular services and there are five routes through the city, which cost ¥10 for a day-pass on one route. Although you'll have to endure the guide's blurb in Chinese, these buses make for an easy way to visit a number of the city's sights and discounted sight entrance tickets are available on board. Regular and tourist (T) buses are listed where relevant. If you want to visit one of the Water Towns, Tongli and Zhouzhuang are both easily accessible by bus or taxi (see *Getting Here & Away*, p. 340 for details). The sights below are divided into Gardens, Museums and Pagodas and Temples and, within these categories, they are listed from south to north.

The Gardens

THE GARDENS OF SUZHOU

Moon gates are common in Suzhou's gardens (Tot Foster)

Suzhou's gardens were first developed in the Song dynasty by retired officials and scholars as places of contemplation. On a map they might seem a little small compared with some of the grand parks of the north, but balance, harmony, proportion and variety, not size, are the elements the gardens aspire to. Using moon gates, pavilions, ponds, carved screen windows, vegetation and bizarrely contorted rocks from nearby Lake Tai, the gardens aim to balance these elements and to create a sense of scale by concealment and division. Although the fundamental features of the gardens remain the same, different gardens focus on particular aspects. While some are dominated by water, others, like Lion Grove, offer a labyrinth of rockeries.

Tip: In stark contrast to their intended purpose as places of reflection and tranquility, the gardens can get overrun with visitors. To view them at their most tranquil, arrive as they open and you should have the place to yourself for a precious while.

★★**Canglang Pavilion**, 3 Canglangting Jie (daily 7:30 am-5 pm; ¥20; buses #1, #28, #101, #T2, #T4 & #T5). This quiet retreat at the southern end of Renmin Lu offers a real escape from the tourist-filled gardens of the north. Built by the Song poet, Su Sunqin, it is the oldest remaining garden in Suzhou and was repaired in both the Ming and Qing dynasties. The garden contains a number of man-made stone hillocks covered with bamboo and ancient trees. The centerpiece is the Canglang Pavilion, inscribed with the famous Chinese couplet. "the refreshing breeze and the bright moon are priceless. The near water and distant hills strike a sentimental note." And they do, although you can't visit at night, so you could exchange "bright moon" for hot sun!

The exquisite Master of the Nets Garden

★★★**Master of the Nets Garden**, 11 Kuo Jia Lane (daily 7:30 am-5 pm; ¥30; buses #202 & #T2). Situated on a small lane off Shiquan Jie just west of the Suzhou Hotel, this small but perfectly formed garden is a must-see. Dating back to the 12th century, it was constructed by a retired official who decided he wanted to try his hand at fishing. It was later named "Master of the Nets" during the **Qing Dynasty** by **Emperor Qianlong** (see p. 15) who had it restored after many centuries of neglect. The garden's focal point is a picturesque lily pond, flanked by roofed walkways, pavilions, courtyards, rockeries, flowers and trees. Everywhere you walk there are glimpses of another part of the garden, conveying the impression that it is much larger than it really is. From mid-March to mid-November, the garden also hosts an evening show (daily 7:30 pm-10 pm; ¥80), featuring traditional Chinese music performances (see *Cultural Adventures*, p. 357).

★**Couples Garden**, 5-9 Xiaoxinqiao Jie (daily 7:30 am-5 pm; ¥20; bus #701). Ou Yuan, as the garden is locally known, is on the eastern edge of town and is surrounded on three sides by canals and the moat. It offers a collection of beautiful miniature gardens and limestone rockeries set around a central house. There's a pleasant teahouse and you can also take short canal trips from here (¥10), which depart from the back of the garden.

★**Lion Grove Garden**, 23 Yuanlin Lu (daily 7:30 am-5 pm; ¥30; buses #2, #T1, #T2 & #T5). In the northeast part of town not far from the Humble Administrators Garden, Lion Grove is a man-made maze of caves, rockeries

Facing page: Zhuozheng Garden (S. Laqua)

and pathways that dates back to the 13th century. It was built by a Buddhist monk to honor the memory of his late master. The rocks are said to have come from the nearby Lake Tai and supposedly resemble lions sleeping, fighting and playing, hence the garden's name, although you may need to stretch your imagination to envisage this!

★★★**The Humble Administrator's Garden**, 178 Dong Bei Lu (daily 7:30 am-5 pm; ¥70; buses #2, #3, #T1, #T2 & #T5). One of the most famous in China and, for some, the best, the Humble Administrator's Garden gained UNESCO World Heritage status in 1997. Given that this is the biggest garden in Suzhou, its title seems a little ironic. It stems from a Tang poem which suggested that garden conservation was the work of a humble man. The garden was built by a retired imperial official under the inspiration of this poem, in the belief that withdrawal and retreat were admirable attributes. However, although it's the largest and most famous, I prefer the more intimate Master of the Nets Garden.

Lingering Garden, 338 Liuyuan Lu (daily 7:30 am-5 pm; ¥40; buses #11, #T1 & #T2). The Lingering Garden sits in the far northwest of town and was designed by a retired Ming dynasty minister. Expanded and renovated in the Qing dynasty, it offers a number of picture-perfect gardens set around pavilions and lily ponds. North of the garden's Nanmu Hall you'll find the 21-foot-tall Guanyun Peak – a contorted and potholed rock tower brought here from Lake Tai. Despite its location, the Lingering Garden has become one of the most popular sights in town and can get very busy in the summer.

Entrance to Tiger Hill Garden (Miguel A. Monjas)

★**Tiger Hill**, Huqiu Lu (daily 7:30 am-5:30 pm; ¥60; buses #8, #49, #T1 & #T2). Su Dongpo (see *Poetry*, p. 61) reputedly said "it is a lifelong pity if you have visited Suzhou without an appearance in Tiger Hill" and, while I managed to avoid it the first few times I came to Suzhou and wasn't aware of any lifelong pity, it is a nice place to head for on a bike trip (see *Adventures On Wheels*, p. 355). Located in the northwestern outskirts of the city, Tiger Hill is the resting place of the supposed founder of Suzhou, Emperor He Lu. Legend has it that a white tiger appeared at the top of the hill just days after he was entombed. Inside the park you'll find numerous temples, pavilions and ponds and the 10th-century, 98-foot-tall Yunyan (or leaning) Pagoda, China's version of Pisa, which currently stands at an angle of 15 degrees!

Facing page: The Humble Administrator's Garden (Galen Frysinger)

Museums

Suzhou Opera Museum, 14 Zhangjia Jie (daily 8:30 am-4:30 pm; free; buses #2 & #4). Although a little off the beaten track, the Opera Museum is a hidden gem. Housed in a Ming Dynasty theater made of latticed wood, the rooms are filled with brightly colored costumes, masks and traditional musical instruments. Many of the exhibits were used for performances of Kun Opera, China's oldest operatic form, and there's even a life-sized model orchestra!

The Silk Museum, 2001 Renmin Lu (daily 9 am-4:30 pm; ¥15; buses #1 & #101). This well-laid-out museum traces the **history of silk**, from its beginnings over 3,000 years ago to the present. Clearly labeled in English and Chinese, the informative exhibits give you the chance to see the silk process in all its stages –from **silkworms** happily chewing away on their mulberry leaves to sorting, spinning and production. The museum also has a shop where you can buy just about everything ever made from silk, although the products are expensive.

Suzhou Arts and Crafts Museum, 58 Xibei Jie (daily 9 am-5 pm last tickets at 4:30 pm; ¥15; buses #3 & #T2). Housed in an old courtyard-style house, this museum has a good collection of local arts and crafts. Highlights include a double-sided silk embroidery of Chairman Mao measuring six by five feet. There's also an exquisite wood carving of a "Temple of Ten Thousand Buddhas" and the museum even has a small collection of imperial clothes on display.

Suzhou Museum, 204 Dongbei Jie (buses #2, #3, #T1, #T2 & #T5). Suzhou Museum used to be housed in the former residence of Taiping Uprising leader, Li Xiucheng, but was **closed at the time of writing** for relocation next door. Previously, the residence's history was more of a reason to visit than its poorly labeled displays of ceramics, but this should change in the new building, designed by acclaimed architect I.M. Pei. It will feature both Eastern and Western influences and will include an art gallery and opera hall. Check with the tourist office for the latest.

Pagodas & Temples

★**Panmen**, 1 Dongda Jie (daily 8 am-4:45 pm; ¥25; buses #5, #7, #30 & #T2). In the southwest of town Panmen (Coiled Gate) includes a trio of ancient attractions: land and water city gates, Ruigang Pagoda and Wumen Bridge. There were originally eight gates in the wall around the city but Panmen is the only surviving one. The city gates were first constructed over 2,000 years ago to serve as protection from invaders, but their current form dates from the 14th century. Just inside the gates, the simple seven-story octagonal **Ruigang Pagoda** stands 175 feet tall and was first built over a thousand years ago. You can ascend the pagoda for great views of the area. The most scenic way to approach Panmen is across the high arch of **Wumen Bridge**, which also makes a good spot to watch the canal traffic. The whole area is popular with traditional morning exercise enthusiasts and if you come early enough you'll see graceful sword dancing and tai chi to the backdrop of a rising sun.

Twin Pagodas, 22 Dinghuisi Lu (daily 7:30 am-5:30 pm; ¥3; buses #2, #5, #27 or #T2). These identical slender pagodas are too fragile to climb, but they sit in pretty gardens just south of Ganjiang Dong Lu. The pagodas were built by two brothers to honor their teacher during the Northern Song dynasty (see p. 11) and are meant to resemble a pair of calligraphy brushes painting the sky. **The pagodas were closed for restoration at the time of writing**.

Temple of Mystery, Guanqian Jie (daily

Ruigang Pagoda (Tot Foster)

7:30 am-4:30 pm; ¥20; buses #1, #2, #20 & #101). At the heart of the bustling Guanqian Jie pedestrianised shopping zone, this Taoist temple complex dates back to the third century and has survived the onslaughts of the ages fairly well, only being rebuilt and restored a few times and avoiding much damage in the Cultural Revolution. The Sanqing Dian (Pure Trinity Hall) is the temple's most impressive hall and is the largest ancient wooden structure south of the Yangzi. Inside it you'll find statues of the Taoist Trinity and a stone tablet inscribed with the image of Taoism's founder, Lao Zi (see p. 50).

North Temple Pagoda, 1918 Renmin Lu (daily 8 am-6 pm; ¥15; buses #1, #T1, #T2 & #T4). This impressive pagoda is one of the first things you see as you cross the moat coming from the train station into Suzhou, and has become a symbol of the city. Originally dating from the sixth century, the pagoda is constructed of wood and bricks and stands an impressive 250 feet tall. The grounds below contain temples and gardens, although you can get a good look at the pagoda for free from Renmin Lu. If you do go in, climb up to the eighth floor where you will get excellent views of Suzhou, weather permitting

★★**West Garden Temple**, Xiajinqiao Lu (daily 7:30 am-5 pm; ¥15; bus #6, #10, #11, #17 & #40). Originally established in the Yuan dynasty (see p. 12) the West Garden Temple is a Buddhist complex housing a number of buildings, the most interesting of which is the Hall of 500 Arhats. This hall, first built in the Ming dynasty holds a 1,000-armed Guanyin statue and rows of gold-painted arhats (*luohan*), each with a different and intricately detailed expression, from the humorous to the tortured – it's not hard to spot the "mad monk"! Behind the temple there's a garden with ponds where fish and turtles have been "freed" by Buddhist believers.

Galleries, Shows & Theaters

Kun opera is the local style and is still widely enjoyed in Suzhou. In addition to the performance at the Master of the Nets Garden (see below), there are also plenty of teahouses where you can see Kun opera and traditional storytelling, including Guangyu Storytelling Hall and Pinfang Teahouse, both of which are on Guanqian Jie.

Gold-painted arhat from the West Garden Temple

★★★**Gardens by Night** (daily 7:30 pm-10 pm; ¥80). For a different garden experience, it's definitely worth visiting the Master of the Nets Garden (see p. 346) by night. The garden is transformed by lanterns and the sounds of traditional music fill the air. Each section of the garden shows a different performance and you are free to wander through the areas at leisure. Kun opera is performed and you'll see a number of **traditional** and **local instruments** being played, accompanied by the soft tones of the Suzhou dialect. There are **nightly performances** between mid-March and mid-November. It's worth visiting in the week as shows can be very busy weekends. The show is particularly memorable if you're here for a full moon, which appears three times – in the sky, in the pond and in the reflecting mirror behind the central pavilion.

Health & Relaxation

Suzhou isn't a hectic city, but if you want to take the weight off your feet and relax you'll find a number of ways to do so. The traditional way of taking some time for reflection is over a cup of tea and many of the gardens still have great **teahouses** – try the one in the Shangzhuo Tower at the Couples Garden (daily 8 am-5 pm). If your feet ache from all this walking and cycling, there are plenty of foot massage parlors in Suzhou – prices start at around ¥40 per hour.

Shopping

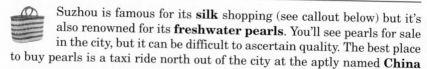

Suzhou is famous for its **silk** shopping (see callout below) but it's also renowned for its **freshwater pearls**. You'll see pearls for sale in the city, but it can be difficult to ascertain quality. The best place to buy pearls is a taxi ride north out of the city at the aptly named **China**

Pearl City (Zheitang Lu, Weitang City) where you'll find over 1,000 shops! Two-thirds of China's pearl trade takes place here and busy days can see 10,000 people eagerly buying and selling.

For **souvenirs**, head to Shiquan Jie where you'll find everything from questionable silk and better quality tea and chopsticks to copy sneakers and DVDs. Or for something a little different, **Tibetan Antelope Culture Development Company** sells an excellent collection of hand-made Tibetan jewelry. Brand name goods and sports shops can be found in the commercial district that surrounds the Temple of Mystery (see p. 351) on Guanqian Jie. There's also the customary **Friendship Store** at 1351 Renmin Lu. For designer wear, try the upmarket **Suzhou Commercial Mansion** at 383 Renmin Lu. Everyday needs can be met in the small supermarket at the eastern end of Shiquan Jie or the legion of **KEDI** 24-hr convenience stores, but if you want a proper supermarket there is a **Carrefour** at 183 Sanxiang Lu in the far west of the city.

SILK SHOPPING

Suzhou has long been famed for its silk. Silk shops and stalls can be found all over the city, but are particularly clustered around the tourist sights. In these places you'll generally find over-priced, low quality goods, so for premium silk it's best to go specialized stores. In better stores the quality is assured but elsewhere you may be fobbed off with a synthetic mix. Wherever you shop it's worth haggling a little. "Fixed price" stores may give you a slight discount, but in smaller stores near tourist sights you should expect to dramatically reduce the asking price.

If you are interested in the silk process it's worth heading to the **Silk Museum** (see p. 350) and afterwards you can check out its shop, which, while a little pricey, has a wide range of products and can give a good idea of what's offered. The **Silk King** next door offers the same at better prices, including the much-touted **silk duvets** which start from around ¥400. For silk undergarments, try **Dong Wu Silk Weaving Mill** at 540 Renmin Lu.

Silk embroidery has a history of more than 2,000 years in Suzhou and, if you want to pick up some embroidered pictures, the **Suzhou Embroidery Factory** at 272 Jingde Lu has won awards for the quality of its craftsmanship (which is more of an art form), but has prices to match.

Adventures

On Foot

Suzhou is a city tailor-made for exploration on foot with **pedestrianised areas** and scenic walkways along its **canals**. It's not always possible to get away from the hustle and bustle of the main streets by bicycle and walking offers a great way to see some of the older sections of town. Some of the best examples of Ming and Qing residential buildings lie along the canal banks and, if you go later in the day, their pavilions and walkways are full of children playing, while older generations sit engrossed in games of Chinese chess. The walk detailed below is my favorite, but any stroll along the smaller streets and canal pathways will yield picturesque scenes of daily life.

★★★ The Canals of Pingjiang (1 hr)

Pingjiang Canal (Tot Foster)

This is an excellent walk that highlights the older side of Suzhou, without the noise, traffic or tourists. The route follows a number of the quietest canals in Suzhou, running from south to north, and can be completed over a leisurely morning of walking. But if you get tired it's easy to cut back west to the town center and catch a taxi back.

Start at the **Master of the Nets Garden** (see p. 346) on **Shiquan Jie** and walk east towards the Suzhou Hotel. From here, you will see a canal running parallel and north of Shiquan Jie. Cross over to the north side of the street and head over the canal, following it eastwards until just before the city moat, where you turn left (north) up **Pingjiang Canal**. From here, it's a simple case of following the canal north for as long as you want. The first sight worth stopping at is the **Twin Pagodas** (see p. 351) on Dinghuisi Lu, a short distance before the first big crossroads where Ganjiang Dong Lu crosses the canal. If you look to the west, you'll see the tops of the ancient pagodas guiding you to their entrance. You can also have a look at the simple Song dynasty Dinghui Temple (daily 7:30 am-5 pm; free) a little before the pagodas on the same side of the road.

Back on the east side of Pingjiang canal, you'll soon reach a large intersection at Ganjiang Dong Lu. Cross over the road and you'll see the continuation of the canal a little to the right, from where you can re-join it heading north. This next section is a must as it contains many of **Pingjiang's older residential buildings**, some of which have recently undergone restoration. It's worth stopping at the **Suzhou Opera Museum** (see p. 350) to your right on the way past. A little farther north, the Pingjiang Canal bends westwards and you'll see another canal starting on your right (east), lined by a row of very bright whitewashed buildings. Follow this east for approximately five minutes and you'll find yourself at the entrance to the **Couples Garden** (see p. 346), where you could stop for a cup of tea.

Once finished, re-trace your tracks back to Pingjiang Lu, and continue northwards, crossing over Baita Dong Lu. Look for the start of Shilinsi Xiang on your left as this will take you down to **Lion's Grove Garden** (see p. 346). If you still have the energy, then continue north and on to Dongbei Jie, where you'll see a string of souvenir shops marking

Suzhou street life (Tot Foster)

the entrance to the **Humble Administrator's Garden** (see p. 348), making a perfect end to your walk. You can take a taxi back from here.

On Wheels

Suzhou is well equipped to deal with bicycles and larger roads have designated cycle lanes, although this may be new information to some of Suzhou's pedestrians, taxi and even truck drivers! In spite of the occasional obstacle, cycle lanes make it easy to travel through the city center, but it's worth conserving your energy for the longer trips out to **Tiger Hill** (see *Sightseeing*, p. 348) and **Precious Belt Bridge**. See *Getting Around, By Bicycle*, p. 342, for rental details.

★ Grand Canal & the Precious Belt Bridge (2-3 hrs)

This picturesque Tang Dynasty bridge's 53 arches span Tantai Lake and make for a scenic backdrop to a picnic or a bit of sunbathing. To get there, ride west along **Shiquan Jie**, turning south onto **Renmin Lu**. Follow Renmin Lu south through the outskirts of the city, crossing over the **city moat**. From here, continue south for another few miles until you see the **Dongwu Tower** (a scale replica of the Eiffel Tower!) in the middle of a large roundabout. Take a left at the roundabout and head east along **Taihu Dong Lu** for about a mile, where you'll find a crossroads. Turn right and ride south onto **Beiyun Lu** and cross the **Grand Canal**. Continue south and over another smaller canal; at the end of the road turn left onto **Shihu Lu**. You should see the Grand Canal at the end and the **Precious Belt Bridge** off to your left. There are plenty of places to stop and relax before heading back to town. If it's all been too much, then ride back to the Dongwu Tower and negotiate a taxi fare back (¥20), for both you and your bike.

★★ Tiger Hill (2-3 hrs)

Starting on **Shiquan Jie**, ride west until you meet **Renmin Lu**, where you turn right, heading north up to the junction with **Daoqian Jie**. Turn left onto Daoqian Jie and go west until you reach canal-side **Jianjinqiao Xiang** off to your right (north). Head up this lane (which changes names to become Shilin Xiang and then Tangjia Xiang), keeping the canal on your left until you reach **Dong Zhong Shi Jie**. Turn left and follow it to the **moat** on the edge of town. Cross over the moat and then turn right (north) across two smaller canals, the latter of which, **Shantang Canal**, you follow northwest. The path runs along the right-hand side of the canal and is marked Shantang Jie. Follow this out of the city, under the railway track, past the park and you'll see the entrance to the pagoda parkland of Tiger Hill on your right after about two miles. Return the same way.

 Tip: For the very energetic, a great escape from the city is to ride out to tranquil Lingyan (daily 7 am-5:30 pm; ¥10) and Tianping Hills (Mon-Fri 8 am-4 pm, Sat & Sun 8 am-5 pm; ¥10), nine miles and 11 miles away respectively. Both offer views of the city, and have temples, pagodas, wooded pathways and streams. If you're not up for the bike ride, tourist bus #T4 heads to both sights.

★★★On Water

Market life along the canal

Suzhou's network of canals has given it the nickname of **Venice of the East**, and although pungently polluted, they still manage to be picturesque and offer a great insight into life around the area. Boats ply their way along the narrow waterways, passing the backdoors of the thousands who still live on their banks and no trip to Suzhou would be complete without a view of life from the water. There are a few different routes to take, but the most common is around the moat. If you want to get off the beaten track, many boatmen will oblige for an inflated cost. To do the entire circuit around the moat takes about 80 minutes and costs ¥38. You can get boats from near the train and bus stations in the north, and at Nanmen Wharf in the south. Another interesting adventure on water is the overnight trip along the Grand Canal to Hangzhou – see *Getting Here & Away*, p. 340, for details.

Cultural Adventures

The Boland School of Cultural Studies (☎ 0512-6741-3422, www.
boland-china.com), at 197 Fengmeng Lu, offers a number of excellent
courses and regular workshops, ranging from **Chinese cooking**, to **traditional musical instrument lessons**. Many of the courses are 'intense' and
can be completed in under two weeks; special packages can be put together
on request. Other courses include **calligraphy, Mandarin lessons, martial arts** and an **introduction to Chinese literature**. For more information, check out the website or pick up your free copy of *What's on in Suzhou*
for current workshops.

Where to Stay

 Suzhou's accommodation options are spread over the city, although
the largest concentration is around Shiquan Jie near the Master of
the Nets Garden.

> **What's it mean?** FC=fitness center; SW=swimming pool; @=in-
> room Internet access; DA=rooms for disabled. For ¥ price codes,
> see page 113.

★**Bamboo Grove**, 168 Zhuhui Lu (☎ 0512-6520-5601, www.bg-hotel.com).
In the south of the city, the Japanese-owned Bamboo Grove offers comfortable rooms set among pleasant bamboo-laden gardens and is popular with
tour groups. The rooms were renovated in 2006 and are light and airy – the
deluxe doubles have excellent views over the pavilion and lake. FC/SW/@
¥¥¥¥

Dong Wu, 24 Shiquan Jie (☎ 0512-6519-3681). Well-located on Shiquan Jie,
the Dong Wu is a large, quiet and reasonably priced option, although it has
seen better days. ¥¥

Friendship, 349 Zhuhui Lu (☎ 0512-6529-1601). This dated hotel has dull
and musty, but functional rooms which are saved by their setting amidst
Chinese gardens, pavilions and bridges and their price! ¥¥

Lexiang, 18 Dajin Xiang (☎ 0512-6522-8888). A well-priced and surprisingly quiet central hotel, the Lexiang is close to the shopping and restaurants around the Temple of Mystery, and has modern, comfortable rooms.
¥¥¥

★**My Hotel**, 263 Shiquan Jie (☎ 0512-6519-3188, www.myhotels.cn). This
is a modern hotel aimed at business travelers, but its cheap rates and handy
location also attract a fair number of budget travelers. Rooms are clean and
well-furnished and service is friendly. @ ¥¥

★★★**Pingjiang Lodge**, 33 Niu Jia Xiang, Ping Jiang Qu (☎ 0512-6523-
3888, www.the-silk-road.com). This 450-year-old building lies in the heart of
old Suzhou. Surrounded by traditional houses, canals and walkways, its
quiet location on the edge of the Pingjiang Canal makes for an excellent

retreat. Built by the Fang family during the Ming Dynasty, the lodge still contains original furniture and pictures. The 42 rooms are clustered around numerous courtyards and traditional gardens, designed to evoke serenity and peace. A number of rooms have windows overlooking the canal. There is also an attractive restaurant serving both Chinese and Western fare. Call ahead before you arrive and they'll arrange a transfer for you. @ ¥¥¥

Sheraton Suzhou Hotel & Towers

★★**Sheraton Suzhou Hotel & Towers**, 259 Xin Shi Lu (☎ 0512-6510-3388, www.sheraton.com/suzhou). Bringing you the high standard you'd expect from this international five-star chain, the Sheraton Garden does so with some Suzhou flavor. The main entrance is modeled on Panmen (see p. 350), just behind the hotel, and the building and grounds are designed to look like a Ming dynasty mansion and contain a number of rock pools, gardens and pavilions. FC/SW/@ ¥¥¥¥¥

Suzhou, 345 Shiquan Jie (☎ 0512-6530-5777, www.suzhou-hotel.com). One of the city's longest-standing hotels, the Suzhou is well-located close to the Master of the Nets Garden. The modern and comfortable, if small, rooms are housed in a bland building set in a large garden. @ ¥¥¥¥

Suzhou Garden View, 66, Luoguaqiao Lu (☎ 0512-6777-8888).This pleasantly situated hotel has well-furnished rooms spread out in low-rise buildings interconnected by quaint walkways. The staff are keen to please, although the restaurants aren't great. FC/@ ¥¥¥¥

Suzhou Youth Hostel, 178 Xiangwang Lu (☎ 0512-6510-9418, www.yhasuzhou.com). This well-located HI hostel has tiny doubles and cramped dorms (¥50) but is about as cheap as you'll find in this part of town. ¥

Where to Eat

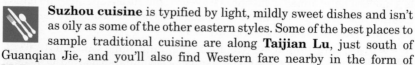

See page 117 for an explanation of the ¥ restaurant price codes.

Suzhou cuisine is typified by light, mildly sweet dishes and isn't as oily as some of the other eastern styles. Some of the best places to sample traditional cuisine are along **Taijian Lu**, just south of Guanqian Jie, and you'll also find Western fare nearby in the form of **McDonalds**, **KFC**, **Pizza Hut** and **Starbucks**.

Shiquan Jie is lined with inexpensive places serving **Chinese favorites** from around the country and most of them have English menus. You'll also find a number of coffee shops here, which are quickly becoming the fashion, although prices can be high. In the listings below, restaurants where reservations are required have telephone numbers detailed.

Deyuelou

★★**Deyuelou**, 27 Taijian Jie (☎ 0512-6523-8940; daily 11 am-2 pm & 5-9 pm). Deyuelou is one of the city's oldest restaurants and is well worth a visit. It's been operating for 400 years and is particularly famous for its "garden food" style of presentation. This style uses food to resemble all the elements of Suzhou's gardens, including flowers, rocks and trees, and includes bizarre dishes such as hedgehog-shaped buns and ham and vegetable fans! If you're keener on eating your food than looking at it, stick to the restaurant's Suzhou specialties – the braised chicken is delicious. ¥¥-¥¥¥¥

★★**Indian at the Cross**, 758 Shiquan Jie (daily 11 am-2 pm & 5 pm-10:30 pm). Don't be put off if this restaurant looks closed from the outside – once inside it is warm and welcoming. The low-lit booths give an intimate feel, and the friendly staff serve a range of Indian favorites, including excellent 100% vegetarian dishes. To enter, go through the hotel on the right, where you'll find the front door of the restaurant. ¥¥¥

Japanese Food, 110 Fenghuang Jie (daily 10 am-10 pm). This low-key Japanese restaurant, just around the corner from the Master of the Nets Garden, offers a quick and tasty lunch option. It has a large selection of Japanese favorites and, if you're feeling indecisive, there are variety boxes of sushi and sashimi. ¥¥-¥¥¥

Indian at the Cross

Sarawak, 516 Shiquan Jie (daily 10 am-2 pm & 5 pm-10:30 pm). If you want to step out of China, but not out of Asia, Sarawak serves good Malaysian fare such as *satay* sticks, *nasi goreng* and *gado-gado*. Staff are friendly and this small restaurant is popular with foreign tour groups. ¥¥

★**Songhelou**, 18 Taijian Jie (☎ 0512-6523-3270; daily 11 am-1:30 pm & 5-8:30 pm). Close to the Deyuelou, this is another of Suzhou's most famous restaurants, with a history of nearly 300 years. The Songhelou (Pine and Crane) is renowned for its boat food, which gets its name from the fact that it used to be enjoyed on board banquet boats. Emperor Qianlong apparently enjoyed the alarmingly named but delicious Squirrel-Shaped Mandarin Fish, and it has remained the restaurant's most popular dish ever since. ¥¥¥

★**SuCa Café**, 357 Shiquan Jie (daily 8 am-12 pm). If it's an American breakfast you want, then this is this place! This quiet Western-style café serves the best coffee on Shiquan Jie and also has a good range of sandwiches, salads and pastas. Its dark wood interior and comfortable sofas and armchairs make for a great place for a leisurely breakfast and a bit of people watching. ¥¥-¥¥¥

Tudori, 251 Shiquan Jie (daily 3 pm-3 am). For something different and some fun, head to this Korean restaurant. Although no English menu is available and no English is spoken, you'll be presented with an extensive picture menu, from which you can select your meal. Try the chicken leg kebabs. ¥¥¥

Xinjiang Yakexi, 786 Shiquan Jie (daily 11 am-late). This cheap and cheerful Muslim restaurant serves up hearty bowls of stretched noodles and is often filled with locals. ¥-¥¥

Yang-Yang "Lonely Planet" Shui Jiao, 420 Shiquan Jie (daily 9 am-3 am). This is the most popular and best of Shiquan Jie's tourist-oriented cheap restaurants and offers tasty Chinese favorites in a comfortable and clean environment. Some staff speak a little English and are very keen to help. Be sure not to get confused with the inferior restaurant next door which also has a Lonely Planet sticker – you want the one on the left! ¥-¥¥

Yunnan Noodles, Shiquan Jie (daily 11 am-late). Near the junction with Fenghuang Jie, this place specializes in Crossing the Bridge Noodles (see *Culinary Experiences Not to Miss*, p. 119), which are worth trying here if you're not heading to Yunnan province. ¥-¥¥

Nightlife

Shiquan Jie has developed nightlife to cater for the number of foreign tourists and businessmen visiting Suzhou. You'll find **American-style bars** with live sports, pool tables and foosball, although some of these places also serve a seedier purpose as pick-up joints for prostitutes. **Pulp Fiction** and **Whiskey Jack's** are popular traveler hang-outs, while **Scarlet**, a little farther east along Shiquan Jie, provides a more comfortable setting for its **live music** (9 pm nightly). Most bars open around 7 pm and won't close until you leave! West of here, the **Shamrock** at 775 Shiquan Jie and the **Blue Marlin** at 261 Fenghuang Jie provide for a more expat crowd of drinkers and the Shamrock also offers free wireless connection.

Hangzhou

Traditionally linked with Suzhou as one of the two paradises below heaven, Hangzhou manages to live up to this claim a great deal more than its northern cousin and is one of China's most beautiful cities. Nestled attractively around the edge of **West Lake** (Xi Hu) and surrounded by **tea-growing**

hills and **grand temples**, Hangzhou's attractions have earned it the dubious title of China's Honeymoon Capital. Hangzhou is my favorite city in this part of China and is well worth a few days break. It's population is about two million. All the usual city amenities are here and Hangzhou has good shopping, restaurants and nightlife, but what sets it apart is the lake. The second you step onto the lakeside it's very difficult to remember you are in a city. Surrounding it are a host of beautiful bike rides and hikes to enjoy, with green tea to replenish you.

History

Leifeng Pagoda on the West Lake (Shizhao)

The completion of the **Grand Canal**, with Hangzhou as its southern terminus in 609 AD, first marked the city on the map, but it wasn't until the Song dynasty (see *History*, p. 11) was ejected from Kaifeng and relocated here that Hangzhou really started to blossom. As the capital of the Southern Song (1126-1279) dynasty, Hangzhou attracted merchants, artisans, poets and artists and its **silk trade** started in earnest. By the time of Marco Polo's supposed visit in the 13th century, the city had a population of a million. Although there is some doubt as to whether Marco Polo actually ever made it to China, his description of Hangzhou sounds accurate and he cites the city as the most opulent in the world! With the fall of the Song some of this splendor was lost, but Hangzhou remained a strategic trading post for silk. It enjoyed revived imperial patronage under the Qing, although the **Taiping Uprising** (1850-64, see p. 16) destroyed most of the city.

These days, as the provincial capital of Zhejiang, Hangzhou thrives upon its reputation as the most romantic city in the country and is a prime weekend getaway destination. But silk and tea are also cornerstones of both tourism and the city's economy, along with more modern industries such as electronics and pharmaceuticals. However, Hangzhou is still part of China and the bright lights have attracted a wave of rural migrants, many of whom end up begging on the streets. If Marco Polo were to visit Hangzhou again he'd see the merchant boats replaced by Ferrari and Porsche showrooms, but he might be surprised by the abject poverty that exists side-by-side with this ostentatious wealth and lakeside beauty.

Getting Here & Away

By Air

As a popular weekend getaway, Hangzhou is connected to airports all over the country and a few Asian destinations such as Bangkok, Osaka and Seoul. The international airport 16 miles north of town is linked by CAAC bus (¥15 for the 50 minute ride to their offices at 390 Tiyuchang Lu) and taxi (¥90). You can buy airline tickets through many hotels and at the CAAC office (☎ 0571-8666-2391) at 390 Tiyuchang Lu.

Destinations, frequencies & durations

Beijing (20 daily, 1 hr 50 mins); **Chongqing** (3 daily, 2 hrs 10 mins); **Guangzhou** (16 daily, 1 hr 45 mins); **Guilin** (2 daily, 2 hrs); **Hong Kong** (12 daily, 2 hrs); **Shenzhen** (11 daily, 1 hr 45 mins); **Xi'an** (5 daily, 1 hr 50 mins).

By Rail

Hangzhou is well-served by trains from all over the country. The vast modern main station is a little over a mile east of the city center and can be reached by buses #K7 and #Y2 or taxi (¥10). You can buy tickets at the station or the booking offices at 149 Tiyuchang Lu in the north of the city.

Destinations, frequencies & durations

Beijing (2 daily, 13 hrs 30 min-15 hrs 20 mins); **Chongqing** (2 daily, 42 hrs 30 min-44 hrs); **Guangzhou** (2 daily, 25 hrs 30 mins); **Guilin** (2 daily, 23-24 hrs); **Shanghai** (10 daily, 1 hr 50 mins); **Shenzhen** (1 daily, 22 hrs); **Suzhou** (5 daily, 3 hrs 30 mins); **Xi'an** (2 daily, 24 hr 30 mins); **Yichang** (1 daily, 25 hrs 30 mins).

There is a planned Maglev high-speed rail link between Shanghai and Hangzhou which will cut the journey time to an incredible 27 minutes and is due to be completed in time for the Expo 2010 in Shanghai.

By Road

Hangzhou has four bus stations simply named after the directions they serve. Thus the west bus station out on Tianmushan Lu serves Huangshan, the east bus station on Genshan Xi Lu operates services to Shanghai and Suzhou and the north station on Moganshan Lu has buses to Nanjing. Taxi is the easiest way to get to the stations, but they are also served by city buses. Take #155, #526 or #555 for the north station, #49 or #803 for the west, #14 or #20 for the south and #31, #55 or #502 for the east station.

Destinations, frequencies & durations

Huangshan (5 daily, 5 hrs); **Shanghai** (frequent, 2 hrs 30 mins); **Suzhou** (frequent, 2 hrs).

By Water

One of the most interesting (but inefficient) ways of reaching Hangzhou is along the **Grand Canal** from Suzhou. Cabins are for two (¥88-95 per person) or four people (¥30-65) and have bathrooms and air-conditioning. Boats leave at 5:30 pm from Wulinmen Passenger Dock (buses #55, #57 & #502) at 208 Huancheng Lu, 1½ miles north of the lake, arriving in Suzhou at 6 am the following morning. You can buy tickets at the dock or Hangzhou Train Station.

Getting Around

Part of the pleasure of Hangzhou is simply getting around, whether walking by the lake, crossing the causeways or cycling out to the tea villages. However, if you just need to get from A to B, the usual range of transport options are available.

By Bus

Buses #Y1, #Y7, #Y9 and #K7 circuit the scenic sites. #Y9 is one of the most useful and simply circles the lake, stopping off at all of its tourist sights, complete with a Chinese-speaking guide. Regular buses cost ¥1, air-conditioned buses are ¥2 and K buses are ¥3-5. Note that buses only accept exact change.

By Buggy

In addition to regular (and mini) buses there are, in true Chinese tourist style, golf buggies that shuttle visitors around the lake and across the causeways. If you're tired after a hot hike around the lake, a buggy ride can take the weight off your legs for a while, although you might have to endure the driver/guide's megaphone. Buggies operate from 8 am-5:30 pm and cost ¥40 for the complete circuit, or ¥10 for any one of the four sections.

By Taxi

Minimum is ¥10 for the first four km (2½ miles) and ¥2 per km (0.6 miles) after that. Few drivers speak much English so, as always, make sure you take your destination written in Chinese.

By Bicycle

Good quality bicycles can be rented all over Hangzhou and most vendors are part of the **Yiyoutang Company**, which enables you to pick up at one location and drop off at another. So, when you get tired, you can just return your bike and take a taxi. However, if you want to do the ride out to Longjing (see *Adventures On Wheels*, p. 376) make sure you get a mountain bike rather than the cute but small-wheeled yellow and pink numbers that most places provide. Prices are ¥5 an hour (plus a ¥200 deposit), but if you haggle hard or take a bike out for a whole day you might get a discount.

By Boat

More sightseeing than practical transport, boats across the lake can be used to get from one side of the lake to the other, but a taxi will be cheaper and quicker. There are also evening canal trips – see *Adventures On Water*, p. 378, for details on both.

Orientation

The modern city and its shopping, restaurants, hotels and amenities are based immediately east of the lake and the train station is farther out this way. **Yan'an Lu** is the main north-south artery in this part of town and holds the bulk of the shops, restaurants and amenities you might need. The entire lake is ringed by roads (Beishan Lu in the north, Xishan Lu in the west, Nanshan Lu in the south, and Hubin Lu in the east). There are also walkways, complete with bars and cafés, so you'll never go thirsty. There are a number of small islands in the lake and it is crossed by three causeways, the **Bai, Su** and **Yanggong**. All of the causeways can be crossed on foot and by bike, but Yanggong is the only one open to cars. Just over halfway up the eastern lakeshore, **Xihutiandi** is Hangzhou's version of Xintiandi (see *Shanghai*, p. 334) and is the city's trendiest dining zone, nestled right next to the lake. North of the lake is the main upmarket hotel area and farther out in this direction you'll find Wulinmen Dock on the Grand Canal. The **Qiantang River** is a couple of miles south of town, and the tea hills and famous village of **Longjing** are to the southwest.

Information Sources

Hangzhou Tourist Information Office (☎ 0571-961-23; daily 8 am-6 pm) has booths around the city, including the airport and the train station. They have a few handy leaflets and maps and also run tours of the city, but the main office is a little out of the way north of the lake on Huanglong Lu, so you're better off dropping in to the booth at the train station when you arrive. The Hangzhou Tourist Committee's website (www.gotohz.com) is a good place to start for pre-trip planning. They have information on sights, walks, tours, hotels and restaurants and they also produce an excellent booklet, *Experience Hangzhou*, which has some great ideas for adventures in the region. On the web, www.hangzhouexpat.com and www.hangzhou.ixpat.com, are also worth checking out and have forums, reviews and up-to-date information on what's hip and what's not in Hangzhou.

Zhejiang Intouch is a local monthly magazine worth picking up and they also have a weekly supplement, *Hangzhou Weekly*, both of which have bar

Shanghai & Around

and restaurant reviews along with the usual listings. They're free and are available from bars and hotels throughout the city.

Events & Festivals

All the main Chinese festivals are celebrated in Hangzhou, and the Lantern Festival (January/February) here is particularly impressive. Unique local festivals and events worth looking out for include:

Dragon Well Tea Festival (April/May) – Celebrates the region's famous green leaves. Picking tea, tea ceremonies and, yes, you eventually get to drink a cup of tea.

West Lake Lotus Festival (July/August) – This annual festival pays tribute to the beautiful lotus flowers that fringe the lake and is also a time for watching local folk drama.

Qiantang River Bore Festival (September) – The natural phenomenon of this impressive tidal river surge attracts thousands of visitors every year and, if you happen to be here, it's definitely worth checking out from Liuhe Pagoda (see p. 371).

Poetic West Lake (Tot Foster)

International Fireworks Show (October) – This annual event illuminates the skies over West Lake with thousands of new fireworks from manufacturers all over the world.

Communications

Post Office: 143 Hefang Lu and 197 Zhongshan Nan Lu.

Telephone code: 0571.

Internet Access: At the Mingtown Hostel (see p. 379), as well as plenty of Internet cafés in the commercial area east of the lake.

Bank of China: Northeast of the lake at 321 Fengqi Lu, and on the western end of Pinghai Lu. Note that most other bank ATMs in Hangzhou won't accept international cards.

Public Security Bureau: A little way east of the lake at 35 Huagang Lu (☎ 0571-8728-0561).

Medical services: Zhejiang number 1 Hospital at 79 Qingchun Lu
(☎ 0571-8723-6666).

Sightseeing

 Hangzhou has a few big drawcard attractions, which include **Feilai Feng, Lingyin Temple, Yuefei's Tomb, Longjing tea village** and the **tea** and **silk museums**, but there are also countless smaller sights dotted around the lake and surrounding countryside. Many have poetically long-winded and flowery titles, such as Autumn Moon on a Calm Lake and Dreamlike Tiger Spring, which are derived from their legendary beginnings. But, whether you remember their names or not, part of the pleasure of Hangzhou is simply strolling among them.

A WEEKEND IN HANGZHOU

Day 1: Head out to **Lingyin Temple** and **Feilai Feng** early to beat the crowds and then spend the rest of the day taking a leisurely amble (or ride) around the lake, making sure to cross either the **Bai or the Su causeways** (or both) and trying to reach **Leifeng Pagoda** or **Shuangtou Bridge** in the southeastern corner of the lake in time for sunset.

Day 2: Set off early to beat the heat and take a bike ride down to the Qiantang River. Visit **Liuhe Pagoda** and ride on to beautiful **Longjing tea village** where you can sample some of the finest green tea in China, maybe stopping at the **Tea Museum** on the way back. Return to your hotel, freshen up and enjoy dinner at Louwailou (see p. 381).

Tours

Unless you're in a hurry, taking a tour around Hangzhou's sights defies the laid-back atmosphere that the lake is all about. However, tourist buses that circuit the main sights are worth taking advantage of (see *Getting Around*, p. 363), as are the boats that ply the lake (see *Adventures On Water*, p. 378). But, if you're set on a tour, ask at your hotel.

West Lake

The two-mile-wide expanse of West Lake dominates and vitalizes Hangzhou. Although there are a number of sights at its edge and on its islands, West Lake is best enjoyed by an amble around its fringes or a stroll across its causeways (see *Adventures On Foot*, p. 375). However, if you want a target for your strolls, the sights below are all worthwhile diversions. The lake is surrounded by a network of paths and trails, which pass lush parks, pavilions and viewpoints.

Hangzhou

1 MILE

2008 Hunter Publishing, Inc.

N

1. Liuhe Pagoda
2. Dreamlike Tiger Spring
3. Nine Creeks & 18 Gullies
4. Longjing Village
5. Felai Feng & Lingyin Temple
6. Pot Peak
7. Tomb of MM
8. To West Bus Station
9. Hangzhou Tourist Information Office
10. To North Bus Station
11. To Wulinmen Passenger Dock
12. To East Bus Station
13. To Airport
14. To Train Station
15. To South Bus Station
16. Traditional Chinese
    Medicine Museum

17. Hanbi Pavilion
18. Silk Museum
19. Huajiashan Villa Hotel
20. Liefeng Pagoda
21. Three Pools
    Reflecting the Moon
22. Ancient Temple Road
23. Yue Fei's Tomb
24. Shangri La Hotel
25. Yellow Dragon Cave
26. Baochu Pagoda,
    Precious Stone Hill
27. Broken Bridge
28. Louwailou Restaurant;
    Solitary Hill Island; Zhongshan Park
    Zhejiang Provincial Museum;
    Seal Engravers' Society

29. Lord Ruan's Mound
30. Mid-lake Pavilion
31. Hubin Park
32. Overseas Chinese Hotel
33. Elan Inn, Hyatt Regency
34. Kuiyuanguan Restaurant
35. Zhiweiguan Restaurant
36. Sofitel
37. Xihutiandi Riverside Complex;
    Crystal Jade Restaurant;
    Jamaica Cofee Shop;
    Va Bene Restaurant
38. Haveli Restaurant;
    Mingtown Youth Hostel;
    Garden of Orioles Singing
    in Ripples of Willows

Causeways & Islands

Sunset from Leifeng Pagoda

West Lake is traversed by three causeways and has several small islands within its expanse, all of which are worth exploring. **Bai Causeway** was named after the famous Tang dynasty poet and governor of Hangzhou, Bai Juyi, and stretches across the north of the lake from the **Broken Bridge** to **Solitary Hill Island**. The **Su Causeway** follows the poet-governor theme and takes its name from another of China's most famous wordsmiths, Su Dongpo. The Su runs from north to south across the west of the lake and, at nearly two miles, is over twice as long as the Bai. As a result, it's a quieter place for a stroll and enjoys equally expansive views. Both the Bai and Su causeways can be traversed on foot or by bike, but the third, **Yanggong** (after Governor Yang) in the far west, is the only one open to cars. That makes it a less attractive proposition for a stroll, although it offers some tranquil views over **Maojiabu Lake** to the west. For walks on the causeways see *Adventures On Foot*, p. 375.

There are three islands within the central lake, which can all be visited on boat trips from Solitary Hill as well as on tours (see above). Tiny **Lord Ruan's Mound** (daily 8 am-5 pm; free) sometimes hosts nighttime opera performances and the **Mid-lake Pavilion** is worth a brief stop, but the Three Pools Reflecting the Moon has a little more to see.

The causeways are great for a bike ride or a stroll

★**Three Pools Reflecting the Moon** (Santanyinyue; daily 8 am-5 pm; ¥20). This pretty little island in the center of the lake holds ponds, pavilions and pagodas, which are shown on the back of the new green ¥1 notes. The man-made island encircles a central lake, which is divided into four ponds by bridges. The three stone pagodas were first built in the 17th century and are lit up by candles for the autumn full moon. The small holes in the pagoda allow this light to shine out onto the lake and mingle with the moonlight, creating the Three Pools Reflecting the Moon and the island's name. To get to the island take a boat from Solitary Hill Island, Hubin Park or the southern end of Yanggong Causeway.

Northern Shore

★★★**Solitary Hill Island** (Gu Shan; bus #Y9). At the western end of the Bai Causeway, Solitary Hill Island (Gu Shan) has a long imperial tradition and offers a number of worthwhile attractions as well as being a great place to find a shady spot to soak up the fine views over the lake. First favored during the Tang dynasty, the Qing emperors Kangxi and Qianlong (see *A Golden Age*, p. 15) also enjoyed time here and the **Autumn Moon on a Calm Lake Pavilion** in the southeast of the island is a testament to their fondness for the area. West of here in the pristine **Zhongshan Park** you'll find the **Zhejiang Provincial Museum** (Mon noon-4:30 pm, Tues-Sun 8:30 am-4:30 pm; ¥10), housed in a wing of the old imperial palace, which holds a good collection of ceramics and Shang (1600-1122 BC) and Zhou (1122-221 BC) bronzes. West again, Louwailou is a great spot for some local culinary specialties (see p. 381). On the hill above, the Seal Engraver's Society (daily 8:30-4:30 pm; ¥10) occupies a small shrub-filled park and offers a collection of ancient inscribed stone stelae as well as excellent lake views.

★**Yue Fei's Tomb** (daily 7:30 am-5:30 pm; ¥25; buses #K7, #Y1 & #Y9). Dedicated to the legendary Song dynasty General **Yue Fei** (see p. 11), this temple is set on the other side of Beishan Lu from the lake and is worth a visit if you're passing by. Yue Fei fought relentlessly against the invading Jurchen Jin but was falsely accused of treachery and executed. Twenty years later the claims were rescinded and Yue Fei was re-interred at this site. To reach the tomb, proceed through the temple, over a small bridge and along the customary avenue of statues where you'll see the Chinese characters meaning "Loyal to the End" on the front of the tomb, allegedly the phrase Yue Fei had tattooed on his back before his execution. The four kneeling statues near his tomb represent the shamed courtiers who betrayed him.

★**Precious Stone Hill** (Baoshi Shan; buses #K7 & #Y9). East of Yue Fei's Tomb, Precious

Baochu Pagoda (Chris Guilbeau)

Stone Hill looms over the lake's northern shore and its famous **Baochu Pagoda** can be seen from all over the lake. The slender 125-foot-tall pagoda (daily 7:30 am-5 pm; ¥15) was originally built in 970 AD, although the current version dates from the 1930s and affords fabulous views over the lake. Above the pagoda the hill is covered in small walkways linking its numerous Buddhist and Taoist shrines and temples. It's definitely worth exploring on foot.

Yellow Dragon Cave (Huanglong Dong; daily 7.15 am-6 pm; ¥15; bus #Y5). On the northern side of Precious Stone Hill, the Yellow Dragon Cave is famous for its never-ending stream of water, which purportedly started spouting from a crevice in the rocks in answer to a monk's prayer for rain. To celebrate the event a golden dragon was built around the spring. If you time your visit right you can see one of the Shaoxing Opera performances that take place here (see *Galleries, Shows & Theaters*, p. 373).

Eastern Shore

★**Orioles Singing in Ripples of Willows Garden** (Liuyang Wenying). Once the imperial garden, this charming and tranquil park on the southeastern lake shore is surprisingly expansive and is a great place to watch locals passing the time of day, along with some impromptu opera performances. The park's lengthy name comes from the orioles that used to flutter freely around the gardens – these days they sing from cages!

Southern Shore

★★**Leifeng Pagoda** (daily 8:30 am-5 pm; ¥50). This sturdy pagoda stands atop a wooded hill at the southern end of the lake and offers excellent sunset vistas. The pagoda was reconstructed in 2002 on the site of the 976 AD original. While the escalator and lift to the top of the pagoda certainly offer easy access to the stunning views, they do little to convey the pagoda's thousand-year history. For a sense of this, a look around the halls at its base will reveal a miniature silver pagoda, which supposedly contains a lock of Buddha's hair.

In Town

★**Traditional Chinese Medicine Museum** (daily 8 am-5:30 pm; ¥10; bus #5). This fascinating museum is hidden down a small alley just off Hefang Lu. The museum is housed in a Qing-era building that used to be a TCM shop, but was converted in 1991. It now details the history of Chinese medicine and also offers consultations, treatment and even medicinal food.

South of the Lake

★**The Silk Museum** (daily 8 am-4:30 pm; free; bus #3). A little south of West Lake, Hangzhou's Silk Museum traces the history of silk production and cultivation throughout the region. Its displays are labeled in English and Chinese and track the silk process from beginning to end. You'll see silkworms happily munching away at mulberry leaves as well as examples of Chinese imperial dress (both original and reproductions) and some beautiful weaving. Upstairs there's an interesting art gallery and a shop, which is a good place to buy lengths of silk as prices are fixed and the quality is guaranteed.

★**Dreamlike Tiger Spring** (daily 6:30 am-6:30 pm; ¥15; bus #Y5). Halfway between the lake and the Qiantang River, this pretty park on Hupao Shan has a liberal sprinkling of shrines, waterfalls and teahouses, which serve *longjing cha* using the park's famed spring water. Legend holds that a Tang dynasty monk wanted to build a temple here but had to move on due to lack of water. Later, he dreamed that a spring had been moved here from afar and sure enough on his return he witnessed two tigers digging the spring!

★**Liuhe Pagoda** (daily 6 am-6:30 pm; ¥20 entry, plus ¥10 to ascend the pagoda). Two miles south of the lake, the six-story Six Harmonies Pagoda affords good views over the Qiantang River and can be visited as part of bike ride out to Longjing (see *Adventures On Wheels*, p. 376). The pagoda was originally built in the Song dynasty as an attempt to quell the river's forceful tidal surges, seemingly to little avail as it is now a popular place to watch the famous tidal bore on the 18th day of the eighth lunar month (see *Holidays & Festivals*, p. 73).

West of the Lake

★★★**Feilai Feng and Lingyin Temple** (daily 8 am-5 pm; buses #Y1, #Y2 & #K7). A couple of miles west of the lake, this large temple complex and the adjacent statue-laden hillside comprise Hangzhou's premier attraction and are both must-sees. Unfortunately, this popularity means the area is no longer the place of tranquil retreat it once was and can swarm with huge

Buddhist carvings at Feilai Feng caves (Miguel A. Monjas)

crowds of domestic tourists – try to come early morning on a weekday. Nevertheless, the collection of ancient (and newer) Buddhist carvings and the grand temple itself makes it worth enduring the masses.

Feilai Feng (¥35). Feilai Feng means the "hill that flew from afar" – named by an Indian monk who visited the region and thought he recognized the limestone hill from back home! On entering the complex to your left you'll find a collection of Buddhist statues which are modern replicas of famous examples from around the country. While these are impressive and fun, if

Carving at Feilai Feng (Tot Foster)

you proceed a little farther and take any of the narrow trails leading up the slope, you'll start to uncover what all the fuss is about – the genuine articles. There are 338 Buddhist images carved into the limestone hillside, many of which date from the Song and Yuan dynasties. This is one of the few southern examples of Buddhist cave architecture and, although many were defiled during the Cultural Revolution, they are certainly worth the climb. The higher up the slope you go, the fewer visitors you'll find and on weekdays you may gain some semblance of the peace for which the site was intended.

Lingyin Temple (¥30). Back on the main thoroughfare, continue for a few more minutes and you'll reach the grand Lingyin Temple. Lingyin Si means "Temple of the Soul's Retreat" and, although it's hard to find any kind of retreat in the ever-crowded temple, it is definitely worth a visit. The temple follows the standard Buddhist temple layout (see *Visiting Temples*, p. 51) and, despite the vast number of visitors, is still a fully functional place of worship with hundreds of monks in attendance. On entry you'll be greeted by the ever-smiling face of Maitreya, flanked by the imposing Four Heavenly Kings. The temple's most impressive hall contains a 78-foot-tall statue of Sakyamuni, which was rebuilt in 1956 after the central beam fell onto it. In fact, few parts of the temple are original and it has been restored and reconstructed countless times through history, although Lingyin managed to survive the Cultural Revolution intact, thanks to the intervention of Zhou Enlai.

★★**The Tea Museum** (daily 8 am-4:30 pm; free; bus #27). A mile southwest of the lake, this interesting museum details the history of tea and tea culture in China and is well worth the trip out of town. The museum's exhibits are well-labeled in English and are divided into a

Tea production (Tot Foster)

number of themes covering topics such as tea etiquette, cultivation techniques, varieties of tea and traditional Chinese tea houses. You'll even find a number of mocked-up traditional teahouses, including Yunnanese and Tibetan examples. If you don't want to take a bike out, then take bus #27 from downtown and get off in front of the Zhejiang Hotel. From here you can see the museum and walk the remaining half-mile.

★★★**Longjing Village** (Dragon's Well Village; bus #Y3 or #27). Longjing village is one of the most famous tea-producing areas in China, renowned for its light, health-giving brew. In spite of the tea's high acclaim, Longjing village remains relatively quiet and is a great place to come on a bike ride (see *Adventures On Wheels*, p. 376). Tea is a way of life out here and you'll smell it in the air, see it on the terraces and doubtless be offered a taste, in the hope you'll buy some. Visiting the village also offers a glimpse into tea production, and provides the opportunity to see leaves being cut, dried, graded and stored in traditional fashion.

Galleries, Shows & Theaters

Shaoxing Opera

Local Shaoxing Opera is enduringly popular and can be seen everywhere from lakeside parks to full-blown theaters. One of the best venues is in the Huanglong Dong Yuan-yuan Mingshu Yuan Theater (☎ 0571-8798-5860) at the Yellow Dragon Cave (see p. 370). Performances are free although you'll have to pay ¥15 for the park entrance, and happen twice daily (8:45-11:45 am & 1:45-4:45 pm). For something is little grander, the

Opera in the park

Dongpo Grand Opera House at 17 Dongpo Lu (☎ 0571-8708-5992; ¥60-80) has a nightly show at 7:30 pm.

Movie Theaters

Hangzhou is a place to enjoy the great outdoors rather than the movies but if it's too hot and you want a couple of hours of air-conditioned entertainment there are a few places that screen movies in English:

UME, 4F West Town Plaza, 551 West Wen'er Xi Lu (☎ 0571-8810-0999)

West Lake Cinema, 113 Pinghai Lu (☎ 0571-8706-1050)

For Families

Hangzhou is tailor-made for a family break and, as long as you throw in some boat and bike rides to offset the museums or temples, you should manage to keep the kids happy.

Health & Relaxation

Hangzhou has a long history as a retreat and its lakeside parks, pagodas and pavilions are great for unwinding, but if you seek deeper relaxation there are some good massage places. Try **Shannana** at 27, Pinghai Lu (☎ 0571-8716-1106), which offers quality foot therapy, and ★**Guoyitang** (☎ 0571-8782-0409) at 58 Yan'an Nan Lu, where you can enjoy herbal massages in traditional surroundings. The **Traditional Chinese Medicine Museum** (see p. 370) also offers consultations and treatment.

Shopping

Hangzhou's shopping scene has become a lot more international in the last few years. Silk and tea have always been popular buys, but these days there are also Ferrari and Porsche dealerships and upscale new shopping centers housing the likes of Gucci and Prada. Most of the shopping is east of the lake along Yan'an Lu. There are local clothing outlets and international sports stores, along with tea shops. You may also be approached by vendors with pictures of their wares that are hidden away nearby, and in the evenings street hawkers offer cheap jewelry. The **nightmarket** on Huixing Lu has all the usual trappings of replica watches, sunglasses and DVDs, along with trinkets, but is more fun for looking than buying. To stock up on picnic goodies there's a **Carrefour** at 135 Yan'an Lu.

Silk & Tailoring

You'll see silk for sale all over Hangzhou but the widest choice of quality items is found at **China Silk Town** on Xinhua Lu, northeast of the lake (bus #8, #11 or #28). This street is packed with silk shops selling all manner of fabrics and garments – try **China Silk World** at number 253. For guaranteed quality, the **Silk Museum** (see p. 370) is another good bet, although prices are higher.

Tea

Tea is big business in Hangzhou and tiny Longjing (Dragon's Well) village is at the center of this. If you really want to see the way tea finds its way into your cup, take a bike ride (or bus) out through the neatly ordered tea hills to Longjing (see p. 373 and *Adventures On Wheels*, p. 376) where you'll see everything from picking to drying and, of course, you can drink and buy tea, but be sure to bargain hard! You can also buy tea throughout the city, but if you want assured quality it's best to head to the **Tea Museum** (see p. 372). Longjing tea comes in five main varieties, the most prized of which is "Before Tomb Sweeping Day," which is picked in early April and commands prices of up to ¥100 an ounce. But if you like green tea, you'll find it's all very drinkable and the later picks can be bought for as little as ¥5 an ounce. If you buy in the village (or on the streets), make sure the tea is packed in front of you to ensure you get the variety you pay for and for the pleasure of watching the expert process of cramming as much into the container as possible without breaking the leaves.

Adventures

On Foot

Any walk around the lake or across its causeways is a rewarding experience and the readily available transport means that you can stroll until you're tired and then hop in a bus, taxi or onto a boat. The following makes for a great half-day's walk, but it could also be covered by bike.

★★★ Causeway Circuit (2-3 hrs)

This walk takes in the Bai and Su Causeways, along with a few historic sights, and ends at one of Hangzhou's most photogenic vistas, the Shuangtou Bridge. The walk can be lengthened or shortened to suit your needs simply by altering your start or finish point but, if you choose to walk only one causeway, the Su is the quieter and more scenic of the two.

Take a taxi, buggy (or walk) to the **Broken Bridge** and stroll across the **Bai Causeway** to **Solitary Hill Island** (see p. 369). There are a few things to see here, including the **Zhejiang Provincial Museum**, before continuing from the northwest side of the island across **Xiling Bridge** back onto the lake's edge. After only a few minutes westwards on **Beishan Lu** you'll come to the **Su Causeway** off to your left. If you want to visit Yuefei Tomb (see p. 366), then continue along Beishan Lu for another five minutes. There are also a few restaurants here (including a KFC) if you're hungry. Otherwise, head back to the Su Causeway. It's worth buying a drink before you begin the two-mile crossing, as there are no vendors on the causeway and Hangzhou can get very hot.

The main path is flanked by two smaller paths that have great views and the causeway's greater length makes it less popular and thus quieter. There are also plenty of benches on the side-paths, which make great picnic spots. When you reach the far side, bear left onto **Nanshan Lu**. After a few minutes you'll pass the entrance to the **Leifeng Pagoda** complex (see p. 370), which is worth ascending for the fine views of the lake. Plus you don't even have to climb the pagoda – there's an escalator and then an elevator to one floor below the top!

Continuing around the lake on the path that runs on the lake side of Nanshan Lu, you'll soon reach the **Shuangtou Bridge**, favored by photographers as the place to get sunset shots with the Leifeng Pagoda in the foreground. If you still have the legs for it and want some dinner, you could carry on for another 20 or 30 minutes to trendy **Xihutiandi**. Otherwise, hop in a taxi back to your hotel.

On Wheels

Hangzhou is a great place for a bike ride, whether just around the lake or for a hilly excursion out to Longjing – *see Getting Around*, p. 363, for rental details.

Lake Loop

You are allowed to take bicycles across all of the causeways and cycling around the lake is an easy and quick way to do it, although I prefer the country route out to Longjing, choosing to walk the lake. The best parts of the lake to ride are the causeways – you can follow the walking route detailed above in the Causeway Circuit.

★★★ Nine Creeks & 18 Gullies Tea Trail (3-4 hrs)

Tea pickers

This is my favorite bike ride in this part of the world and gives a glimpse of life in a Chinese tea village. It's a long, hilly ride so make sure both you and your bike are up to the job. There are places to buy drinks and snacks along the way but there are some good picnic spots so it might be worth taking some supplies with you.

Starting from the southern end of the **Su Causeway** (where you can rent bikes), head west along **Nanshan Lu**, turning left down onto **Hupao Lu** after a few minutes. The road gradually ascends for five or 10 minutes before descending past the zoo and Dreamlike Tiger Spring (see p. 371), down to the **Qiantang River**. A little before the river you'll pass a road off to the right, but continue on, following signs for Liuhe Ta (**Liuhe Pagoda**). You'll pass under a small bridge and then the substantial road and rail bridge before emerging onto **Zhijiang Lu** by the lofty Liuhe (Six Harmonies) Pagoda (see p. 371), where you could stop for a look around and, if you really want to tire yourself out, ascend the steps here before continuing on your ride.

Turning right from the pagoda, you'll have to endure 10 or 15 minutes of traffic zooming by you before bearing right by a small cluster of shops and a circular green bus shelter. Here is a good place to stock up on some cold drinks before leaving the traffic behind and heading into the tea hills beyond. Follow the narrow lane signposted **Nine Creeks and 18 Gullies**, passing a teahouse and a couple of simple restaurants. After 20 minutes, you'll see a small park to your right. The lane diverges here – bear right through a car park of sorts onto a cobbled path that leads up into the woods, running alongside the stream which gives this track its name. It's a gradual climb through the woods and after about 20 or 30 minutes you'll emerge at the bottom of **Longjing Village**, a picturesque mélange of new concrete and older ramshackle wooden houses. This is one of China's most esteemed tea villages and almost every villager will try and persuade you to sit down for a refreshing cup in their home before pressing you to buy. It can be difficult to ascertain quality here, but if you know your stuff then it's certainly cheaper than in the emporiums. Regardless, you may well be tired enough for a break and sitting down for a drink gives you the opportunity to taste some local tea and see them process it in the various stages.

At this point in the ride a few bike repairs may be in order and folks in the village can help – just show someone the problem and you'll be pointed in the right direction. If you can wait for a break, though, it's worth continuing through the village and up the steep hill to the junction with Longjing Lu.

Had Enough? If you're too tired, turning right at this junction will take you back to Hupao Lu, where you turn left again and then right down to where you started, the Su Causeway.

Turn left onto **Longjing Lu** and up hill for another agonizing 10 minutes whence you'll emerge in the upper part of the village. Here there are more teashops with terraces and it's worth stopping to look back over your achievements and perhaps asking to sit on one of the upper floors that enjoy fine views.

The good news is that it's all downhill from here – check your brakes! Once you arrive at the bottom of the hills, you'll soon pass the **Tea Museum** (which closes at 4:30 pm), a couple of minutes along a small road off to your left. After a little tea education and drinking, head back onto Longjing Lu and five or 10 minutes later you'll arrive at the lake, where you turn right again to head back to the **Su Causeway**.

On the Green

Hangzhou has a couple of golf courses – the stunning ★★**Fuchun Resort** (☎ 0571-6346-1111, www.fuchunresort.com, ¥¥¥¥), 40 minutes southeast of Hangzhou, has an award-winning 18-hole course which non-guests can use for ¥2,080. Even if you're not a golf fan, the resort is worth considering for its serene setting among the tea hills and its quality rooms, facilities and services. A similar distance to the southwest, the **Westlake International Golf and Country Club** (☎ 0571-8732-1700) was

designed by Jack Nicklaus and has a varied 36-hole course. Rounds cost
¥680 during the week or ¥880 on the weekend.

On Water

Taking a boat out on the lake is the perfect way to appreciate its
serene beauty and there are a variety to choose from. For ¥45
(including entry fees) you can be part of a wooden motorboat trip
that stops at the Mid-Lake Pavilion and the Three Pools Reflecting the
Moon. These trips take a couple of hours and depart from various points,
including Solitary Hill Island and Hubin Park on the northeastern
lakeshore. Far better, though, is to rent a private boat and be taken around
the lake. It should cost around ¥50 for an hour, but you'll have to haggle.
Alternatively, you can rent electric motorboats (¥30-50 an hour) from the
Broken Bridge, although, oddly, rowboats are only rented to foreigners if
they are accompanied by a Chinese friend (or guide). Finally, if you want to
see the **Grand Canal** (see Suzhou callout, p. 340), so important in
Hangzhou's history yet little visited from the city, there are night
waterbuses (6:30, 7:30, 8:30 pm; ¥15) from Wulinmen, as well as overnight
services to Suzhou (see *Getting Here & Away, By Water*, p. 363).

The modern city of Hangzhou looms over the eastern shore of West Lake

Where to Stay

Hangzhou has a reasonable selection of places to stay, including
some fine upscale hotels, although at the other end of the scale
there is a definite paucity of options.

What's it mean? FC=fitness center; SW=swimming pool; @=in-room Internet access; DA=rooms for disabled. For ¥ price codes, see page 113.

Elan Inn, 1 Putisi Lu (☎ 0571-8778-1234, www.elaninn.com). If you don't mind staying a few minutes back from the lake, you'll find great rooms at bargain prices in this newly established business hotel. All rooms have Internet connection and free in-house movies, although storage space is a little sparse. Note that most of the cheaper rooms are windowless, so it's definitely worth paying extra for that. @ ¥¥

★★**Fuchun Resort**, Fuyang (☎ 0571-6346-1111, www.fuchun-resort.com) – see *Adventures On the Green* for review. ¥¥¥¥

★**Huajiashan Resort**, 25 Santaishan Lu (☎ 0571-8797-6688. Attractively grouped around a small pond southwest of West Lake, this hotel complex designed in chalet-style offers a pleasant alternative if you don't mind being a bit remote from town. Of the two buildings, the triangular number one is the best. Its rooms are light, comfortable, spacious and have balconies. The hotel also rents

Terrace at Fuchun Resort

bicycles and is well-situated for rides to Liuhe Pagoda and Longjing village. The hotel has restaurants and there are a batch of small canteens a few minutes walk away, but you're better heading into town for dinner. ¥¥¥

Hyatt Regency, 28 Hubin Lu (☎ 0571-8779-1234, www.hangzhou.regency.hyatt.com). This new concrete block on the edge of the lake doesn't look that promising from the outside, but the location, rooms and facilities easily make up for this. The rooms have a simple, modern elegance and the lake-view rooms certainly deliver. FC/SW/@/DA ¥¥¥¥¥

Mingtown Youth Hostel, 101-11 Nanshan Lu (☎ 0571-8791-8948, www.hostelz.com/hostel/43025-Mingtown-Garden-Youth-Hostel). Right on the lake near trendy Xihutiandi, this place is a budget traveler's favorite and has dorm beds for ¥45 (eight-bed room) or ¥50 (four-bed room), as well as doubles with lake views for ¥280. However, if you don't want a dorm and can't afford the lake-view rooms, the basic rooms without bathrooms, views or much furniture are just that and you're better off heading into town a little. ¥-¥¥

★**Overseas Chinese Hotel**, 39 Hubin Lu (☎ 0571-8768-5555). The lake-view rooms in this place are a bargain at ¥488. They are comfortable, spacious, well-equipped and have large windows that maximize the view. The rear-facing rooms, by contrast, are smaller and overpriced at ¥388. @ ¥¥-¥¥¥

Shangri-La

★★**Shangri-La**, 78 Beishan Lu (☎ 0571-8797-7951; www.shangri-la.com/hangzhou/shangri-la/en/index). Just northwest of the lake and set in hilly, verdant grounds the Shangri-La is the best hotel in Hangzhou. The sixth floor of the East Wing is the place to stay. Rooms are as large and plush as you'd expect but the highlights are the balconies, which enjoy outstanding views of the lake. Guests can also take breakfast on the sixth floor terrace café – the perfect way to start your day. FC/SW/@ ¥¥¥¥¥

★**Sofitel**, 333 Xihu Dadao (☎ 0571-8707-5858, www.sofitel.com). The Sofitel is a recent addition to Hangzhou's high-end hotel scene and comes up a winner with its lakeside location next to the dining options of Xihutiandi. Rooms are elegantly styled and most enjoy good lake views. FC/SW/@/DA ¥¥¥¥-¥¥¥¥¥

Bedroom at the Sofitel

Where to Eat

With its long imperial history and modern popularity as a weekend escape, Hangzhou has garnered quite a collection of restaurants, some of which are must-sees on the domestic tourist circuit. While less international than nearby Shanghai, Hangzhou has the usual Western offerings of KFCs. McDonald's, Pizza Huts, Starbucks and even Haagen Dazs, along with some worthwhile one-off establishments.

See page 117 for an explanation of the ¥ restaurant price codes.

★★**Crystal Jade**, Xihutiandi (☎ 0571-8702-6618; daily 10 am-10:30 pm). Part of the international chain, this is one of Crystal Jade's finest offerings, exquisitely set amidst the greenery of Xihutiandi. The staff are friendly and all their dishes are good, but the duck is recommended. ¥¥¥

★**Haveli**, 77 Nanshan Lu (☎ 0571-8707-9677; daily 11 am-11 pm). This authentic Indian restaurant on the lake serves good North Indian fare.

There is an extensive menu with vegetarian and meat dishes. The chicken *tikka masala* is recommended. There are also tasty desserts such as *rasgulla* and *gulab jamun* and they have a nightly belly dance show at 7 pm. ¥¥¥

Jamaica Coffee Shop, House 12, Xihutiandi (☎ 0571-8702-6598; daily 8 am-midnight). Another of Xihutiandi's trendy little coffee shops, this place also serves juices, shakes and excellent sandwiches but, despite the location, it lacks atmosphere. ¥¥

★**Kuiyuanguan**, 154 Jiefang Lu (☎ 0571-8702-8626; daily 9 am-9 pm). This local restaurant serves up exceptionally tasty noodles at appealing prices. Kuiyuanguan restaurant has been preparing noodles for over 100 years and offers more than 40 different varieties, from classics such as beef noodle soup to the slightly more refined taste of shrimp and fried eel (a house specialty). ¥¥

★★**Louwailou**, 30 Gushan Lu (☎ 0571-8796-9682; daily 10:30 am-2 pm & 4:30-9 pm). Set on the southern shore of Solitary Hill Island, this plush yet affordable restaurant has a history of over 150 years and is deservedly Hangzhou's most famous offering. Inside, it's all gold and chandeliers, but you'll still find main dishes for as little as ¥12, although specialties such as Beggar's Chicken and King Prawns run to more. The lotus

Louwailou

root is excellent and if you're feeling brave you could try the delicacy of sea cucumber. ¥¥-¥¥¥

Va Bene, House 8, 147 Nanshan Road, Xihutiandi (☎ 0571-8702-6333; daily 11 am-10:45 pm). As one of many new restaurants popping up in the area, Va Bene's excellent Italian dishes and quaint setting overlooking West Lake are proving popular with the local community. Downstairs serves great pizzas, while the upstairs restaurant has a host of pasta classics. ¥¥¥¥

★★**Zhiweiguan**, 83 Renhe Lu (☎ 0571-8706-5871; daily 10 am-9:30 pm). This large restaurant is another institution in Hangzhou, popular for its cheap and tasty local cuisine. Downstairs you'll find *dim sum*, wonton and dumplings and a very local clientele, while the higher levels provide pleasant lake views, a little more comfort and substantial meals. ¥¥-¥¥¥

Zhiweiguan

Teahouses

There are teahouses throughout Hangzhou and these refined havens are great places to enjoy a cup of *longjing cha*. Shuguang Lu has a good selection, including **Fenghe** at #184, **Yellow Dragon** at #57 and **Ziyige** at #172, all of which charge around ¥50 per person.

Nightlife

Hangzhou has a burgeoning nightlife scene and there are a string of bars and pubs around the lakeside, particularly clustered along Nanshan Lu on the lake's southeastern shore. Near the Mingtown Youth Hostel (see p. 379) on Nanshan Lu you'll find regular club players such as Babyface, plus a few less generic offerings, while north from here Xihutiandi is more about dining than drinking, but also has some decent bars.

Where to Drink

Bather Club, 4 Luyang Lu (daily 6:30 pm-2 am). One of many clubs along this stretch just off and along Nanshan Lu, Bather Club is a hip modern nightclub that bangs out a mixture of beats for the enthusiastic crowds. Hip hop, house and Latino sounds are among the favorites and lineups include both foreign and local DJs.

★**Kana**, 152 Nanshan Lu (daily 6:30 pm-3:30 am). The Kana Bar remains one of Hangzhou's top drinking spots and offers some of the best cocktails in town, along with live music. It attracts locals and tourists alike and you may even be lucky enough to meet Burundi-born Kana himself!

Paradise, 36 Hubin Lu (daily 11 am-2 am). Near the lakefront this upmarket pub-style bar is decked out in wood and has a good roof terrace and friendly staff. They have draught Carlsberg and serve bar snacks and set meals.

Shamrock, 70 Zhongshan Zhonglu (daily 10 am-2 am). Currently, the Shamrock is Hangzhou's only Irish pub and its setting in a restored building on a Qing dynasty street makes a great place to relax after a day of sightseeing. Draft Guinness and Kilkenny are just a couple of the choices in the Shamrock's collection of beers.

Zenzibar, House E, 147 Nanshan Lu, Xihutiandi (daily 10 am-2 am). Above Zen restaurant in trendy Xihutiandi, Zenzibar is a cool spot for a quiet drink.

Huangshan & Around

Towering over the south of **Anhui** province, the Huangshan range are arguably China's most beautiful mountains and are definitely worth putting on your itinerary if you're in the area. In developed eastern China, countryside is a rare treat and the fresh air and stunning scenery makes the **Yellow Mountains** a highlight of many visitors' trips to this part of the country. There are 72 peaks in all and the highest is only a little over 6,100 feet, but what the Yellow Mountains lack in stature they more than make up for in scenery. Lone pines perched on jutting crags mystically disappear and

The Yellow Mountains (Tot Foster)

re-emerge from behind swirls of mist. The whole scene is fresh from a scroll painting. Huangshan is China as you dreamed it might be – images of *Crouching Tiger, Hidden Dragon* spring to mind and it's no surprise that parts of the movie were shot in the area. Although the top can be reached by cable car, the tough climb up adds to the sense of reward. It's worth staying on the mountaintop to maximize your chances of some good weather and to enjoy Huangshan's famed sunrise. There are also a host of other scenic spots in the vicinity and you can easily spend a few days here exploring the mountain, waterfalls and wildlife.

Huangshan's accessible beauty has only one major drawback – it is one of the most visited spots in the country and on summer weekends, paths, hotels and restaurants are packed. So it's best to visit during the week but, if that's not possible, it's worth making hotel reservations. Fortunately, the mountain itself is ringed by enough trails so you can always find a spot for yourself and, if you have the stamina and time for the longer western path, you'll see few folks the whole way.

This part of Anhui is not only famous for its natural scenery – **Shexian** and **Yixian** counties are both within easy reach of either Tunxi or Tangkou and offer pretty, time-trapped (but touristy) villages worth visiting for their distinctive architecture.

History

The modern regional hub, **Tunxi**, with 150,000 residents, is located at the confluence of two rivers. It has a long history as a trading town and today retains some of the traditional Huizhou architecture for which the region is famous. The historical heart of this part of Anhui lies halfway between Tunxi and Huangshan at Shexian (formerly known as **Huizhou**). Both Shexian and Yixian were prosperous as salt trading towns during the Ming dynasty (1368-1644, see p. 13) and the surrounding villages still hold many examples of their traditional architecture. The beautiful houses constructed by wealthy merchants were so well-designed that they set the standard throughout central China, while the memorial arches (*paifang*) they built illustrate the social values of the time (for both see *Huizhou Architecture*, p.000).

Huangshan was named in honor of the great Emperor Huangdi and has long been revered as one of China's most bewitching sights. The mountain's steep slopes have been trodden by both emperors and party leaders and were also sought out by Chan Buddhist recluses. Painters have long been captivated by Huangshan's mystical beauty and if you get a sense of *déjà vu*, you've probably seen an artistic impression of the mountain before. The mountain continues to draw eager visitors and Huangshan's presence on the must-see tourist circuit allows the region some wealth in otherwise poor Anhui province.

Tunxi

Getting Here & Away

 Getting to Huangshan is fairly easy, although mildly confused by the fact that most transport labeled Huangshan actually arrives in Tunxi (aka Huangshan City), an hour and a half south of Tangkou, which sits at the base of the mountain.

By Air

Huangshan Airport is just a few miles west of Tunxi, and is served by flights from: **Beijing** (1 daily; 2 hrs); **Guangzhou** (2 daily, 2 hrs 30 mins); **Hong Kong** (1 daily, 1 hr 50 mins); **Shanghai** (3 daily, 1 hr 10 mins); and **Shenzhen** (1 daily, 1 hr 30 mins).

Buses and taxis (¥15-20) run from the airport to Tunxi and take around 10 minutes.

By Rail

 Tunxi is on the main Shanghai-to-Fujian rail line and is well-served by trains. The train station is in the south of town, from where it's a 30-minute walk, or ¥6 taxi into the center. Destinations, frequencies and durations are as follows:

Beijing (1 daily, 19 hrs 20 mins); **Guangzhou** (1 daily, 20 hrs 20 mins); **Guilin** (1 daily, 20 hrs 20 mins); **Shanghai** (1 daily, 11 hrs 10 mins); **Suzhou** (1 daily, 10 hrs).

By Road

 Tunxi's **bus station** is on Fushang Lu, just east of the train station and has buses to **Hangzhou** (hourly, 3 hrs 30 mins); **Shanghai** (6 daily, 6 hrs); and **Suzhou** (2 daily, 7 hrs), as well as local destinations. Buses to Tangkou run from the train station in the mornings, but after that you'll have to head to the bus station where services run every 20

Huangshan

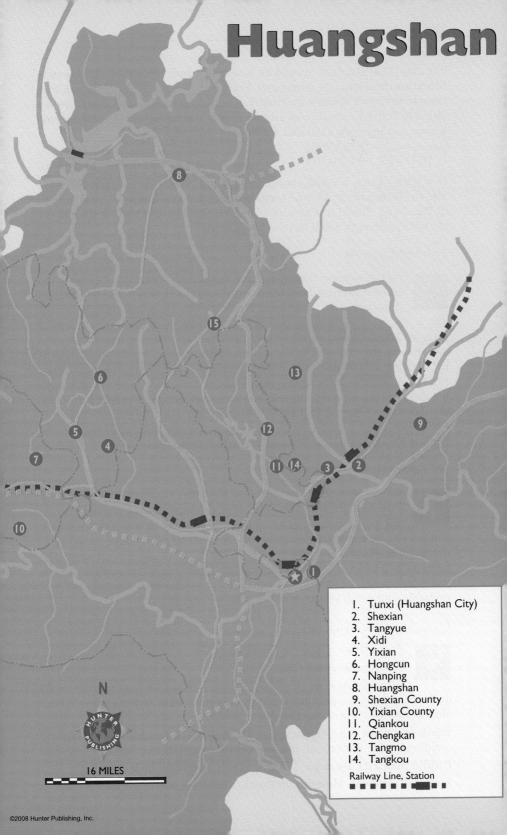

1. Tunxi (Huangshan City)
2. Shexian
3. Tangyue
4. Xidi
5. Yixian
6. Hongcun
7. Nanping
8. Huangshan
9. Shexian County
10. Yixian County
11. Qiankou
12. Chengkan
13. Tangmo
14. Tangkou

Railway Line, Station

N

HUNTER PUBLISHING

16 MILES

minutes (¥13) and take around an hour and a half. There are also buses to **Shexian** (frequent, 30 mins) and **Yixian** (frequent, 2 hrs). You can hire taxis to take you to these destinations but you'll need to negotiate a rate – Tunxi to Tangkou should cost around ¥100 while round-trips to Shexian and Yixian cost between ¥150 and ¥300.

Getting Around

Downtown Tunxi is small enough to get round easily on foot, but there are also **taxis** (minimum ¥5) and **local buses**. **Cycle rickshaws** are abundant in Tunxi and should cost around ¥4 or ¥5 to get from the train station to the old town, although you'll have to bargain hard.

Orientation

 As the nearest transport hub, Tunxi (aka Huangshan City) is the traditional base from which to explore the Huangshan and Huizhou (Shexian and Yixian) area. While the town lacks any major sights it has a couple of original examples of Huizhou architecture, along with a restored Ming dynasty street. When combined with its riverside setting and good hotels, this makes Tunxi a relaxing place to stay. The **train station** is in the north of town just a few minutes walk from the bus station to the east. From the train station, **Qianyuan Bei Lu** runs past a string of budget hotels to the junction with the city's main street, **Huangshan Xi Lu**. Heading west along here, you'll reach restored **Lao Jie** (Old Street), which is lined with tourist shops. It winds through the old town and down to the **Xin'an River**, where you'll find a few better places to stay.

Information Sources

 Tunxi doesn't have an official tourist office so your best bet is asking for information at your hotel. If you're looking to book a tour, hotels can also arrange this or, alternatively, **CTS** (☎ 0559-522-649) at 1 Binjiang Xi Lu can help. For backpackers, another great source of information is local **Steven Huang** (☎ 139-0559-4053; steventour@163.com), who owns a small bed and breakfast and can help to arrange transport as well as guided tours of Shexian and Yixian. Steven speaks good English and will probably find you if you arrive by train!

Communications

Post Office: Opposite the Bank of China on Xin'an Nan Lu. **Telephone code**: 0559.

Internet Access: The Youth Hostel (see p. 389) has Internet for ¥5 an hour and there's another Internet café just south of the square where Huangshan Xi Lu becomes Lao Jie.

Bank of China: On the junction of Huangshan Xi Lu and Xin'an Nan Lu, and there's another branch just west of the bus station.

Public Security Bureau: 108 Chang'an Lu (☎ 0559-2314-191).

Medical services: Huangshan People's Hospital on Huangshan Xi Lu.

Sightseeing

Tunxi itself doesn't have much in the way of sightseeing but, if you won't be visiting Shexian or Yixian (see p. 398), then you might want to hunt out a couple of the remaining Huizhou-style houses in the old town. **Cheng Dawei's Abacus Museum** (daily 8:30 am-5 pm; ¥30), off Chang'an Dong Lu, is of more interest for its architecture than its contents and, as one of the few foreigners who came out here, you'll probably make the curators day! Cheng Dawei was a renowned Ming dynasty mathematician and his houses, while in a sorry state of repair, offer some classic elements of Huizhou architectural style (see p. 399), including horse-head gables, butterfly tiles and intricate wood carvings. Half a mile west of here there's an even more dilapidated Ming residence, the **Cheng Family House**

Local crafts, Tunxi (Tot Foster)

(daily 8:30 am-5 pm; ¥30) which is charmingly ramshackle. Both houses take some finding – make sure you have the language box on hand. If scouring the backstreets isn't your thing, Lao Jie (Old Street) has a collection of restored shops that will give you some idea of the Huizhou style.

ESSENTIAL ANHUI

If you've made the trek out to this part of Anhui it's worth making the most of it. Of course, Huangshan is the main drawing card and you should spend at least a night atop the mountain, but you should also take a day to explore the surrounding area and its legion of **charming old Huizhou-style villages**, pleasantly scattered between hills, bamboo thickets and rivers. A good trip would be to arrive in Tunxi, spend a day visiting Shexian or Yixian, then proceed on to Tangkou the following day, perhaps going bamboo rafting in the afternoon and enjoying a hearty dinner in preparation for a tough day of climbing ahead. The next day, wake early, climb up the eastern trail, check into a hotel and **spend the rest of the day appreciating Huangshan's majesty**. The following morning, take the western trail down to Mercy Light Temple and then back to Tangkou or Tunxi for a well-earned night's rest before moving on to your next destination.

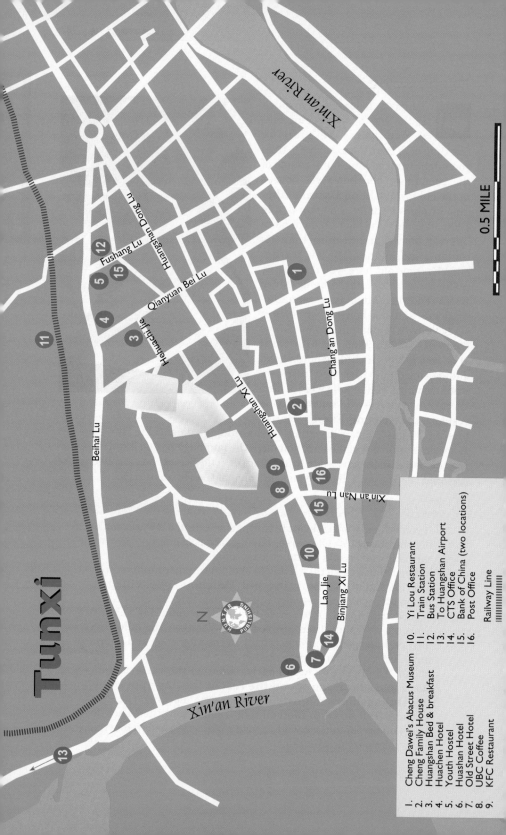

Tunxi

Xin'an River

Xin'an River

Huangshan Dong Lu

Fushang Lu

Qianyuan Bei Lu

Chang'an Dong Lu

Beihai Lu

Heqiachi Jie

Huangshan Xi Lu

Xin'an Nan Lu

Lao Jie

Binjiang Xi Lu

0.5 MILE

N

HUNTER PUBLISHING

1. Cheng Dawei's Abacus Museum
2. Cheng Family House
3. Huangshan Bed & breakfast
4. Huachen Hotel
5. Youth Hostel
6. Huashan Hotel
7. Old Street Hotel
8. UBC Coffee
9. KFC Restaurant
10. Yi Lou Restaurant
11. Train Station
12. Bus Station
13. To Huangshan Airport
14. CTS Office
15. Bank of China (two locations)
16. Post Office

Railway Line

Where to Stay

Tunxi's accommodation is neatly divided into budget lodgings near the bus and train stations and more expensive and pleasantly located hotels in the old town.

What's it mean? FC=fitness center; SW=swimming pool; @=in-room Internet access; DA=rooms for disabled. For ¥ price codes, see page 113.

Huachen, 18 Qianyuan Bei Lu (☎ 0559-2345-188). The Huachen is the best option near the train station and has spacious, if slightly musty rooms, some of which enjoy pleasant views. ¥¥-¥¥¥

Huangshan Bed and Breakfast, Flat 504, 5F, Building 11, Tea Market (☎ 0559-2528-609 or ☎ 0139-0559-4053, www.huangshanbedbreakfast. com). This B&B near the train station is more of a homestay and offers the chance to interact with a local family. Rooms are good value and comfortable, although the construction site over the road will make it a noisy option for the foreseeable future. The owner, Steven Huang, also runs guided trips to Shexian, Yixian and Huangshan at very competitive prices (see *Information Sources*, p. 386 & *Shexian and Yixian*, p. 398). It's difficult to find the B&B, so if you want to stay here call Steven and he'll come and find you. ¥-¥¥

★**Huashan**, 3 Yan'an Lu (☎ 0559-2328-888). This is Tunxi's most upscale hotel and enjoys a pleasant location by the river and close to the shopping and dining of Lao Jie. The Huashan has clean, new and well-fitted rooms and a good range of facilities. FC/SW/@ ¥¥¥-¥¥¥¥

★★**Old Street**, 1 Lao Jie (☎ 0559-2534-466, www. oldstreet-hotel.com.cn). Old Street is a great addition to Tunxi's hotel lineup and offers great value, well-furnished, comfortable and spacious rooms, some of which have river views. The hotel is housed in a mock Huizhou-style building at the western end of Lao Jie and there's also a good foot massage parlor here. @ ¥¥¥

Old Street

★**Youth Hostel**, 58 Beihai Lu (☎ 0559-2114-522, www.yhahuangshan. com). Only a few minutes walk from the train and bus stations, the Youth Hostel is an excellent budget option with friendly and helpful staff and bright and airy rooms. There's also a good café here and a DVD room upstairs. Dorm beds are ¥35. ¥

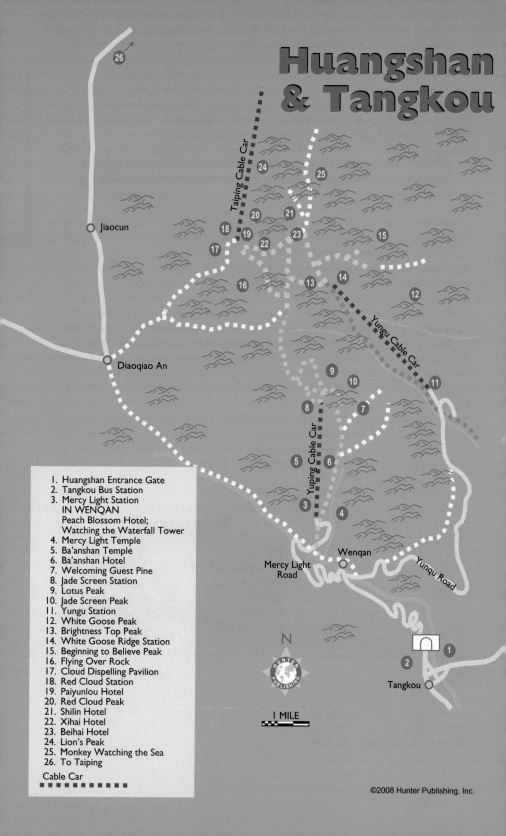

Huangshan & Tangkou

26 (To Taiping, top left)

Taiping Cable Car

○ Jiaocun

24
25
20 21
18   23
19 22
17
16   13   14   12
Yungu Cable Car
○ Diaoqiao An
9
10
11
8
7
Yuping Cable Car
5   6
3   4

Wenqan ○
Mercy Light
Road
Yunqu Road

1. Huangshan Entrance Gate
2. Tangkou Bus Station
3. Mercy Light Station
   IN WENQAN
   Peach Blossom Hotel;
   Watching the Waterfall Tower
4. Mercy Light Temple
5. Ba'anshan Temple
6. Ba'anshan Hotel
7. Welcoming Guest Pine
8. Jade Screen Station
9. Lotus Peak
10. Jade Screen Peak
11. Yungu Station
12. White Goose Peak
13. Brightness Top Peak
14. White Goose Ridge Station
15. Beginning to Believe Peak
16. Flying Over Rock
17. Cloud Dispelling Pavilion
18. Red Cloud Station
19. Paiyunlou Hotel
20. Red Cloud Peak
21. Shilin Hotel
22. Xihai Hotel
23. Beihai Hotel
24. Lion's Peak
25. Monkey Watching the Sea
26. To Taiping

Cable Car
■ ■ ■ ■ ■ ■ ■

N

HUNTER PUBLISHING

1 MILE

15

1
2
○ Tangkou

Where to Eat

Tunxi has a limited selection of restaurants, but there are some places worth seeking out along Lao Jie. Qing-furnished **Yi Lou** (daily 11 am-1:30 pm & 5-8:30 pm) is just inside the *paifang* (memorial arch), which marks the start of Lao Jie and serves local specialties, including Anhui Tofu and Drunken Fish, the latter of which is cooked in Shaoxing wine. For budget meals, **Hehuachi Jie,** just west of Qianyuan Bei Lu toward the station, is known locally as Break-

Huangshan Mountains

fast Street and has a host of cheap eateries. If you're waiting for a train, you could also try the Youth Hostel café (see p. 397). For Western food, there are branches of UBC Coffee and KFC on Huangshan Xi Lu.

Tangkou & the Mountain

Getting Here & Away

There are direct buses to Tangkou from Hangzhou (3 daily; 5 hrs) but, from farther afield, expect to arrive in Tunxi. To get from **Tunxi** to Tangkou there are a number of tourist buses that meet the morning trains, but if you arrive in the afternoon you'll have to walk left out of the train station down Beihai Lu, then turn right to get to the bus station on Fushang Lu.

Tangkou & the Mountain (Tot Foster)

In **Tangkou** you can just flag buses down on the main road, but for local destinations (other than the mountain itself) go to the small station at the southern end of the town by Mr. Hu's restaurant (see p. 398). **Shexian** (1 hr 30 mins) is served by four buses a day and **Yixian** (1 hr) only two, or you can take a taxi for around ¥150-200.

Getting Around

Old Tangkou is a small settlement which you can walk around in half an hour. **Buses** up the mountain cost ¥10 for the 20-minute ride and will pick you up along the main road until about 9 am, after which you'll need to go to the bus depot a mile or so north of the town. A **taxi** up the mountain should charge around ¥20 but drivers will try for as much as they can! For the host of sights within a few miles of Tangkou, taxis will charge around ¥60, including waiting time and return.

Orientation, Communications & Information Sources

Tangkou is a tiny but expanding ramshackle country town, attractively set on a river at the foot of Huangshan. New Tangkou is the name given to the development of hotels on the approach to the old town but, while the hotels here are more modern, there is little else to recommend staying in this part of town. Old Tangkou is small enough that in a short stroll you'll come across most of its hotels, restaurants and shops. Tangkou's principal street, **Yangxi Jie**, runs alongside the river and can be reached by steps down from the bridge on the main road. You can also get down into town along old **Qingtun Lu**, which branches off the main road on the Tunxi side of town, and holds Tangkou's **Bank of China** (no ATM). Unbelievably, there's another Bank of China with an ATM on the mountaintop at Beihai! Continuing upward for another six miles, the mountain's main entrance is at **Yungu Temple**. For help with mountaintop hotel reservations, onward travel tickets and local sightseeing, contact the helpful **Mr. Hu** (☎ 139-5626-4786), who has a small restaurant near the Bank of China and local bus station,

Sightseeing

The reason to come to this region is to climb the mighty mountain, but if you have more time there are a host of other sites that can be visited from either Tunxi or Tangkou. Foremost among them are the charming old villages in Shexian and Yixian counties (see p. 398). However, if you want natural rather than manmade splendor, the countryside around Tangkou has plenty to keep you occupied, including nature's own movie sets, wildlife and bamboo rafting – ask Mr. Hu (see above) for details.

Adventures on Foot

As one of China's most famous mountains, Huangshan can be accessed by a variety of different routes, but these effectively boil down to a choice between hiking or taking a cable car up or down. Either way, you'll have to walk the circuit around the top. Regardless of which way you choose to ascend the mountain, it's worth taking **sunscreen**, a **hat** and a **light jacket** for the summit **in summer**, and lots of **warm**

Forest near Huangshan (Tot Foster)

clothes in winter. If you decide to climb, wear a comfortable pair of walking shoes or sneakers; otherwise, pack as light as you can. There are plenty of places to get drinks and snacks along the way, but if you're on a tight budget you might want to carry some supplies, since prices increase the higher up the mountain you get.

Getting Up the Mountain

There are plenty of different ways to ascend Huangshan. However you choose to go, you'll need to get to one of the park's main access points. The principal gate is at **Yungu Temple**, where the eastern trail and a cable car lead up to White Goose Ridge. To access the western cable car and trail, you'll need to go to **Mercy Light Pavilion** (Ciguang Ge), reached by a road that branches off the Yungu Temple road. Buses to Yungu Temple and Mercy Light Pavilion will pick you up on the main road in Tangkou before 9 am or you can take a taxi for ¥20. Or you can approach the mountain from the north on the Tangkou to Jiuhua Shan road at **Taiping**, from where another trail and cable car lead to the top at Red Cloud Pavilion. Wherever you access the mountain, you'll need to pay the hefty ¥200 **entrance fee** (daily 6 am-4:30 pm).

Hiking Routes

In a country that boasts the Himalaya, at a little over 6,000 feet, Huangshan barely qualifies as a mountain, but your legs will certainly feel as if you've climbed Everest if you choose to ascend and descend the seemingly endless steps on foot. There are four routes up the mountain, two of which are described below. The quickest and most commonly used is the **eastern route**, which starts from **Yungu Temple**, as does the most popular cable car (daily 6 am-5 pm; ¥65). If you're fit and quick, you can get up to the top at **Bai'e Feng** in less than two hours, but more usually it takes between 2½ and four hours. If your idea of hiking up a mountain is all about peace and tranquility, think again on this route – hordes of visitors take the eastern trail, as do porters and in summer there can be traffic jams at certain points in the day!

The **longer western trail** starts from **Mercy Light Pavilion** and its quiet paths afford broad vistas, but note that this route is a much longer and tougher ascent, taking at least four hours to **Brightness Top Peak** (Guangmingding), although you can reduce this by taking the cable car to Jade Screen Pavilion (Yuping Lou; daily 6 am-5:30 pm; ¥65).

A PORTER'S LIFE

If the climb up the mountain seems tough on your legs or lungs, spare a thought for the porters! In spite of the various cable cars up Huangshan, it's cheaper to transport goods up to the summit by foot and you'll see porters straining under incredible loads on the way up – I've even seen fridge freezers carried up here! The toll of this arduous work is almost certain knee and back problems in later life and, while porters are comparatively well-paid, careers are often short. In spite of their hard lives many porters still find time for a cheeky smile on the way up, and on their unburdened return journey you'll see them bouncing down the steps as light as a feather!

The Peak Circuit

Whether you ascend by cable car or on foot you'll find yourself on the main peak circuit which takes two to three hours to complete. Although the spectacular highlights of the circuit are more than worthwhile, if it's solitude you're seeking then some of the side-trails from this route or the western area might be more appealing. The circuit is described heading counterclockwise starting from White Goose Ridge (Bai'e Feng) at the top of the eastern trail and Yungu cable car.

Shortly after **White Goose Ridge** you'll see a trail leading off to the right to a host of sights, including **Beginning to Believe Peak** (Shixin Feng) where you'll find a series of viewing platforms to gaze out over the rocky spires to the lowlands. Back on the circuit you'll quickly reach the **Beihai Hotel** (see p. 397), famous for its Northern Sea of Clouds sunrises. If you want a quick break, the hotel has a good coffee shop and you'll also find the first aid center, police station and a Bank of China with an ATM here. From here it's worth a short diversion north past the Shilin Hotel (see p. 397) along a spectacular ridge to **Lion Peak** (Shizi Feng) and **Monkey Watching the Sea** (Houzi Guanhai), two of the mountain's most celebrated sights.

LOVELOCKED

At the top of Huangshan (and many of China's other famous mountains) you'll see padlocks secured to almost every available piece of railing. The padlocks are placed by families and young couples wishing to display the strength of their loving bond and to bring future health and happiness. If you look carefully you'll see many of them are inscribed with names and messages. If you want to lock yourself in eternal mountain-top love you'll see plenty of padlock vendors who can also etch a message for you.

Back at Beihai, continue round the circuit to the **Western Sea of Clouds** where there's another hotel (Xihai, see p. 397) with a pleasant restaurant and more splendid views. You'll pass down through the hotel's divided complex and then up some steps on the far side toward the **Cloud Dispelling Pavilion** (Paiyunlou). There's yet another hotel here and the pavilion itself enjoys engaging views down through a craggy gorge. From here there's another cable car that runs down to Songgu, although, unless you're pre-

Huangshan's rock towers frame the lowlands

pared to take a bus from Taiping back to Tangkou or have all of your bags with you, this is of little use. The trail starts back east from the Cloud Dispelling Pavilion and climbs up to the **Flying Over Rock**, an isolated stone tower that affords more "sea of clouds" views if the weather is complicit. From here, the trail gently leads round to **Brightness Top Peak** (Guangmingding) and a decision awaits:

IF YOU'VE GOT THE STAMINA ...

If you have the stamina for the western route down, turn right at Brightness Top Peak for a knee-jarring but beautiful and tranquil three hours of steep downhill steps. The trail takes in a mix of landscapes from narrow gorges to broad open vistas and will take you past some of the mountain's most famous sights, including the daunting rock expanse of **Lotus Peak** and the **Welcoming Guest Pine**, which has featured in paintings, adverts and even on cigarette packs. You could half this hike if you walk as far as the Yuping cable car and then ride down to Cigugang Ge, from where you can get a taxi.

Otherwise, bear north past Brightness Top Peak and, after not too long, you'll find yourself back at White Goose Ridge, where you can either take the cable car (until 5 pm) or hike back down.

Where to Stay

Tangkou

 Tangkou's hotel selection principally consists of budget lodgings, although a few mid-range places have opened on the main road and more are in the pipeline, including a five-star affair on the river. Tangkou depends on the tourist trade and it's worth bargaining hard if

@=in-room Internet access. For ¥ price codes, see page 113.

places look quiet, as there are substantial discounts to be had. If you come in winter, something else to bear in mind is the availability of **hot water and heating** – check to see if the a/c unit will blow hot air as it can get very chilly here. When arriving in Tangkou, show your bus driver the name of the hotel you want in Chinese and you'll be dropped at the nearest point.

Yingqiao, Old Qingtun Lu (☎ 0559-5562-968; ¥¥). This is the best of the group of hotels found just off the main road down Old Qingtun Lu. To escape the road noise and look out onto a farmed slope behind, ask for a room on the Yingqiao's sixth floor, although there's no elevator, so this will be some early training for your hike! If the Yingqiao is full, the **Hong Da** (☎ 0559-5562-577; ¥¥) next door has acceptable rooms and is preferable to the **Zhounan** (☎ 0559-5562-387; ¥¥), a little farther on.

Youth Hostel, next to the main road bridge (no phone). This is the cheapest place to stay in town and has very basic dorms for ¥30.

Xingang, Main Road (☎ 0559-5562-648). This is probably the best of the new hotels on the main road and has a few more pretensions than places down in the valley, although the carpets could do with a clean and the rooms are nothing special. ¥¥-¥¥¥

On the Mountain

If you're not on a tight budget then staying on the mountain itself is definitely the way to go, since it affords the opportunity to see Huangshan at sunset and sunrise and allows you to spend a leisurely day exploring the summit area. Given the quality of the rooms, hotels on the mountain are expensive, but you're paying for the location and the opportunity to take a moonlit stroll through the peaks free from the madding crowds of the day. On summer weekends it's definitely worth booking in advance. Conversely, in winter there are huge discounts to be enjoyed, but it's still worth calling ahead as some places close down for the season. In winter, check that the heating and hot water are working before you check in. The list below isn't comprehensive but includes the best of what's available.

Banshan Si Zhaodaisuo (☎ 0559-5584-008), This is by far the cheapest option on the mountain, although it's only a little over an hour's hike up the longer western route, so it's still a long way to the top from here. Very basic rooms (two beds and a wash bowl) and ¥100 dorms are all that's offered. This said, it has a pretty location and if you want to get the most out of your ticket, staying within the park means you can continue to explore the mountain for a few days, using the Yuping cable car to give your legs a break every now and then. ¥¥

Beihai (☎ 0559-5582-555). This is touted as the premium hotel on the mountain and is where party officials stay when they come. It is well located halfway between the cable car stations at White Goose Ridge and Paiyunlou. Although some rooms have reasonable views, they could do with an overhaul. @ ¥¥¥¥¥

Paiyunlou (☎ 0559-5588-581, www.huangshan.com.cn). At the top of the Taiping cable car station, the Paiyunlou is a little smaller and cheaper than the other mountain-top offerings. Although its rooms are of a similar standard, service can be slack. Dorm beds are around ¥150. ¥¥¥¥

Xihai

Shilin (☎ 0559-5581-562, www.shilin.com). A little north of the Beihai, the Shilin's rooms are a bit smaller, but this makes them cozy in winter. Dorm beds are about ¥150. @ ¥¥¥¥¥

★**Xihai** (☎ 0559-5588-888, www.xihaihotel.cn). The Xihai enjoys the best location of any of the mountain-top hotels and has a great sun terrace from which to soak it all up. However, rooms in the lower wing are a bit small and damp; it's better to stay in the upper wing where the new rooms enjoy reasonable views. Dorm beds are ¥120. ¥¥¥¥

Where to Eat

Tangkou

There are a host of cheap eateries dotted around Tangkou, many of which have English menus. The greatest concentration of restaurants lies along the river on Yangxi Jie, where you'll be offered a meal every few yards. Other than the one listing below, none of these places is worth a special mention – just pick one you like the look of and choose from the standard Chinese dishes, such as sweet and sour pork and *gongbao jiding*.

★★**Mr. Hu's**, next to Xiao Yao Hotel (daily 6 am-midnight). Great food, cheap prices and friendly service make Mr. Hu's a favorite on the backpacker circuit. The bargain ¥6 eggs and coffee breakfast will set you up nicely for the hike up Huangshan, while the mixed vegetables and sweet and sour pork are a treat after a hard day on the mountain. If you're still hungry, the traveler-inspired fried banana and apple will please sweet-tooths. Mr. Hu speaks good English and can help with travel arrangements, trips to local sights and general advice on the mountain. His uncle does finger paintings of local scenery, which are for sale. ¥¥

On the Mountain

Once up the mountain, meals are restricted to the hotel restaurants. Snacks (mainly pot noodles, biscuits and seasonal vegetables) and drinks are available from stalls dotted along the paths. Note that you'll pay much more for everything up here – a small bottle of water goes for a minimum of ¥5, so if you're on a budget it's worth carrying what you can. Huangshan is a great place for picnicking and there are supermarkets and bakeries in Tangkou that can supply you with the makings of a basic pack lunch.

Shexian & Yixian

For a trip into olde worlde China, you can't beat Shexian and Yixian counties, where you'll find some excellently preserved **Huizhou architecture**. Although the towns of Shexian and Yixian themselves are worth a quick peek, the real interest lies in the surrounding villages. Yixian is a UNESCO World Heritage Site. Many of the most famous villages have been heavily restored and require some steep admission fees.

In Yixian district, **Xidi's** (¥80) riverside collection of 18th-century dwellings has been converted into an antiques market and, while the village remains attractive, it swarms with visitors in the summer. **Hongcun** (¥80) is renowned for its bull-shaped streetplan, while ★**Nanping** (¥36) was the setting for Zhuang Yimou's acclaimed movie, *Judou*. Shexian county offers a quieter, less gentrified selection of villages, including ★**Chengkan** (¥35), ★**Qiankou** (¥50), **Tangmo** (¥46) and ★★**Xucun** (¥38). Shexian is also where you'll find the bizarre sight of seven commemorative arches (*paifang*) standing in a field at **Tangyue** (¥35).

HUIZHOU ARCHITECTURE

Today Anhui is one of the poorest states in China, but, during the Ming dynasty, the districts of Shexian and Yixian prospered from salt trading, and wealthy merchants built fine houses, some of which are still standing today. Formerly known as Huizhou, the region developed its own unique architectural style with a number of design elements that would go on to set the standard throughout central China. Huizhou houses always have at least one central courtyard, around which there are a series of galleried rooms. From the outside, the houses are easily identifiable by their horse-head gables, which were designed as fire baffles. Typically, the style also incorporates the use of ornate roof tiles, with fine wood carving and lattice work. If you venture out to the villages around Shexian and Yixian, you'll also see huge wood or stone *paifang* – memorial arches. These were constructed to commemorate important historical events and figures, as well as to honor virtuous behavior. The most famous examples are found at Tangyue (see above).

Visiting the Villages

You can make your way out to either Shexian or Yixian by bus from Tunxi or Tangkou (see *Getting Around*, p. 386), but since the villages are quite spread out it's simpler to hire a taxi for the day (Shexian ¥200 or Yixian ¥300). Or take a guided tour, which will also reveal some interesting information about the villages. You can arrange tours at Tunxi's better hotels, through **CTS** (☎ 0559-522-649), at 1 Binjiang Xi Lu, or with **Steven Huang** (☎ 1390-5594-053). Steven is used to dealing with foreigners who want to see the villages at their own pace. He charges ¥60-100 for a day's guiding, on top of which you'll have to pay for entrance fees and local buses or taxis. Entrance fees vary from ¥35-80 (see above) and all the villages are open daily from 6 am to 5:30 pm. Given the higher entrance fees to Yixian's villages, Shexian is a better bet if you're on a budget. Until recently, to visit the villages around Yixian you required a **police permit** (¥50) from the Public Security Bureau, but this had been waived at the time of writing.

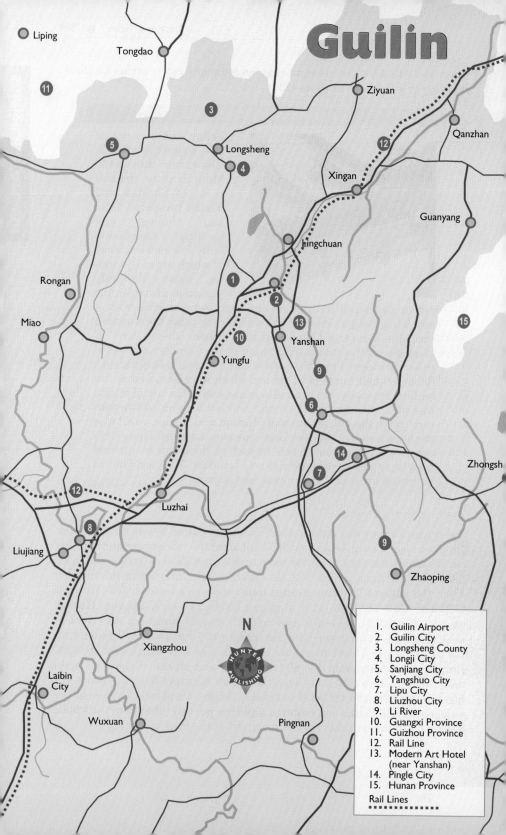

Guilin

1. Guilin Airport
2. Guilin City
3. Longsheng County
4. Longji City
5. Sanjiang City
6. Yangshuo City
7. Lipu City
8. Liuzhou City
9. Li River
10. Guangxi Province
11. Guizhou Province
12. Rail Line
13. Modern Art Hotel
   (near Yanshan)
14. Pingle City
15. Hunan Province

Rail Lines ▪▪▪▪▪▪▪▪▪▪▪

N

HUNTER PUBLISHING

Guilin & Around

This enchanting hideaway is set around the attractively revamped city of **Guilin**, in the heart of rural **Guangxi Province**. **Yangshuo**, a little to the south, makes for a low-key introduction to the area, and offers a

picture-postcard view of what is, to many, the essence of this vast country in which 60% of the population still live on the land. Water buffaloes toil in paddies amidst towering limestone outcrops and the landscape seems to come fresh from a scroll painting. A number of China's ethnic groups can be found in Guangxi, as indicated by its long-winded official moniker, **Guangxi Zhuang Autonomous Region**, reflecting the fact that the most prevalent minority are the Zhuang people. The hills around **Longji**, north of Guilin, are the place to witness hilltribe lifestyles unchanged for centuries, the impossibly steep rice terraces making for an awe-inspiring backdrop to the simple wooden villages and their impressive traditional architecture.

The Li River's enchanting scenery is fresh from a fairytale (Ewen Bell)

History

Guangxi's for the most part has remained a rural backwater on the fringes of the country. The beautiful mountains, which visitors flock to see today, were appreciated as far back as the Tang dynasty, but have long been a hindrance to development, limiting both agriculture and transport links. Guilin first became the provincial capital in the 14th century when the Ming emperor Hongwu appointed one of his relatives to rule the region from here. The city maintained its pole position until 1914, when it was superceded by southerly Nanning. Of the region's other brief moments in the spotlight, Guilin managed to stave off a siege during the 1851 Taiping Uprising, which started in nearby Guizhou province. Moving into the 20th century, after a defeat near Guilin, the First Front Army was prevented from proceeding north by the superior numbers of the Guomindang, forcing them west into Guizhou and Szechuan, before crossing the mountains on their epic **Long March** (see p. 19).

More recently still, Guilin served as an escape from the **Japanese occupation**, and the city was bombed relentlessly until the invading forces arrived – many refugees hid out in the legion of caverns that lie beneath the limestone towers in the region, most famously at Reed Flute Cave. Thus, while its natural splendor remained, the city itself was badly damaged. Ironically, it was the influx of modern friendlier invaders, **tourists**, that led the government to beautify the city in the 1990s. Contrived as this is, it works and makes Guilin a pleasant place to stay, though the main reason for coming here is to see the famed limestone tower karst scenery.

A GOOD GUANGXI TRIP

If you're suffering from an overdose of urban China, a trip to the rural riverside retreats of Guangxi could be the perfect antidote. While Guilin is the customary base from which to explore the region, Yangshuo is more relaxed and closer to the countryside. It also offers the opportunity to study many of China's traditional arts. If you're a keen hiker, cyclist or rock climber you could spend weeks exploring the magnificent terrain, but you can get a feel for the area in the space of a few days.

A good trip would be to fly into **Guilin** and spend a day exploring the sights, dining at Yiyuan and maybe enjoying a drink on Yiren Lu. The following day **take a cruise down the poetically beautiful Li River to Yangshuo**, disembark and check into your hotel. Spend a few days soaking up the laid-back small-town atmosphere, maybe gorging on some Western food, along with the **local delicacies such as beerfish**. There are so many activities available in Yangshuo that it's really up to you what to choose – from tai ji **to cookery courses, balloon rides or just plain old shopping**. But you should certainly take in at least one **bike ride or hike** into the countryside. If you have time, a trip up to the stunning rice terrace scenery of **Longji** is definitely recommended, and from here you could continue back to Guilin and on to your next destination.

Guilin

Guilin, with a current population of 650,000, took a long time to recover from the ravages of the Japanese invasion and it subsequently developed into a minor industrial center. After the economic liberalization of the 1980s Guilin quickly gained ground as a tourist destination. To fit this new purpose much of the city's industry was moved to other parts of the province and the city began a radical program of transformation. During its reinvention in the 1990s, Guilin was often described by local guides as a city "under reconstruction," and that's exactly what it felt like – a building site, albeit with a beautiful backdrop. Since the process has been finished, Guilin is a different city altogether. While it is still plagued by hawkers and rip-off merchants, the redesigned riverside promenade and city center are pleasant places for a stroll and highlight the sights, natural and manmade. As development in Yangshuo spirals it into something of a small city itself, Guilin has once again become a more attractive proposition, although ideally you'd spend time at both.

Getting Here & Away

Guilin is easily accessible by air and rail from all the destinations in this book, while buses are a good option from Shenzhen, Guangzhou or Hong Kong.

By Air

Guilin offers flights to most major cities in China and a few Asian countries, including Japan, Korea and Thailand. Many people make Guilin their first or last stop on their way into or out of Hong Kong and there are several daily flights that take just an hour and a half. Some of the better hotels provide a shuttle bus service to the airport from their doors or you can take the bus (¥20) from the Air China offices in the south of town at Minhang Dasha on Shanghai Lu (☎ 0773-2866-567), where you can also buy air tickets. The airport trip takes about 40 minutes from downtown and if you want to take a taxi, expect to pay ¥80-¥100.

Flight destinations, frequencies & durations

Beijing (5 daily, 3 hrs); **Chongqing** (2 daily, 1 hr); **Guangzhou** (10 daily, 1 hr); **Hangzhou** (2 daily, 2 hrs); **Hong Kong** (3 daily, 1 hr 30 mins); **Shanghai** (2 daily, 2 hrs 10 mins); **Shenzhen** (7 daily, 55 mins); **Xi'an** (5 daily, 2 hrs).

By Rail

Guilin is reasonably connected by rail and has two stations, the old South Station on Zhongshan Lu near the center of the city, and a newer terminal out in the north, a ¥20-30 taxi ride away.

Destinations, frequencies & durations

Beijing (3 daily, 22-29 hrs); Guangzhou (2 daily, 13hr); **Hangzhou** (4 daily, 24-31 hrs); **Huangshan** (1 daily, 22 hrs 30 mins); **Shanghai** (3 daily, 27-29 hrs); **Shenzhen** (1 daily, 15 hrs 40 mins); **Suzhou** (1 daily, 30 hrs); **Xi'an** (1 daily, 28 hrs).

By Road

 Although it looks like a long distance on a map, an overnight bus trip to Guilin (or Yangshuo) by road is a good option from Shenzhen and Guangzhou – it's both quicker and cheaper than the train, there are more services and some of these are very comfortable. There are also regular services to Yangshuo and Longsheng. All of the buses mentioned leave from the depot on Zhongshan Nan Lu, north of the train station.

Bus destinations, frequencies & durations

Guangzhou (several daily, 8-9 hrs); **Longsheng** (several daily, 2 hrs); **Shenzhen** (several daily, 12 hrs); **Yangshuo** (frequent until 8 pm, 1 hr).

Getting Around

If you stay in the center, walking is a good way to get around the sights, but for trips to nearby sights there are buses and taxis.

By Bus

 While plenty of buses ply Guilin's streets, routes can be complex and taxis are cheap, so you're better off using these. However, if you're feeling impecunious, the following may be of use:

- #2 runs from the bus and south train stations into town, along Nanhuan Lu and up Binjiang Lu.
- #10 heads from the bus and south train stations through the center of town and to Zhengyang Lu.
- #11 goes from the bus and south train stations through the center of town and then out to Seven Star Park.
- #58 circuits the main tourist sights, but gets very busy as it's a free service.

By Taxi

 Guilin itself has a host of **taxis**, which cost ¥7 for the first 2 km (1.2 miles) and then 1.6 per km (0.6 miles) after this. Unfortunately Guilin has seen too many visitors for too long and you'll need to be wary of drivers not using the meter. If you're traveling by yourself, or just want a speedy and fun way of getting round the city, there are **motorbike taxis** waiting at almost every junction, but you'll need to bargain hard to get a fair price – trips within town shouldn't cost more than ¥5.

By Bicycle

Given the great bike rides in Yangshuo, riding around Guilin seems less worthwhile, but you could take a ride out to Seven Star Park. You can rent bikes from **Backstreet Youth Hostel** (see *Where to Stay*, p. 412) for ¥20 a day.

By Boat

The boat trip from Guilin down to Yangshuo is covered under *Adventures On Water*, p. 429.

Orientation

Situated amid impressive tower karst scenery and well placed for trips south to Yangshuo and north to Longji, Guilin is the traditional base from which to explore the region. Guilin is an easy city to tour, predominantly contained by the **Li River** to the east, and mountains to the north and west. Most scenic spots are either on the river or within a few minutes' walk of it, as are the hotels listed. The main thoroughfare is **Zhongshan Lu**, which runs north to south, parallel to the western bank of the Li River, down to the south train station. The heart of the commercial district is focused around Central Square, where you'll also find some of the best shopping in town. There's a good selection of restaurants on riverside **Binjiang Lu**, with another pocket west of Elephant Trunk Hill on Nanhuan Lu, while central **Yiren Lu** and **Zhengyang Lu** host Guilin's nightlife. The city's **principal bus station** and one of its **two train stations** are located near to the downtown area, while the second train station and the airport are about 30 minutes out to the north and west respectively.

Information Sources

There are branches of the **Guilin Tourism Information Service Center** (☎ 0773-2800-318, www.guilin.com.cn) dotted around the city, including one at Elephant Trunk Hill, one in Central Square and another at Wave Subduing Hill. Staff are generally helpful and speak English.

Events & Festivals

All the regular Chinese festivals are celebrated in Guilin and if you come around the time of the Moon Festival you'll find the osmanthus trees (from which the city derives its name) in bloom.

Communications

WWW

Post Office: One on Binjiang Lu and another just north of the train station on Zhongshan Nan Lu.
Telephone code: 0773.

Internet Access: There's an Internet café on Nanhuan Lu near the junction with Wenming Lu and there are computers with web access at the Backstreet Youth Hotel (see p. 412), which also has wireless connection.
Bank of China: Between the bus and train stations on Zhongshan Nan Lu. Another branch is on Jiefang Dong Lu.
Public Security Bureau: 16 Shijiayuan Lu (☎ 0773-5829-930).
Medical services: The Renmin Hospital, between Wenming Lu and Binjiang Lu (☎ 0773-2823-767).

LEARNING THE LINGO

Starting on page 598, there's a language section with useful phrases written in Chinese characters, should verbal communication fail! Chinese vocabulary specific to the **Guilin** area begins on page 623.

Sightseeing

The city has undergone a major facelift, adding a few new tourist sights to its natural attractions. While places such as Banyan and Cedar Lake are pleasant enough, the hills beckon. The central sights are close enough together to comfortably walk between them, but if you get tired you could hop on free bus #58 which travels to all the major attractions, or take a taxi.

Camel Hill at Seven Star Park, Guilin

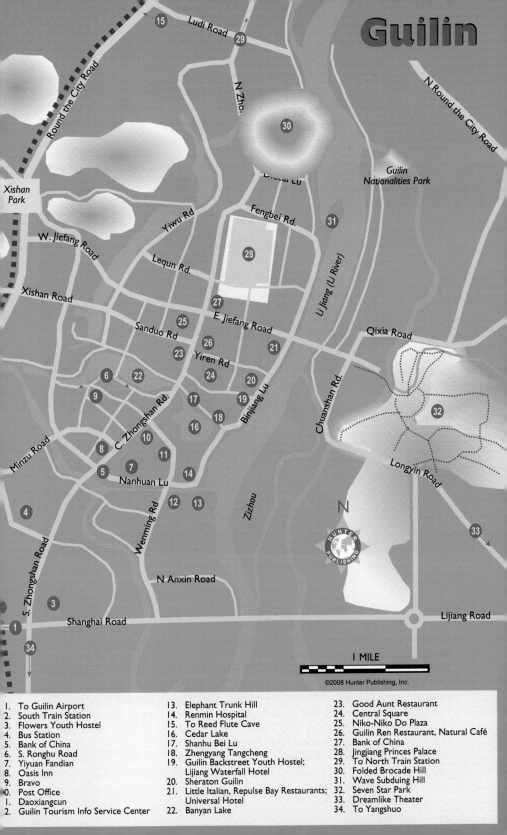

Guilin

I MILE

©2008 Hunter Publishing, Inc.

1. To Guilin Airport	13. Elephant Trunk Hill	23. Good Aunt Restaurant
2. South Train Station	14. Renmin Hospital	24. Central Square
3. Flowers Youth Hostel	15. To Reed Flute Cave	25. Niko-Niko Do Plaza
4. Bus Station	16. Cedar Lake	26. Guilin Ren Restaurant, Natural Café
5. Bank of China	17. Shanhu Bei Lu	27. Bank of China
6. S. Ronghu Road	18. Zhengyang Tangcheng	28. Jingjiang Princes Palace
7. Yiyuan Fandian	19. Guilin Backstreet Youth Hostel;	29. To North Train Station
8. Oasis Inn	Lijiang Waterfall Hotel	30. Folded Brocade Hill
9. Bravo	20. Sheraton Guilin	31. Wave Subduing Hill
0. Post Office	21. Little Italian, Repulse Bay Restaurants;	32. Seven Star Park
1. Daoxiangcun	Universal Hotel	33. Dreamlike Theater
2. Guilin Tourism Info Service Center	22. Banyan Lake	34. To Yangshuo

You really don't need a tour to see the best of Guilin, but for Li River cruises (see *Adventures on Water*, p. 429) you might want to enlist the help of your hotel booking desk or **CITS** at 11 Binjiang Lu (☎ 0773-2861-623). If you want a qualified local guide, **Lily** (☎ 135-5813-6825) speaks good English and has sound knowledge of Guilin.

Elephant Trunk Hill lives up to its name (Tot Foster)

The West Bank

Elephant Trunk Hill (Xiangbi Shan), Binjiang Lu (daily 6 am-6 pm; ¥25, bus #2). There are no prizes for guessing the reason for this hill's name, and for once it really is easy to see – the rock truly looks like an elephant taking a drink from the river. It's so famous that it has become the Guilin city logo.
Banyan Lake (Rong Hu) and Cedar Lake (Shan Hu). These two lakes were originally part of the city moat during the Tang dynasty, but have been recently rehashed as an attractive addition to Guilin's myriad of sights. The two lakes are joined by the Sun Bridge and there's now a pair of pagodas (¥30) gracing Cedar Lake and, to the north, a series of replicas of world-famous bridges – the Golden Gate is here among others!
★**Jingjiang Princes' Palace**, Jiefang Dong Lu (daily 8:30 am-5:30 pm; ¥50). When Emperor Hongwu appointed **Zhou Shouqian**, a distant rela-

tive, to preside over this southerly region, he began a legacy that would last 300 years. The Jingjiang Palace was built in the late 14th century, around the same time as the Forbidden City (see p. 155-57). While its smaller stature reflects Guangxi's minor vassal status, parallels with the Beijing monument are obvious. Inside, you'll find modern portraits of each of the 14 Jingjiang Princes along with relics unearthed from their tombs, which lie un-restored, a few miles out of town. To the north of the palace, **Solitary Beauty Peak** (Duxiu Feng; daily 6 am-6 pm; ¥15) offers another of Guilin's short, steep climbs – as usual, rewarded with fine views.

★**Wave Subduing Hill** (Fubo Shan), Binjiang Lu (daily 6 am-6 pm; ¥15; bus #2). At the northern end of Binjiang Lu you'll find the quiet and atmospheric Fubo Hill, which makes for a great sunset spot. The peak has a number of caves and paths running to the top and although it's only a short ascent be prepared for a steep climb. At the top you are rewarded with excellent views over the area including the city and Elephant Trunk Hill.

Folded Brocade Hill (Diecai Shan), Diecai Lu (daily 6:30 am-6 pm; ¥20; bus #2). Folded Brocade Hill gets its name from the impression that it is comprised of several hills folded into one another. The hill is famous for its Wind Cave which gusts cool breezes and can be very refreshing on a hot day. Unfortunately, the cave is fairly near the bottom of the hill, so no matter how cool you feel, you've still got a short steep climb ahead of you.

Other Sights

★**Seven Star Park**, Ziyou Lu (daily 6:30 am-7 pm; ¥35; bus #58). On the eastern side of the river, you'll find the attractive Seven Star Park, which contains a series of paths running between and up to the seven lush peaks that give the park its name. Many of the peaks are capped by poetically placed pagodas, and from here it's hard to believe there are taxis and buses busily rumbling along the other side of the river. While the real pleasure of a visit here is soaking up the landscape, there is also a temple, a collection of stelae and the Seven Star Cave (daily 8 am-6 pm; ¥30).

★★**Reed Flute Cave**, Ludi Lu (daily 8 am-5:30 pm; ¥60; bus #3 or #58). Some 10 miles out of Guilin lies this most famous of Guangxi's grottoes. A vast complex eventually opening out to a huge central cavern, it was used in the past as a refuge from Japanese bombs, but now sees visitors who come for plea-

Reed Flute Cave

sure, not protection. Its name derives from the reeds that grow near the cave. They are converted into tiny flutes and sold as souvenirs to tourists. In true Chinese style all of the stalagmites and stalactites (just remember mites go up and tights come down) have been given names and are brightly lit to try and reinforce (or create) this appearance – my favorite is New York Skyline in the central cavern. The cave can get very busy and you're supposed to go in a group with a guide (Chinese-speaking unless you wait for a foreign group to assemble), who turns on the lights as you go round. If you want to see the cave in more peace, drift back from your group and wait until the next one comes to light the cave up again, and so on. The temperature remains a pleasant 72°F throughout the year, but the path can be slippery so wear good shoes. Trips can be arranged through your hotel or a travel agent in Guilin. Or negotiate directly with a taxi driver – the ride out there should cost around ¥20.

Galleries, Shows & Theaters

Guilin has a few cultural shows to offer, the best of which is the **Dreamlike Lijiang Show** (☎ 0773-5858-018, www.heaven-creation.com/sube/producing/lijiang1) which features acrobats and ballet and takes place at 8 pm nightly at the Dreamlike Theater, 95 Qixing Lu. Tickets are ¥120-150 and there are even TVs in the bathroom so you don't miss any of the show!

Shopping

 Both Yiren Lu and Zhengyang Lu have trendy handicrafts shops selling bamboo, wooden and wicker items as well as paintings and pottery. Items of more dubious quality can be found at the **nightmarket**, which sets up along Zhongshan Lu between the Sun Bridge and the Niko-Niko Do Plaza every evening from 7 pm. However, it's worth bearing in mind that the same market handicrafts can usually be found for less money in Yangshuo.

For more mundane requirements, the **Niko-Niko Do Plaza** at the junction of Zhongshan Lu and Jiefang Lu is a modern shopping center where you'll find all your daily needs and more. There's also a bizarre warren of clothing stores in an underground shopping center beneath Central Square.

Adventures

On the Green

 Golf has taken hold in Guangxi and there are a few good courses that offer stunning views of its famed scenery. You can rent clubs from the club shops. Below are a couple of courses to try:

Guilin Li River Country Golf Club, Zhujiang Dock (☎ 0773-3609-080). This 7,100-yard, par-72 course is a 40-minute drive from the city.

Merryland Golf Club, Xin'an County (☎ 0773-622-988, www.merry-land. com.cn). Thirty miles northeast from Guilin, the Merryland is a USGA-approved 7,073-yard, par-72 course and there's also a theme park here to keep the kids happy. To get here take the bus from Guilin's bus terminal to Xin'an, then a taxi.

On Water

In Guilin

If you want to take a short motorboat trip around Guilin, the 90-minute **Two Rivers and Four Lakes** trip (¥150) runs daily – you can book tickets through your hotel and CITS. You can also take boat trips to watch **cormorant fishing** (see p. 431) from Guilin, although you'll find more authentic options in Yangshuo – ask at your hotel for details.

★★★Guilin to Yangshuo

The famed journey from Guilin to Yangshuo takes between three and five hours depending on the water level and certainly offers the spectacular scenery people come to see. However, this trip is marred for some by the sheer number of boats (sometimes as many as 50, traveling in convoy) and the

A cruise along the Li River is a must

obsession of some Asian tourists with having their photo taken in every conceivable place, thinking nothing of shoving you out of the way to do so! This, along with the price (¥400-540), including lunch (though specialties such as snake wine are extra), dissuades some more thrifty travelers, who choose to take a shorter boat ride from Yangshuo or Xingping instead. Nonetheless, it is a stunning voyage and, if you choose to skip the lunch, you'll have the open deck to yourself for half an hour or so. The various peaks along the way have all been given imaginative names (meaning you have to use your imagination), such as "Lion Watching the Nine Horses." These are the highlight for many domestic tourists.

You can arrange this trip from all travel agencies and many hotels in Guilin and the price includes transfer to the **Zhujiang Dock** (about 45 minutes from your hotel) and the round-trip bus ride from Yangshuo to Guilin – though you're far better off staying on in Yangshuo, if you have the time, as the day-trip only offers you a few hours. If you decide to stay, either take your luggage onto the boat if they'll let you, or keep it on the bus and collect it in Yangshuo. Most boats leave between 9 and 10 am with buses picking up an hour beforehand.

Cultural Adventures

Guilin is a major producer of osmanthus tea and if you want to learn more about this you can take a trip to the ★**Tea Cultural Institution** at Yashan, which you can arrange through CITS or local guide Lily (see *Sightseeing*, p. 406, for contact details). Another interesting trip is out to ★★**Yuzi Paradise** (☎ 0773-3869-009, www.yuzile.com; ¥80) halfway to Yangshuo, which is claimed to be the largest artistic park in the world. Once there, you'll find the grounds littered with interesting sculptures, set to the backdrop of nature's own creations, the contorted limestone tower peaks. You can also see artists at work on bronzes, ceramics and glass sculptures. There are also tai chi and yoga classes. Shuttle buses from Guilin bus station run to the park, and, if you want to stay, there's an ultra-modern hotel on-site (see p. 413).

Where to Stay

Guilin has been a tourist destination for some time and hosts a wide range of accommodations, from international five-star chains to youth hostels. All of the following have their own travel desks.

What's it mean? FC=fitness center; SW=swimming pool; @=in-room Internet access; DA=rooms for disabled. For ¥ price codes, see page 113.

★**Bravo**, 14 Ronghu Nan Lu (☎ 0773-2823-950, www.glbravohotel.com). Pleasantly situated on the edge of attractive Banyan Lake, the Bravo has good rooms, friendly staff and a reasonable Chinese restaurant. @ ¥¥¥¥

Flowers Youth Hostel, 6 Shangzhi Lane, Block 2, Zhongshan Nan Lu (☎ 0773-3839-625, www.yhaguilin.com). This hostel is just a few minutes from the bus and south train stations and thus is handy for transport, although it's a little far from the central sights. The hostel's dorms and rooms are clean and you can even rent DVD players to watch movies. The usual transport and tour booking facilities are available and there's Internet access. Dorm beds are ¥40. ¥

★**Guilin Backstreet Youth Hostel**, 3 Renmin Lu (☎ 0773-2819-936, www.hostelling.cn; bus #2). This modern hostel enjoys a great location close to the river and has tastefully decorated basic but clean doubles and dorms (¥40). The communal areas are stylishly decked out and the hostel has Internet access, booking facilities and bike rental. @ ¥

Lijiang Waterfall Hotel, 1 Shanhu Bei Lu (☎ 0773-2822-881, www.waterfallguilin.com). This new five-star place claims the world's largest hotel waterfall which flows over the entire back surface of the hotel every night at 8:30 pm! The rooms are light and comfortable and some enjoy views over the lakes and river. FC/SW/@ ¥¥¥¥¥

Oasis Inn, 4F Wuzhou Building, Zhongshan Zhong Lu (☎ 0773-2580-215, www.guilinhome.com). The Oasis is a good budget choice, slightly more upscale than the hostels, but still very competitively priced. It enjoys a central location and there are a range of light and airy rooms. ¥-¥¥

Sheraton Guilin

★**Sheraton Guilin**, 15 Binjiang Lu (☎ 0773-282-5588, www.sheraton.com/guilin; bus #2). Well-positioned next to the river and close to Elephant Trunk Hill, this hotel affords all the usual five-star amenities, and is the place to stay if money isn't an issue. The better rooms enjoy views over the river to Seven Star Park. FC/SW/@/DA ¥¥¥¥¥

★**Universal**, 1 Jiefang Dong Lu (☎ 0773-2828-228; bus #2). Well-located, comfortable and friendly, this hotel has good double rooms, the more expensive of which enjoy views over the river. The hotel also has a couple of restaurants, one of which serves reasonable Western fare. ¥¥¥-¥¥¥¥

Out of Town

★★**The Hotel of Modern Art**, Dabu Town, Yanshan (☎ 0773-3865-555, www.yuzile.com; shuttle bus from Guilin bus station). The angular Hotel of Modern Art lies within the weird and wonderful Yuzi Paradise (see p. 412), a half-hour drive from Guilin. Rooms at the hotel are beautifully designed and there's also a great spa on-site, along with plenty of restaurants. SW/@ ¥¥¥¥¥

Where to Eat

Southerners have long been renowned for their love of all culinary things weird, wonderful and sometimes grotesque. Guilin is no exception to this southern eating style, and is influenced by Cantonese cuisine. The variety of foods that are consumed here and the freshness of the produce is astounding and sometimes alarming! If you're into food exploration, there's plenty to keep you busy along Nanhuan Lu where you'll find restaurants with caged animals outside. If that's not your cup of

Guilin & Around

tea there are also plenty of restaurants serving simpler dishes, as well as a handful of Western cafés and the ubiquitous fast food chains, including a McDonald's on Central Square and a KFC in the Niko-Niko Do Plaza. Unless otherwise mentioned, all the places below have English menus and don't require reservations.

See page 117 for an explanation of the ¥ restaurant price codes.

Daoxiangcun, Wenmin Lu (daily 11 am-10 pm). This traditional restaurant serves delicious Guilin cuisine in its large dining hall and they also have some private rooms. ¥¥-¥¥¥

★**Good Aunt**, Bagui Dasha, opposite Center Square, Sanduo Lu. Similar to Guilin Ren (see below), Good Aunt is a popular buffet-style eatery that serves tasty dishes from around the country. ¥¥

★★**Guilin Ren**, 128 Zhongshan Zhong Lu (daily 11 am-10 pm). This enormous buffet-style eating emporium has a fantastic array of foods from the region and indeed the world. You can watch the preparation and cooking process. The stretched noodles are excellent. ¥¥

Little Italian, Binjiang Lu (daily 11 am-11 pm). This tiny café-bar is decked out in bright colors and Bruce Lee pictures. It serves good Italian dishes to the backdrop of African beats – very cross-cultural. ¥¥

Natural Café, 24 Yiren Lu (daily 11 am-1 am), Natural is a pleasant and comfy café with low coffee tables and armchairs which serves a mix of Asian and Western dishes and is a popular evening drinking spot. ¥¥

Repulse Bay, 6F, 18 Binjiang Lu (daily 10 am-2 am). This open-kitchened sixth-floor restaurant enjoys good views over the river and serves the usual mix of Asian and Western dishes. Set menus from ¥35. ¥¥-¥¥¥

★★★**Yiyuan Fandian**, 106 Nanhuan Lu (daily 9 am-2 pm & 4:30-9 pm). This is a great place to sample delicious fiery Szechuan *gongbao jiding*, fish-flavored pork and a host of vegetable dishes. They even use genuine Szechuan flower peppers, which create a fragrant tingling sensation in your mouth. Of course, if you don't like it hot, they can tone it down, and the helpful staff in this popular restaurant can speak some English. Booking ahead is advised in the evenings. ¥¥-¥¥¥

Zhengyang Tangcheng, Zhengyang Lu (daily 11 am-3 am). This specialty soup-house makes a good stopping-off point after some shopping on Zhengyang Lu, particularly on a chilly winter's day. ¥¥¥

Nightlife

Yiren Lu and **Zhengyang Lu** are at the center of Guilin's lively night scene and there are bars and clubs to suit a variety of tastes – try **Sunshine Bar** near the back entrance to the Sheraton on Zhengyang Lu.

Yangshuo

Some 40 miles south of Guilin, Yangshuo sits amid some of the most spectacular karst scenery in the region. Stretching along the west bank of the **Li River**, Yangshuo is still a small rural town, with a population of 32,000, but it's developing fast as a tourist resort and sees hordes of Chinese and overseas visitors during the summer. Like much of Guangxi province, Yangshuo was traditionally a poor rural area where farming was hindered by the countless limestone towers dotting the landscape, but ironically it is this same landscape that now brings so many visitors to the region.

While no longer the backwater it once was, Yangshuo still offers quaint old streets and has an amazing array of trendy shops, bars, cafés and restaurants serving everything from steak to snake along with an ever-expanding range of good-value places to stay, some of which are beautifully located out in the countryside. There's also the opportunity to study traditional arts and partake in adventurous activities such as climbing and kayaking. Most importantly, this pretty little town still has immediate access to some of the most beautiful countryside in China, maybe the world.

*Bike rides are a great way to explore
the countryside around Yangshuo (China Climb)*

Getting Here & Away

Road and river are the only ways to reach Yangshuo itself, but Guilin airport and train station are both only a little over an hour away by bus.

Guilin & Around

By Road

There are a number of overnight buses running to Yangshuo from **Shenzhen** (12 hrs; ¥230) and **Guangzhou** (8-9 hrs; ¥140). Several companies operate these routes and, although standards vary, buses are usually very comfy, spacious and modern. You can buy tickets from the travel agents mentioned under *Adventures* (p. 410) and from the bus station itself.

From **Guilin**, mini-buses ply the road to Yangshuo throughout the day. It's about an hour's drive and the road passes through some breathtaking scenery. It's worth having your camera in hand, especially as the bus makes a number of stops along the way. Local buses from **Guilin** train station run to Yangshuo's bus depot on **Pantao Lu** every 10 minutes, or when full. The standard bus fare is ¥15 and it takes about one hour. There is also an express bus (¥18), which is more comfortable but no quicker and leaves from the Guilin bus station every 20-30 minutes. If you arrive in Guilin after 8 pm and want to get to Yangshuo that night, you'll need to take a taxi at a cost of about ¥200 (from either the airport or the train station).

For the three-hour journey to **Longji** there are a number of options from Yangshuo. There is a daily tourist bus that departs at 7:30 am (¥150 round-trip), which also includes the entrance fee to the area. It returns in the evening but, if you want to stay overnight there, tell your agent when you buy your ticket and you'll be given a slip of paper that will allow you to return the following day. You can also ask to be dropped at Guilin on the return leg of your journey. If you don't want to take the tourist bus from Yangshuo to Longji, you can get a regular bus to Guilin and then another bus to Longsheng from where you can get a minibus into the hills.

By River

See *Guilin, Adventures On Water* (p. 411) for the cruise from Guilin to Yangshuo.

Getting Around

Yangshuo itself is small enough to negotiate on foot and outside of town the road network is improving all the time, making for easy access to the incredible countryside. Most streets around town are clearly labeled in English and signs out on the larger roads will often guide you to the more remote sights.

From Yangshuo there are buses and **electric golf buggies** that shuttle people to and from the main sights, but the best way to get around Yangshuo and the surrounding countryside is definitely on foot, by **bicycle** or **bamboo raft** (see *Adventures On Foot*, p. 424, *On Wheels*, p. 425, and *On Water*, p. 429), which provide the pace and solitude that this part of the country is all about.

By Bus

Local buses and minibuses run frequently throughout the day from the station on Pantao Lu out to the surrounding villages. Note that these are very 'local' buses and can get filled with people, animals and luggage. But they are certainly worth a try – even if it is only once. Destinations and durations are as follows: **Baisha** (30 mins); **Fuli** (30 mins); **Gaotian** (20 mins); **Puyi** (1 hr); **Xingping** (1 hr), **Yangdi** (1 hr).

By Taxi

Yangshuo has various vehicles that serve as taxis, including official red metered cars. However, the meters are seldom used and you'll need to negotiate a price with your driver before departure. As a guideline, a one-way trip to Moon Hill should cost about ¥20, although you'll have to pay extra for them to wait. Another fun way to get around is by local **motorbike taxi**, which you'll find clustered around the junction of Diecui Lu and Xianqian Jie – expect to pay ¥3 around Yangshuo and ¥10 for most of the sights out of town. Most cafés and hotels can pre-arrange both forms of transport and are a good way of making sure you get a reliable driver. If you are traveling in a larger group, mini-vans and buses can also be hired and start from around ¥40 for a six-seater to the Mountain Retreat or Moon Hill.

By Bicycle

One of the best ways of experiencing the stunning scenery around Yangshuo is by bike. With a vast network of local routes running along predominantly flat terrain, bicycles offer the perfect way to explore. You can't walk more than a few yards in Yangshuo without stumbling on a bike rental stall, but note that prices vary depending on the bike's condition and age. Expect to pay ¥10 for a standard bike or ¥20 for a mountain bike in good repair. **Magnolia Hotel** rents bikes, all of which are in excellent condition and prices are a fixed ¥10 per day. Top-quality mountain bikes can be rented from **Bar & Café 98** for ¥30 a day – the bikes are provided by **Bike Asia** (see *Travel & Living, Specialized Tours*, p. 77) upstairs. See *Adventures On Wheels* for cycling routes and guided rides. If your own steam power doesn't provide enough pace, you can also rent **electric bicycles** throughout Yangshuo for ¥40 a day, but note that they'll run out of power after 20 to 25 miles.

By Boat

If you didn't take the boat from Guilin down here then you should make sure you get out on the water from Yangshuo – see *Adventures On Water*, p. 429.

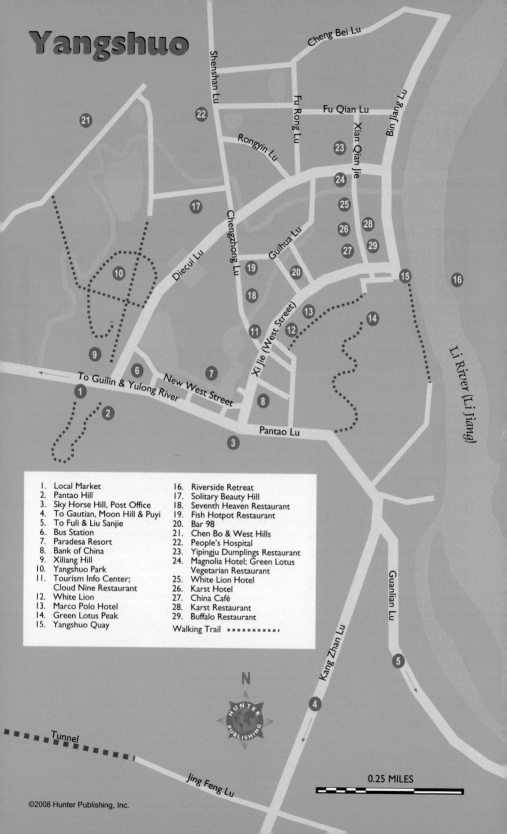

Yangshuo

1. Local Market
2. Pantao Hill
3. Sky Horse Hill, Post Office
4. To Gautian, Moon Hill & Puyi
5. To Fuli & Liu Sanjie
6. Bus Station
7. Paradesa Resort
8. Bank of China
9. Xiliang Hill
10. Yangshuo Park
11. Tourism Info Center;
    Cloud Nine Restaurant
12. White Lion
13. Marco Polo Hotel
14. Green Lotus Peak
15. Yangshuo Quay

16. Riverside Retreat
17. Solitary Beauty Hill
18. Seventh Heaven Restaurant
19. Fish Hotpot Restaurant
20. Bar 98
21. Chen Bo & West Hills
22. People's Hospital
23. Yipingju Dumplings Restaurant
24. Magnolia Hotel; Green Lotus
    Vegetarian Restaurant
25. White Lion Hotel
26. Karst Hotel
27. China Café
28. Karst Restaurant
29. Buffalo Restaurant

Walking Trail ▪▪▪▪▪▪▪▪▪

N

HUNTER
PUBLISHING

0.25 MILES

Orientation

From the river, **West Street** (Xi Jie) and **Diecui Lu** run southwest to meet busy **Pantao Lu**, with a warren of narrow cobbled lanes between them and the mountains. The bulk of shops, cafés, Internet places, hotels and amenities can be found on or around pedestrianized West Street, Chengzhong Lu and Xianqian Jie. The **bus station** is on Pantao Lu, near the junction with Diecui Lu in the center of town, and **boats** from Guilin arrive at **Yangshuo Quay**, located at the eastern end of West Street.

Information Sources

The small **Yangshuo Tourism Information Center** (☎ 0773-6912-773; daily 8 am-11 pm) is on the corner of West Street and Chengzhong Lu and has a reasonable amount of local information available in English. The staff can also book tickets for the Liu Sanjie cultural show (see *Galleries, Shows & Theaters*, p. 420). For information before you get here, try the excellent website, **www.yangers.com**, produced by the owner of Buffalo Bar & Guest House, Alf (☎139-7733-1334). You'll find just about anything you need here with up-to-date listings on hotels (including a reservation service), restaurants, outdoor activities and local maps. The best local map is *Trax2*, available from bars, hotels and cafés.

Communications

Post Office: Pantao Lu, opposite the West Street junction.
Telephone code: 0773.
Internet Access: Below Cloud 9 Restaurant on the corner of West Street and Chengzhong Lu and plenty of places on Pantao Lu.
Bank of China: At the southern end of West Street, opposite the Paradesa Hotel and another at the western end of Pantao Lu. To change foreign cash you'll need a photocopy of your passport, for which you'll be charged ¥0.5.
Public Security Bureau: To extend your visa you'll need to go to Guilin.
Medical Services: The People's Hospital on Shenshan Lu is Yangshuo's best medical facility, although it is not recommended for serious health problems unless you really have no choice. For minor conditions and a medical opinion, **Dr Lily** on Guihua Lu is a fantastic advisor and healer; she practices Chinese medicine and will know who to contact for more serious conditions. She also provides some of the best massage and acupuncture in town (see *Health & Relaxation*, p. 420).

Sightseeing

Yangshuo's sights are in the surrounding countryside (see *Adventures*, p. 422-32), but if you don't want to leave town, **Yangshuo Park** (daily 6 am-9 pm; ¥10), across from the bus station, is pleasant for a stroll (or hike if you choose to climb a peak). It's also a good place to witness, or participate in, morning exercises, ranging from ballroom dancing to tai chi.

Guilin & Around

Galleries, Shows & Theaters

The Liu Sanjie show

To complete Yangshuo's aspirations as an all-round resort, the town now has a cultural show, **Liu Sanjie**, which was choreographed by the master moviemaker and cinematographer, Zhang Yimou (see *Film, The Fifth Generation*, p. 67), who is also overseeing the opening ceremony of the 2008 Olympics. The show centers on the tale of Liu Sanjie, a farming girl from the nearby city of Liuzhou. Liu Sanjie sang to pass the time in the fields and became famous for her beautiful voice. One day she took a bamboo raft to Yangshuo and fell in love with a local boy. The story is acted out on the river and features bamboo rafts, cormorant fishermen and dramatic lighting. Tickets cost ¥188, although you may be able to find them cheaper if you hunt around the agents in town, and the show lasts an hour. Golf buggies are provided to shuttle people to and from the show on the river and cost ¥2 each way for the 10-minute journey.

For Families

Yangshuo is one of the most family-friendly places in China and most of the activities detailed below are suitable for all ages. If you want to put together a family adventure tour, **China Climb** (☎ 0773-8811-033, www.chinaclimb. com) is experienced at coordinating all the activities you might want during your trip, from bamboo rafting to hiking or climbing.

On the Yangti to Xingping trail with China Climb

Health & Relaxation

After a hard day of outdoor pursuits, a great way to relax is to try one of the many types of massage available in Yangshuo for as little as ¥30 an hour. One of the best choices is **Dr Lily Li** (☎ 0773-8814-

625), who specializes in acupuncture, hot cupping (see *Traditional Chinese Medicine*, p. 71), massage and foot reflexology. She is very professional and informative but be warned that her style of massage is on the hard side, and she'll really work out those knots! The clinic is easy to find, located on the small side-street just a few doors down from Bar & Café 98 on Guihua Lu and treatments cost from ¥30-60. The **Paradesa Hotel** also offers good Chinese and Korean massage from ¥120 an hour, with discounts for residents.

Shopping

In Yangshuo you can find an extensive collection of handicrafts from all over the country, as well as the usual plethora of Mao nicknacks, outdoor clothes and tacky t-shirts. Just make sure you buy before or after the big boats appear, as the shops will be packed with people ready to pay Guilin hotel gift shop prices. It's far more soothing to gently accumulate over the course of a few days, gradually chipping away at prices.

Many goods here come from other parts of the country but, if you're after more of a sense of authenticity, you can buy original works from painters here and in Fuli (see *Adventures On Wheels*, p. 425), and even have them painted onto t-shirts! Look out for the Chinese Picasso (or Forest to his friends)

Guangxi market life

who has a small stall that sets up after 5 pm outside Café China on West Street. Forest can and will paint just about anything onto a T-shirt; they cost ¥60 and usually take about 15 minutes. Yangshuo's local crafts include oil-painted umbrellas and wood and bamboo carving, all of which can be found on West Street and the riverside market.

Markets

For a touch of local life, Yangshuo's lively **produce market** on Pantao Lu is where local farmers come to trade their goods, and is a colorful and noisy spot where you can watch the locals haggling over their shopping. Besides the foods on sale, you'll see a number of caged animals and birds, some of which are for consumption while others are to be bought as pets. You'll also get the chance to see some of the more exotic fruits grown in the region, including pomelos, persimmons, kumquats and rambutans – why not sup-

Local fan-making, Fuli

port local farmers by buying some as a healthy snack? Of the various other markets around Yangshuo, **Fuli** (see *Adventures On Wheels*, p. 425) is probably the liveliest and operates on days ending in 2, 5 and 8, while **Baisha** (days 1, 4, 7) and **Xingping** (days 3, 6, 9) are also worth a visit – buses run to all three from Yangshuo's bus station.

Everyday Goods

For more everyday goods, your best choice is Diecui Lu where you will find **pharmacies**, a **supermarket** and general stores. There's also a **book exchange** at the pleasant Café Too on Chengzhong Lu.

Adventures

Despite ever greater numbers of Chinese tourists, Yangshuo first developed as a foreign backpacker's haven and this 20-year history of exchange has seen locals embracing this interaction. There are places organizing everything from balloon rides to climbing, and tai chi to cookery courses. Most hotels can arrange activities, but if you want a general agent who can help you put together an adventurous few days here, **Light Travels** at 3 Chengzhong Lu (☎ 0773-8811-939, www.ysholiday.com; daily 8 am-9 pm) provides a good and well-priced service, and the owner, Bill and his wife, Cathy are a good source of information. Another good general agency is run from **Buffalo Bar & Café** (☎ 13977330345) at 50 Xianqian Jie, where you'll find Aussie Alf and his team. He can arrange all the activities listed throughout the chapter and, as a foreigner who's been living here for a number years, can offer useful advice about the area and what's offered. Many of the companies operating the more specialist adventure sports are well-run and have high standards of safety, but if you're thinking of getting involved it's worth sticking with places recommended in this book, as there are a few cowboys out there. While cultural adventures are unlikely to be dangerous, for assured quality of service it's also worth heading to recommended operators.

Around Yangshuo

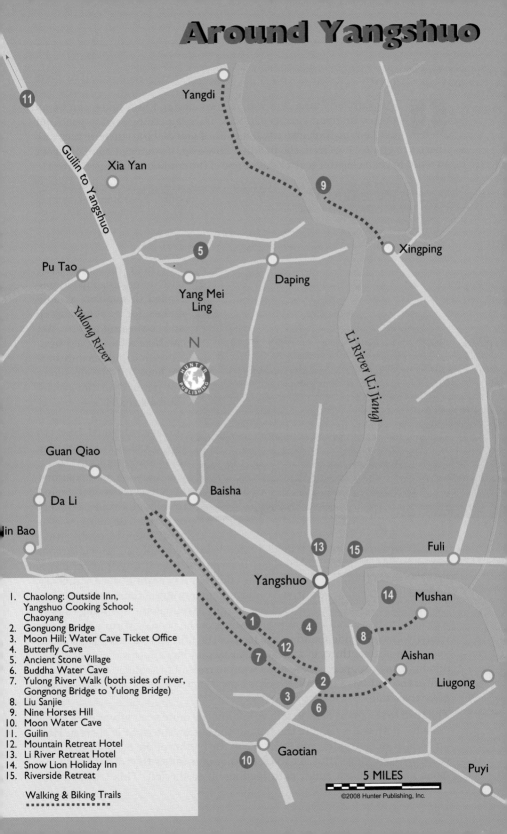

11 Guilin to Yangshuo

Yangdi

Xia Yan

9

Xingping

Pu Tao

5

Yang Mei
Ling

Daping

Yulong River

N

Li River (Li Jiang)

Guan Qiao

Da Li

Baisha

in Bao

13   15

Fuli

Yangshuo

14   Mushan

1. Chaolong: Outside Inn,
   Yangshuo Cooking School;
   Chaoyang
2. Gonguong Bridge
3. Moon Hill; Water Cave Ticket Office
4. Butterfly Cave
5. Ancient Stone Village
6. Buddha Water Cave
7. Yulong River Walk (both sides of river,
   Gongnong Bridge to Yulong Bridge)
8. Liu Sanjie
9. Nine Horses Hill
10. Moon Water Cave
11. Guilin
12. Mountain Retreat Hotel
13. Li River Retreat Hotel
14. Snow Lion Holiday Inn
15. Riverside Retreat

   Walking & Biking Trails

1

4

8

12

Aishan

Liugong

7

2

3

6

10   Gaotian

Puyi

5 MILES

©2008 Hunter Publishing, Inc.

On Foot

This part of China is a walking wonderland and hikes can be as relaxed or strenuous as you like. There's nothing to stop you from just heading out into the fields until you feel like turning back, as there are great views from the paddies. However, if you need more of a goal or want to get a sense of scale, hike up one of the ominous-looking outcrops.

Sunset Magic: If you want a bit of exercise without leaving Yangshuo, try climbing **Green Lotus Peak**, *in the heart of the town, just behind West Street. It only takes about 30 minutes to ascend and offers superb vistas over the town and surrounding area.*

★★ Moon Hill (90 min up and down)

Moon Hill

This huge limestone peak with a moon-shaped hole eroded through its middle makes for a short, steep and rewarding ascent. You can take a bus or taxi from Yangshuo, but it's only half an hour by bicycle along the main road (longer by the backroads, see *Adventures On Wheels*, p. 425). On arrival you'll have to buy a ticket (¥15) and, as on so many walks in China, you may be accompanied by a farmer/vendor trying to sell you drinks, trinkets or postcards. Unless you want them to lead you all the way to the top (which they will happily and helpfully do, providing you buy something), make it very clear that you don't want anything, or buy a drink at the bottom and save them the effort. Or if you want to see a bit more of rural life after your climb, you could accompany one of them to their home for a meal (around ¥20). The food is generally excellent and spending time at a local farm gives real insight into the lives of the people. **Mama Moon** is a friendly farmer guide found at the base of the hill who can arrange this for you – she is something of a local celebrity and has appeared on television and in the newspapers! If you don't want to trek off to a village there's also a café at the bottom of the hill, which is a good spot to enjoy a well-earned beer after the climb.

The trail to the top is easy to follow, but divides quite soon after you start to ascend – both trails head to the top but the one on the right is shorter. Half an hour to an hour later, you'll emerge at the bottom of the moon from where there are good views. But, for the full panorama, follow the trail through the moon and look for a small path leading off to the left. This track can be muddy and slippery and there are some steep drops, so don't attempt it if you don't have the energy or are worried by heights. That said, if you continue, 15 minutes later you'll find yourself in a Chinese poem, with the river often glimmering in the sunlight, meandering its way through the patchwork of paddies, all of it dwarfed by the limestone towers stretching as far as the eye can see in every direction. This little excursion ties in well with a swim or a snack at the Mountain Retreat (see *On Water*, p. 429, & *Where to Stay*, p. 437), a mile or so back toward Yangshuo, on a small track signposted from a bridge over the river.

★★Yangdi to Xingping (5-6 hrs)

This is a beautiful hike that takes in some of the Li River's finest karst scenery. The riverside trail is mostly flat, but it's a long hike and there are some beautiful spots along the way so it's worth taking a picnic with you to enjoy en-route. Although you'll find a few villages along the way, make sure you stock up with water, particularly in summer.

To begin the hike you'll need to take a local bus to **Yangdi**, which takes around an hour. At Yangdi you'll need to buy a Li River entrance ticket, which costs ¥16, and then take a boat across the river where the southward trail begins. You'll need to cross the river another couple of times on the route down, once at Wave Stone Hill and then again when you reach Nine Horses Hill a little before Xingping. The first two crossings are included in the ticket price but the last one costs ¥4. At **Xingping** you could stop for a drink or a snack at one of the cafés near the docks before taking another hour-long local bus back to Yangshuo.

On Wheels

In spite of the other-worldly tower karst peaks of the region, the area around Yangshuo actually offers quite flat terrain and a maze of cart tracks, which are ideal, if bumpy, for explorations by bicycle. As with walking, you can just head out into the fields and be prepared to get lost, but for guaranteed picture-postcard moments and closer cultural interaction, a **local guide** is a good idea. Such guides normally speak basic English, can help you to arrange bicycle rental and will be able to take you to Qing Dynasty villages, ancient bridges and to eat in farmer's houses, along with the more easily found caves and beauty spots. The real advantage of these guides lies in their ability to help you get away from it all. As soon as cycle route becomes established, postcard vendors and more tourists find their way there. Local guides are continually developing new "secret" routes to stay ahead of the pack and the contact you have with locals along the way will be more genuine and facilitated by translation. Such guides congregate at the junction of West Street and Pantao Lu and generally charge around ¥30 per person for a half-day excursion. For a cut above the average, ★**Rose Mo** (☎ 137-6871-7894; rosexiaomo@hotmail.com) is a qualified guide with excellent English who also runs a cooking school out at Gaotian village near Moon Hill. For a full-day trip Rose charges ¥100 for one or two people, or ¥50 per person for three or more.★**Jessie Lu** (☎ 138-0783-0981; jessilu714@

yahoo.com) is another great guide with excellent English who can help you arrange almost any kind of trip; she charges ¥50 per person and can be found at either Seventh Heaven or Buffalo Bar.

If you'd rather enjoy the scenery by yourself, there are a variety of reasonably easy trails to follow (see below), and if you choose to come in winter, you should have these all to yourself. **Bike Asia** is another good source of information on local routes and has the best rental bikes in town (see *Getting Around, By Bicycle*, p. 417, for rental options). You can also combine bike rides and bamboo rafting trips – see *Adventures On Water, Bamboo Rafts*, p. 429.

★★★ Moon Hill (2-hr circuit)

On the main road, the journey to Moon Hill is only 20 to 30 minutes by bike, and some people choose to take this easy option since the climb on foot is fairly strenuous in itself. However, the back route is far more rewarding and takes around an hour.

Out of Yangshuo

Turn left at the end of West Street onto **Pantao Lu** and continue up the hill, down the other side past a Y-intersection. After a few minutes you'll reach a large traffic circle. Turn left here and already you're leaving the hubbub behind. As the narrow road undulates, you'll pass rice paddies and duck ponds, wizened old men in Mao jackets and tractor rickshaws full of faces. After 15 minutes you'll cross a bridge and then, just before Aishan village, you'll see **a small road** leading off to your right along the river. Turn down this road and soon you'll come to a weir that you can walk down to. In the foreground you may see water buffalos wallowing on the water's edge, with phoenix tail bamboo giving way to the mighty oddities of the peaks themselves – it's no wonder this is the subject of many a postcard. Back on your bicycle, the track winds its way through the paddies, which are beautiful at any time of year, whether burned yellow by the summer sun or a waterlogged mirror image of the grand scenery in spring. Less than half an hour later, you should find yourself back on to the main road to Moon Hill and Gaotian. Turn left and after 10 minutes you'll see the entrance to Moon Hill on your right. See the description under *Adventures On Foot* for details of the climb itself (p. 424)

To get back, head left out of Moon Hill and follow the main road all the way back to the traffic circle where you first deviated from it on the way out. Yangshuo is straight over.

★★ Puyi (2-hr round-trip)

Follow the instructions for the Moon Hill bike ride out of Yangshuo as far as Aishan village, but don't turn off the road. Instead, continue along this slightly hilly road for another 45 minutes to the tiny market settlement of Puyi on the river and just out from the tower karst peaks. You'll see all manner of things for sale, from fruits and vegetables to dogs and cats (not the pet variety...) and traditional medicines. Market days here are those ending with 3, 6 and 9. A few years ago it was possible to take a boat here and back from Yangshuo, but the local government has put a stop to this, although inquiries by the river might yield a result if you're lucky.

★★★Fuli (3-4-hr circuit)

This charming old market town lies just seven miles south of Yangshuo on the Li River. As with Puyi, in the past you could take small boats down here from Yangshuo, but now, while you can take a boat here, you can't get off. Check with local agents to see if this has changed, but if not you have a choice of bus, taxi or cycling, the latter offering an exciting jaunt through the countryside. Market days here are those ending with 2, 5 and 8. You can cycle the following route in either direction, though it's preferable to take the main road there and the country tracks back, as you may have little energy left for the market itself if you do the reverse. Note that if it's been raining heavily over the past few days the tracks can become a muddy impasse and you're better taking a bus or taxi or cycling the road both ways.

Out of Yangshuo

Again, starting from West Street, turn left onto **Pantao Lu**, up the hill, down the other side and then immediately as the road levels bear left onto **Guanlian Lu** toward a huge bridge in the distance. Go over the bridge, which gives good views of Yangshuo, and continue along the road for around 30 minutes. While the scenery is still unquestionably beautiful, you'll have to pass through quite a long tunnel and avoid the large trucks and buses that ply the route (it's better to get this part of the ride over quickly – the treasure lies at the other end and on the return leg). Fuli is the second settlement of any size you'll see along the road and it extends from the road down to the river.

Guilin & Around

FULI MARKET

On market days you'll know you've arrived by the hordes of locals carting their wares to and from the market. The market is best visited in the morning, which sees most of the action before it gets too hot. It's divided into a covered section nearest the road and open-air stalls beyond. Not a place for the faint-hearted, Fuli market is the archetypal south Chinese market. Hot, busy and packed with people and produce of every conceivable variety, it can be disarming at first, so mentally prepare yourself, lock your bike and be on the lookout for pickpockets. Carry your valuables in front of you and keep your money in your front pockets. People are friendly and helpful, however, all the more so if you buy something from their stall! There's a huge variety of enormous and colorful fruits and vegetables, fly-infested meat, chicks, dogs, cats and snakes for the eating, along with electronics, clothes, local tobacco, the cheapest (and possibly the worst) haircuts you'll ever have, traditional healers using bamboo suction cups, fortune tellers, and hundreds of eager shoppers. The market still performs an important social function in such places – it's a gathering place and maybe the only occasion old friends see one another. This is evident in the crammed teahouses, canteens and open-air pool halls that skirt the market.

The Village

The cheapest haircuts in town – Fuli Market

Once you've seen enough of the market you can follow the track that runs from the open-air end of the market through tiny flagstoned alleys passing Qing Dynasty structures and temples, down to the river. As an antithesis to the bustle of the market, the **Three Sisters Café** makes a great place to unwind over a drink and some food before the strenuous, but stunning, journey back. There are also a few arts and crafts stores here where you can watch artists painting and traditional paper umbrellas being made.

Back to Yangshuo

From the café you need to maneuver your bicycle onto a **local ferry** across the river (this should be ¥2, but they'll try and charge you as much as ¥10) for the five-minute journey to the other side. Back on land ride up the hill away from the dock to a trail that leads through a village to the open country. At the end of the village cross over the basketball court and soon you'll join a wider track running along a raised embankment between the paddies. Follow this for a few miles until it abruptly stops and you're faced with a **choice of three smaller paths** – take the middle one up the hill. It soon widens. Bear right at a Y-junction and then right again at a T-junction, after which you'll enter a village where there's a small shop selling much-needed cold drinks. Just beyond the shop you'll meet the river – magnificently ensnared by the giant peaks. The grit track runs along the river for a little over a mile and then moves inland and into the villages. The track is pretty clear – **turn left at the only notable junctions**, one in the village and the other at the end of the settlement, which is easily identifiable by the large stone tablet facing you when you reach it. From here it's only 10 or 15 minutes until you'll arrive beneath the bridge you crossed on the way out. Turn right onto the main road and you'll be back in Yangshuo.

★ Climbing

In spite of the obvious opportunities this tower karst region presents for climbing, the sport has only been around a few years in Guangxi, and is now really taking off. There are literally thousands of potential first ascents just waiting, but if you're less of a superhero there are a few pegged routes to scale. Yangshuo has a couple of climbing walls to get a bit of practice in (try the one at China Climb), and then when you're ready there are a host of climbing outfits to help get you to the top of a real mountain. **Karst Café** (www.karstclimber.com) at 42 Xianqian Jie, is owned by Echo, a climber from Yunnan, who combines excellent local knowledge and expertise to offer safe and quality climbing trips. Expect to pay from ¥180-220 for a half-day guided climb and ¥300-400 for a full day. Prices include transfer, instruction and all equipment. Another recommended company is **China Climb** (☎ 0773-8811-033, www.chinaclimb.com). They specialize in tailor-made group trips and can arrange adventure packages, including transfers, accommodation and activities.

It's possible to climb year-round, although routes can be slippery during the rainy season. To meet fellow rock enthusiasts, head for one of the climbing cafés on and around Xianqian Jie – Karst Café, China Climb, Spiderman and Black Rock are popular hangouts.

★★Caving

Limestone is easily eroded and all this tower karst makes for a lot of caves to explore – almost every peak is thought to have one. **Butterfly Cave** (¥35) is an easy and accessible option which is actually two caves linked by a bridge, halfway along the road between Yangshuo and Moon Hill. For more adventure you could try one of Yangshuo's three water caves – ★★**Water Cave** (¥168/¥128 – full route/half-way), ★**Buddha Water Cave** (¥128) and ★**Moon Water Cave** (¥128), all of which are near Moon Hill. These caves offer an intimate (maybe claustrophobic) look inside a karst tower and are much more a voyage of discovery than the others. Inside you'll find **underground rivers, clear springs and mud pools to wallow in**, along with the usual passageways and stalagmites.

Trips around the caves are guided and include a torch and protective helmet and you should **wear clothes you don't mind ruining and pack a bathing suit** and a sense of adventure. The caves are best visited in summer when there's more water around and it's warm enough to swim and cake yourself in mud. You'll see the Buddha Water Cave signed off the road near Moon Hill and the Moon Water Cave and Water Cave have ticket offices here but you'll need to take a minibus (included in the ticket price) for a couple of miles along the road to reach the actual caves themselves.

On Water

Branching off from the Li River, waterways are an obvious way to see the area and there are a variety of ways to do so, from cormorant fishing crafts to bamboo rafts, kayaks and tourist boats.

All boat trips can be arranged in advance through the travel agents listed in the introduction to the *Adventures* section (p. 422).

★★★Boat Trips

Tourist boats offer a fantastic way to see and experience the area, allowing you sit back and watch the majestic peaks drift by. In addition to the famous Guilin to Yangshuo cruise (see *Guilin, Adventures On Water*, p. 411), there are a number of routes that operate around Yangshuo. One of the most sce-

Boat on the River Li (Galen Frysinger)

are a number of routes that operate around Yangshuo. One of the most scenic stretches is between **Xingping** (which President Clinton visited in 1998) and **Yangdi** (¥50). The return boat trip takes 1½ hours and passes through some of the most spectacular areas on the Li River. Another nice option is to take a boat from **Fuli** downriver to **Liougong** (¥150-200 for a 10-seater boat), a journey that takes two hours round-trip. Buses run to both Fuli and Xingping from Yangshuo bus station.

Another great way to travel on the river is by **fishing boat**. Although officially illegal, small local motor boats still take tourists out for early morning trips to Fuli and Xingping. Trips usually leave in the early morning to miss the water police, last about an hour for the one-way trip (you can take a bus back) and cost ¥50 to ¥150 per person, depending on the number of passengers.

★★★ Bamboo Rafts

A much more sedate view can be found by taking a ride on one of these slender craft along the Yulong River, a tributary of the Li River. There are various places where you can rent bamboo rafts for a short half-hour excursion (from ¥60) including the Mountain Retreat (see *Where to Stay*, p. 437). However the river can get busy at these spots and its far more tranquil to cycle out to the river at **Chaoyang** (30 mins), put your bicycle on the boat and then be punted for an hour and a half (¥150 for two people) down to **Gongnong Bridge** on the Moon Hill Road. From there it's a 20-minute cycle ride back to Yangshuo. As you slowly punt along the shallows, you have the leisure to really soak up the scenery and a feeling for rural Chinese life. You can stop for a swim if it's hot.

A cormorant fisherman (Ewen Bell)

★ Cormorant Fishing

While you can see this time-old method of fishing in many parts of China, it is particularly associated with the west and especially with **Guangxi**. The birds are excellent hunters and the fishermen use them to their advantage. Their necks are constricted so that they can't swallow any fish, and each time they make a catch they return to the boat where the fisherman collects the bounty. Why, you might ask, do the birds continue to serve their masters? Every seventh fish is given to the bird – just enough to keep them going. Cormorants are prized possessions and fishermen select the eggs before hatching and then nurture, rear and train them – a process that takes years. A successful fisherman may have up to a dozen birds working for him, which can provide a healthy income. Traditionally, the birds waited on the still bamboo raft and then darted in for the kill, but since the advent of motorboats, a new method where the cormorants swim ahead of the moving boat, catch their prey and then return to their perch, has emerged. In days gone by the fishermen were clad in reed rainproof clothing, but these days the only place you'll see this is at tourist-oriented cormorant fishing shows.

Around Yangshuo the majority of organized tourist trips are indeed just that and, while they show you how the process works, these fishermen make the bulk of their money from tourism, not fishing. A typical trip costs ¥30, leaves at sundown and lasts an hour. Take plenty of insect repellent! If you want to see something more authentic, contact **Light Travels** (see p. 422) – trips cost ¥150 for a boatload of five; be aware that while the fishermen respect and care for their birds, their handling of them can seem a little rough.

★★ Kayaking & Inner-tubing

For more of an adventure on the river, you can arrange kayaking trips through a number of agents in town. While there's no whitewater, seeing the landscape from your own vessel is an exhilarating way to experience the area. Trips typically last three or four hours and cost ¥150, including equipment and transfers to and from the river. The routes are generally easy, traveling downstream, though during the rainy season the currents are stronger.

Inner-tubing is another option, although it has been **officially banned because of the danger posed by strong currents**. You can rent inner tubes from some places in town and then just walk north up the river and hop in, but be sure to **check the river conditions** before you do so – the best time is after 3 pm, when all the cruise boats have left.

★★★ Swimming

If it's all too hot, then a swim could be in order and there are some beautiful spots to do this. One of the best of these is the **Mountain Retreat** (see *Where to Stay*, p. 437), a couple of miles off the Yangshuo to Moon Hill road, where you can enjoy a meal or a drink after a dip in the river, as well as bamboo rafting. Bathing in the clear, calm waters, protected from the flow of the river, and surrounded by a forest of peaks, including Moon Hill, is truly one version of paradise. If you don't want to trek out into the countryside, there are also spots closer to Yangshuo – just walk north along the river, past the market and you'll see a path leading down to the water. On most days, the water here is crystal clear, but the current can be strong so follow the locals' example – if they are swimming, it should be OK, but take care.

★★ In the Air

If you have a head for heights, then taking a **hot air balloon** is one of the best ways to see this magical and mystical landscape. It makes you realize that the peaks just keep going on and on and on. There are two companies operating balloon flights from Yangshuo. **1 Flying Balloon Club** (☎ 0773-8828-444, www.xaballoon. com) is a highly professional outfit and charges ¥1,200 for a 45-minute flight over the area, or ¥120 for a tethered flight up to 330 feet. The **Guilin Flying Hot Air Balloon Club** (☎ 0135-9703-9600, www.chinahotair-balloon.com) is the other option; while their flights (¥600 for 30 minutes) are much cheaper the landings can be a little bumpy. Flights are dependent on weather conditions so it's best to wait until you arrive before you make your booking.

Cultural Adventures

Yangshuo was China's first real backpackers' haven, and this has resulted in the availability of a disproportionate range of cultural pursuits for such a small town. From Chinese cooking to calligraphy, painting, pottery and kung fu, it's all here. All the below options can be booked through hotels, cafés and travel agents around town or directly from the businesses themselves

★Calligraphy & Painting

The dramatic limestone scenery of this area has been attracting painters to Guangxi for a long time. Some of the Chinese scroll paintings you might see around the country, and indeed, the world, were inspired by these hills, the swirling mists adding depth and mystery to the landscapes. Traditional scroll paintings are a very stylized art form, but contemporary painters are also attracted to the area, so you can choose the technique you want to learn. To try your hand at either discipline, seek out **Forest**, an eccentric painter/calligrapher who likes to be known as Yangshuo's Picasso and sells his wares from 5 pm on the corner of West Street and Xianqian Jie, just outside Café China. Forest can also teach those who wish to study calligraphy, the artistic portrayal of Chinese characters. Half-day lessons for either calligraphy or painting cost ¥50 per person, including materials.

★★★Chinese Cooking

If you want to learn more about the delicious dishes you enjoy on your trip, Yangshuo has several good cooking schools. Classes are hands-on, with each student getting their own ingredients, stove and utensils. After you've cooked your dish, you'll then get to eat it and can ask the master chefs where you went wrong! Of the schools, **Yangshuo Cooking School** (☎ 1378-8437-286, www.yangshuo cookingschool.com) is the most professional and is run by an Australian lady, Pam, although the instructors are all local. The school is located in a converted farmhouse a few miles out of Yangshuo at Chaolong and the classes, which also include shopping for your ingredients at the local market, start at 9:30 am and 3:30 pm. Classes cost ¥100 per person (including transfer) and must be booked by 6 pm the day before. Another great cooking school is run by the owners of Cloud 9 and Seventh Heaven (see *Where to Eat*, p. 439, for both), William and Linda. Linda (☎ 135-0783-8851; cloud9restaurant03@yahoo.com) is an excellent cook and has even appeared on TV with famed Hong Kong chef Martin Yan. Their classes are equally good. The school is located above **Cloud 9 Restaurant**. Classes start at 9:30 am and 4 pm daily, costing ¥80 for three hours, including a shopping trip to the local market. A recent addition to the cooking school scene is **Sunlight Farmhouse**, out by Moon Hill, which is operated by Rose

Guilin & Around

Mo (☎ 137-6871-7894; rosexiaomo@hotmail. com). Classes here cost ¥80, including being driven to and from the school, and you could even ascend Moon Hill after the lesson if you want to burn off some of the calories you just acquired.

Will yours look as tempting as this? (Tot Foster)

★ Fengshui

If you want to learn a little about the art of geomancy, **William** (☎ 135-1763-9591) from Seventh Heaven (see *Where to Eat*, p. 439) runs guided tours of local villages where you can see traditional fengshui in practice. Tours cost ¥200 regardless of the number of people in your group.

Language

As one of the first places many people visit on a trip to China, Yangshuo makes a good place to pick up a bit of the lingo, though don't expect miracles overnight. While far from impossible, Chinese is nonetheless a tough language to learn (see *Language* p. 598, for more). There are a number of small "schools" providing everything from private classes to full-blown courses. Of these, the most professional is **Omeida** on Pantao Lu (☎ 0773-8827-705, www.omeida.com.cn). They run a variety of courses, of which the four-hour "50 most popular Chinese sentences," costing ¥160, is of most use to short-term visitors. If you're interested in staying for longer, Omeida also runs exchange programs, as long as you're prepared to commit to at least eight weeks. These programs allow you to study Chinese (and other traditional Chinese pursuits) for two-four hours a day in return for teaching English for a similar period time. Include are accommodation, lunch and dinner. Fees start from US$420 for four weeks, up to nearly US$3,000 for 40 weeks.

Teaching English

Teaching English is an option that will allow you to replenish your travel funds a little and maybe pick up some Chinese as well. Most schools around town welcome help, whether you just attend an evening English session in exchange for a free pizza, or spend a few weeks teaching for a (minimal) salary along with a free room, meals and maybe a bicycle. It's technically illegal for foreigners on a tourist visa to teach for money, but it's commonplace – watch for notices in cafés.

Volunteer English Teachers (☎ 0773-8811-420) is a local organization that runs unpaid placement programs. They post you out to local village schools where you'll teach English to kids who would otherwise have no opportunity to learn the language. VET is run by a Canadian couple, Laurie and Betts, who are happy to receive any kind of help, whether that means just an hour of your time, a month or a financial donation.

Martial Arts

Yangshuo has a number of martial arts schools teaching both kung fu and tai chi. Of these, the most renowned is **Long Tou Shan** (☎ 0773-8812-329, www.longtoutaichi.com), a little out of town near the Li River Retreat (see *Where to Stay*, p. 436), which offers Chen and Yang style tai chi, fan and sword work and *qigong* (an aspect of traditional Chinese medicine involving the coordination of different breathing patterns with various physical postures). Classes are taught by English-speaking qualified national instructors, including Lou Mei Juan who studied under Chen Zheng Lei, one of China's most highly regarded tai chi practitioners. Lessons can be taught in Yangshuo for ¥50 an hour, but for courses it's better to stay at their retreat as exercises begin early and include five to six hours of practice per day. Residential courses are available from ¥1,100 per week, which includes accommodation and three vegetarian meals a day.

Another good school is the **Lijiang School of Culture and Art** on Diecui Lu (☎ 0773-6912-121, www.lijiangschool.com), which is run by the affable master, Henry Huang, who speaks fluent English and also offers instruction in calligraphy, mah jong and painting. Henry teaches a number of kung fu styles including shaolin longquan and tai chi.

Wushu in the park with Henry Huang (Tot Foster)

Classes are taught in Yangshuo Park and down by the river, or indoors if it's too hot. They cost from ¥50 an hour for tai chi and ¥80 an hour for kung fu.

Where to Stay

Yangshuo's accommodation scene has really picked up in the past decade and the number of hotel beds in the town has increased from 3,000 to 20,000 to deal with the increasing number of visitors. On summer weekends hotels can fill up quickly and during the three week-long national holidays, all places double or triple their rates. But outside of these times you'll have a great selection of options. As Yangshuo has grown into a tourist resort, staying on West Street is no longer the quiet option it once was. You'll find quieter and often cheaper rooms a short walk away on sidestreets. But if you want real rural seclusion it's worth opting for one of the many countryside hotels, none of which is more than half an hour away from Yangshuo by bicycle. If everywhere seems to be full, note that some of the cafés such as Buffalo and Seventh Heaven also have good rooms upstairs. You can book many of the hotels listed below through www.yangers.com.

What's it mean? FC=fitness center; SW=swimming pool; @=in-room Internet access; DA=rooms for disabled. For ¥ price codes, see page 113.

In Yangshuo

Karst Hotel, 66 Guihua Lu (☎ 0773-8814-370, www.karstclimber.com). Owned by Echo of the Karst Café and located in the heart of town, this budget hotel has simple but attractively decorated rooms and a good, cheap dormitory (¥20-35 per person). @ ¥

★★**Magnolia**, 7 Diecui Lu (☎ 0773-8819-288). This boutique hotel offers a stylish environment and good rooms. The larger suites have garden rooftop verandas. All rooms are decked out with paintings by local artists and have wireless Internet. There is also the excellent **Green Lotus** vegetarian restaurant downstairs (see *Where to Eat*, p. 439). @ ¥¥-¥¥¥

Lounge at Magnolia

Marco Polo, 85 West Street (☎ 0773-8827-544). The Marco Polo has spacious, attractively furnished rooms with balconies looking over West Street and the peaks, although rooms can get very noisy on weekends. ¥¥

★**Paradesa Resort**, West Street (☎ 0773-882-2109, www.paradiseyangshuo.com). At the junction with Pantao Lu this is still Yangshuo's premier place to stay and is popular with tour groups. The resort is set in spacious gardens, including a small lake complete with a cormorant fisherman! The rooms are pleasant and comfortable, and there's a swimming pool, climbing wall and a gym. FC/SW/@ ¥¥¥

★**White Lion**, 103 West Street (☎ 0773-8827-778). Near the junction with Chengzhong Lu, this characterful hotel has a cozy wooden interior, a friendly staff, and offers comfortable doubles, some triples and a laundry service. Excellent value. ¥-¥¥

Out of Town

★★**Li River Retreat**, north along the Li River (☎ 139-7733-1334, www.li-river-retreat.com). Owned by Alf and Ming Fang, who also own Buffalo Bar & Café, the Li River Retreat offers the best of both worlds. It is only a 20-minute walk out from Yangshuo, but enjoys a glorious setting amidst a pomelo orchard looking out over the limestone peaks. The bright and airy rooms make the most of the views and there's a large terrace. For transport to the hotel (¥20) head to the Buffalo Bar. ¥¥

★★★**Mountain Retreat**, near Moon Hill (☎ 0773-8777-091, www.yangshuomountainretreat.com). To really feel like you're in the midst of the karst scenery, this is the place, set on the river's edge and engulfed by the forest of pinnacles. They have attractive, simple rooms with jaw-dropping

Patio at Li River Retreat

views, a restaurant serving both Chinese and Western fare and welcoming staff. In addition to swimming, you can also go bamboo rafting, rent bicycles, arrange climbing trips and Chinese cooking classes and there's wireless Internet throughout. To get out to the retreat call in advance and they will arrange someone to pick you up from Yangshuo. If you want to make your own way here by bike, it's signposted off to the right from a bridge a mile before Moon Hill, then it's two miles along a bumpy track – the ride takes half an hour from Yangshuo. @ ¥¥

Mountain Retreat

★**Outside Inn**, Chaolong Village (0773-8817-109; herbertchina@hotmail.com). The Outside Inn is a charming converted farmhouse in Chaolong village. Rooms are simple but attractively furnished and there's a pleasant patio where you can enjoy meals. Call for a transfer (¥30). ¥

★**Riverside Retreat** (☎ 0773-882-6879, www.blog.163.com/rivershelly). The original Riverside Retreat was just off the Moon Hill road and was Yangshuo's first countryside hotel. It closed down a few years ago. The local owner, Shelly, has now established this new place, just over the river from Yangshuo, in the same vein, but with far better rooms than the original and wireless Internet throughout. The ground floor rooms are perfectly comfortable but don't have views, while the higher floors command excellent views and correspondingly higher prices. There is a lovely suite on the third floor which is definitely worth splashing out on and the fourth floor has family rooms. Call Shelly for a pick-up from Yangshuo. ¥-¥¥

★**Snow Lion Holiday Inn**, Mushan Village (☎ 135-1763-9591). This is another new countryside retreat with a lovely location amid the pomelo trees a little way back from the river near Mushan village, a 20-minute bike ride out of Yangshuo. The rooms are large and spacious and enjoy pleasant pastoral views. You can wander around the traditional Qing dynasty houses in Mushan from the hotel and can also ascend the peak that gives the hotel its name. From there you can get a sneaky peek at the Liu Sanjie Cultural Show. ¥¥

Where to Eat

This small town now has so many bars, cafés and restaurants that you could spend several weeks here and never eat in the same one twice. While there's plenty of Chinese cuisine to be enjoyed, after months of rice, noodles and dumplings many backpackers choose to indulge their Western palates and now there's even a KFC, although their burgers pale in comparison to some of the tasty versions found at the better cafés! Cafés come and go quickly, but there are some longstanding places in the listings below. Some cafés (such as Seventh Heaven) will serve local specialties such as snake, if requested, and all stay open as late as people keep eating and drinking. Many also have DVD players where you can select your own movies.

See page 117 for an explanation of the ¥ restaurant price codes.

If you'd rather stick with Chinese food in China, you'll find plenty of local places on Diecui Lu, New West Street and Pantao Lu. There are also a number of local **food stalls** that set up early in the evening by the lake on Chengzhong Lu and offer cheap and tasty snacks until the small hours. For a local **breakfast** of rice noodles, *baozi* and *congee* (rice porridge), you'll find a few places just off Diecui Lu, by the junction with Rongyin Lu. If you're feeling the need for some fresh fruit, there are plenty of vendors who wander up and down West Street, trying to drum up business with the now infamous cry of "Hello Banana." There's also an excellent juice bar opposite Buffalo Bar.

★★**Buffalo**, 50 Xianqian Jie (☎ 0773-8813-644, www.guilin-yangshuo.com/WBG; daily 8 am-late). Buffalo is a friendly place run by an Australian, Alf and his Chinese wife, Ming Fang. It serves delicious Aussie meat pies, burgers, sandwiches, steaks and Chinese dishes. As a former tour operator, Alf knows plenty about the area and is a great source of local information. There's also wireless Internet connection, a pool table and a computer with scanner and CD burner so you can save your digital pictures. Buffalo is a popular evening drinking spot and also has **four comfortable rooms** if you need a place to stay. ¥¥

★★★**Café China**, 34 West Street; (daily 8 am-late). Toward the river end of West Street, Café China offers some of the best Chinese food in town. Along with the excellent Chinese dishes such as clay-pot duck and roast goose, Café China also serves good Western food, including tasty cheesecake, and rounds it all off with quality coffee. The restaurant also has wireless Internet connection and during the daytime the roof-top terrace is open, which provides fantastic views of the peaks. The proprietor, Malcolm, also owns Magnolia Hotel, Green Lotus Vegetarian Restaurant (see below) and another eatery down the river in the charming rural village of Liougong. If you want to visit the latter, which serves an excellent spread of traditional dishes, speak to Malcolm and he can arrange a boat down there (¥50 per person for food and ¥150-200 for the 10-seater boat). ¥¥

★★**Cloud 9**, 1F, 1 Chengzhong Lu (☎ 0773-8813-686; daily 9 am-11 pm). Cloud 9 offers excellent Chinese food, which you can enjoy on its balcony overlooking West Street. Both local and Szechuan food are served and are equally good. Try the *yuan-yuang huoguo* (hotpot divided into two sections – spicy and vegetable broth), or one of the specialty medicinal dishes. The owner, Linda, also runs a cooking school above the restaurant (see *Cultural Adventures*, p. 433). ¥¥

Fish Hotpot, on the corner of Guihua and Chengzhong Lu (daily 9 am-midnight). For a different take on hotpot this place offers delicious thin strips of fish which you dip into the boiling pot for a few seconds before eating. ¥¥

Green Lotus Vegetarian Restaurant, Diecui Lu (daily 11 am-2:30 pm & 5-9 pm). This elegant restaurant serves 100% vegetarian, 100% delicious dishes such as steamed stuffed bamboo mushrooms. ¥¥

★★**Karst**, 42 Xianqian Jie (daily 7:30 am-late). Karst is a cozy climber's café on Xianqian Jie, serving the best pizzas in town, along with excellent hoagies (grilled beef, green pepper and cheese baguettes). Karst is owned by Echo, who also runs good climbing trips to the surrounding peaks (see *Climbing*, p. 429). ¥¥

MC Blues, 40 Xianqian Jie (daily 7 am-2 am). Opposite Karst Café, MC Blues is run by a local guy, Mickey, and has some of the best burgers in town, although other dishes and service can be more hit and miss. Mickey's is a popular place for an evening drink. ¥¥

★★**Seventh Heaven**, 2 Chengzhong Lu (daily 7 am-2 am). Seventh Heaven used to be one of the mainstays of West Street but has moved out to quieter Chengzhong Lu where it enjoys a prime position next to the lake, with plenty of outdoor seating and wireless Internet connection. The café serves up tasty Chinese and Western fare, including falafels, and can also prepare local specialties such as snake. Seventh Heaven has **good rooms** upstairs if you need somewhere to stay and is run by the same couple, William and Linda, who own Cloud 9 and the Snowlion Holiday Inn. William can also arrange tours of the region, including trips that focus on *fengshui* (see *Cultural Adventures*, p. 433). ¥¥

★**Yipingju Dumplings**, Xianqian Jie (daily 7 am-midnight). This tiny dumpling joint offers a delicious array of inexpensive *jiaozi* and noodles, perfect for a snack. ¥

Nightlife

As Yangshuo has become more focused on its Chinese weekend visitors, the nightlife has also taken a turn this way and West Street now has several clubs, complete with blaring tunes, neon lighting and plenty of dancing. So if you want a quieter drink you're better off heading to one of the side-streets such as Xianqian Jie, Guihua Lu or Chengzhong Lu. Most of the places listed in the *Where to Eat* section above also serve as bars in the evenings and **Buffalo**, **Karst** and **MC Blues** are popular spots, as is **Bar 98** on Guihua Lu, which also has a pool table, wireless Internet and decent food.

Longji (The Dragon's Back)

Pretty villages engulfed by rice terraces in Longji (Light Travels)

A couple of hours north of Guilin, **Longsheng** marks the start of the hilltribe region that stretches west across Guizhou to Yunnan. This is an area inhabited by **Dong, Yao** and **Zhuang** peoples and their villages are stunningly picturesque, especially when compared with the bland concrete modernism of China's cities. While the most accessible villages such as **Ping'an, Longji** and **Dazai** bear the signs of tourism, a few hours hiking into the valleys beyond will find you in dwellings unchanged since time immemorial. It can be hard work, but the views are a spellbinding fusion of man and nature, the already stunning hills contoured by slivers of rice terrace with simple wooden villages sitting comfortably here and there. More than anywhere else, these hills bring into focus how every strip of land is used to feed the people of this most populous of nations.

Winter Woolies: *Many of the villages in this region are over 3000 feet up in the mountains, and without central heating, it can feel decidedly cold here in the evenings, so remember to bring some warm clothes if you come in fall, winter or spring.*

Transport & Arrival

Longsheng used to be the a necessary transport hub on the way to the villages, but since the region has developed as a tourist destination there are now direct buses from Guilin and Yangshuo to Ping'an. Tourist buses depart from both towns and cost ¥150 for the round-trip day-trip from Yangshuo and ¥180 from Guilin. If you want to stay overnight you need to tell the agent when you book. To cut costs you can take a two-hour bus ride from Guilin to Longsheng (¥17), where you can store any unwanted luggage and then a bus (¥7, every two hours) or minibus for the last half-hour or so (¥40 for the whole minibus). You'll need to **buy a ticket (¥70** – make sure they actually give you the ticket) a little before the turn-off for Ping'an and may have to change to a mini-van (¥5) for the short ride up

Old terraces etch the scenery around Longsheng

the hill – this should be included if you're on a tourist bus or tour. If you need a taxi to take you anywhere while you're staying in Ping'an, this can be arranged through the Liqing guesthouses.

Orientation

Once the bus has dropped you below Ping'an it's all on foot, although you can rent a sedan chair (¥50), or someone to carry your bags (¥10) for the short walk over the Wind and Rain Bridge and uphill to the village. **Wind and Rain bridges** are traditional Dong and Zhuang structures, named for the respite their roofs provide from the elements; they also serve as a meeting place for villagers. Once over the bridge, continue up and to the right and soon you'll arrive in the charming Zhuang settlement of Ping'an, set high on the valleyside. Though comparatively new to tourism, almost every one of its attractive wooden dwellings seems to be a café or guesthouse, but there are still chilies and corn drying on their rooftops, with pigs and chickens running along the steep, narrow alleys below. Although there are countless small alleys, Ping'an only has one main thoroughfare and you'll find the bulk of places to eat, stay and shop here. A few miles along the valleyside, Longji is another pretty village, while over the crest of the hill, Zhongliu is halfway to Dazai – see *Adventures On Foot*, p. 442.

Information Sources

The place where you stay is likely to be your best source of information once you're here – Yibeng and Keying of the Liqing family (see *Adventures On Foot*, below, and *Where to Stay & Eat*, p. 444, for details) are helpful and can act as guides into the surrounding hills.

Communications

Telephone code: 0773.

WWW **Internet Access**: There are computers with Internet access at the Ping'an Guesthouse halfway up the village.

Bank of China: There are **no** money changing facilities in Ping'an so make sure you bring enough cash with you, but in an emergency you could head to the Bank of China in Longsheng.

Medical Services: If you need to see a doctor, the nearest facilities are in Longsheng, but you're better off heading back to Guilin.

Shopping

The local population is intent on selling their **handicrafts**, which can be something of an annoyance if you don't want to buy. Items include dubious quality jewelry, better embroidery, reed sandals and chilies. For **everyday needs** there are a few shops stocking basic provisions and snacks but, if you have any special requirements, you'd better bring them with you.

The Yao are reknowned for their weaving and embroidery (Light Travels)

Adventures on Foot

These hills offer steep but very rewarding hikes between the villages, which are connected by surprisingly good footpaths up to the tops of ridges and down to the bottoms of valleys, up to the tops of ridges, and down to the bottoms of valleys... and so on. It makes for strenuous hiking, but the views and villages more than compensate. However, if you've got limited time or energy, there are a few short walks in the terraces above Ping'an.

Local Walks

The one- to two-hour circuit up to ★★★**Dragon's Backbone** provides spectacular scenery, cultural interest and in itself justifies the journey from Guilin. You may well end up being guided by Yao women, keen to sell you silver and show you their incredibly long hair, of course, at a price – ¥5 to be precise! Dragon's Backbone (which is the Chinese name for the area around Ping'an, *longji*) and the **Moon and Seven Stars** are names derived from the way the terraces look from above and, for once, you don't have to use your imagination too much. They're incredible in any season, but spring sees the waterlogged terraces sparkle silver, highlighting the result of hundreds of years of human toil. For a less strenuous, equally short hike, walk along the valleyside to the pretty village of Longji, where you can enjoy a meal at a local farmer's house.

Yao women at home on the steep slopes of Longji (Ewen Bell)

Hikes

If you want to get farther into the area, it's probably better to go on a tour or hire a guide in Ping'an. Although the paths are easy under foot, there are a bewildering array of them. A guide can arrange somewhere to stay in more remote villages and help bring you closer to the environment you're passing through. One of the first villagers to take tourists hiking through the area was Liqing, and his son-in-laws have now taken over the family businesses, charging around ¥150 per day. There are endless possibilities in the hills around here, but some good options include the hike up to the Yao village of Zhongliu and then down to Dazai (which is linked by a rough road) – this takes around four hours. There are a few places to stay in Dazai (around ¥50) or you could continue down to Ban Nui and on to Si Shui, from where there are buses to Longsheng. You can buy water and supplies in Zhongliu and Dazhai, but you should make sure to carry enough water as it can get very hot in summer.

Where to Stay & Eat

 There are plenty of decent, but basic guesthouses in Ping'an. Prices (around ¥50) and standards vary little although some enjoy better views than others. They all have basic twin rooms and serve cheap, delicious local fare – you may see your dinner running around outside only a short while before it is served to your table! The roasted bamboo tubes of rice (*kao zhutongfan*) are definitely worth a try. In recent times some of the guesthouses have also started offering Western food as well and the pizzas aren't bad. If you arrive with a group tour, your accommodation is usually pre-arranged. If not, the **Liqing Guesthouses**, run by Liqing's son-in-laws, Yibeng (☎ 138-7835-2092; ¥50 per room) and Keying (☎ 135-1763-0321; ¥50 – non a/c or ¥80 with a/c) are a good bet. They are both toward the upper end of the village. These two guesthouses also offer massage (¥50) and a cultural show of sorts, which costs ¥200-250 – ask around to see if anyone's interested in splitting the cost.

The Pearl River Delta

he economic heart of South China, the Pearl River Delta is both agriculturally and financially fertile and is one of the most developed parts of China. Intensely cultivated land is interspersed with some of China's newest and fastest-growing cities, which are linked by some of the country's best and most integrated transport services. The Delta's location makes it a popular trip from Hong Kong and a **major gateway to enter China** itself. Foremost among the Delta's gang of youthful upstart cities is **Shenzhen**, which was the first of China's Special Economic Zones (SEZs) and has grown from nothing to challenge the traditional heart of the region, **Guangzhou**, in less than 30 years. While Shenzhen has little in the way of historic sights, it offers shopping, skyscrapers and theme parks along with some insight as to what China's future looks like. Seventy miles to the north, Guangzhou has a longer history, but is also reaping the economic whirlwind. It's definitely worth a quick stop for its blend of Cantonese cuisine, markets, colonial relics and the gritty taste of a real Chinese city.

Guangzhou

With a population of seven million and long known in the West as **Canton**, modern Guangzhou provides many visitors with their first glimpse of a mainland Chinese city. Frenetically busy, polluted and steamily hot in summer, Guangzhou's conventional sights are comparatively sparse, but the city is **renowned worldwide for its cooking** and is worth visiting on these grounds alone. Before Hong Kong rose to prominence, Guangzhou was one of China's primary trading posts and as a result it has a wide ethnic diversity, including a large Hui (Muslim) population, and a smattering of colonial architecture, much of which is found on charming **Shamian Island**. Guangzhou is at the heart of the south's economic revolution. Although it is still undoubtedly a polluted city, attention is being paid to the environment, albeit often only in the most aesthetic sense. Every time I visit I notice new areas of greenery and the city is becoming more and more visitor-friendly. There is an ever-expanding subway network, a new airport and improved links with other Pearl River Delta destinations. There are also a host of sights to visit within a two-hour transport radius of Guangzhou and the city makes a good base from which to explore smaller towns such as Huizhou and Zhaoqing.

Pearl River Delta

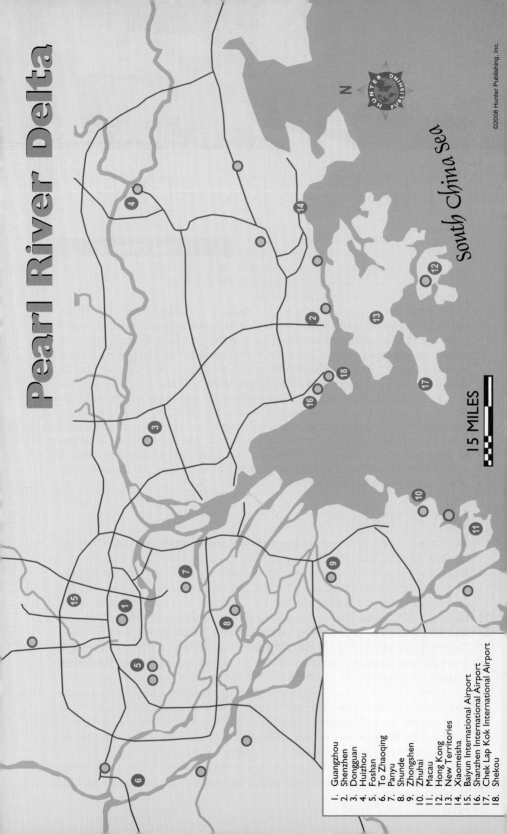

N

South China Sea

15 MILES

1. Guangzhou
2. Shenzhen
3. Dongguan
4. Huizhou
5. Foshan
6. To Zhaoqing
7. Panyu
8. Shunde
9. Zhongshen
10. Zhuhai
11. Macau
12. Hong Kong
13. New Territories
14. Xiaomeisha
15. Baiyun International Airport
16. Shenzhen International Airport
17. Chek Lap Kok International Airport
18. Shekou

Guangzhou

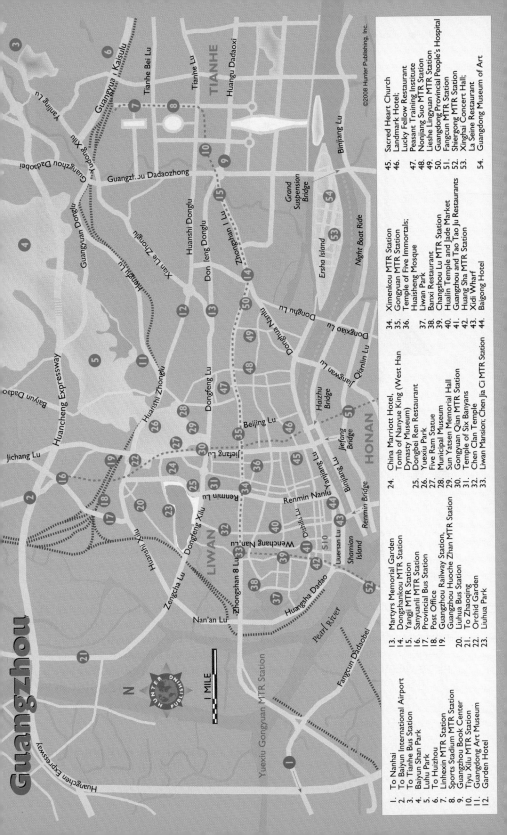

©2008 Hunter Publishing, Inc.

1. To Nanhai
2. To Baiyun International Airport
3. To Tianhe Bus Station
4. Baiyun Shan Park
5. Luhu Park
6. To Huizhou
7. Linhexin MTR Station
8. Sports Stadium MTR Station
9. Guangzhou Book Center
10. Tiyu Xilu MTR Station
11. Guangdong Art Museum
12. Garden Hotel

13. Martyrs Memorial Garden
14. Dongshankou MTR Station
15. Yangji MTR Station
16. Sanyuanli MTR Station
17. Provincial Bus Station
18. Post Office
19. Guangzhou Railway Station;
    Guangzhou Huoche Zhan MTR Station
20. Liuhua Bus Station
21. To Zhaoqing
22. Orchid Garden
23. Liuhua Park

24. China Marriott Hotel,
    Tomb of Nanyue King (West Han
    Dynasty Museum)
25. Dongbei Ren Restaurant
26. Yuexiu Park
27. Five Ram Statue
28. Municipal Museum
29. Sun Yatsen Memorial Hall
30. Gongyuan Qian MTR Station
31. Temple of Six Banyans
32. Chen Clan Temple
33. Liwan Mansion; Chen Jia Ci MTR Station

34. Ximenkou MTR Station
35. Gongyuan MTR Station
36. Temple of Five Immortals;
    Huaisheng Mosque
37. Liwan Park
38. Banxi Restaurant
39. Changshou Lu MTR Station
40. Hualin Temple and Jade Market
41. Guangzhou and Tao Tao Ju Restaurants
42. Huang Sha MTR Station
43. Xidi Wharf
44. Baigong Hotel

45. Sacred Heart Church
46. Landmark Hotel;
47. Peasant Training Institute
48. Nonjiang Suo MTR Station
49. Lieshe Lingyuan MTR Station
50. Guangdong Provincial People's Hospital
51. Fangcun MTR Station
52. Shiergong MTR Station
53. Xinghai Concert Hall;
    La Seine Restaurant
54. Guangdong Museum of Art

Tai chi by the Pearl River (Lonnie Hodge)

History

Goat City

Legend has it that Guangzhou was founded by the Five Immortals who arrived riding rams and planted rice to ensure ongoing prosperity, a story that gives Guangzhou its nickname – **Yangcheng** (Goat City). In the third century BC Guangzhou served as capital of the **Nanyue Kingdom**, which was founded by a rebel Qin commander. The city soon utilized its position in the far south of the country as a trading post and, by the Tang dynasty (618-907 AD, see p. 9), ships were leaving for ports as far away as the Middle East. In the Ming dynasty Guangzhou became China's only officially sanctioned international trading port and it prospered as a result. However, British frustration with Chinese reluctance to trade for goods (rather than precious metals) led to the introduction of opium from India and the resulting addiction and demand soon depleted the imperial coffers. The highly principled commissioner, **Lin Zexu**, was sent to remedy the situation, which he did by blockading the British concession and destroying their opium. The result of this was the **First Opium War** (see p. 16) that eventually led to China opening five treaty ports to the British in 1842, one of which was Guangzhou.

Revolutionary Center

A long way from the historic capitals in central and northern China, Guangzhou has often served as the focus of anti-imperial movements. **Sun Yatsen** spent time here and attempted a coup at the start of the 20th century. When the nationalists finally ascended to power, Sun chose Guangzhou as their **capital**. During the failed Communist-nationalist alliance of the mid-1920s **Mao Zedong** taught at the **Peasant Training Institute** here, which helped to convince him that China's revolution must be born in the fields. In 1927, the same year as the Communists were massacred in Shanghai, a Communist coup failed in Guangzhou. During the war the city fell first into the hands of the Japanese and, after they were defeated, the nationalists controlled Guangzhou, until it was "liberated" in 1949.

Factory of the World

Since economic reforms Guangzhou and the whole Pearl River Delta, untethered by the regulations of the north, have been at the heart of south China's financial revolution. Factories use cheap labor, which swarms in from the rural provinces. Guangzhou, Shenzhen SEZ and a host of other industrial towns like Dongguan in the Delta region now produce most of the goods that are shipped from an ever more tertiary services-oriented Hong Kong. Guangzhou is currently embroiled in a battle for economic supremacy with its upstart neighbor Shenzhen. All the while it revels in its wealth with exotic feasts of the freshest foods known to man.

Getting Here & Away

By Air

Guangzhou is linked to almost every city in China with an airport, along with a growing number of Asian and international destinations. The new **international airport**, 12 miles north of the city at Baiyun, is designed to rival Hong Kong's and has a capacity of 25 million passengers per year, a figure which is set to rise to 80 million with the completion of its third runway in 2010. The principal regional carrier is China Southern and their main 24-hour offices are on the eastern side of Guangzhou Train Station (☎ 020-950-333, www.cs-air.com/en). There are shuttle buses from the China Southern offices to Baiyun International Airport (¥16) or a taxi should cost around ¥100 from downtown. You can buy flight tickets through travel agents in most hotels and at the airport. Look in *that's PRD* or see the websites listed on p. 83 for airline offices in Guangzhou.

Destinations, frequencies & durations

Beijing (23 daily, 2 hrs 45 mins); **Chongqing** (11 daily, 2 hrs); **Guilin** (10 daily, 1 hr); **Hangzhou** (16 daily, 1 hr 45 mins); **Hong Kong** (7 daily, 45 mins); **Huangshan** (2 daily, 2 hrs 30 mins); **Shanghai** (23 daily, 2 hrs 25 mins); **Xi'an** (8 daily, 2 hrs 45 mins); **Yichang** (2 daily, 1 hr 40 mins).

By Rail

Guangzhou has two train stations, the vast and recently renovated **Guangzhou Train Station** in the north of town which serves most mainland destinations, and out in the east, modern **Guangzhou**

East Train Station, which operates trains to Shenzhen, Hong Kong and increasingly more central and eastern cities, including Shanghai. Note that trains leaving Guangzhou can book up quickly, particularly hard sleeper class and it's worth reserving your ticket as soon as you can. Queues at the main station can be monumental so it's worth paying the extra fee (usually around ¥30-50) to get an agent to book for you. All of the hotels listed have train-booking facilities.

Guangzhou Train Station

To buy your own ticket you'll need to head to the eastern part of the station (on the right as you look at the station) where you can ask which windows serve your destination and then settle in for some serious queuing. Departures are from both floors of the western part of the station – look at the board on the entrance to determine your waiting room.

Guangzhou East Train Station

Buying a ticket to Hong Kong from Guangzhou East's second floor is fairly straightforward and doesn't take long. Or you can book online (www.throughtrain.kcrc.com). Trains to Hong Kong depart from the second floor, while Shenzhen services leave from the ground floor opposite their designated ticket office and departures to other areas are on the third and fourth floors.

Guangzhou Train Station is served by subway line #2 and Guangzhou East is the terminus for lines #1 and #3. Both stations have major city bus depots (for routes see *Getting Around, By Bus*, p. 452). A taxi to Shamian should cost around ¥18 from Guangzhou Train Station or ¥35-40 from Guangzhou East.

Services to areas covered in this book

Beijing (5 daily, 22-23 hrs); **Chongqing** (5 daily, 30-38 hrs); **Guilin** (2 daily, 13-14 hrs); **Hangzhou** (3 daily, 23-25 hrs); **Hong Kong** (14 daily, 1 hr 30 min-2 hrs); **Huangshan** (1 daily, 20-21 hrs); **Shanghai** (4 daily, 23-51 hrs); **Shenzhen** (71 daily, 1-2 hrs); **Suzhou** (1 daily; 29 hrs); **Xi'an** (2 daily, 26-28 hrs); **Yichang** (3 daily, 17-22 hrs).

By Road

Guangdong is well-served by bus and for shorter hops that can be the quickest way to go, particularly if you pay a little extra for an express service. Two of the principal bus stations are just west of the main train station on Huanshi Xi Lu. The modern **Provincial Bus Station** on the northern side of the road serves day-trip destinations like Huizhou and Zhaoqing, plus cities as far afield as Shanghai. Go to the second floor and ask which window serves your destination at the information desk. Queues are seldom long and services are plentiful. Departures are from the ground floor.

Just over the road, **Liuhua Bus Station** serves local destinations and is comprised of a collection of depots with its ticket office at the eastern end.

For some longer journeys you'll need to head for **Tianhe Bus Station**, four miles east of town in the new city. You can buy tickets for buses leaving from Tianhe in advance at the Provincial Station and there is a free shuttle bus (30 minutes) for which you must have your ticket stamped.

Provincial Bus Station

Guilin (5 daily, 10 hrs); **Huizhou** (frequent, 2 hrs 30 mins); **Shenzhen** (frequent, 3 hrs), **Zhaoqing** (frequent, 1 hr 30 mins).

In addition to the stations, **China Travel Service** runs buses from several of the upmarket hotels to **Shenzhen** (2 hrs, ¥70), **Hong Kong** (4 hrs, ¥100), **Hong Kong Airport** (4 hrs, ¥250) and **Macau** (3 hrs 30 min, ¥70). There are several different routes that pick up and drop off from the China Hotel, the Landmark, and a few go from the White Swan on Shamian Island. You can buy tickets from any of these hotels or call ☎ 020-8337-2626 for the latest schedules and fares.

By River

Guangzhou is also linked to Hong Kong by **fast ferry** along the Pearl River from Panyu, 15 miles to the south, and Nanhai, 25 miles south of the city. **CKS** boats to China-Hong Kong City Terminal run twice daily and take 2½ hours (¥190), although the 40-minute drive to either dock from central Guangzhou makes the train a quicker option.

Getting Around

Despite its size, population and increasing vehicle ownership, Guangzhou is a fairly straightforward city to get around. There has been much investment in public transport infrastructure of late and the **subway subway system** makes for easy access to many of the city's key attractions.

By Subway (www.gzmtr.com)

Guangzhou's modern subway system now has four lines. Lines #1 and #2, which intersect at Gongyuan Qian, are of most use to visitors. Line #1 runs from Guangzhou East Train Station to Xilang in the west, while line #2 extends from Sanyuanli in the north past Guangzhou Train Station to Wanshengwei in the southeast. The system is still expanding and, having reached

Panyu in the south, it will eventually extend north all the way to the new international airport at Baiyun. The above-ground symbol for stations looks like a Y, which has been vertically divided in two and is usually yellow on a red background. Tickets cost ¥2-8, depending on the length of your journey and can be bought from the easy-to-use machines, which accept small bills and coins. Tickets come in the form of small plastic disks which you scan at the entry gates and deposit on exit. There are line maps on the trains, but stations are poorly marked from the carriages so listen for the stops being announced in English. Both train stations have subway stops.

Pearl River Delta

By Bus

Guangzhou has an extensive and cheap bus network, although destinations are only marked in Chinese, so knowing the bus number you need is of key importance. Tickets are bought on the bus and cost ¥1-2. The main bus depots are just outside the two train stations. From Guangzhou Train Station bus #103 runs to Liuersan Lu for Shamian Island, bus #30 heads east to Huanshi Dong Lu and #271 goes to Guangzhou East Station. Bus #209 runs from Guangzhou East Train Station to Liuersan Lu.

By Taxi

Guangzhou's metallic green taxis are abundant. Minimum charge is ¥7 for the first two km (1.2 miles) and ¥2.2/2.6 (non ac/ac) for every km (0.6 miles) after that. Most taxi drivers don't speak much English so it's essential to take along your destination written in Chinese.

By Bicycle

Guangzhou isn't a good city to negotiate by bike although there are cycles and tandems for rent on Binjiang Lu – see *Adventures On Wheels*, p. 466.

LEARNING THE LINGO

Starting on page 598, there's a language section with useful phrases written in Chinese characters, should verbal communication fail! Chinese vocabulary specific to the **Pearl River Delta** begins on page 626.

Orientation

Guangzhou is divided by the **Pearl River**, China's third-most significant watercourse, and is bordered to the north by the **Baiyun** (White Cloud) hills, which offer a refreshing escape from the seething streets. The city's historic heart lies in central **Yuexiu** and western **Liwan** districts, although its modern business center is now found in eastern **Tianhe** and is gradually creeping east from there, the only direction in which there is free land to develop. South of the river and west, Honan, once home to brothels and opium dens, these days has a few parks and markets and a thriving underground art scene, but little else of interest for visitors.

As for accommodation, eating and day-to-day services, you can find almost everything you need on tiny **Shamian Island** (see *Sightseeing*, p. 455), which lies in the west of the city just off the north bank of the Pearl River. The bulk of tourist sights are within a 20-minute taxi ride of Shamian, but for nightlife you might want to head along the river to Yanjiang Lu, or northeast to Huanshi Dong Lu. Larger **Ersha Island**, east of Shamian, holds the Guangdong Museum of Art, Xinghai Concert Hall and its peaceful environment has attracted a large expat community.

Information Sources

 Guangzhou's excellent webzine, www.thatsgz.com, offers useful listings and reviews for bars, clubs restaurants and cultural events. The printed version is called *that's PRD* and is available from bars and hotels, along with *City Weekend*'s *Guangzhou and Shenzhen Guide*. For news in English, seek out the *Guangzhou Morning Post*.

Events & Festivals

 Guangzhou hosts all the usual annual events on the Chinese festival calendar. If you're here in May, the **dragon boat races** along the Pearl River are worth watching, while the **trade fairs in April and October** are worth avoiding unless you're attending them. Guangzhou Trade Fair is the biggest in China and attracted over 170,000 visitors in October 2005! The whole city is twice as busy and hotel rates rise markedly during these times (check www.thatsgz.com for exact dates).

A dragon boat before the festival (Fanghong)

Communications

 Post Office: On the western edge of the Guangzhou Train Station and a smaller branch on Shamian 3 Jie.

Telephone code: 020

Internet Access: Blenz Coffee at 46 Shamian Dajie offers free Internet to customers. Over by Renmin Nan Lu there's a small Internet café on Xihao Er Ma Lu.

Money

Bank of China: Shamian Island branch next to the White Swan Hotel.

Western Union: Next to the post office at Guangzhou Train Station, with another branch in Shamian Post office.

Consulates

Australia, Room 1509 15F Main Tower, Guangdong International Hotel, 339 Huanshi Dong Lu (☎ 020-8335-0909).

Canada, Room 801, Wing C, China Hotel, Liuhua Lu (☎ 020-8666-0569, ext. 0).

UK, 2F Main Tower, Guangdong International Hotel, 339 Huanshi Dong Lu (☎ 020-8314-3000, www.uk.cn/gz)
US, 1 Shamian Nan Lu, Shamian Island (☎ 020-8121-8000, www. usembassy-china.org.cn/guangzhou).

Medical & Safety

Public Security Bureau: 89 Huanghua Road (☎ 020-8311-9147).
Medical Services: Guangdong Provincial People's Hospital on Zhongshan Er Lu (☎ 020-8382-7812) or Changjiang Global Doctor Medical (☎ 020-3884-1452, www.globalifeline.com; consultations cost ¥550).

Sightseeing

While not as overrun with major monuments as some Chinese cities, Guangzhou has sights ranging from **traditional Chinese temples** to **colonial churches, lively markets** such as **Qingping** and the **Jade Market** (see *Shopping*, p. 461) and contemporary art displays. Sightseeing in Guangzhou has been made much easier with the advent of the subway system – closest stations are listed where convenient. However, if you've only got limited time, then a **city tour** could help you to get the most out of the city. Most hotels have travel desks and can arrange tours – be sure to check that guiding is in English, how many people will be in the group, how long you'll have at the sights, and if there are any hidden costs.

Colonial buildings line the leafy streets of Shamian (Tot Foster)

Through history Guangzhou's distance from the northern capitals has seen it operate variously as a breakaway kingdom and more recently as a revolutionary center. While hardly laden down with historic sights, this turbulent past has left Guangzhou with a few monuments worth seeking out.

GETTING THE MOST OUT OF GUANGZHOU

Many people spend less than 24 hours passing through Guangzhou. If you have limited time but still want to get some Canton city flavor, the first thing to do is try some dim sum – Banxi, Guangzhou and Tao Tao Ju restaurants are all winners. Once you've sated your culinary needs, head for the fascinating and sometimes alarming **Qingping Market**, which is wonderfully offset by the quaint colonial charm of **Shamian Island** across the road. Other sights to seek out are the **Tomb of the Nanyue King** and the atmospheric **Temple of Six Banyans**. Finally a **Pearl River cruise** should round your trip off nicely.

★★★ Shamian Island

(Huang Sha subway)

This quaint green island, ceded to the British under the 1842 Treaty of Nanjing, is an architectural testament to bygone days. When the British and French set up here they built grand villas, churches and embassies, planting trees that have now become giant banyans overhanging the streets. There were gates barring entry to Chinese just as foreigners had been denied access to Guangzhou. Discontent with foreign influence led to a protest demanding the return of Shamian, which resulted in 50 people being shot by colonial troops on June 23, 1925, giving **Liuersan (6/2/3) Lu** its name. Although Shamian lies just a few yards of muddy water from the flyovers of Liuersan Lu, it manages to completely separate itself from the dynamism of downtown, and everything moves a little slower.

The island is only half a mile long and half as wide. Traffic is restricted and the main thoroughfare, **Shamian Dajie**, is pedestrianized, which makes Shamian a great place to explore on foot. Five numbered smaller streets run south from Shamian Bei Jie, bisecting Shamian Dajie and continuing to Shamian Nan Jie, where you'll find the dominating White Swan Hotel. If you're staying on the island (see p. 467 for accommodation options) chances are you'll come across most of its sights, which are detailed in *Adventures On Foot, Shamian Stroll*, p. 464. However, there are a few targets you could try and aim for, foremost of which are the **Anglican and Catholic churches**, set at opposite ends of the island. Both can be visited during services.

Strolling around Shamian you'll be confronted by two recent phenomena – the sight of American moms and dads with their newly adopted Chinese babies (see *Adoption* callout in the *Travel & Living* section, p. 108) and an abundance of bronze statues commemorating Shamian's colonial past as well as its cosmopolitan present. Although there are so many statues that you struggle not to trip over them, some give particular insight into China's changing social world. Opposite **Shamian Park** you'll see a statue that traces the development of women in China – from the traditionally dressed,

Pearl River Delta

The statue on Shamian Island represents a changing China (Tot Foster)

shorter and repressed woman of yesteryear, to the scantily clad, taller and confident Chinese woman of today.

Peasant Training Institute

Zhongshan Lu (Tues-Sun; ¥5; Nongjiang Suo subway)

During the failed Communist-nationalist alliance of the mid-1920s, both Mao Zedong and Zhou Enlai taught at the newly established Peasant Training Institute, housed in a former Confucian academy. The institute aimed to educate and thus liberate and empower the rural masses. Mao's time here helped to formulate his views on Socialist revolution, based on rural rather than urban support. Although the buildings remain attractive, there is little to see here, except for a few photos of Communist martyrs who were executed in the 1927 Shanghai massacre. However, the site still manages to draw scores of domestic tourists, principally for its connection with the late, Great Helmsman.

Sun Yatsen Memorial Hall

Dongfeng Zhong Lu (daily 8 am-6 pm; ¥5; Jiniantang subway)

On the northern side of Dongfeng Zhong Lu you'll see the grand, cylindrical Sun Yatsen Memorial Hall, constructed in 1931 on the spot where Sun took the presidential oath in 1912. The hall is set in parkland just south of Yuexiu Park and its blue-tile roof covers an auditorium that can seat thousands.

★★ Tomb of the Nanyue King

Jiefang Bei Lu (daily 9 am-5:30 pm, last admission 4:45 pm; ¥12 and another ¥5 to enter the tomb itself; Yuexiu Park subway)

Located on Jiefang Bei Lu, the tomb of Zhao Mo, discovered in 1983, dates back to the Han dynasty (see p. 8) and is Guangzhou's premier historic sight. Zhao Mo was the second ruler of the Yue, a breakaway southern kingdom,

The Tomb of the Nanyue King

and he was buried in grand fashion, complete with an entourage of concubines and slaves. There are over 500 artifacts on display, including the burial suit itself, which is made up of countless tiny jade tiles. The entire exhibit is well-presented and organized and there is an English language video.

Temples, Mosques & Churches

With its international history, Guangzhou has places of worship for many denominations, but if you only have limited time, Six Banyans and Hualin temples are the ones to search out.

★ Chen Clan Temple

Yin Long Li (daily 8:30 am-5 pm; ¥10; Chen Jia Ci subway)

Set in the west of the city, this temple was founded in the late 19th century with money collected from families with the surname Chen (a common Cantonese family name). It was designed as both a place of ancestor worship and an educational center for future generations of Chens and managed to escape the ravages of the Cultural Revolution. The temple holds a series of colorful and ornately decorated courtyards with fine stonework and carved screens.

Huaisheng Mosque

Guangta Lu (no entry to non-Muslims; Gongyuan Qian subway)

Huaisheng Mosque reflects Guangzhou's long trading history with the Arabic world and is the spiritual home of Guangzhou's Hui people. Although access is restricted to Muslims, you can get a peek at Guangta, allegedly China's oldest minaret, built by Abu Waqas in the seventh century. This area was known as Fanfang, or the foreigners' enclave during the Ming dynasty and it remains a Muslim part of town with some good *halal* restaurants and *niurou mian* (beef noodle) canteens.

Huaisheng Mosque

★ Hualin Temple

Hualin Xin Jie (daily 8 am-5 pm; free; Changshou Lu subway)

Hualin Temple was founded by the Indian monk Bodhidharma (see *Buddhism*, p. 46, and *Martial Arts*, p. 65) in 526 AD, although the version you can see today dates from after the Cultural Revolution. The 500 life-size *arhats* that line the walls were added in the 17th century. Hualin is one of Guangzhou's most vibrant and lively temples, especially if you visit during a festival.

Temple of the Five Immortals

Huifu Xilu (daily 9 am-noon & 1:30-5 pm; ¥5; Gongyuan Qian subway)

Dedicated to the mythical five characters who supposedly founded Guangzhou, this temple was first built in 1377, although it has recently had a major overhaul. Of most interest is the lofty bell tower, which contains a clapper-less five ton bell; if you hear this bell ringing, head for the hills as it's supposed to mean impending disaster!

★★ Temple of the Six Banyans

Liu Rong Lu (daily 8 am-5 pm; ¥1 entry, ¥10 to climb the tower; Gongyuan Qian subway)

Just off Jiefang Bei Lu and set amidst a crop of religious stalls and shops, this is one of Guangzhou's most celebrated and active temples. It was named in the 11th century by the poet Su Dongpo (see *Culture, Poetry*, p. 61) for its six banyans (*liu rong*), all of which have subsequently died. There is also a Guanyin Temple within the grounds, but these days, Liu Rong Temple is more famous for the towering Flower Pagoda (Hua Ta) which stands beside it. Although it appears as if there are only nine stories from the outside, there are actually 17 levels to this 187-foot tower. The stairway is cramped and the upper floors were **closed at the time of writing**, so check before paying the extra ¥9 to ascend the tower, but if you can get all the way to the top you'll be rewarded with good views.

The Flower Pagoda

Parks

Guangzhou has a league of large parks which can make for the perfect retreat from the heat and smog of the city. If you just want to take a quick break from the stress of the street, then western Liwan and central Liuhua or Yuexiu parks are close at hand, while the Orchid Garden is more of a treat. For greater escapes and a bit of hiking, Baiyun Shan, north of the city, is the place to go.

★★ Orchid Garden

Jiefang Bei Lu (Mon-Fri 8 am-6 pm, Sat, Sun 8 am-7 pm; ¥8 or ¥20 with tea in the central pavilion; Guangzhou Huochezhezhan & Yuexiu Gongyuan subway)

Nestled just off busy Jiefang Bei Lu, the Orchid Garden is a bastion of tranquility with a wonderful collection of orchids, lilies and palms dissected by meandering stone paths. Next door you can peek at the Islamic cemetery, which isn't open to non-Muslims but holds the tomb of Abu Waqas who established the Huaisheng Mosque (see p. 457).

Yuexiu Park

Jiefang Bei Lu (daily 6 am-9 pm; ¥5; Yuexiu Gongyuan subway)

A little east of Liuhua Park, Yuexiu Park covers some 220 acres and has everything from pavilions and pagodas to statues and a museum. Most of all, Yuexiu is a place to get away from the crowds, although domestic tourists flock to the **Five Rams Statue** in the south, which commemorates the city's mythical foundation. A little more worthwhile is the **Municipal Museum** (daily 9 am-5 pm; ¥5), which traces Guangzhou's history from the Stone Age and is housed in a surviving part of the Ming city walls in the center of the park.

The Five Rams Statue

Baiyun Shan Park

9 miles north of city center (daily 8 am-6 pm; ¥5; buses #11 & #24)

The White Cloud Mountains barely qualify for their title given their maximum height of only 1,250 feet, but their 12 square miles offer some respite from Guangzhou's polluted and steamy streets and are close enough to visit comfortably in a day-trip. The bus drops you near **Yuntai Gardens** where there's a cable car (¥25) to the **Cheng Precipice** (aka White Cloud Evening View), halfway up the hill from where there are great views if the weather is clear. Or you could hike up to the Cheng Precipice in a couple of hours. There are a range of other attractions here, including **Mingchun Valley Aviary** (daily 8 am-6 pm; ¥10) and the restored **Nengren Temple** (same hours; ¥5), which gives some idea of what the forested hills were like in the past when their slopes were scattered with monasteries and temples.

From the Cheng Precipice it's another hour or so up to the top at **Moxing Ling** (Star Touching Summit). It's a hot hike in summer so make sure you drink enough water on your way up, although there are teahouses and rest-stops dotted along the trails, so there's no need to carry much in the way of supplies. You can return by cable car or, if your legs are up to it, take the path back down.

Pearl River Delta

Little Guilin & Little Hangzhou

If you're in Guangzhou and don't have time for trips farther into the mainland, you can get a sense of the wonders that await your return by taking day trips to Zhaoqing and Huizhou, both served by bus from the Provincial Bus Station. Zhaoqing lies an hour and a half to the west of Guangzhou by bus and offers a picturesque collection of karst peaks set around a lake which have been compared to the landscapes of Guangxi. A couple of hours to the east of Guangzhou, Huizhou is an attractive lake town which has coined the nickname Little Hangzhou for its likeness to China's honeymoon capital (see p. 361).

Lake in Zhaoqing (Berthold D)

Galleries, Shows & Theaters

Guangzhou's cultural scene isn't much to write home about but the city is home to Cantonese Opera, while the arts have benefited from the recent addition of two art museums.

Art

★**Guangdong Museum of Art**, Yanyu Lu, Er Sha Island (www.gdmoa. org; Tues-Sun 9 am-5 pm; ¥15; bus #131 from Yanjiang Lu). The GDMOA was established in 1997 and is housed in a modern building on upmarket Ersha Island, near the Xinghai Concert Hall (see *Music*). The museum holds one of China's largest contemporary art collections and also has worthwhile temporary exhibits from China and overseas – check the website for schedules.

★★**Guangzhou Art Museum**, Luhu Lu (daily 9 am-5 pm; ¥30; bus #10 from Renmin Square). Out in the north of the city by Luhu Lake, this museum was only opened in 2000 but is already a big success. The museum's fusion of traditional and modern design is also reflected in its exhibits, which range from Cantonese calligraphy and painting to contemporary sculptures.

Music

Cantonese Opera can be enjoyed at the ★**Jiangnan Theater** on Jiangnan Nan Lu (☎ 020-8436-0044; ¥30-40). Other refined options include classical music at the modern ★**Xinghai Concert Hall** (☎ 020- 8735-2222) on Ersha Island. It regularly hosts national and international orchestras. A trip here can be combined with a trip to the Museum of Art next door, or dinner at La Seine (see *Where to Eat*, p. 470).

For Families

★★**Chime Long Night Zoo**, out in Panyu (15 miles south of Guangzhou), is reputedly the first night zoo in the world. Chime Long offers the opportunity to see wildlife from around the globe on evening safaris! There are also rollercoasters, cafés and a luxurious hotel (☎ 020-8478-6838, www. chimelonghotel.com; FC/SW ¥¥¥¥ including two night safari tickets). The parks make for another good family trip, particularly **Baiyun Shan** (see p. 459), as does a **river trip** (see *Adventures On Water*, p. 466). If you have an infant child you'll find plenty of facilities, such as stroller rental and cafés (like Lucy's) with babyfood on Shamian Island. They have developed to serve the needs of overseas couples adopting Chinese babies.

Health & Relaxation

The ★**Shamian Traditional Chinese Medicine Center** on Shamian Bei Jie claims "we cure your pain and care about your spondyle" – whatever that may be! They offer everything from consultation (¥10) and prescription to ear-cleaning, foot massage (¥48-88 dependent on duration) and ginger wraps (¥12)! The doctor is available from 8 am to noon but all other treatments can be enjoyed from 11 am-2 am. Some English is spoken.

Shopping

Many of the goods you buy back home are made within 100 miles of Guangzhou and this is reflected in the range of products offered here. Guangzhou is a great place to shop, with giant malls, plus exciting markets, new and old, which can make the shopping as much about sightseeing as spending.

Markets

Nowhere is the diversity of products available more evident than at the **Haizhu Wholesale Market**, where you can find anything and everything. The market is northwest of the Haizhu Bridge and just south of Yide Lu (Haizhu Guangchang subway). The Cantonese love of ultra-fresh food and medicinal herbs is also very much a part of shopping in Guangzhou's markets as a trip to Qingping will demonstrate, while the Jade Market is equally bustling but less gruesome.

★★**Qingping Market**, Liuersan Lu (Huang Sha subway). Just a few years ago this was one of China's goriest markets, where you'd see everything you could imagine and more – from dogs and dried seahorses to scorpions and snakes! The market opened in 1979 and flourished under economic reforms, but in the 1990s it became renowned for the availability of endangered animal parts and the government instituted a crackdown. This has seen many of the stalls, which were spread out over a network of streets, moved into one central building on Liuersan Lu, which pri-

Picking scorpions at Qingping Market (Tot Foster)

marily sells dried goods and herbs. But, while not as stomach-churning as it once was, in the streets around the building you'll still see scorpions being carefully picked out of plastic bowls using chopsticks, live eels being sliced in two, and bags of frogs, snakes and turtles. On the footbridge leading from Qingping to Shamian you'll also see tiger parts for sale, and, whether genuine of otherwise, interest is alarmingly keen.

The Jade Market (Tot Foster)

★★**Jade Market**, off Changshou Lu (Changshou Lu subway). Less than a mile north of Qingping, the Jade Market's entrance is signed in English from Changshou Xi Lu. If you want guaranteed quality it's easier to buy from an officially sanctioned shop, but the market is definitely worth a visit just to admire the pieces on display and perhaps pick up a few small gifts. North again from the Jade Market brings you to the small "antiques" market on Dai He Lu where you can pick up replica Qing pieces for low prices.

Shopping Streets & Malls

A stroll along crowded ★**Shang Xia Jiu** (Changshou Lu subway) should manage to fill your shopping bags. If not, **Beijing Lu** (Haizhu Guangchang or Gongyuan Qian subway) in the center of town is another bastion of modern consumerism. Increasingly, Guangzhou's shopping is shifting into air-conditioned malls and in the heat of the summer these make for a more appealing option. The gleaming **China Plaza** next to Lieshe Lingyuan metro station in the east of town gives a window into China's future

Facing page: Advertising on the busy shopping streets of Guangzhou (Tot Foster)

Shamian Souvenirs

Shamian Island is bursting with souvenir stalls selling items from all over the country and, while the quality is sometimes suspect and the prices are a little high, it's convenient and if you bargain hard you won't do too badly. If you want a tea break with a difference, head to **Taoran Tea House** at 58 Shamian Dajie (daily 9:30 am-11 pm). Housed in a historic building, this charming teahouse offers a full Chinese tea ceremony in the hope that you'll be so encap-

Bamboo and wicker stall, Guangzhou (Tot Foster)

sulated by the flavors and ritual that you'll buy some. They also serve desserts made from green tea. The teahouse is packed with antiques, porcelains, calligraphy and tea-drinking apparatus, much of which is for sale.

Everyday Needs

Everyday needs can be met at the **7-Elevens** and other 24-hour convenience stores found around the city. If you're staying longer or cooking for yourself, it's worth visiting the French supermarket chain, **Carrefour**, although most of their outlets are on the edge of town. The closest branches are in the Everbright City Plaza at 656 Kangwang Zhong Lu (Chen Jia Ci subway) or on the second floor of Wanguo Plaza at 40 Qianjin Lu in southeast Guangzhou. The Victory Hotel also operates a small **imported goods** store on Shamian 4 Jie.

Adventures

Guangzhou isn't brimming with adventures but the older western part of the city has some good walks, while boat rides on the Pearl River beckon.

On Foot

★★★ Shamian Stroll (45 mins)

Shamian is a great place for a stroll and, given its miniscule size, it's difficult to do more than just that. The best way to see Shamian is on a lackadaisical amble along its streets taking in the colonial splendor of its buildings and stopping for the odd drink or snack in one of its many eateries.

Start at the **White Swan Hotel** (take a taxi or line #1 to Huang Sha subway and walk for 15 minutes, or bus #103 from the center of town) with maybe a quick coffee or snack at The Deli Shop. Proceed west along Shamian Nan Jie, stopping to take in the **Anglican Christ Church** on your right side. Continue on, past the **American Consulate** on your left and follow the road as it loops around the edge of the island to become Shamian Bei Jie. You'll

Shamian garden (Cabincam)

pass the Shamian Traditional Chinese Medicine Center (see *Health & Relaxation*, p. 461) on your right. After that, take the second street on your right, Shamian 4 Jie. After passing the Victory Hotel's Annexe, you'll soon arrive at the central boulevard of Shamian Dajie, where you turn left. Immediately on your left you'll see Blenz Coffee (see *Where to Eat*, p. 469), which offers a good latte in a historic building. Alternatively, if you want some Eastern refreshment, head west back along Shamian Dajie to the Taoran Teahouse (see *Shamian Souvenirs*, p. 464). Continue past countless bronze statues to the **French catholic chapel** at the eastern end of Shamian Dajie. Turn right at the end of the road which bends round the eastern tip of the island to become Shamian Nan Jie. Turn left at the tennis courts and then right a few yards later when you hit the river and you'll see two cannons that were forged in nearby Foshan and used against "imperial invaders," although they were only moved to Shamian in 1963. Soon after the cannons you reach **Shamian Park** with its lazy riverside feel, full of card games and tai chi practitioners. Leaving the park onto Shamian Nan Jie, if you turn left, you'll arrive back at the White Swan. If you want to continue onto the Western Wander detailed below, head north up Shamian 3 Jie straight across the island, over the canal and then up and down the footbridge to Qingping Market.

★★Western Wander (45 min one-way or 90 min round-trip)

This wander through western Guangzhou takes in aspects of the city's past as well as its neon-clad future. Starting from **Qingping market** (see *Shopping*, p. 462), have a meander through the main buildings and surrounding streets, gradually working your way north until you meet **Dishifu Lu** (around 10 minutes walk with no photo stops). You could take a meal at one of this bustling district's fine eateries, such as Guangzhou or Tao Tao Ju

Pearl River Delta

(for both see *Where to Eat*, below), before continuing north up Wenchang Nan Lu to **Hualin Temple** (see *Sightseeing*, p. 457) on Hualin Xin Jie on the right-hand side. Just east of the temple, the **Jade Market** (see *Shopping*, p. 462) occupies a number of streets between **Changshou Lu** and Xiajiu Lu and is definitely worth a browse. Unless you want to nose around Dai He Lu's *faux* antiques market, turn west onto Changshou Lu, one of Guangzhou's busiest shopping streets. Walk to Changshou Lu subway station at the end of the street and either take line #1 or a taxi home, unless you're staying on Shamian and are up for the walk back.

On Wheels

Although Guangzhou's hectic traffic is enough to discourage most visitors from getting around by bike, you can rent bicycles (¥5 per hour or ¥10 for tandems) on riverside Binjiang Zhong Lu, just east of the Haizhu Bridge. The road here isn't too busy and you could have a relatively panic-free hour's ride. For a real ride you're better off heading out of the city – check www.groups.msn.com/GZCycle for information on routes and organized weekend rides.

On Water

★★River Cruises, Yanjiang Lu

A Pearl River cruise (Lonnie Hodge)

You can take a cruise along the Pearl River's murky course, which somehow springs to life in the evenings as the water catches the lights of the city. Most cruises depart from **Xidi Wharf** on Yanjiang Xi Lu. Ninety-minute cruises leave in the evenings from 7 pm and cost ¥33 for the lower deck and ¥48 for the upper. The **Lan Hai Tun Yacht Corporation** (☎ 020-8101-1806), farther east at 406 Yanjiang Dong Lu, runs more upmarket cruises, which include dinner (¥68-98) from 6:30 pm onwards and also has luxurious crafts available for private rental. Routes for all crafts generally go up to Shamian and then head back, under Renmin and Haizhu Bridges to the **Grand Suspension Bridge** at the far end of **Ersha Island**.

Where to Stay

Guangzhou has a good selection of hotels in both its new eastern and old western districts. Shamian's peaceful atmosphere, colonial buildings and good hotels make it the obvious choice for many visitors, but, if you want to pay a little less, there are also a few options around nearby Renimin Lu. If you've come on business, then hotels in the east along Huanshi Dong Lu may be more convenient for you. Note that hotels can be full to bursting during the two annual trade fairs in April and October and you should book as far in advance as possible. During winter it's possible to get discounts of 25-50%. Nearest subway stations are listed where appropriate.

What's it mean? FC=fitness center; SW=swimming pool; @=in-room Internet access; DA=rooms for disabled. For ¥ price codes, see page 113.

Shamian Island

For a short visit, Shamian Island certainly makes a great place to stay. In spite of growing tourist numbers and its location near the traditional heart of the city, the island manages to maintain an air of tranquility. There are hotel options to suit most budgets and plenty of restaurants and amenities, including laundry, close at hand. All the hotels listed below can be reached by a 10- to 15-minute walk from Huang Sha subway station on line #1 or bus #103 from Guangzhou Train Station or #271 from Guangzhou East.

★**Guangzhou Youth Hostel**, 2, Shamian 4 Jie (☎ 020-8121-8606). This well-located budget hotel has nothing to do with Hostelling International, but offers a few dorm beds (¥50) nonetheless. There are also more comfortable double and twin rooms, some of which enjoy good river views. Staff aren't always as helpful as they might be but this is Shamian's best budget option and it's usually full of backpackers. @ ¥¥

Shamian Hotel, 52 Shamian South Street (☎ 020-8121-8359, www.gdshamianhotel.com). Opposite the White Swan and just round the corner from the Guangzhou Youth Hostel, this place is something of a halfway house between the two with comfortable, spacious doubles, some of which enjoy good views of the river and cheaper, but much smaller standard rooms. ¥¥

★★**Victory Hotel**, 53 Shamian Bei Jie & Shamian 4 Jie (☎ 020- 8121-6688, www.vhotel.com). An old favorite, this charming historic building has

Victory Hotel

a range of rooms in its two buildings and makes for a very relaxed stay on Shamian Island. It also has a recommended dim sum restaurant and an imported food store. FC/SW/@ ¥¥¥

★White Swan Hotel, 1 Shamian South Street, Shamian Island (☎ 020-8188-6968, www.white-swanhotel.com). Once Guangzhou's finest hotel, the White Swan still enjoys an excellent location and its facilities remain impressive, but these days there are better top-end options. They have two swimming pools, squash and tennis courts and even a golf driving range. The central atrium's waterfall,

Waterfall at White Swan Hotel (Cabincam)

now somewhat dated, still manages to please visitors, increasingly more of whom are foreigners coming to Guangzhou to adopt Chinese babies. FC/SW/@ ¥¥¥¥¥

Western & Central Guangzhou

Aside from Shamian, western Guangzhou has a plethora of places to stay, from the train station down to the river.

Baigong, 13 Renmin Nan Lu (☎ 020-8192-5999, www.baigong-hotel.com). This budget bargain has spacious, clean and comfortable rooms, even if they are a little past their best. Located on busy Renmin Nan Lu, the Baigong is well-placed for visits to Shamian, Qingping market, strolls along the river and north to Changshou Lu. ¥¥

China Marriott, Liuhua Lu (☎ 020-8666-6888, www.marriotthotels.com; Yuexiu Gongyuan subway). Some 20 years old and still one of Guangzhou's premier hotels, the China is in the heart of the conference district and offers all the opulence you'd expect, along with its fine facilities and shopping mall. FC/SW/@/DA ¥¥¥¥

CITS Hotel Guangdong, Guangzhou Train Station Square, 179 Huanshi Xi Lu (☎ 020- 8666-6889; Guangzhou Huoche Zhan subway). Bland but comfortable enough, this budget hotel is well-located for early morning buses and trains and offers good value twins, although the double rooms are overpriced. ¥¥

★Landmark, 8 Qiao Guang Lu, Haizhu Square (☎ 020-8335-5988, www. hotel-landmark.com.cn; Haizhu Guangchang subway). The business-oriented Landmark is pleasantly located on Haizhu Square and is convenient for the river, restaurants, rambles through town and the subway. Rooms are modern, refined and comfortable. FC/SW/@ ¥¥¥¥

Eastern Guangzhou

If you come here on business or want modern shopping, facilities and nightlife, then staying in one of the upmarket hotels on Huanshi Dong Lu might fit your needs better.

★**Garden Hotel**, 368 Huanshi Dong Lu (☎ 020-8333-8989, www.thegarden-hotel.com). Although its setting is functional rather than beautiful, the Garden is at the heart of the eastern business district and serves as a center for expat life. The hotel offers excellent accommodation, facilities and service and is also home to a

Garden Hotel

number of the city's consulates. The Peach Blossom restaurant on site offers excellent Cantonese cuisine. FC/SW/@/DA ¥¥¥¥

Where to Eat

As the center for *guangdongcai* or Cantonese food (see *Food & Drink, The Four Major Styles*, p. 116), Guangzhou is renowned for its culinary scene and it's certainly worth checking out some of its southern delights, especially dim sum, which is generally served from morning until late afternoon. When you've had your fill of Cantonese, there is other cuisine from around the world to be enjoyed. All the restaurants listed below have English menus unless otherwise specified and reservations aren't usually necessary.

Shamian Island

If you're not staying on Shamian, all of the cafés and restaurants can be reached by a 10- to 15-minute walk from Huang Sha subway station on line #1.

Blenz Coffee, 46 Shamian Dajie (daily 7:30 am-11:30 pm). Housed in a late Qing dynasty edifice, which was the US City Bank, this grand green building has good coffee, croissants and a range of Western snacks and free Internet access for customers. It's a great place to take a break from sightseeing and watch the world wandering by. ¥¥

Cow and Bridge, 54 Shamian Bei Jie (☎ 020-8121-9988; daily 11 am-11 pm). Considered one of the prime Thai offerings in Guangzhou, this modern restaurant presents fine green and red curries, which are well washed down with a cold bottle of Singha beer. Although the setting is a little bland, the service is friendly and the food is excellent. ¥¥¥

The Deli Shop, 1 Shamian Nan Jie (daily 7 am-11 pm). When you've had your fill of Cantonese cuisine and need some Western input, the Deli Shop comes through with fine croissants and sandwiches. You can take them out or there's a small indoor bar and some pleasant tables outside. ¥¥

Lucy's, 3 Shamian Nan Jie (daily 11 am-2 am). A good place for a drink by the river, Lucy's also serves up fairly tasty Western meals, including fish and chips or steaks, to the backdrop of some cheesy tunes. Lucy's also offers a range of baby meals. ¥¥-¥¥¥

★★**Victory Hotel**, Shamian 4 Jie (daily 7 am-5:30 pm). The Victory's Cantonese restaurant has fine dim sum and is often full to capacity. Just choose what you like the look of from the passing trolleys. Remember to ask the price of each, as they can quite easily add up. ¥¥¥-¥¥¥¥

Ying Hua restaurant at the Victory

Western & Central Guangzhou

★★**Banxi**, 151 Longjin Xi Lu (☎ 020-8181-5719; daily 6:30 am-11:30 pm). Banxi is one of the city's most acclaimed and longstanding Cantonese eateries. It enjoys a lovely location on the edge of Liwan Lake and its dim sum is popular with locals and tourists alike. ¥¥

★**Dongbei Ren**, Renmin Bei Lu (daily 10 am-10:30 pm; Jinian Tang subway). Part of a nationwide chain, Dongbei Ren means Northeastern People, which is where the Manchurians, who ruled China as the Qing dynasty between 1644 and 1911, are from. The food, décor and staff's apparel all pay homage to this. Dishes to try include steamed chicken with mushrooms. ¥¥-¥¥¥

★★**Guangzhou**, 2 Wenchang Nan Lu (daily 7 am-10 pm). One of the city's most famous eateries, Guangzhou has outlets all over town, but this is the original and best. The menu can seem a little overwhelming, but pick one of the Cantonese specialty dishes such as crispy chicken and you won't go far wrong. ¥¥¥

★**La Seine**, Xinghai Concert Hall, 33 Qingbo Lu, Ersha Island (daily 11 am-2 pm, 6 pm-1 am; bus #131 from Yanjiang Lu). An upmarket place on Ersha Island, La Seine presents good French fare in elegant surroundings and fits in well with a trip to the Xinghai Concert Hall or the Museum of Art. ¥¥¥¥

★★**Lucky Fellow**, 6F, 111 Taikang Lu (daily noon-2:30 pm & 6-12 pm; Haizhu Guangchang subway). Owned by the same people as the excellent Tao Tao Ju (see below), Lucky Fellow is a little less ostentatious but the menu is the same and the food is equally good. It's signed from the street but you need to head inside the shopping center and take the elevator to the sixth floor. See below for recommended dishes. ¥¥-¥¥¥¥

★★**Tao Tao Ju**, Dishifu Lu (11:30 am-2:30 pm & 5:30-9:30 pm; Changshou Lu subway). Excellent Cantonese fare in opulent surroundings at moderate prices makes this place popular with locals and tourists. Specialties include roast goose, golden suckling pig and a range of Cantonese sand pots. Service is attentive and there is a full English menu. ¥¥-¥¥¥¥

Tao Tao Ju

Nightlife

Long held to be a city of work and no play, these days Guangzhou's nightlife is waking up to be ever more diverse and cosmopolitan, although it is still some way behind Hong Kong, Shanghai and Beijing.

Where to Drink

Shamian Island

Immediately east of the White Swan Hotel, there is a pleasant riverside beer bar where you'll be accosted by the beer girls trying to sell you their brand. A little farther to the east, **Lucy's** (see *Where to Eat*, p. 470) is another decent place for a drink, but for anything more energetic you'll have to head across to either Yanjiang Lu or Huanshi Dong Lu.

Yanjiang Lu

The north bank of the river has a collection of drinking holes and a few tacky clubs up toward the Haizhu Bridge.

★**1920 Café**, 183 Yanjiang Lu (daily 11 am-2 am, happy hour 5-8:30 pm, www.1920cn.com; Haizhu Guangchang subway). A sophisticated bar on riverfront Yanjiang Lu with a stylish interior and a few tables on a pleasant outdoor patio. Excellent German food using imported ingredients is served – try the sausage platter (¥68). Happy hour is from 5-8:30 pm.

★★**Tayin Mansion Lounge**, 58 Yanjiang Xi Lu (daily 5 pm-2 am). This stylish yet relaxed wine bar is a fantastic place for a riverside drink. Housed in the 1919 mansion of one of Sun Yatsen's collaborators, Chen Shao Bai, this five-storey building stands alone on the riverside promenade, a solid island of sophistication somehow cut off from the traffic rumbling along Yanjiang Lu. Outside, there's a pleasant plant-filled patio but the real delights are found inside – five floors of beautifully fused Asian minimalism and Qing elegance provide plenty of quiet nooks to enjoy a fine bottle of wine and good river views. There are wines from France, Australia and South America, although they don't come cheap (¥318-1388). Beer, soft drinks and light snacks (¥25-48) are also served.

Huanshi Dong Lu & Huale Lu

The modern east is where most of Guangzhou's clubs and bars are found these days, especially along Huanshi Dong Lu, Jianshe Liu Ma Lu and an offshoot, Huale Lu. There are no convenient subway stations near here so a taxi is your best bet. If you're staying at the Holiday Inn on Huanshi Dong Lu, you'll find a collection of bars right outside the hotel door on Heping Lu.

B-Boss, 5F Ocean Commercial Plaza, 414 Huanshi Dong Lu. The current in-place to party, B-Boss offers live music and gets particularly busy on Wednesdays for Ladies Night.

The Elephant and Castle, 363 Huanshi Dong Lu (daily 5 pm-2 am). A long-time haunt of local expats, this pub is a good place to catch live sports matches. It also has an outdoor area with a rickety old pool table and is a good place to meet people in the know about Guangzhou.

★**The Paddy Field**, Ground Floor, Central Plaza, 38 Huale Lu (daily early until late). The dark wooden interior of this Irish-owned pub offers a cozy place to enjoy a pint of Guinness (¥50) and some hearty food such as bangers and mash (¥38). It's worth visiting on Sundays to enjoy the weekly roast.

Tang Club, 1 Jianshe Liu Ma Lu (www.tangclub.com.cn; daily 7 pm-3 am). Renowned for its elegant décor and varied sounds, the Tang Club's labyrinth of hallways and rooms only really start to get busy after 11 pm.

Yes Club, 2F Liuhua Square, 132 Dongfen Xi Lu (daily 8 pm-2 am). Recently revamped and now attracting foreign DJs, Yes is one of Guangzhou's premier nightspots and is renowned for its thumping acoustics.

Shenzhen

Thirty years ago Shenzhen was a village surrounded by paddy fields and hills, but now it is China's fastest-growing city, with a population of five million, and vying with Guangzhou for economic supremacy in Guangdong's Pearl River Delta. Brash, edgy, materialistic and modern, Shenzhen initially seems to have little to offer the casual visitor. But it is worth a quick stop on your way to Guangzhou, if only to see the face of the new, not-so-Communist China. Shenzhen is only a little over a half-hour by train from downtown Hong Kong and this proximity has made it a popular day-trip for residents and visitors alike. They flock to the city for its **cheap shopping** and maybe to take in one of the city's **theme parks**. Shenzhen is a gateway city to China and many tourists pass quickly through on their way to Guangzhou or Guilin, possibly taking advantage of the **lower airfares** found here compared with Hong Kong. As a business traveler, you may also find yourself here in the "factory of the world" and will find plenty of options to fill any down-time you might have, from fine dining to shop-

Construction in Shenzhen (Rüdiger Meier)

ping and golf. So, while Shenzhen is hardly a must-see, a brief stop makes for a fascinating insight into one of the driving forces behind China's emergence onto the world economic platform and will forever dispel any preconceptions you might have had about the PRC's Communist legacy.

History

From Farm to Financial Hub

 Aside from a few ruined settlements here and there, Shenzhen's history is fairly simple – it was just another rural backwater until 30 years ago. Where farmers once ploughed fields, today city slickers seal deals amidst an expanding forest of skyscrapers. So how did the phenomenon that is Shenzhen come to be? It all comes down to Deng Xiaoping's **economic liberalization** in the 1980s. Deng had always been in favor of a free market economy to promote growth and, after Mao Zedong died in 1976, Deng began putting his plans for economic reform into practice. The Pearl River Delta had some of the longest-standing international trading links and its position in the south of Guangdong, far from the watchful eye of Beijing, made an excellent testing ground. Shenzhen was designated as China's first **Special Economic Zone** (SEZ) in 1979, and its location just along the river (and over the border) from Hong Kong gave the fledgling city a natural advantage as a manufacturing hub. Since its inauguration as an SEZ, growth has remained at an astounding 30% and by the 1990s Shenzhen was responsible for making nearly half the world's watches and toys. Many of these products were shipped from **Shekou**, Shenzhen's principal dock which was reported to be the world's fourth-largest container port in 1999. While the growth rate has remained stable, business itself has gone through substantial changes; Shenzhen developed as a cheap production center in lieu of Hong Kong and its early days were characterized by migrant workers, sweatshops and seemingly endless construction. However, as the city became more developed and hence more expensive, production moved outwards again and Shenzhen reinvented itself as a financial center, home to South China's bourse, and has continued to prosper in its redefined role.

The Downside of Development

Shenzhen's get-rich-quick reputation still endures, however, and this has had some drawbacks – every hustler this side of Beijing has tried to establish himself in this financial frontier town and the city has a decidedly materialistic, edgy feel to it. Crime is higher here than in any other part of China and the hunger for money is almost tangible on the streets. While the environment hasn't suffered as much as in some of China's heavy industry zones, it was neglected in the early years of Shenzhen's development. This is now being remedied to some extent with a wave of new measures – from seawater flushing toilets to energy-saving building projects.

The Future

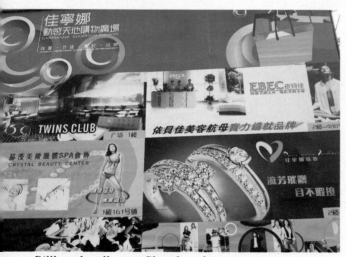

This miracle city is now firmly entrenched in people's minds as an example of everything that is good about China's modern economic policy. Shenzhen is youthful in every way (the average age of residents is just 30) and, like all kids, little by little, the city is coming of age. With this maturity has come stability and a sense of identity that was lacking in the early years. It is still

Billboards call out to Shenzhen shoppers (Tot Foster)

difficult to predict where Shenzhen will be 50, 20 or even 10 years down the line, although one thing seems certain – its days as a rice-farming backwater are well and truly over!

Getting Here & Away

As a key city in the vibrant economic Pearl River Delta, Shenzhen is well-connected by all modes of transport – it's just a case of choosing which is best for your journey. Coming from Hong Kong, the train is certainly the quickest

Shenzhen

1. To: Overseas Chinese Town, Shekou Port, Fuyong Port, Bao'an International Airport
2. To: Splendid China, Window of the World
3. Jin Bo Yang, Shangri-La & Xiangpeng Hotels
4. Qiaoshe Bus Station
5. Luo Hu Border Crossing
6. Lio Hu Commercial City (LCC) & Luo Hu Bus Station
7. Train Station
8. Bank of China
9. Century Plaza Hotel
10. Biefang Fengwei Restaurant
11. Petrel Hotel
12. Guangdong Hotel
13. Made in Kitchen Restaurant
14. Sunshine Hotel
15. Bank of China; Spice Circle & Tangle Palace Restaurants
16. Post Office
17. To: Minsk World, Dapeng Bay
18. Yinhu Bus Station
19. Donghu Bus Station

⊛ Metro Station   ▬▬ Railway Line

1 MILE

©2008 Hunter Publishing, Inc.

and easiest way to get here, while boat is the best way to arrive from Macau. Moving on into the rest of China there are good bus and rail links to Guangzhou and Guilin. For destinations farther afield, flying is the way to go.

If you're arriving from Hong Kong or overseas you will have to clear immigration and customs, which can take anything from just a few minutes to an hour – see *Travel & Living, Customs & Immigration*, p. 83. The Luo Hu border crossing is open from 6:30 am to midnight every day.

By Air

Plane

You'll find substantially lower airfares from Shenzhen than over the border in Hong Kong and many travelers come to Shenzhen purely for this reason – the airport sees nearly 10 million passengers per year and has managed to attract a number of international carriers, which predominantly serve Asian destinations. You can buy airline tickets from hotel travel desks, the airlines (see the websites listed in *Travel & Living* on p. 83), the CAAC (☎ 0755-8334-5000) at Room 615, Hualian Mansion on Shennan Zhong Lu, or at the airport itself. **Bao'an International Airport** (www.szairport.com) is located 12 miles west of the city center and can be reached by regular buses: #K568 runs from the square west of the train station or bus #330 departs from the CAAC on Shennan Zhong Lu.

Flight destinations, frequencies & durations

Beijing (20 daily, 3 hrs); **Chongqing** (10 daily, 1 hr 40 mins); **Guilin** (7 daily, 55 mins); **Hangzhou** (11 daily, 1 hr 45 mins); **Shanghai** (23 daily, 2 hrs 25 mins); **Xi'an** (6 daily, 2 hrs); **Yichang** (1 daily, 1 hr 30 mins).

Helicopter

If you're feeling flush, **Heli-express** (☎ 0755-7778-333, www.heliexpress. com) operates helicopter services between Shenzhen's Bao'an Airport and Macau's Ferry Terminal. There are five flights daily that take between 15 and 25 minutes and cost around ¥1800.

By Rail

Chances are you'll arrive in Shenzhen by train from either Guangzhou or Hong Kong, both of which have good rail connections. The KCR (Kowloon-Canton Railway) from Hong Kong takes less than 40 minutes, after which you'll have to clear immigration and the journey from Guangzhou is only a little longer.

Shenzhen's **efficient new train station** is just over the Luo Hu border from Hong Kong and has well-signed designated areas for buying Guangzhou tickets, another for Hong Kong tickets and then a general ticket office for long-distance destinations. There are even automated machines for tickets to Guangzhou, but they weren't working at the time of writing.

The station is on the subway line and is next to both the local bus station and the intercity terminal.

Destinations, frequencies & durations

Beijing (2 daily, 23 hrs 30 min-29 hrs 30 mins); **Guangzhou** (71 daily, 1 hr 10 min-1 hr 40 mins); **Guilin** (1 daily, 16 hrs 30 mins); **Hangzhou** (1 daily, 22 hrs); **Hong Kong** (every 3 minutes, 40 mins); **Shanghai** (1 daily, 25 hrs).

By Road

 Shenzhen is connected to destinations around the country by bus and for once it's actually preferable to use the bus over the train for a long-distance journey – modern and comfortable overnight buses to Guilin and Yangshuo take around 12 hours and leave at 7:30 pm. The main **Luo Hu bus station** is just east of the train station, but Guilin and Yangshuo buses leave from the **Qiaoshe station** across the overpass to the west. There are also luxury buses (¥180) to Hong Kong Airport from some of the upscale hotels, including the Century Plaza, Guangdong, Landmark and the Shangri-La.

Destinations, frequencies & durations

Guangzhou (frequent, 3 hrs); **Guilin** (several daily, 12 hrs); **Hong Kong** (frequent, 1 hr); **Yangshuo** (1 daily, 12 hrs).

By Boat

You can also get here by boat from Hong Kong or Guangzhou, with services to **Shekou**, Shenzhen's principal port 10 miles west of the city, as well as **Fuyong** port which is out by the airport.

Regular boats from Shekou run to **Hong Kong's China Ferry Terminal** in Kowloon and there are also several daily services to the **Macau Ferry Terminal** on Hong Kong Island. Both trips take about 50 minutes with services operating from 8:20 am to 7:45 pm. Shekou is connected to the city center by bus #204, which runs from Jianshe Lu.

From Fuyong, Turbojet (☎ 0755-2777-6818, www.turbojet.com.hk) runs regular boats out to **Hong Kong Airport** (40 mins) and three ferries daily to **Macau** (1 hr). Fuyong can be reached by a five-minute bus trip from Shenzhen's Bao'an Airport.

Getting Around

By Subway

Shenzhen's brand new, efficient subway line #1 runs north from the border at Luo Hu and train station to Lao Jie, where it turns west and heads out to Windows of the World, home to some of Shenzhen's theme parks. Plenty more lines are planned but so far only a short stretch of line #4 has been completed. Tickets cost between ¥2 and ¥5 and the symbol looks a little like a white spider on a green background. Service hours are from 6:30 am to 10:30 pm.

Shenzhen Subway

By Bus

Shenzhen has an extensive bus service and tickets cost from ¥2. Useful bus numbers are mentioned where relevant.

By Taxi

Metallic maroon taxis ply the streets of Shenzhen and have the highest starting price in the country – ¥12.5 for the first three km (1.9 miles) and ¥2.4 per km (0.6 miles) thereafter.

Orientation

Shenzhen is a vast, sprawling conurbation made up of several sections, but the area of most relevance to short-term visitors is **Luo Hu** (Lo Wu in Cantonese), north of the Hong Kong border. In Luo Hu you'll find the bus and train stations, some good hotels, restaurants and shopping. From the border, Jianshe Lu runs north, parallel with the train tracks to Shennan Lu. Northeast of the train station, **Dongmen Lu** is another popular dining and shopping district of Luo Hu. A few miles west of Luo Hu, Nanshan district contains the **Overseas Chinese Town** (OCT), where you'll find many of the city's theme parks, along with restaurants, hotels, galleries and some nightlife.

Information Sources

The tourist office website (www.shenzhentour.com) has some useful information and there are five branches around the city. The most helpful are at the border (☎ 0755-8234-4253), in the eastern part of the train station exit hall (☎ 0755-8236-5043) and at the airport (☎ 0755-2777-7571). All of the tourist offices are open from 9 am to 6 pm daily. For information on restaurants, clubs and bars as well as expat services, try *that's PRD*, part of *that's magazines* nationwide group, or *City Talk,* both of which are available for free in major hotels, bars, restaurants and cafés, including Starbucks.

Communications

Post Office: Jiangbei Lu, located next to the Face Café.

Telephone Code: 0755.

Internet Access: Pioneer Internet Café (2F & 3F) on Shennan Lu; walk east along Shennan Lu, over the Dongmen Lu junction and it's on your right.

Bank of China: There's a convenient branch next to the Shangri-La on Renmin Nan Lu and another on Dongmen Lu next to the Panglin Hotel.

Public Security Bureau: 4018, Jiefang Lu (☎ 0755-9500-0100).

Medical Services: Bao'an People's Hospital at 118 Longjing Er Lu (☎ 0755-2778-2405).

Sightseeing

Shenzhen's youthful status means that the bulk of its sights are of the modern variety, and most of these are outside of the city center. The most famous of Shenzhen's attractions are its theme parks, many of which are found in the newly developed **Overseas Chinese Town** (OCT), west of the center and linked by subway and bus #T1. There are another couple of theme parks out to the east where you'll also find a beach or two.

★**Splendid China**, OCT, Nanshan District (☎ 0755-2660-0626, www.chinafacv.com; daily 9:30 am-9:30 pm; ¥120). Splendid China prides itself as a portal into the vast history of the nation and contains over 100 exhibits placed according to their location within the country. The entrance ticket also includes the Folk Culture Village, which focuses on China's 56 minority groups. Cultural shows (¥35) and shopping take center

Miniature Great Wall at Splendid China (Dmpendse)

stage here but, despite its touristy air, Folk Culture Village offers a good introduction to the ethnic minorities of China.

Eiffel Tower replica at Window of the World (Arman Aziz)

★★**Window of the World**, OCT, Nanshan District (☎ 0755-2660-8000, www.szwwco.com; daily 9:30 am-10:30 pm; ¥120). Located next to Splendid China, Window of the World houses a collection of recreated world wonders and is currently one of the most visited attractions in China, representing the burgeoning interest in what lies beyond the Middle Kingdom after so many years of isolation. In the park you'll find replicas of the Eiffel Tower, Niagara Falls, the Taj Mahal and even Mount Rushmore, as well as a few rides and activities – try the Grand Canyon Flume Ride! There are also shows and dance performances throughout the day and there's even a wedding ceremony show held in the European-style church!

Shenzhen's Art Scene

Painting by He Xiangning

Places without any inherent culture can invent their own and Shenzhen is a living, breathing example. Free from traditions or history, artists in Shenzhen depict life as they see it, reflecting the stark contrasts that typify Shenzhen the fledgling city. The Overseas Chinese Town (OCT) neighborhood is the hub of Shenzhen's art world, where you'll find galleries such as the **OCT Contemporary Art Terminal** on Enping Lu (☎ 0755-2691-6199; daily 10 am-5:30 pm). It features exhibitions by both Chinese and international artists.

Nearby, the **He Xiangning Art Museum**, at 9013 Shennan Dadao (☎ 0755-2666-4540; daily 10 am-5:30 pm), displays works of art by one of the nation's most acclaimed female artists, Madame He Xiangning, who was also a friend of the late, great Dr. Sun Yatsen.

The East

For something a little different **Minsk World** (☎ 0775-2525-1415; daily 9:30 am-6 pm; ¥110) is China's only military theme park and centers on a Russian aircraft carrier (the fifth-largest in the world) which is permanently docked in Shenzhen! You can get to Minsk World by taking bus #202 or #205. If you're in town for longer you might also want to explore the area of Dapeng Bay, some 20 miles to the east of Shenzhen and accessible by buses #103 or #364. At Dapeng you'll find Shenzhen's **Sea World** (☎ 0755-2506-2986; daily 9:30 am-6 pm; ¥100) and reasonable stretches of sand at **Dameisha** and **Xiaomeisha** beaches, although they can get very busy on summer weekends.

Shopping

Shenzhen at night (Joe HK)

Pearl River Delta

Many Hong Kong visitors (and residents) make the 40-minute journey to Shenzhen specifically for the shopping, which benefits from the cheaper prices of the mainland as well as the proximity of many of the factories where the goods are made. Shenzhen is overloaded with shopping centers, one of the best and most convenient of which is the Lo Wu Commercial Center (LCC), just over the border from Hong Kong and next to the train station. If you're not just here for a one-stop trip at the LCC you'll find other good shopping areas around **Huaqiang Bei Lu** and **Shennan Zhong Lu**. They have numerous malls, department stores and clothing outlets.

The Lo Wu Commercial Center

Stairway to shopping heaven at Lo Wu Commercial Center (Tot Foster)

The LCC has five teeming floors of shops selling everything from artwork to tailor-made suits (the latter a real bargain). Although it's a bit of a mish-mash, the fifth floor has mainly clothes shops and tailors, the fourth has more clothes and (fake) sunglasses, the third sells bags, the second sells shoes and the ground floor has a bit of everything. The center's location next to the bus and train station makes it a prime spot for pickpockets – keep your eyes on your belongings at all times.

Everyday Needs

There is a convenient branch of **Wal-Mart** next to Starbucks on Renmin Nan Lu and you'll find **Watson's** in just about every shopping mall throughout town.

Adventures

On the Green

★★★**Mission Hills Resort**, 1 Mission Hills Road (☎ 0755-2802-0888, www.missionhillsgroup.com/en/). Shenzhen's moneymen need somewhere to unwind a little and so a number of golf courses have grown up around the city's fringes. Mission Hills is by the far the most famous of them. It is currently the world's largest golf course,  employing over 2,500 caddies on its 180 holes! The 10-course club was designed by a veritable Who's Who of the golfing world, from Nick Faldo to Jack Nicklaus and Vijay Singh. There's also a lovely hotel on site (¥¥¥¥¥), with elegant rooms looking over the fairways and surrounding hills. There's also a spa and outdoor pool if you've played one round too many. For golf-hotel packages check out the website.

Where to Stay

As one of China's financial hubs Shenzhen used to have a reputation as an expensive place to stay but, while there are certainly plenty of top-end options, there are also cheaper hotels, predominantly in the budget enclave of Realty House, immediately north of the Shangri-La.

What's it mean? FC=fitness center; SW=swimming pool; @=in-room Internet access; DA=rooms for disabled. For ¥ price codes, see page 113.

Century Plaza, 1 Chunfeng Lu (☎ 8232-0888, www.szcphotel; Luo Hu subway). The Century Plaza is an upper mid-range place with higher aspirations, but which nevertheless offers comfortable stylish rooms with opulent bathrooms and is handy for the train station. Standard reductions cut around 40% off the price. FC/SW/@ ¥¥¥¥¥

★★**Guangdong**, 3033 Shennan Dong Lu (☎ 8222-8339, www.gdhhotels.com; Guomao subway). The Guangdong is a great-value mid-range place. Rooms are comfortable, spacious and tastefully styled in muted colors and staff are friendly and helpful. FC/@ ¥¥¥¥

Jin Bo Yang Hotel, 8F, Realty Building, Renmin Nan Lu (☎ 8234-7022; Luo Hu subway). The Jin Bo Yang is one of the better choices in this budget block which is due north of the Shangri-La and train station. While it won't win any awards for style, the Bo Yang has cheap and comfortable rooms although they are a little damp. ¥

Lounge at Mission Hills Resort

★★★**Mission Hills Resort**, 1 Mission Hills Road (☎ 0755-2802-0888, www.missionhillsgroup.com/en/) – see *Adventures On the Green*, p. 482, for review. ¥¥¥¥¥

Petrel, Jiabing Lu (☎ 0755-8223-2828, www.petrel-hotel.com; Guomao subway). The Petrel offers good value, given its convenient location and clean and functional rooms, some of which offer views over the city. ¥¥-¥¥¥

★**Shangri-La**, 1002 Jianshe Lu (☎ 0755-8233-0888, www.shangri-la.com; Luo Hu subway). While the Shangri-La's regular rooms don't quite live up to the brand's usual high standards, the hotel's great facilities, restaurants and location make up for that. FC/SW/@ ¥¥¥¥¥

★**Sunshine**, 1 Jiabin Lu (☎ 0755-8223-3888, www.sunshinehotel.com; Guomao subway). This was Shenzhen's first five-star hotel and it's keeping

Pearl River Delta

Sunshine lobby

well. Rooms are stylish and comfortable and the hotel's location is excellent. FC/SW/@ ¥¥¥¥-¥¥¥¥¥

Xiangpeng, 15F & 16F, Realty Building, Renmin Nan Lu (☎ 0755-8232-1919; Luo Hu subway). Another budget choice in the Realty Building, the Xiangpeng has smaller rooms than the Jin Bo Yang but is comfortable enough and slightly cheaper. ¥

Where to Eat

While Shenzhen has no cuisine to call its own, the city's explosive growth and the influx of people from around the country (indeed the world) has led to a diverse range of culinary offerings, although eating is unlikely to be a highlight here.

See page 117 for an explanation of the ¥ restaurant price codes.

★★**Beifang Fengwei**, Chungfeng Lu (☎ 0755-8223-9325; daily 11 am-2:30 pm & 5-10 pm; Guomao subway). Although it specializes in northern cuisine, you'll also find tasty southern delicacies here. Dishes to try include stewed king prawns in brown sauce and Beijing duck. There's no English-language name on the door so you'll have to look for the ornate red and gold doorway just opposite the Century Plaza Hotel on Chungfeng Lu. ¥¥¥

★★★**Café 360°**, 31F, Shangri-La Hotel, 1002 Jianshe Lu (☎ 0755-8296-1380; daily 11:30 am-2:30 pm & 5 pm-1 am; Luo Hu subway). Even if the food was no good it would be worth heading up here for the fine views over the city and south across the hills to Hong Kong. As it happens, the food is excellent, whether from the international menu or the temporary menu, which is refreshed every month. They also serve dim sum at lunch, plus a smattering of Chinese dishes. ¥¥¥¥-¥¥¥¥¥

★**Laurel**, Suite 5010, 5F Lo Wu Commercial Center (☎ 0755-8232-3668; daily 7 am-midnight; Luo Hu subway). After some rigorous bargaining in the LCC (see p. 482), a bit of dim sum at Laurel should replenish and refresh, without overfilling you, meaning you'll emerge fighting fit and ready to flex your yuan. The far end of the restaurant also offers good vistas over the nearby hills. ¥¥¥

Made in Kitchen, 7F, 2028 Renmin Lu, Kingglory Plaza, Luo Hu (☎ 0755-8261-1866; daily 10 am-midnight; Guomao subway). This fusion restaurant sits on the top floor of the flashy Kingglory Plaza and is a popular choice with hungry shoppers. The extensive menu covers just about everything from prime Angus beef to Thai fried frog with green vegetables. The restaurant also offers good views around the area and has a fine collection of international wines. ¥¥¥-¥¥¥¥

★**Spice Circle**, 1F Tianjun Mansion, Dongmen Nan Lu (☎ 0755-8220-2129; 11 am-10 pm; Guomao subway). Spice Circle offers innovative Indian cuisine in a stylish, contemporary setting complete with funky wrap-around booths. ¥¥¥-¥¥¥¥

★**Tangle Palace**, 3012 Dongmen Nan Lu, Luo Hu (☎ 0755-8223-3688; daily 7:30-11 pm; Guomao subway). This excellent Cantonese restaurant is easily identified by its glamorous gold façade and serves up well priced and tasty dishes. Although there's no English menu, there is a picture menu and you'll also find the staff speak a little English and are keen to help. ¥¥¥

Nightlife

With so many young people living in Shenzhen, the city is rapidly developing a buzzing nightlife and bars and clubs are popping up all over (check www.shenzhenparty.com for the latest). **Shekou** is a sleazy, but popular night spot where you'll find a number of bars clustered around Taizi Lu, some of which are savory enough to be worth venturing into. A little nearer to downtown, the **Overseas Chinese Town** also has its share of after-hours life. The **Luo Hu** district offers a more limited selection of bars and many of the best are in the larger hotels – try **Henry J. Bean's** on the second floor of the Shangri-La.

Where to Drink

Luo Hu

Face Café, 66 Jiangbei Lu (Luo Hu subway). Part of the nationwide chain, Face Café is one of the better dancing spots in Luo Hu and is popular with the 20-something crowd.

Overseas Chinese Town

★**Browne's Wine Bar and Cigar House**, 55-56 Commercial Street, Portofino International Apartments (Overseas Chinese Town subway). Browne's refined elegance offers some of the best cigars available in China and its wine list is a connoisseur's dream.

V-Bar, 3F Crowne Plaza, Shennan Lu (Windows of the World subway). V-Bar is a stylish poolside bar and club, but be prepared for huge crowds over the weekends.

Shekou

(bus #204 from Jianshe Lu in Luo Hu)

Soho, 1F, Bitao Club, Taizi Lu. Soho is a modern Western bar and offers good food and ambient music away from the less salubrious establishments nearby.

Ex-Ta-Sea, Room A,1F, Yin Bin Building, Taizi Lu. Another of Shekou's more savory choices, Ex-ta-Sea is a popular expat hangout owned by an American sports fan, and is an ideal place for sports lovers, with ESPN coverage for all major events.

Hong Kong & Macau

Whether flying into the vast, ultra-modern Chek Lap Kok Airport and being whisked into the city center on the hi-tech, ultra-fast Airport Express, or arriving by boat at the

China Ferry Terminal, **Hong Kong**, with its population of seven million, never fails to impress. You instantly know you're somewhere special, particularly the first time you lay eyes on the spectacle of the skyscraper-filled island from the Kowloon side. After weeks or months on the road in China, Hong Kong is the perfect spot for some dining, shopping and splurging. But if it's the great outdoors you're after, there are plenty of hikes and beaches in the territory as well. Hong Kong is a place where even the mildest exploration can offer stark contrast and both traditional Chinese and colonial history lurk beneath the city's slick modern exterior. Whether swimming in the sea or hiking an island trail to a small shrine through lush tropical undergrowth on one of the outlying islands, it's difficult to imagine that the gleaming skyscrapers are only a short boat ride away.

Forty miles across the water, **Macau** also served its time as a colony and its Portuguese history has engendered a laid-back ambience unique in China, which remains to this day despite a recent building boom. Walking through the architectural monuments of Macau's stunning historic center you'd easily believe you were in Lisbon, were it not for the occasional Taoist temple. Con-

Victoria Harbour (Tot Foster)

versely, a trip out to the islands will take you on a journey into Macau's casino-laden future at Cotai and then back to its past amidst the small fishing villages and beaches of yesteryear on Coloane.

Hong Kong
History

Up to the Arrival of the Europeans

 While Hong Kong's development is a comparatively recent thing, humans have inhabited the region for millennia, a fact underlined by the discovery of various ceramics, bronzes and tools, including a 6,000-year-old stone hammer on Lamma Island. However, little of note occurred until the arrival of the Europeans in the 1500s. Portuguese mariner Jorge Alvarez first visited the Pearl River Delta in 1513, although initial foreign incursions focused on Macau and Canton (present day Guangzhou), while Hong Kong remained little different from anywhere else along this stretch of coastline, comprised of islands, farms and fishing villages until the First Opium War (see p. 16). As a result of the war, Hong Kong was ceded to the British under the 1841 Convention of Chuen Pi, although this wasn't legally binding since it was never signed. Still, the British raised their flag at Possession Point on Hong Kong Island and Henry Pottinger was appointed as the first governor. The **1842 Treaty of Nanjing** officially ceded the island to the British and also entailed the opening up of five other strategic ports around China to international trade. Thereafter, this small island, formerly known as Heung Gong (Fragrant Harbor), became British Hong Kong. From humble beginnings, this little harbor, less than a mile from the Chinese mainland, embarked on a colonial voyage that lasted over 150 years and saw the colony grow to become one of the most successful trading ports the world has ever known.

Early Days of British Rule

Traders from Canton and Macau moved to Hong Kong Island and land sales were held which resulted in the development of Central as a trading hub, while government and military buildings were erected nearby. The Second Opium War gave the British further concessions in Kowloon on the mainland, although it was the Portuguese who took the lead in colonizing the area. As the increasing economic potential of Kowloon was recognized, more businesses were established there. Meanwhile, over on Hong Kong Island, as the heat of the sticky summers took its toll, the Brits were retreating for the hills and Victoria Peak became *the* place to escape. In 1888 the Peak Tram funicular railway opened to ease the journey up to the hillside residences and it remains in use today. However, while coolies carried government officials and foreign traders around, the lot of the everyday Chinese was far less luxurious and in the humid lowlands disease was rife.

Racial Tensions

By the end of the 19th century, British administrators had begun to learn Cantonese and include the local community in government affairs – attempting to bridge the gap between themselves and the Chinese. But relations were still frosty and this lack of cultural interaction bred misunderstanding and fear on both sides. With the rise in Chinese Nationalism the British feared that Hong Kong was indefensible from the mainland, so they acquired a 400-square-mile plot of land north of Kowloon. The aptly named **New Territories** were secured under a 99-year lease in 1898. That deal ultimately led to the return of the entire colony to China in 1997.

Made in Hong Kong

Although racial tensions remained, it was money that held Hong Kong together and, as the economy began to embrace industry, business picked up. When the rest of China became locked in civil war, Hong Kong continued to prosper and many wealthy businessmen from the mainland relocated here. However, Hong Kong's perceived invincibility was shattered when the **Japanese invasion** stretched into the territory in 1941. The British troops were supported by a number of Indian and Singaporean regiments, as well as the first Canadian forces to see active service in World War II. After the Japanese invasion began on December 8th, 1941, their superior numbers quickly forced the British to retreat from Kowloon and, a couple of weeks later, to surrender on Christmas Day. However, Japanese rule was short-lived and the British re-established themselves in 1945, quickly quelling moves to independence. The formation of the PRC in 1949 further swelled Hong Kong's population with political refugees and entrepreneurs from Shanghai. This added labor force and business acumen made for a powerful cocktail that would soon project Hong Kong to the forefront of the Asian economy. Hong Kong's industrial development began with textiles in the 1950s and by the end of the following decade there were factories producing everything from plastic toys to clothes and watches. All of a sudden the world was awash with "Made in Hong Kong" products. While China was undergoing the famines of the Great Leap Forward, Hong Kong was crowded, but prosperous. In response to the growing housing shortage, the first of numerous land reclamation projects were undertaken and buildings began to focus on the vertical – it was in the 1970s that Hong Kong really started to develop its skyline.

The Handover

By the 1970s Hong Kong was a regional financial hub and started to move into the tertiary sector, which was well-timed given Deng Xiaoping's opening up of the mainland economy and the resulting industrial shift to north of the border. However, the question of what would happen when the British lease on the New Territories expired in 1997 was looming ever larger and the uncertainty this caused hindered investment. In 1984 the situation was resolved by the **Joint Declaration**, which assured the return of the entire territory to China in 1997 with a tacit understanding (but no guarantee) that its democratic system of government would remain in place for at least 50 years. This sent shivers up the spine of many Chinese who had fled here in 1949, and there was large-scale emigration to Australia, Canada, New Zealand and the USA. The flood of people leaving Hong Kong peaked after the Tian'anmen Square Demonstrations in 1989. Some of the student pro-

Hong Kong & Macau

tests in Beijing were organized from Hong Kong and the most vehement condemnation of the brutal Chinese response came from here – candle-lit remembrance vigils are still held in Victoria Park on June 4th every year. Relations with the mainland were further strained when Chris Patten, the last British governor appointed to Hong Kong in 1992, introduced expansive electoral reforms, which gave a voice to a much greater percentage of the population, without backing from the Chinese government. However, contrary to the expectations of some, when the giant handover countdown clock in Beijing's Tian'anmen Square finally reached zero, the return of Hong Kong passed without incident. The British sailed away on *HMS Britannia* and there were huge celebrations around China, but otherwise business in the territory carried on as usual. Patten's electoral reforms were reversed and Tung Chee-hwa, a shipping magnate, was appointed as the first chief executive of **Hong Kong Special Administrative Region** (SAR), running the territory under the **"one country, two systems" policy**, which Beijing is still trying to repeat in Taiwan.

Competition, Democracy & Disease

However Hong Kong's days as the economic top dog of the region were numbered, particularly after the designation of Shanghai as China's financial capital. Shortly after the handover, the **Asian Financial Crisis** hit Hong Kong hard. Skyrocketing property prices and labor costs pushed more and more businesses north of the border into the Pearl River Delta and cities such as Shenzhen sprung up almost overnight. In spite of continued infrastructure investment (most notably the completion of the Sir Norman Foster designed international airport at Chek Lap Kok), the scale of development was more than matched over the border in the Delta, which was increasingly challenging Hong Kong's role as the region's primary trading hub. Added to this increased competition, the recent **SARS and Bird Flu** scares stopped the territory's tourist trade in its tracks. Government corruption has been another major source of contention and, while some argue that the right to protest is an indication of political freedom, others point out that this is only valid if opposing viewpoints are actually listened to. For Hong Kong to achieve the democratic society it aspires to it needs to satisfy the populace at large. In 2003 a half-million-strong protest took to the streets of Hong Kong and their calls for Tung Chee-hwa's resignation were eventually answered in 2004 when he was replaced by the long-term civil servant, Donald Tsang.

The Environment

For all its first-rate public services, futuristic skyscrapers, fancy restaurants, theme parks and international visitors, Hong Kong is rated as one of the most polluted cities in the world, thanks in no small part to the thousands of factories just over the border. While the environment was previously treated as a resource to be exploited, greater awareness and concern have led to a stronger environmental movement in the territory, which has been incorporated into policy (see www.epd.gov.hk for more). However, when there's lots of money at stake, nature still seems to get a rough deal, as evidenced by ongoing land reclamation projects. Of the many issues that might frustrate residents (and visitors), the environment is most regularly cited. If Hong Kong wants to continue attracting international businesses and their employees, it urgently needs not only to acknowledge the problem, but also to ensure that appropriate action is taken.

The Future

In summary, although Hong Kong is facing ever more competition and is no longer the only boomtown in the region, it is by far the most developed part of China. Today there is a first class infrastructure, people enjoy greater social freedom than they do just over the border and the government is committed to making Hong Kong a truly developed international city – look no further than the overload of public infomercials relating to health, safety and good conduct for a view of where they would like Hong Kong to be in the future. The return to China is only a decade old and the region is still trying to define its role within the burgeoning Chinese economy which undoubtedly makes for uncertain times. If the authorities can successfully walk the fine line between pleasing the people and keeping Beijing happy, as well as clean up the environment, then there's no reason why Hong Kong can't remain the focal point of this part of Asia. For now, the skyscrapers keep getting taller, the malls are full of shoppers flexing their credit cards and all the indications are that this adaptive, resourceful and international community will continue to prosper.

Getting Here & Away

Visas

Citizens of most Western countries do not need a visa for short visits to Hong Kong as long as employment isn't sought. Many nationalities, including Americans, Canadians, Australians, New Zealanders and most Europeans, can stay for up to three months with no visa, while Brits are allowed up to six months. You have to fill in an embarkation card on carbon paper of which one copy is kept by immigration officials while the other is tucked back into your passport – try to hold onto it to avoid having to fill out another one on your departure. To find out more and the latest regulations check out www.immd.gov.hk.

China Visas

Hong Kong is one of the easiest places to get (or renew) a China visa. You can get your visa from the Consulate Department of the Chinese Ministry of Foreign Affairs at 7F, Lower Block, China Resources Building, 26 Harbour Road, Wanchai (☎ 00852-3413-2424, www.fmcoprc.gov.hk; Mon-Fri 9 am-noon & 2-5 pm). However, it's often cheaper and easier to use the visa services offered by most hotels and travel agencies. **China Travel Service (CTS)** at 27-33 Nathan Road (☎ 00852-2315-7188) is conveniently located, and there are also specialized agents such as **Japan Travel Agency**

(☎ 00852-2368-9151) at 509-513, 5F, East Ocean Center, 98 Granville Road in Tsimashatsui. They can arrange a visa in a day if necessary, more usually two. Costs for a standard entry visa through agents range from **HK$200** (three-month single entry) to **HK$650** (one year multi-entry), depending on your nationality, how quickly you want the visa processed, its duration and the number of entries. You can also get visas at the airport if you don't want to come in to the city. Which ever way you apply, you'll need a passport photo and your passport.

By Air

Hong Kong is China's best-served international gateway and some of the cheapest China flights you'll find from North America, Europe and Australasia head here. The airport is also linked to most major cities and tourist destinations on the mainland, although you'll find cheaper onward flights into China from Shenzhen, which is just an hour over the border by boat or bus. For airline offices in Hong Kong see the websites listed on p. 83.

Hong Kong Airport

The award-winning airport (www.hkairport.com) on Chek Lap Kok, north of Lantau Island is said to be the largest covered space in the world, and after a few initial hiccups, it has proved to be a phenomenal success and remains one of the world's busiest airports. The airport was designed by the British architect, Sir Norman Foster (who is also responsible for the HSBC Headquarters on Hong Kong Island) and the sweeping curves of its façade hold a light and airy interior – the antithesis of the crowded and gloomy airports of yesteryear. Relocating the airport here involved not only putting together the enormous edifice of the terminal itself, but the leveling of an entire island and the construction of three bridges, including the impressive Tsing Ma Suspension Bridge.

Inside the airport, the giant terminal has enough amenities and facilities to make it a small city unto itself. Along with banks, restaurants, shops, Internet cafés, foot massage parlors and phone recharging facilities, there are helpful and well-stocked tourist offices between customs and the arrivals hall, which are open from 7 am-11 pm. All passengers leaving Hong Kong by air must pay a departure tax of HK$120, which is usually included in the flight ticket price.

Getting into Hong Kong

There are three main ways of getting from the airport into town – by the airport express train, bus or taxi. The express is the quickest option and my favorite way to get to town, but buses are cheaper, at around HK$30-45, though slower, taking around an hour to reach downtown. While taxis will take you from door to door, they are not much quicker than the bus and they're expensive, costing around HK$280 to Kowloon or HK$340 to Central.

Airport Express

This speedy service takes just 23 minutes from the airport to Central and costs HK$100 to Central or HK$90 to Kowloon. If you're going to be using a lot of public transport and are taking the Airport Express, it makes sense to buy a tourist version of Hong Kong's stored value **Octopus card** (see callout, p. 496). There are free shuttle buses every 15 to 25 minutes (daily 6:30 am-11 pm) from a number of hotels around both Hong Kong Island and Kowloon, which will take you to the nearest station to catch the airport express. In Hong Kong Island, route #H1 stops at the Island Shangri-La, Pacific Place and the Hong Kong Convention and Exhibition Center, while route #H2 goes to the Excelsior in Causeway Bay. There are five shuttle bus routes on Kowloon and stops include Hung Hom Kowloon-Canton Railway (KCR) Station, Jordan Mass Transit Railway (MTR) Station, the BP International Hotel, the Holiday Inn Golden Mile, the Intercontinental and the Peninsula.

Getting to China from the Airport

If you're heading straight into China and don't want to go into Hong Kong, you can arrange both visas and onward transport at the airport. The airport **China Travel Service** (CTS; ☎ 00852-2261-2472; daily 8 am-4 pm) is located at counter A4 in the arrivals hall and should be able to get you a **visa** within a few hours. But the greater cost of getting a visa from the airport and the fact you'll have to sit around here for half a day makes it infinitely preferable to head into Hong Kong, pay less and do some sightseeing or shopping while you wait.

In addition to far-flung Chinese cities served by air from Hong Kong, there are also land and water options for closer mainland destinations. Several companies, including **CTS** at counter A10 in the arrivals hall (same telephone number as above, www.ctsbus.hkcts.com) and **E.E. Bus** at counter A8 (☎ 00852-2261-0176) operate **buses** from the airport to Shenzhen (40 mins, HK$100-120) and Guangzhou (4 hrs, HK$250). There are also **fast boats** from the airport's Skypier to Fuyong (for Shenzhen airport; 40 mins, HK$230) and Shekou (for Shenzhen; 40 mins, HK$200) and Macau (45 mins, HK$180) operated by Turbojet (☎ 00852-2859-3333, www.turbojetseaexpress.com.hk), which avoid Hong Kong immigration. You can buy boat tickets from a counter just before immigration in arrivals and if you have checked baggage it will be retrieved for you and transferred to the boat.

Mainland destinations served by flights from Hong Kong

Beijing (frequent, 3 hrs 40 mins); **Chongqing** (5 daily, 1 hr 50 mins); **Guangzhou** (5 daily, 40 mins); Guilin (3 daily, 1 hr 10 mins); **Hangzhou** (12 daily, 2 hrs); **Huangshan** (1 daily, 1 hr 50 mins); **Shanghai** (11 daily, 3 hrs); **Xi'an** (daily, 2 hrs 30 mins).

Helicopter

For those with money to burn or no time to spare, **Heli-express** has flights to Macau that leave from the Macau Ferry Terminal on Hong Kong Island. Flights on the 12-seater copters take just 16 minutes and offer great views

Hong Kong & Macau

in clear weather, but cost a whopping HK$1,700/1,800 (off-peak/peak). There are flights every 30 minutes between 9:30 am and 11 pm and you need to arrive at least 15 minutes prior to departure. You can buy tickets at the Heli-express office at Room 1603, 6F, China Merchants Tower, 200 Connaught Road in Central (☎ 00852-2108-9898, www.heliexpress.com; Mon-Fri 9 am-6 pm, Sat 9 am-1 pm).

By Water

Hong Kong is a major stopping off point for cruise liners in this part of the world (see *Travel & Living, Getting Here & Away, By Water*, p. 86), but there are also regular boat services from Macau, Shenzhen and Guangzhou. There are two principal docks, the **China Ferry Terminal** in Tsimshatsui and the **Macau Ferry Terminal** in the Shun Tak Centre on Hong Kong Island, although there are also services to Macau and Shenzhen from the Skypier near the airport (see *By Air, Getting to China from the Airport*, p. 493). On arrival at either end you'll have to clear customs and immigration. The easiest way to get to or from the China Ferry Terminal is to take a taxi, but it is also accessible by bus #14 in Kowloon. Macau Ferry Terminal on Hong Kong Island is close to Sheung Wan MTR station. Boats are operated by two principal carriers, Turbojet and First Ferry, but **CKS** has two daily boats to Guangzhou (2 hrs 30 mins, HK$190) that leave from the China Ferry Terminal.

Turbojet (☎ 00852-2859-3333, www.turbojet.com.hk) offers speedy jetfoils from both terminals. The one-hour trip to Macau from the Macau Ferry Terminal leaves every 15 minutes between 7 am and 1:30 am, with a few services running through the night. Tickets cost HK$138 for economy class and HK$240 for super class, which offers more comfortable seating and includes a newspaper, drink and snack. Turbojet also operates seven services a day to Fuyong (for Shenzhen; 1 hr) that leave from the China Ferry Terminal.

First Ferry (☎ 00852-2131-8181, www.nwff.com.hk) runs slightly slower catamaran services for HK$137 (1 hr 10 mins) to Macau every 30 minutes from both the China Ferry Terminal on Tsimshatsui's Canton Road and the Macau Ferry Terminal.

By Rail

Hong Kong's trains serve three regions on the mainland. There are intercity passenger services to the Pearl River Delta (Shenzhen and Guangzhou), and long distance lines to Beijing and Shanghai. The principal station is at Kowloon's **Hung Hom**, and this is the only station that serves mainland destinations, but you can buy tickets at Mongkok and Kowloon Tong stations or online (www.kcrc.com). The easiest way to get to Hung Hom is by taxi, though if you're in the south of Kowloon the KCR from Tsimshatsui East runs there, as does bus #8 from the Star Ferry terminal.

Destinations, frequencies & durations

Beijing (1 every other day, 24 hrs, HK$601/934 hard-sleeper/soft-sleeper); **Guangzhou** (12 daily, 1 hr 45 min, HK$145); **Shanghai** (1 every other day, 24 hrs 30 min, HK$530/825 hard-sleeper/soft-sleeper); **Shenzhen** (frequent, 40 min, HK$34).

By Road

Various companies run buses from Hong Kong to Pearl River Delta destinations, including Shenzhen and Guangzhou. For services to Guangzhou you'll have to get off the bus at the border and proceed on foot through immigration and customs with your bags, then you change buses. You'll be labeled with a sticker which will help the staff on the other side of the border get you to the right bus.

Both **E.E. Bus** (☎ 00852-2723-2923) and **China Travel Service** (CTS, ☎ 00852-2365-0118, www.ctsbus.hkcts.com) run services to Shenzhen (1 hr, HK$35-50) and Guangzhou (4hr, HK$100). E.E buses leave from outside the BP International Hotel on Austin Road and from the Concourse by Prince Edward MTR station. CTS also use the Concourse, but has other services from the Coliseum by Hung Hom KCR Station, CTS House on Connaught Road and the MTR Park Hotel on Tung Lo Wan Road in Causeway Bay. The same companies also run buses to Shenzhen and Guangzhou from the airport – see *By Air, Getting to China from the Airport*, p. 493, for details.

Getting Around

Getting around Hong Kong is easy, inexpensive and often a pleasure. In spite of the vast number of people crammed into this small area, the excellent and integrated public facilities cope comfortably and modes of transport range from enormous escalators to high-speed subways (MTR). As it has acquired wealth, the city has invested heavily in its infrastructural systems, which it hopes will continue to bring visitors to this Asian transport hub. Along with its speedy, efficient services, Hong Kong also offers slower, more traditional transport such as the Peak Tram and Star Ferry, both of which have become tourist attractions in their own right.

By MTR

M-Train (Moktzekin)

Hong Kong's Mass Transit Railway (MTR or subway) system is cheap at only HK$4-26 per journey, but it can get very busy at peak times (7-10 am, 11 am-1 pm and 4-7 pm). There are six routes, the most useful being the Sheung Wan (red) and the Island (blue) lines. The **Sheung Wan Line** runs from Central on Hong Kong Island under the harbor, following Nathan Road north until Prince Edward, where it bears west out to Tsuen Wan. The **Island Line** goes from Sheung Wan in the west of Hong Kong Island past Central, Admiralty, Wanchai and Causeway Bay out as far as Chai Wan in the east. Route maps are plastered all over the MTR system as well as on the trains themselves. They also show which is the next station, where the train is heading and which side of the carriage the next exit will be. Stations often have a bewildering choice of street exits – where appropriate the best exit is listed after the station name in the Sightseeing descriptions below. Using the ticket machines is fairly straightforward, but you need coins or small

Hong Kong & Macau

notes (HK$20 or less) to use them – there are change kiosks in the stations. Tickets are in the form of plastic cards. If you plan to use the MTR a lot in one day you can also buy day-passes for HK$50.

Octopus Cards

If you're going to be in Hong Kong for a substantial period it is certainly worth buying an Octopus card. The stored-value cards can be used to pay for most forms of transport in Hong Kong as well as at certain stores and restaurants, including McDonalds, Starbucks, Circle K and 7-Eleven. You can obtain the smart cards for HK$150 (including HK$50 deposit) from MTR stations and then top them up at the aforementioned stores. The deposit is non-refundable if you return the card within three months, which makes the cards not really suited for short-term visitors. Still, if you don't want to have to wait in line to buy tickets for your stay, it could be US$6 well spent. There are now also **tourist-friendly** versions of the card available. For HK$220 you get to travel one way on the airport express (HK$300 for round-trip) and then enjoy unlimited MTR transport for three days as well as HK$20 credit for other transport services. You can buy the passes at Airport Express Stations. See www.octopuscards.com for more details.

By Rail

In addition to its MTR system, Hong Kong also has an effective rail network, which is useful for getting out to the New Territories. The **Kowloon-Canton Railway** has several branches and runs as far as the Lo Wu (Luo Hu) border with Shenzhen in the north, Tuen Mun in the west and Ma On Shan in the east, with a light rail line (and the airport express) going out to Lantau. For more on these lines see *Getting to the New Territories*, p. 525.

By Tram (www.hktramways.com)

Trams have operated here since 1904 and are still a common feature on the streets of Hong Kong Island. Trams follow several overlapping routes along the north shore of Hong Kong Island, of which the most useful run along Queensway and Hennessy Roads. They are in service from early morning until midnight and cost HK$2. They are a fun way to get around the city, offering good views from the upper deck. Get on at the back of the tram and pay as you alight. If you're really fond of tram

Tram (Richard Gallagher)

travel you can even rent trams for private tours of the city, although it's not cheap (HK$570-2,800 per hour) – check out the website for more.

By Bus

Hong Kong has an efficient and extensive double-decker bus and minibus network that covers the major sights on Hong Kong and Kowloon as well as destinations in the New Territories. There are also services on some of the larger Outlying Islands such as Lantau. However, given that the MTR covers many of the sights close to Kowloon's Nathan Road and Hong Kong Island's downtown zone, buses are most useful for trips to more distant parts of Hong Kong Island and into the New Territories. The major hubs are outside of the two Star Ferry terminals and at Exchange Square in Central. Buses tend to be comfortable but can be slow, especially during rush hour. Services operate from 6:30 am to midnight and cost between HK$3.5 and HK$6. Bus numbers are listed in the Sightseeing section where applicable.

By Taxi

Easily identifiable bright red taxis are everywhere on Hong Kong Island and in Kowloon, though you'll have trouble finding an empty one in the rain. Cabs are green in the New Territories and blue on Lantau. Fares are HK$15 for the first two km (1.2 miles), and then HK$7 per km (0.6 miles) beyond this, with a fee of HK$5 per piece of luggage placed in the trunk. If you go through any of the Kowloon-Hong Kong Island tunnels you'll have to pay the HK$20-30 toll, which will be added to your fare at the end of the journey. Likewise, the ride to the airport involves extra charges. Many drivers speak a smattering of English but it's best to get the name of your destination written in Chinese at your hotel, or make sure know where it is on the map.

By Car

Although you can rent cars in Hong Kong, its small size, excellent public transport facilities and the amount of traffic make it more hassle than it's worth, even for residents. What's more, car rental isn't cheap (starting at around HK$500 a day) and many of the places you might want to escape to, such as the Outlying Islands, are inaccessible by car. If all this isn't enough to discourage then try Avis (www.avis.com.hk) at Shop 46, Peninsula Centre, 67 Mody Road (☎ 00852-2890-6988; Mon-Fri 9 am-6 pm, Sat & Sun 9 am-4 pm). You need a **valid international driver's license** to rent vehicles.

By Bicycle

Downtown Hong Kong is not fun to negotiate by bike, but once out in the countryside or on the outlying islands it can be a great way to get around. You can rent bikes on Cheung Chau Island (see p. 524)

and at Tai Po KCR Station in the New Territories for around HK$50 per day. See *Adventures on Wheels*, p. 544, for more.

By Ferry

★★★Star Ferry (www.starferry.com.hk)

Star Ferry (Mailer diablo)

Despite the construction of several tunnels linking Hong Kong Island and Kowloon, the Star Ferry, in service since 1888, remains one of the principal carriers for this route and offers 10 minutes of spectacular harbor views in the bargain. Divided into a pricier upper deck and a cheaper lower level, the Star Ferry has featured in many a movie and is a must for any traveler to Hong Kong. The ferries run from Tsimshatsui and Hung Hom in Kowloon to both Wanchai and Central on Hong Kong Island. The Central Pier was just moved, amid much controversy, from its old locale due north of Statue Square, to a new spot half a mile to the north, next to the Outlying Islands Ferry Pier. Fares range from HK$1.7 to HK$5.30, depending on route and class. It's best to have exact change, although there are change booths at the toll gates. If you want to see more, the Star Ferry also runs harbor cruises (see *Adventures On Water*, p. 545).

Outlying Islands Ferries

Hong Kong has countless small islands and to reach many of them you'll need to come to the Outlying Islands Ferry Pier, next to the Star Ferry terminal on Hong Kong Island. There are frequent and inexpensive services to Cheung Chau, Lamma and Lantau. Although journeys can be a little choppy, the crafts are fairly modern and comfortable. Note that during severe weather, such as typhoons, these services may be suspended, so check before you head out to the islands if you've got a plane to catch. See the descriptions of these islands below for durations and frequencies of services.

Orientation

If you limit yourself to the principal downtown zones, as many visitors do, then you could be forgiven for thinking that Hong Kong is little more than a densely crowded city. But it is actually comprised of Hong Kong Island, Kowloon, the New Territories and some 235 islands. Of these islands, Hong Kong is the most densely populated, while **Lantau** is the largest and is home to the impressive modern airport, Disneyland, the serene seated Buddha at Ngong Ping and plenty of beaches and hikes.

The center of Hong Kong is spread between the northern side of Hong Kong Island and Kowloon, just across the harbor. Downtown **Hong Kong Island** is divided into several districts, which stretch east from **Sheung Wan** through **Central**, **Admiralty** and **Wanchai** out to **Causeway Bay**, south of which the lowlands are home to Happy Valley racetrack (see *Gambling*, p. 547). These five districts make up the heart of Hong Kong's business and shopping center and there are countless bars, cafés, hotels and restaurants nestled in and around the hundreds of skyscrapers. This narrow strip of modernity is currently being expanded by the most recent of Hong Kong's land reclamation projects, which will take a swathe of sea between Central and Causeway Bay. Near the shore, streets in this section of town predominantly run east-to-west, changing names as they pass through different districts. But the farther from the sea you travel, the less ordered the roads become, as they negotiate the increasingly steep hills that rise to the south, the loftiest of which, **Victoria Peak**, enjoys amazing views over this man-made magnificence.

A bus ride away on the other side of the island, you'll find some retreat from the madness at **Stanley**, which has a couple of beaches and a good market. Not far away, **Aberdeen** is renowned for its floating restaurants, while nearby Ocean Park is Hong Kong's original theme park. Across the harbor from Central, **Kowloon** has more hotels, restaurants and shops and offers breathtaking views back across to the island. The southern part of Kowloon is known as **Tsimshatsui**, which leads north along its bustling neon-lit main artery, **Nathan Road**, to **Jordan**, **Yaumatei** and **Mongkok**, where you'll find many of Hong Kong's best markets and the blurry boundary with the New Territories.

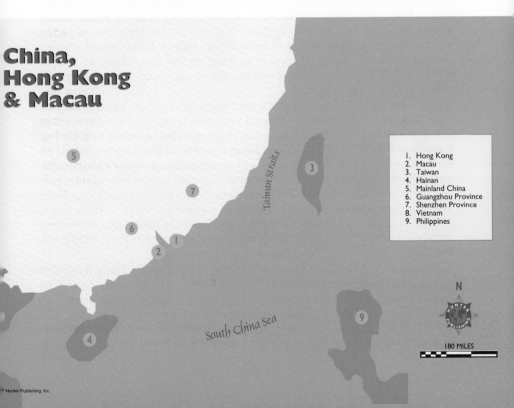

China, Hong Kong & Macau

1. Hong Kong
2. Macau
3. Taiwan
4. Hainan
5. Mainland China
6. Guangzhou Province
7. Shenzhen Province
8. Vietnam
9. Philippines

Taiwan Straits

South China Sea

N

180 MILES

© Hunter Publishing, Inc.

There is more than enough to keep you occupied for a few days (if not weeks) in the two key zones of Hong Kong Island and Kowloon, but it is only when you step outside of these areas that you will witness the true diversity Hong Kong has to offer. The **Outlying Islands** and **New Territories** contain beaches, hiking trails, small fishing villages and temples. To gain a true sense of Hong Kong (and a break from the fast-paced metropolitan life), a visit to at least one of these areas is imperative.

A "ladder street" in Aberdeen (K.C. Tang)

Information Sources

i **Information Offices & Publications** (www. discoverhongkong. com): Hong Kong is one of the few places in China that has first-rate tourist information services and, whether you visit their offices or just pick up some of the multitude of brochures and pamphlets, you're certain to find them useful. If you only want to carry around one of the tourist office's booklets, the *Hong Kong Leisure Guide for Business Travelers* has most of the information found in their other leaflets. If you're just passing through for a few hours, it's worth picking up the *Hong Kong In-Transit Guide*, which has a selection of quick sightseeing routes that can be completed in half a day or less.

If you want advice in person you'll find the tourist offices equally helpful. One of the most conveniently located branches is in the Tsimshatsui Star Ferry Terminal (daily 8 am-8 pm), but there are also branches by Exit F of Causeway Bay MTR station (same hours), at the Lo Wu (Luo Hu in pinyin) border crossing (daily 8 am-6 pm) and just before the arrivals lounge in the airport (daily 7 am-11 pm). There is a multilingual tourist information hotline on ☎ 00852-2508-1234. For more detailed information on Hong Kong (including government statistics) and good maps of the whole of Hong Kong, you can visit the Government Publications Centre at Room 402, 4F Murray Building, Garden Road, Central (☎ 00852-2537-1910; Mon-Fri 9 am-6 pm & Sat 9 am-1 pm).

Audio and PDA Guides: Showing its technological colors, Hong Kong also has an audio guide service that can be accessed through your cell phone. The service provides tourist information about many of Hong Kong's sights and also keeps you posted on events and promotions. To access the service, simply dial ☎ 454 (but you'll have to pay roaming charges) or pop into the tourist offices at Causeway Bay or the Tsimshatsui Star Ferry Terminal and pay

HK$60, which gives you three days of unlimited access, free from roaming charges. Tech-travelers might also want to take advantage of the PDA Hong Kong Leisure Guide, which also provides basic Cantonese phrases and GPS mapping – you can download the package for free at www. discoverhongkong.com/pda.

Magazines, Newspapers & Television: Beyond the tourist information brochures (see above) there are also a host of expat-oriented magazines such as *City Life*, *Hong Kong Where*, *HK Magazine* and *The List*, which are free and can be picked up from bars, hotels and restaurants. Hong Kong's more liberal social stance means that the territory has China's only gay city magazine, *G Magazine* (www.gmagazinehk.com), which you can find at bars and clubs. To keep up to speed with world events there are two local English newspapers – *The South China Morning Post* and *The Standard*. If you'd rather watch than read there are two English-language TV channels, ATV World and Pearl.

Maps: Free maps of Hong Kong are available at tourist offices and hotels across the territory. Of the many versions available, the *City Life* map and the one produced by the tourist office are the best. If you want good maps for a trip out to the New Territories, then try the Government Publications Center (see *Information Offices & Publications*, above for details).

Events & Festivals

 Reflecting its history of both Chinese and Western influence, Hong Kong celebrates festivals from both calendars – Christmas, Buddha's Birthday, and a series of modern events designed specifically to draw visitors! All of the regular Chinese festivals are held (see *Holidays & Festivals*, p. 73) along with a host of other traditional celebrations. If you're going to visit during a festival month and want to attend, check out www.discoverhongkong.com for exact dates (which change from year to year) and information on associated tours.

Rugby Seven's (March/April) – The Sevens is a major event on the world rugby circuit and sees hordes of fans from around the globe converge on Hong Kong. Hotels are booked to capacity and everything is busier so, unless you're coming to watch the matches, it's a period worth avoiding.

Hong Kong International Film Festival (April) – One of Hong Kong's most prestigious events, this attracts film lovers from around the world. It last two weeks and features screenings of local and international movies around the city. Check out www.hkff.org.hk for more.

Buddha's Birthday (April/May) – Although this day is celebrated at Buddhist temples throughout Hong Kong, it's worth heading to Po Lin Monastery on Lantau to watch worshippers bathing Buddha's statue.

Tin Hau's Birthday (late April/May) – Tin Hau is the local goddess of the sea (also known as A-Ma in Macau and Mazu on the mainland and in Taiwan) whose importance in Hong Kong is signified by the fact that over 100 temples in the territory (and an MTR station) are dedicated to her. Tin Hau's Birthday is celebrated by processions laden down with religious icons and brightly decorated paper offerings, which make their way to the various temples around the territory. Once at the temple, there are fireworks and further festivities. The Tin Hau Temple in the district of the same name on Hong Kong Island is a good place to witness the celebrations.

Cheung Chau Bun Festival (May) – The origins of this unique festival are somewhat uncertain but it falls on the birthday of another important regional deity, Pak Tai, and is held on the small island of Cheung Chau. The festival sees enormous bamboo towers festooned with traditional Chinese buns and in the past these structures were ascended by the brave, who grabbed as many buns as they could on the way up. The festival culminates in a colorful street procession featuring children on stilts. Thousands of residents and tourists alike flock to see the festival.

Shopping Festival (August) – The annual shopping festival combines promotional rates and shows to attract visitors to Hong Kong's legion of malls.

Mid-Autumn Festival (September/October) – This is celebrated with the usual mooncakes, along with lanterns and a giant dragon dance in the district of Tai Hang south of Causeway Bay. The dance originated over 100 years ago when the inhabitants of Tai Hang were struck by a plague and then a typhoon a few days before the festival. They say that bad things happen in threes and while the villagers were repairing the typhoon damage a snake came and ate their livestock. To overcome their run of bad luck the villagers made an enormous straw dragon, lit firecrackers and danced for three days. Sure enough, all their problems were solved and they have been performing the dance for the Mid-Autumn Festival ever since.

Quiksilver Hong Kong Surfing Cup (December) – This annual surfing tournament draws ever larger crowds to Big Wave Bay on Hong Kong Island (see p. 547).

Communications

 Post Office: On Hong Kong Island the principal **post office** is at 2 Connaught Place, while Kowloon's main office is at 405 Nathan Road in Jordan.

Telephone code: 00852.

Internet Access: There are Internet cafés dotted around Hong Kong, and if you have a laptop, many coffee shops, malls and hotel rooms have **wireless connection**, but you may have to pay for access (generally about HK$0.50 per minute). Internet cafés charge upwards of HK$20 an hour, while hotel business centers charge significantly more. But there are places where you can surf for free for a limited period – try the access points in the **Hong Kong Convention and Exhibition Center** at 1 Harbour Road in Wanchai. Net cafés to try on Hong Kong Island include one opposite Habibi (see p. 557) on Wellington Street and another near the junction with Luard Street on the south side of Lockhart Street in Causeway Bay. There are also plenty of places in Chungking Mansions on Nathan Road – City Cyberworks charges HK$20 an hour, which includes a drink and they also have photocopying, printing, scanning and fax services.

Money

Banks: Hong Kong is one of Asia's financial hubs and this shows itself in the number and range of different banks you'll find here – even up on Victoria Peak you can get hold of cash from an ATM! Main branches include the Bank of America (Bank of America Tower, 12 Harcourt Road, Central), the Bank of China (1 Garden Road, Central) and HSBC (29 Queen's Road, Central). They all have ATMs, offer money exchange and are open Monday to Friday, 9 am-4 pm and Saturday 9 am-noon. ATMs generally accept most major international cards, but check before putting your card in the machine. The territory is also fairly switched on to payment by credit card – most major hotels, restaurants and shops will take plastic.

Exchange Offices: For those who prefer to pay with paper, you'll find Hong Kong overflowing with exchange offices – the ground floor of Chungking Mansions on Nathan Road has some of the best rates, but make sure you compare a few places. Shops tend to be open from early in the morning until 9 or 10 pm.

Consulates

Australia, 23-24F, Harcourt Centre, 25 Harbour Road, Wanchai (☎ 00852-2827-8881, www.australia.org.hk).

Canada, 12F, One Exchange Square, 8 Connaught Place, Central (☎ 00852-2847-7555, www.hongkong.gc.ca).

China, 7F, Lower Block, China Resources Building, 26 Harbour Road, Wanchai (☎ 00852-3413-2424, www.fmcoprc.gov.hk).

New Zealand, 6508 Central Plaza, 18 Harbour Road, Wanchai (☎ 00852-2525-5044, www.nzembassy.com).

United Kingdom, 1 Supreme Court Road, Admiralty (☎ 00852-2901-3000, www.britishconsulate.org.hk).

United States, 26 Garden Road, Central (☎ 00852-2523-9011, www.hongkong.usconsulate.gov).

Emergency & Medical Services

In case of emergency you can call 999 and be connected to all services, but if you need the **police** specifically call the hotline on ☎ 00852-2527-7177. Hong Kong has the best medical facilities in China and if you have any health problems it's worth seeing a doctor here rather than on the mainland. Healthcare is cheap and most **hospitals** here are of a good standard – **Queen Elizabeth** at 30 Gascoigne Road in Kowloon (☎ 00852-2958-8888) is one of the best and has a 24-hour accident and emergency wing. Alternatively, call or check out www.ha.org.hk for the nearest facilities. There are also several private options, such as **Matilda International Hospital** at 41 Mount Kellett Road in Central (☎ 00852-2849-0123, www.matilda.org), which offer first-rate but expensive care (although the cost should be covered by your insurance).

Sightseeing

 For such a small place, Hong Kong has an amazing array of sights, ranging from the ultra-modern **Symphony of Lights** show which illuminates the harbor every night at 8 pm, to historic temples, **colonial remnants** and nature's own attractions, including some fine beaches. With so many things to see, it can be difficult to know where to begin, but the good news is that even getting there is often part of the experience in Hong Kong. Whether riding the **historic Peak Tram** or crossing the harbor on the **Star Ferry**, the incredible skyline dominates. What's more, the territory's small size and excellent modern transport connections make seeing a lot in a short space of time perfectly feasible. If you have limited time, then it's worth starting with the triple-starred attractions, but if you have longer you can pick and choose to suit your tastes, mood and the weather!

First impressions of Hong Kong are of the spectacular skyscrapers, the scenery of the harbor and the hustle and bustle of its neon-clad streets. But to really gain some insight into the contradictions that typify the territory you should take a trip to the south of Hong Kong Island or, if you have more time to spare, go over to one of the **Outlying Islands** or into the **New Territories**.

The Essential Day Trip

Take a harbor-side stroll from the **Avenue of Stars** along the harbor to the **Star Ferry**. Sit on the upper deck and enjoy the 10-minute trip across to Central. Jump on the #15C bus up to the **Peak Tram** terminal and marvel at the views (and impossible angle of the tram). Enjoy a walk around the **Peak Circuit** and then finish with dinner or a drink at Café Deco, overlooking Hong Kong. If you still have the time or energy, head for a drink at **Lan Kwai Fong** and then take the MTR to Kowloon's **Nathan Road** for a dash of neon and maybe some night shopping.

Tours

As mentioned above, Hong Kong's sights are fairly easy to negotiate on your own, but if your time is very limited then a tour can offer the opportunity to pack a lot into a short period. Furthermore, some tours will take you to places that would otherwise be difficult to reach and can offer detailed guidance to help you fully understand the sights.

Gray Line operates some of the best city trips, but there are a host of more specialized operators who organize harbor cruises and cultural and adventurous tours – see *Adventures*, p. 539, for details.

Gray Line tours (☎ 00852-2207-7235, www.grayline.com.hk) can be booked through the tourist office and many of the major hotels. For a brief trip around the main sights, try the Deluxe Hong Kong Island tour which runs twice daily (8 am and 1 pm) from major hotels and costs HK$295. The tour visits Victoria Peak, Man Mo Temple, Aberdeen, Repulse Bay and Stanley market, lasting around five hours. If you want to see the New Territories, Gray Line's Land Between tour introduces some of Hong Kong's wide-open spaces and operates twice daily (8:30 am & 1 pm), costing HK$395 for a host of sights, including Tai Mo Shan and Fanling walled village. The Heritage tour (Mon, Wed & Fri 8:45 am; HK$295) opens the door to Hong Kong's traditions and takes in a variety of the New Territories' cultural sights, such as the Lo Wai walled village, the Man Mo Temple and wishing trees at Tai Po.

Hong Kong Island

This small and spectacular mountainous island remains at the heart of Hong Kong's economy and has a plethora of attractions, both manmade and natural, foremost of which is the looming hulk of Victoria Peak. There is plenty to see within the downtown area of Central, Admiralty, Wanchai and Causeway Bay, while to the west Sheung Wan and Kennedy Town afford a more traditional flavor. Over on the other side of the island beaches, markets and a theme park await.

★★★Victoria Peak (www.thepeak.com.hk)

Victoria Peak looms 1,800 feet over Hong Kong and has long been home to many of the city's wealthiest residents. Its name is taken from the British Queen, from the time when having a house on the Peak was very much "the done thing" in order to escape the teeming heat and hustle below. Although powers have changed hands and the property market has flattened out, Victoria Peak remains an exclusive residential area and land prices are still some of the highest in the world. Fortunately, you don't have to be one of the Hong Kong elite to ascend to the summit of the Peak and if there's only one thing you do in Hong Kong it should probably be this. Six million visitors take to the Peak annually but, despite the crowds, the outstanding views north over Hong Kong's forest of skyscrapers and the bustling harbor to Kowloon in the distance are unmissable. Just make sure you pick a clear(ish) day, or you might see nothing at all!

The Peak Tram

You can take a taxi or bus #15 from Exchange Square all the way to the top of the Peak, but the historic tram makes for a much more dramatic and memorable journey. The tram is actually a funicular railway and was first constructed in 1888 as commuter transport. Before the tram, residents used to ascend the Peak in sedan chairs carried by two coolies. After its construction, the tram initially had three classes – first class was reserved for government officials and Peak residents, second was for policemen and soldiers and third was for servants.

Originally steam-powered, the tram is now electric and runs up and down the mountain at seemingly impossible angles. The cost is HK$30 round-trip or HK$20 one-way for the 10-minute journey. Trams run every 10-15 minutes between 7 am and midnight. Try to get seats at the front on the right-hand side for the journey up. Bus number #15C runs from the Star Ferry terminal to the bottom station, or you can take the MTR to Central and walk there in about 10 minutes. If the heat isn't too much for you, there's also the option of walking up the entire way, but you'll need plenty of water and at least an hour. You're probably better off saving your energy for the walk around the top or back down the Peak.

On the Peak

Although you'll generally find the clearest skies in the morning, my favorite time to visit is mid- to late afternoon, which allows you enough time for a walk around the circuit or up to the highest point (see *Adventures On Foot*, p. 540) in the warm glow of afternoon light. After that you can sit and watch the sunset before taking dinner on the terrace at Café Deco (see p. 560;

Dusk view from the Peak (Tot Foster)

reserve a table before you set out on the walk). Try to choose a clear day to ascend the Peak, but if this isn't possible and clouds obscure the view, it's worth sticking around for a while as you may get a breathtaking few moments of respite.

Once at the top there are two major buildings, the Peak Galleria and the Peak Tower, which contain more cafés, restaurants, shops and attractions than some small towns. Fortunately, they also offer viewing decks with incredible vistas. You don't need to worry about taking supplies with you as there is everything from atmospheric restaurants to Burger King, McDonalds, Haagen Dazs and even a supermarket and an ATM at the top. The distinctive Peak Tower was built in 1996 and is both loved and hated for its unusual design, which has been compared to a giant wok straddling Victoria Gap. The Peak Tower's observation decks were closed for renovation at the time of writing, but you'll find equally jawdropping views from the platforms at the top of the Galleria, which tend to be a bit quieter. The Galleria also has viewing decks with more natural views south over to Lamma Island.

If there aren't any views or you have kids, you could visit **Madame Tussaud's Waxworks Museum** (daily 10 am-10 pm; HK$115 or HK$120 including the Peak Tram) or **Ripley's Believe It or Not** (daily 10 am-10 pm; HK$90) which has a bizarre collection of oddities, including a 20-foot-tall replica of the Eiffel Tower made from toothpicks! Both are found in the Peak Tower.

Hong Kong

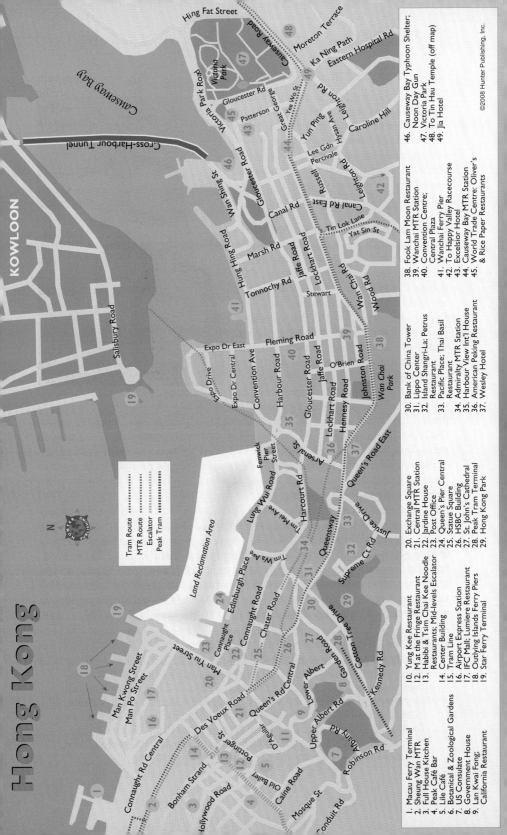

KOWLOON

Causeway Bay

Cross-Harbour Tunnel

Streets and landmarks (labels on map):
Hing Fat Street, Moreton Terrace, Ka Ning Path, Eastern Hospital Rd, Causeway Road, Victoria Park, Victoria Park Road, Gloucester Rd, Patterson, Great George, Lee Wo St., Yun Ping, Hysan Ave, Leighton Rd, Caroline Hill, Lee Gdn, Percivale, Russell, Canal Rd East, Tin Lok Lane, Yat Sin St, Canal Rd, Marsh Rd, Jaffe Road, Lockhart Road, Wan Shing St, Hung Hing Road, Gloucester Road, Wan Chai Rd, Wood Rd, Tonnochy Rd, Stewart, Wan Chai Park, O'Brien, Johnston Road, Hennesy Road, Fleming Road, Expo Dr East, Expo Dr Central, Convention Ave, Harbour Road, Gloucester Road, Jaffe Road, Lockhart Road, Expo Drive, Fenwick Pier Street, Arsenal St., Queen's Road East, Wesley Hotel, Lung Wui Road, Tim Mei Ave, Harcourt Rd, Tim Wa Ave, Supreme Ct Rd, Justice Drive, Queensway, Edinburgh Place, Connaught Place, Connaught Road, Chater Road, Cotton Tree Drive, Garden Road, Lower Albert, Upper Albert Rd, Albany Rd, Kennedy Rd, Robinson Rd, Queen's Rd Central, Des Voeux Road, Man Yiu Street, Connaught Rd Central, Man Kwong Street, Man Po Street, Bonham Strand, Pottinger St., D'Aguilar, Old Bailey, Caine Road, Mosque St, Conduit Rd, Hollywood Road, Salisbury Road, Park Road, Victoria Park

N

Legend:
Tram Route
MTR Route
Escalator
Peak Tram

©2008 Hunter Publishing, Inc.

Land Reclamation Area

1. Macau Ferry Terminal
2. Sheung Wan MTR
3. Full House Kitchen
4. Peak Café Bar
5. Lile Café
6. Botanical & Zoological Gardens
7. US Consulate
8. Government House
9. Lan Kwai Fong; California Restaurant
10. Yung Kee Restaurant
11. M at the Fringe Restaurant
12. Habibi & Tsim Chai Kee Noodle Restaurants; Mid-levels Escalator
13. Habibi & Tsim Chai Kee Noodle Restaurants; Mid-levels Escalator
14. Center Building
15. Tram Line
16. Airport Express Station
17. IFC Mall; Lumiere Restaurant
18. Outlying Islands Ferry Piers
19. Star Ferry Terminal
20. Exchange Square
21. Central MTR Station
22. Jardine House
23. Post Office
24. Queen's Pier Central
25. Statue Square
26. HSBC Building
27. St. John's Cathedral
28. Peak Tram Terminal
29. Hong Kong Park
30. Bank of China Tower
31. Lippo Center
32. Island Shangri-La; Petrus Restaurant
33. Pacific Place; Thai Basil Restaurant
34. Admiralty MTR Station
35. Harbour View Int'l House
36. American Peking Restaurant
37. Wesley Hotel
38. Fook Lam Moon Restaurant
39. Wanchai MTR Station
40. Convention Centre; Central Plaza
41. Wanchai Ferry Pier
42. To Happy Valley Racecourse
43. Excelsior Hotel
44. Causeway Bay MTR Station
45. World Trade Centre: Oliver's & Rice Paper Restaurants
46. Causeway Bay Typhoon Shelter;
47. Noon Day Gun
48. To Tin Hau Temple (off map)
49. Jia Hotel

Victoria Park

Central, Admiralty & the Mid-Levels

This was the original heart of colonial Hong Kong which housed many of the most important government and trading buildings. Today it retains its financial significance and now holds some of the most impressive skyscrapers found anywhere in the world (see *The Sky's the Limit*, below). Although there are a few historic buildings such as **Government House** and **St. John's Cathedral** dotted around, they seem uncomfortably out of place, surrounded by the glass and metal towers that define Central and Admiralty. Getting around this part of town can be a confusing business, with the quickest routes often running along raised walkways and through shopping malls, but fortunately there are plenty of signs to guide you. However, some of this district's claustrophobia may be relieved when the land reclamation

The Lippo Center

project currently underway is complete: a swathe of sea stretching from the Outlying Islands Ferry Pier across to Causeway Bay will soon be watery no more, but exactly what the land will be used for is a source of contention. Although civil right groups want the area to provide an open-plan promenade offering a much-needed sense of space, commercial interests often seem to win out in Hong Kong.

As you ascend away from the narrow strip of coastal Central through the nightlife zone of Lan Kwai Fong (see *Where to Drink*, p. 564) there is some respite from the skyscrapers, elevated walkways and congestion in the form of Hong Kong Park and the Zoological and Botanical Gardens. To the west, the Mid-Levels has long been a favorite expat residence, and is now served by the world's longest outdoor escalator, which stretches some 2,600 feet up the slope and takes 20 minutes. The **Mid-Levels Escalator** runs downwards from 6-10 am and upwards from 10:20 am-midnight.

THE SKY'S THE LIMIT

The large population and lack of land in the British colony of Hong Kong led to land reclamation projects as early as the late 19th century and, once advances in architecture allowed buildings to reach skywards, Hong Kong focused on the vertical. Although there have been tall buildings in Hong Kong since the 1930s, the territory's first real skyscraper, **Jardine House**, was built in 1973 and, though now dwarfed by surrounding buildings, its unique porthole windows make it stand out over three decades later.

Today there are so many tall buildings in Hong Kong that, to make their mark, new skyscrapers have to be significantly higher than their neighbors (the 1,362-ft **IFC2** and Kowloon's new **International Commerce Centre** for example) or feature eye-catching shapes. Hong Kong may be an ultra-modern financial hub, but *fengshui* (see p. 54) still has its part to play, and geomancy experts are consulted on architectural design even on projects as unerringly Western as Disneyland! Architectural design has often been interpreted as a reflection of the owner's future prospects or intentions. Thus the **Bank of China**'s dagger like angles were perceived to illustrate the mainland's attitude toward the returning colony! Other buildings to look out for include the Sir Norman Foster-designed industrial-looking **HSBC Building** which features on some of the territory's banknotes, the mirrored bulges of the **Lippo Centre** and the unmissable **Center Building** which blazes with color at night.

Until recently Kowloon was hindered in the race for the sky by restrictions placed on building height to allow aircraft to land at Kai Tak airport. But, with the completion of the new airport at Chek Lap Kok on Lantau, these have been lifted and there are now construction projects afoot that will see superskyscrapers extend to both sides of the harbor. These days, all of the world's great cities have tall buildings, but, despite fierce competition from Shanghai, Hong Kong continues to stretch for the sky.

★**Zoological and Botanical Gardens**, Albany Road, Central (☎ 00852-2530-0154; daily 6 am-7 pm; free; Admiralty MTR, Exit B & C1). The Hong Kong Zoological & Botanical Gardens are on the northern slopes of Victoria Peak and provide a soothing break from the city below. The extensive gardens were originally built in 1871 and are divided by Albany Road with an underground walkway joining the two sections. In the park you'll find over 1,000 different plant species on show. The park is also home to a number of animals and birds, including orangutans, monkeys, a tree kangaroo and pink flamingos – whose sounds are very welcoming after the noise of car horns downtown.

★**Hong Kong Park** (daily 6 am-11 pm; Admiralty MTR, Exit C1). This large park is just east of the Botanical Gardens and makes a pleasant diversion from shopping at nearby Pacific Place mall. Inside the park you'll find scenic gardens, a small lake, a children's playground and, of most interest, the ★★**Edward Youde Aviary** (daily 9 am-5 pm; free). The aviary is discreetly housed under an arched swathe of mesh and its raised walkways allow you to traverse the tropical foliage, which is alive with the color of its 150 species of Southeast Asian birds. Birdspotters might also want to come to the park on Wednesday mornings as there are guided tours (see B*ird Watching*, p. 540, for more). Also within Hong Kong Park you'll find the **Flagstaff House Museum of Teaware** (Wed-Mon 10 am-5 pm, free), which is worth a visit as much for its architecture and history as its contents. The building was originally constructed in 1846 and is Hong Kong's oldest remaining colonial building. Inside, you'll find an extensive collection of teaware spanning from the Tang dynasty to the 20th century.

West to Sheung Wan & Kennedy Town

If you want to escape the mirror-clad monoliths of modernity, a trip west toward Sheung Wan can supply a more traditional feel and older buildings that still (just about) fit their surroundings. **Hollywood Road** was used to film scenes for the movie *The World of Suzie Wong* and also has the **Man Mo Temple** (see below) along with antique shops galore (see *Shopping*, p. 538). Back down toward the harbor, the **Western Market** is housed in a three-storey Edwardian-style building, although its renovated interior sells arts and crafts rather than food as it used to. Some of Hong Kong's most interesting streets lie within a few minutes of Sheung Wan MTR station and, even if you're not in the market for traditional herbal remedies, exotic animal parts or name stamps, Wing Lok Street and Wan Ma Lane make for an intriguing walk.

Farther west, the tram lines extend out to **Kennedy Town** and, while there's little specific to see here, **Mount Davis**, which rises nearly 900 feet, is worth climbing for the views, and has one of Hong Kong's best youth hostels.

Incense coils in Man Mo Temple (Mike McD82)

★★**Man Mo Temple**, 126 Hollywood Road, Sheung Wan (daily 8 am-6 pm; free; Sheung Wan MTR, Exit A2). Although not as grand as some temples in Hong Kong, the Man Mo Temple is one of the most atmospheric you're likely to encounter here. It unites an unlikely pairing of gods, Man, the God of Literature and Civil Servants, and Mo, the God of War and Martial Arts. It's situated in a very traditional part of town and just the walk there is enough to transport you to a different era. The streets outside sell religious items and inside you'll see elaborately carved wooden chairs formerly used to transport the gods in processions, along with some of the longest incense coils in the territory, which can burn for up to three weeks! At the far end of the temple, you'll find statues and altars to the two gods presiding over the temple.

Wanchai

East of Admiralty, Wanchai was once home to brothels notorious among sailors and the area's seedy ambience and charms form the setting for Richard Mason's novel about a Wanchai prostitute, *The World of Suzie Wong*. The book was later made into a movie, although much of this was actually shot around Hollywood Road. These days only an inkling of Wanchai's former iniquity remains in the form of a few girlie bars which are outnumbered by a newer collection of pubs, clubs and restaurants, all set amidst the obligatory sea of skyscrapers. The most impressive of Wanchai's buildings are near the harbor. The **Hong Kong Convention and Exhibition Centre** at 1 Harbour Road resembles anything from a manta ray to lotus petals, depending on your perspective, and was where Hong Kong was formally returned to China in 1997. Outside the building, **Golden Bauhinia Square** holds daily flag

Wanchai's Lee Tung Street (Jerry Crimson Mann)

raising and lowering ceremonies popular with mainland tourists. Behind the Exhibition Centre, **Central Plaza**'s golden glow is unmissable and you can ascend to the 46th floor for good views over the harbor.

Causeway Bay

East along the tramlines from Wanchai, Hennessy Road becomes Yee Woo Street and you'll approach Causeway Bay, which seems to be inaccurately named until you realize that this bustling district was under water until the 1950s! While there's plenty of eating and shopping to be done in Causeway Bay, along with a range of accommodation options, there is little to see. Down on the waterfront the Causeway Bay Typhoon Shelter is full of yachts and sampans. Nearby the **Noon Day Gun** still sounds daily in homage to bygone days. Victoria Park (see below) in the east also affords some respite from Causeway Bay's hustle and bustle. Farther out, the 200-year-old **Tin Hau temple** (daily 7 am-5 pm) by the MTR station of the same name (exit B) is also worth a look. The temple was built by a Hakka family who found a statue to Tin Hau among some rocks on the shore and so they erected a shelter to house it. Over time that became the temple you can see today. Aside from these "sights," activities focus on shopping and one of the best places to do this is Times Square, which is actually a couple of modern towers packed with shops and restaurants.

Victoria Park, Causeway Bay (daily 24 hours; free; Tin Hau MTR, Exit B). The green open spaces provided by Victoria Park are some of the largest in the city and it is a popular *tai chi* spot. There are a number of recreational facilities (including a public swimming pool and a boating lake). On June 4th every year, the park is transformed into a sea of candles in remembrance of the Tian'anmen Square Incident, testimony to Hong Kong's relative free-

Causeway Bay shoppers (mailer_diablo)

dom from mainland authority. If you're visiting during Chinese New Year it's worth paying a visit as the park hosts the annual flower fair.

Happy Valley, 2 Sports Road, Happy Valley (☎ 00852-2895-1523, www.hkjc.com; tram or Causeway Bay MTR). The colonial institution of Hong Kong's first race track was established in 1846 when the land on which it now stands was just a mosquito-infested marsh. Racing was a popular pastime for the British and, ever since its opening, Happy Valley has generated huge revenue. It still remains one of *the* places to be seen. Racing season is from September to June and if you're a racing enthusiast you may find the **Hong Kong Racing Museum** (Tuesday to Sunday 10 am-5 pm; free) of interest. It offers a detailed history of horseracing in Hong Kong, the history of Happy Valley and even houses the skeleton of one of Hong Kong's best-loved racehorses, Silver Lining. For more on the races see *Gambling, The Races*, p. 547.

South of the Island

One of the easiest and quickest escapes from the metropolitan mayhem is to take a short bus ride across to the south side of Hong Kong Island where you'll find beaches, markets, restaurants and temples set amidst pretty coastal scenery. The unhurried pace of life can come as something of a culture shock after the bustle of downtown, but it highlights the amazing contrasts even Hong Kong Island has to offer. Added to the aforementioned attractions, the south of the island also includes the dramatically located theme park of Ocean Park (see *Theme Parks*, p. 531).

★**Aberdeen** (bus #75 from Exchange Square in Central, or #4 & #4A from Lockhart Road in Causeway Bay). With a population of over 60,000 Aberdeen is not the quiet fishing village it once was, but it still offers an interesting glimpse into a fishing community, albeit one now surrounded by high-rises and shops. Formerly a pirate haven, these days Aberdeen is renowned for its **floating restaurants**, particularly Jumbo (see p. 561). Far more interesting are Aberdeen's **floating communities**. These communities include Tanka boat people and once numbered in the hundreds, but today only a few families live on the water. While you're here it's also worth checking out the lively wholesale fish market on the western side of the harbor. If you want to get a closer look at the harbor you can take a sam-

pan trip for around HK$60, or the trip out to one of the floating restaurants will give you a glimpse on the way to your lunch or dinner.

Deep Water Bay and Repulse Bay (bus #6, #6A and #260 from Exchange Square in Central). Of the many beaches dotted along the island's coastline, Deep Water Bay and Repulse Bay are two of the most accessible, attractive and expansive and can make the perfect antidote to an overdose of downtown smog. Both golden sand beaches were extensively cleaned up in the 1990s and today provide clean and safe swimming. They offer barbecue facilities and are backed by trees and a number of cafés and restaurants. However, the good transport links to downtown make both very popular with locals, particularly on weekends when they are packed with Filipino and Indonesian domestic workers enjoying their day off.

Putting Something Back: If you want to spend a bit of time on the beach and help make it cleaner for those who come after you, the Civic Exchange runs coastal clean-up projects. Check out www.civic-exchange.org for more.

★★**Stanley** (buses #6, #6A, #260 from Central or minibus #40 from Causeway Bay). Less than half an hour from Central, Stanley feels a world away from downtown and has all the ingredients for a great day-trip. There are **beaches, markets, temples**, a few **historic buildings**, and a smattering of **cafés** and **restaurants**. Although modern developments have eroded some of its former charm and it swarms with tourists on weekends, Stanley's relaxed seaside ambience still prevails and it makes for a thoroughly worthwhile trip.

Buses drop you opposite the entrance to the market (daily 11 am-6 pm) from where you can wander through its motley range of shops and stalls selling everything from mock Terracotta Warriors to designer sunglasses. At the end of the market you'll emerge onto Stanley Main Street which fronts the ocean and includes a number of restaurants, cafés and bars, the best-known of which is the Smugglers Inn (see p. 561). As always in Hong Kong, there's a shopping mall, the Stanley Plaza, at the far end of the street, but for once it is fairly discreet. Continuing around the bay you'll see the grand colonial building of **Murray House**, which was originally constructed as army quarters in Central in 1846 and stood there until 1982, after which it was placed in storage until 1998 when it was moved here. On the ground floor there are a few photographs and exhibits tracing the building's history. Murray

St. Stephen's Beach

House also now contains a selection of restaurants, some of which offer great ocean breezes and views. If you carry on past Murray House there's a trail that runs a few minutes along the coast to the tiny **Pak Tai temple** (daily 7 am-5:30 pm), where incense sticks burn against the backdrop of the South China Sea. Back in town the atmospheric **Tin Hau Temple** (daily 7 am-5:30 pm) was originally built in 1767 and, amidst the usual incense coils and statuary, it also has the skin of a prowling tiger which was shot by local police in 1942!

On the eastern side of the peninsula, Stanley Bay has a reasonable stretch of beach and more bars and cafés. But if you want a swim and some sunbathing, the pretty cove of **St. Stephen's Beach** is a nicer spot. It's a 10- or 15-minute walk south of the market to St. Stephen's and there are changing facilities, a watersports center (see *Adventures On Water*, p. 545) and a small kiosk that sells drinks and basic snacks.

Above the beach, **Stanley Military Cemetery** is a moving place, set on the hillside overlooking the bay. In the early days of colonial rule many British stationed in Hong Kong were buried here, but the cemetery was then closed for 70 years before re-opening in 1942 to bury those who lost their lives in World War II. Over 4,500 British, Canadians, Chinese and Indians died in Hong Kong during World War II, many of them during the fighting of December 1941, and 691 of them are buried here. There's a central memorial cross and plaque detailing the Allied resistance as well as a register of

Sampan boats in Victoria Harbour (Flizstiff)

those interred here. Beyond the cross, the grassy slopes are lined with gravestones, many of them hewn in rough stone, and there are several tombs for unknown soldiers.

Shek O and Big Wave Bay (bus #9 from Shau Kei Wan MTR). At the southernmost point of Hong Kong

Island, this sleepy, quaint fishing village is as far removed as you can get from city life and offers excellent beaches and a stunningly rugged coastline. Most of the houses you'll find here are made of stone, which gives Shek O a decidedly Mediterranean feel. To get to the beach, just walk east over the roundabout from the bus stop for about five minutes and you'll also find a number of shops and restaurants in the same area. From the promontory, there's also a small footbridge leading out to **Tai Tau Chau Island**, providing excellent views of the New Territories. A lit-

Shek O Beach (Alan Mak)

tle farther north will bring you to one of Hong Kong's few surfing spots at **Big Wave Bay**, where it's possible to rent body boards and surf boards (see *Adventures On Water*, p. 545).

A GOOD HALF-DAY TRIP

You can quite easily come to Stanley for just a couple hours, but to make a fuller day of it I'd recommend the following itinerary. Take a picnic lunch to enjoy by the beach (if you like to barbecue there are cooking pits at St. Stephens, but they are hard to come by on the weekends) and stop for a swim before a few moments reflection at the cemetery, then head back to town for a look around the markets and Tin Hau temple, out to the Pak Tai temple for sunset and then back to Murray House for dinner before taking the bus back to Central. You can also combine a trip to Stanley with a visit to Aberdeen, which can be reached by minibus #52 from outside Stanley Plaza.

Kowloon

Kowloon means Nine Dragons, a name that supposedly relates to the range of eight hills snaking around the north of the peninsula – the ninth dragon is in reverence to the emperor himself. While the south of the peninsula is dominated by the harbor and its manifold attractions, farther north you'll find Kowloon Park, hidden old temples and lots of markets that offer both shopping and the chance for a taste of an older Hong Kong.

The Harbour

Victoria Harbour, enjoyed from Kowloon, offers one of the world's greatest cityscapes. Arresting by day, the view intensifies with the addition of neon at night, and becomes a blaze of lasers and light during the nightly 8 pm Symphony of Lights and at Christmas and New Year. If you can tear your eyes away from the harbor view, looking inland you'll see a number of significant buildings. Heading east from the Star Ferry Terminal, you'll pass the **Kowloon-Canton Railway Clock Tower**, which was built in 1921 and is the only remaining relic of the old train station. Immediately to the east you'll see the sweeping curves of the **Hong Kong Cultural Center** (see *Galleries, Shows & Theaters*, p.000 for events). However, despite its fantastic location, the Hong Kong Cultural Center appears a little drab in comparison with the architectural monuments that surround it and is considered by many to be a wasted plot of extremely valuable land. This aside, its roofline and use of angles can provide some good photos, especially on blue-sky days. Next is the **Museum of Art** (see *Galleries, Shows & Theaters*, p.000), behind which sits the shiny white dome of the Space

Hong Kong Cultural Centre

Museum (see below). A little farther along the shoreline you'll come to the Avenue of Stars (see below), which follows an elevated walkway out over the waters of the harbor. Walking along the harbor's edge and raised pathways is a popular evening pastime and you might also see impromptu plays or musical performances as well as *tai chi* (see *Adventures*, p.000) and ballroom dancing. If you want to get out onto the water, either take the Star Ferry (see *Getting Around*, p.000) or go on a harbor cruise (see *Adventures On Water*, p.000), many of which leave from this vicinity.

Hong Kong Space Museum and Stanley Ho Theater, 10 Salisbury Road, Tsimshatsui (☎ 00852-2721-0226, www.hk.space.museum; Mon, Wed, Thurs & Fri 1-9 pm, Sat & Sun 10 am-9 pm; HK$10; Tsimshatsui MTR, Exit F). This informative museum offers a number of interactive exhibits and is divided into two sections, with Space Science located on the ground floor and Astronomy on the first floor. Both have some fun interactive features, including a gravity machine that simulates movement on the moon. Still, much of what you'll see is a little worn and the museum could definitely do with a revamp. The attached **Stanley Ho Space Theater** is more worthwhile and offers larger-than-life Omnimax movies covering a range of topics that change monthly. The permanent 'Sky Show' on the Hubble Space Telescope (daily 2:40 pm & 6:10 pm; HK$12-HK$32) takes you on a journey into outer space and will leave the kids wanting to become astronauts!

Avenue of Stars (Tsimshatsui MTR, Exit F). Acknowledging Hong Kong's significant movie business (see below), the Avenue of Stars includes paving stones, hand prints and a couple of statues paying tribute to the territory's greatest stars. Although you may not recognize many of the names, ones to look out for include Jackie Chan's handprints and a large bronze statue of

Bruce Lee. Thus Hong Kong's Avenue of Stars doesn't really match up to the US original, but the elevated promenade affords great views across the harbor.

Hong Kong Hollywood

Hong Kong is the world's third-largest movie town after Bombay and Hollywood. Its comparatively liberal governing stance has over the years allowed it to become the center of Chinese movie-making and Hong Kong is noted for its martial arts films. Bruce Lee (see p. 69) and Jackie Chan both rose to fame in Hong Kong and *Crouching Tiger, Hidden Dragon*'s Chow Yun-fat was born on Lamma Island. Hong Kong's movie year reaches its zenith with the annual Film Festival (*Holidays & Festivals*, p. 73).

North from the Harbor

Set a little back from the harbor, Salisbury Road is home to one of Hong Kong's most famous historic buildings, the Peninsula Hotel (see p. 554), which sits behind bubbling fountains and green Rolls Royces (the hotel has a fleet of them). Immediately east of here, **Nathan Road** is Kowloon's primary artery, run-

Shopping frenzy (Ewen Bell)

ning south-to-north all the way to the New Territories through some of Hong Kong's busiest shopping districts.

Heading north from the harbor along Nathan Road, you'll pass the infamous **Chungking Mansions** (see *Where to Stay*, p. 553) on the right and the History Museum (see below). A few hundred yards farther on from Chungking Mansions, stretching north from westerly Haiphong Road, lies the green expanse of Kowloon Park (see below). On the southeastern corner of the park, the re-built **Kowloon Mosque** was originally constructed by the British for its Indian troops stationed here and remains a hub of Islamic life in downtown Hong Kong, although access is denied to non-Muslims. From the mosque, Nathan Road continues its shop-happy northward journey into Jordan, where you'll find **Temple Street Market**, **Yaumatei Market**, the **Jade Market** and a Tin Hau Temple, all to the west. From here on up, this

Kowloon Peninsula

Playing Field Rd
Flower Mkt Rd
Yuen Po St.,
Bird Garden
Prince Edward Road East
Prince Edward Road West
Arran Street
MONGKOK
Bute Street
Nathan Road
Argyle St
Dunbar
Ivy Street
Tong Mi Road
Mongkok Rd
Goldfish Market
Fa Yuen Street Market
Sai Yee Street
Anchor St
Cherry Street
Argyle Street
Sai Yeung Choi (Electronics)
Tung Choi (Ladies Goods)
Yim Po Fong Street
Waterloo Road
Pui Ching Road
Shantung Street
Soy Street
Ferry Street
Dundas Street
Hoi Wang Road
Pitt Street
Nathan Road
Wylie Road
Princess Margaret Road
Chung Hau St
Waterloo Rd
Shek Lung St
Ching Ping St
Tung Kun St
King's Park Rise
Hong Chong Road
Wylie Road
YAUMATEI
Public Square St
Kansu St
Canton Road
Shanghai St
Gascoigne Road
JORDAN
Jordan Road
Jordan Path
Bowring St
Cheong Wan Rd
Yuk Choi Road
TSIMSHA TSUI EAST
Austin Road
Hillwood Rd
Cheung Wan Rd
Hung Hom S Rd
Tak Fung Street
Canton Road
Observatory Rd
Science Mus Rd
Carnarvon Rd
Kimberley Rd
Kowloon Park Drive
Granville Rd
Chatham Road South
Cameron Rd
Nathan Rd
Prat Ave
TSIMSHA TSUI
Haiphong Rd
Mody Road
Salisbury Road
Peking Rd
Middle Rd
Mody Road
Promenade
Salisbury Road
Cross-Harbour Tunnel
Canton Road
Salisbury Road

1. Mongkok MTR Station
2. Yaumatei MTR Station
3. Yaumatei Market
4. Jade Market
5. Tin Hau Temple; Post Office
6. Temple Street Market
7. Eaton Hotel
8. Queen Elizabeth Hospital
9. KCR Rail Line
10. Hung Kom KCR Station;
    The Coliseum
11. Star Ferry Terminal
12. Rent-a-Room Hotel
13. Jordan MTR Station
14. BP International Hotel
15. Kowloon Park
16. China Fery Terminal
17. Kowloon Mosque
18. Tsimshatsui East KCR Station
19. Star Ferry Terminal;
    Tourist Office
20. Avenue of Stars
21. Tang Court Restaurant
22. Aqua and Hutong Restaurants
23. Tsimshatsui MTR Station
24. Holiday Inn Golden Mile and
    Mirador Mansions Hotels
25. Chungking Mansions Hotel;
    Post Office
26. Tsimshatsui East KCR
    Station; Mariners Club
27. Intercontinental Hotel
28. Stanley Ho Theatre
29. Hong Kong Museum of Art
30. Kowloon Pier; Kowloon-Canton
    Railway Clock Tower
31. Hong Kong Cultural Center
32. Hong Kong Space Museum;
    Salisbury YMCA
33. Peninsula Hotel; Felix and
    Spring Moon Restaurants
34. China Travel Service

N

0.5 MILES

©2008 Hunter Publishing, Inc.

part of town is all about markets and, progressing northwards through Yaumatei and into Kowloon's northernmost district, Mongkok, you'll come across the electronics market, **Flower Market** and the **Bird Market**, all to the east of Nathan Road (see *Shopping*, p. 534, for more on all markets). **Hong Kong History Museum**, 100 Chatham Road (Wed-Mon 10 am-6 pm; HK$10; Tsimshatsui MTR, Exit B2, or Jordan MTR, Exit D). This is an easy place to while away a few hours with fascinating, well-designed displays that trace Hong Kong's history from earliest times. The museum is divided into four sections: Natural History, Archeology, Ethnography and Local History. Highlights are traditional local garments, photos of Olde Worlde Hong Kong and extensive dioramas.

★**Kowloon Park**, 22 Austin Road, Kowloon (daily 6 am-12 pm; free except swimming pools; Tsimshatsui MTR, Exit B1). After the British gained Kowloon they were quick to see the military advantage of this hilly location overlooking the harbor and established the Whitfield Barracks on the site of the current park. It remained a military domain until 1971 when it was opened as a public park by the governor of the time, Sir David Trench.

In Kowloon Park
(Magalie L'Abbé)

The HK$300 million cost of the transformation was donated by the Royal Hong Kong Jockey Club and the park has flourished as a haven from the hustle and bustle ever since.

Deliberations outside Tin Hau Temple (Tot Foster)

More than just an open space, Kowloon Park is also a center of recreation, with excellent public facilities, and if you'd like a swim and some sunbathing there are good indoor and outdoor pools (see *Swimming*, p. 545, for details), although the cheap price and central location mean that they can get very busy. In the park you'll find a pleasant fitness trail, eight fitness areas, a maze, a number of gardens (including a Chinese traditional garden and a sculpture garden) and a bird lake with aviary. Bird-watching is popular here and, if you arrive at 7:30 am on a Friday, you'll find a keen group who will help you understand some of the local species (for more on bird watching, see p. 540).

★**Tin Hau Temple**, Public Square Street, Kowloon (daily 8 am-5 pm; free; Yaumatei MTR, Exit C). This small temple, dedicated to Tin Hau, Goddess of the Sea, offers a quiet escape from the busy market area surrounding it.

Inside, you'll find giant incense coils hanging from the ceiling, which fill the small temple with smoke. Despite its small size the temple is a popular place of worship and you should be careful not to offend with your photography. The temple is surrounded by a small square, often filled with crowds of old men playing intense games of Chinese chess and mah jong.

★★**Wong Tai Sin Temple** (☎ 00852-2328-0270; daily 7 am-5:30 pm; free; Wong Tai Sin MTR, Exit B). Although it's actually in the New Territories, this striking temple is most easily accessed from Kowloon. Taoist, Buddhist and Confucian worshippers all come here to pray and it's also a popular spot for divination. If you're interested in having your face or palm read (HK$100-200) you might even be able to find an English-speaking teller to decode your fate. To see the temple at its best, visit on the weekend, when you'll be greeted by clouds of thick incense burning from the massive ceiling coils, and the clatter of bamboo pots filled with divination sticks as people keenly await their fortunes.

Outlying Islands

The Outlying Islands are the antithesis of what you might expect from the modern metropolis of Hong Kong. Quiet, secluded and traditional, they offer beaches, hikes, temples, fishing villages and some fine seafood restaurants. If you're in Hong Kong for anything more than a couple of days it's certainly worth taking a boat out to one of the islands and, for more of a break, maybe staying overnight. The Outlying Islands are actually part of the New Territories, but the three described below are best accessed from Hong Kong's Outlying Islands Ferry Pier, next to the Star Ferry Terminal in Central.

★★★ Lamma Island

(Boats from Pier 4 run at least hourly to both Yung Shue Wan and Sok Kwu Wan between 7:30 am and 10:30 pm; 20-35 mins, HK$11-20). Lamma is a gem, only 30 minutes from Hong Kong Island by boat, but a million light years away in terms of pace and atmosphere. The island is only five square miles but it offers a range of attractions, including excellent hiking paths, beaches, quaint towns and renowned fish restaurants. All can be linked in a lovely short hike (see *Adventures On Foot*, p. 540).

Yung Shue Wan was once just a fishing community which developed small-scale industry in the post-war period, but later became popular for young foreigners to live away from the city and developed something of a hippy culture. Although most of this scene moved on post-handover, the legacy continues in the form of a number of cool cafés and bars and a few long-term expat residents. There are also a few hotels and

The fishing boats and restaurants of Sok Kwu Wan (VirtualSteve)

apartments in the town that offer lower rates than the city. Yung Shue Wan is a relaxed place to base yourself if you don't mind the half-hour boat ride every time you want to go downtown. On the other side of the island **Sok Kwu Wan** is famous for its fish restaurants and is connected to Yung Shue Wan by a paved hiking trail. With no public transport on the island, walking and cycling are the only options for getting to its beaches and hilltop pavilions – a refreshing change after the traffic-laden streets back in Central.

If you're too hot for a hike, help is at hand in the form of **Hung Shing Ye** and **Lo So Shing** beaches, only a 15-minute walk from Yung Shue Wan and Sok Kwu Wan respectively. Both have good swimming, offshore pontoons, changing facilities, lifeguards and shark nets. Lo So Shing is the prettier of the two, especially since there is a power station marring the view at Hung Shing Ye. During the week you might have the beaches more or less to yourself, but on the weekends they can get busy. If the main beaches are packed, **Hung Shing Ye** has a northern section, known as Tai Wan To, which isn't shark-netted, and if you're willing to take the risk you'll find it quieter here.

★★★ Lantau

Lantau is the largest of Hong Kong's islands, famous for its rugged highlands, quiet beaches and three (very different) constructions that reflect the dynamic balance between traditional and modern in Hong Kong. The award-winning **airport** designed by Sir Norman Foster and the brand-new **Disneyland** are both built on reclaimed land and lie on Lantau's north and east coasts respectively. In the far west sits the world's largest seated bronze Buddha on the Ngong Ping Plateau, now linked by the 360° Skyrail. **Tsing Ma Bridge**, which links the airport to the mainland, is the world's longest road and rail suspension bridge. At the eastern end of the island the utopian suburbia of Discovery Bay is home to many of Hong Kong's expat families, who relish its man-made beach, car-free environment and modern housing complexes, which are linked to Central by fast ferry.

The main reasons to come to Lantau are the Giant Buddha at Ngong Ping, the stilted fishing village houses of Tai O and the island's beaches. Many of the sites detailed can be linked on foot and Lantau offers some of Hong Kong's best hikes, including the 44-mile Lantau Trail or shorter routes such as the Fanlau Trail from Shek Pik Reservoir around to Tai O (see *Adventures On Foot*, p. 540 for more).

A GOOD DAY-TRIP

Take the ferry to Mui Wo then take bus #2 to **Cheung Sha Beach** for a swim, sunbathe and maybe a snack at Stoep (see p. 562), then continue on by bus through glorious countryside to the Po Lin Monastery at the foot of **Lantau Peak**, Hong Kong's second-highest mountain, at 3,064 feet. Alight here and enjoy the setting of the world's largest seated bronze Buddha before taking bus #21 to Tai O and checking out the stilted houses and old fishing village atmosphere. From Tai O, take bus #11 to Tung Chung and then take the MTR back to Hong Kong. Now that the Ngong Ping Skyrail is open, you could do this route in reverse, starting at Tung Chung and taking the cable car up to Ngong Ping, maybe doing a side-trip to Tai O, before heading round the island for a swim and sunset drinks at Stoep and then the ferry back to Central from Mui Wo.

View from Ngong Ping

Po Lin Monastery (daily 9 am-6 pm) and the ★★★**Giant Buddha** (10 am-5:30 pm; both free; bus #2 from Mui Wo or #23 from Tung Chung). Lantau's isolated hills first attracted monks to the **Ngong Ping plateau** in 1927, although the construction of the Giant Buddha in 1993 and the Skyrail in 2006 has put the monastery firmly on the tourist map, and so it has lost some of its tranquility. Still, the monastery remains a genuine place of worship and meditation and its gardened complex is certainly worth a look around. There's also a great **vegetarian restaurant** (see p. 562) in the monastery, which serves inexpensive meals between 11:30 am and 5 pm. If you want to stay and hike in the surrounding hills, the SG Davis Hostel (see p. 555) is basic but beautifully located. The reason that most people come to the Ngong Ping plateau, though, is to admire the enormous seated bronze **Buddha**, which at 85 feet is the tallest of its kind. There are 268 steps to the top, from where you'll properly appreciate its size as well as enjoy fine views across the island's mountainous interior and out over the South China Sea. If it's a foggy day in winter, though, the plateau can resemble Scotland more than Hong Kong. The long-awaited

Po Lin Buddha

Ngong Ping 360° Skyrail (www.np360.com.hk; HK$58/88, one-way/round-trip) has finally opened and presents a stunning 20-minute ride from Tung Chung MTR station up to the monastery. Not only is the journey beautiful, it also makes for an easy day-excursion, maybe taking the cable car up and walking down (around 90 minutes).

★**Tai O Village** (bus #1 from Mui Wo, 40 mins, or #11 from Tung Chung, 40 mins). Tai O is one of the last remaining places in Hong Kong where people still live in stilt houses, which are raised above the salty creek to prevent tide damage, although this watery location didn't stop a fire which raged through the village in the year 2000. Tai O today is far from small, but the once-nomadic Tanka boat people have retained much of their traditional lifestyle and they still make the pungent shrimp paste and dried fish products they have survived on for hundreds of years. The salt trade, which used to be a mainstay of the Tanka, has declined to nothing, however. If you want to eat but aren't so keen on the dried fish, then there are a few basic Cantonese restaurants that serve fresh seafood. The quickest way to get to Tai O is by bus #1 from Mui Wo, but there are also #21 buses linking it with the Ngong Ping plateau. Note that Tai O can get very busy on weekends, so a mid-week trip is advised.

Getting to Lantau

Ferries from the Outlying Islands Pier take 40 minutes to arrive at Mui Wo, aka Silvermine Bay (daily 7 am-11:30 pm; HK$11.30), and from here there are buses and taxis to the rest of the island. There are no private vehicles, which makes the island's roads substantially quieter than the rest of the territory. There are also boats around the clock to Discovery Bay, but there's little to see there so you're better off sailing to Mui Wo. If you're not fond of boat travel, another way to get to the island is to take the MTR line to Tung Chung and then take a bus (or the cable car) to Ngong Ping or Tai O.

★★Cheung Chau Island

Street in Cheung Chau (Tsui SIng Yan Eric)

(Boats from Pier 5 run every 30 minutes between 6:30 am and 11:30 pm; 40 mins-1 hr; HK$11.30-HK$22.20). South of Lantau Island, Cheung Chau (Long Island) is a tiny dumbbell-shaped speck in the sea measuring less than a square-mile, yet it is one of the most densely populated places in Hong Kong. Its current population is about 30,000 but, unlike nearby Lamma and Lantau, there are very few expats. Most residents commute into the city to work, which can leave the island feeling decidedly empty, except on the weekends when locals and tourists flock. Even when it's busy, the island retains a certain charm and its main promenade,

Praya Street, even manages to feel a little Mediterranean on a summer evening. Cheung Chau also has some good beaches, lively temple festivals and even a few pirate legends. Cheung Chau is said to be one of the longest inhabited islands in the area, and during the 18th century it was a safe haven for pirates attacking the busy trading waterways between Macau and Guangzhou. There's a cave out on the south island where **Cheung Po Tsai**, the Delta's most notorious pirate, is alleged to have hidden and perhaps even stashed his treasure!

Exploring the Island

Boats arrive at the narrowest part of Cheung Chau, from where you can access both of its two formerly separate islands. Cheung Chau is motor-vehicle-free (apart from its mini fire engines) and so small that the best way to enjoy its manifold minor sights is to amble (or cycle) along the network of paved trails that run across the island. Before long you'll have stumbled into everything. Cheung Chau is an easy place to keep on exploring and might be worth an overnight stop if you want a break from the city – note that prices can halve during the week (see p. 555 for accommodation options). While the food scene isn't fantastic, there is still plenty of good and reasonably priced seafood found in the restaurants lining the harbor. If you come on a day-trip there are also some good picnic spots. After an amble across the island you might feel like relaxing on a **beach** and Cheung Chau has plenty of these – **Pak Tso Wan** and **Tung Wan** are two of the best, although note that shark nets are removed from the latter in winter.

You can rent **bikes** for HK$50 per day from numerous shops on Cheung Chau (see *Adventures On Wheels*, p. 544, for details). Whether on foot or wheels it's easy to find remote spots and the whole island is scattered with small shrines and temples, the most impressive being **Pak Tai Temple** at the top of Pak She Street. This 200-year-old temple is the center of the lively **Bun Festival**, which attracts thousands and is worth visiting if you're going to be here in late April or May (see *Events & Festivals*, p. 73 for more). Another place to head for is the small village of **Sai Wan**, where you'll see junks and sampans being made, traditional fishing techniques in practice and the alleged Cheung Po Tsai pirate cave. From Sai Wan you can hop on a locally made sampan (HK$2.50) for the short trip back to the ferry port and then back to the city.

New Territories

The New Territories is the name given to the part of Hong Kong ceded to the British as a buffer zone in 1898. The New Territories accounts for 40% of Hong Kong's total area and, although this figure is matched in ratio by its population, the majority of inhabitants live in the bigger cities, which allows the rest of the region to maintain the feel of a rural backwater. The territories also include the Outlying Islands but the bulk of its landmass stretches north from Kowloon to the border with the mainland. In recent years a series of **new towns** have been built in the New Territories to act as satellite and commuter cities for the overflow from Hong Kong and Kowloon. They now house over three million residents. In cities such as Sha Tin and Tsuen Wan, you'll find the same modern services, shops and facilities as downtown, and you'll get an idea of how half of Hong Kong's people live. However, the real reason to come to the territories is to explore the **unspoiled countryside**, dotted with **traditional villages, ancient temples** and **pretty beaches**, many of which are connected by **hiking trails**. There are pockets of interest spread over most of the territories, but the least developed and most beautiful parts lie to the east and include the beautiful **Sai Kung peninsula**.

In spite of grand incursions by the New Towns, as environmental consciousness develops in Hong Kong, the New Territories are benefiting from increasing interest in their natural habitats. Much of the region is protected as **country parks** and **wildlife centers** such as the new **Wetlands Park** (see below) and the **Mai Po Marshes** (see *Bird Watching*, p. 540). These are helping to highlight the importance of protecting the "other" Hong Kong. The great news is that the mountains, valleys, rivers and country parks of the New Territories see far fewer visitors than the central hub of Hong Kong and Kowloon. If you're in Hong Kong for more than a few days and want a taste of the old Hong Kong and some adventure, the New Territories is a must. You could quite easily spend a few days out here and there are basic hostels dotted about the countryside as well as hotels in the New Towns. But if time is limited you can take one of Gray Line's New Territories tours (see *Tours*, p. 504). It's also feasible to do a day-trip to the New Territories independently if you limit yourself to a short excursion out from one of the major transport hubs or rent a private vehicle to take you (see below).

Getting to the New Territories

The major New Towns of the territories are well-connected to Kowloon and Hong Kong Island by MTR, rail, buses and boats. Heading north from Tsimshatsui East through Kowloon to the Central New Territories and out to the border, the Kowloon-Canton Railway (KCR) takes in Sha Tin, Tai Po, Tai Wo, Fanling and the last stop before Lo Wu, Sheung Shui. For trips to the west, the West Rail

Sha Tin on Shing Mun River (Tsui SIng Yan Eric)

and MTR lines extend out to Tsuen Wan. The less developed eastern part of the territories, including the Sai Kung peninsula, are reached by bus from Diamond Hill MTR on the Kwan Tong line or from Ma On Shan via a branch line which extends east from Tai Wai on the KCR. The New Territories are also served by boats to **Tuen Mun.**

If time is of the essence, then hiring a private car and driver can be an efficient way to see the territories and most hotels can arrange this for you, although prices are hardly cheap, starting at around HK$500 for a half-day .

Central New Territories

Due north of Kowloon, this part of the New Territories is little more than a continuation of urban Kowloon, which begins with Tai Wai before arriving at the original and still bustling Hong Kong new town, **Sha Tin**. While there's nothing remarkable about Sha Tin, it enjoys a pleasant riverside setting, holds Hong Kong's second racecourse, a fine Heritage Museum, the atmospheric 10,000 Buddha Monastery and all of this is less than half an hour away by KCR.

Hong Kong Heritage Museum, 1 Man Lam Road, Sha Tin (☎ 00852-2180-8188, www.heritagemuseum.gov.hk; Wed-Mon 10 am-6 pm; HK$10; Sha Tin KCR). Opened in 2006, the modern Hong Kong Heritage Museum offers six permanent exhibitions, all of which are clearly labeled in English. The museum is a good place to visit on your way to the New Territories as its exhibits provide a detailed history of the area from prehistoric times to modern.

At 10,000 Buddhas
Monastery (Magalie L'Abbé)

★★**10,000 Buddhas Monastery**, Sha Tin (☎ 00852-2691-1067; daily 9 am-5 pm; free; Sha Tin KCR, Exit B). Although it's a comparatively new monastery, the 10,000 Buddhas is certainly worth the climb. The path is lined with golden *arhats* and when you arrive you'll be greeted by the arresting sight of a vast collection of miniature statues of Sakyamuni, actually numbering 13,000. Many of the statues are quite unusual – look out for the statue of Sakyamuni astride a dog. In the small annex behind the main temple, you'll find the body of the temple's founding monk, now enshrined in gold leaf, whose mole reputedly continues to grow hair! You'll also find it hard to miss the bright red gleaming pagoda that dominates the complex and even features on some Hong Kong HK$100 bank notes. If the walk up to the monastery has stimulated your appetite there's also a good vegetarian restaurant (set meal HK$50) on-site. To get to the monastery look for the IKEA store just outside the KCR station where you'll see the first sign and from here it's about a 30-minute walk.

Sha Tin Racecourse (☎ 00852-2966-8065; Sha Tin Racecourse KCR). Sha Tin racecourse was built in 1978 and may not have quite the history of its older sister, Happy Valley on Hong Kong Island, but the atmosphere at the 83,000-capacity course is electric nonetheless. You can also see the world's longest video screen here, extending an amazing 257 feet. Race schedules vary so it's best to check in advance – see *Gambling, The Races*, p. 547, for more.

Western New Territories

The western part of the New Territories has experienced a great deal of change over the last 25 years, due to the rapidly inflating population in Kowloon and new towns have quickly developed. Only eight or nine miles from Kowloon, Tsuen Wan is the biggest new town in this part of the territories, while Tuen Mun is another new center out in the northwest and marks the end point of the cross territory **MacLehose Trail** (see *Adventures On Foot*, p. 540). While neither town is a particularly interesting place to visit, Tsuen Wan is well connected by MTR, KCR West Rail and boat. It offers a few worthwhile destinations, including an ancient walled village and a couple of religious sights that can make for an easy day-trip. North of here, 3,140-foot **Tai Mo Shan** is Hong Kong's highest peak, making for a steep climb, though the summit itself is fenced off.

★**Sam Tung Uk Museum**, 2 Kwu Uk Lane, Tsuen Wan (☎ 00852-2411-2001; Wed-Mon 9 am-5 pm, free; Tsuen Wan MTR, Exit E). This ancient **Hakka** (see *Minorities*, p. 44) walled village was first built in 1786 by migrants from Fujian and was inhabited until the 1970s, after which it was restored to serve as a portal into the past. Although it seems a bit artificial after restoration, the village is an excellent example of the many Hakka villages throughout southern China. The grandest of these lie on the Guangdong-Fujian border, still housing hundreds of people within their fortified, often circular walls. The rectangular village here in Tsuen Wan contains 12 restored houses and ancestral halls, complete with original furnishings. It's a 10-minute walk west from the MTR station and is clearly signposted.

★**Yuen Yuen Institute**, Sam Dip Tam, Tsuen Wan (☎ 00852-2492-2220, www.yuenyuen.org.hk; daily 8:30 am-5:30 pm, free; Tsuen Wan MTR, Exit B1). For some insight into China's principle three religions, Buddhism, Confucianism and Taoism, the Yuen Yuen Institute is a good place to start, although you won't be alone. The temples are popular with both tourists and locals. The expansive compound enjoys an attractive hillside location and incorporates a host of temples including houses of worship for each of the Chinese birth signs and a main structure resembling Beijing's Temple of Heaven. There's also a good vegetarian restaurant here. To get here, take minibus #81 from Shiu Wo Street near Tsuen Wan MTR.

★★**Chuk Lam Shim Yuen Monastery**, Fu Yung Shan, Tseung Wan (☎ 00852-2490-3392; daily 9 am-5 pm; free; Tsuen Wan MTR, Exit B1). If you want a quieter religious experience this hillside monastery sees fewer tourists and seems like a much more authentic place of worship. The monastery is contained within tranquil grounds and you'll often see monks chanting prayers in the temple at the far end of the compound. To get here take the MTR to Tsuen Wan then a taxi or minibus #85 from Shiu Wo Street.

Northern New Territories

The northern New Territories are accessed easily by the KCR and stretch up to the Hong Kong border at Lo Wu, offering distractions such as the Wishing Trees at Tai Po, Kadoorie Farm and the walled village at Fanling along the way. In the east, Plover Cove Country Park is a lovely area, while wildlife is the focus of the new Wetland Park in the west, and ornithologists will delight in the Mai Po Marshes (although you'll need to book long in advance for one of their organized tours – see *Bird Watching*, p. 540).

★**Kadoorie Farm and Botanic Garden**, Lam Kam Road, Tai Po (☎ 00852-2488-1317, www.kfbg.org.hk; 9:30 am-5 pm, no entrance permitted after 4 pm; free; Tai Wo KCR). Established in the early 1950s, Kadoorie

Farm and Botanic Gardens is a vast green sanctuary set on one of Hong Kong's highest peaks (Kwun Yum Shan) and gives the opportunity to see some of the region's fantastic flora and fauna. The project was set up by the wealthy Jewish brothers, Horace and Lawrence Kadoorie, with the aim of promoting self-reliance and sustainable agriculture in the dwindling local farming community. All visitors must call in advance to arrange a visit. Guided tours of the park run with a minimum of 20 people or you can join the tourist office's Kadoorie Farm and Botanic Garden Experience Tour on Mondays. To get here without a tour, take the KCR to Tai Wo and then a 20-minute bus ride on route #64K to the park.

★**The Wishing Trees**, Lam Tsuen Village, Tai Po (☎ 00852-2654-1262; Tai Po Market KCR and then bus #64). Just 20 minutes from Tai Po Market, Lam Tsuen valley contains the extraordinary Tai Po wishing trees. These large Chinese banyans (see *Flora*, p. 36) offer the chance for your wishes to come true and are a popular pilgrimage site. To try your hand, you need to throw a brightly colored streamer attached to an orange (known as *bao die*) into the branches. Only if your orange stays in the tree will your wish come true, so it's worth watching the locals first! If your *bao die* falls back to the ground, superstition says you were too greedy with your wish. It's a particularly busy spot throughout the Chinese New Year celebrations, with people from all over the region visiting to make their New Year's wishes come true.

★**Plover Cove Country Park**, Tai Mei Tuk (Tai Po KCR and then bus 75K). This country park centers on a reservoir that was created when a former sea bay was dammed in the 1960s. The park has a variety of hiking trails offering fine views, pretty pools and perhaps even a glimpse of Hong Kong's largest fauna, including barking deer. Routes include the Pat Sin Leng Nature Trail from Tai Mei Tuk to Bride's Pools (where you can camp) and a marked circular walk around the park which takes an hour to complete. There's a hostel (the Bradbury Lodge, see p. 556) and visitor center in Tai Mei Tuk.

Hong Kong Wetland Park

Hong Kong Wetland Park (☎ 00852-2708-8885, www.wetlandpark.com; Wed-Mon 10 am-5 pm; HK$30; Wetland Park Light Rail Station). Hong Kong's Wetland Park opened to great fanfare in May 2006 offering visitors the opportunity to experience some of the region's most precious habitats. Its first few months were marred by the actions of a few visitors who clearly couldn't care less about the environment as they noisily discarded litter into the wetlands. Measures have since been taken to educate the un-environmentally savvy and the park is big enough to ensure that you get a chance to be at one with nature; but try to come during the week to avoid the crowds. The park contains a visitor center and some 150 acres of wetlands to explore, all well laid-out with boardwalks, lookout towers and viewing decks. There are so many different routes through the park that you should pick up a map from the visitors center so you can find your way. To get here you can join the tourist office Wetland Park tour (contact the tourist office) or jump on the KCR to Tin Shui Wai and change onto the light rail to the Wetlands Park.

Eastern New Territories

This is Hong Kong's least developed zone, which makes it an outstanding place to really experience the wilder side of the territory. The Sai Kung peninsula and Clear Water Bay to the south offer Hong Kong's best beaches and a host of kayaking and hiking opportunities (see *Adventures*, p. 539) and if you're seeking serious escape this is the place to come.

The Sai Kung Peninsula

The Sai Kung Peninsula offers some of the best vistas in Hong Kong, full of rugged headlands and clusters of small islands. The whole area is covered with lush vegetation and foliage. The potential for walks through the country is endless. The main town, Sai Kung, is also a pleasant escape, retaining a sleepy laid-back atmosphere, centered on an old fishing port. There are a number of good seafood restaurants, cafés and bars that cater to the expats who have taken up residence in the area. Sai Kung also makes a great place to explore the nearby islands and beaches. You can rent sampans from the harbor (HK$50 per 30 minutes) and a short trip will give you a brief glimpse of the coastline, but you're better off negotiating a price for a half-day so that you can go out and really explore. Two of the best islands to head for are Tai Long Wan and Yim Tin Tsai, which remain quiet and remote.

★★★**Sai Kung Country Park**, Pak Tam Chung, Sai Kung. The highlight of any trip to this spectacular area is a visit to the Sai Kung Country Park (divided into eastern and western sections), which covers a vast part of the eastern New Territories. Virgin Forest and lush grasslands cover the park, dropping down to secluded golden sand beaches. The area has been a country park since 1978 and has escaped the development of the surrounding areas. The country park offers some of the best hiking in Hong Kong and sections of the **MacLehose Trail** (see *Adventures on Foot*, p. 540) pass through here, along with plenty of other rambles. With so many possible options and limited public transport you'll need careful planning in order to maximize your time in the park and it's worth sitting down with the staff at the tourist office before your visit. On arrival you could also pay a visit to the **Sai Kung Country Park Visitor Center** (☎ 00852-2792-7365; Wed-Mon 9:30-4:30 pm) in Pak Tam Chung, which provides a whole range of information about the area, including some free maps. Although it is possible to visit the area in one very long and tiring day, it's best to come for a few nights. Hostels are the order of the day here, and they offer some fantastic locations, along with useful advice about the area (see *Where to Stay*, p. 550, for more). To get to the Sai Kung Country Park, take bus #94 from Sai Kung in the direction of Wong Shek Pier, which takes about 20 minutes.

★★**Clear Water Bay** lives up to its name and offers some of the most beautiful coastline in the New Territories. The terrain that engulfs the bay is rugged and green, providing attractive vistas over the coastal area, especially on clear days. Two of the best and most popular beaches are the originally named Beach One and Beach Two, which offer pristine golden beaches and, you guessed it, clear waters. It's also worth taking a walk to the **Tin Hau Temple**, the oldest in Hong Kong. To get there, walk south along the road from the Clear Water bus stop until you see the Golf and Country

Tin Hau Temple (Sengkang)

Club and follow the signs for the Tin Hau Temple that will lead you along a small path from the club car park. The temple dates back to 1274 and has been re-built and renovated many times over the years. Getting to Clear Water Bay is easy – take bus #91 from Choi Hung MTR or Diamond Hill MTR to the Tai Au Mun bus terminus overlooking Clear Water Bay. It takes about 40 minutes.

Galleries, Shows & Theaters

Hong Kong has a diverse cultural scene and ,whether you prefer contemporary or classic, you should find something of interest.

Art

★★**The Fringe Club**, 2 Lower Albert Road, Central (☎ 00852-2521-7251, www.hkfringeclub.com; daily noon-late night; Central MTR). The Fringe was originally set up as a temporary festival space in 1983, but proved to be so popular and successful that it has never looked back, slowly converting the 19th-century cold storage warehouse into a fully-fledged contemporary creative space. The Fringe offers rent-free space to emerging and established artists and holds regular art and photographic exhibitions, plays and live performances. Members and their friends can enjoy meals at the club's Roof Garden. Check out the website or pop in and pick up a program for more details.

Hong Kong Museum of Art, 10 Salisbury Road, Tsimshatsui (☎ 00852-2721-0116, www.hk.art.museum; daily 10 am-6 pm; HK$10; Tsimshatsui MTR, Exit F). Located next to the Cultural Center in the heart of Victoria Harbour, the Museum of Art houses a collection of art and ceramics from across Asia. The museum has five permanent collections, including Chinese painting and calligraphy, contemporary Hong Kong art and historical pictures. They also host a number of temporary exhibitions. The calligraphy collection on the second floor is well worth a look, as are the classic Chinese ink and brush paintings on the fourth floor. The museum offers helpful free guided tours in both English and Cantonese that leave frequently from the foyer. Headphones for audio tours (HK$10) are available from the first floor. Log on to the website for details of temporary exhibitions.

Music

Hong Kong Cultural Centre, 10 Salisbury Road (☎ 00852-2734-2009, www.hkculturalcentre.gov.hk). Despite its blandly tiled exterior, the Cultural Center houses two theaters and a concert hall within, playing host to some highly acclaimed international performances. It is home to the Hong Kong Philharmonic Orchestra and most Western opera and ballet performances in Hong Kong happen here. Every Saturday (2:30-4:30 pm) and Thursday (6-7 pm) the center holds free traditional Chinese performances in the foyer, which are well worth a visit. All program listings are on the website so check in advance to see what's on.

Movie Theaters

The following theaters screen shows in English and range in cost from as little as HK$30 for matinee performances to HK$60 or HK$70 in the evenings.

IFC Palace, Level 1, IFC Mall, Central (☎ 00852-2388-3188; Central MTR).

UA, Times Square, Causeway Bay (☎ 00852-2317-6666; Causeway Bay MTR).

Grand Ocean, 3 Canton Road, Tsimshatsui (☎ 00852-2186-1313; Tsimshatsui MTR).

For Families

Hong Kong is a kiddies' wonderland and most of its activities are suited to all ages, from days at the beach to theme parks, harbor cruises, interactive museums and shopping. **Disneyland** (p. 532) has grabbed all the headlines recently, but **Ocean Park** (see below) remains a worthy adversary with its fine setting, rides, shows and pandas. If you don't want to splash the cash on theme parks there are free but fun options at Hong Kong Park's **Edward Youde Aviary** (p. 509) and the **Zoological and Botanical Gardens** (p. 509). **The Peak** (p. 506) also has features for all the family – you'll find Madam Tussaud's, Ripley's Believe It or Not, shopping, fine restaurants, walks, and spectacular views (weather permitting). Even the journey on the Peak Tram is fun. If you're going to be spending a substantial amount of time in Hong Kong with your children, it might be worth picking up a copy of *Adventures with Kids* by Sarah Woods (HK$120).

Theme Parks

★**Ocean Park** (☎ 00853-2552-0291, www.oceanpark.com.hk; daily 10 am-6 pm; HK$185 or HK$93 for children aged three-11; bus #629 from Star Ferry Terminal in Central or Admiralty MTR). Built in 1977, this was Hong Kong's first theme park and its array of attractions, mechanical and natural, set near Aberdeen in the rugged south of Hong Kong Island, continue to draw plenty of visitors. The park is divided into several zones linked by gondolas, which soar 100 feet above the mountainside and give great views over

Deep Water Bay. In the Lowland Gardens you'll find long-
term **panda** residents, An An
and Jia Jia, who have recently
been joined by a new pair, Le
Le and Ying Ying, donated by
the Central Government to celebrate 10 years of reunifica-
tion with the motherland. At
the other end of the gondola,
the Headland has a few rides,
which are fairly tame by modern standards, and nearby
Marine Park features regular
dolphin shows that continue to
be a highlight for many visitors despite a rising worldwide
anti-captivity movement.
Marine Park also has an
impressive aquarium that
includes the Jellyfish Spectacular and a shark tunnel, which
might make you think twice
about taking a dip outside of

Ocean Park (Sengkang)

the shark-netted zones next time you're at the beach! Continuing around
the headland, you'll find Ocean Park's best white-knuckle rides in Adventure Land – the 196-foot Abyss Turbo Drop might leave you wishing you'd
gone a little easier on lunch. Despite the large numbers who assail the park
on weekends, lines are seldom longer than an hour and you can often walk
straight onto rides during the week.

Ocean Park was established as a not-for-profit organization and remains so
today, aiming not only to entertain, but also to educate. To this end there are
educational tours, which take visitors to areas that are normally off-limits
and allow closer access to the park's animals, including the opportunity to
feed the pandas. These tours run from 1-2:30 pm, cost HK$70 and can only
be booked on a first-come first-served basis at the main entrance ticket
office from 9:30-11:45 am or from the Pacific Chandlers Souvenir Shop
between 11:45 am and 1 pm.

★**Disneyland** (☎ 00852-1830-830, www.hongkongdisneyland.com; daily
10 am-7 pm, later during peak periods; Mon-Fri HK$295 or HK$210 for children aged three-11, weekends and holidays HK$350/250; Disneyland
Resort MTR). If you're coming from the US, Japan or France, then Disneyland may not be such a big thing but, once it overcame a few initial hiccups
after opening in September 2005, the Hong Kong version has become a big
hit with Chinese tourists and is a great place for a break if you've got kids or
just want to unleash the child in you. Indeed, even those who've grown up
with Mickey at their back door have good things to say about Hong Kong
Disneyland, noting the attractive setting on the ocean and the short lines
mid-week, which is when you should try to come.

The park has several themed areas that offer a range of attractions, from the storybook world of Fantasyland, to the thrill-seeking futuristic Space Mountain and shoot 'em up Buzz Lightyear rides found at Tomorrowland. As well as its Jungle River Cruise, Adventureland also hosts a live version of the animated hit *Lion King*, while Main Street USA harks back to a simpler time and holds daily parades featuring Mickey, Minnie, Donald and Goofy.

Castle at Disneyland (David Quitoriano)

If you've got kids and want Disneyland to feature in your trip you could stay in one of the park's two hotels, with rooms starting from HK$1,000 (check the website for details). The Hollywood Hotel is more fun for kids than the Disneyland Resort Hotel. However, unless you want complete immersion into the world of Disney, a stay isn't necessary. Although the resort is out on Lantau Island, as always in Hong Kong, transport links are excellent. The easiest way to get here is via the Tung Chung MTR line from Hong Kong station out to Sunny Bay and then change onto the Disneyland line for the last stop, a journey of about a half-hour. You can also get here by taxi (around HK$200 from Kowloon or upwards of HK$270 from Hong Kong Island), bus #R11 from Hung Hom (HK$32) or #R21 from Hong Kong Island (HK$38). And a ferry link will soon start running to within walking distance of the park! Ticket prices are listed above and you can obtain them online, at Hong Kong MTR station or at the park gates.

Health & Relaxation

Hong Kong is an intense place and a few days of trawling the city's hot, busy streets can take their toll. A trip out to the Outlying Islands, New Territories, or even just the south side of Hong Kong Island can restore your shopping and sightseeing vigor. But if you don't have time for a trip out of town then a massage or spa might do the trick. There are massage parlors dotted around downtown, particularly clustered south of Haiphong Road but, although they are cheap, the quality of massage can vary. Spas are also growing in popularity and the best ones are often found in the five star hotels – try **Plateau** at the Grand Hyatt. For reliable massages try the **CA Center of Acupressure & Massage of the Blind** (☎ 00852-2721-5989) where the staff's heightened sense of touch really works wonders. Massages are by appointment only and prices start at HK$240. The center is at Room 402, Landwide Commercial Building, 118 Nathan Road in Kowloon (Central MTR, Exit D). If you want to more actively improve your health, there are plenty of adventurous options, which can give you some exercise along with some sightseeing (see *Adventures*, p. 539). If you want to jog, there's a fitness track in Kowloon Park and a running circuit around the top of the Peak.

Shopping

Hong Kong is a shopper's dream: a **tax-free zone** packed with gleaming **shopping malls**, busy **nightmarkets, traditional tailors**, shady **electronics warehouses**, musty **antiques** shops, **designer boutiques** and lively **produce markets**. While prices aren't as cheap as during Hong Kong's manufacturing era, the variety of choice has increased massively. Brands from around the world are represented, along with goods made in China and more traditional items such as **silk**, **jade** and **jewelry, antiques, arts** and **crafts**. Although there are frequent sales, in the malls and most shops, prices are fixed. This said, at markets and many electrical outlets, bartering is standard practice. If shopping is the primary focus of your trip to Hong Kong, then you could try and time it to coincide with the annual **shopping festival** (see *Holidays & Festivals*, p. 73). Whatever you seek from shopping in Hong Kong you're likely to find it if you know where to look. Below is a selection of the latest and greatest, starting with markets, through malls and then shopping for specific items such as antiques, electronics and tailoring.

> **TIP:** For good products and service look for the QTS sticker, which denotes establishments commended by the government. You can pick up a listings booklet of all QTS establishments from tourist offices (see *Information Sources*, p. 500). If you have any problems with things you've purchased contact the Travel Industry Council on ☎ 00852-2807-0707.

Markets

Like the rest of Hong Kong, its markets reflect both its ancient Chinese past and its technologically advanced present. So whether it's antique jewelry or cutting-edge electronics you're after, you'll probably find what you want in one of Hong Kong's numerous markets, even if that's just some insight into what makes this place tick. Most markets are in the northern part of Kowloon, but over on Hong Kong Island there are some offerings, including the touristy (but inexpensive) **Stanley Market**. For a snapshot of local life you could check out the **Bowrington Street** produce market, which runs south off Hennessy Road halfway between Wanchai and Causeway Bay.

★**Sheung Wan Western Market**, Des Voeux Road, Hong Kong Island (daily 10 am-7 pm; Shueng Wan MTR, Exit B). The Western Market is in a beautiful Edwardian building five minutes from Sheung Wan MTR. It was built as a food market in 1906 and until the mid-1990s its three stories were filled with locals haggling over the price of fruit. It has since been restored and now houses a collection of stalls and shops selling art, jade, antiques and fabrics. It's also a good place to find trinkets, memorabilia and quirky antiques.

Temple Street Treats

Temple Street Market comes alive in the evening, and it's a great place to sample local street food. The smells of **seafood skewers** and **sizzling kebabs** make a tempting diversion from shopping so go with an empty stomach and prepare for an excellent, cheap dinner!

Graham Street Market (Magalie L'Abbé)

★★**Temple Street Market**, Temple Street, Jordan (daily 2-10 pm; Jordan MTR Exit A & C2). This bustling market is a must for anyone on a trip to Hong Kong and draws crowds every day. A five-minute walk from Jordan MTR station will bring you to the market, which runs north off Jordan Road just a few blocks west of Nathan Road. Although the market starts in the afternoon, it is best visited in the evening (from 6 pm) when the street is filled with vendors selling anything and everything. You'll find all the usual trinkets here, wedged between stalls selling DVDs, watches, cheap clothes and sunglasses. Be prepared to haggle your hardest and aim to pay a third to a half of the asking price. There are often fortune tellers perched on the roadside at the northern end of the market and you might see street performances of Chinese opera.

★★**Yaumatei Market**, Reclamation Street, Kowloon (daily 6 am-8 pm; Jordan MTR, Exit A). This is one of Hong Kong's biggest fresh food markets and offers a great chance to see local produce including unusual looking fruits and vegetables, local herbs and dried teas, although you may have to hunt around for an English speaker to help determine what they all are! The main market runs along Reclamation Street while the indoor fish market is at the end of the market by the junction with Kansu Street and a number of surrounding streets hold the overflow.

Fish Market in Yaumatei (Tot Foster)

★**The Jade Market**, Kansu Street, Yaumatei, Kowloon (daily 6 am-8 pm; Yaumatei MTR, Exit C). Spread through two covered enclosures, north off Kansu Street, Hong Kong's Jade Market is a lively and colorful place, filled with jade, pearls, beads, antiques and replicas. The market is Hong Kong's main center for jade trading and is often packed with locals, armed with magnifying glasses, intensely examining stones and artifacts – jade is a serious business! As usual, it can be difficult to ascertain quality, but it is said that the finest jade should always feel cool to the touch.

Bird Market (Tot Foster)

★★**Yuen Po Bird Market**, Yuen Po Street, Kowloon (daily 7 am-8 pm; Prince Edward MTR, Exit B1). Hong Kong's bird market is well worth the walk and is right next to the flower market just off Prince Edward West Road. In 1997 a traditional-style Chinese garden was built to house the market and offers a pleasantly shady and restful retreat. The garden now holds about 70 stalls filled with birds and everything associated with them; there are even a number of insect stalls and for once they're not for human consumption! The market is popular with locals who you'll see enjoying the serene atmosphere and shade provided by the garden.

★**Flower Market**, Flower Market Road, Kowloon (daily 7 am-8 pm; Prince Edward MTR, Exit B1). This fresh flower market offers the opportunity to see a vast collection of Asian flowers and is a real feast for the eyes. Shop after shop is filled with orchids, lilies, pitcher plants, *bonsai*, bamboo (the list is endless) and you might wish you had a house here to buy them for. Many of the shop keepers speak English and are keen to provide answers to any questions you may have. For those with green fingers, a number of shops sell local flower, vegetable and fruit seeds, but there may be restrictions on taking them back to your home country.

Shopping Malls

Just about anywhere you go in Kowloon or on Hong Kong Island you'll find legions of air-conditioned shopping malls where you can flex your credit card. In these places you'll find everything from sports shops to designer boutiques, as well as a generous helping of restau-

Guard cat (Magalie L'Abbé)

Facing page: Bowrington Street Market (Tot Foster)

rants, cafés and sometimes free Internet access posts. Some of these places are so big it can be tricky to find specific shops or restaurants, but fortunately there are information counters and maps dotted around. You'll also find a number of the five-star hotels house smaller malls offering designer stores; for the likes of **Gucci** or **Armani** try the **Marco Polo** and **Peninsula** in Kowloon, or the **Landmark** in Central.

Pacific Place, 88 Queensway, Admiralty (daily 10 am-8 pm, www. pacificplace.com.hk; Admiralty MTR, Exit C1). Shops include Dior, Emporio Armani, French Connection, Hugo Boss, Shanghai Tang, Tiffany & Co, Watson's and Zara. Restaurants include Thai Basil (see *Where to Eat*, p. 559).

Times Square, 1 Matheson Street, Causeway Bay (daily 10:30 am-9 pm, www.timessquare.com.hk; Causeway Bay MTR, Exit A). Shops include Birkenstock, Kookai, Mango, Marks & Spencer, Nike and Watson's. Restaurants include WasabiSabi and Water Margin (see *Where to Eat,* p. 556).

IFC Mall, 8 Finance Street, Central (daily 11:30 am-midnight, www.ifc.com. hk; Central MTR, Exit A). Shops include Calvin Klein, CitySuper, Mango, Prada, Watson's and Zara. Restaurants include Lumiere (see p. 559)

Harbour City, 3 Canton Road, Kowloon (daily 10:30-9 pm, www. harbourcity.com.hk; Tsim Sha Tsui MTR, Exit E). Shops include Fortress, Kookai, Michael Kors, Versace and Watson's. Restaurants include Oliver's Super Sandwiches.

Hong Kong's Italian Labels

While moving through Hong Kong's busy streets, you'll inevitably come across **Baleno, Bossini** and **Giordano**. In spite of their Italian-sounding names, all three of these labels are homegrown and offer reasonable quality, inexpensive clothes in current styles for men, women and kids.

Antiques, Arts & Crafts

If you're in the market for antiques, then Hong Kong offers a good selection of Chinese items. Although prices are higher than you'll find on the mainland, it's easier to get assured quality here and prices are still lower than those at home. Rows of antique shops fill the western end of **Hollywood Road** and the surrounding side streets. There are some real treasures found hidden within their doors. **Cat Street** (or Lower Lascar Row) is one of the best roads in the area, with antiques, nicknacks and replicas overflowing from the many shops. It's a great place to buy jade and jewelry. You'll also find some top Chairman Mao memorabilia – make sure you look around first and then negotiate hard over the price!

Tailors

Unlike mainland China, even large Westerners will find sizes to fit, but if you can't there are a host of tailors out there just waiting to take your measurements. Hong Kong is famed for its tailors, many of whom are of Indian descent. Walking past **Chungking** or **Mirador Mansions** on Kowloon's

Nathan Road you'll undoubtedly be approached for a fitting, and most of them will do a fairly good job for not too much money (prices start from about HK$500, depending on time, style and the quality of the fabric). A recommended place to try here is ★**Sam's Tailor**, at 94, Nathan Road (www.samstailor.com). You can see pictures of the celebrities (including Bill Clinton and Princess Diana) that Sam has fitted and he has an excellent collection of fabrics to suit all budgets. A 24-hour suit from Sam's usually starts from HK$2,500, although prices drop the longer you wait. There's also an excellent ladies tailor, ★**Sze Sze**, at 83C Percival Street near Causeway Bay MTR, who specializes in local-style *cheongsam*. Expect to pay from HK$2,000 for the fabric plus HK$3,000 for the tailoring, which will be first class.

Electronic Goods

In the past, as a mass producer of electronics, Hong Kong was renowned as a great place to buy the latest technology at bargain prices, but as manufacturers have moved north over the border to Shenzhen and other mainland Special Economic Zones, this is no longer the case. However, while Hong Kong is no longer the electronics bargain hunter's paradise it used to be, it still offers an enormous variety of the latest technology at competitive prices and, if you stay away from the wheeler-dealers, you can make sure you get the right language settings and warranties for your purchase. **Fortress** sells everything from cameras to laptops and is one of your best bets for reliable service. There are branches of Fortress throughout the city, including one on Peking Road and another on Queen's Road in Central. It's also worth having a look around some of the other larger chains such as **Broadway** (Times Square) and **Citicall** (5-8 Queen Victoria Street), whose prices are all competitive and who stock similar goods. If you're looking for the cheapest deal going and know a little about what you want, you can still find good deals at **Mongkok Electronic Goods Market**, where the sheer variety of choice is mind-boggling. But make sure you don't get fobbed off with end-of-line products. Haggling is very much of the essence here, and make sure that you get a warranty valid for your home country (if this isn't possible but you're still prepared to purchase, you should be able to negotiate a further discount).

Everyday Needs

Most convenience goods can be found in the plethora of **7-Elevens** and **Circle-Ks**, but for a bigger shop try **Wellcome** – there are branches all over the city, including one on Austin Road in Kowloon and a 24-hour branch on Paterson Street in Causeway Bay. For a more upmarket supermarket try **CitySuper**, which has a branch on Podium Level 1 of the IFC Mall. For toiletries, head for one of the ubiquitous **Watson's** in the listed shopping malls.

Adventures

Hong Kong is such a mix of old and new, rural and urban, land and water, that the adventure possibilities are seemingly limitless. Whether it's the great outdoors or China's grand culture that takes your fancy, you'll find something to fit. There are harbor cruises, mountain hikes, tai chi sessions, swimming beaches, fengshui lessons – it's just a case of choosing which is for you.

Hong Kong & Macau

In the Air

Helicopter Tours (☎ 00852-2802-0200, www.heliservices.com.hk). If you really want to come to grips with Hong Kong, one of the best ways to do this is from the sky. From here, you'll get the chance to view the numerous islands and peaks, the sheer scale of urbanization throughout the area and the heavy water traffic that passes through every day. The copters can seat five passengers and costs start at a whopping HK$4,900 for 15 minutes to rent the whole craft. Alternatively, you can combine a flight with a meal at the Peninsula (which has its own heli-pad) where prices start from HK$4,840 for a lunch package including flight and a three-course meal at any of the hotel's restaurants for two people.

Bird Watching

Bird watching in Hong Kong is a popular pastime and yellow-browed warblers, blue magpies and fork-tailed sunbirds are all common sights. If you're lucky, you may catch a glimpse of the striking yellow-crested cockatoo. The **Hong Kong Bird Watching Society** (HKBWS) arranges free tours to learn more about local and migratory birds in the area. The two-hour tours operate at 8 am every Wednesday in Hong Kong Park and at 7:30 am on Fridays in Kowloon Park. They are led by local members of the Society and are well worth the early rise. The Society also arranges bird-watching trips farther afield. Check their website for more (www.hkbws.org.hk) or contact the tourist office. Other areas of interest for bird lovers include the **Wetlands Park** (see *Hong Kong*

Yellow-crested cockatoo

Wetland Park, p. 528), **Kadoorie Farm** (see p. 527) and the many **country parks** in the New Territories. **Mai Po Marshes** are the winter resting ground for black-faced spoonbills and a host of other flora and fauna. The site is managed by the World Wide Fund for Nature and runs guided three-hour tours of the reserve for HK$70, although it is advised to book at least a month in advance due to limited numbers (☎ 00852-2652-0285, www.wwf.org.hk). To get to the marshes, take bus #76K from Sheung Shui KCR.

On Foot

Many people's first thought when you mention walking in Hong Kong are of battling your way through the crowds, with plenty of shopping and coffee breaks thrown in. But if you want strenuous mountain hikes or leisurely country strolls, you'll find them in abundance too. It might seem impossible in downtown Hong Kong but you can be a long way from help in some parts of the territory and, if you're heading into the hills, make sure you take plenty of **water, sunscreen, a hat and sturdy shoes**. If you want to go in a group, the tourist office runs hiking trips to Po Lin Monastery and the South Lantau Country Park. They also produce an excellent brochure entitled *Hong Kong Walks*, which details nine of the best hikes. For good hiking routes, practical information and a general hiker's database, you could also check out www.hkcrystal.com/hiking.

★★★ The Peak Circuit (1 hr)

To see a little more of the Peak, a walk around the upper rim takes an hour and affords views both north over Hong Kong Island across the **harbor** to Kowloon and south to **Lamma**. The walk starts from the **Peak Tram terminal** where you walk due west along Harlech Road until you reach Lugard Road. From here, Lugard Road runs along the northern edge of the Peak and returns to the tram terminal area, making for a short but excellent circuit. If you want to continue you could head up Mount Austin Road which leads to the top of the Peak. There you'll find the **Victoria Peak Garden** which was once the **governor's residence**.

Hong Kong Loop (2 hrs)

With so much to see in downtown Hong Kong, it's hard to know where to start. This route takes in some of the urban highlights and can be completed in two to three hours, depending on where you choose to stop. Start at the **Star Ferry terminal** in Central and walk to **Statue Square** and **Jardine House**. Walk through the square and out the far side, crossing over Des Voeux Road. Directly in front of you you'll see the **Hong Kong and Shanghai Bank** with the **Bank of China** to its left. Turn left onto Des Voeux Road, walking past the banks, the **Cheung Center** and on to the **Bank of China Tower,** where the road turns into Queensway. For excellent views over the harbor, take the express lift to the 43rd floor free viewing deck in the Bank of China Tower (Mon-Fri 8 am-8 pm & Sat 8 am-2 pm).

Lunch Stop

If you want a bite to eat you could continue east along Queensway, past the **Lippo Centre** and soon you'll see the vast **Pacific Place** Shopping Center (see *Shopping Malls*, p. 536) on your right where you could do a bit of air-conditioned shopping before enjoying lunch at Thai Basil (p. 559). You can pick up your walk by entering **Hong Kong Park** through its main entrance on Supreme Court Road, accessible from **Pacific Place**.

Turn right onto Garden Road (just before the Bank of China Tower) and follow it up the hill. If you want to visit **Hong Kong Park** (see p. 509) you'll find an entrance just south of the **Citibank Plaza**. To your right you'll pass **St. John's Cathedral** and the **US Embassy**. Go past the embassy and then turn right onto Upper Albert Road, which will take you around the edge of the **Botanical and Zoological Gardens** (see p. 509). If you want to visit the gardens, then walk down Albany Road, which leads off after about five minutes. Otherwise, continue round until you reach Glenealy Street on your right, which will take you down to **Lan Kwai Fong** where you can round off your walk with a well-earned drink.

Island & New Territories Hikes

Hong Kong has invested heavily in its tourist infrastructure and part of this is its extensive network of well-marked hiking trails. If the pace of the city is getting too much for you, even a half-day trip can reward you with a rejuvenating breath of fresh air. Below are a selection of my favorite island and New Territory hikes, from hour-long strolls to the 60-mile MacLehose Trail. In addition to the walks listed below, Plover Cove Country Park (see p. 528) offers a varied range of hiking options.

★★★Yung Shue Wan to Sok Kwu Wan on Lamma (I hr)

One of my favorite afternoon trips in Hong Kong begins in **Yung Shue Wan**, a 30-minute ferry journey from Central. Turn right from the port and stroll through the trendy little town, with its bars, cafés, hotels and seaside shops. You might want to pick up a sandwich and a drink here for your walk – try the **Bookworm Café** (see p. 562). At the end of the village you'll find a small Tin Hau temple which is worth a quick side-trip before re-tracing your steps and turning uphill onto a paved trail. Ten minutes through banana palms and you'll find yourself emerging out at Tai Wan To beach and, a little farther on, **Hung Shing Ye** beach, where you could stop for a swim. From the beach the path heads steeply up for 10 or 15 minutes to the full height of the island. At the top there's a pavilion, which makes for a good lunch stop with great views in both directions. The path then continues along the backbone of the island for 15 or 20 minutes before descending, at which point there's another well-placed pavilion. From here you can see **Sok Kwu Wan**, where a fish dinner and the ferry home await. A little farther on you'll see a sign for **Lo So Shing** beach diverting right from the main path. It's only a few minutes walk down to the charming little beach and, after a hot hike, a cooling dip might be the perfect thing to really work up an appetite. There are also showers here if you want to freshen up for dinner. Back on the main path it's only 15 minutes to the quaint little fishing town of **So Kwu Wan**. This place is famous for its fish restaurants and is very popular in the evenings, particularly on the weekends. The last boat back doesn't leave until 10:30 pm so you'll have plenty of time to enjoy some great food and maybe a well-earned beer before the half-hour boat ride back to Central – just hope that the water isn't too rough if you've had a lot to eat or drink! This route can also be done in reverse and there are good Western cafés (see p. 556) as well as fish restaurants in Yung Shue Wan or you could even choose to stay here (see *Where to Stay*, p. 550).

THE FANLAU TRAIL, LANTAU (5-6 HRS)

If you don't have time for the Lantau Trail, the one-day Fanlau Trail offers some of the best hiking in Lantau. The trail starts at the Shek Pik reservoir and follows a flat cliff top path all the way around the western coast to Tai O, taking in dramatic ocean scenery and a number of beautiful beaches. Buses #1 and #2 from Mui Wo run to Shek Pik and after the hike you can take #1 back to Mui Wo for boats, or #11 to Tung Chung for the MTR.

★★The Lantau Trail (44 miles)

Lantau Trail (Hong Kong Outdoors)

A great way to take in all the sights that Lantau Island has to offer is to spend a few days completing the Lantau Trail, a hike that circles the whole island. The route is challenging, but offers jaw-dropping vistas over the area, particularly at sunrise and sunset. The trail starts in Mui Wo in the east of Lantau and then loops around the island, crossing Lantau Peak, Ngong Ping, Tai O and then down to Shek Pik before looping back to Mui Wo. Some of the trail is particularly tough, so be prepared and take plenty of water with you. The trail is clearly marked the whole way round and can be shortened by taking buses or taxis for stretches or broken down into smaller sections for day-trips such as the Fanlau Trail (see below). If you're keen to complete the whole circuit, you'll have to spend at least a night en route at the **SG Davis Hostel** (see *Where to Stay, Lantau* p. 555). For more information see www.hkcrystal.com/hiking.

★★★The MacLehose Trail, Sai Kung (5 days)

This superb hike derives its name from a former governor of the colony, Sir Murray MacLehose, who was passionate about the area. It comprises of 60 miles of breathtaking hiking that passes through some of the region's wildest and most rugged landscapes. Starting in Sai Kung, the trail runs from east to west, winding along the coastal scenery and then inland towards the mountains. The trail passes 20 of Hong Kong's mountains (including Tai Mo Shan) before reaching the coast on the western side at Tuen Mun. The route is divided into 10 sections, offering shorter walks although they can easily be combined for overnight hikes. The trail is also popular with charities, and there are annual sponsored walks that aim to complete the trail in one go, usually taking about 48 hours. If you're keen to find out more about the route, then the

The MacLehose Trail (Hong Kong Outdoors)

Hong Kong & Macau

Agriculture, Fisheries and Conservation Department website (www.afcd. gov.hk) offers up-to-date information on trails, along with practical advice about hiking in the area.

On Wheels

Hong Kong and Kowloon are best left to exploration on foot or by public transport, but out on the islands and in the New Territories you'll find more scope for cycling, with a range of trails catering to all levels of skill and fitness, and there are even some that are suitable for families with young kids. Real mountain biking enthusiasts should contact the Hong Kong Mountain Biking Association (www.hkmba.org), who can provide detailed routes and maps, biking tips and advice.

★ Cheung Chau

Cheung Chau is a great biking destination as paths are generally flat and clearly marked, making it popular with families. There are numerous shops renting bikes by the hour (HK$50) and you may get a discount if you're renting for a half-day or more. Try **Hop Cheung Bicycle Shop** (☎ 00852-2896-0816) or **Siu Kee Bicycle** (☎ 00852-2981-1384) for reliable bikes.

A pleasant route to try starts by the ferry pier on Praya Street and heads south towards South Island, taking in the village and its fishing community en-route. You'll go past Tung Wan Beach and onto Peak Road. Peak Road continues around the whole southern island, taking in a number of sea-facing cemeteries, Pak Tso Wan beach, Sai Wan (West Bay), the Tin Hau Temple and the Cheung Po Tsai Cave (see *Cheung Chau*, p. 523).

On the Green

Hong Kong has plenty of golfing opportunities and many of them are set amid stunning scenery. If you don't have much time but want a quick swing, there are a number of driving ranges within the city itself; try the **City Golf Club** at 8 Wui Cheung Road in Kowloon (☎ 00852-2992-3333, www.citygolfclub.com; HK$50 per half-hour) which has good facilities and is in a convenient location, right near Jordan MTR (Exit, C2). For golf courses, you should visit one of the public courses, unless you have the thousands of dollars required for private club membership. Many of the cheaper options are farther away in the New Territories, so expect to pay more downtown. Some to try are:

Discovery Bay Golf Course, Discovery Bay Golf Course Valley Road, Lantau (☎ 00852-2987-7173). Non-members can play on Mondays, Tuesdays and Fridays for HK$1,400.

Jockey Club Kau Sai Chau, Sai Kung (☎ 00852-3390-3344, www.kscgolf. com). The Jockey Club course is located on a private island just near Sai Kung, so you'll have to take their private ferry from Sai Kung to Sai Kung Chau. For both courses you'll need a handicap card. A round costs HK$400 on weekdays and HK$540 on weekends.

On Water

So much of Hong Kong is near water that it's bound to play at least some part in your trip here, whether that's a gentle harbor cruise, the exertion of paddling yourself around its islands, a bit of banana-boating or just a plain old swim in the sea.

Harbor Cruises

The harbor is one of Hong Kong's key attractions and cruises are one of the best ways to experience it. There are a variety of different operators, ranging from the Star Ferry to genuine junks, new and old. Note that Queen's Pier in Central where some of the boats board is due to move to Pier 9, next to the recently relocated Star Ferry Terminal.

★★★**Aqua Luna** (☎ 000853-2116-8821, www.aqualuna.com.hk). One of the most luxurious and stylish options is the traditionally styled junk, *Aqua Luna*, whose red-lit sails are easily identifiable across the harbor. Owned by the same company as the excellent Aqua bars and restaurants (see p. 561), the *Aqua Luna* is comfortably decked out in dark wood and sofas and the HK$150 tariff includes a free cocktail aboard.

If you get hungry, there is also a selection of savory snacks available on board. Cruises operate eight times daily, last 45 minutes and start from the docks outside the Cultural Center on Tsimshatsui, also picking up from the Queen's Pier in Central. You can simply turn up and take the cruise, but on weekends and evenings it's better to book in advance.

★★**Duk Ling** (☎ 00852-2508-1234; Thurs 2 pm & 4 pm & Sat 10 am & noon from Tsimshatsui Pier; Thurs 3 pm & 5 pm and Sat 11 am & 1 pm from Queen's Pier, Central; free). For a cheaper alternative, you can join the tourist office's *Duk Ling* hour-long cruise. The *Duk Ling* is the last authentic Chinese junk in the harbor and, after 25 years at sea, was restored in the 1980s and has been used as a tourist boat ever since. The cruise is free, but you may be asked for your passport to prove that you are a genuine tourist. You should book your place in advance at the tourist office in the Star Ferry terminal in Tsimshatsui.

★★**Star Ferry Harbor Cruise** (☎ 00852-2367-7065, www.starferry.com. hk/harbourtour). If you enjoyed your brief trip across the harbor on the Star Ferry then their harbor cruises, which stop at all the terminals (Central, Tsimshatsui, Central, Wanchai and Hung Hom) might appeal. The hour-long trips cost HK$40 during the day, HK$85 at night or HK$120 during the evening light show. Alternatively, you can buy a half-day (HK$65) or one-day (HK$150) hopping pass which allows you to travel between the piers at your leisure.

★Dolphin Watching

(☎ 00852-2984-1414, www.hkdolphinwatch.com). The discovery of these creatures in the early 1990s came as a surprise to the world, and since then research into their dwindling numbers has continued. These dolphins, actually called Chinese white dolphins, have unique coloration. But, despite their name, they have a pink complexion and are born almost black. Hong Kong's economic development and expansion has left them living between power-plants, factories and the airport and has seen their population dwindle to about 1,000. **Hong Kong Dolphinwatch** was established in 1995 and has been working hard to promote awareness and the protection of these beautiful mammals ever since. To catch a glimpse of Hong Kong's endangered dolphins there are tours on Wednesdays, Fridays and Sundays at 8:30 am from the Mandarin Oriental Hotel, Central, or at 9 am from the Kowloon Hotel, Nathan Road, Tsimshatsui, all arranged by Hong Kong Dolphinwatch. Their staff is extremely knowledgeable and, if you're unlucky enough not to see any dolphins, you can go on the next trip for free. The half-day trips cost HK$320.

Watersports

Hong Kong's beaches get busy on summer weekends and watersports are popular. From jet skiing to banana boating, water skiing to windsurfing, it's all available at most major beaches throughout Hong Kong. Although aimed at local residents, if you're an avid watersports fan and are in Hong Kong for a while, there are government-run watersports centers at five points around the territory, including both Main Beach and St. Stephen's Beach in Stanley and at Tai Mei Tuk by the Plover Cove Reservoir in the New Territories. Prices are far cheaper at these centers than at private rental places and all activities are overseen by qualified experts. But in order to use their equipment you'll need to take along ID, as well as certification that you have attained a certain proficiency with the equipment you would like to rent (for more information check out www.lcsd.gov.hk). They all have windsurfs (HK$24), kayaks (HK$20) and sailing dinghies (HK$30) for rent by the hour.

Kayaking

Kayaks await (Paul Etherington)

This is an excellent way to see the islands from water level and throws in some exercise for good measure. You can rent kayaks from many of Hong Kong's beaches for a cost of HK$20 an hour but to really get away from it all, contact a professional like **Paul Etherington** (☎ 00852-9300-5197, www.kayak-and-hike.com). Paul has been living in Hong Kong for over 25 years and specializes in adventures around the beautiful Sai Kung Peninsula. Trips costs vary from HK$600-800 per day depending on your needs.

Surfing

Hong Kong's waves tend not to be suited to surfing, except during typhoons when you should stay indoors, but there are a few spots where you'll find rides. **Big Wave Bay** is the best known of these and has places like Eric's Shop down on the beach where you can rent body boards (from HK$10) and surf boards (HK$50 plus HK$100 deposit). If you're visiting in mid-December, don't miss the new annual Quiksilver Hong Kong Surfing Cup, which is getting more popular by the year. Bus #9 runs to Shek O and Big Wave Bay from just outside Shau Kai Wan MTR every 15 minutes.

★ Swimming

Hong Kong's steamy summer lasts a good seven months and during this time swimming in its outdoor pools and sea is a pleasure. In the cooler months of winter there are also plenty of indoor pools in which to exercise. Many of the best **pools** are in hotels with access restricted to guests, but if you can't afford their room rate, some of the public ones are also fairly good – the indoor and outdoor pools at **Kowloon Park** (both daily 6:30-noon, 1-5 pm & 6-10 pm; HK$19) and **Victoria Park** (daily 6:30 am-nooon, 1-5 pm & 6-10 pm; HK$19) are both cheap but can get very busy.

While it certainly doesn't have the best **ocean** in Southeast Asia, Hong Kong's outlying islands and New Territories offer pretty coves where you can swim in emerald waters and soak away the stresses of downtown. Since seawater quality testing was introduced, the bulk of the beaches are of an acceptable or better standard, particularly those in the farther flung spots. All designated swimming beaches listed below are demarcated and shark-netted, have lifeguards in attendance at peak times (daily 9 am-6 pm) and many have changing facilities and showers. Shark attack is perceived as a serious threat by the Chinese, although the actual incidence is no higher than elsewhere in the world, and the risk is minimal. Indeed the greatest danger from swimming at undesignated beaches is probably the ocean currents, which can be powerful. If you're not a strong swimmer then it's probably best to stick to the designated areas, and all ocean swimming should be avoided in severe weather. For more on public swimming pools and beaches visit www.lcsd.gov.hk.

TOP FIVE SWIMMING BEACHES

- **Repulse Bay**, Hong Kong Island (see p. 513)
- **St. Stephen's**, Stanley, Hong Kong Island (see p. 514)
- **Lo So Shing**, Lamma Island (see p. 542)
- **Cheung Sha**, Lantau Island (see p. 521)
- **Clear Water Bay**, New Territories (see p. 529)

Gambling: The Races

Happy Valley (see p. 512) and **Sha Tin** (see p. 526) are the only places where it's legal to gamble in Hong Kong and as a result they are enormously popular. More money is bet here on a single race than at many Western tracks in a month, and an estimated HK$91 billion is bet each year. The Chinese are renowned gamblers, sometimes winning big, but all too often losing everything but the shirt on their back. Despite the law prohibiting gambling in China and Hong Kong, it is rampant and can be seen at mah jong tables around the country. This predilection for gambling serves Macau well and its legal casinos (see *Macau, Gambling*, p. 589) are packed with visitors from Hong Kong, Taiwan and the mainland on weekends.

The races themselves are much akin to those you'll find around the world, and the excitement and tension in the air is tangible. The race season is from September to June and meets are usually on Wednesdays and weekends. Basic entrance is HK$10, but if you want to have a trip arranged for you, Race Tour Packages to both courses are available through the tourist office (or call ☎ 00852-2366-3995). They start from HK$580, which includes admission, a welcome drink, souvenir program and a guided tour of the parade ring and winning post. For race schedules and events check out www.hkjc.com/english or contact the tourist office.

Cultural Adventures
★★★ Cantonese Cooking

Cantonese cooking is China's most famous culinary form, exported and modified to appear in restaurants around the globe. But it is at its best and truest in Hong Kong and Guangzhou. As always, the tourist office comes through with the goods and can arrange a number of excellent courses where you will be taught the art of Cantonese food preparation by award-winning Cantonese chefs, either in their restaurant or in a professional cooking school. These courses are not only fun, but will help you to understand more about local produce, techniques and cooking styles. Classes are daily at 10 am or noon and cost HK$620, including your lunch. Contact the tourist office to book.

Fengshui

To understand more about the concept of geomancy (see *Fengshui*, p. 54) you can take a half-day tour to three sites with good fengshui organized by Skybird (☎ 00852-2369-9628, www.skybird.com. hk). Tours cost HK$290 per person and leave on Tuesdays, Thursdays and Saturdays at 8:45 am from the Excelsior Hotel on Hong Kong Island, or 9:15 am from the Salisbury YMCA Hotel in Kowloon. The tour will take you to Lung Cheung Road Lookout in Kowloon, the Nine Dragons Wall in Wanchai and Statue Square in Central, pointing out examples of both good and bad fengshui.

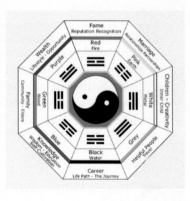

Tai Chi

Hong Kong's rapid pace and large number of people can often leave you feeling fatigued and tai chi is a great way to unwind and relax. And what better place to do it than to the backdrop of Victoria harbour? Free classes are taught by **Mr. Ng**, a famous local master, and take place on the Avenue of Stars every Monday, Wednesday, Thursday and Friday between 8 and 9 am, but it's worth calling the Hong Kong Tourist Board Visitor's Hotline (☎ 00852-2508-1234) to double-check. Or you can head to any of the parks in the early morning and see many locals warming up for the day with tai chi. Tai chi, tea culture and fengshui are covered by **Skybird's** (☎ 00852-2369-9628,

Chinese junk in Hong Kong Harbour (Ken Exner)

Hong Kong market (Galen Frysinger)

www.skybird.com.hk) Traditional Lifestyles tour. The tour costs HK$298 and operates on Mondays, Wednesdays and Fridays from the Excelsior Hotel on Hong Kong Island at 7:30 am, or 7:45 am from the Salisbury YMCA Hotel in Kowloon.

Kung Fu

The city has heavy kung fu connections, so it's not surprising that it's a popular recreational activity. To see some of the local talent and to pick up a skill or two, head to **Kung Fu Corner** (Sculpture Walk, Kowloon Park; ☎ 00852-2724-3344) between 2:30 and 4:30 on a Sunday. Not only will you see some highly skilled demonstrations of different styles, but you may also get the chance to see traditional dragon dances and ceremonial drumming.

Where to Stay

Hong Kong has an enormous range of places to stay, from windowless boxes that cost as little as US$20 to five-star splendor at international prices. However, make no mistake, this is the most expensive place to stay in China and you'll have to pay at least US$70 to get anything vaguely resembling a decent-sized, comfortable and clean room.

HOTEL PRICE CHART	
$	Under HK$300/US$40
$$	HK$301-600/US$41-80
$$$	HK$601-1,000/US$81-100
$$$$	HK$1,001-2,000/US$101-140
$$$$$	Over HK$2,000/US$140

Still, even if you're on a tight budget you can stay in the center of Hong Kong, as long as you're prepared to accept small, if not tiny, rooms. The greatest number of budget options lie in two crumbling old buildings in Kowloon, **Chungking Mansions** and **Mirador Mansions** (see below), but there are other pockets, notably across the water in the bar, restaurant and shopping district of **Causeway Bay**.

While all of these places are fine for a few days, anything longer can leave you feeling distinctly claustrophobic. If you have more time some of the secluded spots in the **New Territories** and on the **Outlying Islands** can make for a more relaxed break and are cheaper too. If you're going to spend a little more on your accommodation anywhere along your China trip, make it **Hong Kong** – those extra dollars will buy you a heap more comfort and security and, at the top end, the territory has some of the finest hotels in the world.

In upscale hotels there are additional taxes of 13% added to the room rate, but these are usually offset by discounts of up to 30% off the published rack rates.

Hong Kong Island
Central & Admiralty

★**Ritz-Carlton**, 3 Connaught Road (☎ 00852-2877-6666, www.ritzcarlton. com; Central MTR, Exit J3). The Ritz-Carlton is undeniably plush, and its comparatively small number of rooms makes it feel intimate for a five-star.

The hotel's location is great for trips around the territory, very close to both the MTR and ferry terminals, but if you just want to relax, the outdoor swimming pool is a lovely spot. FC/SW/@ $$$$$

★★**Island Shangri-La**, Pacific Place, Supreme Court Road (☎ 00852-2877-3838, www.shangri-la.com; Admiralty MTR, Exit C1). The Shangri-La, as ever, exudes class, and offers some of the most spacious and scenic rooms in Hong Kong. The higher harbor-view rooms have panoramic vistas over the bay from their giant windows – ask for the 50th floor or above. As you'd expect, the hotel has plenty of amenities, including the excellent

> **What's it mean?** FC=fitness center; SW=swimming pool; @=in-room Internet access; DA=rooms for disabled.

Petrus restaurant (see p. 559), but if you need more diversions, the mega-mall of Pacific Place and its upmarket international shops and restaurants is right next door. FC/SW/@/DA $$$$$

Wanchai (Wanchai MTR with the exception of the Wesley)

★★**Grand Hyatt**, 1 Harbour Road (☎ 00852-2588-1234, www.hongkong.grand.hyatt.com). As usual the Grand Hyatt comes through with the goods, from the art-deco opulence of the lobby to the simple, modern styling of the rooms. The hotel boasts a good

Island Shangri-La

location and many rooms enjoy harbor views. There are a host of dining options, notably **Grissini** (see p.559), which serves quality Italian cuisine, and **Tiffin**, with a fine afternoon tea selection. Health facilities are also up to par and **Plateau**, the hotel's 80,000-square-foot spa, has an enormous swimming pool. FC/SW/@/DA $$$$$

Harbour View International House, 4 Harbour Road (☎ 00852-2802-0111, www.harbour.ymcaorg.hk). Like its sister over the water, the Y on Hong Kong Island is more of a hotel than a hostel and, although it's

Grand Hyatt

hardly plush, some rooms have good harbor views. The staff are friendly and the "hostel" is well-located. Combined with the affordable prices, this makes it popular with tour groups. @ $$$-$$$$

Wesley, 22 Hennessy Road (☎ 00852-2866-6688, www.hanglung.com; Admiralty MTR, Exit C1). The reasonably-sized, functional rooms at the Wesley are a fairly good deal, particularly for stays of a month or more (from HK$10,800), and attract a string of long-term residents. Although there are rooms at a range of different budgets, it's worth noting that, aside from the Deluxe Plus, the rooms are all the same – the higher price just denotes a higher floor. $$$

Causeway Bay (Causeway Bay MTR)

★**Excelsior**, 281 Gloucester Road (☎ 00852-2894-8888, www. excelsiorhongkong.com). Comfortable, plush and well-located, the Excelsior's excellent staff add to the experience and facilities are also good, although there isn't a pool. Many of the hotel's rooms enjoy harbor views. FC/@ $$$$

Jia studio

★★★**Jia**, 1-5 Irving Street (☎ 00852-3196-9000, www.jiahongkong.com). This Philippe Starck-designed boutique hotel has taken Causeway Bay by storm and is *the* place to stay, offering tastefully styled, comfortable, relaxed and spacious rooms with ultra-modern amenities. That has made it a favorite with tourists and business travelers alike. There are three categories of rooms – studio, one-bedroom suites and penthouse suites. All are divided into living, dining and working areas, making the Jia feel more like an apartment home than a hotel. There are also a couple of great restaurants on site – **OPIA** offers excellent Australian Asian fusion food. Hotel guests enjoy use of the nearby California Fitness Club. FC/@ $$$$-$$$$$

★**Noble Hostel**, Flat A1, 17F, Great George Building, 27 Paterson Street (☎ 00852-2576-6148). In the heart of Causeway Bay, the Noble offers small but clean and functionally well-designed rooms, all of which have windows. Reception is on the 17th floor. $$

Elsewhere on Hong Kong Island

Mount Davis Hostel, Mount Davis Path, Mount Davis, Kennedy Town (☎ 00852-2817-5715, www.yha.org.hk; Sheung Wan MTR and then bus or taxi). This is one of Hong Kong's best hostels and enjoys a stunning setting atop Mount Davis above Kennedy Town. Facilities are good and the hostel has recently been expanded to deal with its increasing popularity. To get here you'll need to take the hostel shuttle bus; otherwise it's a steep 40-minute climb! Dorm beds are HK$65. $$

Kowloon
Tsimshatsui (Tsimshatsui MTR)

CHUNGKING & MIRADOR MANSIONS

Both of these enormous crumbling old buildings are found at the southern end of Nathan Road, in the heart of Kowloon's shopping district. The lower two floors are taken up with shops and restaurants of every description, which are predominantly run by Indians and Nepalis. Walking along the warren of narrow lanes that dissect the ground floors, you'll come across moneychangers, *chai* (Indian milk tea) vendors, cell phone dealers, backpackers, traditional tailors and Internet cafés! This intense blend of cultures formed the backdrop for Wong Kar-wai's movie *Chungking Express*. However, while the multicultural ambience is fascinating and the location excellent, rooms can be miniscule, may not have a window, security can be lax, and the complexes are infernos just waiting to happen. This said, if you want to be in the heart of Kowloon for US$20, this is the place, and there are a few better hotels within the complex that charge a little more. Of the two, Chungking has a greater selection of places to stay, but Mirador is a little less cramped and hectic.

★**Harbour Guest House**, 4F Block B, Chungking Mansions, Nathan Road, Kowloon (☎ 00852-2721-2207). Rooms are nicely decorated, clean and comfortable and Mrs. Francis is an attentive host. She can also offer helpful information on Hong Kong. $ ★★**New Garden Hostel** and **USA Hotel**, 13F, E1 & F1, Mirador Mansions, Nathan Road (☎ 00852-2311-2523). Run by Mr. and Mrs. Li, the New Garden Hostel is one of the better options in Mirador Mansions. Offering a range of different priced rooms and dorms, facilities are clean and modern and the staff are friendly, although bathrooms are shared. You'll also find the USA Hotel (run by the same couple) just next door, which offers better and more expensive rooms with en-suite bathrooms. They also have rooms on the 5th and 8th floors. Laundry service and Internet are both available. @ $

Taiwan Hotel and Oriental Pearl, 3F A-Block & 11F E-Block respectively, Chungking Mansions, Nathan Road (☎ 00852-9858-5034; taiwan_hotel@hotmail.com). If you're set on staying in Chungking Mansions then these two hotels are more secure, larger and better equipped than the standard places. Both hotels are owned by a helpful Taiwanese man named Peter. Although you pay a little more than you might at other places, it is money well spent. @ $

★**Holiday Inn Golden Mile**, 50 Nathan Road (☎ 00852-2369 3111, www.holiday-inn.com/hongkong-gldn). The excellent location of this hotel, combined with its roof-top pool and reasonable prices make the Holiday Inn a good option. Although the rooms are fairly standard, the facilities and excellent service compensate. SW/@/DA $$$$

★★★**Intercontinental**, 18 Salisbury Road, 18 Salisbury Road (☎ 00852-2721-1211, www.intercontinental.com). The Intercontinental's lobby is one

Intercontinental

of the most impressive in the world, not so much for its décor which is low-level and subdued, but for the spectacular floor-to-ceiling views over Hong Kong's gleaming cityscape. Facilities match the lobby with a stunning infinity spa pool on the third floor, an around-the-clock fitness center and quality rooms, the very best of which have private jacuzzis overlooking the harbor. FC/SW/@ $$$$$

★★★**Peninsula**, Salisbury Road (☎ 00852-2920-2888, www.peninsula.com). Built in 1928, the Peninsula remains the grandest hotel in Hong Kong and has been graced by presidents, film stars and royalty from around the world. In spite of a 30-floor extension in 1994 to regain the view over the harbor (after the construction of the Cultural Center) the "Grand Dame of the Far East"

retains her elegance and character. Rooms are large and light and offer all modern comforts with a stylish blend of European and Eastern design elements. Service is impeccable and the list of facilities available to guests includes a fleet of Rolls Royces, private helicopters from the hotel's helipad and personalized courses in Hong Kong's culture, cuisine, arts and history, along with more usual options like the first-rate spa and excellent indoor Romanesque swimming pool which enjoys breathtaking

Peninsula

views over the harbor. Even if it's a little out of your price range the Peninsula is worth a visit – try one of its fine restaurants (see **Spring Moon**, p. 562), bars (see **Felix**, p. 562) or hark back to the old days with some afternoon tea in the lobby. FC/SW/@ $$$$$

★★**Salisbury YMCA**, 41 Salisbury Road (☎ 00852-2268-7000, www. ymcahk.org.hk). Given its prime location, good facilities and prestigious neighbor, it's hard to fault the Salisbury. While the rooms aren't anywhere close to the standards of the Peninsula, the vistas from the higher rooms are, and it's worth paying a little more for one of these. $$$

Jordan (Jordan MTR)

BP International, 8 Austin Road (☎ 00852-2376-1111, www.bpih.com.hk). BP stands for Baden Powell, the founder of the Cub Scouts Movement, which gives this hotel a decidedly institutional feel. Nevertheless the BP offers a fairly good location, small, but well-equipped rooms and moderate prices, which make it popular with tour groups. @ $$$$

★★**Eaton**, 380 Nathan Road (☎ 00852-2782 1818, www.eaton-hotel.com). It's a fair walk from the Eaton down to the harbor, but this hotel is worth considering for its well-priced and comfortable (if small) rooms, excellent staff and lovely rooftop pool. One advantage of the location is that it's just a five-minute walk from Temple Street Market. FC/SW/@/DA $$$$-$$$$$

Eaton

★**Rent-a-Room**, Flat A, 2F, Knight Garden, 7-8 Tak Hing Street (☎ 00852- 2366-3011, www.renta-roomhk.com). A 20-minute walk back from the harbor, the rooms in this family-run place are a cut above anything you'll find in Chungking or Mirador Mansions and are, accordingly, a little more expensive. In spite of the miniscule size of many of the rooms there's an array of amenities encapsulated within them, including fridge, hairdryer, kettle, safe and TV. They have a wide variety of room shapes and sizes so it's worth asking to have a look at a few if you're not happy with the first one you see. $$

The Outlying Islands

Lamma

★★**Concerto Inn**, 28 Hung Shing Ye Beach (☎ 00852-2982-1668, www.concertoinn.com.hk). This small hotel offers a real escape from downtown and its location near a small and secluded beach makes for a romantic choice. $$-$$$

Lantau

★★**SG Davis Hostel**, Ngong Ping (☎ 00852-2985-5610, www.yha.org.hk; bus #2 from Mui Wo, bus #23 from Tung Chung MTR or Ngong Ping 360° Skyrail). The SG Davis Hostel offers good facilities in an excellent location. It's situated near Po Lin Monastery up in the hills and provides a breath of fresh air after the city, although you will need some warmer clothes during the cooler winter months. It's also a great place to start hikes from and you'll find the staff has plenty of helpful tips for walking routes. The hostel has kitchen facilities but there's also the excellent vegetarian restaurant at Po Lin (see p. 562) just down the road. The hostel is well sign-posted from Po Lin and takes about 10 minutes to walk to. Dorm beds from HK$45. $

★**Silvermine Beach Hotel**, 648 Silvermine Bay, Mui Wo (☎ 00852-2984-8295, www.resort.com.hk). The Silvermine Beach Hotel's quiet rooms offer beautiful views and its beachfront location means the lack of swimming pool is no problem. The hotel also has an outdoor terrace restaurant and is just a short walk from the Mui Wo Ferry Pier. SW/FC/@ $$$$

Cheung Chau

★★**Warwick**, East Bay (☎ 00852-2981-0081, www.warwickhotel.com.hk). This once-dated hotel has recently undergone restoration to give it stylishly furnished rooms, some of which offer fantastic views over Cheung Chau's

Hong Kong & Macau

main beach to the ocean. Prices are heavily discounted during the week, although it's worth paying extra for a balcony with seaview. The hotel also has a host of recreational activities, including bike rental, water sports and fishing trips. FC/SW/@ $$$

Warwick

New Territories

While the cities of the New Territories hold little worthy of an overnight stay, there are a number of inexpensive and basic hostels, which provide access to the beaches and hikes in the wilder parts of the territory. Make sure you call in advance to arrange pick-ups and directions to the following hostels as they can be a little off the beaten track and some are only accessible by foot. All of the following have dorm beds for around HK$50.

Bradbury Lodge, 66 Tai Mei Tuk Road, Tai Mei Tuk, Tai Po (☎ 00852-2662-5123; Tai Po KCR, then bus #75K).

★★★**Pak Sha O Hostel**, Hoi Ha Road, Sai Kung; (☎ 00852-2328-2327; bus #92 from Sai Kung).

Sze Lok Yuen Hostel, Tai Mo Shan, Tsuen Wan (☎ 00852-2488-8188, www.yha.org.hk; Tsuen Wan MTR, then bus #51).

Where to Eat

Hong Kong is one of the world's culinary capitals, most famous for its Cantonese cuisine, but other Chinese and Southeast Asian styles such as Thai and Vietnamese are also well-represented. Hong Kong is far too cosmopolitan to limit itself to just one continent though and you'll find some of the greatest culinary diversity on the planet, available day and night, cheap and expensive. Although you can often walk into many of the restaurants listed below and get a table immediately, it's worth calling in advance to be sure, particularly for the better establishments and those with views.

Although Hong Kong offers fine **Cantonese cuisine**, if you've come from Guangzhou and the mainland and want a break from unfamiliar food, you'll find plenty of Western options to sate your palate – from the usual overload of McDonald's, Pizza Hut and Starbucks, to excellent sandwich chains like Oliver's and Prêt a Manger, as well as a host of other choices from steak to *haute cuisine*.

While Hong Kong is certainly expensive when compared to China, the good news is that eating here doesn't have to break the bank. Of course, there are places where you can spend international prices on an exquisite meal, but there are also plenty of cheap cafés and canteens with tasty sustenance from China and Southeast Asia for under US$6. Streetfood is another cheap, tasty option and can be

RESTAURANT PRICES	
$	Under HK$50/US$6
$$	HK$50-120/US$6-15
$$$	HK$121-240/US$16-30
$$$$	HK$241-400/US$31-50
$$$$$	Over HK$401/US$50

found in nightmarkets around the territory. Kebabs, seafood and vegetable skewers are all common sights and you'll also find stalls selling dim sum, varieties of tofu and *yudaan* (fish balls). One of the best places to try is Temple Street Night Market, where you'll find all the aforementioned plus a whole lot more. The real-life surroundings and interaction can also come as a bit of a reminder that this is still China despite the slick service and hygienic sterility of some of the (top class) mall restaurants. Price codes are based on the cost of a meal for one along with a beer or soft drink.

Hong Kong Island

Lan Kwai Fong, Soho & Mid-Levels

(Central MTR except for Full House Kitchen)

California, 30-32 D'Aguilar Street, Lan Kwai Fong (☎ 00852-2521-1345; daily noon-midnight). This café in the heart of Lan Kwai Fong serves healthy and tasty monster burgers, pastas, pizzas and good wines in a modern American diner where Wong Kar-wai saw fit to film scenes of *Chungking Express*. $$$

★★★**Full House Kitchen**, 13 Queen's Road West, Sheung Wan (☎ 00852-2851-7631; daily, early till late). This atmospheric local restaurant serves up some excellent Cantonese food all day long. Not only does it offer 40 varieties of *congee* (including preserved egg and frog congee) but the *wonton* noodle soup (only HK$16) is some of the best in Hong Kong. $

★★**Habibi Café and Restaurant**, 112-114 Wellington Street (☎ 00852-2544-3886/6198; daily 11 am-midnight; Central MTR, Exit D2). Habibi is a fantastic little café and restaurant offering a genuine taste of Middle Eastern cuisine, including delicious mezze such as *babaganoush*, *hummus* and *tabouleh*, as well as healthy and hearty mains like *koshari* (mixed pasta and rice with lentils and chickpeas). The café's earthy desert tones and dome are complemented by its pictures of Egyptian movie stars, and you can enjoy an apple *shisha* (water pipe) after your meal if that's your thing! Habibi restaurant next door is equally tasteful but in somewhat more refined style. $$

★**Lile Café**, 10 Shelley Street, Soho (☎ 00852-2810-9777; Mon-Fri 8 am-midnight, Sat & Sun 10 am-midnight). The interior of Lile is as wholesome as the food and you start to feel healthier just by walking through the door (plus you can walk up the hill to get here if you choose not to take the Mid-Levels Escalator). Lile is the brainchild of the folk from Lamma's Bookworm Café and serves a delicious and nutritious range of organic foods, including tasty wraps and sandwiches, as well as juices, beers and wines. They also have gluten-free, wheat-free and yeast-free options. $$-$$$

★★**M at the Fringe**, 2 Lower Albert Road, Central (☎ 00852-2877-4000; Mon-Fri noon-2:30 pm & 7-10:30 pm, weekends evenings only; Central MTR, Exit K). M at the Fringe offers some of the most mouth-watering continental food in Hong Kong in an eclectically styled dining hall. Although it doesn't enjoy the same fantastic views as its Shanghai counterpart, it manages to avoid the pretensions of M on the Bund and the service is first-rate. Most importantly, the food is delicious, whether you choose the daily specials or the time-honored favorites like the Salt Encased Slowly Baked Leg of Lamb. $$$$

Peak Café Bar, 9-13 Shelley Street, Soho (☎ 00852-2140-6877; Mon-Fri 11 am-2 am, Sat & Sun 9 am-midnight). The Peak Café lost its lease atop Victoria Peak and was replaced by the Peak Lookout, but rather than pack up shop completely the restaurant retained its name and opened at the bottom of the Peak in Soho. The café still offers the refined style and expansive blend of Western and Asian dishes, from pizza to tandoori dishes, which first made it popular and it continues to draw crowds today. The café also offers wireless Internet connection throughout. $$$-$$$$

★**Tsim Chai Kee Noodle**, 98 Wellington Street, Central (daily 10 am-9 pm; Central MTR, Exit D2). This is a popular lunchtime spot and serves up some tasty Cantonese *wonton* for as little as HK$11. Don't be put off by the lengthy queues as it really is worth the wait. $

Yung Kee *(Simon Shek)*

★★★**Yung Kee**, 32-40 Wellington Street, Central (☎ 0852-2522-1624; daily 11 am-11:30 pm, *dim sum* Mon-Sat 2-5:30 pm, Sun 11 am-5:30 pm; Central MTR, Exit D2). Yung Kee has a long history of serving fine Cantonese food, notably the delicious crispy goose (HK$180 for a half-bird which will serve up to six people). The restaurant started as a roadside stall before World War II and subsequently moved thrice, each time to a building with the number 32! These days Yung Kee is an opulent affair, which has been acclaimed by no less than *Fortune Magazine* and is certainly worth a visit for the superb Cantonese fare. $$$

Central & Admiralty

★**Lumiere**, 3101-3107, Podium Level 3, IFC Mall, Central (☎ 00852-2383-3933; daily noon-2:30 pm & 5:30-11:30 pm; Central MTR, Exit D2). You may well be ready to eat by the time you've hunted out Lumiere in the heart of the IFC Mall, but it's certainly worthwhile for the innovative blend of South American and contemporary Szechuan dishes they offer – try the Szechuan Chicken Salad. To add to the experience, the stylish restaurant also enjoys good views over the harbor. $$$-$$$$

Thai Basil, Lower Ground Floor, Pacific Place, 88 Queensway, Admiralty (☎ 00852-2537-4682; daily 11:30 am-10 pm; Admiralty MTR, Exit C1). This modern and spacious mall restaurant serves reliable Thai fare with plenty of fresh flavors at affordable prices – great for a break from shopping. $$-$$$

★★**Petrus**, 56F, Island Shangri-La, Pacific Place, Supreme Court Road (☎ 00852-2820-8590; daily 7 am-10 am, noon-3 pm & 6:30-11 pm; Admiralty MTR, Exit C1). This is Hong Kong's premier French restaurant and also offers some of its best harbor views from the oversized windows of the elegant dining halls. All the dishes are excellent, but the langoustines served with a lemon confit are superb. Petrus also has one of the city's best wine selections. $$$$-$$$$$

Wanchai (Wanchai MTR)

American (Peking) Restaurant, 20 Lockhart Road (☎ 0852-2527-7277; daily noon-11 pm). It may not look much like a northern Chinese restaurant, but the American has been pulling in the crowds for years and continues to serve reliably good Beijing duck. $$$

Petrus

★**Fook Lam Moon**, 35-45 Johnston Road (☎ 00852-2866-0663; daily 11:30 am-3 pm & 6-10:30 pm). This upscale dining hall is renowned for its exquisitely presented Cantonese fare, including stuffed crab, abalone and delicious suckling pig. The latter must be ordered a day in advance. The crispy chicken also comes highly recommended. $$$-$$$$

★★**Grissini**, 2F Grand Hyatt Hotel, 1 Harbour Road (☎ 00852-2588-1234; daily noon-2:30 pm & 7-11 pm). This is one of the best Italian restaurants in the city, serving traditional Italian dishes and delicacies. Homemade pastas and quality seafood are just some of their mouth-watering specialties and they can all be enjoyed with a bottle of equally fine wine from the extensive cellar. $$$$-$$$$$

Causeway Bay (Causeway Bay MTR)

Oliver's Sandwiches, GF World Trade Center (daily 10:30 am-10 pm). Found across Hong Kong Island and Kowloon, this chain serves excellent freshly made sandwiches along with a host of other goodies. There's a branch in the World Trade Center, right next to the Excelsior Hotel. Oliver's also has branches in Harbour City Ocean Terminal (Kowloon). $-$$

★**Rice Paper**, Shop P413-18, 4F World Trade Center, 280 Gloucester Road (☎ 00852-2890-3975; daily 11:30 am-11 pm). Rice Paper serves fine Vietnamese dishes full of fresh and punchy flavors in a light and bright restaurant, which enjoys good views and has funky wraparound two-person booths built into the walls. The slow-cooked duck in coconut is excellent. There's another branch at Shop 3319, Level 3 Gateway Arcade, Harbour City in Tsimshatsui (☎ 00852-3151-7801). $$$

★★**WasabiSabi**, 13F Food Forum, Times Square, 1 Matheson Street (☎ 00852-2506-0009; daily noon-3 pm & 6-11 pm). A

WasabiSabi

great name for a great place which offers an unlikely fusion of Japanese and Italian cuisine with dishes such as Wagyu Beef Teriyaki served in an Italian sauce and a dessert list that includes wasabi ice cream! The cool, refined and stylish restaurant has a sushi bar, wraparound circular booths and a velvet lounge for drinks. WasabiSabi certainly isn't cheap, but its set lunches are a good value. $$$$

★**Water Margin**, Shop 1205, 12F Food Forum, Times Square (☎ 00852-3102-0888; daily noon-3 pm & 6-11 pm). Although it's a bit too contrived, Water Margin's rustic decoration and low lighting just about manages to make you forget you're in a Hong Kong mall and transport you north to a Shandong village. But the real reason to come here is for its quality northern cuisine, which includes Shandong and Szechuanese specialties, such as Diced Chicken in a Sea of Red Peppers. $$$-$$$$

Elsewhere on the Island

★★**Café Deco**, Level 1 & 2, The Peak Galleria, 118 Peak Road (☎ 00852-2849-5111; daily 11:30 am-11 pm, Sun opens at 9:30 am for breakfast; Peak Tram). Although there are plenty of cafés and restaurants on the Peak, this is the best, both in terms of its unparalleled views and its quality international fare. There's live music nightly, and the pick of tables are those on the sliver of first-floor outdoor ter-race – the ones towards the right-

Café Deco

hand end offer the best vistas. I've never eaten a bad meal here, but service can be slow, as the café gets very busy – reserve in advance. $$$-$$$$

Jumbo Kingdom

Jumbo Kingdom, Shum Wan Pier Drive, Wong Chuk Hang, Aberdeen (☎ 00852-2553-9111, www.jumbo.com.hk; Monday to Saturday 11 am-11 pm & Sunday 7 am-11 am; bus #75 from Admiralty bus terminal). The Jumbo Kingdom floating restaurant is possibly the most touristy eatery in Hong Kong and its flashy lights and casino-like air continue to draw in the crowds – an estimated 30 million visitors have dined here since the 1970s. But you'll find few locals here, as the seafood is far from exceptional and it's heavy on the wallet. However, this doesn't stop a mass of hungry mainlanders from keenly munching away and, if you're heading to Aberdeen, Jumbo is worth a visit for the experience, if not the food. $$$

King Ludwig Beerhall, Shop 202, Murray House, Stanley (☎ 00852-2899-0122; daily noon-midnight; bus #4 or #4A, Lockhart Road, Causeway Bay).

King Ludwig sits at the top of Stanley's Murray House and serves a range of tasty German dishes – the Sausage Sampler offers several delicious kinds of bratwurst and will feed two. The dark wooden interior leads out to a terrace that has good ocean views. $$$

★Peak Lookout, 121 Peak Road (☎ 00852-2849-1000; daily 10:30 am-midnight; Peak Tram). The Peak Lookout has taken the place of the beloved Peak Café, which has now moved downhill to the Mid-Levels and, while the food is certainly good and the patio is very atmospheric, a lookout is about all you get in terms of views. If you want more vista with your vino, try Café Deco (see above). $$$-$$$$

Smugglers Inn, 90A Stanley Main Street, Stanley (☎ 00852-2813-8852; daily 10 am-late; bus #6 or #6A, Exchange Square, Central). This small pub in the center of Stanley Main Street serves tasty and reasonably priced meals, including fish and chips and sandwiches and is a popular drinking haunt in the evenings. $$

Kowloon
Tsimshatsui (Tsimshatsui MTR)

★★★Aqua, 29F & 30th, 1 Peking Road, Tsimshatsui (☎ 00852-3427-2288, www.aqua.com.hk; daily noon-3 pm & 6 pm-midnight). This ultrastylish Kowloon restaurant offers some of the best vistas and finest food around. The restaurant has an entirely glass façade and mirrors in the interior. It has exquisite Italian and Japanese cuisine to accompany the excellent harbor views. If you just want a

Aqua

drink, the Aqua bar is on the 30th floor and overlooks the restaurant and the harbor. The Aqua group also owns Hutong in the same building (see below), Wasabisabi and Water Margin on Hong Kong Island and operates junk cruises aboard the *Aqua Luna* (see p. 545). $$$$

★★Delhi Club, 3F C-Block, Chungking Mansions, Nathan Road (☎ 00852-2368-1682; daily noon-3:30 pm & 6-11:30 pm). This is the best of

Chungking Mansion's collection of Indian restaurants and serves up a mean *jalfrezi*. You can take the edge off of that with a cold bottle of Kingfisher. $$

★★★Felix, The Peninsula Hotel, Salisbury Road (☎ 00852-2315 3188; 6 pm-2 am). The

Felix

classy Phillip Starck-designed interior gives way to some of the best views Hong Kong has to offer. The refined and romantic restaurant serves top notch Western food, including tasty rib-eye steaks, while the slightly elevated tear-shaped bar is all peaches and cream. The only disappointment with this place is that the trendily designed blinds obscure some of the view. $$$$-$$$$$

★★★**Hutong**, 28F, 1 Peking Road, Tsimshatsui (☎ 3428-8342; daily 12 am-3:30 pm & 6 pm-12 pm). One floor down from Aqua and under the same ownership, Hutong is equally good in a thoroughly different way. It shares the same excellent views and its interior offers a modern take on classical Chinese style, while the delicious specialty cuisine is decidedly northern – try the crispy lamb ribs. If you're in a group of six or more, the Japanese low tables are a good option. $$$$

★★**Spring Moon**, 1F Peninsula Hotel, Salisbury Road (☎ 00852-2920-2888; Mon-Sat 11:30 am-2:30 pm & 6-11:30 pm, Sunday 11-2:30 pm & 6-10 pm). As is to be expected, Spring Moon rises above most other restaurants in Hong Kong and serves some of the best Cantonese cuisine available. Its classic Cantonese teahouse style oozes quality and sophistication and the chefs make over 12,000 individual dim sum every day! Each one is created to perfection and the famous pork-filled pumpkin dumplings are mouth-watering. $$$$$

★★★**Tang Court**, 1F Langham Hotel, 8 Peking Road (☎ 00852-2375 1133; daily noon-3 pm & 6-11 pm). This award-winning Cantonese restaurant offers the finest quality Cantonese food available in Hong Kong, served in a grand imperial setting. Dishes are cooked to perfection with presentation to match, and the staff are trained to these same high standards. If you want the best in town, then this may just be it. Highly recommended. $$$$$

The New Territories & Outlying Islands

★★★**Bookworm Café**, 79 Main Street, Yung Shue Wan, Lamma Island (☎ 00852-2982-4838). This cozy café is well worth a stop if you're visiting Lamma, and provides healthy, organic food in a relaxing environment. It serves quality vegetarian cuisine and a number of exotic juices and drinks, including soya milk lattes and dandelion coffee. Bookworm Café also provides free Internet and a number of books for leisurely reading. If you like it here and want more of the same in town, Lile Café (see p. 558) is run by the same folks. $$

Po Lin Monastery entrance *(Dennis Moynihan)*

★★★**Po Lin Monastery Vegetarian Restaurant** (☎ 00852-2985-5248; daily 11:30 am-5 pm) Any visit to the Po Lin Monastery wouldn't be complete without a meal at its famous vegetarian restaurant. The canteen serves up every type of soybean creation, offering excellent imitations of fish and meat and all the meals are prepared using traditional Buddhist techniques. The restaurant has no menu and you eat what's been prepared for that day. Choose between the basic (HK$60) or deluxe meals (HK$100). $$

Rainbow Restaurant, 23-24 First Street, Sok Kwu Wan, Lamma Island (☎ 00852-2982-8100; daily 11 am-11 pm). This enormous seafood restaurant is Lamma's biggest, seating over 800 people. But, despite its size, it still has excellent seafood at reasonable prices; set menus for two are a particularly good value and include delicacies such as crab soup and fried lobster. The restaurant also offers free shuttle ferries that run between Queens Pier in Central and Sok Kwu Wan. $$$

★★**Stoep**, 32 Lower Cheung Sha Village, Lantau Island (☎ 00852-2980-2699). Stoep's stunning beachside location provides the perfect setting for its excellent South African cuisine which has been infused with Malay spices. The beach patio is a great place to enjoy their mixed grill barbecue platter – which goes well with a bottle of South African wine. $$$

Nightlife

Hong Kong was once notorious for its raucous nightlife and this reputation spawned books such as *The World of Suzie Wong* and the movie appearance of the Bottoms Up strip club in *The Man with the Golden Gun*, but redevelopment and regulation have cleaned up much of its seediness. These days Hong Kong is still a 24-hour city and its nightlife is the most developed of any city in China, although Shanghai is giving it a run for its money. You'll find everything from jazz bands to opera performances, noisy pubs and all-night clubs.

Wanchai was the city's original den of iniquity, renowned for its brothels, bar fights, drugs and sailors. The bars and clubs remain, but it's a much calmer scene today. These days Hong Kong's prime drinking district is out to the west at **Lan Kwai Fong** and stretches uphill to the Mid-Levels and Soho. Over the water in Kowloon there are also drinking options, but they are more limited and principally confined to **Knutsford Terrace**, a small lane just off Kimberley Road, which is filled with bars and restaurants and is crowded most evenings.

Where to Drink
Hong Kong Island

Lan Kwai Fong (Central MTR)

Blue Door, 5F, 37 Cochrane Street (Saturday 10:30 pm-12:30 am). The Blue Door was established in 2001 and has since become *the* jazz club. It provides excellent live jazz on Friday nights with a lineup that includes both local and international musicians.

C-Club, 30-32 D'Aguilar Street (Mon-Thur 6 pm-2 am). There's standing room only at this hip and happening nightspot, which enjoys a prime location between California (see *Where to Eat*, p. 557) and Lux. The curvaceous bar and red lighting act as an atmospheric backdrop to the pumping hip-hop, soul and Latino tunes.

D'Apartment, 34-36 D'Aguilar Street (Mon-Sat 6:30 pm till late). This funky basement bar offers all the pleasures of a luxury apartment and has a number of rooms kitted out like a home; a sitting room, complete with armchairs and comfy sofas, a bedroom, where you can lie around and watch TV and a library with some quality reading! When you combine this with the banging tunes provided by the house DJ (Thurs-Sat), you'll feel as if you've come to a house party.

D26, 26 D'Aguilar Street (Mon-Sat noon till late). D26 makes a great place to start your evening as it offers a quieter vibe and is one of the few bars along this stretch where you can actually have a conversation without shouting over the music.

Insomnia, 38-44 D'Aguilar Street (daily 9 am-6 am). With its stone arches and long drinks, from the outside Insomnia gives the impression that its seeking a little more sophistication than some of its neighbors but, once you reach the cavernous interior, you'll realize it's all about drinking and dancing. Live music is offered nightly from 10 pm.

Wanchai

Delaney's, One Capital Place, 18 Luard Road, Wanchai and 71-77 Peking Road, Kowloon (daily noon-2 am; Wanchai & Tsim Sha Tsui MTR respectively). This Irish pub has branches on Hong Kong Island and Kowloon and offers the usual pub fare along with Guinness and a host of other draught beers.

★★**Old China Hand**, GF, 104 Lockhart Road (Sun-Thu 8-5 am & Fri-Sat 24 hours). The Old China Hand is an institution in Wanchai and has been serving pints since 1977. The friendly pub has an excellent beer selection and traditional British pub grub (fish and chips, pies, etc.), making the China Hand popular with expats. It has been named one of Asia's top bars. They also offer tasty early morning full breakfasts.

Kowloon

Bahama Mama's, 4-5 Knutsford Terrace (daily 4 pm-2 am; Tsim Sha Tsui MTR, Exit B2). One of a number of bars and restaurants along Knutsford Terrace, Bahama Mama Caribbean bar is a pleasant place for a drink, replete with lanterns and dark wood. Cocktails and shooters are a popular happy hour choice (4 pm to 9 pm) and tasty bar snacks are available.

Kangaroo Downunder, 53-55 Chatham Road (daily 11 am until late; Tsimshatsui MTR, Exit G). For a taste of Australia, head to this bar and restaurant in downtown Kowloon. The pub-style interior and good Aussie tucker make it a popular choice with expats.

PJ Murphy's, Basement, 32 Nathan Road (daily 11-1 am; Tsimshatsui MTR, Exit E). This cozy basement bar is one of many Irish pubs in Hong Kong and offers a tasty range of pub snacks along with its selection of beers, including Guinness on tap.

Macau

Macau, though often mentioned in the same breath as Hong Kong, is an intrinsically different place and worthy of a trip in its own right. Occupying just 10 square miles on the other side of the Pearl River Delta from Hong Kong and due south of mainland Zhuhai, Macau has a population of 500,000. It is comprised of the **Macau Peninsula** and two small islands, **Taipa** and **Coloane**, linked to the mainland by bridges and increasingly more reclaimed land. But they say beautiful things come in small packages and Macau's period of Portuguese rule has lent it a distinctly European flavor, which complements its natural beauty. It has a range of attractions, from stunning **Portuguese architecture** to beaches, temples and, most importantly for the Chinese, casinos. For this reason, and its annual November **Grand Prix**, Macau has been labeled "the Monte Carlo of the Orient." Despite its international airport, its grand prix and much recent construction since gambling laws were liberalized in 2002, Macau retains an enchantingly slow pace, making it a great place to unwind for a few days.

History

The Portuguese

Though archeological finds indicate that Macau has been continuously inhabited for the last six millennia, until five hundred years ago, its history was little different from that of any other coastal area along the South China Sea. However, the expansion of European seafaring saw Portuguese traders reach the Pearl River Delta in 1513, having founded colonies in **India** in 1510 and Malaysian **Malacca** in 1511. In 1542 they also secured a settlement in **Japan** and, this being an awfully long hop from Lisbon, the Portuguese wanted a staging port along the way. In 1557 they finally managed to negotiate themselves a strategic piece of land at the entrance to the Pearl River Delta, known as Macau (or Aomen in Mandarin). Nearly 300 years before the British acquired Hong Kong, Macau was a flourishing international port, which superseded the **Silk Road** as Europe's trading gateway to China. With the Portuguese came **Christianity** and many of the ruined churches you can see today were built in Macau's brief heyday in the late 1500s. However, the good times were short-lived and Japan's expulsion of the Portuguese from Nagasaki in 1637 and the Dutch capture of Malacca in 1641 saw the trade network collapse, leaving Macau to fall into decline.

Gambling, Gangsters & Return to the PRC

In the mid-19th century the Portuguese **legalized licensed gambling** in an attempt to generate funds. Although this may be Macau's best bet for the future, it did little to improve the situation at the time. Hong Kong's rise to glory only furthered Macau's demise and it gained a reputation as a sleazy gangster town, which it is still trying to shrug off today. Macau's perceived value was humiliatingly shown when China refused to accept Portugal's offer to return the territory in 1966 and again in 1974. An agreement was finally signed in 1987, but when it actually happened in 1999, despite being the final piece of Asian soil to be ceded by European powers, Macau's return was a far quieter affair than that of its noisy neighbor two years earlier.

Modern Macau

While Macau holds the same **SAR** (**Special Administrative Region**) status as Hong Kong, economic dividends have been slower in coming. But this may be about to change, once again with the help of the Chinese obsession for gambling. In 2002 Macau's gambling laws were relaxed and in 2005 the first Vegas-funded casino, Sands, opened its doors. Now the financial tides are turning Macau's way, heralded by ever-grander construction projects like the

Macau Tower and the Venetian Casino development on **Cotai**, between Taipa and Coloane. But this recent building boom could spell the end for Macau's gentle island pace and wonderfully decrepit old buildings. This said, although modern Macau becomes more Chinese day by day, its Portuguese legacy endures, not only in its architecture and **trade-route influenced cuisine**, but also in the several thousand **Macanese residents** numbered among its population of 500,000, some of whom still speak Portuguese.

Getting Here & Away

The most common way to arrive in Macau is by boat from Hong Kong, but it also has an international airport with flights from other Asian cities and increasingly more Chinese cities, as well as a land border with China.

By Air

Plane

Macau's underused **international airport** on Taipa Island is trying to step up its game of recent and with its lower airport fees has managed to attract budget carriers like Air Asia (www.airasia.com) and Tiger Airways (www.tigerairways.com). If you're coming from elsewhere in Asia using one of these airlines can substantially reduce your airfare with round-trip flights from Singapore for as little as US$150 and Bangkok from US$100. Air Macau offers the widest variety of flights, but Eva Airways, Silk Air and TransAsia also serve Macau's airport. You can buy air tickets through travel agents and upscale hotels in town and at the airport. Leaving Macau, there is a departure tax of MOP$90, which is usually included in the ticket price.

The airport is fairly small but has a food court, luggage storage and post office on the departures floor and a bureau de change, hotel booking desk and tourist information office (daily 9 am-10 pm) in the arrivals section below. If you're heading into China there are a number of companies operating from the airport (see *By Road*, p. 568). Taxis from the airport to old Macau cost around MOP$65, including a MOP$5 airport charge (only payable when leaving the airport). But if you're on a tighter budget, bus #AP1 (MOP$4) covers the route.

Flights into China

There are flights to a number of mainland cities including:
Beijing (2 daily, 3 hrs); **Hangzhou** (3 daily, 1 hr 50 mins); **Shanghai** (6 daily, 2 hrs 15 mins); **Shenzhen** (2 daily, 30 mins); and **Xi'an** (1 daily; 4 hrs).

Helicopter

If you're really in a hurry or just want a different transport experience, **Heli-express** (☎ 00853-727-288, www.heliexpress.com) runs a helicopter service between Macau, Hong Kong and Shenzhen. While hardly cheap, at between MOP$1,700 and MOP$1,800, both trips take a mere 16 minutes and offer great views en route. Helicopters seat 12 and services to Hong Kong operate every 30 minutes between 9:30 am and 11 pm. There are five services a day to Shenzhen. Departures are from Macau Ferry Terminal and you need to arrive at least 15 minutes before your flight.

By Sea

The commonest way to arrive in Macau is by boat from Hong Kong or Shenzhen using one of the three companies that serve these routes. Note that while Turbojet and First Ferry operate from **Macau's Ferry Terminal**, Yuet Tung boats run from the **Porto Interior** on the other side of the Macau peninsula.

TurboJet (☎ 00853-790-7039, www.turbojet.com.hk) offers speedy jetfoils (1 hr) to and from Hong Kong's Shun Tak Centre every 15 minutes between 7 am and 1:30 am, with a few services running through the night. They also have less frequent jetfoils from Hong Kong's international airport (45 mins). One-way jetfoil tickets cost from MOP$134 for the cheapest daytime economy service to MOP$272 for super class evening journeys. There are four jetfoils a day to and from Fuyong terminal, close to Shenzhen airport, taking around an hour and 20 minutes and tickets cost MOP$166 for economy and MOP$263 for super class. Super class offers more comfortable seating and includes a newspaper, drink and snack.

First Ferry (☎ 00853-727-676, www.nwff.com.hk) runs slower catamaran services (1 hr 10 mins) every 30 minutes from the HK China Ferry Terminal on Tsim Sha Tsui's Canton Road. Ticket costs range from MOP$136 to MOP$267, depending on what time of day and in which class you travel.

Yuet Tung (☎ 00853-574-478) runs three boats a day from the Porto Interior to Shekou terminal for Shenzhen. Services take 80 minutes and cost MOP$116.

Whether traveling to or from Macau, you should arrive at the ferry terminal 30 minutes prior to departure. On arrival, you'll have to clear customs and immigration. Baggage collection can be somewhat chaotic and you'll have to show your luggage ticket. The Macau Ferry Terminal is spread over three floors, with arrivals at the bottom, departures and ticket offices on the middle floor and a restaurant at the top. There's also a tourist office (daily 9 am-10 pm), hotel booking desk, Avis counter and luggage checking. There are taxis and buses from here – #3, #3A and #10A will take you to the center of town.

By Road

You can also travel to and from Zhuhai, Macau's mainland neighbor, due north of the peninsula. The **Barrier Gate border crossing** is open from 7 am to midnight, and emerges into an enormous shopping center on the Zhuhai side. If you plan to head to China you'll need a visa, which can be obtained from Macau's China Travel Service (see p. 566 for details) on Rua Nagasaki. Buses #3A, #5 and #10 link the border with the peninsula, or there are **China Travel Service buses** from the Grandview and Landmark hotels on Taipa to equally upscale hotels in Guangzhou (hourly; 3 hrs 30 mins, MOP$100) – call ☎ 00853-7980-877 for more information. A number of companies also operate from the airport: **Gogo Bus** (☎ 00853-881-228) offers four buses a day to Zhuhai (MOP$25; 15 mins), Dongguan (MOP$106; 2 hrs 30 mins) and Guangzhou (MOP$101; 3 hrs).

Getting Around

Macau is a small place with ever more roads and bridges and an efficient public transport system. Getting around the peninsula itself is often best done on foot (see *Adventures On Foot*, p. 585, for walking routes), but for longer journeys there are buses, taxis and cycle rickshaws. If you want to explore the islands at your own pace there are bikes and cars for rent.

By Bus

Macau bus (Kamsand23)

Macau has an extensive, inexpensive bus network that runs from 6:30 am to midnight. Within the Macau Peninsula journeys cost MOP$2.50, while services to Taipa cost MOP$3.30 and MOP$4-5 to Coloane. Some useful routes include:

#10 and #10A runs from the ferry terminal, past the Lisboa casino to the Largo do Senado and then along Avenida de Almeida Ribeiro and down to the A-Ma Temple. #10B departs from the China border down past the ferry terminal to the Lisboa casino. #21A leaves from A-Ma Temple and goes past the Largo do Senado before going down to Coloane, stopping at Seac Pai Van Park, Coloane village and Hac Sa beach. #AP1 starts at the airport and passes the ferry terminal before going to the China border.

By Taxi

Taxis are either yellow or black and cost MOP$10 for the first 1.5 km (0.9 miles) and then MOP$1 for each 200 m (656 ft) after this. Waiting is charged at MOP$1 per minute and there are additional charges of MOP$3 for each piece of baggage placed in the trunk, MOP$5 leaving the airport, MOP$2 coming to or from Taipa and MOP$5 for Coloane.

By Cycle Rickshaw

More sightseeing tour than effective transport, cycle rickshaws offer a slow, pleasant pace, allowing you to really take in the street life. They cluster outside the ferry terminal and the Hotel Lisboa, costing around MOP$150 for an hour. Make sure you establish the price at the beginning of the journey, but by the end you'll agree that they've earned the price.

Rickshaw driver takes a break (Tot Foster)

By Bicycle

Bicycle offers a good way to get around parts of Macau, but isn't recommended on the peninsula and, as there are no designated cycle paths, you'll have to ride on the road. Taipa village is easily explored by bike, although much of the rest of the island is highly developed and roads are busy. Coloane's roads are quieter but there are a lot of hills and to really get into the countryside you're better off on foot.

Bikes can be rented from some of the upscale hotels like the Hyatt on Taipa and the Westin on Coloane (MOP$50/hour), or from a kiosk near the Tin Hau temple in Taipa village (MOP$15 per hour). Note that you're not allowed to cross any of the bridges between the peninsula and Taipa by bicycle.

By Car

Though Macau's tiny size almost makes vehicle rental seem excessive, the fact that they have soft-top **mini Moke jeeps** adds a little island flavor. Battered old Mokes can be rented for MOP$350 per day from **Happy Mokes** (☎ 00853-439-393) on the ground floor of the ferry terminal, although most of

Mini Moke

Hong Kong & Macau

the vehicles are so old that the company may well cease to operate soon. Much newer Cubs (similar to Mokes) can be rented for MOP$450 from **Avis** at the Mandarin Oriental Hotel (☎ 00853-336-789), where you'll also find more everyday automobile options. All prices include third-party insurance; drivers must be at least 21 years old and possess a valid driver's license. You need to bring along your passport and a credit card as deposit. Note that in Macau cars drive on the left.

Orientation

The bulk of amenities and sights are enclosed within the shoe-shaped parcel of land that is the Macau Peninsula. The peninsula is a patchwork of modern casinos, hotels and skyscrapers, at odds with the cobbled streets and Portuguese architecture of yesteryear, whose center-pieces are the imposing **Leal Senado**, the **Ruins of St. Paul's Basilica** and, looking over it all, the **Mount Fortress**. The principal street in this area, **Avenida de Almeida Ribeiro**, is locally known as **San Malo** and lends its name to the surrounding area, which encapsulates most of Macau's historic sights. **San Malo** runs southeast from the Porto Interior and is where you'll find much of the city's budget accommodation. It leads to the focal point of the old city, the open plaza of **Largo do Senado** (*largo* means square in Portuguese) and then continues onto the grand and gaudy **Lisboa Casino**. In the southwest of the peninsula, **Penha** and **Barra hills** have many of the territory's grandest residences and lead to the manmade **Sai Van** and **Nam Van lakes**. On the triangle of land between the lakes you'll find Macau's tallest building, the **Macau Tower**, which is over 1,100 feet tall.

Much of the peninsula's modern growth has been focused on an oblong strip of reclaimed land on its eastern flank known as Nape. This is Macau's business district but is also home to the bar strip of **Avenida Dr. Sun Yatsen**, a new restaurant development at **Fisherman's Wharf**, the ferry terminal and the territory's grandest casino to date, Sands.

Not so long ago the small islands of Taipa and Coloane and their smattering of beaches, farmland, fishing villages, ruined churches and temples were blissfully free of development. However these days **Taipa** is little more than a continuation of the peninsula, although there are still quaint pockets of decaying architecture and some good restaurants. Another reclamation project, the Cotai strip between Taipa and Coloane, will bring a string of new casinos and promises to make Macau "Asia's Las Vegas." **Coloane** itself has thus far escaped the attention of developers and still offers a slice of rural life along with a few good hotels and restaurants.

Information Sources

The Macau Tourist Office website is a good starting place for pre-trip research (www.macautourism.gov.mo). If you want information on Macau while you're still in **Hong Kong** try the **Macau Tourist Offices** at Chek Lap Kok Airport (☎ 00852-2769-7970) or at the Macau Ferry Terminal in the Shun Tak Center (☎ 00852-2857-2287).

The main **tourist offices** in the Largo do Senado (daily 9 am-6 pm; ☎ 00853-315-566) and on the 12th floor of Alameda Dr. Carlos D'Assumpcao (Mon-Fri 9 am-1 pm & 2:30-5:45 pm; same telephone number) have helpful staff, maps and leaflets covering the bulk of Macau's attractions. There are also tourist offices at the airport, ferry terminal and Gongbei border crossing and small kiosks at the Guia fortress or just inside the Basilica of Sao Paulo façade. Dotted around the peninsula there are also computerized information points ("City Guide Kiosks") with details on the main sights and hotmail access (for a charge). In the future you should also be able to download the city guide onto a pocket PC or smartphone from the kiosks. There is a tourist hotline (☎ 00853- 333-000) which operates between 8 am and 7 pm and provides recorded information around the clock. *Macau Talk*, a monthly publication, offers listings and information on upcoming cultural events, while the *Macau Post* (MOP$5) can keep you up to speed with happenings in the territory.

Events & Festivals

Macau's varied cultural history has given it a full schedule of events and festivals throughout the year and, although a visit during these times is likely to be busier, the rewards often outweigh the costs. Macau's Christian history means that Christmas and Easter are celebrated with more gusto here than on the mainland. Other events and festivals of note include:

New Year's Eve (December 31st) – Marked by impressive fireworks over Nam Van Lake and big crowds in the illuminated Largo do Senado.

Procession of the Lord of Steps (Lent, February/March) – A huge procession of clergy in full regalia carries the statue of Christ on the cross in a circuit from St. Augustine's Church.

Arts Festival (March/April) – Various acts from hip-hop to Cantonese opera are staged nightly for nearly a month in the atmospheric Largo do Senado. There are also plays staged in theaters around the peninsula and painting exhibits at the Cultural Center. Some shows are free, others require tickets – for more information check out www.icm.gov.mo.

Tam Kung's Birthday (May) – This Taoist deity is particularly important to fishermen and is celebrated by temple processions and performances of Chinese opera, particularly in Coloane village.

Procession of Our Lady of Fatima (May 13th) – Catholic girls clad in white carry the statue of Our Lady from St. Dominic's church to the chapel on top of Penha hill, accompanied by chanting clergy.

Macau Open (May) – One of the more dramatic courses on the Asian Golf Tour.

Dragon Boat Races (May) – Nam Van Lake is a great place to enjoy these traditional longboat races with teams strongly but calmly paddling to the steady beat of a drum (see *Holidays & Festivals*, p. 73, for more on the history of Dragon Boat racing).

International Fireworks Contest (September/October) – This incredible display sees international contestants trying to outshine each other.

Macau Grand Prix (November) – The climax of the Formula 3 calendar.

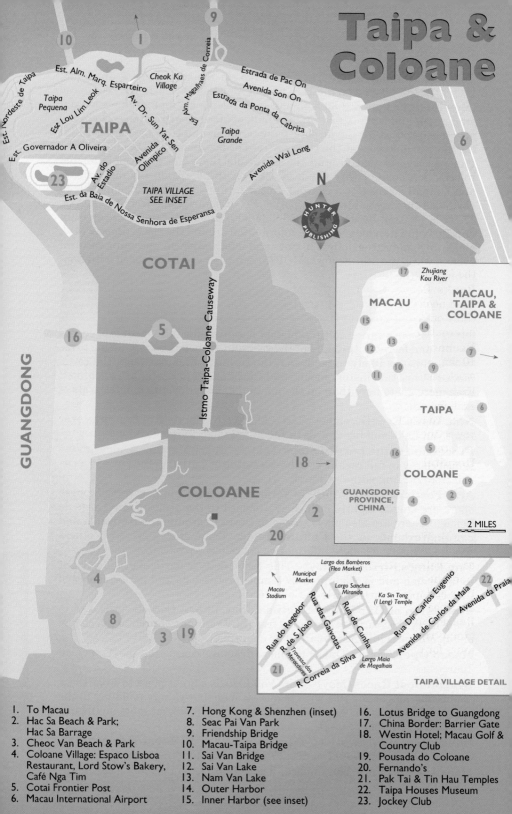

Taipa & Coloane

N

Zhujiang Kou River

MACAU, TAIPA & COLOANE

MACAU

TAIPA

COLOANE

GUANGDONG PROVINCE, CHINA

2 MILES

Largo dos Bomberos (Flea Market)

Municipal Market

Macau Stadium

Largo Sanches Miranda

Ka Sin Tong (I Leng) Temple

Rua do Regedor
Rua das Gaivotas
R de S Joao
Rua de Cunha
Travessa dos Mercadores
R Correia da Silva
Largo Maia de Magalhais
Rua Dir Carlos Eugenio
Avenida de Carlos da Maia
Avenida da Praia

TAIPA VILLAGE DETAIL

1. To Macau
2. Hac Sa Beach & Park; Hac Sa Barrage
3. Cheoc Van Beach & Park
4. Coloane Village: Espaco Lisboa Restaurant, Lord Stow's Bakery, Café Nga Tim
5. Cotai Frontier Post
6. Macau International Airport
7. Hong Kong & Shenzhen (inset)
8. Seac Pai Van Park
9. Friendship Bridge
10. Macau-Taipa Bridge
11. Sai Van Bridge
12. Sai Van Lake
13. Nam Van Lake
14. Outer Harbor
15. Inner Harbor (see inset)
16. Lotus Bridge to Guangdong
17. China Border: Barrier Gate
18. Westin Hotel; Macau Golf & Country Club
19. Pousada do Coloane
20. Fernando's
21. Pak Tai & Tin Hau Temples
22. Taipa Houses Museum
23. Jockey Club

Communications

Post Office: on the corner of Largo do Senado.
Telephone code: 00853
Internet Access: **EJ Internet Café** and **Chinoy Express** on Rua dos Cules, just a few minutes uphill from the Largo do Senado.

Money

Macau's currency, the *pataca*, usually written as MOP$, is worth fractionally less than the Hong Kong dollar, which is also universally accepted. The rate at the time of writing was eight *pataca* to the US dollar.

Banks: Banks are generally open from 9 am-5 pm Mondays to Fridays, and 9 am-noon on Saturdays. They can be found throughout the peninsula, especially on Avenida Infante Domingo Henrique. Most have **ATMs** that accept international cards.

Exchange Offices: On Avenida de Almeida Ribeiro, they stay open until 9 or 10 pm, but they can be fussy about which bills they accept. If you're really stuck, some of the casinos such as the Lisboa have around-the-clock facilities.

Emergency and Medical Services: Macau has a reputation as a Mafia enclave, which is not wholly undeserved but, unless you are in a gang, have gambled enough to owe someone big, or go out of your way to make trouble, you're unlikely to have any problems here. If you should need emergency services, call 999, 110 or 112. For medical assistance head to **Kiang Wu Hospital** (☎ 00853-371-333) on Estrada do Repouso.

Sightseeing

Central Macau's architectural wonders were listed as a **UNESCO World Heritage** site in 2005 and with good reason. The bulk of Macau's sights are found on the Macau Peninsula, many within easy walking distance of the central Largo do Senado. For sights farther from the center, bus numbers are given. However, if you only have a short time and want a guide to show you round the sights, most hotels have travel agencies who can arrange **private and group tours**. Or try **Gray Line** on Rua do Campo (☎ 00853-336-611) who run a variety of half-day and full-day group trips costing from MOP$68-200, as well as private chauffeur-driven tours for a minimum period of three hours.

MACAU IN A DAY

Macau's heady mix of splendid colonial architecture, pretty beaches, evocative temples and fine food are certainly worthy of a few days of your time. But if you only have a day you should not miss a walk through the historic center to the **Ruins of St. Paul's Basilica** and the **Mount Fortress**, a trip to the **A-Ma Temple**, some sumptuous **Macanese food** and, if you're feeling lucky, a trip to the **casino**.

Hong Kong & Macau

Macau Peninsula
Architectural Treasures

Much of Macau's appeal and charm comes from its Portuguese architecture, which was, until recently, being quietly left to rot away. Even the shortest of strolls through historic San Malo will unveil a host of buildings unrivaled in style or grandeur elsewhere in China. Many of them are churches, while the fringes of the peninsula are dominated by the architectural superlatives of the modern era, notably the Macau Tower, the Friendship and Taipa Bridges and the Kun Iam Statue.

★**Leal Senado**, 163 Avenida de Almeida Ribeiro (daily 9 am-9 pm; free). Originally built in 1784, this whitewashed Portuguese building is one of the most prominent examples of Macau's historic architecture. It takes its name from Macau's loyalty (*leal*) to the true throne during the Spanish occupation and still looms large over the Largo do Senado. Inside there are beautifully tiled halls and courtyards, a contemporary exhibition center and an exquisite wood-paneled library (Mon-Sat 1-7 pm). This high-ceilinged book trove has works dating back to the 17th century and is wonderfully calm after the hustle of the Largo do Senado over the road.

★★★**Ruins of St. Paul's Basilica**, Rua de Sao Paolo. This ghostly and imposing structure, looming over the old city, is rightly one of the most popular sights in Macau. The Basilica of St. Paul was originally built by the Jesuits in the early 17th century and was used as a training center before sending missionaries off into

Art imitates life below the ruins of St. Paul's Basilica (Tot Foster)

the "wilds" of mainland China. Its architecture represents a fusion of Eastern and Western styles and is unique in East Asia. Japanese craftsman were recruited to carve the classical religious scenes from stone, but the majority of the church was built from wood and only the façade survived a fire in 1835. Restoration and excavations in the early 1990s led to the opening of the Museum of Sacred Art (daily 9 am-9 pm; free) directly behind the façade. The museum holds a small collection of relics, including bones of the followers of St. Francis Xavier.

Old City Walls, Rua de Sao Paolo. Just next to the Ruins of St. Paul's you can see a short stretch of the old Portuguese city wall. The Portuguese constructed a wall around the city in 1569 and, while the project was never completed, it used to circle three-quarters of the city, although little remains today. Using a unique mix of clay, sand, soil, rice straw, crushed rocks and oyster shells (known as *chunambo*), the mixture was compacted into several layers, which you can still see.

★★**Mount Fortress**, Praceta do Museu de Macau (daily 7 am-8 pm; free). Even without its European-style fortress it's worth climbing the hill for views over the city and, once you're here, there's also the Macau Museum to peruse (see *Museums*, p. 580). The *Fortaleza do Monte* was built by the Jesuits in 1617 to provide protection from invaders and it served as their headquarters. The fortress was reinforced by the Portuguese before becoming the official residence of the Governor of Macau. It subsequently housed a prison, army barracks, observatory and now a museum!

★★★**Guia Fortress**, Chapel and Lighthouse, Estrada de Cacilhas (daily 9 am-5 pm; free; buses #6 & #28C). Standing at the top of Guia Hill (see *Parks*, p. 581), the Guia Fortress was constructed in the first half of the 17th century and offers aspects of Macau's trio of principal historic themes – military, missionary and maritime. Within the fortress walls, the highest point of the hill is capped by a small, whitewashed chapel established

The façade of St. Paul's (Tot Foster)

by Clarist nuns and which contains an interesting blend of Chinese and Christian art. Next to the chapel is the quaint lighthouse, built by Carlos Vicente da Rocha and first operated in 1865. There are excellent views of the city from here and consequently it's a popular spot for wedding photographs! You can get here by bus, a short, steep climb, or by cable car from Flora Gardens (Tues-Sun 8 am-6 pm; MOP$2 each way or MOP$3 round-trip), followed by a short walk.

Kun Iam Statue, Avenida Dr. Sun Yatsen, Nape (Sat-Thur 10 am-6 pm; free; buses #1A, #8, #12, #17 & #23). Though hardly worth a trip in its own right, the graceful 66-foot-high bronze figure of Kun Iam (or Guanyin), the Buddhist Goddess of Mercy, is worth checking out if you're in the area. The statue, which was

The classical lines of Guia Chapel

created by a Portuguese sculptor and

Hong Kong & Macau

Macau Peninsula

CHINA

Canal dos Potos

Estrada Marginal

da Ilha Verde

N

Reservoir

Nam Van Lake

Macau-Taipa Bridge

Grand Prix Circuit

Avenida de Amizade

Outer Harbor

Bars

0.5 MILES
©2008 Hunter Publishing, Inc.

Barra Hill

Sai Van Lake

To Airport, Taipa & Coloane

Kum Iam Statue

1. St. Lawrence's Church
2. Macau Tower, Café180, Café 360
3. Posada de Sao Tiago Hotel
4. Ritz Hotel
5. Maritime Museum
6. A-Ma Temple
7. O Porto Interior and Lorcha Restaurants
8. Penha Chapel
9. Henry's Galley Restaurant
10. Lilau Square (Largo de Lilau)
11. Lisboa Hotel and Club Militaire Restaurant
12. Macau Tourist Office
13. Carlos Restaurant
14. Kum Iam Statue
15. Macau Museum of Art & Cultural Center

16. Mandarin Oriental Hotel; Sands Casino
17. Grand Prix & Wine Museums
18. Guia Hotel
19. Guia Hill
20. Guia Cable Car
21. Macau Ferry Terminal
22. St. Augustine's Church; Dom Pedro V Theater
23. Leal Senado: Largo do Senado; Post Office; Tourist Office; Singing Bean Restaurant
24. Safari Restaurant
25. Pawnshop Museum
26. Sun Sun & Man Va Hotels
27. Hou Kong Hotel
28. East Asia Hotel

29. Portuguese Consulate
30. Ruins of St. Paul's Basilica; Na Tcha Temple & Old City Walls
31. St. Anthony's Church
32. Kiang Wu Hospital
33. Old Protestant Cemetery
34. Luis de Camoes Gardens
35. Lou Lim Ieoc Garden
36. Montanha Russa Garden
37. Kun Iam Temple
38. Canidrome (Dog Track)
39. Dr. Sun Yat Sen Park
40. Barrier Gate
41. Ilha Verde Hill
42. New Yaohan Shopping Center
43. Fisherman's Wharf & Floating Casino

cast in China, stands in a lotus flower, under which is a space for meditation. There are also good views of Taipa from here if the weather is willing.

★★★**Macau Tower**, Largo da Torre de Macau (www. macautower.com.mo; buses #23 & #32). At over 1,100 feet, this is Macau's tallest structure. The observation decks on the 55th and 61st floors (daily 10 am-9 pm; MOP$70) offer unparalleled views out over Macau and, if the weather and smog permit, as far as the Chinese border. If you want to

Largo de Senado (Tot Foster)

enjoy more than just the views, there are some truly breathtaking adventure sports options, including skyjumping, mast climbing and skywalking, run by the expert crew from A.J. Hackett (see *Adventures in the Air*, p. 585 for details). If you'd rather fill your stomach than lose it, the tower also boasts a number of cafés and restaurants. Two of these, the Café 180° and

The Macau Tower

revolving Café 360°, located on the 59th and 64th floors respectively, will allow you to sate your appetite and do a bit of sightseeing at the same time (see *Where to Eat*, p. 592, for more). There are also a few shops, a movie theater and, this being Macau, plenty of slot machines.

Churches & Temples

The Portuguese period has left Macau with a legion of grand and beautiful churches, while its Chinese history provides a host of atmospheric temples, many dedicated to gods associated with the seafaring nature of the territory.

★★★**A-Ma Temple**, Rua de Sao Tiago de Barra (daily 8 am-5:30 pm; free; buses #2, #5, #10, #10A & #21A). At the southern end of Rua do Almirante Sergio, this picturesque temple was originally founded in 1555 and is dedicated to A-Ma (also known as Mazu), the Goddess of Fishermen and the Sea, one of the principal Taoist deities in Guangdong, Fujian, Hong Kong and Taiwan. The temple is said to have given Macau its name (A-Ma Gao means

Incense coils at A-Ma Temple

A-Ma Bay in Cantonese) and was painted by the landscape artist George Chinnery whose works can be seen at the Museum of Art (see p. 583). The temple consists of a principal building at the base of the hill and then a smattering of smaller shrines and statues nestled among the boulders and banana palms of the hillside. A distinctive feature of Macau's temples is the giant incense coils which you will see hanging almost anywhere there is space in A-Ma Temple. While the temple looks back to Macau's past with its seafaring imagery, the pots full of Chinese coins with water trickling over them for good luck are an indication of the territory's mainland financial future.

St. Augustine's Church, Largo de Santo Agostinho (buses #10, #10A & #21A). Originally built by Augustinian friars from Spain in the late 16th century, St. Augustine's has been reconstructed and the current building dates back to 1814. A church legend states that whenever the central statue of Jesus carrying his crucifix is moved to the cathedral, it magically returns home to its altar overnight. If you're visiting around Lent, then don't miss the **Procession of the Lord of Steps**, where Catholic devotees carry the famous crucifix from the church to the cathedral, before returning it the next day (ask at the tourist office for details).

A shrine at A-Ma Temple

★★**St. Dominic's Church**, Largo do Domingos (daily 6 am-7 pm; free). Built by Dominican priests in 1587, this church still dominates the small square just north of the Largo do Senado. The church was restored in 1997 and now houses the "Treasure of Sacred Art" display upstairs (daily 10 am-6 pm), a collection of chalices, paintings and statues. If you happen to be here in May it's worth heading to the church on the 13th to witness the white-clad procession that carries the image of Fatima from here to the chapel on Penha hill.

★**Kun Iam Temple**, Avenida do Coronel Mesquita (daily 7 am-6 pm; free; buses #12, #17 & #19). Dedicated to the Goddess of Mercy (Guanyin), this atmospheric temple complex was originally built in the 13th century, although its current form dates from 1627. At the center of the temple's banyans, ornately tiled roofs and shrines is the main hall, which contains a clothed statue of Kun Iam. To the rear of this there are 18 statues – see if you can spot the one reputed to be Marco Polo. The temple is also famous as the site where the US and China forged their first trade agreement in 1844. You can still see the table where the Chinese viceroy and US Minister Caleb Cushing signed the treaty.

★**St Lawrence's Church**, Rua de Sao Lourenco (daily 10 am-6 pm, closed Mon 1-2 pm; free; buses #9, #16, #18). Macau's third-oldest church, St. Lawrence's was first built using wood in the1560s. In 1801 it was rebuilt in stone and recent renovations have restored it to its original beauty. Set amidst palms, St. Lawrence's cream and white exterior is strikingly Neo-Classical while the interior boasts gold beams, large chandeliers and impressive stained-glass windows. One of its two bell towers was once used as an ecclesiastical prison.

Na Tcha Temple, Rua de Sao Paolo (daily 8 am-5 pm; free). This tiny temple, just to the left of the Ruins of St. Paul's, was built in 1888 and, although overshadowed by its towering neighbor, it presents an interesting contrast. Dedicated to the mythical character Na

Tiny red shrines featuring incense and miniature statues of deities are seen outside many houses in Hong Kong and Macau.

Tcha, it was constructed to try and put a halt to the plague savaging the city at the time. The collection of huge spiraling incense coils from the ceiling and intricate painting add some color to the otherwise gray square.

Penha Chapel, Calcada da Penha (buses #6, #9 & #28B). The imposing **Bishop's Palace** stands at the top of southern Penha Hill, and looks out over Praia Bay. Within the palace, the small Penha Chapel is the finishing point of the May 13th procession of Our Lady of Fatima, which starts at St. Dominic's church. In Macau's maritime past, adventurers and sailors came to the chapel to pray for safe passage on the hazardous seas.

Museums

Macau has a collection of museums covering everything from its maritime tradition to the Grand Prix and wine. You can buy a five-day pass for MOP$25, which covers some of the main museums (detailed below).

★★**Macau Museum**, Mount Fortress, Praceta do Museu de Macau (Tues-Sun 10 am-6 pm; MOP$15/Museum Pass). Located within the walls of the Mount Fortress (see p. 577) and accessible by an outdoor escalator from the Ruins of St. Paul's, Macau Museum focuses on the territory's cultural traditions and has an excellent collection of local craftwork. The first floor tracks the relationship between the Europeans and Macanese and displays a reproduction of a classic Macanese street, while the second floor concentrates on everyday life and traditional crafts. Contemporary exhibitions are held upstairs every four months.

Maritime Museum, 1 Largo do Pagoda da Barra (Wed-Mon 10 am-5:30 pm; Mon-Sat MOP$10, Sun MOP$5/Museum Pass; buses #2, #5, 10,

Hong Kong & Macau

#10A & #21A). Spread out over three floors, this well-laid-out museum, next to the A-Ma Temple, has an interesting range of exhibits from Macau's maritime history and also includes an aquarium. Built on the site where the Portuguese first landed in Macau, the museum's shape is supposed to resemble a moored ship, although, as often is the case in China, you might need to use your imagination to see this!

★**Grand Prix Museum**, 431 Rua de Luis Gonzaga Gomes (Wed-Mon 10 am-6 pm; MOP$5/Museum Pass; buses #10 & #10A). Built to commemorate the 40th anniversary of the Macau Grand Prix, this interactive and lively museum opened in 1993 and offers a range of exhibits and experiences, including a simulated drive around the Formula 3 track. The Macau Grand prix started when a group of Macanese residents held a friendly race on the streets of Macau, driving course similar to the circuit in Monaco. Many of the pieces on display (including race cars and motorbikes) have been donated by ex-competitors and winners, and will be greatly appreciated by car lovers. For more on the Grand Prix check out www.macau. grandprix.gov.mo and, if all this looking at cars has you ready to race, there's go-karting available on Coloane (see *For Families*, p. 582)

Wine Museum, 431 Rua de Luis Gonzaga Gomes (Wed-Tues 10 am-6 pm; MOP$15/Museum Pass; buses #10 & 10A). This entertaining exhibition was opened two years after its neighbor, the Grand Prix Museum, and covers all areas of wine production, including a detailed history of wine in Portugal. Clearly labeled and well planned, it makes for an interesting visit (especially given the scarcity of good wine on the mainland) and you'll also get a chance to do some tasting at the end to help you on your way.

Pawnshop Museum, Avenida de Almeida Ribeiro (daily 10:30 am-7 pm, closed first Mon of every month; MOP$5). Pawnbroking originated in China and this tiny museum pays homage to that fact. Housed in a century-old fortress of a pawnshop, its granite-walled storage tower was capable of withstanding fires, floods and robbers. Items on display include a ledger of pawned items and a gold testing stone.

Parks

Macau gets very hot in summer and its parks offer respite from the sun, a few historic monuments and lots of good people-watching opportunities.

★★**Luis de Camoes Gardens**, Praca de Luis Camoes (daily 6 am-11:30 pm; buses #8A, #17 & #19). This green haven, just 15 minutes walk from the town center, makes for a welcome break from the city. Walkways, pavilions and large shady trees provide a cool escape and give a good excuse for some serious people watching. There's always a lot happening, with martial arts, exercises and power-walking all being practiced throughout the day. You'll find a bronze bust hidden in a grotto up on the hillside, depicting Portugal's famous poet, Luis de Camoes and a number of different trails leading off around the park. Don't worry about getting lost as it isn't huge and the area is well sign-posted. After a stroll through the park, make sure you don't miss the Old Protestant Cemetery.

★★**Old Protestant Cemetery**, Luis de Camoes Gardens, Praca de Luis Camoes (daily 6 am-11:30 pm; free; buses #17 & #19). Built in 1821, this was Macau's first Protestant cemetery and is the final resting place of many adventurous 19th-century Americans, British and Germans. Headstones to seek out include the first Protestant missionary in China, Dr. Robert Morrison, and the landscape painter, George Chinnery, whose works can be seen at the Museum of Art (see p. 583). The tranquil, reflective setting makes for a great retreat from the noise of the city and is well worth a trip in conjunction with the Luis de Camoes Gardens (see *Adventures On Foot, Historic San Malo*, p. 585). Just next door to the cemetery you'll find the Neo-Classical mansion of the **Casa Garden**, once headquarters of the British East India Company.

Guia Hill, Estrada de Cacilhas (daily 6 am-6 pm; free; buses #6 & #28C). Looming large over the Macau peninsula, Guia Hill offers a breath of fresh air from the seething streets below. The southern entrance is at the top end of Estrada San Francisco and brings you into the park just below the fortress and lighthouse. There's a northern entrance by the Flora Gardens off Avenida Sidonio Pais. From either entrance it's a short but steep climb to the upper section, but if you're not up for this there's a cable car from the Flora Gardens (Tues-Sun 8 am-6 pm; MOP$2 each way or MOP$3 round-trip).

Most of the upper part of the hill is parkland and is very popular with fitness enthusiasts. The top of the hill is surrounded by the canon-bearing walls of the Guia Fortress (daily 9 am-5 pm), which contains a historic lighthouse and chapel (see *Architectural Treasures*, p. 575).

★**Lou Lim Ieoc Garden**, Estrada de Adolfo Loureiro (daily 6 am-9 pm; free; buses #16 & #22). Lou Lim Ieoc is a traditional Chinese garden in the Suzhou style (see *The Gardens of Suzhou*, p. 345), complete with bamboo groves, lotus ponds and rockeries – a popular retreat from the streets. The garden was created in the late 19th century for a wealthy Chinese family. The family lived in the adjacent Victorian-style house and on occasion entertained Dr. Sun Yatsen (see p. 18), who used to live nearby.

Taipa

Connected to the mainland by three bridges, these days Taipa is little more than an extension of the peninsula. The island is home to **Macau's horse-racing track** and a couple of large parks, along with the international airport and an ever-increasing number of high-rises. However, while much of Taipa's character has been lost, there are still some parts worth seeking out and its development has led to a burgeoning restaurant scene.

Taipa village lies south of the original island (these day reclaimed land links Taipa and Coloane) and its collection of narrow lanes houses the lion's share of the island's remaining old buildings. The highlight is the ★**Taipa Houses Museum** on Avenida da Praia (Tues-Sun 10 am-6 pm; free; bus #30). House number one contains a blend of European and Chinese furnishings reflecting the territory's mixed lineage. Other spots to walk to from here include the **Church of Our Lady of Carmel** just along the road, **Rua do Cunha** food street (see *Where to Eat*, p. 593) in the center and **Pak Tai** and **Tin Hau temples** to the west.

Coloane

This small island and its quaint namesake village give an idea of what much of Macau must have been like not so long ago. Coloane has Macau's best beaches, ★**Hac Sa** and ★★**Cheoc Van**, a good **golf course** (see *Adventures on the Green*, p. 587), some great restaurants and hotels and a number of pleasant hiking trails around **Seac Pai Van Park** and the **Hac Sa barrage** (see *Adventures on Foot*, p. 585). A-Ma is memorialized here by the 65-foot statue to her atop Coloane Hill.

If you want to enjoy some peace and quiet, but still have the splendor and shopping of downtown Macau within reach, Coloane is a great place to base yourself. In the southwest of the island, ★★**Coloane village** offers a rustic reminder of fishing village life and is a popular place to live for expats looking to escape the developing peninsula. The pretty **Chapel of St. Francis Xavier** in the village center looks very old but was actually built in 1928 to

Tam Kung Temple

enshrine a relic of the saint's arm. Just a few minutes walk to the south you'll find the **Tam Kung temple** (Tues-Sun 10 am-6 pm) on the waterfront, dedicated to the storm-quelling god. The village also has some great places to eat and drink (see *Where to Eat*, p. 593). Buses #15, #21A, #25 & #26A run to Coloane.

Galleries & Shows

If you're after something more refined than a nightclub, Macau has plenty of cultural entertainment, much of which can be found at the ultra-modern **Cultural Center** on Avenida Xian Xinghai. It presents plays, classical music (check *Macau Talk*'s *What's On* section for performances) and includes Macau's Museum of Art. The Hong Kong-produced *Art Map* is another good source of information for cultural offerings and is available from the tourist office.

★**Macau Museum of Art**, Cultural Center, Avenida Xian Xinghai (Tues-Sun 10 am-7 pm; MOP$5/Museum Pass; buses #8, #12 & #17). This is Macau's only art museum and boasts an excellent collection of classical Chinese art and calligraphy. Its five floors are filled with artifacts from all periods of Macanese history, including exceptional ceramics and paintings, along with works by the famous China landscape artist, George Chinnery who is buried at the Old Protestant Cemetery. The museum also has frequent contemporary exhibitions so it's worth calling ahead (☎ 00853-7919-814) to see what's on.

For Families

In spite of Macau's UNESCO listing for its heritage buildings, it's not all old architecture and there are plenty of activities to keep the kids happy. Indeed some of Macau's modern buildings are designed for kids (and the kid in all of us).

Fisherman's Wharf

Fisherman's Wharf, next to Sands Casino on the outer harbor, is a Vegas-style wacky wonderland of scaled-down architectural marvels, including Lhasa's Potala Palace. While hardly Disneyland, there are a few rides, including a "volcano float," and plenty of cafés to sit in while the kids have their fun.

Go-Karting

If the Grand Prix Museum unveiled your racing colors there's a go-karting track at the **Macau Motorsports Club** by Seac Pai Van Park on Coloane (☎ 00853-882-126; MOP$100/180 for 10/20 minutes) where you can see who's number one (buses #21A and #25).

Macau Tower

On rainy days the **movies** are always a good option. There's a theater screening films in English at the Macau Tower, and if the weather picks up you could ascend the tower itself (see *Sightseeing*, p. 577), maybe even taking in some **adrenaline sports** (see *Adventures in the Air*, p. 585), although note that your kids must be over 10 years old for the Sky Jump and over 12 for the Sky Walk. Down at "Base Camp' there are some lower but still exhilarating entertainments, including a bungee trampoline (MOP$30) and a climbing wall (MOP$50).

Cheoc Van Beach

The steamy days of summer are perfectly suited to lazy days at the beach – Hac Sa is large and popular with domestic tourists, but I prefer smaller Cheoc Van beach less than a mile away. Aside from the usual swimming in the sea (and in beachside pools) and sandcastle building (with black sand on Hac Sa), there are also watersports to be enjoyed (see *Adventures on Water*, p. 587). Both beaches also have great restaurants to take a break from the sand (see *Where to Eat*, p. 591-93).

Cheoc Van Beach

Hac Sa Barrage

Macau's parks (see *Sightseeing*, p. 581) offer another escape from the city and if you head to the Hac Sa Barrage you can rent pedal boats (Tues-Fri 2-6 pm, Sat 1-6 pm & Sun 11 am-6 pm; MOP$10) as well as enjoying a walk (see *Adventures On Foot*, p. 585).

Shopping

 Although it doesn't live up to the heady heights of neighboring Hong Kong, Macau has a variety of shops offering just about anything you might require, along with plenty that you probably don't! From electrical goods and antiques to designer clothes, Macau stocks it all. However, while there are bargains to be had, there are also pitfalls – if you have any problems contact the Consumer Council Hotline (☎ 00853-9889-315).

Markets

For market shopping try the **Red Market**, which seems to have every kind of food known to man, while small streets around it sell everything from clothes to cameras. The market is by the intersection of Avenida Almirante Lacerda and Avenida Horta e Costa. Other weird and wonderful offerings can be found along **Rua de Felicidade**, from pressed meats to custard tarts and even live snakes.

Antiques

Rua de Santo Antonio runs between the Ruins of St. Paul's and St. Anthony's Church and has dozens of antiques shops offering a large variety of goods from the mainland and Tibet. Be wary of some unscrupulous shop owners who try and pass off mass-produced repro antiques as genuine – check your item carefully! Shops are jam-packed with larger items like cabinets, wardrobes and tables but there are also more portable pieces. Larger items will need shipping at an extra price; make sure you check all the costs as you may have to pay an extra charge when you return home in order to actually retrieve the goods from their handlers and this can increase the price substantially. Most shop owners speak some English and it's advised to bargain hard.

Clothes

There's no shortage of clothes shops in Macau and they offer designer labels, cheaper copies and standard inexpensive clothes. The area around **Largo do Senado** is the central shopping zone, offering many of the favorite Asian chains such as Giordano and Bossini, along with the more familiar Mango and Esprit. For designer names, head to **Avenida Infante Domingo Henrique** just to the east of Largo do Senado. The **New Yaohan** shopping center close to the ferry terminal stocks a similarly familiar line-up of international brands.

Electronics

Macau also offers competitively priced electronic goods although be sure to buy only recognized brand names from chain outlets, as cheaper local products could be difficult to repair at home. **Fortress**, which has a branch in the Largo do Senado, is a good place to try.

Everyday Needs

For basic daily items there are plenty of small supermarkets and 7-Elevens. Toiletries can be found at **Watson's** – there's a branch in the Largo do Senado.

Adventures

Macau has an abundance of adventures from city strolls to quiet hikes, clifftop golf to gambling at casinos and racecourses, or the adrenaline rush of adventure sports.

In the Air

The construction of the **Macau Tower** in 2002 provided bungee king A.J. Hackett with an opportunity to take Macau's adventure sports scene sky high. At base camp there are a range of activities, including a bungee trampoline, tower climbing wall and a zip line, but the real action is at the top of the tower. From here there are three options, the least vertigo-inducing of which is the **skywalk** (MOP$198), a harnessed stroll around the outer rim 764 feet above ground. The **skyjump** (MOP$588) from the same height offers a controlled descent taking 15 seconds, but you'll still travel around 50 miles per hour! The **mast climb** (MOP$688) is the most exhilarating of the three, as it takes a couple of hours to ascend and descend the final 328 feet to the tower's summit. Though not recommended for the fainthearted or unfit, from 1,108 feet you really feel you're on top of the world. Buses #23 and #32 run to the tower.

On Foot

Macau is small but diverse enough to allow even short walks to take in a range of scenery, though for wilder trails you're better off going to Coloane. The tourist office's *Walking Tours by Day and Night* details walks throughout Macau and is worth picking up. In addition to the options detailed here, a walk up to the Guia Fortress is worthwhile (see *Sightseeing*, p. 577), as is a stroll around the edge of Sai Van Lake.

★★★ Historic San Malo (1 hr)

This walk takes in a huge helping of Macau's Portuguese past, starting with the grand plaza of **Largo do Senado**. Walk through the square, past the McDonald's and up to the right. Head past the recently restored **St. Dominic's Church** (p. 579) onto Rua de Sao, then bear left up the hill onto Rua da Palha which soon becomes Rua de Sao Paulo and leads to the towering façade of the **Ruins of St. Paul's** (p. 574). Here is a good spot for a drink and there's a juice shop at the bottom of the steps, but make sure you get them to make it fresh for you. From here you can climb up to the right to the **Mount Fortress** (daily 7 am-8 pm, see p. 576), which guards the hilltop and is home to the **Macau Museum** (MOP$15; Tues-Sun 10 am-6 pm; p. 582). After visiting, return to the Ruins of St. Paul's to continue the walk. Take the lane from the northwestern corner by the small temple of **Na Tcha** and an original section of wall (p. 579), which leads down to Rua de Santo Antonio, lined with antique shops. Turn right up the hill and follow the road until you reach the church of St. Antony. You'll see the entrance to **Luis de Camoes Garden**s up to the left. Before you go up the hill, though, check out the **Old Protestant Cemetery** (p. 581), just to the east, full of deceased voyagers from yesteryear. **Luis de Camoes Gardens** (daily 6 am-10 pm; p. 581) offers a short, steep ascent through wonderful tropical foliage to the peaceful pavilions above, a world away from the busy streets not so far away. From here, a taxi, or bus #8A or #19 can take you back to the Largo do Senado.

★★Churches & Temples
(45 min-1 hr one-way or 90 min- 2 hr circuit)

This short ramble takes in some of Macau's finest churches, along with the charming A-Ma temple and nearby Maritime Museum. It also includes some good dinner options. Starting in **Largo do Senado**, cross Avenida de Almeida Ribeiro and walk south down Rua Dr. Souares. Bear left onto Calcada do Tronco Velho, at the end of which you'll see **St. Augustine's Church** (p. 578). Here you'll also find **Sir Robert Ho Tung's Library** and the **Dom Pedro V Theatre**, the oldest European theater in China. To the left there's a cobbled ramp leading onto Rua Central, which becomes Rua de Sao Lourenco; off to the right lies the grand **St. Lawrence's church** (daily 10 am-4 pm; see p. 579 for more). This road soon becomes Rua de Padre Antonio and leads into pretty Lilau Square. From here it's just a short walk down Calcada de Barra to the picturesque **A-Ma Temple** (p. 578) and the **Maritime Museum** (p. 580).

After visiting them you could enjoy a meal in one of the fine restaurants like **A Lorcha** or **O Oporto Interior** (bookings are advisable, see p. 592-93), both of which are only a few minutes walk up **Rua do Almirante Sergio**. You can end your walk with a taxi or bus #2 or #5 back to the Largo do Senado. But, if you've got the energy, you could continue north up Rua do Almirante Sergio and experience modern Macau without any of the glory. Car parts and shipping machinery outlets are interspersed with dried fish stalls, street canteens and tiny winding lanes crammed with ancient houses that are slowly decaying, their elderly residents sitting outside passing the time of day. Twenty minutes or so along this street (which becomes **Rua das Lorchas**) will bring you to the junction with **Avenida Almeida de Ribeiro** – turn right here and it's only 10 minutes back to the Largo do Senado.

Coloane Walks

Coloane has a host of connected walking trails running between Seac Pai Van Park in the west and Hac Sa in the east. You can do the whole circuit or just short stretches. The walk detailed below offers a range of scenery and wildlife and is one of my favorites.

★★Beaches, Mountains & Reservoir
(1-3 hrs depending on which route you take)

This short walk on Coloane Island takes in a reservoir, some hilly forest and beaches. If you come during the week when there are fewer visitors you might spot wildlife ranging from giant butterflies to snakes. The walk starts from the coastal road between Cheoc Van and Hac Sa, which can be reached by buses #15, #21A, #25 and #26A. Get off the bus by the large wooden arch marked **Parque Naturel de Barragem de Hac Sa**. Head up the steps and toward a circular yellow building with a soft drink machine. Bear left at the building and up the steps. Soon you'll see the milky green waters of the **reservoir** and a path off to your left across the barrage. Don't take this, but continue along the edge of the lake. Once you lose sight of the reservoir, the path divides. Turn left (signposted 1,100 m) rather than going straight ahead and a few minutes later you'll come to a small, sturdy **suspension bridge**. Cross this and turn left. A little farther on there's a place you can rent pedal-boats (Tues-Fri 2-6 pm, Sat 1-6 pm & Sun 11 am-6 pm). You'll see a pavilion up to your right, which offers views over the reservoir. Turn right just past the pavilion and proceed up the steps. A short climb later you'll find yourself on a yellow perched pavilion sitting atop a giant boulder with fine views over Hac Sa beach. It makes a great spot for a picnic.

You could turn around here, taking a shortcut across the barrage on your return, which would make for around an hour circuit. Or if you've still got some spring in your legs you could take the 450-m (1,475-ft) path uphill to the 65-foot A-Ma statue, from where you can connect to the trails of Seac Pai Van Park. Alternatively, if you'd like to close your hike with a swim and some fine food, proceed straight ahead from the yellow pavilion. Follow the main path and don't take any of the side trails until you see a signpost marked **Parque de Merenda de Cheoc Van** leading down to the left. Take the steps steeply down for a few minutes and you'll soon reach the road.

Across the road you'll see a sign and steps heading to **Pousada de Coloane** where you could get a drink and meal before ordering a taxi home (see *Where to Stay* and *Where to Eat*, below). You could also take a swim on pretty little **Cheoc Van beach** (p. 583). Or to take a bus straight back to the peninsula turn left from the park and cross the road – after a couple of minutes you'll see a bus stop on your right where you can take buses #15, #21A, #25 or #26A. If you want to continue the hike, carry on walking left along the road past the wooden arch you started from until you reach the turn for **Hac Sa beach** off to your right. Head down to the beach and either take a bus once you are finished here (same bus numbers) or walk left all the way along the beach to the **Westin Hotel** where you could enjoy a drink with views over the South China Sea in the Porto Bar (see *Where to Drink*, p. 594) before ordering a taxi home.

On the Green

Despite its small size, the territory boasts a fine golf course – the short but hazardous cliff-top par-71 **Macau Golf and Country Club** (☎ 00853-871-188, www.macaugolfandcountryclub.com). The course hosts the Asian Tour's Macau Open in May, which has attracted the likes of golf legends Fred Couples and Nick Faldo. The club is next to the Westin Hotel on Hac Sa beach and is open to hotel guests and members only. The weekday green fee is MOP$800 but it leaps to MOP$1,500 on the weekends. Clubs can be rented for MOP$280. Good value overnight golf packages can be booked through the Westin Resort (see p. 591).

On Water

Coloane's **Cheoc Van** and **Hac Sa beaches** are the best places for a swim in the sea and both have lifeguarded sections during the summer. Although the water appears a little on the brown side, this is due to Pearl River silt rather than pollution, and the water is pleasant for a dip from May to November. If the ocean doesn't appeal there are outdoor pools at both beaches open during summer.

There are also **watersports** facilities at both beaches, including jet-skis, kayaks and windsurfs, although you must be a member of the nautical club to use Cheoc Van's equipment. The Hac Sa reservoir also has a few pedal boats for rent and is a good area for a hike (see *On Foot, Beaches, Mountains & Reservoir*, p. 585). Both beaches and the reservoir are served by buses #15, #21A, #25 and #26A.

Gambling

Casinos

In 1847 legalized gambling was introduced to Macau in a desperate attempt to bolster the economy, and it remains enduringly popular with the gambling-mad Chinese to this day. Every weekend the casinos are full of Chinese from Hong Kong, Taiwan and the mainland, oblivious to the quaint decaying European streets, churches and fishing villages around them, intent only on making their million. Until recently, all of Macau's casinos were controlled by **Dr. Stanley Ho** and the most famous of his establishments was the garish **Lisboa**, which still packs in the punters today. In 2002 gambling laws were liberalized, which was immediately followed by large-scale investment from a Las Vegas consortium and the opening of Macau's slickest joint, **Sands**, which is a great spot for a drink to take in the glitz of it all, even if you don't gamble a dime. Hot on its heels are a string of further casinos, foremost of which will be the **Venetian**, another Vegas development currently being built on reclaimed land between the peninsula and Taipa, an area known as **Cotai**.

Once inside, the seriousness of the business at hand is immediately striking and casinos are alive with the electricity of fortunes coming and going. As long as you're not betting your pension, then gambling here can be fun, and Macau certainly has plenty of places ready to help you stake your money. You can bet on everything from baccarat to blackjack, roulette and even worldwide sports games, but you must be 18 years old to gamble in Macau.

Horseracing

Along with the 30 or so casinos in Macau, there is also a horseracing track at the Macau Jockey Club (☎ 00853-820-868, www. macauhorse.com) on Taipa. The **Jockey Club** is one of the largest private employers in Macau, with over 1,400 staff and it has racing all year round. Races are usually held on Tuesday nights and one day during the weekend, although during the height of summer (June to August) meets take place on Wednesday and Saturday nights to avoid the heat. You should call to check in advance. Free shuttle buses are provided both to and from the club on race days, with pick-ups from the Lisboa and the ferry terminal. Numerous buses, including #11, #15 and #22, also stop at the track. Most mid-range and upscale hotels can arrange racecourse packages, which cost MOP$100 and include a MOP$50 betting voucher.

Dog Racing

Macau offers Asia's only greyhound track, the **Canidrome**, one of the largest and best equipped in the world. Over 300 dogs compete on race nights (tickets MOP$20), which start at 7:45 pm four nights a week (always Thursdays and Sundays). The Canidrome is at Avenida do Almirante Lacerda in the north of the city and is serviced by buses #1A, #3 and #5.

Where to Stay

Macau has a good range of places to stay, many of which offer more character than their counterparts in Hong Kong or on the mainland. Prices are cheaper than in Hong Kong but more expensive than the mainland. Macau lives and dies by its weekend trade. Therefore, if you're staying mid-week, it's certainly worth negotiating the room rate – discounts of up to 50% are common. Unless otherwise mentioned, all the hotels below have air conditioning, television and en-suite bathrooms.

HOTEL PRICE CHART	
$	Under MOP$300/US$40
$$	MOP$301-600/US$41-80
$$$	MOP$601-1,000/US$81-130
$$$$	MOP$1,001-2,000/US$131-250
$$$$$	Over MOP$2,000/US$250

What's it mean? FC=fitness center; SW=swimming pool; @=in-room Internet access; DA=rooms for disabled.

Macau Peninsula

East Asia, 1A Rua da Madeira (☎ 00853-922-433). A long established and well-located budget option housed in a historic building, the East Asia offers reasonably comfortable and spacious, if faded and slightly musty, rooms with a friendly, helpful staff. $

Guia, 1 Estrada do Engenheiro Trigo (☎ 00853-513-888). This newly renovated hotel is well-located for Guia Hill and lies just above the Grand Prix Circuit but is a 20-minute walk from San Malo. Although rooms are a little small, they are well-equipped and some have balconies enjoying fine views. $$$

Hou Kong, 1 Travessa das Virtudes (☎ 00853-937-555). This newly renovated hotel has a reasonable location at the western end of Avenida de Almeida Ribeira. Although the hotel is a bit bland, paintings of old Macau add a hint of character and rooms are tiled, clean, spacious and a great value. $

★**Lisboa**, 2-4 Avenida de Lisboa (☎ 00853-377-666, www.hotelisboa.com). As you'd expect at Macau's most famous casino hotel, rooms here are gaudily opulent – from the black marble bathrooms to the free mini-bar. Although the hotel can get overwhelmingly busy with weekend gamblers, if you want the real Macau casino experience this is the place. FC/SW/@/DA $$$$

★★**Mandarin Oriental**, Avenida de Amizade (☎ 00853-567-888; www. mandarinoriental.com/macau). The Mandarin Oriental is on the east of the peninsula and offers the usual impeccable service and facilities, particularly its first-rate health spa. The extensive grounds also include a large, attractive swimming pool and tennis courts. FC/SW/@ $$$$$

Hong Kong & Macau

Mandarin Oriental

Man Va, 30 Rua da Caldeira (☎ 00853-388-656). This is a good, inexpensive option with clean and modern, if small, rooms, on a narrow atmospheric street running parallel to Avenida de Almeida Ribeiro. $$

★★★**Pousada de Sao Tiago**, Avenida da Republica (☎ 00853- 378-111, www.saotiago.com.mo). It's housed in a historic 17th-century Portuguese fort overlooking the sea; you can almost taste the history here. This is certainly Macau's most charming hotel and offers traditional comfort in each of its 24 rooms, as well as more modern ameni-ties like wireless Internet connection. Along with its excellent terrace res-taurant, garden and pool, it also has a small 18th-century chapel devoted to Sao Tiago, the patron saint of the Portuguese army. The Pousada is a bit of a hike from Sao Malo, but reception can arrange taxis or there are buses (#6, #9 or #28B). SW/@ ¥¥¥¥¥

Ritz, Rua do Commendador Kou Ho Neng (☎ 00853-339-955, www.ritzhotel.com.mo). The Ritz has a quiet and pleasant location in a smart res-idential area overlooking Sai Van Lake. Although the rooms are a little bland, they are comfortable and some enjoy great harbor views. FC/SW/DA $$$$

Sun Sun, 14 Praca Ponte e Horta (☎ 00853-939-393). This Best Western chain hotel has comfortable rooms, some of which have good harbor views, although its location isn't great. Staff are friendly and there is wireless Internet connection in the lobby. DA $$$

Coloane

Pousada de Coloane

★★**Pousada de Coloane**, Cheoc Van Beach (☎ 00853-882-143, www.hotelpcoloane.com.mo). This small family-run hotel offers 30 comfort-ably furnished Portuguese-style rooms in a long low-rise modern building nestled into the hillside. All rooms have double Jacuzzi baths and balconies looking over Cheoc Van beach. There is a good restaurant, pool and terrace and the beach is just a couple of minutes walk. It's a 20-minute drive from the penin-sula, but staff can organize taxis and car rental. SW $$$

★★**Westin Resort**, 1918 Estrada de Hac Sa, Hac Sa Beach (☎ 00853-871-111, www.westin-macau.com). The

Westin Resort

Westin is a far more luxurious and ostentatious option than the other beach choice at the Pousada de Coloane and it dominates the eastern end of Hac Sa beach. Rooms are very comfortable and have enormous balconies, the more expensive of which give good ocean views. The Westin has international facilities and allows access to the Macau Golf and Country Club (see *Adventures, On the Green*, p. 587) along with its health club, tennis courts, three pools and restaurants. FC/SW/@ $$$$$

Where to Eat

Macanese & Portuguese Cuisine

Macanese cuisine is a unique blend of Chinese, African, European and Indian influences and is definitely worth sampling. This fusion is one of the enduring legacies of Portugal's worldwide trade network in its maritime heyday. After the austerity of many of mainland China's restaurants, the relaxed European

DINING PRICE CHART	
¥	Under MOP¥50/US$6
¥¥	MOP¥51-120/US$6-15
¥¥¥	MOP¥121-240/US$16-30
¥¥¥¥	MOP¥241-400/US$31-50
¥¥¥¥¥	Over MOP¥401/US$50

atmosphere of Macau's eateries comes as a welcome break, and the food is often excellent – **African chicken, *bacalhau* (salted cod), curry crab** and **suckling pig** are must-tries. If you've been craving desserts after a stint on the mainland, Macau can also meet your needs with fine delicacies such as *serrdurra*, literally translated as sawdust pudding, but actually a delectably sweet and simple mix of creamy condensed milk sprinkled with biscuit crumbs.

Asian & Western

There are also some great Chinese and Thai restaurants, and there is good quality wine found even in these places. Conversely if it's Western fast food you want, there are the usual collection of McDonalds and Pizza Huts, many of which are found around the Largo do Senado. There's also a Starbucks here, which makes for a great spot to people-watch – many of the regular clientele are southern European expats and thus even this bastion of modern life manages to feel very old-world. For ice cream fans there's a Haagen-Dazs just a little up the road, next to St. Dominic's Church.

Snacks & Tea

Once again showing Macau's place at the crossroads of civilizations, not far from its modern coffee shops there are **traditional Chinese teahouses** and street tea vendors. The main tea is *guangdongcha* and for a particularly authentic experience it should be drunk while listening to operatic singing, which you'll sometimes find at the **Tai Long Fong Casa de Cha** on Rua de Cinco de Outubro, near the East Asia Hotel. **The Casa de Cha Long Wa** on Rua Norte do Mercado Almirante, near the corner of the Red Market, is another great teahouse. The Long Wa also serves dim sum and is alive with tweeting birds brought in by their elderly owners after a morning walk! If you're just after a snack, Macau has lots of great little treats like ***natas***

(Portuguese custard tarts) and almond cakes, both of which can be found at *pastellarias* throughout the old city. Macau is also famous for its **pressed roast meats** – Rua de Felicidade is particularly good for these. You'll also see crispy stuffed crêpes and fantastic tropical fruit cocktails – the shopping center a little before the grand Portuguese Embassy on Rua de Pedro Nolasco da Silva has both.

Food is a big deal in Macau and there are countless restaurants; below are some of the best, incorporating all of Macau's culinary forms. For more detail check out local magazines like *Macau Food Guide* or *Dining in Macau* (www.dininginmacau.com) – available from restaurants. Where telephone numbers are given, reservations are advised (especially at night and on weekends). There are cheap eats to be enjoyed, but it's worth splashing out a little at some of the better restaurants. The price codes above are based on a standard meal for one (meaning a single dish with a beer or soft drink).

Macau Peninsula

★★★**A Lorcha**, 289 Rua do Almirante Sergio (☎ 00853-313-193; Wed-Mon 12:30-3 pm & 6:30-11 pm). A bastion of Macau's culinary world a stone's throw from A-Ma Temple, this award-winning restaurant consistently serves up excellent Portuguese and Spanish fare. The clams, grilled prawns and African chicken are all excellent and the atmosphere isn't bad either. $$$

★★**Café 180° & 360°**, Macau Tower, Largo da Torre de Macau (☎ 00853-933-339; daily noon-2:30 pm & 6:30-10 pm). These two cafés boast outstanding views of Macau and a classy ambience with some fine food thrown in. The Macau Tower entrance ticket is included in the meal price, although there is a minimum of MOP$100 at Café 180°. The 360° Café offers panoramic views from the sleek revolving 64th floor of the Macau Tower. There's an à la

Café 180°

carte menu as well as the seafood buffet (MOP$158/228 for lunch/dinner). Five floors down, the Café 180° serves light snacks, or set meals for MOP$148, but is more popular for its drinks in the evening. $$$-$$$$

★**Carlos**, Rua Cidade de Braga (☎ 00853-751-838; Tues-Sun 11 am-3 pm & 6-11 pm). A block back from the main bar strip, this white-walled, high-ceilinged restaurant serves tasty Portuguese and Macanese food in a convivial environment. Try the African chili chicken or deliciously different sweet and sour pork with a carafe of the house wine. $$-$$$

★★**Club Militaire de Macau**, 975 Avenida da Praia Grand (☎ 00853-714-000; noon-3 pm & 7-11 pm). Housed in the grand Macau Military Club, this formal dining affair is worthwhile for the architecture alone, restored to its original 1870 splendor. Though the Portuguese food doesn't quite live up to the setting, it is good nonetheless

Club Militaire de Macau

and the restaurant has a fine wine list. The dress code states no sportswear! $$$$

★**Henri's Galley**, 4 Avenida de Republica (☎ 00853-556-251, www. henrisgalley.com; daily noon-10 pm). This is another Macau institution, serving splendid curry crab since 1976, along with the usual host of specialties. Although it has lost some of its character through renovation in recent years, the restaurant is still comfortable, low-lit and decked out with maritime paraphernalia. There are also a few tables outside on the tranquil Avenida da Republica with fine views. $$$

★★**O Porto Interior**, 259 Rua do Almirante Sergio (☎ 00853-967-770; noon-11:30 pm). For fine wine and Macanese and Portuguese cuisine this restaurant, close to A-Ma Temple, is one of the best. Though the antique Chinese wooden screens, porcelain and historic photographs make the ambience feel a little contrived, the food and service are unquestionably good. The succulent sea-bass is well-accompanied by the *vino verde*. $$$

★★**Pousada de Sao Tiago**, Avenida da Republica (☎ 00853-378-111, www.saotiago.com.mo; daily 7:30 am-10:30 pm). Fine food and an enchanting ambience make the terrace restaurant a great choice for dinner or just a cup of tea. Though not cheap, the excellent Asian and Portuguese cuisine is surpassed only by the sea views. Piri-piri chicken is the specialty. $$$-$$$$

Safari, 14 Patio do Cotovelo (daily 11 am-11 pm). This cheap eatery offers many of the classic Macanese dishes in simple surroundings. Although the food isn't up to the high standards of some Macau restaurants, it is tasty, filling and good value – set meals cost from MOP$30. $

Singing Bean, Largo do Senado (daily 10 am-10 pm). Just off the Largo do Senado, this modern place is mainly visited for its fine coffees, including continental blend, allegedly Dr. Stanley Ho's favorite. They also serve fairly good sandwiches, crêpes (MOP$42) and cakes, which might be just the replenishment you need after a few hours' sightseeing and shopping. $$

Taipa

Taipa's restaurant scene has really taken off in recent years and there is some fine cuisine from around the globe to be enjoyed here, along with a variety of street snacks found on **Rua do Cunha**, nicknamed Food Street.

Mix Asian, Mei Keng Gardens, Rua Braganca (☎ 00853-842-724; daily noon-3 pm & 6-11 pm). Mouth-watering curries with ingredients from Nepal and India make this new addition to Taipa's eating scene worth seeking out. Friendly staff and good imported wines complete the package. $$$

★★**O Manel**, 90, Rua Fernao Mendes Pinto (☎ 00853-827-571; daily noon-3 pm & 6:30-10:30 pm, closed every first and fourth Tues of the month). Renowned for its *bacalhau* (salted cod), which is imported from Norway and salted in Portugal, this cozy restaurant has a good selection of cheeses and wines to accompany the fine food. $$$

Coloane

★★★**Café Nga Tim**, 8 Rua Caetano (☎ 00853-882-086; daily noon until late). Atmospherically located in the square next to the pretty chapel of St. Francis Xavier, this place has an enormous menu covering Chinese, Macanese, Portuguese and Western fare. Recommended dishes include curried crab and baked seafood rice and pineapple, but the house specialty is undeniably the flamboyantly prepared Sauna Prawns. $$$

★**Espaco Lisboa**, 8 Rua das Gaivotas (☎ 00853-882-226; Mon-Fri 11 am-3 pm & 6-11 pm, weekends 11 am-11 pm). This intimate little restaurant set in a Chinese village house near Coloane's bus stop serves fine Portuguese food and is renowned for its grilled seabass and *bacalhau con natas* (salted cod with cream). $$$

★★★**Fernando's**, 9, Praia de Hac Sa (☎ 00853-882-264; daily noon-9:30 pm). Legendary among expats, this place offers excellent and affordable Portuguese fare and good wine. The combination of a relaxed, airy atmosphere and simple but attractive rustic brick and beam décor really leaves you wondering if you've somehow stepped through a portal into Portugal. Of particular note are the wonderfully crispy suckling pig (MOP$100 per person) and delicious charcoal pork ribs. $$$-$$$$

★**Lord Stow's Bakery**, Coloane Village Square (Thu-Tue 7 am-11 pm & Wed 7 am-6 pm). It's worth dropping into this little bakery for its famous *natas* (custard tarts). $

Nightlife

Centered on the casinos, Macau has a reputation for unseemly nightlife, dating back 150 years. Along with the casinos there are a host of bars and nightclubs, some of them little more than fronts for brothels. Many of the best bars and clubs are in the big hotels, although more diversity has been added of late along the bar street of **Avenida Dr. Sun Yatsen** (known as Lan Kwai Fong in homage to Hong Kong's bar street) and there are some good watering holes out on the islands.

Where to Drink
Macau Peninsula

Bar Nova Guia, Mandarin Oriental Hotel, Avenida de Amizade (daily 5 pm-3 am). A pleasant, comfortable and refined spot for a drink.

Casablanca, Avenida Dr. Sun Yatsen, Nape. One of a dozen or so options on Macau's bar strip, this place has a pool table, pleasant outdoor seating and pricey drinks.

★**Xanadu, Sands Casino**, Largo de Monte Carlo, Nape (24 hour). Set in the center of Sands main casino hall, this is a great place to soak up the slickness of Macau's gambling scene and has live shows throughout the day.

Taipa

★**Old Taipa Tavern**, 21 Rua dos Negociantes, Taipa Village (daily noon-1 am). In spite of its name this place is only a few years old but its pub atmosphere has already attracted a following. The pub is right next to the Pak Tai temple, serving a range of draught beers and showing live sports. Though principally a drinking establishment, the pub grub is fairly tasty and there's a dining area upstairs – try the fish and chips (MOP$75) or deep-fried brie (MOP$74). Happy hour offers a 25% discount from 4-8 pm.

Coloane

★★**Porto Bar**, 3F, Westin Resort, 1918 Estrada de Hac Sa (daily 5 pm-1 am). Harking back to Macau's pre-casino past, the Porto Bar offers fine Portuguese wines, spirits and cigars, accompanied by South China Sea views and a touch of class.

Appendix
Bibliography & Recommended Reading

The following books are all worth reading, particularly the triple-starred works, and have been of use and interest during my travels in China and the compilation of this book. For more on Chinese literature see p. 61. You'll find reviews for most of the titles below at www.amazon.com.

Biographies

★★★Jung Chang, *Wild Swans*
★★Jung Chang & Jon Halliday, *Mao: The Unknown Story*
Richard Evans, *Deng Xiaoping and the Making Of Modern China*
★★Ma Jian, *Red Dust: a Path Through China*
John Man, *Genghis Khan*
★★Anchee Min, *Red Azalea: Life and Love in China*
Philip Short, *Mao: A Life*
Marina Warner, *The Dragon Empress*
★Adeline Yeh Mah, *Fallen Leaves*

Classics

Li Bai & Du Fu, *Endless River*
Wu Cheng'en, *Journey to the West*
Confucius, *The Book of Songs*
Luo Guanzhong, *Romance of the Three Kingdoms*
Luo Guanzhong & Shi Nai'an, *Outlaws of the Marsh* aka *The Water Margin*
David R. McCraw, *Du Fu's Laments from the South*
Arthur Waley (trans) *Monkey* – an abbreviated version of *Journey to the West*
Cao Xueqin, *The Dream of the Red Chamber*
Sun Zi, *The Art of War*

Culinary

Francine Halvorsen, *The Food and Cooking of China*
★★Nina Simonds, *The Food of China: a Journey for Food Lovers*
★★Martin Yan, *Martin Yan's Culinary Journey Through China*

Culture & Society

★★Ian Buruma, *Bad Elements: Chinese Rebels from LA to Beijing*
★Tom Clissold, *Mr China*
Ted Fishmen, *China Inc*
Oded Shenkar, *The Chinese Century*
Kenneth Wilkinson, *World Cultures: China*
★Xue Xinran, *The Good Women of China*

Fiction

Andrea Barrett, *The Middle Kingdom*
Carolyn Choa & Su Li-Qun, *The Picador Book of Contemporary Chinese Fiction*

★Wei Hui, *Shanghai Baby*
★★Lao She, *Rickshaw Boy*
★★Wang Shuo, *Please Don't Call Me Human*
Sid Smith, *A House by the River*
★Annie Wang, *People's Republic of Desire*
★★★Mo Yan, *The Garlic Ballads*

History

Patricia Ebrey, *Cambridge Illustrated History of China*
Peter Fleming, *The Siege at Peking*
Larry Habegger & James O'Reilly, *Travellers Tales: China*
★★Ann Paludan, *Chronicle of the Chinese Emperors*
★★★J.A.G. Roberts, *A History of China*
Mao Zedong, *Quotations of Mao Tse-Tung* aka *The Little Red Book*

Historical Accounts

★★Zhang Boli, *Escape from China: the Long Journey from Tian'anmen to Freedom*
★Jenni Daiches (aka Jenni Calder), *Letters from the Great Wall*
★Peter Hopkirk, *Foreign Devils on the Silk Road*
★Julia Lovell, *The Great Wall*
★★Gavin Menzies, *1421, The Year China Discovered the World*
★★★Anchee Min, *Empress Orchid*
★★Yan Mo, *Red Sorghum*
★Marco Polo, *The Travels*
Sun Shuyun, *The Long March*
★Edgar Snow, *Red Star Over China*
★★Lu Xun, *Diary of a Madman & other stories*

Hong Kong & Macau

★★Austin Coates, *Myself a Mandarin*
★Jonathan Dimbleby, *The Last Governor*
★★Richard Mason, *The World of Suzie Wong*
Paul Theroux, *Kowloon Tong*
Frank Welsh, *A History of Hong Kong*

Martial Arts

★Kumar Frantzis, *The Power of Internal Martial Arts*
Bruce Lee, *Tao of Jeet Kune Do*
Erle Montaigue, *Power Taiji*
Bruce Thomas, *Bruce Lee: Fighting Spirit*
Religion & Philosophy
Kenneth Ch'en, *Buddhism in China*
★Confucius, *The Analects*
★Martin Palmer, *Travels Through Sacred China*
Lao Zi, *Tao Te Ching*

Travel Literature

Raymond Barnett, *Jade and Fire: a Novel of Emerging China*
Polly Evans, *Fried Eggs with Chopsticks*

★Peter Fleming, *One's Company: a Journey to China in 1933*
Polly Greeks, *Embracing the Dragon: a Woman's Journey along the Great Wall of China*
★Peter Hessler, *Oracle Bones: Journey between China & the West*
★★Peter Hessler, *River Town: Two Years on the Yangtze*
★W. Somerset Maugham, *On a Chinese Screen*
★★Simon Myers, *Adrift in China*
★★★Paul Theroux, *Riding the Iron Rooster*
★Colin Thubron, *Behind the Wall*
★Lulu Wang, *The Lily Theater: a Novel of Modern China*
★★★Simon Winchester, *The River at the Center of the World: a Journey up the Yangtze and Back in Chinese Time*
★★Gao Xingjian, *One Man's Bible*

Glossary

Arhat	Buddhist saint (*luohan* in Mandarin)
Cheongsam	Traditional Chinese women's dress (*qipao* in Mandarin)
Dharma	Buddhist path to enlightenment
Hutong	Narrow alley
Laowai	Foreigner (old outsider)
Luohan	Chinese word for *arhat*
Mah Jong	Traditional Chinese board game
Mandala	Mystical geometric diagram representing the cosmos
Paifang	Memorial arch
Pinyin	Romanization of Chinese characters
Putonghua	Mandarin Chinese (normal language)
Qilin	Mythical creature associated with good luck
Siheyuan	Courtyard house
Sinicized	Made Chinese
Stele (stelae)	Commemorative stone tablet
Tai Chi	Style of Martial Art (see p. 66)
Wushu	Martial Arts

Acronyms

CAAC	Civil Aviation Authority of China
CCP	Chinese Communist Party
CITS	China International Travel Service
CTS	China Travel Service
KCR	Kowloon-Canton Railway
KMT	Kuomintang (Guomindang in pinyin) – Nationalist Party
MTR	Mass Transit Railway (subway)
PLA	People's Liberation Army
PRC	People's Republic of China

PRD	Pearl River Delta
PSB	Public Security Bureau
RMB	Ren Min Bi (People's Money)
ROC	Republic of China (Taiwan)
SEZ	Special Economic Zone
WHO	World Health Organization
WTO	World Trade Organization
WWF	World Wildlife Foundation
Hotel Abbreviations	
SW	Swimming Pool
FC	Fitness Center
@	Internet access in rooms
DA	Rooms suitable for disabled people available

Language

Chinese initially seems a baffling cacophony of tones and a labyrinth of characters, but with a little effort, a good sense of humor and the odd hand gesture you should be able to make yourself understood. Even the tiniest bit of spoken Chinese will help traveling in practical terms, but will also be widely appreciated by anyone who you try it out on. Learning **Mandarin Chinese** is no easy feat – the tones and the characters see to that, however, the grammatical structure is comparatively simple and even just a few hours study should yield some results, if only in your understanding of the tenets of the language rather than practical usage.

Dialects

There are countless different dialects of Chinese (known as *hanyu* or *zhongwen* in China and *guoyu* in Taiwan) which can sound as unalike as a deep southern drawl and a New York accent, and there are also a host of other spoken languages amongst the ethnic minorities. The prevalent form of Chinese on the mainland is *putonghua* (normal language), the Beijing dialect which has clearly defined tones and a tendency to add "er" to the end of words. In the far south and Hong Kong, *guangdonghua* or Cantonese is the prevalent tongue and with its garrulous nine tones, feels a world away from the refined north. Other major dialects include Shanghainese and Hokkien (minnanhua) which is spoken in Fujian. Some of the most widely spoken ethnic languages are Hakka (kejia), Mongol, Uyghur and Tibetan. Putonghua is understood throughout China and Taiwan, although in remote rural areas older people may only speak their regional or ethnic dialect.

The Spoken Word

Chinese is a tonal language, meaning that any character can have many different meanings according to its tone and the character it is connected to. There are **four principal tones** (1- high flat, 2 - low rising, 3 - like a Chinese hat upside down, and 4 - abrupt falling) and a fifth "toneless" tone. This means that any one character can have many different meanings depending upon its tone and the character it is linked with. Thus: *mā* (1 - mother), *má* (2 - hemp), *mǎ* (3 - horse), *mà* (4 - scold).

Unless you are a natural linguist the tones take some mastering, but don't be shy to try – if you have context (you're in a bar and you ask for a beer for example) you're likely to be understood even if your tone is a little off. However, be prepared for a few blank faces too! Even if you have good Mandarin many people just won't expect you to speak Chinese and are convinced they won't be able to understand you – repeating yourself should do the trick. Amusingly if you manage to get into a conversation but then hit a linguistic stumbling block some people will write the Chinese character in the belief that this will be easier to understand. This offers some insight into the diversity of the language – people from far flung parts of the country may not understand eachother's dialects, but if they can read they'll be able to communicate.

Practicing the tones for some basic phrases and then trying them out in context makes a good way to start teaching yourself Chinese, although understanding the responses can be more problematic! If you're really keen to learn the language then there are plenty of great places to do just that all over the country, from short lessons to entire courses (see *Studying and Working in China*, p. 105, and individual chapter listings). For me though the best way to learn a language is to absorb yourself in a country – gradually the strings of unintelligible sentences start to break down into words and once you've heard the word enough times to repeat it, ask what it is and that's your word for the day...

The Written Word

You need to know around a couple of thousand Chinese characters to be able to read a newspaper and learning to write Chinese takes years of study. However, even for the short-term visitor there is insight found through understanding a few of the characters. The Chinese written language was originally a pictographic language and this can still be seen in some of its more elemental symbols such as fire, middle and mountain. In 1956 as part of Chairman Mao's drive to increase literacy, the Chinese written form was simplified and thousands of characters were lost or altered. This system has indeed facilitated learning but in Hong Kong and Taiwan the original characters remain in use and are admired for their elegance and sense of history. As a language without an alphabet Chinese has to adapt itself and create new character combinations to deal with modern inventions. Thus train literally translates as fire-car and computer means electric brain!

Chinese has been Romanized into a system called **pinyin** (spellsound) which also incorporates the tones (see *The Spoken Word* for more on the tones) and is far more effective than the dated Wade-Giles transliteration still used in Taiwan. Many of the letters are pronounced in the same or a similar way to their English sound, however there are a few notable exceptions:
c (ts, thus *cun* is tsun) / q (ch, thus *qin* is Chin) / x (sh, thus *xie xie* is she she) / z (ds, thus *zai* is dsai), zh (j, thus *zhong* is jong).

Grammar

Chinese grammar offers some light relief from the complexity of the tonal and written language and is fairly simple compared with English. Sentence order generally follows the subject verb object format and a few basic words offer the key to changing tenses and altering sentences from statements to questions or demands. If **ma** is added to the end of any sentence it makes it into a question (*ni yao ma* = "Do you want?"), or alternatively the verb can simply be repeated after a negative (*ni yao bu yao* = you want not want meaning "Do you want?"). There is no conjugation of verbs and to change tenses you simply start the sentence with the relevant one of the following (*yiqian* or *zhiqian*=before/ *yi hou* or *wei lai*=after or in the future).

Basic Words & Phrases

SOME OF THE MOST BASICS VERBS ARE:

drink	喝	hē
eat	吃	chī
have	有	yǒu
hear	听	tīng
know	知道	zhīdào
know (a person)	认识	rènshí
like	喜欢	xǐhūan
love	爱	ài
see	看	kàn
understand	懂	dǒng
want	要	yào

THE BASIC PRONOUNS ARE:

I	`我	wǒ
you	你	nǐ
he/she	他/她	tā
we	我们	wǒmén
you (plural)	你们	nǐmén
they	他们	tāmén

BASIC PHRASES
Meeting People

Hello	你好	nǐ hǎo
How are you?	你好吗	ní hǎo ma
I'm fine	我很好	wǒ hén hǎo
Thank you	谢谢	xìe xìe
You're welcome	不客气	búkèqì
Goodbye	再见	zài jiàn
How old are you?	你多大/你几岁了	ní dūo dà/ ní jǐ sùi le
What's your name?	你贵姓?	nǐn gùi xìng?
My name is...	我叫…	wǒ jiao …
Do you have any children?	你有没有小孩子	ní yǒuméiyǒu xiǎo háizi
Are you married?	你结婚了吗	nǐ jíehūnle ma
I would like….	我要…	wǒ yào
I don't understand	我不懂.	wǒ bù dǒng
Where are you from?	你从哪里来?	nǐ chóng ná lǐ lái?
I'm …	我是…人	wǒ shì … rén
American	美国人	měiguó rén
Canadian	加拿大人	jīanádà rén
British	英国人	yīnggúo rén
Australian	澳大利亚人	àodàlìyà rén
a New Zealander	新西兰人	xīnxīlán rén
South African	南非人	nán fēi rén

Getting Around

Excuse me	请问	qǐngwèn
Where is the ...?	...在哪里	... zài ná lǐ
Airport	机场	jīchǎng
Bank of China	中国银行	zhōnggúo yínháng
Bus Station	汽车站	qìchē zhàn
Internet Café	网吧	wǎngbā
Post Office	邮局	yóujú
Train Station	火车站	hǔochē zhàn
What time is the next service?	下一趟几点开	xìa yī tàng jǐ dǐan kāi
How many hours?	几个小时	jǐgè xǐaoshí
Which platform?	哪个站台	nǎgè zhàn tái
Hard seat	硬座	yìng zùo
Soft seat	软座	rǔan zùo
Hard sleeper	硬卧	yìng wò
Soft sleeper	软卧	rǔan wò
Regular bus	普通车	pǔtōng chē
Express bus	直达快吧	zhīdá kuài bā
Sleeper bus	卧铺车	wòpù chē

Shopping

How much?	多少钱	dūo shǎo qián
That's too expensive!	太贵了	tài guìle
Is a little cheaper possible?	可以便宜一点吗	kéyí piányì yìdǐan ma

Accommodation

Hotel	宾馆	bīngǔan
Single room	单人房	dānrénfáng
Double room	大床房	dàchúangfáng
Twin room	标准房/双人房	bīaozhǔnfáng/shūangrénfán
Dormitory	多人间	dūorén jīan
Air conditioning	空调	kōngtíao
Clean the room	打扫房间	dáshǎo fángjīan
Towel	毛巾	máojīn
Balcony	阳台	yángtái
I want to change room	我要换房间	wǒ yào huàn fángjīan

EATING

Staples

Bread	面包	mìanbāo
Rice	米饭	mǐfàn
Noodles	面条	mìantíao
Rice noodles	河粉	héfěn

Meat	肉	ròu
Chicken	鸡肉	jī ròu
Duck	鸭	yā
Fish	鱼	yú
Goose	鹅	é
Pork	猪肉	zhū ròu
Mutton	羊肉	yáng ròu

Vegetables 蔬菜 shūcài

Beans	豆	dòu
Chili	辣椒	làjīao
Cucumber	黄瓜	húanggūa
Eggplant	茄子	qíezi
Green pepper	青椒	qīngjīao
Green vegetables	青菜	qīncài
Lotus root	莲藕	lían ǒu
White mushrooms	蘑菇	mógū
Brown mushrooms	香菇	xīanggū
Potatoes	土豆	tǔdòu
Tomatoes	西红柿	xīhóngshì
Tofu	豆腐	dòufù

Cooking Methods

Boiled	水煮	shǔi zhǔ
Fried	炒	chǎo
Roasted	烤	kǎo
Steamed	蒸	zhēng

Specific Dishes

Beef noodles	牛肉面	níuròu mìan
Beer Fish	啤酒鱼	píjǐu yú
Beggars' Chicken	叫花鸡	jiaòhùa jī
Beijing Roast Duck	北京烤鸭	běijīng kǎoyā
Braised eggplant with garlic	红烧茄子	hóngshāo qíezǐ
Caramelized apples	拔丝苹果	básī pínggǔo
Crossing the Bridge Noodles	过桥米线	gùoqiáomǐxìan
Dim Sum	点心	dǐanxīn
Drunken Prawns	醉虾	zùixīa
Dumplings	饺子	jiǎozi
Dumpling Banquet	饺子宴	jiǎozi yàn
Egg-fried rice	蛋炒饭	dànchǎofàn
Fish Flavored Pork	鱼香肉丝	yúxīang ròusī
Gongbao Chicken	宫保鸡丁	gōngbǎo jīdīng
Hotpot	火锅	hǔogūo
Mapu Tofu	麻婆豆腐	mápú dòufù

Noodle soup	汤面	tāngmìan
Pancakes	煎饼	jiānbǐng
Plain rice	白米饭	bái mǐfàn
Sand Pot Casserole	沙煲	shā bāo
Scrambled eggs & tomatoes	西红柿炒蛋	xīhóngshì chǎodàn
Sliced Potatoes with vinegar	醋溜土豆丝	cù līutǔ dòusī
Steamed buns	馒头	mántóu
Stuffed steamed buns	包字	bāozǐ
Steamed pork dumplings	小笼包	xǐaolóngbāo
Stir-fried bamboo shoots	炒竹笋片	chǎo zhu sǔn pìan
Stir-friend mixed vegetables	炒什锦菜	chǎo shí jǐncài
Stretched noodles	拉面	lāmìan
Sweet and Sour Fish	糖醋鱼	tángcù yú
Sweet and Sour Pork	糖醋里脊	tángcù lǐ jī
Wonton Soup	混吞	hún tūn
Fruits	水果	shǔigǔo
Apple	苹果	pínggǔo
Banana	香蕉	xiāngjīao
Lemon	柠檬	níng méng
Mango	芒果	mángǔo
Orange	桔子	júzǐ
Peach	桃子	táozǐ
Pineapple	菠萝	bōlúo
Pomelo	柚子	yòuzǐ
Strawberry	草莓	cǎoméi
Watermelon	西瓜	xīgūa
Drinks		
Apple juice	苹果汁	pínggǔo zhī
Beer	啤酒	píjǐu
Rice wine	米酒	míjǐu
Coffee	咖啡	kāfēi
Cola	可乐	kělà
Diet Coke	健怡可乐	jiānyí kělè
Sprite	雪碧	xǔebì
Milk	牛奶	níunǎi
Mineral Water	矿泉水	kùangqúan shǔi
Green tea	绿茶	lù chá
Jasmine tea	茉莉花茶	mòlìhūa chá
Red tea	红茶	hóng chá
Red wine	红葡萄酒	hóng pútáo jǐu
White wine	白葡萄酒	bái pútáo jǐu
Yogurt	酸奶	sūan nǎi

Useful Restaurant Vocabulary

Bill / check	买单	mǎidān
Bowl	碗	wǎn
Can you recommend a dish?	可以介绍一道菜	kéyǐ jièshào yídào cài ma
Chopsticks	筷子	kuàizǐ
English menu	英文菜单	yīngwén càidān
Glass	玻璃杯	bōlí bēi
Knife & fork	刀/叉	dāo/chā
I don't eat meat	我不吃肉.	wǒ bù chī ròu
I'm a Buddhist	我是佛教徒	wǒ shì fójiào tū
I don't want spicy food	我的菜不要辣椒	wǒdě cài bu yào làjīao
I'm allergic to nuts	我对坚果过敏	wǒ dùi jīanguǒ gùomǐn
No MSG	不要味精	bù yào weìjīng
Waiter	服务员	fúwùyúan

Western Food

Chocolate	巧克力	qǐaokèlì
French Fries	薯条	shǔtíao
Hamburger	汉堡包	hànbǎobāo
Pasta	意大利面	yìdàlì mìan
Pizza	比萨	bǐsà
Sandwich	三明治	ānmíngzhì
Carrefour	家乐福	jīalèfú
KFC	肯德基	kěndéjī
McDonalds	麦当劳	màidāngláo
Pizza Hut	必胜客	bìshèngkè
Starbucks	星巴克	xīngbākè

HEALTH

I'm allergic to	我对…过敏	wǒ dùi… gùomǐn
I'm ill	我生病了	wǒ shēng bìngle
Cold	感冒	gǎnmào
Cough	咳嗽	kēsòu
Dentist	牙医	yáyī
Diarrhea	腹泻	fùxìe
Doctor	医生	yīshēng
Fever	发烧	fāshāo
Vomit	呕吐	ǒu tù

EMERGENCIES

Help!	救命啊!	jìu mìng a
Hospital	医院	yīyùan
Police	警察	jǐngchá
Thief	小偷	xǐatōu

Someone has stolen my things	有人偷了我的东西	yǒurén tōule wǒde dōngxī
Public Security Bureau	公安局	gōng ān jú
Report for insurance	保险遗失报告	báo xiǎn yí shī bào gaò

NUMBERS

1	一	yī
2	二	èr
3	三	sān
4	四	sì
5	五	wǔ
6	六	lìu
7	七	qī
8	八	bā
9	九	jǐu
10	十	shí
11	十一	shíyī
12	十二	shíèr
13	十三	shísān
20	二十	èrshí
21	二十一	èr shí yī
22	二十二	èr shí èr
23	二十三	èr shí sān
30	三十	sānshí
40	四十	sìshí
50	五十	wǔshí
60	六十	lìúshí
70	七十	qīshí
80	八十	bāshí
90	九十	jǐushí
100	一百	yī bǎi
200	两百	liáng bǎi
300	三百	sān bǎi
1000	一千	yì qīan
2000	两千	lǐang qīan
3000	三千	sān qīan
10000	一万	yí wàn
½	半	bàn

DAYS

Monday	星期一	xīngqī yī
Tuesday	星期二	xīngqī èr
Wednesday	星期三	xīngqī sān
Thursday	星期四	xīngqī sì
Friday	星期五	xīngqī wǔ
Saturday	星期六	xīngqī lìu
Sunday	星期日	xīngqī rì

TIMES

What time is it?	现在是几点钟	xìanzài shì jídĭan zhōng
It's .... o'clock	现在是......点.	xìanzài shì.......dĭan
It's half past one	现在是一点半	xìanzài shì yī dĭan bàn

MONTHS

January	一月	yī yùe
February	二月	èr yùe
March	三月	sān yùe
April	四月	sì yùe
May	五月	wŭ yùe
June	六月	lìu yùe
July	七月	qī yùe
August	八月	bā yùe
September	九月	jĭu yùe
October	十月	shí yùe
November	十一月	shíyī yùe
December	十二月	shier yùe

Beijing & Around

BEIJING　北京

Practicalities
Beijing International Airport	北京首都机场
Beijing Train Station	北京火车站
Beijing West Train Station	北京火车西站
Deshengmen Bus Station	德胜门公共汽车站
Dongzhimen Bus Station	东直门公共汽车站
Pingguoyuan Bus Station	苹果园汽车站
Qianmen Bus Depot	前门汽车站

Sights & Shops
Ancient Observatory	古观象台
Beihai Park	北海公园
Bell & Drum Tower	钟鼓楼
Big Bell Temple	大钟寺
Confucius Temple	孔庙
Dazhalan	大栅栏
Forbidden City	故宫
Hongqiao Pearl Market	虹桥市场
Houhai	后海
Jingshan Park	景山公园
National Museum	国家博物馆
Old Summer Palace	圆明园
Ox Street Mosque	牛街礼拜寺
Panjiayuan Antique Market	潘家园旧货市场
Prince Gong's Palace	恭王府
Ritan Park	日坛公园
Shichahai	什刹海
Silk Market	秀水街
Soong Qingling's Former Residence	宋庆林故居
Summer Palace	颐和园
Temple of Heaven	天坛
Tian'anmen Square	天安门广场
Tibetan Lama Temple	雍和宫
Wangfujing Dajie	王府井大街
White Cloud Temple	白云观
Workers' Stadium	工人体育馆
Zhengyang Gate	正阳门

Around Beijing

Badachu	八达处
Botanical Gardens	植物园
Eastern Qing Tombs	青东陵
Fragrant Hills	香山
Jietai Temple	戒台寺
Longqing Gorge	龙庆峡
Ming Tombs	十三陵
Peking Man Site & Museum	北京猿人遗址博物馆
Tanzhe Temple	潭柘寺
Great Wall	长城
Badaling	八达岭
Huanghua	黄花城
Jiankou	箭扣
Jinshanling	金山岭
Mutianyu	慕田峪
Simitai	司马台

Galleries, Shows & Theaters

Academy of Traditional Chinese Opera	中国戏曲学院
Chaoyang Theater	朝阳剧场
Dashanzi	大山子
Liyuan Theater	梨园剧场
Red Theater	红剧场
Shaolin Warriors	朝阳文化俱乐部
Tianqiao Acrobatics	天桥杂技剧场

Hotels

Bamboo Garden	竹园宾馆
China World Hotel	中国大饭店
Downtown Backpackers	东堂客栈
Drum Tower Youth Hostel	鼓韵青年酒店
Far East International Hostel	远东国际青年旅舍
Grand Hotel Beijing	北京贵宾楼饭店
Grand Hyatt	北京东方君悦大酒店
Jade Youth Hostel	智德青年旅舍
Jianguo	建国饭店
Kerry Center Hotel	嘉里中心饭店
Lotus Hostel	莲舍
Lusongyuan	侣松园宾馆
Peninsula Palace	王府饭店

Raffles	北京饭店莱佛士
Red Capital Residence	新红资客栈
Scitech	赛特饭店
St. Regis	北京国际俱乐部饭店
Tiantan	天坛饭店

Hotels Around Beijing

The Commune	长城脚下公社
Fragrant Hills	香山宾馆
Red Capital Ranch	新红资避暑山庄
Simitai HI	司马台青年旅舍

Restaurants

Bento & Berries	缤味美食屋
Café Igosso	冲浪者餐厅
Café Sambal	马来西亚餐厅
Celestial Court	天宝阁
Dadong Beijing Duck	大董烤鸭店
Dong Lai Shun	东来顺
Fangshan	仿膳饭店
Fish Nation	鱼邦
Green T. House	紫雲轩
Jingcai Roasted Duck	精彩烤鸭
Justine's	杰斯汀
Kaorouji	烤肉季
Laoshe Teahouse	老舍茶馆
Li Family Restaurant	厉家菜
Li Qun Beijing Duck	利群烤鸭店
Made in China	摩登中国
Mei Mansions	梅府
Pure Lotus Vegetarian	净心莲
Quanjude Duck Restaurant	全聚德烤鸭店
Red Capital Club	新红资俱乐部
Source	都江源
The Courtyard	四合院
Three Guizhou Men	三个贵州人
Xiao Fei Yang	小肥羊

Bars

Banana	巴那那
Bar Blu	蓝吧
Buddha Bar	不大

Beijing & Around

Centro	炫酷
Drum and Bell	鼓钟咖啡馆
East Shore Live Jazz Café	东岸咖啡
Goose and Duck	鹅和鸭
Hometown Bar	故乡酒吧
Ice House	库冰
Lotus Blue	蘭莲花坊餐吧
Pass By Bar	过客酒吧
No Name Bar	无名酒吧
Poachers Inn	友谊青年吧
Stone Boat Bar	石坊
The Tree	隐蔽的树
What? Bar	什么?酒吧
World of Suzie Wong	苏西黄
Yugong Yishan	愚公移山

CHENGDE 承德

Practicalities

Chengde Train Station	承德火车站
Long Distance Bus Station	长途汽车站

Sights

Bishu Shanzhuang	避暑山庄
Pule Temple	普乐寺
Puning Temple	普宁寺
Putuozongcheng Temple	普陀宗乘之庙
Sledgehammer Rock	棒钟山

Hotels

Garden	园林宾馆
Mongolian Yurts	蒙古包
Sai Bei	塞北宾馆
Shanzhuang	山庄宾馆
Tianbao	天宝假日酒店
Yunshan	云山饭店

Restaurants

Man Han Quan Xi	满汉全席大酒楼
Qianlong Jiaoziguan	乾隆饺子馆
Qingyuanheng	庆元亨大

XI'AN   西安

Dongguangchang Bus Station   东广场汽车站
Xi'an Airport   西安机场
Xi'an Train Station   西安火车站
Beilin Stone Tablets Museum   碑林博物馆
Bell Tower   钟楼
Big Wild Goose Pagoda   大雁塔
City Walls   城墙
Drum Tower   鼓楼
Eight Immortals Temple   八仙宫
Great Mosque   大清真寺
Little Wild Goose Pagoda   小雁塔
Shaanxi Provincial Museum   陕西历史博物馆
Shuyuanmen   书院门
Tang Paradise   大唐圣境

Around Xi'an

Banpo Museum   半坡博物馆
Huashan   华山
Huaqing Pool   华清池
Qin Shi Huang's Tomb   秦始皇陵
Terracotta Warriors   兵马俑
Zhouzhi Panda Reserve   周至熊猫保护区

Hotels

Bell Tower   钟楼饭店
Bell and Drum   钟鼓楼大酒店
Grand Mercure   雅高人民大厦
Han Tang Hostel   汉唐驿
Hyatt Regency   凯悦（阿房宫）酒店
May First   五一饭店
Qixian Hostel   七贤庄
Shaanxi Wenyuan   文苑大酒店
Shuyuan Hostel   书院青年旅舍
Sofitel   雅高人民大厦

Restaurants

Defachang   德发长
Hui Fang   回坊人家
Le Chinois   乐轩华
May First   五一饭店
Shaanxi Local Fast Food   陕西风味快餐厅
Tong Sheng Xiang   同盛祥饭庄

Three Gorges

CHONGQING   重庆

Practicalities

Chongqing Airport	重庆机场
Chongqing Train Station	重庆火车站
Caiyuan Bus Station	菜园坝汽车站
Chaotianmen Docks	朝天门码头

Sights

Victory Monument (Jiefangbei)	解放碑
Luohan Temple	罗汉寺
People's Concert Hall	人民大礼堂
Three Gorges Museum	三峡博物馆

Around Chongqing

Dazu	大足
Baoding Shan	宝顶山
Bei Shan	北山

Galleries, Shows & Theaters

Huguang Guild Museum	湖广会馆

Hotels

Chaotianmen	朝天门大酒店
Chongqing Guesthouse	重庆宾馆
Harbor Plaza	海逸酒店
Hui Xian Lou	会仙楼宾馆
Marriott	万豪酒店
Milky Way	银河大酒店
Sanxia	三峡宾馆

Restaurants

American Cowboy	美国牛仔烧烤城
Canglong	沧龙火锅
Common Tales	重庆刘一手
Daxigoudian Hexi	大溪沟店和喜火锅
Lao Sichuan	老四川大酒楼

THREE GORGES 三峡

Baidicheng	白帝城
Lesser Three Gorges (Daning River)	小三峡
Fengdu Ghost Temple	丰都
Qutang Gorge	瞿塘峡
Shennong Stream	神农溪
Shibaozhai	石宝寨
Three Gorges Dam Site (Sandouping)	三峡大坝区
Wu Gorge	巫峡
Xiling Gorge	西陵峡

YICHANG 宜昌

Practicalities

Yichang Airport	三峡机场
Yichang Train Station	宜昌火车站

Sightseeing

Gezhouba	葛洲坝

Hotels

Heping Jia Ri	和平假日酒店
New Century	新世纪酒店
Taohualing	桃花岭宾馆
Yichang International	宜昌国际大酒店

Restaurants

Beijing Jiaoziguan	北京饺子馆
Zhenjiangge	镇江阁茶楼

Three Gorges

Shanghai & Around

SHANGHAI 上海

Practicalities

Hongqiao International Airport	虹桥机场
International Passenger Quay	国际客运码头
Jinling Pier	金陵码头
Jinmao Docks	金茂码头
Maglev Train Terminal	磁悬浮列车
Pudong International Airport	浦东机场
Shanghai Train Station	上海火车站
Shiliupu Pier	十六浦码头

Sights & Shops

Bird and Flower Market	花鸟市场
Botanical Gardens	植物园
Bund	外滩
Bund Tourist Tunnel	外滩人行观光遂道
Dongtai Lu Antiques Market	东台路古董市场
Former Residence of Mao Zedong	毛泽东故居
Former Residence of Soong Qingling	宋庆玲故居
Former Residence of Sun Yatsen	孙中山故居
Former Residence of Zhou Enlai	周恩来故居
Huangpu Park	黄埔公园
Jade Buddha Temple	玉佛寺
Jewish Refugee Museum	犹太难民博物馆
Jing'an Park	静安公园
Jing'an Temple	静安寺
Jinmao Tower	金茂大厦
Longhua Temple	龙华寺
Lu Xun Park	鲁迅公园
1st National Congress of the CCP	一大会址
Oriental Pearl TV Tower	东方明珠广播电视塔
Renmin Square	人民广场
Science and Technology Museum	科技馆
Shanghai Museum	上海博物馆
Shanghai Ocean Aquarium	海洋馆
Shanghai Urban Planning Center	城市规划中心
Shikumen Open House Museum	石库门博物馆
Yu Gardens	豫园

Xiangyang Market	向阳市场
Xintiandi	新天地
Xujiahui Cathedral	徐家汇天主教堂

Around Shanghai

Tongli	同里
Wuzhen	乌镇
Xitang	西塘
Zhouzhuang	周庄
Zhujiajiao	朱家角

Galleries, Shows & Theaters

Arts and Crafts Museum	工艺美术博物馆
Grand Theatre	上海大剧院
Museum of Contemporary Art	上海当代艺术馆
Propaganda Poster Art Center	宣传画艺术中心
Shanghai Art Museum	上海艺术博物馆
Shanghai Centre Theatre	上海商城剧院
Shanghai Circus World	上海马戏城
Shanghai Concert Hall	上海音乐厅
Yifu Theatre	逸夫舞台

Hotels

Anting Villa	安亭 别墅.花园酒店
Astor House	浦江饭店
Captain Hostel	船长青年酒店
Chun Shen Jiang	春申江宾馆
Classical	上海老饭店
Grand Hyatt	金茂君悦大酒店
Hengshan-Moller Villa	衡山宾馆
Hiker Youth Hostel	旅行者青年旅舍
Jinjiang	锦江饭店
Marriott	万豪酒店
Nanjing	南京饭店
Panorama Century Court	海湾大厦
Park	国际饭店
Peace	和平饭店
Portman Ritz-Carlton	波特曼丽嘉酒店
Renmin	人民大酒店

Ruijin 瑞金酒店
St. Regis 国际俱乐部饭店
Westin 威斯汀大饭店
YMCA 青年会宾馆
#9 九号饭店
#88 新天地

Restaurants

Art Deco Garden Café 瑞金宾馆餐厅
Bali Laguna 宏亚餐厅
Bao Luo 保罗酒楼
Crystal Jade 翡翠酒家
Cupola 望江阁
Element Fresh 新元素
Godly Vegetarian Restaurant 功德林
Guyi Hunan 古意湘味浓
Hongze Jiulou 宏泽酒楼
Huxinting Teahouse 湖心亭茶楼
Kathleen's 5 赛玛西餐厅
Lu Bo Lang 绿波廊
Meilong Zhen 梅龙镇酒家
M on the Bund 米氏西餐厅
Nanxiang 南翔馒头店
New Heights 新视角餐厅
Old China Hand Reading Room 汉源书店
Old Shanghai Teahouse 老上海茶馆
Ren Ren 上海人人菜馆
Shaanxi Noodles 迪檬餐饮店
Shintori 新都里
Simply Thai 天泰餐厅
Suzhou Mian Guan 苏州面馆
TMSK 透明思考
Wagas 我哥四
Whampoa Club 黄浦会
Yang's Kitchen 杨家厨房
Ye Shanghai 夜上海

Bars

Big Bamboo 大竹子酒吧
Blue Frog 蓝蛙
Captain's Bar 船长酒吧

Chez L'Ami	云天吧
Cloud 9	九重天酒廊
Cotton Club	棉花剧乐部
Face Bar	妃思吧
Freelance	自由蓝色
Glamour Bar	魅力酒吧
Mojo Café	海仑休闲吧
rbt Garden	滨江花园
The Blarney Stone	布拉尼司栋

SUZHOU 苏州

Practicalities
Nanmen Wharf	南门码头
North Bus Station	汽车北站
South Bus Station	汽车南站
Suzhou Train Station	苏州火车站

Sights & Shops
Canglang Pavilion	沧浪亭
China Pearl City	中国珍珠城
Couples Garden	耦园
Humble Administrator's Garden	拙政园
Lion Grove Garden	狮子园
Lingering Garden	留园
Lingyan Hill	灵岩山
Master of the Nets Garden	网狮园
North Temple Pagoda	北寺塔
Panmen	盘门
Precious Belt Bridge	宝带桥
Silk Museum	丝绸博物馆
Suzhou Arts & Crafts Museum	苏州工艺美术博物馆
Suzhou Museum	苏州博物馆
Suzhou Opera Museum	戏曲博物馆
Temple of Mystery	玄妙观
Tianping Hill	天平山
Tiger Hill	老虎山
Twin Pagodas	双塔
West Garden Temple	西园

Hotels

Bamboo Grove	竹辉饭店
Dong Wu	东吴饭店
Friendship	友谊宾馆
Lexiang	乐乡饭店
My Hotel	麦禾旅店
Pingjiang Lodge	平江客栈
Sheraton Garden	喜来登大酒店
Suzhou	苏州饭店
Suzhou Garden View	苏州人家大酒店
Suzhou Youth Hostel	苏州国际青年旅舍

Restaurants

Deyuelou	得月楼
Indian at the Cross	玉泉楼饭店
Japanese Food	女秀才
Sarawak	砂拉越餐厅
Songhelou	松鹤楼菜馆
SuCa Café	苏卡意式咖啡
Tudori	土大力
Xinjiang Yakexi	新疆亚克西酒楼
Yang-Yang	洋洋
Yunnan Noodles	云南面馆

Bars

Blue Marlin	蓝枪鱼
Shamrock	三叶啤酒屋
Whiskey Jack's	四季风酒吧

HANGZHOU 杭州

Practicalities

East Bus Station	长途汽车东站
Hangzhou Xiaoshan Airport	杭州萧山机场
North Bus Station	长途汽车北站
Qiantang River	钱塘江码头
Train Station	火车站
West Bus Station	长途汽车西站
West Lake	西湖
Wulinmen Passenger Dock	武林门客运码头
Xihutiandi	西湖天地

Sights & Shops

Bai Causeway	白堤
China Silk Town	中国丝绸城
Dreamlike Tiger Spring	虎跑梦泉
Felai Feng	飞来峰
Leifeng Pagoda	雷锋塔
Lingyin Temple	灵隐寺
Liuhe Pagoda	六合塔
Longjing Village	龙井
Lord Ruan's Mount	阮公墩
Nine Creeks and Eighteen Gullies	九溪十八涧
Orioles Singing in Ripples of Willows Garden	柳浪闻莺
Precious Stone Hill	宝石山
Silk Museum	丝绸博物馆
Solitary Hill Island	独山
Su Causeway	苏堤
Tea Museum	茶叶博物馆
Three Pools Reflecting the Moon	三潭印月
Traditional Chinese Medicine Museum	中药博物馆
Yanggong Causeway	杨公堤
Yellow Dragon Cave	黄龙洞公园
Yuefei's Tomb	岳飞墓
Zhejiang Provincial Museum	浙江博物馆

Galleries, Shows & Theaters

Huanglong Yuanyuan Mingshu Yuan Theater	黄龙剧院
Dongpo Grand Opera House	东坡剧院

Hotels

Elan Inn	怡莱连锁酒店
Fuchun Resort	富春山庄
Hyatt Regency	凯悦酒店
Huajiashan Villa	花家山庄
Mingtown Youth Hostel	明堂国际青年旅舍
Overseas Chinese Hotel	华侨饭店
Shangri La	香格里拉饭店
Sofitel	索菲特西湖大酒店

Restaurants

Crystal Jade	翡翠花园酒家
Haveli	哈唯喱
Kuiyuanguan	奎元馆
Louwailou	楼外楼
Va Bene	华缤霓
Zhiweiguan	知味馆

Bars

Kana	卡那酒吧
Paradise	天上人间
Shamrock	三叶啤酒屋

HUANGSHAN & AROUND

TUNXI (HUANGSHAN CITY)   屯溪(黄山市)
Practicalities

Huangshan Airport	黄山机场
Train Station	火车站
Bus Station	汽车站

Sights

Cheng Dawei's Abacus Museum	程大位居
Cheng Family House	程氏三宅
Lao Jie	老街

Hotels

Huachen	华辰大酒店
Huangshan Bed & Breakfast	黄山自助酒店
Huashan	华山宾馆
Old Street	老街口客栈
Youth Hostel	国际青年旅馆

Restaurants

Hehuachi Jie	荷花池街
Yi Lou	一楼

TANGKOU & THE MOUNTAIN

TANGKOU   汤口
Practicalities

Tangkou Bus Station	汤口汽车站
Yungu Cable Car	云谷索道
Yuping Cable Car	玉屏索道

Sights

Banshan Temple	半山寺
Beginning to Believe Peak	始信峰
Brightness Top Peak	光明顶
Cloud Dispelling Pavilion	排云亭
Flying Over Rock	飞来石
Huangshan	黄山
Jade Screen Peak	玉屏楼
Lion's Peak	狮子峰
Lotus Peak	莲花峰
Mercy Light Temple	慈光阁
Monkey Watching the Sea	猴子观海
Red Cloud Peak	丹霞峰
Welcoming Guest Pine	迎客松
White Goose Peak	白鹅峰
Yungu Temple	云谷寺

Hotels (Huangshan)

Banshan Si Zhaodaisuo	半山寺招待所
Beihai	北海宾馆
Paiyunlou	排云楼宾馆
Shilin	石林大酒店
Xihai	西海饭店

Hotels (Tangkou)

Hong Da	洪大师酒店
Xingang	新港大酒店
Yingqiao	银桥大酒店
Youth Hostel	国际青年旅馆
Zhounan	洲楠大酒店

Nearby Sights & Towns

Chengkan	呈坎
Hongcun	宏村
Nanping	南屏
Qiankou	潜口
Shexian	歙县
Tangmo	唐模
Tangyue	堂越牌坊
Xidi	西递
Xucun	许村
Yixian	黟县

Guilin & Around

GUILIN   桂林

Practicalities
Guilin International Airport	桂林两江国际机场
Guilin South Train Station	桂林火车南站
Guilin North Train Station	桂林火车北站
Bus Station	汽车站
Zhujiang Dock	竹江码头

Sights
Elephant Trunk Hill	象鼻山
Li River	漓江
Banyan Lake	榕湖
Cedar Lake	杉湖
Jingjiang Princes' Palace	靖江王府
Solitary Beauty Peak	独秀峰
Wave Subduing Hill	伏波山
Folded Brocade Hill	叠彩山
Seven Star Park	七星公园
Reed Flute Cave	芦笛岩

Galleries, Shows & Theaters
Dreamlike Theater	梦幻漓江

Hotels
Bravo	桂林宾馆
Flowers Youth Hostel	花满楼
Guilin Backstreet Youth Hostel	后街国际青年旅馆
Hotel of Modern Art	愚自乐园
Lijiang Waterfall Hotel	漓江大瀑布饭店
Oasis Inn	绿洲酒店
Sheraton Guilin	大宇大饭店
Universal	环球大酒店

Restaurants
Daoxiangcun	稻乡村
Good Aunt	好大妈
Guilin Ren	桂林人
Little Italian	这里
Natural Café	闻莺阁
Repulse Bay	浅水湾咖啡厅
Yiyuan Fandian	怡园饭店
Zhengyang Tangcheng	正阳汤城

YANGSHUO　　　　　　　　　　阳朔

Practicalities
Li River　　　　　　　　　　　漓江
Bus Station　　　　　　　　　汽车站
Passenger Ferry Pier　　　　　阳朔外事码头

Sights
Butterfly Cave　　　　　　　　蝴蝶泉
Green Lotus Peak　　　　　　　碧莲峰
Moon Hill　　　　　　　　　　月亮山
Moon Water Cave　　　　　　　月亮水岩
Water Cave　　　　　　　　　龙门水岩
Water Buddha Cave　　　　　　菩萨水岩
Yangshuo Park　　　　　　　　阳朔公园

VILLAGES AROUND YANGSHUO
Aishan　　　　　　　　　　　矮山
Baisha　　　　　　　　　　　白沙
Chaolong　　　　　　　　　　朝隆
Chaoyang　　　　　　　　　　朝阳
Fuli　　　　　　　　　　　　福利
Gaotian　　　　　　　　　　高田
Liougong　　　　　　　　　　留公
Mushan　　　　　　　　　　木山
Puyi　　　　　　　　　　　　普益
Xingping　　　　　　　　　　兴坪
Yangdi　　　　　　　　　　　杨堤

Galleries, Shows & Theaters
Liu Sanjie Cultural Show　　　印象刘三姐

Hotels
Karst　　　　　　　　　　　喀斯特驿站
Magnolia　　　　　　　　　　白玉蘭酒店
Marco Polo　　　　　　　　　马可波羅酒店
Paradesa Resort　　　　　　　百乐来度假饭店
White Lion　　　　　　　　　未来恩饭店

Around Yangshuo
Li River Retreat　　　　　　　水岸花园别墅
Mountain Retreat　　　　　　胜地酒店

Outside Inn   荷兰饭店
Riverside Retreat   东岭别墅
Snow Lion Holiday Inn   雪狮岭度假饭店

Bars, Cafés & Restaurants
Bar 98   酒吧
Buffalo   牛头吧
China Café   原始人
Cloud 9   聚福楼
Fish Hot Pot   富贵楼斑鱼火锅店
Green Lotus Vegetarian   暗香疏影素菜馆
Karst   喀斯特
MC Blues   大逢车中西餐厅
Seventh Heaven   七重天咖啡厅
Yiping Ju   一品居饺子店

LONGJI   龙脊

Practicalities
Longsheng   龙胜

Villages
Dazai   大寨
Ping'an   平安
Zhongliu   中六

Sights
Dragon's Backbone   龙脊
Moon and Seven Stars   七星伴月

Hotels & Restaurants
Liqing Guesthouse   丽晴旅馆

The Pearl River Delta

GUANGZHOU   广州

Practicalities
Baiyun International Airport	白云机场
Guangzhou East Train Station	东方火车站
Guangzhou Train Station	广州火车站
Liuhua Bus Station	流花客运站
Nanhai Ferry Terminal	南海（平洲）码头
Provincial Bus Station	省汽车客运站
Tianhe Bus Station	天和客运站
Xidi Wharf	西堤码头

Sights & Shops
Baiyun Shan Park	白云山公园
Chen Clan Temple	陈家祠
Ersha Island	二沙岛
Huaisheng Mosque	怀圣清真寺
Hualin Temple	化林寺
Jade Market	玉石市场
Orchid Garden	兰圃
Pearl River	珠江
Peasant Training Institute	农民运动讲习所
Qingping Market	清平市场
Sacred Heart Church	圣心大教堂
Shamian Island	沙面岛
Shamian Park	沙面公园
Sun Yatsen Memorial Hall	中山纪念堂
Temple of Five Immortals	五仙观
Temple of Six Banyans	六榕寺
Tomb of Nanyue King	西汉南越王墓
Yuexiu Park	越秀公园

Around Guangzhou
Huizhou	惠州
Zhaoqing	肇庆

Galleries, Shows & Theaters
Guangdong Museum of Art	广东美术馆
Guangzhou Art Museum	广州艺术博物院
Jiangnan Theater	江南剧院
Xinghai Concert Hall	星海音乐厅

Hotels

Baigong　　　　　　　　　　　　　白宫酒店
China Marriott　　　　　　　　　　中国大酒店
CITS Hotel Guangdong　　　　　　广东国旅酒店
Garden Hotel　　　　　　　　　　花园酒店
Guangzhou Youth Hostel　　　　　广州青年招待所
Landmark　　　　　　　　　　　华夏大酒店
Shamian Hotel　　　　　　　　　沙面宾馆
Victory Hotel　　　　　　　　　　胜利宾馆
White Swan Hotel　　　　　　　　白天鹅宾馆

Restaurants

Banxi　　　　　　　　　　　　　泮溪酒家
Blenz Coffee　　　　　　　　　　沙面百怡咖啡
Cow and Bridge　　　　　　　　　泰国牛桥
Deli Shop　　　　　　　　　　　美食屋
Dongbei Ren　　　　　　　　　　东北人
Guangzhou　　　　　　　　　　　广州酒楼
La Seine　　　　　　　　　　　　塞纳河
Lucy's　　　　　　　　　　　　　露丝酒吧餐厅
Lucky Fellow　　　　　　　　　　幸运酒楼
Tao Tao Ju　　　　　　　　　　　陶陶居

Bars

1920s Café　　　　　　　　　　　酒吧
Elephant and Castle　　　　　　　大象堡酒吧
Paddy Field　　　　　　　　　　田野西餐厅
Tang Club　　　　　　　　　　　唐会
Tayin Mansion Lounge　　　　　　塔影楼堤岸咖啡馆
Yes Club　　　　　　　　　　　音乐工房

SHENZHEN　　　　　　　　　深圳

Practicalities

Bao'an International Airport　　　　保安机场
Fuyong Port　　　　　　　　　　福永码头
Luo Hu border　　　　　　　　　罗湖
Luo Hu Bus Station　　　　　　　罗湖汽车站
Qiaoshe Bus Station　　　　　　　桥社汽车站
Shekou Port　　　　　　　　　　蛇口码头
Shenzhen Train Station　　　　　　深圳火车站

Sights & Shops

Dameisha	大梅沙
Luo Hu Commercial Center	罗湖商业城
Overseas Chinese Town (OCT)	华侨城
Minsk World	明思克航空世界
Sea World	海洋世界
Splendid China	锦绣中华民俗村
Window of the World	世界之窗
Xiaomeisha	小梅沙

Galleries, Shows & Theaters

He Xiangning Art Museum	何香凝美术馆
OCT Contemporary Art Terminal	当代艺术中心

Hotels

Century Plaza	新都酒店
Guangdong	粤海酒店
Jin Bo Yang	金波阳宾馆
Mission Hills Resort	骏豪酒店
Petrel	海燕大酒店
Shangri-La	香格里拉大酒店
Sunshine	阳光酒店
Xiangpeng	湘朋宾馆

Restaurants

Beifang Fengwei	中华御膳罗湖大酒店
Café 360°	酒吧酒廊餐厅
Laurel	丹桂轩
Made in Kitchen	厨房制造
Spice Circle	时派圈印度餐厅
Tangle Palace	康乐宫

Bars

Browne's Wine Bar & Cigar House	布朗士葡萄酒雪茄吧
Ex-Ta-Sea	龙宫酒吧
Face Café	菲诗酒吧
Soho	碧涛剧乐部
V-Bar	吧